THE ENCYCLOPEDIA OF HOUSEHOLD HINTS AND DOLLAR STRETCHERS

REVISED EDITION

The Encyclopedia of
HOUSEHOLD HINTS
and
DOLLAR STRETCHERS

by

MICHAEL GORE

Completely revised, and with new material added, by the J. G. Ferguson Publishing Company, a division of Doubleday & Company, Inc.

DOUBLEDAY & COMPANY, INC., GARDEN CITY, NEW YORK
1977

91170

Library of Congress Cataloging in Publication Data

Gore, Michael.
    The encyclopedia of household hints and dollar stretchers.

    1. Home economics. 2. Recipes. I. Ferguson (J. G.)
Publishing Company. II. Title.
TX158.G668 1977   640.73
ISBN 0-385-13005-8
ISBN 0-385-13133-X paperback
Library of Congress Catalog Card Number 77–95

CONTENTS

1. **Your Meat Dollar**   1
   *Listen to the advice of butchers and prize-winning cooks—
   know your meats and save!*

2. **Poultry**   16
   Economy hints, cooking methods, fresh and frozen do's and don'ts

3. **Carve Like a Connoisseur**   23
   It's an art—but here are the ABC's that make it simple

4. **Fish and Shellfish**   28
   There's a world of delicious seafood waiting to be explored

5. **Vegetables**   37
   *All you need to know about wasteless buying, storing,
   preparing, and serving*

6. **Dairy Products and Eggs**   51
   *Basic to the diet, delicious to the taste, but perishable
   if not handled properly*

7. **Soups**   57
   *Homemade, canned, or frozen—here are tips on how to make
   the most out of soups*

8. **Breads, Rolls, and Biscuits**   6
   The staff of life can also be the life of the party

9. **Cakes**   )
   Basics and shortcuts for fine cakes, from baking to cutting

10. **Pies**   82
   *How to make them right—including some different pie ideas—
   plus a P.S. on waffles and pancakes*

11. Sweets and Desserts 92
*Low-cost ways to make new desserts, cookies, puddings, and
other treats—including ice cream*

12. Fruits, Jellies, and Nuts 104
Little-known tips to save money, work, and time

13. Beverages 112
*Coffee, tea, chocolate, and other light drinks to refresh
your taste and budget*

14. Sandwiches, Box Lunches, Picnics, and Cookouts 118
Some treats and tips for adding variety to informal meals

15. A Bouquet of Herbs 122
*Applied properly, these turn flat meals into
pleasurable experiences*

16. The Home Freezer 125
Ways to save money, food, and time with this storage convenience

17. Kitchen Appliances 134
*Ranges, refrigerators, and electrical appliances that make
meal-preparation easier and more pleasant*

18. Kitchen Hints 141
Tricks of the trade that save time, work, and money

19. Nutrition and Dieting 150
Losing—or gaining—weight must be based on sound nutrition

20. Words for the Kitchen 164
*Learning the language of food will help make your meals
easier to prepare, tastier to eat*

21. Measures and Weights 174
*Review familiar measures and get a head start on thinking
metric in the kitchen*

Personal Appearance 178
*A natural approach to cultivating good looks also connects
with health and happiness*

23. Your Wardrobe 207
*How to choose and care for your clothes and shoes to be well-dressed
on a budget*

24. Laundering, Cleaning, Ironing 218
Laboratory-tested directions for taking good care of fabrics

CONTENTS vii

25. Spots and Stains   232
How to remove the most common ones and save many dollars in cleaning bills

26. Luggage   244
Experience-tested tips on how to pack properly and how to care for your luggage

27. Sewing   251
A mini-course in making, remodeling, and mending clothes, with ingenious tips on saving time and money

28. Needlecrafts   270
Crochet, knit, or embroider with the aid of words-and-pictures directions

29. Child Care   288
Hints for raising happier, healthier children—from infancy to teens

30. Home Furnishings   294
How to get better and longer service from the things that make a home

31. Housecleaning   304
How to keep your home clean with less work, less money, and less time

32. Rugs and Carpets   311
Hints on increasing the beauty and life of rugs and carpets—and directions for removing the most common stains

33. Redecorating the Home   319
Be your own interior decorator—work wonders and save money while making your home more pleasant

34. Painting and Wallpapering   345
Practical hints and directions that show how to paint and wallpaper the interior and paint the exterior

35. Household Handyman   355
A miscellany of helpful tips for all those little things that need doing

36. Indoor and Outdoor Gardening   362
How to make your home and garden more beautiful

37. The House   378
Directions and tips for the basics of care and repair of a house, inside and out

38. Heating the Home   391
Simple ways to cut down heating bills without sacrificing comfort

39. Utilities and Services   399
*Reduce those monthly bills with these simple but all-too-often-
overlooked tips*

40. Car Conservation   403
*Add years and enjoyment, reduce costs and headaches by following
these basics of car maintenance*

41. Managing Your Money   415
*Sound tips to ensure that your money comes—and goes—in more
reasonable ways*

42. Your Bank   426
The dollars and sense of its many services

43. Insurance   433
*Sage counsel and handy hints that put insurance into
proper perspective*

44. Safety at Home   445
*Hints for avoiding accidents at major trouble spots
around the home*

45. First Aid   450

Index   463

1

YOUR MEAT DOLLAR

Listen to the advice of butchers and prize-winning cooks—know your meats and save!

Variety is the spice of life. When shopping for meat remember that variety can add appetizing surprises to menus, extra value to your meat dollar. Save money by knowing the different lower-cost cuts which can turn out as well as higher-cost cuts when prepared with imagination and care. Because of the constant changes in supply and demand, one cut may be the best buy one day, while a different one may be a "special" another day. A "special" usually means that a particular cut is more plentiful on the day offered. The lower price helps to keep meat moving while it is fresh. Remember, there are many, many meat cuts from which to choose.

HOW TO COOK BEEF

Broil, panbroil, or sauté: Club, T-bone, porterhouse, sirloin, round steaks; ground beef patties, hamburgers; rump roast, if top quality.

BASIC BEEF CUTS

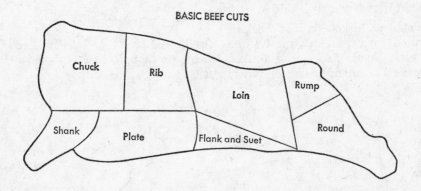

For definitions of cooking terms see chapter 20, "Words for the Kitchen" (pages 164–173).

BASIC VEAL CUTS

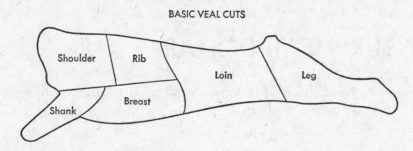

"London" broil (don't panbroil) flank steak, shoulder, or round on preheated broiler pan, as close to heat as possible (first having marinated the meat to insure tenderness and enhance flavor), only long enough to sear the meat. Then cut diagonally across the grain in thin slices.

Roast: Standing or rolled rib roast; rump roast, if top quality.

Braise: Chuck roast, rump roast (both as pot roast), round steak, chuck steak, flank steak (this may also be scored, stuffed, and baked), short ribs, liver, oxtail, kidney.

Simmer: Brisket (corned beef, if cured), plate, all stew meat (from chuck, shank, flank, neck, brisket, or heel of round), and all variety meats (heart, tongue, kidney, oxtail).

HOW TO COOK VEAL

Braise or sauté: Round steak, loin steak, loin chop, rib chop, shoulder chop, sweetbread, scallop.

Roast: Round roast, rump roast, rib, breast (stuffed rolled shoulder).

Simmer: Stewing veal (shank, breast, neck), skillet steak (shoulder).

HOW TO COOK LAMB

Broil, pan-broil, or sauté: Leg steak, rib chop, loin chop, shoulder chop.

BASIC LAMB CUTS

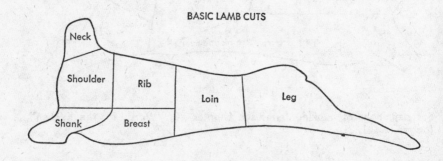

Roast: Leg (American and "Frenched"), loin end of leg, crown roast (rolled or straight), breast, boneless rolled shoulder.

Braise: Leg, shoulder, neck.

Simmer: Stewing lamb (neck, shank; both also for broth).

HOW TO COOK PORK

When really fresh, pork cuts are firm, fine-grained, grayish-pink in color, with a marble design of flecks of fat. On the outside pork is uniformly covered with firm white fat. Bones are pinkish, too, and porous inside when sawed. When you prepare fresh pork cuts they must be cooked until thoroughly well done—that is, to an internal temperature of 170–180° F.

Roast: Loin roast, spareribs, fresh ham, whole tenderloin, fresh shoulder butt, fresh picnic shoulder, whole shoulder, whole or half ham, Canadian bacon (whole or piece), smoked butt.

Braise: Shoulder steak, rib chop, loin chop, tenderloin (whole or fillet), spareribs.

Simmer: Spareribs, boneless smoked butt, smoked picnic, ham shank, pig's feet, hocks.

Fry: Ham slices, bacon, Canadian bacon, sausage, salt pork.

ECONOMY IS OFTEN A QUESTION OF QUANTITY

Have at your fingertips some waste-preventing general rules as to how much meat to buy per serving. This is no problem, of course, when you buy chops or frankfurters: You simply count noses. But other meats require a bit of estimating. Here is a good general guide:

Boneless meat: ⅓ to ½ pound per serving of cutlets, stew meats, ground meat, rolled roasts, boneless round steak, etc. (Steaks for broiling, incidentally, should be one to two inches thick.)

BASIC PORK CUTS

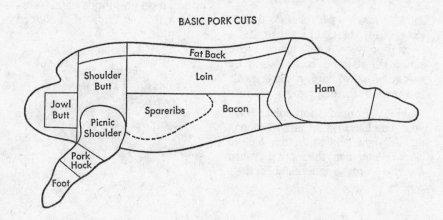

Meat with average amount of bone: ½ pound per serving of bone-in roasts, steaks, ham, etc.

Meat with larger amount of bone: ⅔ to ¾ pound per serving of short ribs, spareribs, pork hocks, etc.

Another way to save is to buy quantity. That is, buy larger cuts. The butcher's "specials" quite often are found among the larger cuts. If your family is not large enough to require that amount of meat at a single meal, you have perhaps felt that these otherwise excellent buys would mean too many meals of the same kind. But there are various ways to get around that.

You don't have to prepare the whole cut at once. You can divide a larger cut into several really different meals. The pictorial directions for each of the money-saving buys that follow will show you how. You can do the cutting yourself, in most cases, but your butcher is usually more than willing to oblige. Tell him how you want your meat cut. Just follow the diagrams.

How to make a rib roast do double duty. Rib roast, of course, is a special-occasion cut. But you can make rib roast a better value by using it for two fresh-cooked meals as shown in the diagram.

Meal 1: Braised short ribs. Have your butcher saw through the bone at "A" and "B" as in the picture above. You can then cut between the ribs to make individual servings

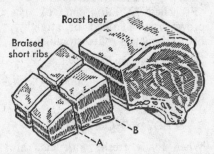

BEEF RIB ROAST

Roast beef

Braised short ribs

B

A

of short ribs. Braise them slowly with vegetables to stretch their good meat flavor further in the meal.

Meal 2: Juicy roast beef. Now, for the roast, you have just the tenderest "heart" of the piece. Follow the directions for roasting on page 7.

From one cut of beef chuck: pot roast, steaks, stew. You may not always find this cut, an arm cut or round-bone pot roast, since beef chuck is cut differently in various parts of the country. When you do buy a round-bone pot roast, however, have it cut thick and use it as follows. Instead of pot roast on Sunday and hash on Monday and Tuesday, you'll have three fresh-cooked

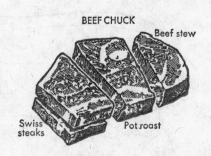

BEEF CHUCK

Beef stew

Swiss steaks

Pot roast

and entirely different meals that you can spread over a week's time:

Meal 1: Beef stew. From the round end of the roast cut off a boneless piece of meat to cube for beef stew.

Meal 2: Pot roast. Cut a piece from the center for a small, one-meal pot roast.

Meal 3: Swiss steaks. With a sharp knife you can easily split the remaining piece to make two attractive Swiss steaks. Braise one to two hours.

Stretch your leg of lamb. This idea works well with a small leg of lamb, but it's especially recommended for use at the time of year when large legs of lamb (seven to nine pounds) are plentiful and featured at a lower price. Below is just one of several good ways to divide a whole (full cut) leg of lamb so you don't have to cook it all at once and can stretch it into three thoroughly luscious meals:

Meal 1: Lamb steaks for broiling. Broil the lamb steaks just as you would loin chops.

Meal 2: Lamb roast. Here's your Sunday roast, just the easy-to-carve center portion of the leg. Make a panful of gravy and serve with potatoes and a fresh vegetable. Remember, you'll get more juicy slices and less cooking shrinkage if you roast lamb at a low temperature (no higher than 325° F.).

Meal 3: Stew or curry. Later in the week cut the meat from the shank into cubes for another freshly cooked meal. Use these boneless cubes of lamb in an Irish stew or in a more glamorous dish, such as lamb curry. Or leave the shank whole and roast it. After cooking until tender, remove the bone and put a whole cooked carrot in the center of the shank. Fasten with toothpicks, dip in egg and crumbs, brush with melted butter or margarine, and bake in a 400° F. oven for ten minutes.

Three fresh-cooked meals from a pork-loin roast. You know the economy of buying half a pork loin and having your butcher cut off a few pork chops for you. Here's an-

LEG OF LAMB

Lamb steaks

Lamb roast

Stew or curry

other good idea, using the rib half of the loin:

PORK-LOIN ROAST

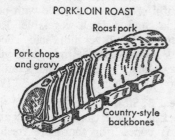

Roast pork

Pork chops and gravy

Country-style backbones

PORK BUTT

Pork steaks

Pork roast

Chop suey

Meal 1: Country-style backbones. Select a rib half of pork loin and have your butcher saw through the ribs high enough to leave an inch-thick layer of meat on the backbones. Ask him to chop these meaty backbones into serving-size pieces. Cook as you would spareribs, barbecued or with sauerkraut.

Meal 2: Pork chops and gravy. Later, cut enough chops for another meal from the remaining piece by slicing between the ribs. (This is as easily done as slicing a loaf of bread, after the backbones have been removed.)

Meal 3: Roast pork. You still have a piece left to cook as a one-meal pork roast.

How to make three fresh-cooked meals from one pork butt. The whole fresh pork shoulder butt is a nearly boneless cut that usually weighs from five to seven pounds. You can divide this economical cut at home into a roast, boneless steaks, or cubed pork for grinding and casserole dishes.

Meal 1: Pork roast. Cut across the roast as shown to divide it into two pieces. Use the piece with the bone for your pork roast.

Meal 2: Pork steaks. The remaining piece is clear, solid meat. From it you can cut boneless pork steaks about a half inch thick. Braise these steaks just as you would pork chops, browning, then cooking them in a covered skillet with or without added liquid.

Meal 3: Chop suey. As you get to the small end of the boneless piece, cut the remaining meat into small cubes. Use the diced pork for a meat-stretching dish of chop suey, or make into a casserole dish.

Four fresh-cooked meals from half a ham. Many who buy half a ham habitually select the butt half. Shank halves, however, usually are

HALF A HAM

Boiled dinner

Boneless ham slices

Baked ham

offered at a lower price. Here's how to make the most of this excellent cut. (Be sure to get a full shank half for this four-way method.)

Meal 1: Boiled dinner. Have your butcher saw off a generous shank end. For lots of flavor in an old-fashioned boiled dinner, simmer it with carrots, onions, potatoes, and wedges of cabbage.

Meal 2: Baked ham. You can easily divide the center part into two portions. Bake the piece with the bone at 325° F. Slices will be small because of the bone in the middle. Delicious, though. And just enough for one meal for a small family.

Meals 3 and 4: Boneless ham slices. The remaining piece is boneless and easily sliced with a sharp knife. To fry or broil, cut thicker slices from the larger end. Cut the smaller end into thinner slices or cubes for ham and scalloped potatoes, or other one-dish meals.

If you have a freezer, you can double-wrap, label, date and freeze any of the cut-up large cuts described above and serve the meat in different form another week or months after you've had the first meal from the large cut.

FIRST-RATE EATING AT CUT-RATE COSTS

For variety: variety meats. Liver, tongue, kidney, heart, brains, sweetbreads, tripe give your meat meals new flavor, often at sizable savings. Variety meats are rich in vitamins and minerals and delicious when prepared in such taste-tempting ways as these:

From the ground meats you can make wonderful treats, such as stuffed peppers, stuffed cabbage, meat loaf, Swedish meat balls, quick beef hash, turnovers, chili, beef drumsticks, and many of your own special recipes.

HOW TO ROAST MEAT

The modern method of roasting meats at low temperatures does away with spattered ovens, cuts down shrinkage, and gives you more and juicier servings per pound. ("Baking" is the term usually applied to roasting smoked hams and picnics.) Here's how to do it:

1. Sprinkle meat with salt and pepper.

2. Place fat side up on rack in open roasting pan. For very lean meats, such as veal, ask your butcher for a piece of pork or beef fat to lay over the top, or use a few strips of bacon or salt pork. Fat will flavor the meat and add juiciness to it while it cooks.

3. If you have a meat thermometer, insert through the outside fat into thickest part of muscle, so point does not rest on fat or bone.

4. Roast at a continuous low heat (300–325° F.). Use this same temperature throughout cooking period. Do not add water, do not sear meat, do not cover pan, do not baste.

5. Remove from oven when meat thermometer registers desired degree of doneness.

Frozen meats may be roasted without thawing, but you must allow about one and one half the usual cooking time. Thawed meats are roasted same length of time as fresh meats.

BAKED HAM

The ham most generally available in markets across the country is the modern, mild, cured, tenderized ham. If it is sold in the packer's wrapping, the type of ham and cooking directions are printed on the outside. But many large chain markets have hams produced on special order, without accompanying cooking directions. Although "ready-to-eat" hams are improved by further cooking or baking, the following directions apply to "cook-before-eating" smoked hams:

1. Wipe ham with clean cloth, rewrap loosely in one of the paper wrappers around the ham or in clean, fresh wrapping paper, and place it, fat side up, on rack of shallow pan. Do not cover pan or add water.

2. Bake in 325° F. oven until within 45 minutes of total baking time for your ham. Remove paper and rind from ham. Make a series of shallow cuts across fat to cut into squares or diamonds. Spread with desired glaze. Insert one clove into each square of fat.

3. Bake uncovered in 325° F. oven for the remaining 45 minutes.

4. To decorate, cut orange peel into five-point stars on each square of fat, using clove as fastening center. Or form flowers with canned peach or apricot slice "petals," using half a maraschino cherry as the center.

Ham baked in aluminum foil. Wrapping the ham snugly in heavy-duty aluminum foil, with four inches of overlap where the ends are joined together, quickens the baking time.

Glazing. If you glaze whole hams with a spicy mixture made with 1 cup of brown sugar, 1 teaspoon of cinnamon, ½ teaspoon ground ginger, ¼ teaspoon ground cloves, and the grated rind of an orange, the flavor gets baked in.

Other tasty glazes can be made by following the imagination. Here are some variations: 1 cup of brown sugar, juice and grated rind of an orange; 1 cup of brown sugar, 1 tablespoon dry mustard; glass of melted currant jelly; ¾ cup pineapple juice, same amount of strained honey, ½ teaspoon dry mustard, cooked together until thick; ½ cup of maple syrup, same of cider or apple juice, 2 tablespoons dry mustard.

BROILING MEAT

What to broil. Broiling is cooking by direct heat. This can be done under a flame in a gas-range broiler, under the broiling element in an electric oven, inside a portable broiler or rotisserie, or outdoors over hot coals. Broiling is recommended for tender cuts of meat with enough fat on them to keep them from drying out as they cook. For best results, therefore, neither veal nor pork should be broiled, although bacon and smoked ham steak may be broiled. Otherwise broiling is meant chiefly for beef (steaks, ground patties, and hamburgers) and for lamb chops.

How long to broil a steak or a chop depends on a lot of things: the thickness, your preference for rare, medium, or well done, and the fact that there are so many different makes and models of ranges, broilers, and rotisseries in use in American kitchens. However, here are some general rules to follow:

1. Before you broil, make these preparations: Wipe meat, do not wash, and make several cuts in the outside fat covering along the edge at one-inch intervals. This is to keep the meat from "cupping" while it is broiling.

2. Set regulator at "broil."

3. Put meat on broiler rack and place under broiling unit so that top surface of meat is about two inches from heat (greater distance for very thick chops or steaks).

4. Broil with door closed if using a gas range, with door slightly ajar if broiling by electricity.

5. Broil until meat is well browned, season with salt and pepper.

6. Turn and brown other side. Only one turning is necessary.

7. Serve broiled meats immediately on hot platter, "to save the sizzle."

Two broiling "tricks-of-the-trade." For three-inch steaks, brown on both sides in hot broiling unit, then place in hot roasting oven to finish cooking. For bacon-wrapped "special," wrap slices of bacon around individual tenderloin or sirloin steaks. Fasten with toothpicks and broil.

Labor- and flavor-saving device. Line the broiler pan with aluminum foil and you do away with the scouring after broiling. The foil is nonflammable and will catch melted fats that drip. Placing steak directly on aluminum foil, whose sides have been folded to stand up and form a very shallow foil pan, will leave broiler pan clean and will help seal in flavor and juice of steak. The melted steak fats and drippings are caught and can be used on the finished steak for extra juiciness.

How to broil over a charcoal fire.

1. Build a big enough fire to have a good bed of coals. Give it plenty of time for all flames to die down to a glowing bed of embers before starting to cook the meat.

2. Trim excess fat from meat. Have grill far enough from coals so that when fat from meat drips and flares up, flames do not char the meat excessively. (Most outdoor cooks consider a little charring desirable.)

HOW TO PAN-BROIL

1. Preheat your heaviest cast-aluminum or iron skillet or griddle.

Do not add fat. (If you're afraid of meat sticking, rub pan with piece of suet or grease lightly with other fat.)

2. When pan is very hot, put in meat, brown quickly on both sides. Do not cover pan.

3. Reduce heat and cook slowly until done. If fat collects in pan, pour it off. Season just before serving.

HOW TO PAN-FRY

Pan-frying, rather than pan-broiling, is necessary when meat has very litle fat or when meat is breaded or floured. Procedure is the same as for pan-broiling except that fat is added first.

Note: Despite what you may have heard to the contrary, fried meats, when properly prepared, are as digestible as meats cooked by any other method. However, smoking fat is harmful. Fat allowed to smoke forms indigestible acids when eaten.

HOW TO BRAISE

Braising is a method of moist-heat cookery in which the meat is browned in a little hot fat, then cooked slowly in a covered utensil, usually with a small amount of added liquid. Here's how:

1. Season meat with salt and pepper. Sprinkle with flour for a richer brown.

2. Brown meat slowly on all sides in a little hot fat.

3. Add small amount of liquid. As liquid cooks away, a little more may be added.

4. Cover tightly. Cook over low heat at simmering temperature on top of range or in 325° F. oven until meat is tender. (Two to 3 hours for pot roast, 1 to 2 hours for Swiss steak.)

5. Vegetables may be added 30 to 45 minutes before meat is done. Continue cooking until meat and vegetables are both tender.

FOIL-ROASTING

Inexpensive meat is coaxed to make gourmet pot roast by the foil-roasting method. This pot roast is not the result of water-braising, but of broiling and baking. The meat, placed on heavy aluminum foil, is first broiled by itself until brown, then turned for second-side browning. Add small onions and other taste-giving vegetables and pull up foil so that meat and vegetables are sealed into an airtight package. Then bake in very slow (300° F.) oven for 3 hours or more. Use no water. The meat and vegetables are "stewing in their own juice," since no liquid can evaporate. But for extra flavor you may add ¼ cup of red wine before sealing and baking.

HOW TO MAKE A STEW

1. Have beef, veal, or lamb cut into uniform pieces, one to two inches square. Season with salt and pepper. Flour meat if you want a deep brown color.

2. Brown on all sides *in hot fat.* Many people brown sliced or chopped onions along with the meat.

3. Barely cover meat with hot water, stock, or other liquid. (To make a quick meat stock, dissolve a bouillon cube or one teaspoon of beef extract in a cup of hot water or liquid from cooking vegetables.)

4. Cover kettle closely, cook slowly until meat is tender. Simmer, do not boil. Add extra liquid if necessary.

5. Add vegetables just long enough before meat is tender to be done but not overcooked.

6. Thicken gravy with a smooth flour-and-water paste, using a few tablespoons of flour and enough water to moisten.

SLOW SIMMERING

This is a method often used for cooking cuts such as corned beef, fresh brisket, hocks, ham shank, smoked tongue.

1. Cover meat with lightly salted water.

2. Add a peeled onion and herbs or spices, if desired.

3. Bring to a boil, then cover and cook over low heat at simmering temperature (just below the boiling point) until done.

4. If vegetables are to be cooked with the meat, add them 30 to 45 minutes before meat is done.

COOKING BACON

Soak the bacon strips in cold water for a few minutes before frying. This lessens tendency of the bacon to shrink and curl. Put the slices into a cold skillet, turn them often, drain off excess grease as it accumulates. You wind up with more of the bacon, and what a difference in its appetizing good looks!

Frying bacon faster. Frying time can be cut down, and more cooked at once, if you crisscross the slices and turn them all at once with a pancake turner.

Easiest way to cook bacon, if you're in no hurry, is in a low-temperature oven. Place strips of bacon on rack in a shallow roasting pan. Cook at 300–325° F. for an hour or more without bacon drying out or scorching. If you want to rush it, raise temperature to 375° F. and cook for ½ hour. This method requires no watching, turning, or other bother. Simply set a timer clock to remind you when the bacon is ready to serve.

CHOPPED BEEF

Have hamburgers whenever you want them. Prepare them well in advance by shaping ground meat into patties and freezing. Wrap individually, or pack several together, separating each patty with double thickness of moisture-vaporproof material. Can be broiled without thawing, though it's necessary to allow more cooking time than for thawed patties.

Everybody's hamburger will be the same size if you measure meat with an ice-cream scoop. Scoop is ideal for this purpose and is easy to clean.

Meat extenders make meat loaf and shopping dollar go further. Double size of meat loaf with soybeans, bread, cracker crumbs, or crushed dry cereal. Interesting idea: stuff meat loaf with the same kind of savory mixture you put into a roast chicken.

Old-world meat loaf with "golden center." Try this. When shaping your meat loaf, put a peeled hard-cooked egg in the center. Makes interesting-looking slices and adds egg nourishment to your meal.

Meat loaf with a party look. Prepare meat loaf with pound of ground meat and your other favorite ingredients. Pack into a clean number-two can (saved from bargain-size can of vegetables) and bake in shallow pan. The round roll loaf will have a different look. Dress it up with simple sauce made by heating a can of mushroom soup.

HOW TO BE A GENIUS WITH LEFTOVERS

Dressed-up leftovers are fun to prepare, fun to eat. They tax the imagination but not the budget.

Leftover roast ends up in hash. But if a small amount of the hash is left over, use it hot as a filler for sandwiches made from well-browned French toast.

New idea for roast-beef bits. Everybody knows about using leftover roast-beef bits in sandwiches and combinations with vegetables in casserole, but here's a new trick: add them to canned chili for a hearty, different, luncheon main dish.

Miniature art. Grind leftover beef roast with a small onion. Store in a small covered dish in your refrigerator for several days. Let the family forget all about it, then spring it on them as midget meat loaves.

Meat-and-mushroom muffins. A small amount of leftover cooked beef may be ground and added to any standard muffin mixture. Serve the meat muffins hot, topped with a quick sauce made from undiluted mushroom soup.

Saucy meat loaf. Leftover meat loaf will seem new and different served the second time if topped with a tasty sauce. For instance, combine 2 cups applesauce, 2 tablespoons dry mustard with horseradish, 2 tablespoons Worcestershire sauce, and 3 tablespoons tomato catsup. Serve hot or cold on slices of the reheated loaf.

Three hard or soft rolls may be used as the basis of a luncheon dish. Scoop out center crumbs after splitting rolls, and save for any crumbing use. Fill the shells with any mixture of leftover meat or fish mixed with a little chopped celery and mayonnaise. Put in 350° F. oven until piping hot and lightly toasted, 25 to 30 minutes.

Part of a can of luncheon meat and leftover mashed white or sweet potatoes may be combined for a savory meat loaf. Slice the meat thin and sandwich it with the potato, mixed with a little mayonnaise. Bake at 350° F. until very hot and lightly browned, about 20 to 25 minutes.

Your stock goes up with meat stock used as the liquid in gelatins for molded meat loaves and aspics.

Don't pour flavor down the sink. Bacon drippings used for frying and for searing meat give it a fine, delicate flavor. But be sure to use a little less salt when you cook with bacon fat.

Additional ways with bacon drippings. Use it as shortening for bran muffins; to make white sauce, onion sauce, tomato sauce; in bread stuffing for veal, poultry, fish; as blend in some vegetables and soups; in bread crumbs or cereals to top vegetable or fish casseroles; to flavor macaroni, noodles, spaghetti; to grease muffin pans, to fry eggs, for flavor and economy; to brown croutons; to add to meat loaves. For shortening, strain through three thicknesses of cheesecloth.

HOW TO MAKE GRAVY

Gravy from oven roasts. Since no water is added to oven roasts, only fat and drippings will be left in the pan. Skim off all but 2 or 3 tablespoons of fat. Stir in 2 or 3 tablespoons of flour and gradually add to it 1½ cups of water or liquids saved from cooking vegetables. Cook over low heat until thick and bubbly, stirring constantly. Season to taste. (Rare roasts yield few drippings and will make less gravy. Why not skip it and simply serve pan drippings with the roast?)

Pot-roast gravy. There are two ways of making this gravy, the dry-flour and flour-paste.

Dry-flour: When cooked, remove meat from cooking liquor and place on hot platter. Pour all liquid and fat into separate container. When fat rises to top, skim off with a spoon, returning only 4 tablespoons to pan. Heat fat and gradually stir in 4 tablespoons of flour. Add 2 cups of cooking liquid and meat juices. (If necessary, add water to make this quantity.) Cook and stir over low heat until smooth and thickened. Scrape bottom of pan to loosen any meat particles.

Flour-paste: Remove meat to hot platter. Skim off excess fat from the cooking-pan liquor. Measure liquor, and for each 2 cups of it measure out 4 tablespoons of flour. Add water gradually to flour, stirring constantly, until a thin paste results. (An egg beater or blender rushes this and insures smooth paste.) Pour a little of the cooking liquor into the flour paste, stirring constantly until smooth. Then add the diluted paste to the meat liquor and cook and stir until thickened.

Keep lumps out of brown gravy. Add liquid slowly, stirring and scraping with spoon. If there are lumps, strain gravy through sieve and reheat.

Using hot water often makes gravy lumpy. You may do better with cold water. A lumpless way to thicken gravy, and use cold water, is to have the water in a jar, adding flour and shaking until smooth, then adding to the meat liquids.

Serve gravy at its best. If gravy is made in advance of serving time, add a little liquid, stir, and heat when ready to serve. Gravy should always be very hot. Reheat for second helpings. If fat has separated out of gravy, stir well with a tablespoon of cold water, then reheat.

POINTERS ON MEAT STORING

1. Fresh meat vs. fresh bacteria. Remember meat is perishable. As soon as you bring it home, put it in the refrigerator until you are ready to cook it. Unwrap the meat, wipe it, but don't wash it. Rewrap meat loosely in market or waxed paper. Another method is to place meat on a clean, dry plate or shallow dish and cover it loosely with waxed paper so air can circulate. If meat is not to be used the same day, put it in the coldest part of your refrigerator. Store prepackaged fresh meat the same way, first loosening original wrapper.

2. Roasts and steaks. The smaller the cut of meat, the sooner it should be used. Steaks and chops should be cooked within two or three days of purchase. Roasts may be stored slightly longer. Store broiling steaks in loose, clean wrapping paper. Keep frozen steaks frozen until you use them. They may be broiled without thawing, but allow longer time.

3. The "cold war" against spoilage of small cuts. It's best to freeze small cuts if they are to be kept more than three days. If you don't have a home freezer, meat may be frozen in the frozen-food compartment or ice-cube section of your refrigerator. Use special freezer wrapping materials for long home freezer storage. For short storage, a week or two, wrapping with aluminum foil is adequate freezer wrapping. Wrap each chop or ground meat separately with the paper. Packed closely, several may be overwrapped with one piece of foil. For refrigerator freezing, turn control to coldest position until meat is frozen.

4. Variety meats are sensitive. They spoil more quickly than other meats. Liver, kidney, sweetbreads, and cubed meat especially should be used within a day of purchase, and meanwhile kept under coldest refrigeration.

5. The smoked-meat department. Smoked hams, bacon, sausage products, such as bologna, frankfurters, etc., require the same cold-storage care as fresh meat. Smoked hams and bacon should be used within a week. All prepackaged smoked meat may be stored in the original wrapper. Be sure package is well sealed to prevent odors from spreading to the other foods in your refrigerator or freezer. However, by wrapping fresh meat tightly with smoked meat, you can give the fresh meat a smoky flavor.

6. Cooked meat is perishable. All cooked meats must be refrigerated. Store in a covered container or wrap tightly in waxed paper or aluminum foil.

7. Are canned meats immune to spoilage? Some are, some aren't. To make sure, check the can labels. The larger-size cans of luncheon meat and canned ham definitely need refrigeration. Smaller canned ham or picnic meat is usually well protected by the can itself, but to stay on the safe side read the labels.

8. Keep frozen meat frozen. Frozen meats packaged in moistureproof wrapping may be stored for fairly long periods, but only in a home freezer and at 0° F. or lower. Once you thaw meat, use it. Never refreeze, except after it's been cooked in a form that lends itself to freezing leftovers.

Note: For general rules on freezing, see pages 125–133.

2

POULTRY

Economy hints, cooking methods, fresh and frozen do's and don'ts

Checking on chicken. The chickens you buy at your local market are ready-to-cook. "Ready-to-cook" chickens are priced after head, feet, and viscera have been discarded. All poultry that moves in interstate commerce is subject to federal inspection to insure wholesome quality.

Chickens should be plump and youthful-looking. When buying chicken there are a number of quality controls you can exercise. Look at the drumstick. Don't buy if the chicken's thigh is thin and the bone heavy. Look at the neck. If it is well-fleshed, the rest of the bird will probably be the same. Be careful if it has a long, scrawny neck, though. White, blue-tinged skin is not the mark of aristocracy in a chicken. The best-meat chickens have creamy or light yellow skin.

HOW MUCH POULTRY TO BUY

When shopping for poultry, allow approximately ½ to 1 pound ready-to-cook bird per person.

Larger birds may mean economy. These are called fowl, hens, or stewing chicken. Their meat is less tender than that of smaller birds, but they are delicious when slow-cooked in moisture and used in stew, fricassee with dumplings, chicken pies, or chicken à la king.

Better buy turkey. Because in larger birds there is less bone in proportion to meat than in smaller birds, turkey often is a better buy than chicken.

The "new look" in turkeys. Some years ago a new style of turkey was developed, a new breed of broad-breasted bird that gives you more white meat, less bone waste with each turkey as compared with traditional turkeys. The Beltsville turkey is one of these new birds. It's a junior size four-to-nine-pound turkey that suits the needs of the small family of three to six people.

FROZEN POULTRY

Several good brands of frozen poultry are available. You may buy whole-chicken broilers, fryers, roasters, Rock Cornish game hens, stewing chickens, assortments of chicken breasts, legs, thighs, wings, chicken livers, giblets, hearts, gizzards—all cleaned and ready to cook, after thawing. You can buy frozen young hen turkeys, young tom turkeys, junior turkeys, Long Island ducklings, and whole frozen capons that weigh about four pounds or over. The capons are castrated male birds that have a large portion of white meat and are packaged and prepared to be eaten as roasters.

Thaw frozen poultry completely before cooking. There are three ways to do this:

1. Place poultry in its original wrapper or box in the regular compartment of your refrigerator for about five to six hours for every pound of bird. (Overnight for a chicken, two to three days for a large turkey.)

2. For quicker thawing, place whole birds in cool running water until just pliable enough to handle. This requires one to three hours. Do not allow to stand in water after thawing.

3. Packages of cut-up chicken or parts should be opened and contents placed on a rack in a shallow pan or tray until pieces can be separated. An electric fan, directed toward the thawing chicken, speeds the process.

To keep it from spoiling—keep poultry frozen in frozen-food compartment of your refrigerator until you plan to thaw and cook it.

COOKING

How to roast chicken or small turkey. Use shallow, uncovered pan. A V-shaped rack placed in the pan will hold the bird in position. Place it breast side up on rack. To give the thin breast skin and the low-fat area under the skin the necessary protection, place on it a double thickness of cheesecloth dipped in melted butter or margarine. Baste with additional butter or margarine during roasting, or, if you prefer, brush the bird with melted fat and protect the breast part and the top of the legs with a square of aluminum foil laid loosely over it. Do not entirely cover the bird with foil.

To roast average- and large-size turkey. Brush bird all over with melted butter or margarine and place breast down on rack. Bird may be turned breast up during the last half hour of roasting time. Follow timetable page 18, but you may also test doneness by moving the turkey's leg. If it moves easily, so the joints seem loose, the turkey is done. For a very large turkey, follow the same procedure. If your roasting pan is not large enough, the drip pan of your broiler is a good substitute.

How to roast duck and goose. Place breast up on rack in roasting pan. If you roast a large goose, prick the breast skin to allow fat to drain away. Do not brush with fat. Protect top during first part of roasting time with square of foil, as with chicken. Remove foil the last half hour of roasting time. Prick skin again.

Baked chicken. Most baked chicken is browned in skillet first, then transferred to covered or open casseroles in oven for baking. Here are a few ideas for variations on this theme:

Chicken baked in sour cream. Dredge chicken pieces in mixture of flour, salt, and pepper. Brown in butter or margarine. Transfer to casserole. Add sliced mushrooms and a cup of sour cream diluted with a cup of water. Cover closely. Bake at 325° F. for one hour.

"Baked broiler sauterne." Refrigerate chicken in sauterne wine three to four hours. An hour before serving time, start oven at 450° F. Pour wine from chicken. Add to wine chopped parsley and scallions. Sprinkle chicken with salt, pepper, and paprika, and coat with softened butter or margarine. Place chicken breast side down in shallow baking pan. Pour on the wine mixture. Bake 25 minutes, basting frequently. Turn and bake breast side up another 20 minutes, or until tender and brown.

Chicken baked in foil. Place chicken halves in center of large square of aluminum foil. Rub with garlic, if desired, and spread with melted butter. Sprinkle with salt, pepper, and any other desired seasonings. Bring foil up over chicken, seal all edges tightly, turning folds up so juices will not escape. Place on cookie sheet and bake at 400° F. for 50 minutes. Open foil and turn back. Brown chicken under broiler, basting with the juices that have accumulated within the foil cover.

Chicken in foil baskets. Use breast, leg, or thigh parts. Rinse, dry, and lightly brown (do not flour). Place two or three pieces on aluminum

YOUR HANDY POULTRY ROASTING GUIDE

BIRD	WEIGHT IN POUNDS	OVEN TEMPERATURE	COOKING TIME IN HOURS
Chicken	2	400° F.	1–1½
Chicken	2½–4	375° F.	1½–2¼
Chicken	4½–7	325° F.	3–5
Turkey	4–8	325° F.	2½–3½
Turkey	9–12	325° F.	3¾–4½
Turkey	13–16	325° F.	4¾–5½
Turkey	17–20	325° F.	5¾–6½
Turkey	21–24	325° F.	6½–7
Rock Cornish Game Hen	¾–1½	400° F.	¾–1
Duck	4–5½	325° F.	2½–3
Goose	4–6	325° F.	2½–3
Goose	7–8	325° F.	3¼–3¾
Goose	9–12	325° F.	4–4½
Goose	13–14	325° F.	4½–5

square large enough to wrap pieces completely but loosely. Add lightly browned small white onions and mushrooms to each "package." Sprinkle with salt, pepper, paprika, and chopped parsley. Add 2 tablespoons light cream to each. Bring up edges of foil and double-fold so each serving is sealed in tightly. Place "packages" on cookie sheet or shallow pan and bake at 450° F. for 1 hour. Fold back foil to form individual little baskets from which to eat.

How to sauté chicken. Have chicken cut up. Flour pieces lightly by shaking them in a paper bag containing flour and seasonings. Brown pieces a few at a time in a large, heavy skillet in which you have heated ½ inch cooking oil. Continue cooking over very low heat, uncovered, for 15–25 minutes on each side. Test with fork for tenderness. You may add a sprinkling of chopped parsley and paprika just before removing from skillet. Serve with pan juices.

Oven-barbecued chicken. First flour and brown pieces as for sautéing, then place in casserole and cover with barbecue sauce. Bake at 350° F., covered, for 1 hour.

Barbecue sauce consists of chopped onion cooked in butter over low heat for ten minutes, chopped celery, sliced green pepper, catsup, Worcestershire sauce, brown sugar, pepper, water.

For deep-fat fried chicken, use small (1½ to 2 lb.) fryers. Fry floured pieces in deep fat, at 350° F., until brown all over, about 15 minutes. Drain on paper toweling before serving.

Fry-'n-freeze. While most fried foods should not be frozen for later use, fried chicken may be, if properly wrapped in moistureproof, vaporproof paper. May be eaten thawed out and cold at picnics, or from lunch boxes.

How to broil chicken or turkey. Use small birds. Have them split in half (lengthwise) and have backbone and neck removed. Or buy chicken or turkey parts. Preheat broiler. Place pieces, skin side down, on lightly greased broiler rack. Brush poultry liberally with melted butter, margarine, or cooking oil. Brush pieces with additional butter, etc., after they have been turned.

To stew chicken. Like all stewing, this is low-heat, simmering water cookery. Place cut-up stewing chicken, seasonings, vegetables in kettle and cover with boiling water. Cover and simmer over low heat 2½ hours, or until tender. Remove vegetables. Measure broth and, for each cup, stir 2 tablespoons of flour into cold water to make a thin, smooth paste. Stir a little broth into the paste and then add to remaining broth. Cook and stir over low heat until gravy thickens and reaches the boiling point. Cook and stir for one more minute.

Use **stewed chicken** in casserole specials, in pies, salads, sandwiches, chicken shortcakes, à la king, Tetrazzini, chicken loaf, with gravies, etc.

How to fricassee chicken. Use chicken parts. Coat pieces with seasoned flour by shaking in paper bag. For appetizing color and extra flavor, give it a slow browning in thin layer of hot fat. Brown on all sides. Drain off (and save) fat. Add 1 cup of water plus 1 cup of flavoring liquid, such as juices (orange, pineapple, tomato), soup, or wine. Add a pinch of dry seasoning, such as onion flakes, nutmeg, curry, or a little grated lemon rind. Cook chicken in this liquid, covered, over low heat, until largest meat part becomes tender (2½ to 3½ hours). Watch it, and add water if necessary while it is cooking. Thicken gravy with flour paste, allowing 2 tablespoons of flour for each cup of cooking liquor.

HOW TO PREPARE POULTRY FOR ROASTING

Rub inside of body cavity with teaspoonful of salt, then stuff. (Careful; don't pack stuffing. It expands in cooking.) Next, stuff neck cavity (loosely), pull neck skin to the back and fasten with long skewer. Fold wings to the back and hold wing tips in place by pulling the neck skin over them. If desired, tie wings close to the body. Now draw body opening together with small turkey skewers or strong toothpicks. Lace it shut with white cord, the way a shoe is laced. Cross long ends of cord to wind around leg ends, then around tailpiece. Draw close to body and tie securely. Truss turkeys even when roasted without stuffing.

STUFFINGS

Kinds of stuffing are as endless as recipes and cookbooks and your own culinary talent and imagination. The table on page 21, however, gives you ingredients and proportions for a basic, all-time favorite stuffing, or dressing.

How to make it. Cook giblets, dice when tender, and save broth. Cut bread into small cubes and toast lightly in oven. Let onion and celery cook in the butter over low heat until clear, about ten minutes. Pour over bread cubes, add remaining seasonings, the chopped giblets, and enough of the broth to moisten very lightly. (Dressing draws moisture from bird as it roasts, and becomes soggy if too much broth is added.)

Pork sausage dressing. Same as giblet dressing, with these differences: Omit butter. Use only half as much salt. One 1-pound pure pork sausage for 12-pound turkey, or ⅓ pound sausage for a chicken. Fry sausage twelve to fifteen minutes, breaking it up as it cooks. Add drippings and meat to the dressing.

Orange stuffing for duck. Place three cups dry bread crumbs in mixing bowl, pour ½ cup melted butter over it. Add teaspoon of salt,

GIBLET DRESSING

	4-LB. CHICKEN	12-LB. TURKEY
Bread cubes	1 quart	3 quarts
Giblets		
Chopped onion	2 tablespoons	6 tablespoons
Chopped celery	¼ cup	¾ cup
Butter or margarine	¼ cup	¾ cup
Salt	1 teaspoon	1 tablespoon
Pepper	⅛ teaspoon	¼ teaspoon
Poultry seasoning	¼ teaspoon	¾ teaspoon
Broth	½ cup	1½ cups

pinch of pepper, 2 cups of chopped celery, pulp and grated rind of 1 orange, and only enough water to moisten lightly. You may add coarse chopped pecans for the final touch, and serve duck with a garnish of orange.

DON'T RISK FOOD POISONING

Stuff bird just before roasting. Don't stuff ahead of time, not even if you are going to refrigerate or freeze it.

Scoop out leftover stuffing from a leftover roast chicken or turkey and refrigerate each separately, in covered dishes or wrapped in waxed paper or aluminum foil. Stuffing should be used within two days. Fowl may be kept four to five days or longer if properly wrapped and frozen.

Never stuff a chicken or turkey with warm stuffing, then hold overnight before roasting.

Never let gravy, dressing, or cooked poultry stand at room temperature for even a few hours. Refrigerate them right after finishing the meal.

Never partially roast a large turkey one day, then leave it out of the refrigerator overnight to be completed the following day. If need be, get up early and put it in the oven before breakfast if you want to serve it at noon.

TIPS FOR ENJOYING POULTRY

Why not experiment with herbs? An easy trick is to tie together several large sprigs of parsley, a small sprig of tarragon, and one of thyme. Then drop this bouquet into a kettle of soup or stew, in fact add it to any meat or fowl dish that is cooked by moist heat. Or try putting a herb bouquet into the cavity of a roasting chicken. It does wonderful flavor things to the meat and eliminates the need for stuffing the chicken.

Use a cigarette lighter to singe pinfeathers left on dressed poultry. Result is neater, safer, quicker, and singeing that doesn't smudge the skin of the fowl.

Place a cored apple inside a roast chicken to keep meat moist and to add piquancy to flavor.

Decorating Christmas turkeys.
Fringe two pieces of white or pink
tissue paper or aluminum foil and
wrap unfringed part around end of
bird's legs. Foil will remain in
place. Fasten paper fringe with fine
thread of matching color.

**If turkey is too large for your plat-
ter,** wrap a tray with aluminum foil
and use it for serving.

If leftover turkey is too big for
your refrigerator, disjoint it, wrap
loosely, and refrigerate.

Cover leftover refrigerated chicken.
Its delicate flavor is lost and absorbs other food flavors easily.
Don't try to keep cooked poultry
more than a few days. Use it up as
soon as possible in interesting leftover dishes, or wrap and freeze it.

3

CARVE LIKE A CONNOISSEUR

It's an art—but here are the ABC's that make it simple

Carving skillfully takes a little practice, but it's neither tricky nor hard. And it's worth a little practicing, because when a perfectly cooked meat is properly carved, it is served at its appetizing best.

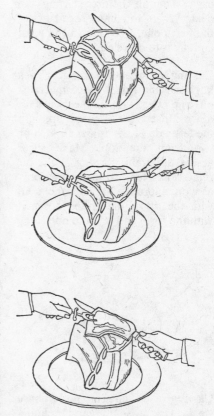

A sharp knife is the first requisite of good carving. Forged carbon steel makes the best, sharpest knife blades, according to chefs and gourmets, but many people prefer good-quality stainless steel because of its easier upkeep. Stainless steel blades do not rust (carbon steel knives must be dried immediately after being washed *because they do rust*) and they rarely need sharpening. Carbon steel blades, when sharp, are sharper than stainless blades, but should be sharpened each time they're used. Sharpen them on a "steel"—a rod of rough-surfaced steel fitted into a handle.

Carving a standing rib roast. It is best to have the backbone loosened by the butcher and then removed in

Acknowledgment is gratefully made to the National Livestock and Meat Board for providing graphic material on which some of the illustrations in this chapter are based.

the kitchen after roasting. Use a large carving knife. Set the roast on the platter as illustrated, rib bones to the left, large end away from carver. Insert fork, guard up, between two top rib bones. Cut slices from outer fat edge to bones, making slices no thicker than ¼ inch.

Free each slice by running the point of the knife along the edge where the meat joins, the bone, and lift each slice off before starting the next. When you have sliced below the first bone, free it from the roast and lay it to one side.

Carving a rolled rib roast. Use a large carving knife. Place the roast on a platter with the cut surface down. Insert fork, guard up, into the left side of the roast, an inch or two from the top. Make slices across the grain, starting at the far right side. Remove each cord only as you approach it. Cut the cord with the tip of the knife, loosen it with the fork, and lay it to one side.

Carving a T-bone or porterhouse steak. Use a small carving knife. Place steak on platter with flank (tail of steak) at carver's left. Cut

around the T-bone to free it from the meat. Lay the bone to one side. Cut clear across the steak, making uniform wedge-shaped portions. Cut the flank into serving pieces. In serving, place on each plate a piece of the larger or top muscle, a piece of tenderloin, and, if desired, a piece of the flank.

Carving a blade-bone pot roast. Use a small carving knife. With the point of the knife, cut around the blade bone and remove it. Trim off other bones. If the roast is thin, slice across muscles. For thicker roasts, turn the section on its side and carve across the grain.

Carving a whole ham. Bring the ham to the table with the "decorated" side up and the shank to the carver's right. The leg bone divides the ham into two unequal portions. The thick or chunky side of the ham will yield larger, more attractive slices called "horseshoe" slices. In order to carve these easily, first cut several lengthwise slices off the thinner side to form a base on which to rest the ham during carving.

Now turn the ham on this base and cut a small wedge-shaped piece from the shank end (where the bone protrudes). This cut should be made just inside the knuckle. Then cut slices right down to bone. When a sufficient number of slices has been cut, slip the knife in at the wedge and cut along the bone to free all of the horseshoe slices at once. For more servings, turn the ham over to its original position and cut slices to the bone.

Carving a pork loin roast. Have the backbone loosened from the roast at market. When you take the roast out of the oven, remove the backbone before sending the roast to the table. Place the roast on the platter with the rib ends up, and rib side of the roast in front of the carver. In-

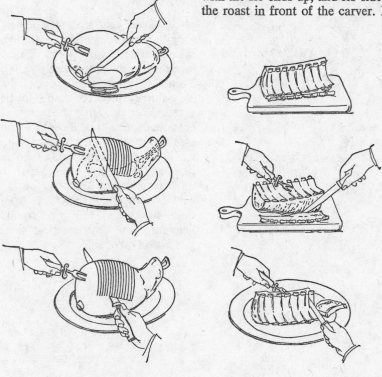

sert fork in the top of the roast. Slice downward between the ribs, to make chop-sized servings. If the loin roast is a large one, it is possible to serve a boneless slice between each rib.

Carving a roast leg of lamb. Bring the lamb to the table on a platter with the shank to the carver's right.

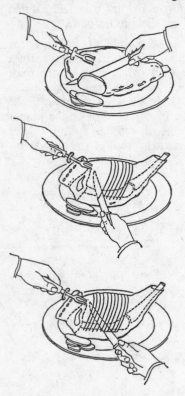

Cut two or three slices lengthwise from the near side. This will form a base to make carving easier.

Turn the meat onto the base and, starting at the shank end, cut slices perpendicularly down to the bone, as shown in the illustration.

Free the slices by cutting under them, following the top of the shank bone. Lift the slices out, transferring them to the platter.

How to carve fowl. Carver places platter so neck of bird is to his left, and sticks fork astride breastbone. Leg and thigh bone are separated from nearest side by cutting at thigh joint (1), pressing leg away from body. With carving fork still in place, carver next separates nearest wing in same manner as he did leg, cutting around wing joint (2) to locate exact dividing point of joint. Then he severs wing completely. Now breast meat is ready to be sliced. Start at angle near tip of breastbone. Cut thin slices of white meat, always working toward joint where wing was removed, as shown in illustration (3). Then separate thigh from leg at joint (4); in the case of turkey, cut thin slices from these two pieces (5). For second helpings, turn platter, repeat same process on other side.

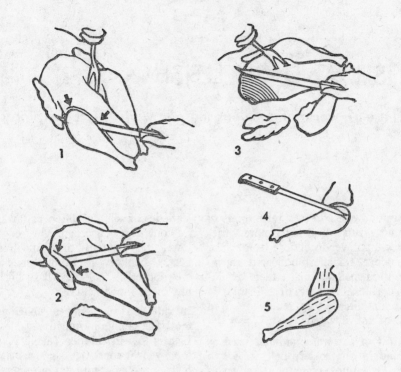

4

FISH AND SHELLFISH

There's a world of delicious seafood waiting to be explored

Seafood can add new taste treats to your menus. You have more varieties than ever to choose from, since modern transportation and refrigeration methods make them available at local markets or fish stores in communities far removed from their native waters.

Most of the water animals used as food in our society belong to two major groups, commonly known as fish and shellfish. The fish, both fresh- and salt-water varieties, are vertebrates—that is, have backbones. They are covered with scales or, occasionally, with just a scaly-looking skin. Shellfish are invertebrates—that is, they lack backbones but are covered with some type of shell.

The shellfish we eat belong to two major subgroups—mollusks and crustaceans. Mollusks, such as clams and oysters, are very soft in their body and are protected by hard shells. The crustaceans, such as lobsters, crabs, shrimps, and crayfish, are covered by segmented, crustlike shells.

Varieties of seafood differ, as far as fat content is concerned. Most have lower fat content than medium beef. Exceptions are salmon, mackerel, butterfish, catfish. All shellfish are low in fat content.

In addition to being a delicious food, fish is high in nutritive values. Fish is low in calories (a big plus for weight-conscious gourmets), high in protein, and high in mineral content. This varies from fish to fish, but most fish are mineral-rich, notably in calcium, phosphorus, copper, and iron. Besides this, fish with a relatively high fat content, like salmon or mackerel, contain some vitamins A and D.

BUYING SEAFOOD

Perhaps even more than with meat, your success in serving tasty seafood depends first upon your buying skill. Fish aren't only seasonal but also regional to some extent. Many varieties are shipped only into the large markets such as New York, Chicago, New Orleans, and San Francisco. In other areas you'll always find the seven favorites— flounder, haddock, mackerel, cod, halibut, ocean perch, and whiting— plus fish from nearby lakes, rivers, bays, or oceans, and a variety of frozen fish and shellfish. As the demand for other varieties increases, they'll become available, so ask for them in your grocery market or at your fish dealer's.

Local descriptive terms add to the confusion in buying fish. To help you in buying, here are individual fish descriptions and market forms:

Whole or round fish. Marketed just as it comes from the water. Fish sold this way must be scaled or skinned, eviscerated, and head, tail, and fins removed, if desired, before cooking.

Drawn fish. Marketed with the entrails removed. Fish must be scaled or skinned and head, tail, and fins removed, if desired, before cooking.

Dressed fish. Marketed scaled and eviscerated, usually with head, tail, and fins removed. These are ready to cook as purchased or, if large, can be split.

Steaks. These are slices, cut crosswise, of larger dressed fish. They vary from ½ to 1½ inches in thickness and are ready to cook as purchased. Chunks are pieces cut from large dressed fish. They vary in size and weight and are usually used for poaching or steaming. They are also usually cut to order.

Fillets. These are practically boneless pieces cut from the sides of fish. They are ready for cooking.

Butterfly fillets. They are two sides of a fish cut away from the backbone but held together by the flesh of the underside of the fish. They are ready for cooking.

Cured fish. Many salt- and freshwater fish are cured by smoking, drying, salting, or pickling in brine. Smoked and dried fish are generally split. Salted and pickled fish are available whole, split, or cut into small pieces.

Cold smoked fish such as finnan haddie and kippered herring are cured and partially dried at about 90° F. for a few hours. These will keep only a short time unless frozen. Cold smoked fish that are processed for a longer time and are drier such as boneless herring will keep longer.

Hot smoked fish are smoked at temperatures from 150° F. to 200° F. and are partially or wholly cooked. They will keep for only a short time unless frozen. Whitefish, lake herring, lake trout, buffalo fish, eels, and sturgeon are typical fish that are hot-smoked. The most popular is herring, called bloater in some areas and buckling in others.

Dried fish may be either air- or heat-dried. Thoroughly dried, salted or not, fish will keep indefinitely. But it must be rehydrated before using. Haddock, cod, hake, pollock, and cusk are fish that are usually dried.

Salted fish is either dry-salted or brine-cured. Brine-cured fish, such as herring, is ready for eating after having been soaked in fresh water. Or it may be pickled.

When buying fresh fish, watch for these signs of real freshness:

Eyes—bright, clear, full, transparent, and somewhat protruding. The eyes of stale fish often are cloudy or pink and somewhat sunken.

Skin—shiny and full-colored. Stale fishskin looks faded.

Gills—red and clean-looking. Gills of stale fish are gray, brownish, or greenish.

Flesh—firm and adhering to the bones.

Odor—fresh. "Fishy" odor associated with fish only develops as fish is stored. It should never be disagreeably strong.

Frozen fish have quality standards too:

Odor—Little or no odor. Poor quality frozen fish has strong fishy odor.

Flesh—solidly frozen with no discoloration or browning. Fish thawed and refrozen is usually poor in quality.

Wrapping—steaks and fillets should be wrapped in moistureproof material with little or no air space between fish and wrapping.

Glazing—whole fish in the round or dressed are often frozen with a glaze of ice to prevent drying and freezer burn. This glaze should be intact.

Shellfish—whether being bought live, fresh, or frozen—present special requirements depending on the variety:

Lobsters when bought alive should show movement of the legs and the tail should curl under the body. When cooked in the shell, lobster should be bright red in color and without strong or disagreeable odor. Cooked meat should be white, sweet-smelling, and always held or displayed on ice.

Lobster tails (rock lobster or spiny) are usually sold frozen. They are sections of ocean crayfish. The meat should be whitish, hard-frozen, and odorless.

Crabs should be alive in the shell as hard-shell the year around, or alive in the shell as soft-shell in warm months only. In-the-shell crabs should show movement of the legs if bought alive. When cooked in the shell, they should be bright red in color and without disagreeable odor. Cooked meat should be milky white, sweet-smelling, and always held or displayed on ice.

Crab meat and lobster meat are sold fresh cooked in pry-open cans, useful in quick main dishes as well as in salads.

Shrimp should have firm meat texture, mild odor. Shells are grayish green, pinkish tan, or pink, depending on variety. "Green" shrimp is a market term for shrimps that have not been cooked. Shrimp are usually priced according to size, the larger ones higher in price. Size, however, does not affect quality.

Scallops are sold shucked, fresh or frozen. Fresh sea scallops are white, larger and less expensive than bay scallops, which are creamy, light tan, or pinkish in color. They should have a sweet, pleasant odor and be practically free of liquid.

Oysters should be alive in the shell, tightly closed. Gaping shells that do not close when tapped indicate dead oysters that should be discarded. Shucked oysters should be creamy in color, plump, with clear

liquor, and free from pieces of shell. The liquor should not exceed ten per cent by weight of the total.

Clams should be alive in the shell. If the shell is open, it should close tightly when tapped. Discard any clams that remain open. Shucked clams should be creamy in color, plump, with clear liquor, and free form pieces of shell.

Mussels should be alive in their shells, which should be closed—or at least the shells should close tightly when tapped. Shucked mussels are not sold in fish stores but may be bought in cans.

QUANTITIES TO BUY

FISH (Fresh or Frozen)		SHELLFISH		
FORM	APPROXIMATE AMOUNT TO BUY PER SERVING	SHELLFISH	FORM	APPROXIMATE AMOUNT TO BUY PER SERVING
Whole fish	1 lb.	Clams	In shell	6
Drawn	¾ lb.		Steamers	9 to 12
Dressed	½ lb.		Shucked	⅓ pint
Steak	⅓ lb.	Crabs (soft-shell)	Live	2 to 3 (depending on size)
Chunks	⅓ lb.			
Fillets	¼ to ⅓ lb.	Crabs (hard-shell)	Live	3 to 12
			Cooked meat	¼ lb.
		Lobsters	Live	1 lb.
			Cooked meat	⅛ to ¼ lb.
		Lobster tails		1 per serving (about ½ lb.)
		Mussels	In shell	⅓ lb.
		Oysters	In shell	6
			Shucked	⅓ pint
		Scallops	Shucked	¼ to ⅓ lb.
		Shrimps	Headless	⅓ lb.
			Cooked, shelled, cleaned	¼ lb.

STORING SEAFOOD

Keep fresh fish fresh. Fresh fish is tastiest when eaten soon after you bring it home. Flavor decreases in a few days, even when fish stays otherwise fresh. Refrigerate to keep but do not freeze store-purchased fresh fish.

Keep frozen fish frozen. Frozen fish should be stored in the freezing compartment of your refrigerator or in your home freezer until ready to use. Once thawed, don't refreeze frozen fish. Don't thaw completely before preparing, only enough to let outside lose its icy rigidity. Flavor drains away with melting ice.

Shellfish: Treat the same as fish. Keep live shellfish in the refrigerator at medium temperature but do not place in water.

When the family fisherman or fisherwoman brings home more fish than you can use conveniently, choose what you want to cook immediately, then freeze the rest.

COOKING SEAFOOD

Fish differs from meat. Though fish is protein food, its water content is higher than that of meat and its extractives are lower. This means that the flavor of fish is delicate. Meat cookery is more concerned with tenderness and the development of flavor. Fish and some shellfish are already tender, so cooking must develop flavor.

Don't turn fish fillets while broiling. Place fish fillets or shellfish, such as shrimps, scallops, split lobsters, or spiny lobsters, on greased preheated broiler rack, 3 to 5 inches from heat source. Brush with butter or margarine. Sprinkle with salt and pepper. Broil 5 to 10 minutes, without turning, until fish flakes easily when pierced with a fork or until shellfish is tender. Well-broiled fish or shellfish is golden brown, juicy, and tender. Use a spatula or pancake turner to place fish on platter and serve immediately after broiling.

Turn thick steaks and whole fish once, when broiling. Follow directions for fillets, broiling 3 to 8 minutes before turning, depending on thickness of fish. Brush with melted butter after turning, sprinkle with seasonings, and broil second side.

Broil fish with imagination. Place tomatoes, mushroom caps, and baked potatoes, split in half and topped with cheese, in broiler pan around your fish. Broil all to a beautiful color picture.

Metal foil boats help eliminate cleaning chores after boiling and baking, help you remove fish unbroken from pan.

Off with its head? Only after baking. If the head is cut off before baking fish, the cut end dries and toughens. Leaving the head on during baking seals in the flavor and juices and shortens cooking time.

How to bake fish. Bake at 350° F. 11 to 19 minutes per pound (for large fish) or 1½ to 2 minutes per ounce for tiny fish. Bake only until fish flakes easily. Then serve at once.

To stuff fish, have fish (3 pounds or more in weight) pocketed for stuffing. Rub inside with salt and pepper. Pack stuffing of your choice lightly into pocket. Use fairly dry and savory stuffings. Fasten openings with strong toothpicks or skewers and lace with white cord. Place fish on greased rack or foil in shallow baking pan. Brush with melted butter and season well. Bake according to directions given above for baked fish.

How to poach fish. Tie fish (fillets, steaks, chunks, split or whole fish) in cheesecloth. Bring Court Bouillon (see recipe, below) to simmer in pan. Lower fish into pan and cover. Simmer until fish is done, 8 to 16 minutes per pound, depending upon thickness and variety of fish. Drain and remove cheesecloth. Well-cooked fish flakes easily when pierced with fork. Serve hot or cold with sauces.

Court Bouillon. Melt a tablespoon of butter or margarine in large saucepan that has tight-fitting cover. In the butter sauté for 10 minutes 1 cup chopped onion, 2 tablespoons chopped green pepper, ¼ cup chopped celery. Add 5 cups water, 1 tablespoon chopped parsley, 2 teaspoons salt, 2 peppercorns, 2 whole cloves, 1 bay leaf, and 2 tablespoons lemon juice. Bring to boil. Then reduce heat and simmer 30 minutes. Strain. May be used for several poachings within a few days.

"Full steam ahead." Fill kettle with enough boiling water to make depth of 2 inches. Tie fish in cheesecloth and place on rack in kettle. Steam until fish flakes easily. Place thin fillets, which tend to fall apart when poached, on foil-covered rack, wrap fish and rack in cheesecloth, and lower into pan.

What causes the fish odor isn't so much the fish itself as the smoking fat. Solution: Be careful to keep the frying fat from reaching the smoking point. (A fat thermometer is surest way to control fat temperature when deep-fat frying.)

For pan-frying, dip fillets, steaks, split or whole small fish, or shellfish into milk or mixture of beaten egg and 2 tablespoons water and then roll in bread or cracker crumbs. Fry on both sides until light brown. And watch that fat! For "sauté meunière," leave out the bread crumbs.

To sauté fish, do not coat but fry in melted butter or margarine, over moderate heat to be sure fat does not burn. Turn only once. Pour pan drippings over fish before serving.

How to deep-fat-fry fish and shellfish. Dip fillets, whole small fish, or shellfish (especially clams, oysters, shrimps, or scallops) into a prepared batter of your choice or a mixture of 1 beaten egg and 2 tablespoons water or milk. Then coat with bread or cracker crumbs, seasoned flour, or a combination of flour and corn meal. (Dip and coat twice if you want a thick crust.) Heat fat in heavy kettle or electric fryer to 365° F. to 375° F. (If you haven't a fat thermometer, a 1-inch cube of white bread browns in 1 minute when fat is right temperature for deep-fat frying.) Place fish in frying basket and lower, a few pieces at a time, into hot fat. Fry 2 to 5 minutes, or until golden brown, turning once. Be sure that fat does not smoke while you deep-fat-fry.

How to plank fish. Brush hardwood plank (family size, or several small planks for individual service) with melted butter or margarine. Lay split fish, skin side down, on plank. Brush fish with melted butter or margarine and sprinkle with salt and pepper. Bake at 350° F. until fish flakes. Baking time varies with size and kind of fish. Prepare vegetables, garnishes, and mashed potatoes while fish bakes. Place potatoes in pastry bag. Remove fish from oven. Flute potatoes around fish in attractive design, leaving room for vegetables and garnishes to be added later. Return plank to oven and bake 10 minutes or until potatoes are lightly browned. Remove from oven, add hot vegetables, such as string beans, tomato slices, peas, lima beans, and garnish with water cress, parsley, capers, etc. Serve at once. Protect your table by placing plank on a trivet or hot pad.

Smellproof baking can be yours if you follow this simple tip. Individ-ual packets of fish and vegetables are best baked in aluminum foil. Each packet is a serving. Place about ⅓ pound frozen cod, had-dock, or sole fillets on aluminum foil square, the fish defrosted just enough to get your knife through it to cut portions. Add tiny peeled or lightly parboiled onions, narrow strips of raw carrot, tablespoon of melted butter or margarine, salt and pepper, and a little lemon juice. Top with a sprinkling of parsley. Bring up edges of foil, double-fold for tight-sealed, loose-fitting wrapping. Place on pan or cookie sheet in preheated oven. Bake at 425° F. for about 40 minutes. Not a smell in the kitchen. You get your first whiff—and a taste-tempting delightful one—when you open your packet to eat.

COOKING SHELLFISH

Know the clam family. Steamers are the largest of the clam family. The chowder clam is prepared steamed in the shell with a butter-base sauce, unshelled and fried, or in soup (chowder or broth). Cherrystones are smaller and hard, usually served on the half shell. They also can be successfully steamed. Littleneck is the smallest clam, used mostly in clam cocktails and clam fritters.

Last in is the oyster. In any cooked oyster dish, oyster is the last ingredient to add. Usually you stew or fry oysters. To stew: best when done with the double boiler method, stewing over boiling water until the edges curl. To fry: give it just 1 minute on each side.

Many oyster fans like oyster best when served raw on the half shell. Oysters are easy to remove from shells if you first soak them in carbonated water. After five minutes of this "effervescent bath," oyster muscles relax and shells open without effort.

Scallops can be so-o-o tender. Don't overcook them. This shellfish is chiefly for sautéing or broiling.

To cook lobster alive, thrust it headfirst into boiling water, using 3 quarts of water with 3 tablespoons of salt for a one-pounder. Cover and simmer 10 minutes if a one-pounder, 3 more minutes for each additional pound. When cool enough to handle, split front from head to tail and force the two halves apart by hand. Take out intestinal vein that runs the length of the tail. Serve with dunking dish of melted butter flavored with drops of lemon juice or with garlic.

Shrimp is easy. Cook and serve cold as shrimp cocktail or salad, serve as curry or casserole dish, combined with rice and vegetables. Fry with or without bread-crumb coating, grill, or bake—but don't overcook. If you buy canned shrimps, soak in ice water for an hour and they'll taste better than fresh from the can.

Deep-fry soft-shell crabs. Dip dressed crabs in beaten egg and roll in a mixture of half corn meal, half flour. Drop crabs, in pairs, into hot fat, deep enough so crabs float as they fry. Fry a few moments, watching over them with care so you don't let them fry past a light brown. Remember, they're tender.

SOME HINTS FOR ENJOYING SEAFOOD

The fish that didn't get away. Those fish needn't be so slippery when you handle them if you first dip your fingers in salt.

Lean fish is clean fish (fat fish, too) and requires only a dip in salt cold water and wiping dry. Don't hold fish or sea food under running water.

"Butter up" your fish by using butter generously in cooking and in fish sauces. Butter brings out the best in every one of them.

Rare tidbit in rarebit: Leftover or canned sea food makes a welcome rarebit difference. Add tomato juice instead of milk and see for yourself.

Fish stock plus gelatin equals aspic. This is a jelly made from fish stock. Stock is boiled down enough to become firm when cold, then is thickened with gelatin. Adds festive touch to salads, side dishes, lunches.

In addition to the fish and shellfish described here, there are many other aquatic inhabitants that many peoples, especially in other parts of the world, enjoy eating. Eels, to name one, are highly prized and make tasty fare: all you need do is get over any prejudices about eels' appearance and reputation. Still another variety of seafood popular among many peoples is squid. There are several ways of serving them but one of the tastiest is to deep fry them like onion rings. Squid are easily cleaned (and virtually odorless). When clean, the hollow body may be sliced in ½–¾-inch bands; these are then tossed in a lightly seasoned flour and placed gently in hot cooking oil; fry 15–20 minutes, remove and drain excess fat, and serve with slice of lemon.

5

VEGETABLES

All you need to know about wasteless buying, storing, preparing, and serving

Careful selection of fresh foods makes all the difference in what your table gains and your wallet loses, and nowhere is this truer than with buying vegetables. When you want vegetables just right—fresh, solid, ripe, attractive—pay for the best: when you start throwing away parts of your "bargain" buys, you are probably losing most of the pennies you saved.

But if the vegetables are to be cooked or prepared in some way, if the appearance doesn't count, perhaps you should look around for cheaper varieties. Vegetable stands sometimes set aside "seconds," slightly bruised vegetables or those that have passed their prime. If the price is considerably less, these may be real bargains.

Refrigerator can revive bargain vegetables. Many food dealers will sell slightly wilted leafy vegetables at reduced price. Before storing, wash them; place in crisper drawer while still moist. Process often restores crispness completely.

Don't throw away beet tops. They are delicious and are rich in vitamins and minerals, especially iron.

Many people discard celery tops. Chop and use them in salads, soups, stuffings, sandwich spreads, and stews. They add flavor.

Don't buy squishy squash. Save money on squash. Select only squash that is heavy for its size, with a clear complexion and a firm, smooth rind. Blemishes and scars and soft rinds may mean you're wasting your money.

Quality counts. In choosing fruits and vegetables for freezing, buy the best. Properly packaged, you get out of the freezer exactly what you put into it. Freezing does not improve low-grade foods.

STORING VEGETABLES

The storing story. Generally, fresh green vegetables are most safely stored in the refrigerator if not used the same day you bring them home. Still there are a few little tricks to know:

Certain vegetables keep better if stored "as is." Peas and lima beans should be stored in the pod and corn in the husk (to preserve full food value and prevent shriveling).

Keep corn on the cob fresh. When you have to keep it a day or longer before serving, corn on the cob can be kept juicy and fresh in this way: Slice a small piece off the stalk end and stand ears in a pan containing an inch of water. Let the outside leaves stay on.

Goes to their heads. The tops of carrots, beets, turnips, and parsnips should be cut off before the vegetables are stored. The tops draw the moisture and food value from the roots, leaving them wilted and limp.

Keeping parsley fresh. Place in a fruit jar, close lid tight, and keep in the refrigerator.

FREEZING VEGETABLES

To freeze or not to freeze, that is the question. Each vegetable reacts in a different way. It's worth knowing for sure.

Let the government help you. Some varieties of vegetables and fruits are better adapted to freezing than others. When planting a garden or buying vegetables for freezing, consult Agricultural Extension Service Department at your state university to learn about varieties grown in your locality that are considered best for freezing.

Do not freeze lettuce, celery, raw tomatoes or carrots. They lose crispness when frozen.

To prepare vegetables for freezing, first sort, then clean and wash in cold water. Work with quantities of no more than a pound at a time. After washing, scald or steam. Either method of heating prevents loss of flavor, color, and texture (because it retards action of enzymes).

Get 'em while they're young. With few exceptions (such as winter squash and eggplant), buy "young" vegetables, before their starch content has developed. Prepare for freezing immediately after harvest or purchase. If this is impossible, store in refrigerator, but not for more than eight hours.

Test corn before freezing. Corn loses flavor rapidly after picking and must be prepared for freezing as soon after harvest as possible. Choose only ears of best maturity and variety. Quality can be determined by testing kernels. Kernels should fill the ear and their "milk" should be thin and sweet, not starchy. Ears chosen for corn on the cob should be even less mature.

Newest wrinkle in freezing corn on the cob. Remove husks from corn and wrap each ear individually in heavyweight freezer aluminum foil. Place wrapped ears in rapidly boiling water and blanch eight minutes. Chill in the refrigerator for an hour. Freeze as usual. To reheat after freezing, place in cold water directly from freezer, then bring to the boiling point. In this way corn thaws while water is heating. (If corn is to be held only one or two months it can be wrapped in lightweight aluminum foil.)

PREPARING VEGETABLES

When washing green vegetables (spinach, kale, broccoli, etc.), add salt to the water and allow to soak for a few minutes. Any foreign matter clinging to them will float to surface.

Laundering spinach. You'll save many, many washings if you soak spinach first in salt water. (P.S. If you like your spinach with a nice, fresh green color, cook it uncovered, in only the water that clings to the leaves after the final rinse.)

Wash leafy vegetables, such as spinach, just before cooking. Add no water; enough clings to the leaves, from washing water, to cook them.

Clean newly dug garden vegetables easily. Place in wire egg-gathering basket and spray with garden hose. Basket holds generous supply of vegetables.

How to "chop" parsley. Away with the tedious old wooden bowl and chopping tool. Separate tufts from stems. Either cut the parsley with one of the new patented cutters or gather it firmly in the left hand, cutting through it with a knife or scissors until it is very fine.

You'll grate carrots without sustaining wounds if you leave at least an inch of the green tops on. Use them as handles and you can grate the vegetable with ease. If you buy the kind of carrot that is packaged without tops, "snack" between meals on the last half-inch bit of raw carrot. It's loaded with vitamin A and has practically no calories. You won't gain an ounce if you eat it.

To extract juice from an onion. Cut a slice and scrape the onion over the finest part of your grater. Or simply scrape a sharp knife across the cut edge, working over a small bowl. You'll soon have that teaspoonful that many recipes call for. Skip the bowl, if you have a sense of adventure, and scrape the juice right into the mixture that calls for onion juice. A few drops more or less don't matter and you save washing one dish.

Know your onions and shed no tears. Next time you slice onions, spear a 1-inch chunk of bread on the point of your paring knife before peeling. Bread absorbs those tear-jerking fumes.

Beets peel easily if they are dipped in cold water immediately after they are boiled. Don't soak 'em, though. They bleed easily. And remember to leave about an inch of stem on beets when you cook them. Cut too close, they really bleed.

For crisp celery, immerse in ice-cold water, with a couple of ice cubes added for good measure, for a few moments before serving.

SALADS

Chances are no salad, however "mixed," will contain all twenty-four basic greens that make up the salad family. But there they are, and one way or another they are all being used in healthful, wonderful green salads.

Roll call. Here are their names: Four kinds of lettuce (iceberg, Boston, leaf, bibb); four kinds of cabbage (savoy, Chinese, green, red); escarole, romaine, chicory, French endive; watercress, mustard greens, dandelion greens, beet greens, field salad, nasturtium leaves, spinach, kale, celery tops, sour grass, turnip greens, finocchi.

You'll serve more salads if you store greens, washed and ready to use, in your refrigerator crisper or wrapped in aluminum foil. Ready enough greens to last a week to ten days by draining them and sealing them into envelopes of foil. They'll remain crisp and garden-fresh for as long as they last and will always be ready for tossing into delicious salad mixes.

Let's talk lettuce. Most frequently used in green salads, it is important to pick out crisp, young, perky heads. Remove outside leaves (but don't throw them away). Cut out core, hold core end under cold running water until leaves are forced apart by water pressure. Shake dry, by hand, on a cake rack or in lettuce basket. Cut or break into shreds. Chill and store in foil. Do not mix ahead of serving. Prepare dressing; do your tossing at the table. All ingredients and serving utensils should preferably be chilled.

Save outer leaves. While salad greens must be kept crisp for last-minute serving, whether as salad, trimming, or in sandwiches, the less crisp outer leaves should not be wasted. Though not as crisp as the inner leaves, they are rich in vitamins and minerals. Unless they are bruised, save them, wash them, and try to liven them up by placing them in a bowl of water to which lemon juice has been added. Then dry leaves and, with kitchen shears, shred right into the salad bowl.

Salads are exciting with non-green extras mixed in or parading on top. Here are a few colorful ideas:

Tomatoes are first choice. Add them at the last minute, so they won't thin dressing. Also, cut them in vertical slices, the way the French do. Keeps more juice in.

Radish roses are most decorative, but thin slices or coarse shreddings perk up salads too.

Celery stalks lend themselves to a variety of strips, depending on whether you cut them thin, diagonal, or lengthwise; or fringe both ends, soak them in ice water, and turn them into celery curls.

Carrots curl around your finger if the shaving is thin. Use a vegetable parer for thin shavings. They chill, in ice water, and stay curled better than a permanent wave.

Mushroom disks are a delicacy. Use fresh, raw, whole, unpeeled, washed, young mushrooms, and slice either lengthwise or crosswise.

Drained canned whole or sliced mushrooms are fine, too, for salads.

Raw cauliflower (or broccoli) yields beautiful, delicious, tiny flowerets. Or slice bigger flowerets into wafer-thin fans.

Cucumber slices for cool summer salads are a natural. Or, to be more festive still, make cucumber curls by slicing unpeeled cucumbers lengthwise, very thin, with a potato or vegetable parer. Spread with cream-cheese spread and roll up jelly-roll fashion. Fasten ends with colored toothpicks. Chill until ready to serve.

Dress up your dressing. Dressing can be bought all prepared. But if you are prepared to mix your own, here's how: French dressing takes one part vinegar or lemon juice to three parts salad oil. After that let it be as spicy as your imagination. If you like just a soupçon—a touch —of garlic, place a small peeled clove of it in a glass measuring cup with a teaspoon of salt. Crush until the garlic is absorbed in the salt. Add ¼ teaspoon dry mustard, large dashes of pepper and paprika, a teaspoon of herb salad seasoning, such as tarragon, basil, dill, chervil, or rosemary. Blend, cover tightly, and chill.

Toss your salad in any kind of bowl —china, glass, earthenware, or a regular wooden salad bowl. Don't soak your wooden salad bowl. Just rinse quickly in clear lukewarm water. Wipe dry with a lint-free tea towel and store in a dry place. In time, garlic and other flavorings from your salads will season the wooden bowl.

MOLDED SALADS

What do all molded salads have in common? Gelatin, of course. How to use it? Simple. Dissolve a package of gelatin (flavored or add your own flavoring) in water, according to package directions. When slightly thickened, fold in your cooked vegetables (and/or fruits). Pour into molds. Chill until firm. Unmold and serve.

Salad molds are healthful. There are two reasons: First, the food value from the vegetables you put in. Second, gelatin is mostly protein.

Add flavor to bland vegetables before adding to gelatin mold (for fruits, add dash of lemon juice, a little salt, a sprinkling of sugar). Heighten vegetable flavors with few teaspoons vinegar, a little salt, some scraped onion, bit of celery seed. Allow to marinate while preparing gelatin.

When using vegetables, choose tart-flavored gelatin, such as lemon or lime. Use the flavor that flatters other ingredients.

Make unmolding easy. Try lightly greasing the inside of the mold with mayonnaise. When you're ready to serve it, presto! the salad slides right out.

Shortcut to tomato aspic. Dissolve one package lemon-flavored gelatin in a pint of hot tomato juice. To speed up chilling process, dissolve gelatin in a cup of heated tomato juice, then add remainder of juice cold.

POTATOES

Cooked potatoes should not be frozen in liquid. They become mushy and grainy, so leave them out of frozen stews and meat pies or casseroles. Mashed and stuffed potatoes, however, can be frozen. For mashed potatoes, cook as usual, but mash through ricer so there will be as little air in mixture as possible; add 1 tablespoon butter for each pound of potatoes used, then add milk as needed. Season with salt and pepper. (Ricer: utensil with small holes through which vegetable is pressed.)

Get the edge on potato slicing. If you dip a sharp knife in boiling-hot water, the potatoes will slice more easily. But if you're lucky you have a slicing attachment with your electric mixer and simply feed the medium-size, whole or cut-up large potatoes into the slicing apparatus. You can also use the slicing side of a four-sided upright grater-slicer.

Preserve full nutritive value of potatoes by cooking them in their skins. Boil in salted water, 2 to 3 teaspoons salt to quart of water. Try parboiling them in salted water for 15 minutes. Then dry as you would mashed potatoes—after you've drained off the water—over low heat, shaking the pan so potatoes dry on all sides. Place around oven roast of any kind during the last hour of roasting, basting several times with pan drippings. You're in for a taste treat if you haven't tried this nutty-flavored way to get full taste and nutritive value from potatoes with their jackets left on.

Milk in boiled potatoes. Add a little milk to the water in which you boil potatoes. Improves tastiness immensely, prevents them also from turning dark. Another way to keep potatoes white is to add a teaspoon of vinegar to the cooking water.

Mashed sweet potato will extend three thin slices of boiled ham to serve lunch to six people. Add to the potato a few finely chopped nuts, some real mayonnaise, and a beaten egg. Roll up this filling in ham slices and bake, surrounded by a little pineapple or other fruit juice. Cut the finished ham rolls in two when ready to serve.

Baked potato gets healthy complexion. When potato skins are well washed and dried, then rubbed with cooking oil or bacon grease and thoroughly pricked with a fork before retiring to the oven, potatoes come out beautifully brown and crisp when baked. That's all there is to it. They can go right on the oven racks while they bake.

Even easier way to bake potatoes. Prepare them as directed above and then place them in oven in muffin tins. It's a handy time-saver that prevents burned fingers when you take out the finished potatoes. Use a pot holder, of course, to remove the muffin tin filled with baked potatoes.

Baked potatoes in half the time. Parboil them about five minutes before draining and drying potatoes and putting them into the oven, and they'll bake in about half the usual time.

For a party look, wrap scrubbed baking potatoes in foil, pop them into the oven, and bake. Serve them right in their shining jackets, cutting a crisscross in the top and squeezing potatoes to fluff up. Add a generous pat of butter to each and a sprinkling of paprika to complete the festive look.

Barbecue-baked potatoes. Wrap scrubbed, whole, well-pricked, medium-size potatoes, thoroughly dry, in aluminum foil. Prick foil with the tines of a fork to allow for escape of steam. Bake over the grill an hour or more, until potatoes are tender when tested with a knife, turning occasionally to bake uniformly. Serve with salt, ground black pepper, and lots of butter or margarine.

LEGUMES

Get acquainted first. Legumes are members of the pulse family, botanically, the seeds of which are commonly classed as vegetables. Beans to you and me: navy or pea, lima, kidney, black, chili, pinto, soy; Italian fava and black-eye; colorful cranberry beans, black-eye peas, lentils; and a variety of dried peas both whole and split, green and yellow.

Beans are easy on the budget, the lowest cost source of protein you can buy, and make wonderful taste treats when you use them with imagination. Dried legumes that have been tenderized need less soaking than formerly. A few hours will do instead of overnight. If package directions are lacking, experiment by cooking a few after a short soaking period. If they aren't cooked reasonably soft in about an hour, soak the rest of the dried legumes overnight.

Home-baked beans. They're also called Boston baked beans. Soak beans overnight. Drain in the morning and cover with fresh water. Cook about an hour or until skins break when you blow on them. Keep the skimmer handy when the beans first begin to cook. You'll need it to remove the foam. Turn beans into bean pot or casserole. Cut up ¼ pound salt pork into half-inch slices and tuck into the top of the beans. Mix 1 teaspoon salt, 2 tablespoons molasses, 1 tablespoon brown sugar, ½ teaspoon Worcestershire sauce, ½ teaspoon dry mustard, and ½ cup boiling water. Pour over beans. Cover and bake at 250° F. to 300° F. 6 to 8 hours, adding water when necessary. Uncover during last half hour of baking.

Baked kidney beans. Soak beans overnight. Drain, re-cover with water, and cook slowly for 2 hours. Combine with 2 slices bacon, diced, and a chopped onion in a greased baking dish. Mix ¼ cup catsup, ¼ cup molasses, 1 teaspoon salt, ½ teaspoon dry mustard, and ½ cup hot water. Pour over beans. Cover and bake 2 hours at 300° F., adding additional hot water when necessary. Arrange frankfurters on top and bake 30 minutes at 350° F.

Cranberry beans are colorful teamed with tomatoes. Shell a pound of them and boil in salted water until tender, about 30 minutes. Drain. Meanwhile, dice ¼ pound salt pork and cook in heavy skillet with just a few drops of olive oil, stirring occasionally, until crisp. Drain off excess fat. Then mix the pork thoroughly with a can of tomatoes and heat. Pour over beans and serve.

Lima beans with mushrooms. Cook fresh or frozen beans until just tender. (If you salt toward the end of the cooking time, beans will stay greener.) Drain, place in top of a double boiler with ½ cup light cream or top milk, and season to taste. Sauté ½ pound sliced mushrooms in 2 tablespoons butter over low heat, until just tender. Pour over beans and stir just enough to blend. Hold over hot water until ready to serve, no longer than 5 or 10 minutes.

Lima-bean chili. Try substituting cooked dried lima beans for the usual kidney beans in your chili con carne. Or use canned limas in place of canned kidney beans.

Black-eye beans Italian. Cut a pound of black-eye beans in small pieces. Cook uncovered in boiling salted water until tender. Drain. Meanwhile, sauté 2 chopped onions in 2 tablespoons olive oil until golden, about 10 minutes. Cut a half-pound veal cutlet in small pieces, dredge with flour, and brown in oil. Add a can of Italian tomatoes with paste, some chopped parsley, a pinch of oregano or thyme, and a little water if necessary. Stir well. Simmer until meat is tender, about 45 minutes. Combine beans and meat mixture and serve with freshly grated Parmesan cheese on top.

Black-eye peas in casserole. Cook frozen or fresh peas until tender. (Soak dried ones a few hours, then cook until tender.) Combine cooked peas with a cup of diced ham, a cup of cooked rice, a can of tomatoes, 1 sliced onion, green pepper cut in strips, and 2 cut-up stalks of celery. A cup of grated cheese is an added taste boost. Mix well. Season to taste. Pour into buttered casserole, cover with buttered bread crumbs, and bake 45 minutes at 350° F.

Final legume suggestion makes a perfect first course: Black bean soup. Soak a cup of black beans overnight. Drain and re-cover with cold water. Sauté a small sliced onion and a diced celery stalk in 2 tablespoons butter until golden. Add to beans and simmer, covered, for 3 hours, adding more water as needed. Sieve. Add ½ teaspoon salt, ⅛ teaspoon celery salt, ¼ teaspoon dry mustard, few grains cayenne, and 3 tablespoons sherry. Reheat, stirring to be sure mixture does not stick to pan. Blend a tablespoon of flour with one of melted butter. Stir in soup and cook and stir 3 minutes over moderate heat. Serve soup garnished with thin slices of hard-cooked egg and lemon.

COOKING TIPS

Preserve vitamins and minerals by cooking vegetables as little as possible. Avoid peeling if you can. If skins must come off, pare thinly. To preserve natural color, leave pot uncovered for first few minutes of cooking.

To cook frozen or fresh vegetables at their best, use smallest practical amount of water. Use saucepan with tight-fitting lid. After cooking and draining (saving cooking liquor for other purposes, such as making soups and gravies), add bit of butter or margarine and keep at warm or simmer heat until serving time.

Food-saver. When food cooked in water has been oversalted, boil a few pieces of raw potato in the pot for several minutes. Most of the excess salt will be absorbed by the potatoes.

Avoid the overflow. A small piece of butter added to the cooking water prevents vegetables, macaroni, or rice from boiling over. Keeping heat low, once boiling has begun, is another trick to control the situation.

Frozen stew. When preparing stew for freezing, do not cook vegetables completely. They will finish cooking when the stew is thawed and reheated. Omit potatoes from frozen stew and add them, fresh-cooked, when stew is ready to use.

Rice trick. Keep rice grains snowy-white and separate, instead of lumpy, by adding a teaspoonful of lemon juice to the water.

Another trick with rice. Place washed rice in a casserole dish, add a can of consommé, cover, and bake at 350° F. for an hour. Rice comes out fluffy without watching. Consommé adds flavor.

Whiter cauliflower. Cauliflower will come to the table much whiter if a piece of lemon is added during cooking. And cook only until tender. Overcooking also tends to darken cauliflower.

COOKING
FROZEN VEGETABLES

For best results, do not thaw out vegetables (except corn on the cob or spinach) before cooking. Cook in a very little water for as short a time as possible, so that vegetables are tender but still slightly crunchy.

To thaw frozen vegetables. Simply put them, package and all, in cold water.

When cooking two packages of a frozen vegetable at once, simply use a pan large enough so the frozen blocks may be placed side by side on the bottom of the pan, not on top of each other.

For faster cooking of quick-frozen spinach and chopped broccoli, cut block into six or eight pieces. There are knives especially designed to do the job for you, though any good, sturdy, sharp knife will do.

Asparagus and broccoli will cook more quickly if you let frozen blocks thaw just enough so stalks separate before your put them in water.

Try a smidgin of sautéed chopped onion or chopped chives stirred into quick-frozen cooked golden squash or whipped potatoes.

You can cook frozen vegetables right in the oven while you're preparing an oven-cooked meal. Just place solidly frozen vegetables in a casserole with a couple of tablespoons of butter and ¼ teaspoon salt. (If cooking lima beans, add about ¼ cup water.) Cover and bake at 325° F. to 375° F. about 40 to 60 minutes.

SOME TASTY VEGETABLE DISHES

Mock eggplant. Try dipping cucumber slices in beaten egg, then in fine bread crumbs. Now fry. They taste like eggplant and add variety to any meal.

Cook cauliflower whole. Cut out as much of the core as you can from a cauliflower and then cook it, in a small amount of salted water, until just tender. Ease it into a heated serving dish, pour white sauce over it, add a good chunk of butter and

a sprinkling of nutmeg, and you dramatize its whiteness.

Piquant flavoring for rice. After cooking, allow to stand about ten minutes, then add orange marmalade, 2 tablespoons to a cup of quick-cooking rice.

Peas—Dixie style. Heat peas to serving temperature, then sprinkle bits of crumpled crisp bacon over them. Absolutely delicious and a grand way to make a daily favorite taste different.

For "different" green beans, add sautéed mushrooms or shaved blanched almonds just before serving.

Onions and peas go together naturally. Cook separately; combine, buttered, just before serving. They're good creamed, too, with a bit of nutmeg sprinkled on top.

Baked acorn or butternut squash. Split acorn squash or small butternut in half lengthwise. Remove seeds. Put 2 teaspoons brown sugar, 1 teaspoon of butter or margarine, a dash of salt, cinnamon, and cloves in each. Place in baking pan containing 1 inch of hot water. Cover. Bake 25 minutes in preheated 400° F. oven. Remove cover. Bake 10 to 15 minutes, or until brown and tender.

Delicious squash casserole. Combine 4 cups mashed winter squash with 3 tablespoons each of brown sugar and butter or margarine, ½ teaspoon each of grated lemon and orange rind, and ¼ teaspoon salt. Turn into a 1-quart casserole.

Brush top with melted butter or margarine. Bake 25 minutes, or until brown, in preheated 400° F. oven. Yield: six servings.

Stuffed peppers, apples, onions and the like will not lose their shape or flavor during baking if you bake them in muffin tins.

Panned or skillet vegetables. French and Chinese cooks are famous for this simple method that produces deliciously flavored vegetables with semi-crisp texture. Vegetables lending themselves to this method are carrots, celery, cabbage, snap or green beans, potatoes, spinach, and other greens. Shred, slice, or dice vegetables and place in heavy saucepan or skillet with 1 or 2 tablespoons melted butter or margarine. Toss lightly. Cook, covered, until vegetables sizzle; then reduce heat. Cook only until crisp-tender, stirring once or twice. The French rinse a couple of lettuce leaves in cold water and place them, dripping wet, over the vegetables. Steam is produced from the moisture given off by the lettuce.

Carrots. Wrap scrubbed, whole, unscraped carrots (two to a package) in aluminum foil. Bake over the grill 25 minutes, or until tender when tested with a knife, turning to cook uniformly.

Snap or green beans. Wash and cut ends off fresh beans. Place each serving on a square of aluminum foil, over which place 1 teaspoon butter or margarine and a sprinkling of salt. Wrap securely. Bake over grill 20 to 25 minutes, or until done, turning to cook uniformly.

Grilled butternut squash. Select squash weighing from ½ to ¾ of a pound. Wash and split in half lengthwise. Remove seeds. Stick a whole clove in each end of each half and sprinkle with a dash each of salt and ground black pepper. Put a teaspoon of butter or margarine and 2 teaspoons brown sugar in one of each of the squash halves. Cover with the other half. Wrap each whole squash in aluminum foil, folding and lapping edges so nothing can leak out. Bake over grill 2 hours or until soft to the touch.

Vegetable scallop. Line a baking dish or casserole with heavy aluminum foil, letting the foil extend above the dish to form a decorative border. Grease foil lightly. In a small amount of boiling salted water carefully cook a small head of cauliflower, separated into flowerets, carrots cut lengthwise, and small white onions. Drain. Arrange the vegetables in the baking dish and pour over them a rich, well-seasoned, not-too-thick white sauce in which the liquor from cooking the vegetables has been used in place of a third of the milk. Grate Cheddar or Parmesan cheese over the top and bake at 375° F. just long enough to heat the mixture and brown the top. Aluminum foil dresses up the baking dish for table service, protects it from burned-on or gummy foods, so that scrubbing and scouring after the food is served is unnecessary.

VEGETABLE SAUCES

Hollandaise is a fine sauce to use for special occasions. Made of eggs, butter, and lemon juice, it can be served hot or cold with vegetables (especially asparagus, broccoli, and artichokes) or fish. Don't try to reheat it, though; it separates.

Cream peas the easy way. A delicious cream sauce for peas is made in a jiffy by heating a can of mushroom soup with a half cup of vegetable liquor. When sauce is hot, add peas.

Creamed string beans. To roux (flour and melted butter or margarine stirred smooth over low heat) add string-bean cooking liquor and enough milk to make a smooth cream sauce. Cook and stir until sauce thickens. Add hot cooked beans. Add salt, pepper, a little lemon juice, and a tablespoon of granulated sugar. Cook and stir until sugar dissolves. Just before serving, add 2 tablespoons sour cream and heat over low flame or simmer setting of electric unit.

IDEAS FOR LEFTOVER VEGETABLES

Leftover vegetables can give you a delicious treat. Place them in layers in a casserole, add cream sauce, sprinkle with grated cheese, and bake.

Peas pep up leftovers. If vegetables such as string beans, broccoli, corn, carrots, or beets are among your leftovers, use them with canned peas in a mixed-vegetable salad served with French or Russian dressing.

Add a few empty pea pods to peas and to soup when cooking; they add flavor. But fish them out before serving either; they're too tough to eat except when they are garden-fresh and cooked with tender young peas, when you eat pod and all.

Cauliflower stalks are usually thrown away from force of habit. They are delicious cooked and served with a cheese or Hollandaise sauce.

A few leftover string beans can be added to chopped celery and finely chopped onion for a nutritious and delicious sandwich filling. Moisten the mixture with mayonnaise or other salad dressing.

A little leftover spinach, finely chopped, adds intrigue and color to the batter for luncheon waffles. Or, mixed with chopped hard-cooked eggs in a white sauce, it becomes part of a topping for waffles.

Save leftover broccoli to decorate next day's casserole of whipped potatoes. Push stems into potatoes, with just the blossoms showing. Brush with melted butter or margarine and put in oven at 350° F., to brown, for about 15 minutes.

Quick oats have many uses as leftovers. Brown some in butter or margarine for "crumbs" to top a vegetable or other casserole dish. Or use the oats instead of part of all the nuts called for in your favorite brownie recipe. Brown and crisp in butter or margarine before using oats as nuts, both on brownies and for topping.

Old friends, new faces. For treat flavor, try dipping tomatoes, eggplant, and such in leftover waffle batter, than sauté lightly. Puts new faces on old favorites and helps the budget no end.

HANDY HINTS FOR WORKING WITH VEGETABLES

Chop, chop—once a week. Why not do the whole week's chopping at one time? Store chopped parsley, peppers, onions, celery, nuts in refrigerator, each in an individually labeled jar.

Corn off the cob. The kernels of sweet corn are a cinch to remove if you use a shoehorn. The wide end of the horn is just right for shearing the kernels off.

An asparagus tip. Always open cans of whole asparagus spears from the bottom so that the tips will not break as you ease the spears out of the can.

Keep the vinegar from sweet pickles (or any other pickles, for that matter). Serve it in a glass jar for pepping up salads and dressings. Awfully good, for instance, when mixed with potato salad.

Note to K.P.s. Don't throw away half of that highly nutritious potato by peeling it. Rub the skin off, instead, with one of those new metal pot cleaners. These are just rough enough to rub off the outer skin without wasting the body of the potato.

Let them catch their breath. Freshly opened canned vegetables, if allowed to stand for 15 minutes before heating, will regain oxygen they have lost by canning. Makes an amazing difference in flavor.

Popcorn à la hurry. Use your pressure cooker without indicator weight for popping corn. Heat small amount of vegetable oil; add enough corn to almost cover bottom of cooker. Shaking isn't necessary. It should take about five minutes to pop a goodly batch this way.

Fingers stained? Remove vegetable stains from your fingers by rubbing them with a slice of raw potato.

Candid advice on candied vegetables. You love 'em. But you hate washing the pan afterward. Who doesn't? Even an electric dishwasher rebels. Heat the greased pan before adding the sugary mixture. Doesn't it wash a whole lot easier?

Don't waste olives. Next time you serve them, pour a little salad oil over the remainder in the jar. Prevents molding, makes them keep a long time in the refrigerator.

Make your own "olive" oil. Soak four large olives (unstuffed) in cup of salad oil, keeping in tightly covered jar, in the refrigerator for a week.

Refrigerate all vegetable oils, including real olive oil. They become rancid in time, especially in warm summer months, if not refrigerated. If you object to the cloudiness that develops if oil is a little too chilled, simply remove the container from the refrigerator an hour before you plan to use the oil and it will be crystal-clear again.

Pliers ply their trade when you open a jar of home-canned vegetables or fruit. Use the pliers to grip the rubber ring and screw cap loosens in a jiffy.

Kitchen shears share kitchen chores. They beat a knife for removing seeds and pulp from peppers you're preparing for stuffing. To save their flavor, cut chives and tarragon with shears, instead of chopping. Use shears in cutting parsley, for dicing cooked meats, giblets, for cutting crusts from bread, and to cut marshmallows and raisins. (Dip shears in flour before cutting sticky substances.)

Identify with glamour. Save those good-enough-to-eat pictures of fruits and vegetables from the magazines, then paste them on the appropriate jars when you do your canning. Makes each one look more appetizing.

6

DAIRY PRODUCTS AND EGGS

Basic to the diet, delicious to the taste, but perishable if not handled properly

Milk stays fresh longer if not allowed to stand at room temperature for any length of time, so don't remove until actually needed. Return unused milk to refrigerator promptly.

Fresh milk stays fresh longer if you add a pinch of salt to a quart of fresh milk.

Store milk in the coldest part of your refrigerator, at about 40° F., to protect its flavor and food value. If it cannot be kept cold, use milk as soon as possible. To save the riboflavin, one of milk's important vitamins, keep container away from strong light.

A partially emptied milk container should be re-covered with the closure provided. Uncovered milk quickly picks up flavors of other nearby foods.

If you use milk for coffee or tea, empty the cream pitcher back into the covered refrigerator container; don't store it in the uncovered pitcher.

Milk in the freezer. Pasteurized, homogenized milk may be frozen for periods up to 2 weeks in original container. Caution: pour off a little before freezing, because you need a 2-inch air space at the top of the container to allow room for expansion during freezing.

Before boiling milk, rinse the pan in cold water. Keeps milk from sticking to the pan. But it doesn't keep it from boiling over, so keep an eye on it and turn off heat the minute milk boils.

Milk may be heated, for yeast-dough making, custards, and other mixtures, in the top of a double boiler set over boiling water. That way you don't have to worry about boiling over or possibly scorching milk over direct heat.

After opening can of evaporated milk, plug the openings with neat little rolls of waxed paper. Keeps can holes from being sealed over with dried milk, lets milk pour freely when plugs are removed. Also, contents are less likely to spill if the can is accidentally tipped—

and the milk won't take on odors from other foods in the refrigerator.

Dying for a glass of milk? Combining ½ cup water and ½ cup evaporated milk makes the equivalent of 1 cup fresh milk.

Cream won't curdle. We've all been annoyed at the way cream tends to curdle when poured over acid berries or fruits, spoiling the appearance though the taste's the same. Avoid this by mixing a pinch of baking soda with the cream before serving.

Cream whips faster. To whip cream in record time, add 6 to 8 drops of lemon juice per pint (2 cups) of cream. Use an eye dropper and count them; too much lemon sours the cream.

CHEESE

Cheese can replace milk. For children (up to 80) who do not like milk, cheese can be used to add flavor and milk values to meals. For instance, 1¼ ounces of yellow cheese equals many of the food values contained in a whole cup of milk. They share many fine nutritive qualities, of course, since cheese is made from milk.

Store perishable soft cheese, as you do milk, in the refrigerator in a tightly covered container. Buy in amounts to be used in a short time. Other cheeses keep well in a cold place if wrapped so that air is kept out. Foil is fine for this.

Refrigerate packaged cheese in its original container, using additional waxed paper or aluminum foil, if necessary, to rewrap the cheese. Wrap unpackaged cheese tightly with waxed paper, laminated foil, a vinegar-dampened cloth, or similar wrapping before refrigerating. An overwrap that's convenient for paper or cloth is non-porous pliofilm bag such as you use in freezer storage.

If mold forms on cheese, it may be scraped away with no harm to the cheese. Should cheese become dry, grate it and keep in covered container. It's good for cooking even if no longer attractive in solid form.

Don't throw away empty candy tins. They're wonderful for storing sharp cheeses in the refrigerator. Cheese stays properly moist yet doesn't impose its odor on other foods in the refrigerator.

Cheese (except cottage) tastes best when served unchilled. Take it from the refrigerator long enough before serving to reach room temperature.

To prevent curdling, scorching, and stringiness in foods made with cheese or milk, cook at low, low temperatures and don't overcook.

Easy-to-cut cheese. Warm the knife and it's no trick at all to slice cheese as easily as butter. But there are cheese cutters, too, that are just as easy to use.

Cheese grates easily if it has been chilled first. So grate it the moment you take it from the refrigerator.

Cheese and fruit. They were "meant for each other." Serve Roquefort cheese with fresh pear sections; Tokay grapes with Liederkranz cheese; orange sections with Swiss and cream cheese; apples with Camembert; pieces of apple, cheese, and pears, speared on toothpicks.

Cream-cheese spread. Soften a 3-ounce package of cream cheese with 1 tablespoon each of tomato catsup and fresh lemon juice. Add a bit of finely chopped parsley for garnish.

Meat-stretcher cheese uses (with a little help from milk). You can get 4 generous servings out of ½ pound hamburger meat if you add 4 ounces of sliced cheese to make four cheeseburgers. By using a pint of milk and ½ pound of cheese for your macaroni-and-cheese main dish, you get better taste, better food value, at very little extra cost.

Cheese pudding. Simply substitute a cup of grated Cheddar cheese for sugar and spices in dessert bread pudding and you have a hearty luncheon dish. Season it, of course, with salt and pepper.

Cheese puffs. An elegant first course made by mixing 2 teaspoons flour with a cup of grated Edam cheese (the kind you buy red-skinned) and ½ teaspoon salt. Fold into a stiffly beaten egg white seasoned with a dash of cayenne and ¼ teaspoon Worcestershire sauce. Roll into small balls, no larger than walnut size. Chill 1 hour. Fry in hot deep fat 1 to 2 minutes, until golden.

Cheese sticks. Remove crusts from 8 slices of white or whole-wheat bread. Cut in ½-inch strips. Spread with softened or creamed butter and sprinkle lightly with cayenne. Dip in grated cheese. Bake on aluminum foil at 350° F. 5 minutes, or until lightly browned.

Roquefort or blue-cheese pinwheels. Roll out plain pastry. Strew crumbled cheese all over it, roll like jelly roll. Chill 1 hour. Cut in ¼-inch slices and bake on very lightly greased cookie sheet at 450° F. 10 to 15 minutes, or until pastry is delicately browned.

Welsh rarebit. Melt a tablespoon of butter over very low heat. Add a cup of grated Cheddar cheese. As the cheese melts, add ¼ cup beer. Add ½ teaspoon salt, ½ teaspoon dry mustard, and a dash of cayenne to a well-beaten egg. Add to cheese-beer mixture (very low heat, remember), stir well, and cook 1 minute longer.

BUTTER

Butter keeps better if you keep it clean, cold, covered, to protect its delicate flavor and texture. Leave it in original protective wrapping until ready to use. Some refrigerators have temperature-controlled butter compartments to keep butter spreadable. Keep only two or three days' supply in such compartments, even though they're sized to fit a pound block of butter.

Easy-to-spread consistency is best achieved by setting on a small plate or butter dish the amount of butter you will require to spread on bread and leaving this at room temperature for about 10 minutes. Melting or quick melting of unnecessarily large quantities spoils freshness of the butter you don't use right away.

Cream butter in a hurry with your electric mixer. First cut up into pieces with a clean knife, to give the mixer a good start. Creamed butter is most desirable when making tea sandwiches. And it's nice for making butter balls, using 2 wooden boards designed for the purpose or a cold metal baller.

EGGS

What are Egg Grades? Eggs are graded according to freshness and quality. (Grade AA represents the freshest, finest quality, Grade A the next lower step, etc.) Prices vary by the size of the eggs within each grade. (Jumbo, Extra Large, etc.) The tables in the next column will help you choose the eggs you want for a particular purpose.

Tips on egg storage. Always keep in refrigerator. Unbroken eggs should be in covered containers; otherwise they lose moisture and absorb odors, because shells are porous. Yolks keep best if covered with water; whites should be kept in a tightly covered jar.

To keep eggs fresh for a fairly long time, rub very fresh eggs with oil, butter, or pure glycerin over the entire surface of the shell.

If you keep all your eggs in one basket, pencil-mark leftover eggs, so that you'll use them up first.

To test the age of an egg, place in deep pan of cold water. If it lies on its side, it is fresh. If it stands at an angle, it is probably 3 or 4 days old. If the egg stands on end upright, it is over 10 days old. If it floats to the top, toss it out!

EGG GRADES

GRADE	DESCRIPTION
AA	Freshest, top quality. Well-rounded yolk is centered, white is firm. First choice for table, cooking, and baking.
A	Fresh, fine quality. Excellent choice for table, cooking, and baking.
B, C	Less fresh and attractive, but fine for omelets or scrambled eggs, as well as for cooking and baking.

Grade AA   Grade A   Grades B and C

EGG SIZES

SIZE	MINIMUM WEIGHT PER DOZEN
Jumbo	30 oz.
Extra Large	27 oz.
Large	24 oz.
Medium	21 oz.
Small	18 oz.

Is that stray egg hard-cooked or raw? To test, place the egg on its side and spin it like a top. If the egg spins on an even keel, it is cooked. If it wobbles, it's raw.

Don't freeze cooked foods containing hard-cooked egg whites. Egg white changes in texture rapidly, toughens, and tends to develop off flavors when frozen.

The least understood and most important rule in egg cookery is—low temperature. The science behind the rule is that the protein in the egg is easily toughened by too-high temperature. This accounts for eggs of unappetizing texture that give away the third-rate cook.

Cold-water start is recommended for simmering eggs if eggs are taken right from the refrigerator, because sudden temperature changes tend to crack shells. If you are in a hurry, though, try running hot water over the eggs and immediately draining it off. That scares them a little but not to the cracking point. Then add more hot water and cook. (Simmering timing given below assumes you start timing just as the water is about to boil and you lower flame or electric-range heating element.)

Simmer eggs. Boiling water is not recommended, since both yolks and whites coagulate at temperatures below the boiling point of water. Simmer soft-cooked eggs 3 minutes for very soft, 4 minutes for firm whites but soft yolks, 5 minutes for folks who like 'em a little longer but still on the soft side. Eggs simmer to hard-cooked stage in 10 minutes, but without any of the usual green division between white and yolks that develops when eggs are boiled. No hard-boiled egg odor either.

"Seal" broken eggshell immediately if it cracks during cooking. How? Just add a little vinegar to the cooking water.

Egg-peeling tip. By adding salt to the water in which eggs are hard-cooked, you harden the shell and make it much easier to peel off. A quick dunk in cold water helps too, as does rolling the egg around to crush the shell somewhat before you begin peeling.

To prevent egg white from spreading when poached, add 1 teaspoon salt or a few drops of vinegar to each cup of water used for poaching. Helps to hasten coagulation of egg white. A little swirl of the water around the egg with a spoon helps too.

To separate egg whites and yolks, the for-sure no-broken-yolk way, puncture a small hole at one end of the shell. This releases the white into a collecting bowl and yolk stays inside. Break shell, remove yolk whole.

It's best to open eggs in separate bowl before adding to mixed batter. Avoids spoiling entire mixture should one egg prove bad. Keeps shells out of batter too.

Best way to divide an egg. After beating the egg, measure it in a measuring cup, pour off half, save the rest for scrambled eggs. Cover the leftover beaten egg, stored in a custard cup, with aluminum foil.

When beating egg whites, be sure to use an enamel, stainless-steel, glass, or porcelain bowl. Never use aluminum, because eggs darken aluminumware.

Egg whites beat up quicker and higher if you add a tiny pinch of salt and let them stand until they're room temperature before you beat them.

How many eggs? Most recipes call for average-sized eggs (medium to large). If using small eggs, allow about 3½ tablespoons slightly mixed whole egg for each egg in the recipe.

7

SOUPS

Homemade, canned, or frozen—here are tips on how to make the most out of soups

Whatever you boil, whether meat, poultry, fish, vegetables, all yield wonderful stock for a soup base. Even if all you can do about soup is to open a can of ready-to-dilute condensation, add liquids saved from cooking. They give you a bonus of extra-fresh flavor and vitamins.

Any French cook will tell you it is an unforgivable waste to throw away those outside lettuce leaves, even when they are wilted. They make a wondrously tasty extra for homemade soup.

Old spice, new tang. Have you tried a few cloves in your vegetable soup? Even to this classic soup they give an exciting new lift in flavor.

To remove fat from soup (and from yourself), dip an ice cube wrapped in piece of clean cloth into soup. Fat congeals quickly on a cold surface.

QUICK AND EASY MEALS WITH SOUP

Save time and please the family by cooking with soup. Here are six one-dish meals that have a soup base:

1. Combine undiluted cream of celery soup with ½ cup milk and 1 cup or more of grated sharp cheese. Heat slowly until cheese melts, stirring frequently. Add 4 cups cooked macaroni, spaghetti, or noodles, and a little chopped, sautéed green pepper and onion. Heat and serve.

2. In a skillet or saucepan combine 1 can cream of mushroom soup, ½ cup evaporated milk, a 7-ounce can drained flaked tuna, 1 cup cooked peas or other vegetable, and 1 cup crushed potato chips. Heat and serve with a generous sprinkling of chopped parsley on top.

3. Sauté 1 chopped onion and a slivered green pepper in a tablespoon of hot fat. Stir in 1 can undiluted chicken gumbo soup and several tablespoons chili sauce. Taste and season. Add 2 cups cooked shrimp. Cook until thickened. Serve over plenty of hot cooked rice.

4. Combine soup with leftovers. Add a can of Scotch broth, undiluted, to leftover diced or chopped cooked meat, vegetables, and gravy. Add a bit of chopped onion for tang, some chopped black olives for glamour. Turn into a casserole or other baking dish and top with mashed potatoes, biscuits, or pastry, and bake, at 400° F., until topping is baked or browned and casserole piping hot.

5. Another casserole idea to please the family. Sauté several strips bacon until crisp. Remove from pan. Brown chopped onion in the bacon drippings. Stir in 1 can undiluted tomato soup, 4 cups cooked drained lima beans, and the bacon, broken up. Turn into a casserole, spread with buttered bread crumbs, and bake until brown.

6. An egg stretcher uses soup. Heat 1 can cream of mushroom soup with ¼ cup milk. Gently stir in 4 or 5 sliced or quartered hard-cooked eggs and some chopped stuffed olives. Heat. Serve on hot buttered toast, toasted English muffins, or hot split biscuits.

Menu planning is easy when you have a variety of canned soups on your pantry shelf. Try serving two soups in a divided dish, to combine or to provide a choice.

Combine two favorite soups to make a fine "supper soupmate." Here are five ideas:

1. Green pea and cream of chicken mixed with milk or cream and topped with a sprinkle of curry makes a combination of flavors that's unusual.

2. Another good combination is onion soup with cream of mushroom, diluted with water. A few added tablespoons of good wine are recommended for that pair.

3. Bean with bacon and vegetable soup are another duo that team well together. Dilute with water or milk and add a sprinkling of grated Parmesan cheese just before serving.

4. Hearty peasant-style soup is yours when you combine beef soup with rich vegetable soup. Remember to float a generous slice of garlicky French bread atop each serving.

5. A rich cream soup combines cream of chicken and cream of asparagus and is diluted with half canned evaporated milk and half water or milk. Stir just a tablespoon or two of finely chopped cucumber into the soup for that extra-flavor touch.

Soup for breakfast. Soup makes a wonderful day starter, and when you add soft rolls, stewed fruit, and eggs sunny-side-up, even the most finicky appetites will be tempted by your unusual menus.

Cereal and soup. Having trouble tempting children into eating a good breakfast? Try floating a shredded-wheat biscuit in a bowl of chicken-with-rice soup. Or top off tomato or vegetable soup with a handful of puffed rice or wheat flakes. Good cold, too.

Soup scrambles for teen-agers. Serve at least four different kinds of combinable soups, buffet-style, surrounded by bowls and bowls of accompaniments such as chopped egg, cereal crunch, chopped nuts, pickle relish, minced parsley, bacon bits, butter pats, a variety of breads and crackers, and anything else you can think of to go with soup. Then let the youngsters take over and serve themselves. Some will mix two soups. Others will combine all four and add a spoonful of everything, a real soup scramble.

OFF-BEAT WAYS WITH SOUP

On a diet? Try soup on the rocks. Simply pour good beef bouillon, your own or right from a can, over ice cubes in a tall glass. Swish around to chill, then drink. You'll find it light and refreshing. Plain, or with a twist of lemon peel, soup on the rocks has become a national favorite beverage.

Don't like eggs? Everyone should eat an occasional egg, at least three a week. For those who don't care for eggs a soupnog may be the answer. Use a rotary beater to blend 1 can cream of chicken, celery, or mushroom soup with 1 can milk. Chill. Just before serving, beat in an egg for each portion. Serve ice cold. Good with tomato soup too.

Purée is pure delight. A delicious soup, made with food put through a ricer and thinned with cream or stock. Example: split-pea soup. Don't let it stick to the pot and burn. Stir frequently while the soup

cooks. And try cooking it in an aluminum pot. Try making puréed soups, too, by using a blender. You can begin with raw foods and liquids if you have a blender and use it to make soup.

Vary your cold-soup story. Stock your refrigerator with cans of consommé, to serve jellied with diced avocado and lemon wedges; bouillon to serve full-strength on the rocks, over ice cubes; cream of chicken to which you add cold milk.

A chilled-soup special. Combine cream of mushroom soup with cream of chicken, 1 can of each. Stir in 1 can of water and 1 can of milk. Add ½ cup chopped shrimp (canned or fresh-cooked), then chill thoroughly before serving. Chill serving dishes too.

"Company" soup. Combine 1 can black bean soup and 1 can condensed tomato soup and dilute with 2 cans water. Add 1 teaspoon sherry for each serving. Chill. When ready to serve, garnish with lemon wedges or chopped hard-cooked egg.

Soup for party dips. Here are three ideas:

1. Combine 1 can condensed bean with bacon soup, ¼ cup mayonnaise or sour cream, 1 small can deviled ham, and a little minced onion. Taste and season. Thin with a little cream, if desired.

2. Stir together condensed tomato soup, sour cream, and a little cream

cheese. Season rather highly and chill thoroughly before serving.

3. Undiluted black bean soup stirred up with a little minced onion, mayonnaise, or sour cream, and a few tablespoons of good sherry makes a deliciously different dunk for crisp raw vegetables.

HEARTY CHOWDERS FROM SIMPLE SOUPS

Chicken-corn chowder. Combine 1 can condensed cream of corn soup, 1 can of cream of chicken soup, 1 or more cans milk, and 1 cup chopped cooked chicken (leftover or canned). Blend and heat. Add a pinch curry, or any favorite herb or spice, for special flavor.

Wonderful fish chowder. Combine 1 can of cream of celery soup with a 7-ounce can drained flaked tuna, a 5-ounce can drained chopped shrimp, and ½ cup clam juice. Stir in 1 cup milk and ½ cup or more finely chopped cooked potato. Simmer until ready to serve, then top each full bowl with a bit of butter and a sprinkle of paprika.

Ever taste mushroom chowder? You'll like it when you do. Combine condensed cream of mushroom soup with 1 can light cream, 1 cup sautéed sliced mushrooms, a few tablespoons lightly sautéed onion, and a sieved hard-cooked egg. Heat and serve.

A rich clam chowder. Combine 1 can condensed clam chowder soup, 1 can vegetarian vegetable soup (for Friday or Lenten observers), a 7-ounce can minced clams with juice, 1 can water or milk, and seasonings to taste. Bring to boil and add 1 cup macaroni shells or elbows. Cover and simmer gently until macaroni is tender, about 10 to 12 minutes. Add more liquid if chowder is too thick. Serve piping hot with pilot biscuits.

For cold winter nights try beef-and-vegetable chowder. Brown ½ pound ground beef and a chopped onion in a little hot fat. Break the beef up with a fork as it cooks. Add 1 can spiced beef soup, 1 can vegetable soup, and 1 can or more of water. Taste and season with favorite herb or spice. For extra thickness, stir in some cooked rice or macaroni. Serve hot, with biscuits or corn bread.

Something new is chicken-cheese chowder. Combine 1 can condensed cream of chicken soup with 1 can chicken noodle soup, 1 can milk, and 1 cup diced, cooked carrots. Heat. Stir in 1 cup grated sharp Cheddar cheese. Simmer and stir until cheese melts and blends. Season to taste with a pinch of mace, or other spice, and salt and pepper. Serve with a garnish of crumbled crisp bacon.

FOREIGN FLAVOR FAVORITES FROM SOUP

Exotic omelet with a Chinese touch. Stir 1 can of undiluted cream of mushroom soup into 6 eggs you've beaten until frothy.

Add seasonings, a finely chopped small onion, ½ cup each minced cooked ham and chicken (or other leftover cooked meat), and a little thinly sliced celery. Cook as usual. This makes four generous servings. Sprinkle with soy sauce when served.

Borsch, almost as good as the real thing, takes a lot less time. It combines bouillon and beets. Chop or grate enough canned beets to make two cups. Combine beets, 1 can undiluted condensed beef bouillon, a little chopped onion, and 1 cup water. Season to taste with salt and pepper and lemon juice. Bring to a boil, then cool and chill. Serve ice cold with a dollop of sour cream and a bit of chopped dill pickle.

Make-believe vichyssoise is good either hot or cold and is made in a jiffy. Combine 1 can condensed cream of chicken soup with 1 can frozen potato soup and 1 cup milk. Add a small whole onion, a pinch of celery seed, and a sprinkling of paprika. Simmer gently. Remove onion before serving. Just before serving, either hot or cold, stir a generous spoonful salted whipped cream into each bowl. A dash of nutmeg makes a final gourmet touch.

An Indian favorite is shrimp Bombay. Combine 1 can condensed cream of chicken soup with curry powder (enough to taste, starting with ¼ teaspoon), a little pepper, and 1 cup evaporated milk. Simmer to blend flavors. Add 2 cups cooked shrimp and heat. Serve with fluffy hot boiled rice, chopped salted peanuts, and diced green pepper and onion.

Hollanders love rich pea soup. They'll like yours, too, if you use this recipe: Have a few thick slices of highly seasoned salami cut in slivers and browned in a little butter. Add 1 can condensed green pea soup, 1 can condensed vegetable soup, 1 can water, and ½ cup evaporated milk. Mix well and simmer until very hot. Add a little more water or milk if a thinner soup is preferred.

South-of-the-border chili con carne. Cook ½ pound chopped beef, 1 large chopped onion, and a minced garlic clove in a few tablespoons hot fat. Stir in 1 can condensed tomato soup, 4 cups undrained canned kidney beans, 1 tablespoon chili powder, and a little salt. Cook to blend flavors. Serve in bowls with toasted crackers and raw relishes. (You may want to adjust amount of chili powder to your own taste.)

USE SOUP TO MAKE GRAVIES THE EASY WAY

Roast-pork gravy. Pour off extra fat in pan. Add undiluted cream of celery soup and stir into the browned drippings. Stir over low heat until smooth and thickened. Serve over hot pork slices.

Wonderful lamb gravy, and so easy, too. When lamb is roasted, skim all fat from drippings left in pan. Then simmer a little, so drippings get good and brown. Stir in undiluted condensed cream of chicken or mushroom soup. Heat until thick and smooth. Not dark enough? A tablespoon or two of strong coffee will darken the gravy with no effect on flavor.

Creamy chicken gravy. For an extra-good extra-chickeny flavor with fried or roasted chicken, add undiluted cream of chicken soup to the browned drippings in skillet or roasting pan. Stir until smooth and heat until thickened. Add a tablespoon or two of heavy cream for that real down-on-the-farm taste.

Not enough gravy? To ½ cup of any leftover gravy add 1 can of undiluted tomato soup. Stir in 1 tablespoon of your favorite meat sauce, such as Worcestershire or A.1., and 1 teaspoon of lemon juice. If desired, a touch of chili powder can go in. Heat. This is good with franks and hamburgers too.

Like gravy with your ham steak? Add undiluted cream of mushroom soup to the skimmed pan drippings after you've cooked the ham. Stir until thick and smooth. A teaspoon of prepared mustard added to this gives a special tang.

Hot, it's gravy; cold, it's sauce. If you like a hot gravy or a cold sauce with your fish, here's a winner that does double duty. In top of a double boiler combine undiluted cream of chicken soup with ¼ cup mayonnaise and 1 or more tablespoons

lemon juice. Stir in generous pinch cayenne pepper. Blend and heat. To serve cold, chill and fold in ¼ cup well-drained chopped cucumber. Good either way, and you'll like it on vegetables too.

SOUP TOPPINGS AND ACCOMPANIMENTS

To top it all. Any canned or home-made soup may be given a company touch by topping the servings with a mixture of beaten egg white, plenty of real mayonnaise, and a dash of salt. Add a spoonful to the top of each serving of soup and garnish with finely chopped parsley.

Different bread sticks to serve with soup may be quickly made from stale bread. Trim crusts and spread both sides of bread with real mayonnaise. Toast in waffle iron until brown. Cut each slice into three fingers.

Heat thin slices of frankfurters in lentil or pea soup for ten minutes. They'll float on top when you serve the soup. They go well with bean soup too.

Two ways with croutons. Cut stale bread into small cubes. Sauté in butter until golden brown, stirring frequently for uniform color. A quick way to make croutons in quantity is to fry them in hot, deep fat. If you have a fat thermometer, heat fat to 375° F. If you haven't, a test crouton should be brown in 1 minute.

Hot popcorn doesn't have to be fresh-popped as a soup topper.

Heat plain or cheese-flavored popcorn in a 350° F. oven, in a brown paper bag, for 5 to 10 minutes. It's a good topper for cream of spinach soup or other bland cream soups.

Whipped cream, lightly salted and sprinkled with paprika, is a quick-and-easy but elegant soup topper.

Sautéed Taylor ham cubes make a hearty topping for rich pea soup, lentil or bean soup. Cut the ham crouton-size and sauté in butter or margarine or in any bacon drippings you may have on hand.

Old-fashioned cracklings for New England fish chowder. Cut ¼ pound salt pork in small pieces and sauté in a large kettle or Dutch oven. Cook and stir until the fat has been extracted. Remove cracklings and drain on paper toweling. Use the fat as the base for making fish chowder. Serve chowder with cracklings sprinkled on top.

Custard garnish. Beat together 3 egg yolks, 2 tablespoons milk, dash of cayenne, and a little salt. Pour into small pie plate or other small oven pan, so that there is a ¼ to ½ inch layer of custard. Set plate in a pan of hot water and bake at 350° F. for 20 minutes, or until set. Cool and dice. Makes a wonderful garnish for a clear consommé.

Pimiento cream. Fold 1 stiffly beaten egg white into 1 cup whipped cream. Then fold 2 tablespoons minced pimientos and a dash of salt. Goes well on top of clam bisque.

Meat-ball garnish. Beat an egg yolk. Add ½ teaspoon onion juice, ½ teaspoon lemon juice, salt, pepper, and thyme to taste. Crumble ½ pound chopped beef into this mixture and stir just enough to combine. Chill ½ hour. Shape into tiny balls the size of a marble, roll in flour, and sauté in butter until lightly browned. Drop into hot consommé about 15 minutes before serving.

Special simple tops for special soups. Chopped chives, of course, for true vichyssoise. Thin slice of avocado for chilled tomato soup containing a bit of whipped cream. Thin slice of lemon and another of hard-cooked egg for black bean soup. Sliced cucumber for beet soup or borsch.

8

BREADS, ROLLS, AND BISCUITS

The staff of life can also be the life of the party

Tips that keep bread fresh. If you store bread in a room-temperature place, such as your breadbox, it will stay soft but may not keep too long, especially in warm weather. If you store it in your refrigerator it will be safe from mold but will not remain soft. Compromise is to store bread in the refrigerator but wrap it first in waxed paper or other moisture-proof paper and then tuck it into a pliofilm bag. Double wrapping keeps moisture in, refrigerator temperature keeps mold out.

If you use lots of bread, store it in your breadbox. But be sure to keep the box clean and free of old pieces of bread. Scald and/or sun it weekly.

If you use little bread, but have a freezing compartment in your refrigerator, double-wrap the bread as directed for refrigerator storage and store bread in the frozen-food compartment. You can keep several kinds of bread frozen simultaneously, have a choice of breads, and use only as much as you need for one meal.

Can you freeze bakery bargains? Baked foods (including yeast rolls, yeast bread, quick breads, cookies, unfrosted cakes and some frosted ones, and cupcakes) can be frozen for from two to three months. Buy them when your baker features specials, eat them when you want them. (See pages 125–133 for more details on frozen foods and home freezers.)

Know your bread flours. Flour milled from hard wheat is best for bread baking. (Leave the soft wheat type of flour for fine-textured cakes.) For quick breads, biscuits, muffins (and some pastries), the "all-purpose" flours are well suited.

Whole-grain flours for highest food value. Whole-wheat, graham, and rye flours have exceptionally high nutritional content. They're a better buy, nutritionally, than white flour, better even than "enriched" white flour. Soya flour, generally used in combination with wheat flours for home baking, adds valuable protein content. Use ratio of one part soya flour to nine parts wheat flour.

To prevent bread crust from cracking, shelter fresh-baked bread from cold gusts of air or sudden drafts and winds on the heated surface.

It does not matter how you slice it. If sliced too soon after it has been removed from the oven, fresh bread tends to compress and collapse. Be patient—and gentle. Then use a serrated bread knife, and you should be able to slice the bread as smoothly as if it were done by a machine.

To freshen French bread, Italian bread, hard rolls, cover crusts with cold water, using a pastry brush. Then place in 350° F. oven until crisp again, about 10 minutes. Cool before slicing.

Savory French bread, hard-long or junior-length loaf, is prepared by slashing, not slicing, the bread into diagonal portions an inch wide. Slash it not quite through to the bottom crust. Spread the inside cut surfaces with melted butter in which you placed a garlic clove as it melted. Bake at 325° F. 15 to 20 minutes.

Use leftover bread slices to make bread sticks, croutons, bread crumbs, meat loaves, and for pudding.

New twist on good old bread pudding. Beat an egg white stiff and season with sugar and spice. When pudding is ready to remove from oven, cover it with this meringue and bake until puffy and light brown, about 15 minutes.

Roll your dried bread crumbs or cereal crumbs the easy way. Place them between folds of a clean towel or sheets of waxed paper, then roll them. Let no crumbs scatter when grinding dried bread. Catch them in a paper bag. Fasten opening of bag firmly around grinder outlet with tightly tied cord or a rubber band.

Salt cartons into bread-crumb boxes. Empty salt cartons with spouts make excellent containers for bread crumbs ground from dried bread. Use funnel to get crumbs into carton.

ROLLS

To heat ready-to-eat bread and rolls, wrap bread slices or rolls snugly in aluminum foil. Bake at 350° F. about 15 minutes, or until hot. If served in the foil wrapping, turn foil edges down to form a basket; they'll keep hot to the last crumb.

Add your own trimmings to hot-roll mixes. Make hot-cross buns from hot-roll mix by adding raisins to the dough as well as chopped citron, granulated sugar, cinnamon. Then let rise as directed on package, until double in bulk. Shape ball-like buns. Place in greased cake pan. Let rise in warm place for another 30 to 60 minutes. With scissors, cut small cross in each bun. Bake at 400° F. 15 to 20 minutes, or until done. Combine confectioners' sugar with a little warm milk and vanilla extract to dip over hot bun and fill crosses.

Brown 'n' serve rolls come raised and almost completely baked. You bake them another few minutes, following package directions, to bring out the golden color in the crust. You may bake them with your special sweet-mixture topping made with honey, nuts, caramel, orange, brown sugar, or cooked prunes.

Brioche—a famous favorite. To make that light and flaky French delicacy and wonderful companion to afternoon tea or coffee do this: In warm water, dissolve yeast from packaged roll mix as directed. Add a slightly beaten egg and mix well. Blend in the roll mix and mix thoroughly; cover. Let rise until double in bulk. Shape three-quarters of the dough into 18 rolls, place in greased 2½-inch muffin-pan cups, and press large indentation into top of each roll. Brush with butter. Divide remaining dough into 18 parts and shape into balls, then press a ball flat into each indentation. Again let rise in warm place for 30 to 60 minutes, until light. Bake at 375° F. for 15 minutes.

BISCUIT WIZARDRY

For light, flaky biscuits, this is the way to handle ingredients: As milk is added to dry ingredients, work latter lightly away from the bottom of mixing bowl with a fork. Then press the bits of dough into a ball. Do not knead. Pat out dough on floured board and roll lightly, outward from center. Never roll back and forth.

Biscuits bake best on baking sheet without sides. To insure proper heat circulation, sheets should be small enough to leave one or two inches of space between edges of sheet and sides and back of oven.

No more pale-face biscuits. Wan-looking baking-powder biscuits turn a healthy golden brown if you simply add a teaspoonful of sugar to the dry ingredients.

Start with a biscuit mix and use your imagination. You can make quick and succulent breakfast hot bread this way: Roll a recipe of biscuit mix into rectangular shape, about ¼ inch thick. Spread with melted butter or margarine. Sprinkle with brown sugar, raisins, and chopped nuts. Roll as you would a jelly roll. Cut into ½-inch slices. Bake on a greased cookie sheet, cut side up, at 425° F. for 15 to 18 minutes.

Leftover biscuit pinwheels. You can use up leftover cooked meat, chicken, or fish and make good use of leftover gravies by using prepared biscuit mix. Roll out a recipe ¼ inch thick, in oblong shape. Grind up leftover meat or other protein with a small raw onion. Add a little tomato catsup, seasonings, and a little leftover gravy. Mix well. Then spread on biscuit dough. Roll as for jelly roll. Cut in ½-inch slices. Bake on greased baking sheet, cut side up, at 425° F. for 15 to 18 minutes. Serve with leftover gravy, mushroom or tomato sauce.

The biscuit mix need not make biscuits. Waffles, pancakes, dumplings, nut bread, fudge cake, chocolate-chip cookies, and breakfast crumb cake are only a few of the goodies you can make with biscuit mix. Simply follow package directions at first, then let yourself go on other uses for biscuit mix.

Bake 'n' eat biscuits come mixed, rolled, and cut, ready for the oven. If you keep a package on hand, store it in the refrigerator, never on the pantry shelf or in your home freezer. It needs refrigerator cold and no more. Before baking, you may add your own sharp or sweet topping, or sprinkle butter-brushed top with poppy seed, caraway or celery seed. Bake at 425° F. for 10 to 15 minutes, or as package directs.

Kitchenette pizza before you say good night. Place three bake 'n' eat biscuits on cookie sheet, with sides touching, cloverleaf fashion. Place ½-inch cube of cheese on each. Top each cube with teaspoonful of chili sauce. Sprinkle with grated Parmesan, garlic salt, dried thyme, salt, pepper. Drizzle on a little salad oil. Bake at 550° F. 5 to 8 minutes.

Coffee-ettes after you say good morning. First dip bake 'n' eat biscuits into melted butter, then into mixture of granulated sugar, cinnamon, chopped nuts. Bake in greased pan or cookie sheet at 425° F. for 20 to 25 minutes.

LET YOURSELF GO WITH BAKING SHORTCUTS

Mixes mix in good company. Even though you're pressed for time, you can still have home-baked hot biscuits, muffins, and other breads if you begin with a mix. All you do is follow package directions and bake. Make hot rolls and buns with mixes too. Just mix and bake as package directs.

Super bread sticks can be made from frankfurter rolls by quartering them lengthwise. Spread cut slices, on all sides, with soft butter or salad oil. Roll in minced parsley, chives, or grated Parmesan cheese. Bake at 425° F. for 5 to 10 minutes.

Don't halve English muffins with a knife. To split, insert fork into side of English muffin until fork reaches center, then repeat all around. Spread torn surfaces with butter or margarine. Toast in toaster or broiler. Or spread first with cream cheese topped with jelly or grated Cheddar cheese, crumbled blue cheese, or cinnamon mixed with sugar and topped with chopped nuts, or nippy soft cheese topped with sliced olives. Then toast in broiler.

Corn muffinettes. Split corn muffins. Top with drizzle of molasses, add chopped nuts, and broil.

Petite toast, as new for breakfast as the morning headlines. Slice hard rolls or French bread into rings ½ to ¾ inch thick. Dip into your favorite French-toast mixture and sauté as usual. This is particularly good with whole-wheat rolls.

Toast for taste. Cut loaf of unsliced raisin bread into squares. Brush cut square surfaces, as well as top and bottom, with melted butter. Sprinkle with sugar and cinnamon. Bake at 375° F. for about 15 minutes, or until golden.

TRY YOUR HAND AT PARTY TREATS

Crosscut cocktail canapés. One square slice of bread makes eight triangular canapés with four cuts—two cuts across, two diagonal cuts. Before cutting, spread each large slice with different cocktail spreads. After cutting, top each triangle with olive, black or red caviar, chopped egg, anchovy, pimiento, or other tasty ornament, and you'll have a trayful of elegant canapés.

Devil's-food sandwich cake. Take thin-sliced pumpernickel or dark rye bread; prepare a spicy cream-cheese base spread. Spread this filling on seven pieces of bread, then place slices on top of each other, pressing down slightly to make filling stick to bottom of each slice. Spread the rest of the filling on the four vertical sides of the "cake," in the manner of a cake frosting. Top with salted nuts, black olives; chill, serve cake-fashion. Cross section will be good-looking black-and-white stripe. Good on buffet tables, with salads, tea, light suppers.

Seven-layer sandwich cake. Prepare same as above, but use different kinds of bread (white, rye, wheat, pumpernickel) and different kinds of spreads. Good way to use up leftovers, in spreads.

Toast de luxe four ways:

1. In oven: Butter thin bread slices, spread with cream cheese, top with bits of blue cheese, bake 8 minutes at 425° F.

2. In broiler: Toast bread on one side in broiler, turn, butter broiled side, then add cheese and anchovy paste mixture, top with chili sauce, finish broiling.

3. In skillet: Melt butter or margarine in skillet, sprinkle it with paprika or celery, garlic, or onion salt. Sauté bread slices in this mixture until golden on both sides.

4 In waffle iron: Bake unbuttered bread slices in iron until golden brown. Waffle pattern is pretty on bread, too.

Sardine sophisticates. For evening snacks, a three-decker sandwich with two fillings: one is made of mashed sardines, curry, minced onion, mayonnaise; the other ax-sharp cheese spread. Bake flat, at 425° F., for 8 minutes. Combine just before serving, hot.

Ever hear of sandwich kabobs? Try this idea and you'll never hear the last of how good it is. Make four-decker sandwich with buttered bread and a filling of deviled ham with mustard or soft cheese with mustard; or, if you plan something sweet, coconut with brown sugar, nutmeg, or cinnamon sugar. Trim the crusts, cut each bread slice into four squares, string on skewers by twos, and bake 8 minutes at 425° F., or toast in broiler, turning when necessary.

Muffin-pan rolls make another sweet idea. Cut crusts from fresh white or wheat bread slices. Spread slices with margarine or butter. Cut each into two strips. Spread three bread strips with jelly. Roll up one, roll another around it, and the third around the second. Place finished individual portion of jelly wheel in muffin cup, cut side up. Bake at 425° F. for 10 minutes. Wonderful with tea.

9

CAKES

Basics and shortcuts for fine cakes, from baking to cutting

Mixes are time- and money-savers. Follow package directions and you'll bake a perfect cake every time you use a mix. You can even buy them complete to foil pan, made to fit the recipe for a modest-size cake that serves four nicely, and with another container that has frosting ingredients in it.

Take your pick of mixes. You have a choice of white, gold, chocolate, spice and various other mixes.

When you're a good mixer, have become familiar with a particular cake mix, you may want to vary it slightly by adding ¼ to 1 teaspoon of additional flavoring. And as long as you chop nuts fairly fine and cut up any fruits you may elect to put in the batter, the resulting cake becomes your special creation.

So you mix your own cake? Start with a sound recipe from a reliable tested source. Follow it exactly, without making changes or substitutions, unless you have made a particular recipe often enough to risk experimenting. Even then, only change flavoring or add solids such as chopped nuts and fruits. Why bother to change a recipe you know is good when you can simply select another from the many thousands published?

You need a baking routine. Read recipe carefully, start only when you really understand it. Determine how you will combine ingredients, assemble ingredients, assemble utensils, prepare pans for baking, making sure they're the proper size and kind.

Do first things first. Chop nuts, heat oven to specified temperature, sift the flour just before measuring it, separate eggs, etc.

Have standard measuring equipment and use it scrupulously, accurately. Never guess. Measure.

Important measuring tools. Two measuring cups (one for dry ingredients, the other for liquids) and one or two sets of measuring spoons are basic when you bake.

Ways to measure shortening. Press into measuring cup or tablespoon and pack lightly, scraping top flat with a spatula or straight knife. Another method is by water displacement. To measure ½ cup shortening, for example, first half fill cup with water. Add shortening by spoonful until water rises to the top of cup. Then drain off water.

In measuring butter, allow ½ pound for 1 cup.

Melted butter or shortening is measured like any liquid.

FLOUR AND BAKING POWDER

Know the role of the different flours in cake baking. Cake flour usually comes boxed, is specially milled for cakes, adds much to their delicacy.

All-purpose flour is used for pastries, biscuits, and breads, and for cakes that require moist, sturdy texture.

Self-rising flour contains leavening and salt and should be used only as per the instructions on the package.

Special bread flour is just that and nothing else, so must never be used in baking cake.

As a general rule, where a recipe specifies the kind of flour you are to use, use it.

Storing rule. To keep cake flour, close package flap securely after use and store in cool, dry place.

Keep your baking powder dry, too, as well as tightly closed and in a cool place. Long storage may reduce its strength too; better date the can so you may know when you bought it and replace if it's been on your pantry shelf for a year or more.

Two speeds of baking powder. Double-acting, in spite of its name, is actually the slow-acting powder because part of its content doesn't begin to work until the cake is actually in the oven and baking. The fast powder is labeled "tartrate" on the can, and if your recipe calls for that kind of baking powder, don't dawdle over getting the cake into your preheated oven.

Heed recipe specifications on the kind of baking powder to use, because the amount needed varies with the type of baking powder. It's generally safe to assume, however, that the one to use is the double-acting if the recipe simply calls for "baking powder."

In measuring flour, remember it has a tendency to pack. To avoid using more than necessary, sift flour before measuring. (A piece of waxed paper is a good base for the sifted flour, saves washing an extra bowl.) Lift sifted flour lightly by spoonfuls into cup, level off by drawing edge of spatula or flat knife across top. Never press flour or shake it down in cup.

Measure baking powder carefully. Even a small amount too much or too little can give disappointing results. Use dry standard measuring spoon. Dip spoon into baking powder, then level off lightly with edge of spatula or straight knife.

PANS ARE IMPORTANT

Let the pan fit the cake. For best results, cake batter should only half fill the pan. If you haven't the size pan a recipe calls for, however, select one of the same depth and approximately the same area (length times width).

Warped baking pans cause uneven baking. Warping may cause batter to run to one side of pan and spoil not only the appearance but also the quality of the finished product.

Metal pans of light materials are generally best for cakes. They heat quickly, yet reflect heat so that cakes brown delicately.

If cake pan is too shallow, you can build up the sides by lining with a "collar" or strip of heavy brown paper, to give desired height. Paper should be smoothed against greased sides of pan, then the paper itself well greased.

For attractive layer cakes: Insure uniform layers by using straight-sided pans and, if you're a true perfectionist, weighing batter, spooning it into each pan until weights are equal. A household scale works with you on this tip.

Baking insurance. Temper new metal pans before using. Grease them lightly, place in 300° F. oven for an hour or two. Insures better baking results.

If baking recipe calls for greased pan, use very soft or melted shortening. (Butter may be preferred, for flavor.) Dip pastry brush or small piece of crumpled paper toweling in shortening, rub over inside of pan to cover bottom and corners with thin grease film. Greasing sides of baking pans isn't necessary, wastes money and spoils cake's appearance.

Special note for angel-food and sponge cakes. Never grease the pan. These batters need to cling to sides of pan to reach full height. Batter, made up largely of beaten egg whites, is too delicate to hold up and give cake its full volume without support of sides of ungreased pan, to which cake clings during baking and cooling (in inverted pan). Greasing would cause such cakes to fall out of inverted pan while cooling, thus making them flat and soggy.

If you want to bake special-shaped cakes for festive occasions, yet haven't the space to store a lot of special-occasion cake pans, try shaping cake "pans" out of aluminum foil. Using heavy foil double, you can mold it into a heart for an engagement party, a Christmas tree for the Yule season, a star for the Fourth of July, and so on.

Bake 'em oblong, shape 'em later. Another way to have fancy cake shapes is to bake sheet cakes, cut paper patterns in the desired shape, lay the pattern on the cake, and carefully cut cake, using a hot knife, by following the edge of the pattern as you cut. Use leftover pieces of cake for petits fours and in cake-base desserts where the shape's unimportant.

Liners for cake pans. For a good fit, place your pan on several thicknesses of large pieces of waxed paper. Trace around pan with sharp knife. Cut out circle, or the shape pan you've traced. Place one sheet of paper in bottom of pan for one baking. It will be a luxury to have several spare liners handy for future bakings.

IN THE OVEN

Prepare the oven for baking. Be sure oven racks are correctly placed before heating oven. Place racks where heat is most even, so baked product will rise evenly and brown perfectly. Start heating oven early enough before baking so you have even heat of the right temperature before placing in oven to bake. If your oven isn't automatically heat-controlled, keep a reliable oven thermometer handy.

Don't crowd your oven. Never try to bake too much at once or place pans too close to oven wall. Heat must circulate freely on all sides of baking pan to give evenly baked results. When using two racks at the same time, do not place one pan directly over the other but stagger them on each rack.

"Baking-is-finished" signals. Usually the time in recipes is exactly right if your oven heat is correct. But, as safeguards, make these tests:

1. Product should have risen to full height and have delicately browned crust.

2. Insert wire cake tester or toothpick near center. It should come out clean and dry.

3. Cake (except sponge cake) should have shrunk away slightly from sides of pan.

4. Press top surface gently with finger. Surface springs back and leaves no imprint if cake is done.

Exceptions: Very rich cakes or chocolate cakes. On these, use only test 1 or 3, because such cakes sometimes cling to tester or may dent slightly when pressed, even though they are thoroughly baked.

THINGS THAT MAKE OR BREAK A CAKE

Cake won't break if you don't try to remove it from the pan before it is sufficiently cooled or cut it while still hot. Otherwise it may crumble.

Cake won't stick. Before placing that delicious cake masterpiece of yours on the plate, spray some powdered sugar over the plate. Keeps the cake from sticking and renders it as maneuverable as it should be.

"Life preserver" for sinking fruits and nuts. If you heat them in the oven, then dust with flour, before adding to cake batter, fruits and nuts won't go to the bottom of the pan.

Your cakes will be light and fluffy if you avoid overstirring or beating batter. Unless cake is very rich, stir after each addition of ingredients only until well blended and smooth.

Another precaution: guard against use of too much sugar or liquid, or too little leavening.

Your cake's appearance will be enhanced if you take this simple precaution when putting batter into baking pan: spread batter evenly and away into the corners.

Coarse grain spoils the appearance of angel or sponge cake. It is usually caused by underbeating egg whites or improper folding when added to the batter. Large holes come from air folded into batter as it is poured into pan. After batter is poured, cut through it with spatula to break large air bubbles and thus eliminate holes.

THE TOP'S THE BEST PART

Frosting—your cake's crowning glory. There are several "basics" you want to know about, and vary.

Seven-minute frosting. Combine 2 egg whites, 1½ cups granulated sugar, ½ cup water, a tablespoon white corn syrup, ½ teaspoon salt in double-boiler top. Place over rapidly boiling water. Beat at medium electric-mixer speed for 7 minutes, or as steadily as you can by hand with an egg beater. Remove from range. Add a teaspoon vanilla extract and continue beating until mixture forms stiff peaks. This makes enough frosting for top and sides of two 8- or 9-inch layers.

Chocolate seven-minute frosting. When frosting is done, fold in 2 squares of melted, cooled, unsweetened chocolate.

Velvety frosting. Melt package of semi-sweet chocolate pieces over hot water. Cool slightly. Separately, mix ½ cup soft butter with 2 unbeaten eggs. Add chocolate, beating until smooth and firm enough to hold peaks.

Quick fudge frosting. Melt 2 packages semi-sweet chocolate pieces over hot water. Add 3 cups sifted confectioners' sugar, ¼ cup soft shortening, ½ cup hot milk. Remove from heat. Beat with spoon until smooth.

Bittersweet frosting. Combine 2¼ cups sifted confectioners' sugar, ¼ cup hot water, 9 squares melted, unsweetened chocolate. Stir only enough to dampen sugar. Add 3 unbeaten eggs, one at a time, beating vigorously with spoon until smooth. Add ½ cup plus 2 tablespoons butter, then beat until melted and smooth. Add dash of salt and 1½ teaspoons vanilla extract.

Whipped-cream frosting. Sprinkle ½ teaspoon unflavored gelatin over 2 tablespoons cold water in small bowl. Let stand a few minutes. Scald 2 tablespoons heavy cream and pour over gelatin, stirring to dissolve. Chill. When mixture is thick, but not stiff, beat. Whip cup of heavy cream (less the 2 tablespoons scalded). Fold in whipped-cream gelatin mixture. Add dash of salt, 2 tablespoons confectioners' sugar, ½ teaspoon lemon juice.

Chocolate whipped cream. Same as whipped-cream frosting, omitting lemon juice and substituting a package of cooled, melted, semi-sweet chocolate pieces. Fold melted chocolate into whipped-cream frosting.

Orange whipped cream. In whipped-cream frosting, leave out lemon juice and substitute teaspoon of grated orange rind.

Coffee whipped cream. To whipped-cream frosting add teaspoon of instant-coffee powder.

Chocolate curls are most festive, especially on whipped cream and marshmallow frostings. Allow square of unsweetened chocolate to stand where it will warm up but not melt. Using a vegetable parer or sharp paring knife, shave off very thin slices from the back of the chocolate square. Chocolate curls automatically if you slice it thin enough.

Butter frosting without cooking. Cream sifted confectioners' sugar into butter or margarine. Add cream, milk, fruit juice, or other liquid—enough to give it spreading consistency. Be sure to use XXXX (confectioners') sugar.

TOPPING TIPS

Cooked cake frostings spread smoother if you cool cake thoroughly before frosting. Then brush off all loose crumbs and trim off ragged edges. Use spatula to spread frosting.

Hint on tints. To tint frostings, add vegetable coloring, a few drops at a time, and mix frosting until evenly tinted. Light, delicate shades are usually more appetizing and attractive than bright colors.

For "different" cake toppings, after the cake is frosted add such extra touches as chopped nuts, walnut halves arranged attractively, shredded coconut, cocoa sprinkled around a cardboard pattern or through a paper doily over white frosting, vanilla sugar on dark frosting, candied fruit.

When using pastry bag, fill only half full of frosting at a time for best results. Use one hand to guide tip and other to force frosting out gently. If in doubt about results, practice first on a piece of waxed paper. You can scoop up the practice frosting and put it back in the pastry bag, and if it becomes a little too thick, dilute with a drop or two of hot water.

Make your own pastry bags out of paper or cloth. Here's how:

1. Paper. Cut rectangle, 10 inches by 8 inches, of sturdy waxed paper or thin parchment paper. Cut rectangle diagonally into two triangles. Roll each into cone shape and fold down top points of cone to hold in place. Snip off top of cone to provide small opening. It's nice to have the spare pastry bag when you're doing a lot of cake decorating.

2. Cloth. Shape bag from muslin or light canvas, then stitch. Metal tips of varying sizes and patterns can be inserted at bottom of either cloth or paper cone. You'll find them in

some hardware stores and in house-wares sections of department stores.

Tip to keep top from tipping. If the top layer begins to slide when you frost a cake, insert wire cake tester or thin knitting needle through both layers to keep top layer in position. Remove wire or needle before frosting top layer. Or else leave it in until frosting is set, then cover mark with cake decoration.

Very special cakes. It pays to frost smoothly first with a thin layer of frosting, to hold down any crumbs and to give an even base coat. When set or firm, the final frosting will spread more evenly and easily.

New use for toothpicks. When trimming cake frosting, use toothpick to trace design lightly. Then apply trimming, such as tiny candies, nuts, melted jelly.

HOW TO BE AN ARTIST WITH CAKE

Take a piece of cake, whether you or the baker baked it, and start creating. You can work miracles with it in no time at all. Here are a few to start you off:

Baked Alaska. Spoon 1 pint ice cream on cake; cover with meringue topping. Bake at 450° F. 5 minutes. Serve at once, cut in wedges, with or without sauce.

Lemon cream cake. Split cake layer into two layers. Fill with packaged lemon-pudding pie mix made as label directs. Sift confectioners' sugar over top of cake.

Quick banana lemon cream cake. Slice ½ large banana over individual sponge cakes. Make lemon pudding from pudding mix, following package directions. Spoon over the bananas and cake. Garnish with fresh raspberries.

Tea toasties. Spread cake slices with butter or margarine; sprinkle with nutmeg or combined sugar and cinnamon; broil until bubbly and brown.

"Poached egg on toast." Place canned peach half, with cut side down, on cake square. Surround with almond-flavored whipped cream.

Cream topper. After whipping heavy cream, fold in rum or rum flavoring, grated lemon rind or chocolate, or applesauce. Use to top cake squares.

Chocolate whipped-cream cake. Split two cake layers, making four in all. Whip 1 cup heavy cream until it thickens; add ½ cup canned chocolate sauce all at once. Beat until mixture mounds. Fill and frost cake layers. Chill 24 hours before serving.

Star cake. Cut filled and frosted two-layer cake into wedges. Arrange wedges in circle, on a large platter, with points out. Fill center with balls of ice cream. Serve with sauce, if desired.

Fruit cheesecake. Top wedges of cheesecake with canned crushed pineapple, sliced peaches, fresh or frozen strawberries.

Cake shortcake. Split two layers, making four in all. Fill and top with one of these fruits: crushed raspberries or strawberries (fresh or frozen), canned crushed pineapple, berries and sliced peaches combined, canned fruit cocktail, sliced fresh or canned peaches, spiced apple-sauce, orange sections, canned cranberry sauce. Serve cut in wedges, with cold custard sauce or whipped cream.

Cake pudding. Heat cake slices in double boiler. Serve with coffee ice cream or hot lemon sauce. For firm slices, simply heat them in your toaster. Another way is to sauté them in the skillet in a little butter. This is particularly good for poundcake, both raisin and plain.

Ablaze. Place around cake six cubes of sugar dipped in lemon extract. Light cubes with a match and serve cake in a blaze of elegance.

Pineapple dream. Fold drained, crushed pineapple into whipped cream. Serve over squares of gingerbread or poundcake.

"Terrific" trifle. Sprinkle cake crumbs with sherry, top with custard sauce. Chill. Garnish with bits of bright jelly, nutmeg, or chocolate shavings or curls.

PARTY CAKE FOR CHILDREN, BIRTHDAYS, OR OTHER "OCCASION" DAYS

You can make petits fours. Cut a slice of cake into bite-size squares or in the shape of diamonds, circles, etc., and give each piece a topping. Just start and then let your imagination carry you the rest of the way. Any good cookbook will give you frosting recipes.

Balloon cake. Set gumdrop slices, with cut sides down, on angel, sponge, or chiffon tube cake frosted with white icing. Paint strings with toothpick dipped in food coloring. Add green and yellow candles.

Tic-tac-toe. Frost 9-inch by 9-inch by 2-inch cake with white icing. Outline 2-inch squares by drizzling melted chocolate thinned with corn syrup on icing. Set tiny yellow candles diagonally across top. Place inside each 2-inch-square gumdrop rings (with cut sides up), tiny candy balls or gumdrops, and candles.

Sweet sixteen. Frost angel cake with white icing tinted pink. Press spatula on icing, then lift to make peaks. Insert candy wafers around edge. Group sugar cubes, tied with ribbons, around cake.

Minted cake. Fill and frost chocolate cake layers with white icing tinted green. Coat all except center top with coconut. Brush mint sprigs with water, dust with granulated sugar, tuck around edges. Set candles in center.

Butterfly cakes. Make butter frosting. Reserve ⅓ cup. Halve jam-filled layer cake. Frost halves. Set each at angle. Place half a paper doily (with plain center) on each; sift sweetened cocoa; lift off doily.

Add melted chocolate to remaining frosting. With cake decorator, add two names in plain areas left when doily halves were removed. Antennae are colored pipe cleaners.

Roly-poly. Frost jelly roll or two from baker (set end to end) with white icing tinted green, reserving ⅓ cup. Add melted chocolate to remaining icing. With cake decorator write guests' names on each portion of jelly roll.

WIN A CUP FOR CUPCAKES

A champion cupcake maker provides fun as well as delicious dessert food with the fabulous variety you can get from just one baking. The trick is in frostings and individualized decorations.

Clown cupcake. Here is fun indeed. Frost top of cupcake with an orange cream or butter frosting. Make eyes, nose, mouth out of bits of candied cherries. Serve cupcake turned on its side and decorate with a colorful "hat" made of paper nut cup.

Butterfly cupcake. With paring knife remove cone-shaped piece from top center of cupcake. Fill hollow with whipped cream, cream filling, or white frosting. Cut cake cone in half. Press the two halves into filling to look like butterfly wings. Use stems of maraschino cherries for antennae.

Tips for tiptop tops. To get perfectly shaped cupcakes, grease just the bottoms of cupcake cups. This helps keep cupcakes from running over. Or buy packaged paper liners for your cupcake cups. Then you'll have no greasing or scouring to do, no rough edges, and no chance of cake's sticking to the bottom. Just peel off paper liners when cupcakes are cool. Never fill cupcake cups more than half full. Fill a cupcake cup with water, measure the water, then use half that amount of batter for each cupcake. Cup from graduated set is good for pouring batter. So is a small soup ladle.

TIME-SAVERS AND STORAGE HINTS

Electric mixer saves time, energy, does variety of jobs for you. It not only mixes perfect cake batters but also provides short cuts to dozens of interesting desserts, frostings, beverages, and soufflés, chops fruits better than you can by hand.

To maintain freshness, cover any kind of cake, either with a special cover designed to go over a cake pan or with waxed paper. Large cakes may be halved and wrapped for home freezer storage or in the freezing compartment of your refrigerator.

Melt chocolate the easy way. Grease the pan in which you melt chocolate; makes dishwashing easy afterward. Or melt chocolate in little cup made out of two thicknesses of aluminum foil.

Cakes take to freezing. You may bake your cake ahead of time for parties or box lunches, or for unexpected guests.

Frost cake before freezing, if you wish, but remember not all frostings freeze well. If saving time is your motive and you must frost before freezing, don't use seven-minute or egg-type frostings; they become rubbery when frozen.

Frozen cakes will thaw rapidly at room temperature. For best eating quality, they should be served the day you thaw them.

Always refrigerate whipped-cream-frosted cakes, cream-filled cakes, or puff pastries.

Leave fruitcake in original wrapper until ready to serve. Briefly stored, fruitcake may be wrapped in a lint-free cloth. Sprinkle a few drops of brandy or cider over the cloth occasionally to keep cake moist and fresh. For long storage, keep cake in covered metal container that is not entirely airtight.

Serve stale cake fresh, with orange slices, for a quick, attractive hot dessert. Slice cake and top each slice with two slices of orange. Arrange in shallow pan. Cream together a little butter and sugar, stir in an egg yolk and grated orange rind, and spoon over cake and orange slices. Run under broiler five minutes, or until delicately browned.

To freshen stale cake, wrap it in a towel, then put it into a slightly warm oven for a few minutes before serving.

For a novelty dessert treat, try new flavor combinations in your next cake. Delicious blends result from combining two flavors, such as lemon with vanilla, or rose with almond extract.

Use spices sparingly in baking. Measure amounts accurately, because too much spice disguises delicate flavor of baked goods. Sift spices with flour to blend well with other ingredients.

Choose the proper cake plate. Plate should "frame" the cake, be as flat as possible, and extend about two inches beyond edge of cake all the way around. If too large or deep, plate will dwarf the cake. If too small, cake will look giant-clumsy.

THE ART OF CAKE CUTTING

Use long, sharp knife in cutting cake to be sure you don't spoil its looks. If cake is frosted, rinse knife in hot water before using. Cut with gentle, sawing motion. Do not press down.

For sponge cake or angel food, cut lightly with very sharp or serrated knife, or gently "tear" off each piece, using two forks or a cake breaker.

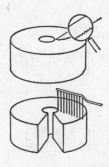

The following diagrams illustrate methods of cutting cakes of various sizes and shapes.

Sheet Cakes

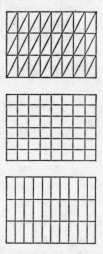

Layer Cakes

Square Cakes

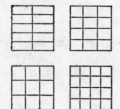

Loaf Cakes

TIER CAKES

The average number of portions that various sized layers will yield are as follows:

14-inch layer will yield approximately 40 servings.

12-inch layer will yield approximately 30 servings.

10-inch layer will yield approximately 20 servings.

9-inch layer will yield approximately 16 servings.

8-inch layer will yield approximately 12 servings.

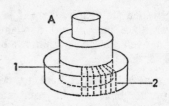

A—Cut vertically through the bottom layer at the edge of the second layer as indicated by the dotted line marked 1; then cut out wedge-shaped pieces as shown by 2.

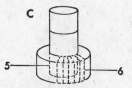

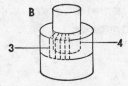

B—When these pieces have been served, follow the same procedure with the middle layer; cut vertically through the second layer at the edge of the top layer as indicated by dotted line 4; then cut out wedge-shaped pieces as shown by 3.

C—When pieces from the second layer have been served, return to the bottom layer and cut along dotted line 5; cut another row of wedge-shaped pieces as shown by 6.

D—The remaining tiers may be cut into the desired size pieces.

10

PIES

How to make them right—including some different pie ideas—plus a P.S. on waffles and pancakes

Crust is the crux of the pie matter. For flaky, tender-crust pastry that nevertheless has body, use all-purpose flour, sometimes called "family flour." Sift it just before making level measurements.

To make a shortening story long. The right kind of flour isn't enough to make pie pastry tender and flaky; you need the right kind of shortening too. The following types serve the purpose well:

1. All-vegetable shortening. Excellent, needs no refrigeration.

2. Lard, traditional. (Regular lard must be refrigerated, new-type lard need not be.)

3. Meat-and-vegetable shortening. The name is self-explanatory. Where a recipe specifies the kind of shortening or oil to be used, follow directions for best results.

Liquid assets. Liquid is the cement between flour and fat. The amount is, therefore, most important for consistency. Follow specifications carefully. If there's too little liquid, dough falls to pieces. If there's too much, the pastry will be tough. Where the recipe says "about," start with less liquid, then add the rest gradually and cautiously. Most frequently the liquid is water: cold water from the tap, or boiling water, as directed by the recipe. Sometimes recipe calls for milk.

Easy steps to flaky crust. Sift together 2¼ cups enriched all-purpose flour and a teaspoon of salt. Sift into bowl. Spoon ¼ cup flour mixture into a cup or bowl. Measure shortening (not butter, margarine, or salad oil) in ½-cup and ¼-cup parts of your measuring-cup set. Pack well; level with spatula. Drop shortening into flour; scrape the cups clean with a rubber spatula. Cut in shortening with pastry blender or with two knives, until all parts are the size of small peas. Mix the reserved ¼ cup flour with ⅓ cup water. With a fork, stir into pastry until particles cling together when pressed gently. Make a smooth ball of the dough, then divide in two. Roll half of dough to 12-inch circle. Fold it in half toward you. Center the fold on 9-inch pie plate. Unfold the circle away from you. Fill. Trim lower crust even with edge of pie plate. Save trimmings for decorative edging.

ROLLING CAN MAKE OR MAR A PIE

Roll right. Unless recipe says otherwise, use a stockinet-covered rolling pin and flour lightly. Use a cloth-covered board. Roll the floured pin over the board twice, to rub the flour off on it lightly. Shape half of the dough into a ball on cloth. Flatten with patting motion of pin. Now make a circle by rolling lightly from the center of the dough in all directions. As you approach the edges, lift the rolling pin, to avoid splitting the edge of the dough or thinning it down too much. Occasionally lift dough to give it a quarter turn, but do not turn it over. If it seems to stick, lift it gently by slipping rubber spatula under edge and sprinkling a little flour on the cloth on the board. Not much, though, as too much flour toughens pastry. Continue to roll out until the circle is 12 inches in diameter. Make sure there are no cracks or holes into which the filling can later seep.

No rolling pin handy? Well, what's wrong with a nice big soda bottle? Just slip a stockinet cover over it and you have a reasonable facsimile of a rolling pin, if one not quite as handy as if it had two handles.

The upper crust. A pie should be perfect right up to the upper crust.

To proceed: roll the other half of the pastry into another 12-inch circle. Fold it in half. Take a knife and make several slits to serve as vents to let the steam escape when you bake the pie. Moisten edge of bottom crust with water. Place top crust over the filling, centering the fold, then unfold to make complete

circle. Fasten edges down by pressing. Cut excess dough off top of crust. Glaze. Another way to place top crust over filling, after rolling out top circle: roll it onto pin and unroll it over the filling. Then make slits for vents. Glaze.

Slitting pretty. You can make these slits whether you do it over the filling or by first folding the upper crust in half. If you use the folding method, you can make the cuts through both halves of the circle, like cutting a paper doll. Cut in pattern shown by dotted lines. This way the slits will form an exactly symmetrical design. If you make the slits after the top crust is in place over the filling, you can still follow the designs. Just disregard the fact that half of each design consists of dotted lines.

Let off steam from your pie another attractive way: Place top crust on

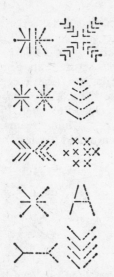

there are bubbles, prick the shell again. Cool on rack before filling. If filling is to bake with shell, don't prick shell at all.

Here are some pretty, yet easy, edgings you can give your pie masterpieces. Caution: Where you use fork or skewer, dip it in flour before using.

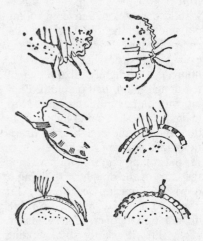

filling, secure it at edge of lower crust. Then, with a small cutter in the shape of a heart, star, or bunny, make six cutouts evenly spread in a circle all through the top crust but do not remove the cutouts.

Whether you make your own crust dough or use a packaged pie crust, you will want to bake to a beautiful shape. Here's how: Place bottom crust in pie plate loosely. Then, with your hands or with balls of pastry, pat out air, so that pastry fits snugly. Trim the overhang, leaving a ½- to 1-inch edge. If baking involves only the shell, and filling is added later and is not to be baked, take a four-tined fork and prick the lower crust closely and deeply around sides and in bottom of shell. After chilling shell for a half hour, bake for 12 to 15 minutes at 450° F. Look in on it after five minutes of baking, though. If

When it's not a double-crust pie or an open-top or deep-dish pie, what is it? Well, it may be a trellis pie. And here's how to make it: Roll-cut ½-inch-wide pastry strips, 10 in all.

Take a strip, attach to edge of pie shell; press. Twist strip across filling. Attach strip to pastry on opposite side, then press firmly. Attach 4 more strips parallel to the first. Then repeat with the remaining strips, so they cross the first ones. Turn overhang up over the rim, press and seal each strip tightly to rim. Flute the edge, brush strips with melted butter or cream. A lattice pie is made the same way, except that you don't twist strips.

Baking day is decoration day. Illustrations show the unusual decorative effects you can achieve with pastry strips.

A variation on the basic crust: Nut crust. Make mixture of a cup of finely ground almonds, walnuts, pecans, or Brazil nuts and 2 tablespoons of granulated sugar. Use the back of a tablespoon to press mixture into pie plate, bottom and sides only, not the rim. Bake at 400° F. for 8 minutes.

Another variation on standard crust: No-bake graham crust. Make crumbs of graham crackers, then mix 1⅓ cups graham-cracker crumbs, ⅓ cup brown sugar, ½ teaspoon cinnamon, ⅓ cup melted butter. With back of a tablespoon, press mixture into 9-inch, well-greased pie plate, bottom and sides only, not the rim. Chill very well, fill, then cover with 3 tablespoons of the graham-cracker crumb mixture.

THE FINE POINTS IN PIE BAKING

Reason for tough pastry may be in mixing it too long, or handling it too heavily, or using too much water, or not enough shortening. Good pastry is the result of speed, a light hand, and not much rolling.

Extra pie-crust mix is a must. Keep one on your shelf as emergency measure. The late hour when you'll be grateful to have it may come early.

Avoid warped pie shells by remembering to add enough prebaking fork pricks and to inspect the pie after five minutes of baking to see if any blisters have appeared that have to be pricked while baking.

Slouching pie shells are a sign of one of two omissions: flutes may not have been pressed to plate firmly enough, or pie has not been chilled for a half hour before baking.

Good pastry greases itself, does not rely on a greased pie plate.

Safe transfer of bottom crust. To eliminate the annoyance of having a fragile round of pie crust break as you are lifting it into the pie plate, roll your crust out on a piece of aluminum foil cut to a circle about 2 inches wider than the pan. With the foil as a guide, you'll find it easy to roll the crust to the right size and shape. Then lift the foil, with the crust on it, and place both in the pie pan with no danger of the crust tearing. You can trim the crust with scissors to the proper size, but leave a fringe of aluminum foil an inch or two wide to catch any juices that may leak from pie and try to run over. And, best of all, the pie plate won't need washing.

To line casseroles and baking dishes with aluminum foil, mold foil over back of utensil, then fit inside. Smooth out and arrange decorative ruffle around top edge of utensil.

Glass bakeware has advantages in pie baking. It gives pie nice, even, brown undercrust. Glass pans are as safe to use as metal ones if oven temperature is kept slightly lower than called for in recipe.

Overjuicy pies need not run over. Suggestions: Before baking, insert 1½-inch pieces of uncooked macaroni in several of the slits in the top crust. Remove macaroni before serving, of course. Or wrap wet pie tape around the rim before putting the pie in the oven. Or cut the vent slits nearer the center of the top and away from the edges. Or make fluted or forked edge, illustrated on page 84, to help seal in the fruit juices. If fruit juice insists on drip-ping, bake pie on upper rack of oven and catch juices on pan, cookie sheet, or aluminum foil placed in the bottom of the oven. If juices don't run, but you prefer thicker filling, cool pies for 2 or more hours between finishing and serving.

To make fruit pies less juicy, try this: When preparing the filling, beat 1 egg white stiff, mix with the amount of sugar required for the filling, add 1 tablespoonful of flour, then mix thoroughly with fruit and other ingredients, if any.

MERINGUE TOP SECRETS

For an honest, upstanding meringue, set out 3 eggs to warm to room temperature, as egg whites can then be beaten to greater volume. Turn on oven, set at 400° F. Separate eggs. (If you're not using the yolks, add a little water, cover, and store in the refrigerator. They go fine as part of scrambled eggs another day. Water prevents hard crust from forming on yolks, may be poured off if you've managed not to break the yolks.) Beat eggs until frothy but not stiff. Gradually add 4 tablespoons granulated sugar, beating after each addition. Beat until stiff peaks form. Peaks should be so stiff they stand upright and don't curl over. Spoon meringue onto filled 9-inch pie. Spread with a spatula so that meringue touches inner edge of crust all around. This avoids shrinkage when baked. Pull up points all over the meringue, with your spatula, to make it attractive. Bake at 400° F. 8 to 10 minutes, until it turns a very delicate brown. It's done if it's dry to the touch. Cool on a rack and keep out of drafts.

Hurry-up lemon-meringue pie. Combine 1⅓ cups canned, sweetened condensed milk with ½ cup lemon juice, a teaspoon grated lemon rind, and the yolks of 2 eggs. Blend and cook over low heat, stirring constantly, until thickened. Pour into 8-inch baked pie shell. Top with meringue made with the 2 egg whites. Bake until meringue is golden brown. Cool.

"Meringue lemon" pie. That's not a printing error, but a different kind of pie. It's made with a meringue shell that brims out to a luscious, crinkly-looking picture-frame border. The meringue shell is filled with a velvety lemon cream. The edge of the shell is sprinkled with toasted shredded coconut. The delicious concoction then goes into the refrigerator for at least 12 hours, preferably overnight. For a real effect, decorate top with fresh strawberries in center and blobs of sweetened, freshly whipped cream "petals" with toasted shredded coconut "dew" on them.

Meringue shells. It's easiest to order them from your bakery. But they're fun to make. Beat 4 room-temperature egg whites until frothy. Sprinkle ¼ teaspoon salt on top and beat until stiff. Gradually beat in ½ cup sugar, adding 2 tablespoons at a time. Add ½ teaspoon vanilla,

then fold in another ½ cup sugar, gradually, but stop beating. Color with vegetable coloring if you wish, just a few drops; they should be pastel colored at most. With pastry bag or spoon shape mounds of the meringue on ungreased, paper-covered baking sheet. Bake at 275° F. 45 to 60 minutes, or until very delicately browned and dry on surface. Remove from paper while warm and cool on cake rack. If meringues stick to paper, moisten bottom side of paper by placing on wet towel, then remove meringues with spatula. Recipe makes 3 dozen large or 5 dozen small meringues.

Don't weep over "weeping" meringue. Remember never to add more than 2 tablespoons of sugar per egg white. And be sure to beat as directed and to spread it so it gets into every nook and cranny of the pie-crust edges. Cool it slowly, too.

Fractureproof meringue cutting. To keep your fragile, precious meringue topping from breaking up, come cutting time, sprinkle a little granulated sugar over it before cutting.

PIE IDEAS THAT ARE DIFFERENT

Instant apple pie. If you have a baked-and-stored pie shell handy, ready for just reheating in the oven, you can make a quick filling with cooked canned pie apples. They come all prepared, precooked, sliced, cored, and delicious. Use a can of pie apples, ⅓ to ½ cup granulated sugar, a teaspoon of lemon juice, ¼ teaspoon nutmeg, a dash of salt, ¼ teaspoon grated lemon rind, ¼ teaspoon cinnamon, 1½ teaspoons butter or margarine, ½ tablespoon flour. Fill shell, put the pie in preheated 350° F. oven for ten minutes.

Mince-apple pie. Make as usual, but in preparing filling, combine 2 cups of pared, cored thin apple slices with two cups of mincement.

Mock pumpkin pie. Few can tell the difference, yet this "pumpkin" pie is made from sweet potatoes or steamed squash. For an egg, substitute a tablespoon of cooked oatmeal beaten into the custard mixture.

Spirited apple pie. When pie is baked, slowly trickle 3 tablespoons of brandy through the slits in the crust.

1-2-3 pie. Step 1: Bake (or have ready) a 9-inch pie shell. Step 2: Fill shell with 3 cups sliced strawberries or peaches. Step 3: Top with whipped cream, sweetened or not. And there you are!

Strawberry-rhubarb pie. It's really just like apple pie, except you use 3 cups frozen rhubarb, just thawed, and 3 cups sliced fresh strawberries. Also ¾ cup granulated sugar, ⅛ teaspoon salt, ¼ teaspoon nutmeg, ½ teaspoon cinnamon, 4 tablespoons flour, 1 tablespoon butter.

Blueberry pie short cut. Line a 9-inch pie plate with vanilla wafers or lemon snaps. Make an instant vanilla pudding from a package. Pour it into the wafer-lined pie plate. Chill. Just before serving, cover top with washed-and-dried fresh blueberries.

Apricot-cheese pie. Blend ¾ package cream cheese and a cup of sour cream into a smooth mixture. About half an hour before serving, spread mixture into a baked pie shell. Top it with well-drained canned apricots. Sprinkle with combination of ⅓ cup granulated sugar and a teaspoon cinnamon. Chill.

Deep-dish apple pie. Heat oven to 425° F. Combine cup of granulated sugar (or ½ cup granulated and ½ cup brown sugar) with 2 tablespoons flour, ⅛ teaspoon salt, ¼ teaspoon nutmeg, ¼ teaspoon cinnamon, teaspoon lemon juice, 2 teaspoons butter. Mix with 6 cups sliced apples and turn into a baking dish 10 by 6 by 2 inches. Roll crust pastry on top of dish, to fit loosely, leaving ½-inch overhang. Make slits or cutout vents. Fold overhang under and press firmly onto the rim with a floured fork. Glaze. Bake at 425° F. for 40 minutes, or until done. Toppings: cream or ice cream with dash of nutmeg, whipped cream with chopped nuts, hard sauce.

The chocolate chiffon pie. Place 24 vanilla wafers in 2 rows on a large piece of waxed paper. Fold paper over wafers and tuck under so that wafers are wrapped. With rolling pin roll wafers gently until reduced to fine crumbs. Now measure 1⅓ cups of crumbs into 2-cup measuring cup. Add ¼ cup soft butter. Mix with fork until crumbly. Set aside 3 tablespoons of this mixture. Spread the remainder of crumbs into the bottom and on sides of a 9-inch pie plate. Press crumbs evenly to the plate with the back of a tablespoon, press to the rim with your other hand. Then soak an envelope of plain gelatin in ¼ cup water. Melt 2 squares chocolate in ½ cup water, double-boiler method. Into melted chocolate stir 3 egg yolks. Cook and stir, over boiling water, until creamy. This should take about 2 minutes. Add gelatin and stir until dissolved. Pour into mixing bowl. Add ¼ teaspoon salt, 1 teaspoon vanilla, and stir. Fold in a stiff meringue made of 3 egg whites and ½ cup sugar. Spoon final mixture into crumb crust and chill until set. Serve with whipped cream made from ½ cup cream, then top with 3 tablespoons of the crumb mixture reserved for this moment.

All that's pie isn't pie-size. Don't forget you can make little pies and tarts too. They're lots of fun and, in a small way, are made the same way as big pies are.

Turnovers made of pie dough are wonderful for picnics and lunch boxes. Cut pie crust in 4-inch squares or 4½-inch circles. Fill half the area with fruit or mince or cheese filling. Turn pastry over to form triangle or half-circle respectively. Seal in filling by pressing the edges together with a fork. Slit the tops and bake 15 minutes at 450° F.

Leftover pastry dough may be pressed together, rolled into a ⅛-inch-thick sheet. Top it with butter or margarine, creamed with brown sugar and chopped nuts, or with a mixture of sugar and cinnamon, or with grated cheese. Cut pastry into strips, rounds, or squares, or roll it up like a jelly roll and slice roll ¼ inch thick. Bake at 400° F. 8 to 10 minutes. Nice with tea, salad lunch, midnight snack.

HOW TO FREEZE—HOW TO THAW

Frozen unbaked pie shell. Leave shell in pie plate. (Bake it in a metal-edged paper freezer pie plate so you don't tie up your regular baking equipment.) Freeze shells, properly wrapped for freezing, one at a time. Later stack frozen shells, separated by paddings of crumpled waxed paper, overwrapped with moisture-vaporproof material.

How to freeze baked pie shell. Cool baked shell at room temperature. Freeze, then wrap. Store with or without pie plate. Stack in freezer, if you have several, well wrapped during storage.

Freezing pie shells, generally. It's best to freeze shells already baked. They are then ready for filling at a moment's notice. But, baked or unbaked, pie shells are fragile, so get them into a sheltered area of the freezer and don't store too many at the same time.

How to thaw that frozen unbaked pie shell. Unwrap. Bake at 450° F. 5 minutes. Prick again, if necessary, and bake 15 minutes longer. Or allow shell to remain wrapped at room temperature for a half hour. Then bake 5 minutes, check for further pricking, and bake another 7 minutes.

How to thaw frozen baked pie shell. Unwrap. Heat at 375° F. for 10 minutes, or until thawed. Or leave on wrapping and thaw at room temperature.

How to freeze unbaked fruit pies. Don't make slits in the top crust. Leave in pie plate and cover with an inverted pie plate, preferably a paper one. This protects the pie and allows you to stack another on top of it. Wrap covered pie with moistureproof, vaporproof foil or freezer paper. Label, date, and freeze. Use within 2 months, while they are at their best in quality and flavor. (Cherry pie is not recommended for freezing unbaked.)

How to freeze baked fruit pies, including cherry pie. Cool pies at room temperature, then wrap like unbaked pies, and freeze. Be sure pies stay level inside freezer, so fruit juice won't drip. Use within 4 months.

How to thaw frozen unbaked fruit pies. Take off wrapping. Make slits in top crust. Bake at 425° F. 40 to 60 minutes if it's a deep-dish pie, 45 to 60 minutes for a double-crust pie.

How to thaw frozen baked fruit pies. Remove wrapping. Heat in 375° F. oven for 30 to 50 minutes for deep-dish pie, 35 to 50 minutes for double-crust pie.

How to freeze chiffon pies. Lemon, orange, chocolate, and nesselrode pies may be frozen only in baked shells. After filling has set, wrap as described for freezing fruit pies and freeze. Use within 4 months.

How to thaw chiffon pies. Unwrap and leave at room temperature for an hour or two. If it thaws before you are ready to serve it, put it in the refrigerator until serving time. Add whipped-cream topping either while pie is thawing or just before serving. If necessary, cut one or more wedges from the frozen, unthawed pie and return pie itself to the freezer—wrapped, of course.

Not recommended for freezing. Cream or custard-type pies tend to become grainy and crack when frozen. Some curdle, become lumpy. Meringue toughens and shrinks.

NON-FREEZER REFRIGERATED STORAGE

Two-day-old fruit pies taste ovenfresh if stored in the refrigerator and reheated at 350° F. for 7 to 10 minutes before serving. Pies just brought home from the bakery are also restored to original oven-fresh flavor if heated for about 3 minutes before serving.

Right way to keep pie shells fresh. Pie shells may be made in advance of baking and stored by covering with foil or waxed paper and refrigerated for 2 or 3 days. Or bake pie shells in advance of filling and store, covered; then reheat for 5 minutes at 425° F.

Pie, unless served fresh-from-the-oven warm, must be kept cold. If you don't serve it right after baking, store it in the refrigerator. Once served, whether it came from the oven or refrigerator, don't let pie stand on table. Slip it right back into the refrigerator.

BREAKFAST PIES: PANCAKES AND WAFFLES

Double-acting baking powder is a time-saver. When used in preparing waffle or griddle-cake batter, mixture can be made ahead of time and stored several hours in refrigerator, because powder releases only about one third of its leavening action when cold, remaining two thirds during baking process.

Tastier waffles. Instead of using milk, try making waffles with cold water and see how nicely crisp and appetizing they turn out.

Waffles won't stick to grids after this procedure: Clean grids with baking soda. Apply soda with stiff, wire-bristled brush. Removes all discoloration.

Easy way to keep pancakes from sticking. Fill small cheesecloth bag with table salt. Just before pouring batter, rub salt bag over surface of hot skillet or griddle. Not only keeps batter from sticking, but does away with need to grease utensil.

For extra-tasty pancakes, add a tablespoon of pancake syrup to the batter.

Fresh-raspberry pancakes. Fold a cup of fresh raspberries into batter of your favorite breakfast pancake recipe, using 2 cups flour.

11

SWEETS AND DESSERTS

Low-cost ways to make new desserts, cookies, puddings, and other treats—including ice cream

Go easy on sugar when you make refrigerator desserts. Too much sugar prevents proper freezing.

Store brown sugar in refrigerator. Moist cold prevents sugar from hardening.

To keep brown sugar soft and moist, place a cut apple or a slice of bread in the container and cover it.

If brown sugar has hardened, rub the solid chunk of sugar back and forth against a kitchen grater placed over a bowl. A kitchen sieve does the trick too.

Store honey in a warm, dry place. If kept in cellar or other damp spot, it is likely to absorb moisture and ferment.

Best way to measure syrups. Thick liquids and syrups (molasses, honey, etc.) should be poured into a measuring cup or spoon from their original containers. If cup has already been used to measure shortening or water, syrup will empty out readily. Don't dip measuring spoon into sticky liquids, for too much will cling to the underside of the spoon, causing overmeasurement or waste.

Measure molasses the easy way. First dip measuring cup full of flour. Empty it back into flour sack (or tin) and you leave a coating that prevents molasses from sticking to the glass. Every drop comes out cleanly.

NEW AND UNUSUAL DESSERTS

Banana "whipped cream." Add sliced banana to white of an egg and beat until stiff. Sugar according to taste. Tastes every bit as good as whipped cream, costs less, provides novel dessert topping.

Black-and-white creams. Cut chocolate cupcakes part way down the center. Fill gash with whipped cream, sprinkle with toasted shaved almonds.

Orange fluff. Whip 1 cup heavy cream, mix with 1 cup coconut shreds, 2 tablespoons orange juice, 1 teaspoon orange rind. Top sponge-cake wedges with it.

Prune cream. Pit and slice 1 cup unsweetened cooked prunes. Beat 2 egg whites, gradually beat in ½ cup granulated sugar. Fold into whipped cream (from 1 cup heavy cream) together with dash of powdered cloves, 1 teaspoon vanilla extract, 1 cup of coarse graham-cracker crumbs, and the prunes. Spoon into sherbet glasses. Refrigerate.

Always-fresh doughnuts. To recapture that "just-out-of-the-kettle" flavor of plain cake doughnuts, place them in a covered casserole and bake at 400° F. for 5 minutes. For an added touch of spice that's nice, roll them immediately afterward in sugar-cinnamon mixture.

Short-cut strawberry shortcake. Roll a batch of biscuit-mix dough into a ½-inch-thick oblong. Spread with melted butter or margarine and fold over. Bake at 450° F. 10 to 12 minutes. While shortcake is still hot, cut into 4 portions. Split each portion, pile sweetened berries, fresh or thawed frozen, on lower half. Add upper part of each, top with whipped cream, and garnish with whole berries if you have fresh ones on hand.

Nippy apple dumplings. Combine ¾ cup granulated sugar, 1 teaspoon cornstarch, ½ teaspoon cinnamon, 1 cup water. Cook and stir until mixture boils. Then simmer 10 minutes. Roll bake-and-eat biscuits (or your own biscuit mix rolled out ½ inch thick and cut to size) to a 4-inch circle. Slice 2 pared, cored apples. Place a small amount of sliced apple in center of each stretched biscuit. Dot with butter. Gather up dough over apple and seal at center. Place in greased baking dish. Pour syrup around them. Bake at 400° F. for 25 minutes. Serve with syrup spooned over dumplings and garnish with whipped cream if you wish.

Mincemeat dumplings. Instead of apple and butter, fill stretched-out biscuits with a cup of prepared mincemeat, reducing sugar to ½ cup.

Fresh fruit cobbler. Combine 1½ cups thinly sliced fresh or thawed frozen fruit (peaches, strawberries, blueberries, blackberries, or apples); ½ cup granulated sugar (unless you use sweetened frozen fruit, in which case add no sugar); and ¼ cup water. Stir, bring to boil, then keep hot. In a bowl beat 1 egg, ½ cup granulated sugar (this in any case), and 1 tablespoon shortening until fluffy. Use spoon for beating. Now add 1 tablespoon milk. Then stir in ½ cup all-purpose flour, ½ teaspoon baking powder, and ¼ teaspoon salt, sifted together. Spread resulting batter in baking dish and pour hot fruit over the batter's entire surface. Bake at 375° F. 25 to 30 minutes, or until tender. Serve warm, with cream.

Gingerbread as an emergency dessert. Keep a package of gingerbread mix on hand and you'll never be caught empty-handed, come dessert time, when you have these topping ideas:

1. *Canned crushed pineapple* and whipped cream.

2. *Ice cream* covered with chocolate sauce.

3. *Custard sauce* and grated orange rind.

4. *Mincemeat* folded into whipped cream.

5. *Lemon sauce* with nutmeg.

6. *Applesauce* sprinkled with sugar and cinnamon, poured on gingerbread, and placed under broiler until sauce bubbles.

7. *A combination* of ⅓ cup brown sugar, 2 teaspoons cinnamon, 3 tablespoons butter or margarine, ⅓ cup chopped nuts. Mix well. Sprinkle on top of hot gingerbread, then return it all to the oven for another 5 minutes.

Tutti-frutti rice. Prepare ⅔ cup packaged precooked rice, with ½ cup water, ¼ cup syrup from pineapple, and ½ teaspoon salt. Otherwise boil as package directs. After it has been standing away from heat for 10 minutes, add 6 diced maraschino cherries, an 8-ounce can of drained pineapple pieces, and a diced, medium-size banana. Add a tablespoon of granulated sugar, a cup of whipped heavy cream, and fold into the rice mixture. Refrigerate before serving.

Fruit basket. You can use the same tutti-frutti mixture to fill a shell basket made from split ladyfingers lining your individual dessert serving dishes.

Modern angel cake is heaven-sent, quick, delicious, and easy to make from a packaged angel-cake mix or fresh from the freezer. For an unusual frosting, add instant-coffee powder to heavy cream and whip. Sweeten to taste. For chocolate flavor, add instant cocoa.

Marbled marvel in tapioca. Prepare tapioca cream as directed on package, then spoon it into tall glasses. Between spoonfuls, add marbling layers such as: melted semi-sweet chocolate and chopped nuts, syrupy melted brown sugar and butter, melted currant jelly tossed with coconut, or baby-pack strained peaches flavored with almond.

Speaking of peaches (and cream of any sort), peach is one of the most delicate fruit flavors in light puddings or whips. Make these three the stars in your repertory:

Peach fluff. Whip ½ cup heavy cream, then beat in 1 tablespoon sugar. Fold in 4 diced, canned, cling-peach halves and a cup of cubed 2-day-old cake. Chill before serving.

Frozen peach whip. Set your refrigerator at its coldest control point. Beat 1 egg white until stiff but not dry. Beat in ⅓ cup sugar and a cup of strained peaches (just rob baby's shelf). Whip a cup of heavy cream and fold into the peach mixture, finishing by adding ½ cup orange juice and 1 tablespoon lemon juice with a light touch. Pour into freezing tray. Freeze until firm, stirring once. (Remember to return refrigerator temperature control to normal after you've served this dessert.)

Mocha peach cream is a subtle dessert for gourmets. In top of double boiler soften an envelope of unflavored gelatin in ½ cup water. Set it over boiling water and stir until dissolved. Stir in ⅓ cup sugar, ⅛ teaspoon salt, 1 cup strong black coffee, and 1 teaspoon lemon juice. Remove from range. Or, for quick chilling, empty bottom half of boiler and half fill it with ice cubes, add some cold water and 2 tablespoons salt. Set double-boiler top on ice. Stir gelatin frequently until it reaches the consistency of unbeaten egg white. Whip ½ cup heavy cream; fold gelatin mixture into cream. Flavor with ¼ teaspoon almond extract. Serve topped with 1½ cups sliced fresh peaches or 1 package thawed frozen peaches.

STYLISH PUDDINGS

Cornstarch pudding goes elegant when you make it into black-on-black chocolate pudding by adding a square of melted chocolate. Serve warm, with chocolate ice cream on top.

Dream pudding is simply cornstarch pudding chilled, then beaten with an egg beater and ½ cup whipped heavy cream folded in. Flavor with a dash of almond or rum extract.

Hawaiian pudding is the same old cornstarch pudding, fixed like dream pudding but flavored with vanilla extract and served over pineapple chunks, fresh or thawed frozen.

"Mousse au chocolat" is French for this: Melt ½ package semi-sweet chocolate over hot water. Remove from heat. Beat in 3 egg yolks with a spoon. Add teaspoon vanilla extract. Beat 3 egg whites until stiff but not dry. Fold into chocolate mixture. Spoon into sherbet glasses. Refrigerate. Garnish with whipped cream.

Chocolate soufflé is another educated pudding for educated tastes. Combine a package of chocolate pudding with 1¼ cups milk and a dash of salt. Cook and stir, over medium heat, until mixture boils. Cool 5 minutes, stirring once or twice, adding 1 teaspoon vanilla extract. Add pudding to beaten yolks of three eggs and stir well. Beat 3 egg whites until stiff but not dry. Gently fold in pudding. Pour into 8 greased custard cups, place cups in pan of hot water, and bake 25 minutes at 350° F. Serve hot, with whipped cream on top.

"A pint a package" is a simple formula to remember for perfect proportion of liquid to prepared puddings and gelatin mixes. For vanilla, chocolate, tapioca, and similar puddings, liquid should be milk. For gelatins, use water or fruit juices.

CUSTARDS

Fanciful custards. To maple rennet custard, add teaspoon of sherry. To chocolate custard, add instant-coffee powder, then rum extract. To chocolate custard, add almond extract for exotic flavor.

No-bake custard. Packaged custard-dessert mix cooks in about 7 minutes, and you cannot tell it from the baked custard in a million years.

Custard sauce tops any dessert. Make it from ½ package vanilla pudding, 1½ cups milk, and cook and stir over low heat until mixture coats the spoon. Flavor with almond, vanilla, or sherry extract. Refrigerate. Or make it with a baby pack of strained custard pudding lightened with ½ cup whipped cream.

Curdled custard may result from overcooking or from overhot baking. Baking temperature should be no higher than 325° F. to 350° F. And always bake custards in a pan of hot water. Cooked custard is done the moment the mixture coats the spoon, should be removed from heat immediately afterward and allowed to cool.

GELATINS

To loosen gelatins from mold, dip small, pointed knife in warm water and use to loosen firm gelatin from around edge of mold. Then quickly dip mold just to the rim in warm water. Shake mold slightly, cover with serving plate, then invert both plate and mold. Lift off mold.

Value of molds in gelatin desserts. Metal molds not only give the dessert attractive appearance, but, since metal itself chills quickly, dessert becomes firm more quickly than if left in bowl.

Avoid gummy gelatin molds by making sure the powdered gelatin is completely dissolved. Stir all crystal-like particles carefully from sides and bottom of mixing bowl. Keep stirring until completely clear when dipped up in a spoon.

For extra-fast chilling of gelatins, set mold in pan of ice and water. This is a special boon when kitchen time is limited. Also helpful when making layered gelatin molds.

Vary gelatin flavors with liquids. Interesting flavor variation can be created with orange-flavored gelatin. Instead of using full pint of water, mix cup of water with ½ cup grape juice and ½ cup orange juice.

Sink or swim. Some fruits sink, some swim, in gelatin mixtures. These sink: canned apricots, Royal Anne cherries, peaches, pears, pineapple, raspberries; fresh orange sections, grapes; cooked prunes and plums. These float: apple slices and cubes, banana slices, grapefruit sections; fresh peaches, pears, raspberries, strawberry halves; marshmallows and nut meats float too.

Orderly fruit layers. Take advantage of floating and sinking qualities of fruits you combine with gelatin desserts by starting with a layer of sinking kind, then add a layer of the floating kind, and continue until you finish with the sinking kind to hold everything in position, the way you want it.

Dessert supreme. Whipped gelatin. And it's economical, too: stretches a pint of dessert to serve 8 or 10. Chill gelatin dessert until thickened to syrupy state. Set in bowl in somewhat larger bowl partly filled with ice and water. Ice cubes may be used, but be sure bowl of gelatin rests firmly on bottom of larger bowl, to prevent slipping. Whip with rotary egg beater or your electric mixer until mixture is fluffy, like whipped cream. Turn into molds and serving dishes at once and chill.

Important note on gelatin whips. If egg whites are used, add to cold, thickened gelatin before whipping; cream or other ingredients are added after whipping.

"Marble" effect with gelatin desserts. Mold colorful gelatin dessert in parfait glasses. When firm, pour 2 tablespoons light cream or custard sauce on top. Cut gelatin in several places by inserting flat side of knife deeply near edge of glass, allowing cream or sauce to trickle down through the cuts.

Gelatin cubes rival restaurant fare. Mold gelatin in shallow metal pan about 8 inches square and 2 inches deep. Chill until very firm. Cut in cubes, using very sharp knife

warmed in water (to avoid tearing edges of cubes). Unmold on waxed paper or remove from pan with spatula. Pile into serving dishes and garnish with whipped cream or plain sweet cream. For extra appeal, add grated coconut, finely chopped nuts, or maraschino cherry.

"Desserted" floating island. Make creamy packaged gelatin pudding, increasing milk to 3½ cups. Chill in covered bowl. Beat slowly with rotary egg beater until smooth and creamy. Turn into shallow serving dish and top with blopping "islands" of whipped cream.

COOKIES

Mixes make prize packages of mixed cookies. Cookies made from package mixes are always good. They contain finest ingredients and a great variety potential for any cookies you or your recipe book can think of.

In a cookie mix the basic ingredients are in the box of mix. The outside of the box lists simple recipes for making many of your favorite cookie types, such as brownies, refrigerator cookies, crisp cutouts, and so on.

Cake mix makes good cookies too. Did you know that? Try it. Cakemix manufacturers provide many excellent cookie recipes, often on the cake-mix box.

Add glaze for the professional touch. You can do this before baking, by brushing cookies with cream or egg yolk, or egg white diluted with a little water. Or you can do it after baking, while cookies are still warm, with a sugar glaze mixed from ¾ cup sifted confectioners' sugar and 3 to 4 teaspoons water. Mix until smooth and of frosting consistency, adding a few drops more water if needed.

YOUR COOKIE SAMPLER

New-fashioned sugar cookies. Made with a mix, of course. Blend ½ cup shortening, ¼ teaspoon vanilla extract, one egg yolk, until smooth and creamy. Add a package of cake mix (white, silver, devil's food, or fudge). Work until firm and pastrylike. Shape, wrap, chill as refrigerator cookie dough. When chilled, slice dough ⅛ inch thick and place slices on ungreased cookie sheet. Sprinkle with granulated sugar, decorate with sliced candied cherries or with raisins. Bake at 375° F. 8 to 10 minutes. Cool before removing from cookie sheet.

No-bake wine balls. Mix well 2½ cups finely crushed vanilla wafers, 1 cup confectioners' sugar, 2 tablespoons cocoa, and 1 cup finely chopped walnuts. Then add 3 tablespoons corn syrup, ¼ cup wine. Roll into 1-inch balls. Roll in powdered sugar. No baking.

No-bake chocolate cookies. In double boiler melt ½ pound milk chocolate, a package of semi-sweet chocolate pieces, 2 squares un-sweetened chocolate, and 1 tablespoon butter or margarine. Cool. Chop 1½ cups shredded coconut and mix with chocolate. Stir in 4 cups crushed cornflakes. Drop onto cookie sheet and allow to set in refrigerator. Makes about 50 "cookies."

Cookie sandwiches. From your favorite cookie mix rolled ½ inch thick cut an equal number of 2½-inch circles and circles with ¾-inch circles cut from the center. Bake until done, following package directions for baking. Cool. Spread solid disks with currant or other jelly and top with cookie rings. Sprinkle with confectioners' sugar.

Whee! Pinwheels! Roll a batch of vanilla cookie-mix dough ¼ inch thick. Do the same for a batch of chocolate dough. Place on top of each other, roll securely with the help of waxed paper, wrap, chill. Cut in ¼-inch slices, bake cut side up on ungreased cookie sheet, following package directions for baking time and temperature.

Holiday ribbons. Slice lengthwise, into 3 equal parts, a batch of rolled, chilled vanilla dough. Do the same with a batch of chocolate cookie-mix dough. Brush surfaces with hot milk. For one ribbon, alternate in this order: chocolate, vanilla, chocolate. For another ribbon, alternate in this order: vanilla, chocolate, vanilla. Wrap, chill, cut into strips just before baking according to package directions for time and temperature.

Checkers, anyone? Start as with ribbons, cutting vanilla and chocolate doughs into thirds lengthwise. Then cut each slice into lengthwise thirds again, so you now have 9 lengthwise slices each of vanilla and chocolate dough. Brush surfaces with hot milk. To make a bar of checkerboards, place side by side a vanilla and a chocolate strip. Then place a vanilla strip on top of the chocolate, a chocolate on the vanilla. Wrap, chill. Cut into slices before baking according to package directions for time and temperature.

Bridge cookies. Slice 2 rolls of chilled cookie dough, of contrasting shades such as chocolate and vanilla, or butterscotch and coconut. With small cutters, remove centers with heart-, diamond-, spade-, and club-shaped cutters, so you have the same quantity of each shape in both colors of dough. Place light cutouts in dark cookies, dark cutouts in light cookies, and bake according to package directions.

Other inlay shapes, such as circles, stars, triangles, bells, oblongs, etc., can be cut out for holidays and other occasions. Just try to keep your pairs matched so you waste no cookie dough, though a few silhouettes might be fun too. And you can always reroll bits of leftover dough and recut them. You can also use the short-cut method that follows.

Short cut to roll-and-cut cookies. Instead of rolling and cutting, you can drop spoonfuls of chilled dough on greased cookie sheet, 1 inch apart, then flatten each drop by pressing with a fork dipped in sugar or flour. Or you can drop spoonfuls of dough 2 inches apart on greased cookie sheet and flatten each with bottom of tumbler dipped in sugar or flour or covered with damp cloth.

The dough for these cookies can be any variety of your own. Or basic cookies can be made an easier way too. Choose your favorite cookie mix, dark or light in color. Make it according to package directions. Roll about ⅛ inch thick. Cut out shapes. Bake as package directs, then decorate.

Exterior decorating. For quick white frosting, combine sifted confectioners' sugar, a drop of cream of tartar, an egg white, a little vanilla or almond extract. Beat until a spatula leaves a path in its wake. Tint with food color if you wish. For dark designs, use melted semisweet chocolate.

Save the shape. Roll dough on a sheet of aluminum foil, remove dough from around cookies with a knife, then slip a cookie sheet under the foil and bake. Since you don't have to pick up the cut-out cookies, you can roll the dough as thin as you like and still get distinct outlines.

DROP COOKIES

Grease cookie sheet only lightly, where called for, and only in spots where dough is to be dropped. Allow for spreading, though.

When dropping dough in center of greased spot, use another teaspoon to help you drop mounds of the same size.

If you have no cookie sheet, turn your baking pan upside down, dropping dough on bottom.

Evenly baked cookies depend on heat circulation. That is why your ideal cookie sheet is about 2 inches narrower and shorter than your oven.

If you need an extra cookie sheet, cut aluminum foil the size of your cookie sheet. Cut several pieces. Place foil on sheet, drop cookies on foil. While those are baking, drop dough on another sheet of foil. When the first batch comes out, simply slip off the sheet of baked cookies, slip the cookie sheet under the second piece of foil and cookies, and bake.

Cool cookies on wire racks. Place them next to each other—never overlap or place on top of one another—until they are cool.

STORING COOKIES

Storage. Airtight, cold, or freezing. Store crisp cookies in a container with a loose-fitting cover. To re-crisp in humid weather, place cookies in an open shallow pan in a 300° F. oven for 3 to 5 minutes.

Empty butter cartons are fine for molding and storing cookie dough in the refrigerator. The cartons come waxed, so they need no greasing. In addition, when the dough is sliced for cookies, each will be uniform in size.

Refrigerator cookies are refrigerated as dough. Wrap roll of dough in wax paper or in frozen-juice can from which both end disks have been removed, chill in refrigerator or freezer until dough is firm, then slice and bake the quantity you need.

Cookie doughs are roll-wrapped for freezing the same as for refrigerating, but it's well to overwrap with freezer foil to be sure no moisture is lost during freezing. If roll is difficult to slice when you remove it from the freezer, "thaw" it in the refrigerator for an hour. Freeze drop or roll cookie dough; store in waxed freezer containers or in plastic ones. Thaw before handling, until manageable.

To freeze baked bar and drop cookies, arrange on waxed paper, pack in layers inside a plastic bag or cardboard box. Wrap in freezer paper. You may also use covered, well-sealed plastic boxes. Allow about 15 minutes for thawing.

Other baked cookies are mostly packed in waxed freezer containers or tin boxes with covers. Fill air spaces between cookies with crumpled foil or waxed paper.

Molded cookies are best stored when carefully fitted into cardboard freezer boxes, as they won't break and yet fill box completely.

When sending home-baked cookies to camp or school, aluminum-foil packing is a smart idea. Being grease-proof, odorproof, and moisture-proof, foil insures that the cookies (or cake) arrive in perfect condition, moist and fresh. And since aluminum is in the nature of a soft suit of armor, your baking will arrive unbroken and uncrushed if packed right, with air spaces properly filled.

ICE CREAM AT YOUR FINGERTIPS

You can make ice cream in a crank freezer, hand or electric. Let's see how it works with banana ice cream. Mix together 2 cups mashed ripe bananas (made from 5 or 6 bananas), 1½ tablespoons lemon juice, ½ cup granulated sugar. Add ½ teaspoon salt, 2 beaten eggs, 1 cup milk, 1½ teaspoons vanilla extract. Stir in 2 cups heavy cream. Freeze in 2-quart freezer until it becomes hard to crank, using 8 parts ice to 1 part ice-cream salt. Makes 2 quarts.

Make ice cream in your refrigerator ice-cube tray too. Take peach ice cream as an example. Turn refrigerator temperature control to coldest setting. Then combine ⅔ cup canned sweet condensed milk, ½ cup cold water, ⅛ teaspoon salt, 1½ teaspoons vanilla extract. Add 2 cups sieved fresh or thawed frozen peaches, 1 or 2 drops of almond extract, 1 teaspoon lemon juice. Refrigerate. Whip 1 cup heavy cream to custardlike consistency, then fold into chilled mixture. Turn into chilled bowl. With egg beater or electric mixer, beat until smooth but not melted. Quickly fill freezer tray and freeze until firm. Makes about 6 servings.

Use package pudding to make ice cream. Pick your flavor. To package of gelatin prepared pudding add ¼ cup sugar and a dash of salt. Chill. Fold in cup of heavy cream, whipped. Turn into freezer tray and freeze for 1 hour at coldest refrigerator temperature. Turn into bowl, beat with an egg beater until smooth but not melted. Return to tray, freeze until firm, about 3 or 4 hours. Makes 1 quart.

Make your own sherbet in your refrigerator's freezing tray. For orange sherbet, first turn refrigerator temperature control to coldest setting. Then combine 1½ cans of undiluted evaporated milk, 1 cup granulated sugar, and ⅛ teaspoon salt. Gradually stir in ½ cup fresh orange juice, 2 tablespoons lemon juice, 1 tablespoon grated orange rind. Pour into freezing tray, freeze until firm. Turn into chilled bowl (chill egg beater, too, right in the bowl). Beat until smooth and fluffy. Return at once to tray. Freeze until firm, stirring once. Makes 3 to 4 servings. (Don't forget to reset temperature control of refrigerator at normal setting.)

Ice cream is sensitive. It loses most of its velvety texture if handled too much. The richer the cream, the colder is the freezing and storing temperature it requires, especially for long storage. Ice-cream desserts need low temperatures even more. Unless stored at zero freezer temperature, don't keep ice cream longer than a few hours.

Who wants to wait for ice cream? When the ice-cream carton is hard to pull off, just cut through the rim with a knife and your ice cream is ready to serve.

Ice cream is good for a month in your home freezer, if you follow the instructions you received with your freezer on storing ice cream.

Store unopened containers of ice cream in the coldest section of your freezer. To keep at serving consistency, store one or two cartons away from the freezing coils or in the special ice-cream compartments that modern freezers provide. Opened cartons are best covered by a double thickness of cellophane first, then tightly resealed to avoid loss of flavor and the formation of ice crystals.

In refrigerator-freezer combinations the normal setting is at zero, just right for storing ice-cream desserts hours ahead. The freezer part of the combination can be set at coldest point without affecting the temperature of the refrigerator itself.

ICE-CREAM SENSATIONS THAT ARE EASY TO CREATE

Flaming mincemeat. Spoon heated prepared mincemeat on that vanilla or coffee ice cream. Top with cube of sugar dipped into lemon or rum extract, then light a match to it.

Snowballs. Roll balls of ice cream in shredded coconut or chopped nuts. Serve on top of a serving of chocolate sauce or pour canned crushed fruit sauce over balls.

Frozen angel cake. Split angel cake in 3 layers. Fill with ice cream. Slice. Serve chocolate sauce on the side.

Chocolate parfait. Alternate chocolate ice cream, whipped cream, and canned crushed pineapple in parfait glasses.

Ice-cream cookie sandwich. A favorite among young fry. From cylinder container, slice ice cream ½ inch thick. Place slices between large sugar cookies or wafers, sandwich-fashion.

Four-layer ice-cream cake. Cut baker's poundcake into 4 layers. Reassemble, spreading ice cream between layers, after sprinkling with chopped nuts. Serve sliced, with dessert sauce.

Don't give pie à la-mode monopoly. Other desserts that are special and delicious with ice-cream topping include hot gingerbread, chocolate or butterscotch pudding. Dutch apple or plum cake, bread pudding, fruit cobblers, fruit Betties, toasted spongecake or angel-cake slices, cold brownies, shortcakes, fruit tarts, Indian puddings, honeydew melon or cantaloupe.

Your "**sundae best.**" Actually, a sundae consists of ice cream, sauce, whipped cream, and a cherry. But many shortcut sundaes can be made with a fancy topping. For instance:

Peanut pebbles. Crushed peanut brittle over chocolate, coffee, or vanilla ice cream.

Cherry plus. Crushed Bing cherries and syrup over strawberry ice cream.

Almond supreme. Pistachio ice cream topped with chocolate sauce and whole salted, toasted, blanched almonds, the nuts still warm from the toasting.

Brazil delight. Coffee ice cream sprinkled generously with chocolate and Brazil-nut shavings. Add a little shredded coconut too, if you like.

Semi-sweet sauce. In double boiler combine 1 package semi-sweet chocolate pieces, ½ cup white corn syrup. Heat until blended. Stir in ¼ cup light cream, 1 tablespoon butter, ¼ teaspoon vanilla extract. Pour warm over coffee, chocolate, or vanilla ice cream. Wonderful with butter pecan too.

Date sauce. In saucepan combine 7 ounces snipped pitted dates, a dash of salt, ½ cup water. Heat to boiling point, then remove from heat. Stir in ½ cup white corn syrup, ½ cup chopped walnuts. Cool. Serve over vanilla or coffee ice cream.

IDEAS THAT MAKE YOU A WIZARD TO YOUR CHILDREN

Malt topping. Sprinkle cocoa or chocolate-flavored malted-milk powder over ice cream, with or without chocolate sauce. (Most youngsters will vote "with" on the sauce.)

Clown cone. On large chocolate cookie or chocolate-covered doughnut place a round ball of vanilla ice cream topped with inverted cone wafer hat. Make a face on the ice cream, using chocolate candy bits for eyes and nose and a snipped maraschino cherry for the mouth.

Potted heart. Plant a red heart-shaped lollipop in a fluted, colored party cup filled with choclate ice cream. For the leaves, use long green gumdrops, sliced lengthwise.

Jolly jalopy. Cut away the upper left-hand corner from a square of ice cream. For the wheels use marshmallows. Install windows with whipped-cream tubing.

Snow man. Top a large vanilla ice-cream ball with a smaller one, both rolled in shredded coconut. For eyes and buttons, raisins. For mouth, a cherry. For the hat, an inverted paper party cup. For the broom, a lollipop.

Valentine bouquet. With scotch tape, fix paper doily, from which center circle has been cut, to edge of ice-cream cone. Fill cone with ice cream, top with another scoop, insert colored gumdrop "flowers."

12

FRUITS, JELLIES, AND NUTS

Little-known tips to save money, work, and time

Fruits are one of those foods that are both delicious and nutritious, and few people need persuading to eat them. But why not consider some new and less familiar kinds along with your favorites? As with so many food items today, the consumer has a wide choice of fruits throughout the year (and when the fresh aren't to be had, there are always canned fruits). The only drawback with modern methods of distributing fresh produce is that, in concentrating on varieties that transport well and survive long, we have sacrificed flavor and texture. But you can still have the best of both worlds if you take the trouble to learn when the best local fruits and imported varieties are on the stands and in the stores. Learn the names of the varieties and the sources of the fruit you find best, make a list, and then hold out each year until these are available. Resist buying the "first of the season"— unless you know they are truly good—for you will pay dearly for the privilege.

Save time when peeling pears or peaches. First scald the fruit with boiling water, then peel. Skins come off much easier that way.

Apple to the rescue. A slice of apple added to each pint of cranberries before cooking will greatly improve the flavor without sacrificing any of the tartness.

Place a cut apple in your cookie jar or fruitcake box. It will keep soft cookies soft and fruitcake moist. Caution: don't store apples with crisp cookies.

Leftover fruit juices have many uses. They make fruit gelatin desserts more fruity, and they can "make" the sauce you pour over ice cream, pudding, or cake. They improve the tang of French dressing. Fruit syrup has same usefulness. Also, try mixing it into mayonnaise or with cream cheese.

Leftover fruit goes over big when added to chilled summer drinks, when found atop a mound of dish dessert, when crushed into cake-drenching sauce, when used mixed in gelatin, when mixed with peanut butter as sandwich filling.

Salt enhances sweet flavors. The proper function of salt is to develop and bring out natural food flavors, not to make foods taste salty. Sprinkle a small amount in fruit juices; it decreases sourness of acids and increases sweetness of sugars.

CITRUS FRUITS

To keep lemons, limes, oranges fresh, wrap them in tissue or oiled paper and keep them in dry, cool place or on low shelf in refrigerator. Or keep them in a closed fruit jar in refrigerator.

To keep lemons for months, after you buy them at a bargain, put the whole lemons into sterilized canning jars, cover with cold water, adjust rubber rings, and screw covers down tightly. Not only will they stay fresh for months, they will yield much more juice than when you first bought them.

Get more juice. Even when you do no long-term storing you get more juice from lemons, limes, and oranges if you soak them in a pan of water for a while before squeezing. Then, before cutting, roll the fruit around on the table with your hand.

Citrus bonus. For more flavorful fresh-fruit drinks, place orange and lemon rind in cold water so that rind is fully covered. Bring to boiling point. Remove rinds. Add fruit-flavored cooking water to fruit juices.

Strain without strain. Moisten cheesecloth in water and wrap around end of lemon. Juice will strain-as-you-squeeze.

Lemon-aid in fruit chopping. Before you chop sticky fruits, put a few drops of lemon juice into the food to be chopped. Makes cleaning easy.

Beat life into canned orange juice. Wonder why canned orange juice may lack that "fresh-squeezed" taste? It's because, during canning, air is removed. That's why economical canned orange juice should be stirred vigorously, or aerated with a rotary beater, an electric blender, or poured several times between two containers.

Fresh orange fizz. Mix 1 cup sugar, 1 cup water, and heat to boiling point. Cool. Add 1 cup unstrained fresh orange juice, ¼ cup unstrained fresh lemon juice, 2 teaspoons grated orange rind, and ½ teaspoon grated lemon rind. Pour into freezer tray. Freeze until firm. Pour tall glasses ¼ full with frozen mixture. Fill up glasses with ginger ale. Garnish with fresh mint. Serves 6 to 8.

Fresh grapefruit compote. Peel fresh grapefruit and cut into sections, being sure to remove membrane and white inner portion of rind. Place sections in sherbet glasses. Add 2 teaspoons grenadine to each serving. Sprinkle with shredded coconut. One large grape-fruit yields 3 servings.

Orange peel, a de luxe flavor. It's smart, it's thrifty, it's a treat to use orange peel in your puddings, cake batters, and cookies. Simply grate the rinds and use. Or grate the orange peel, dry in oven, save in tight-covered containers for future flavor flourishes.

To peel an orange without spattering, dig heel of paring knife into skin and draw it backward around middle of orange. Then insert smooth teaspoon handle into the cut and work it around until you pry the skin loose. Remove one half at a time.

When grating rind of lemon or orange, be sure not to grate too deep. The colored part of rind gives the flavor while the white part causes food to taste bitter.

For trim orange or grapefruit sections, set fruit on board; then, with a sharp knife, whittle off peel in strips, cutting from top to bottom and deep enough to remove all white membrane. Next cut along both sides of such dividing membrane and lift out each section. Work over a bowl at this point, so you save all the juice.

FRUIT NOVELTIES

To cut up fresh pineapple, cut washed pineapple into ½-inch crosswise slices. Remove core from each slice with a pointed sharp knife or the "hole" part of a dough-nut cutter. Next peel outer edge of slices, cutting deep enough so you remove the eyes. You can serve the pineapple sliced or cut the slices into thin wedges.

Pineapple used in gelatin desserts should be either canned or cooked. Raw pineapple and fresh-frozen contain an enzyme that prevents proper jelling.

Crushed pineapple. A clever way to crush pineapple is to run it through your meat chopper. Looks wonderful. Be sure, of course, to trap the juice. And with a little liquid added, you can crush pineapple in seconds in an electric blender.

Frosted grapes, unusual garnish for fruit-salad molds. Beat egg white until just foamy. Dip small bunches of white grapes into beaten egg white, then in powdered sugar; let dry on paper toweling. Another way: Dip tiny red grape bunches, one by one, into lemon juice, then sprinkle with granulated sugar. Dry on cake rack.

Other ways with garnishes. Try prunes or dates, plain or stuffed; a few berries or cherries, stems on; kumquats, whole or sliced; rhubarb curls; figs, crab apples, sliced pickled peaches.

To make melon balls, or apple, cantaloupe, avocado, canned jellied cranberry sauce balls, use French ball cutter. If you haven't one, the teaspoon of your measuring set (or the ½ teaspoon size if you like smaller ones) is an excellent tool, too.

If you enjoy avocado, here's a deliciously different way to serve that leftover turkey. Make your usual creamed turkey, but stir a cup of diced avocado into each 3 cups of turkey mixture just before serving.

Avocado cocktail dip. Mash and put ½ large avocado through a sieve. Mix with 1 tablespoon each of fresh lemon juice and mayonnaise, ¼ teaspoon salt, and ⅙ teaspoon each of powdered dry mustard and ground black pepper. (Actually, a pinch of each of those last two ingredients is all you need.) Serve in a dish surrounded by potato chips, crackers, and raw vegetable strips. Makes ¾ cup of dip.

Avocado mayonnaise. Combine ½ cup avocado purée with ½ cup mayonnaise, ¼ teaspoon grated onion, and 1 to 2 teaspoons fresh lemon juice. Serve over vegetable salads.

Make rhubarb sauce, using 3 cups diced unpeeled fresh rhubarb cooked with 2 tablespoons water in covered saucepan over low heat. Add ½ cup sugar. Cool. Serve over squares of freshly made gingerbread, made from your favorite mix. Top with whipped cream.

Fruit purée for dessert. Purée, a pulpy fruit juice, may be frozen and stored for long periods. Makes delicious sauce for ice-cream sundaes and puddings, also fine as flavoring for ices, sherberts, and fruit ice creams.

For good-looking baked apples, prick their skins beforehand.

They'll bake without bursting. Extra-flavor tip: a dried apricot or a few raisins in the core with the sugar and spices.

Apple-ball sauce. For a variation from the usual applesauce, make apple balls with a round cutter. Cook the rest of the apple, not formed into balls, as usual. Simmer the balls in a little orange juice to which you've added some bright red jelly such as strawberry or currant. Save the juice for another dessert. Combine the little red balls with the usual sauce and you have a festive dessert, with some left over for topping another dessert another day.

COOLING AND FREEZING FRUITS

Fresh berries. Spread berries out on tray and store in refrigerator on an open sheet. Chill, but do not wash until shortly before using. Then place in colander and run cold water gently over berries. If there are hulls, remove after washing, to save flavor.

Keep strawberries firm even if you must store them several days before using. Put them in the refrigerator in a colander. The cold air, circulating through the berries, will keep them firm and fresh.

Cold, but not too cold. To enjoy its full flavor, remove fruit from refrigerator a little ahead of serving, so that it can warm up a bit. (Remember not to store bananas in the refrigerator.)

Before freezing berries or cherries, wash them in ice-cold water. Better results, less waste.

Prevent darkening of fruits. For those fruits that have a tendency to darken in freezing, add ¼ teaspoon ascorbic acid (vitamin C) to each cup of syrup. You can buy the ascorbic acid at the drugstore.

During fresh-fruit season, freeze fruit in half-pint containers, for lunches at later date. Consult your Agricultural Extension literature on how to freeze fruits.

When thawing time is short, put unopened carton of quick-frozen fruit in a bowl of water and let it stand about 25 minutes. Fruit will be thawed and ready to serve when you open the container.

Frozen fruit looks best, tastes best if served when just thawed, while there are still a few ice crystals left.

FRUIT SALADS

Ambrosia salad. A de luxe main dish served in a large, shallow glass bowl to show off the colors. In center set small glass bowl of coconut cream-cheese topping, made with soft cream cheese, ½ cup cream, dash of salt, ¾ cup coconut, whipped smooth with a fork. Around this arrange following fruits in groups, tucking watercress in between: chunks of fluted banana dipped in lemon juice; watermelon scoops; cherries stuffed with almonds, walnuts, or pecans; pineapple or cantaloupe cubes; strawberries or raspberries; seedless grapes. *Voilà!*

Golden fruit salad. For each serving, fill half a seeded cantaloupe with canned or frozen pineapple chunks, top with cream-cheese dressing prepared with mayonnaise, chopped walnuts, orange juice, lemon juice, sugar, and salt. Serve with toasted corn muffins and a French dressing alternate.

Waldorf salad. Toss pared or diced apple, pear, pineapple, or banana with lemon juice, sugar, and mayonnaise. Before serving, add thinly sliced celery, coarsely chopped walnuts, more mayonnaise, and toss again. Serve in crisp lettuce, sprinkle with French dressing.

Pineapple-shrimp salad. Cooked or canned cleaned shrimp, plus fresh, frozen, or canned pineapple chunks, with chopped walnuts, sliced stuffed olives, mayonnaise, and French dressing, combine into a sea-food salad supreme.

Low-calorie salad dressing. Combine ⅔ cup cottage cheese, ⅓ cup fresh grapefruit juice, 2 tablespoons fresh lemon juice or lime juice, 1 teaspoon grated lemon rind, ½ teaspoon salt, ⅛ teaspoon each ground black pepper and paprika. Beat with an electric or rotary beater. Serve over mixed salad greens or fruit salad. Makes 1¼ cups.

Avocado side dish. Halved, pared and pitted, the avocado may hold any of these fillings: apple and pineapple; grapefruit with flaked crab; fruit cocktail plus diced oranges; cottage and Roquefort cheese.

Fruit medley mold is a harmonious final chord to any meal. It is made with lemon-flavored gelatin, can of fruit cocktail and syrup drained from fruit cocktail, diced banana, and raspberries or sliced strawberries. Jell in fancy mold, serving with lemon-cream sauce made of mayonnaise, lemon and orange juice, confectioners' sugar, and cream. Or omit cream and fold in whipped heavy cream, for light richness.

Set fruit-flavored gelatin in 30 to 60 minutes. Make it with a block of frozen fruit. Use 1½ cups water (instead of 2) to dissolve gelatin. Then add frozen fruit to warm gelatin and stir until fruit thaws and gelatin begins to set. Chill.

MAKING JELLIES AND JAMS

Any fruit can be jellied if three basic essentials are present in the right proportions: fruit acid, sugar, and pectin. Good jelling fruits contain enough natural acid and pectin to form jelly with addition of sugar and boiling. Only a few fruits (sour apples, currants, wild plums) have the right proportions when fully ripe. In the case of most fruits, the amount of fruit acid in proportion to natural pectin or sugar decreases when they are at their peak of flavor richness. Solution: add small amount of lemon juice.

Commercially prepared pectin assures perfect jelly for every variety of fruit, retains flavor of full ripeness, and insures successful jelly making. Pectin gives greater jelly yield and may also be used in relishes.

Jelly making is easier today than in Grandma's day. Grandma's formula demanded "good jellying fruit, plus the right amount of sugar." Today there's no limit; all fruits are "good jellying fruits" with the aid of inexpensive products found on your grocer's shelves.

New short-boil method vs. old-fashioned jelly making. In old-fashioned, long-boiling method it was necessary to have fruit either underripe or part ripe and part underripe, to have sufficient natural pectin and fruit acid to insure jellying. Long boiling cooks away the flavor, darkens color, and causes evaporation. Modern short-boil method uses fully ripe fruit, thus obtaining full food value and flavor.

Use potato masher to stir jelly. Saves time and trouble. The handle keeps your hand cool and its shape prevents it from slipping into the pot as spoons often do.

Sugar saver. When making jam, let the fruit boil for about 10 minutes before adding the sugar. About half the usual amount will be needed.

The children's marbles go to work. Sounds silly, but try and see. Place several marbles in your kettle when you're making jelly preserves, apple butter, or anything that requires continuous stirring. Marbles will roll constantly across the bottom and prevent sticking.

Don't get into this jam. To prevent jam from sticking to the bottom of the pan, rub the inside of your cooker with a little cooking oil just before making jam.

Fill jam and jelly jars without dripping. Use your gravy boat for the job, because its long spout fits easily into any size of jar opening.

SOME ANSWERS TO JELLY-MAKING PROBLEMS

Tough jelly? Probably you are using too little sugar to balance the recipe proportions.

To keep fruit from floating in jam, use fully ripened fruit, crush it thoroughly, cook sufficiently, and, when ready, cool and stir for 5 minutes before filling jars. Skim foam from top and stir thoroughly, then fill jars.

When jelly will not jell, place the glasses in the oven, at 250° F., for about an hour. This saves the time and effort needed to remove the jelly from jars and reboil and does the trick just as nicely.

Jelly gets cloudy if poured too slowly or too late (jelly has started to form and particles hold tiny air bubbles), juice is pulpy (avoid this by straining through clean, wet jelly bag), setting is premature because recipe has not been followed carefully and accurately.

Mold forms on jelly if imperfectly sealed. You can cut out mold and use remainder of jelly, since mold does not penetrate below the surface of the jelly. Or do this: pour ¼ teaspoon brandy or grain alcohol over jelly, roll glass so liquid covers the entire surface, then light it. When alcohol has burned off, mold is gone. Apply new coating of paraffin at once.

If homemade jelly changes color, here's the possible reason: darkening at top is caused by air getting through paraffin. You then need tin or paper covers in addition to paraffin. Fading, especially in berries, occurs if jelly is not stored in cool, dark place.

What makes jelly "weep"? Unbalanced recipe, with surplus acid (possible with high sugar solids in original juice), too-heavy layer of paraffin (⅛-inch layer offers best protection), too-warm storage (keep below 65° F.), changes in temperature.

Syrupy jelly is caused when there is too little pectin, acid, or sugar to balance the proportions.

Crystals in jelly, caused by any of these: too much sugar, too slow or too long cooking (evaporation), too little cooking (insufficient inversion of sugar), evaporation due to uncovered jelly.

Too-stiff jellies result from over-balance of pectin or sugar in mixture. Happens when fruit is not fully ripe or when overcooking causes excessive evaporation. Latter can be avoided by boiling at high heat and cooking quickly.

Gummy jelly is caused by overcooking. Acid may affect the action of pectin.

NUTS

Nuts we use the most include almonds, Brazil nuts, butternuts, cashew nuts, chestnuts, filberts or hazelnuts, hickory nuts, pecans, pine nuts, pistachios, and the different varieties of English, black, and other walnuts.

Hotel chef's trick. Ever wonder how hotel chefs make those delicious long slivers of Brazil nuts in their salads and desserts? Here's their secret: cover shelled Brazil nuts with cold water, bring slowly to a boil, simmer two or three minutes, then cool. Shells come off easily afterward and you'll find you can slice the shelled nuts in long slivers just as you find them in expensive restaurants.

Blanching almonds. Pour boiling water over shelled almonds, permitting them to stand until the brown skin has loosened. Usually by the time the water has cooled the nuts are ready for you to remove that brown skin. To whiten blanched almonds, soak in cold water in the refrigerator.

Toasted blanched almonds, a wonderful topping for desserts and a piquant addition to green beans and other vegetables. Using a very sharp knife, cut blanched almonds into as thin slivers as you can. Melt some butter or margarine in a large pie plate and stir the almonds around in the butter. Use only enough butter to lightly coat the almonds. Bake at 350° F. for 15 minutes, or until almonds are golden, "toasted" the easy way.

Toasted coconut adds festive touch on puddings, cakes, and custard pies. Spread packaged or freshly grated coconut in thin layers in pan or cookie sheet. Place in 350° F. oven. Toast until golden, stirring or shaking frequently to make coconut toast evenly.

Another chef's trick, with almonds. Try toasting them with the skins left on. Melt butter in a pie plate and stir almonds until they're thoroughly coated with butter. Bake at 350° F. 15 minutes. Sprinkle lightly with salt. Makes a wonderful cocktail accompaniment, just as served in fine restaurants.

13

BEVERAGES

*Coffee, tea, chocolate, and other light drinks
to refresh your taste and budget*

Tired of the same old drinks? Why not start today to experiment with different brands, varieties, and beverages. There are far more choices available even on supermarket shelves than the standard kinds. Some may cost a bit more, but some cost less; over the long run, they shouldn't add that much to your budget, and you'll certainly get more pleasure out of what you do drink.

COFFEE

Most of the coffee we drink comes from only a few places, even though the standard brands are usually blends. But there are many different coffee beans grown around the world. Even with the commercially available standard brands, you can make your own blends. For instance, next time you go to brew a pot, use a teaspoon or two less of your regular brand and substitute an equivalent amount of one of the espresso brands. These are darker, finer-ground, and have a

slightly different taste. See if you like what it does to your regular coffee. If you don't, try other combinations.

True coffee connoisseurs will insist that the only way to get good coffee is to start with the freshly roasted bean. Specialty stores often sell a variety of coffee beans—expensive, perhaps, but worth trying. Then some of the large supermarket chains still sell the beans that they can grind to order. These are often cheaper.

Or you can grind your own at home. Only the purest of the pure insist on grinding coffee by hand. There are several fine electric grinders that do the essential job: provide fresh coffee in the exact quantity as you want it.

An electric coffee grinder holds a pound of bean coffee. If you keep a spare pound on hand, you're always prepared to make perfect coffee. Beans keep best in the refrigerator or freezer, but short-time shelf storage is satisfactory too.

If you don't want to be bothered with searching for different beans or grinding your own, at least keep what you do buy as fresh as possible. Once exposed to the air, coffee tends to go stale in about 10 days. Two rules for keeping vacuum-packed coffee fresh: Seal the lid tightly after withdrawing coffee to use. Keep the closed container in your refrigerator. If lid is bent or hard to tamp down tightly, try using a jar for coffee storage. The lid is easier to turn tight.

Everyone has the secret for making the best cup of coffee—yet somehow everyone has a different secret. Experiment and find your own way. Unfortunately, too much experimentation would involve too many different and expensive kinds of equipment. So use the coffeemaker you have and see if you can produce more desirable results by varying amounts of coffee or water, cooking longer or shorter periods, mixing blends as suggested.

A clean pot makes good coffee. One thing everyone agrees on: the coffeepot should be cleaned of old coffee oils, stains, and any other remains. Run your automatic coffeemaker through a perking or other brewing cycle occasionally with water and baking soda in the pot. Clean it thoroughly afterward with clear water to be sure no trace of the taste of soda remains in the pot.

Fill it with cold water between brewings if you use your automatic coffeemaker every day. Water absorbs unwanted odors and flavors that may develop in the coffeemaker if stored dry.

Plug your coffeemaker, filled with water and coffee, into your range timer outlet or into a similar outlet of a wake-up-to-music radio at night; set the timer a little earlier than you get up in the morning and you can have coffee waiting when you wake up.

Drip coffeemakers undoubtedly leave the least grounds and sludge. And if you are able to buy the newer and better models, you now have considerable control over the strength of the coffee you can make. One drawback for the budget is the constant expense of buying filters. But look in the papers or magazines, or inquire around and find where you can buy the standard filters in large quantities at considerably less cost.

One cup of coffee coming up, in a hurry. Why bother brewing even in a 2-cup pot when boiling water and a spoon is all you need for a quick cup of excellent coffee made with instant powdered coffee? There are a wide variety of brands to choose from, and the "freeze-dried" do seem to produce a more natural coffee taste. If you know that you are going to be drinking instant steadily, buy in as large a quantity as reasonable, because you pay a disproportionate sum for the small sizes.

Use instant coffee in your coffeemaker, too. Simply make the number of cups you want, in quantity in the coffeemaker, with spares for seconds, and serve from the coffeemaker instead of making individual servings in coffee cups.

Coffee substitutes taste much like coffee and are available for people for whom coffee is too stimulating or who are on special diets that do not include coffee.

Decaffeinated coffee. This is true coffee but with most of the caffein, the part that stimulates, taken out. It's also for people who can't drink coffee. Brew it just as you do ordinary coffee.

Café au lait. Make strong or double-strength coffee by any method you prefer. Have ready an equal amount of freshly scalded milk. Simultaneously pour coffee and milk in equal amounts in heated cups. For a richer drink, add 1 tablespoon butter to each cup of milk or top each cup with 1 tablespoon whipped cream.

Iced coffee with chocolate. Beat or blend (electric equipment is easiest) 1 cup strong coffee, 1 tablespoon chocolate syrup, 2 tablespoons whipped cream, and ¼ cup chipped ice. Serve immediately. Makes 2 servings if you use a standard 8-ounce measuring cup.

Frosted coffee. Almost fill tall glasses with chipped ice or ice cubes. Pour strong hot coffee over ice until glasses are three quarters full. Top each with a scoopful or a heaping tablespoonful of vanilla ice cream.

Frozen coffee. Why waste left-over coffee when you can pour it into your ice-cube tray, freeze it, and have flavored cubes for use in iced coffee?

TEA

As with coffee, there are far more varieties available even on supermarket shelves than most people realize. Unless you are absolutely positive you have found your tea-of-paradise, try some of the different kinds. You may be in for some pleasant surprises, teas that will turn a routine cup into a delightful experience.

In addition to the classic teas, there are the herb teas. Many peoples around the world drink them, and in recent years they have become more widely appreciated and available here. Some are imported, but others are domestic, and if they cost more than standard brands, you may find yourself drinking less but enjoying it more. And even if they don't have all the medicinal or health properties claimed by some, they at least provide a pleasant change.

A good cup of tea. Personal preferences vary widely, but there are general rules for making good tea:

When kettle water boils, pour a cup of water into a china or earthenware teapot. (Glass is a good teapot material too.) Let stand for a minute, to warm pot, then empty out the heating water.

Measure desired amount of tea leaves (2 teaspoonfuls of tea leaves to 2½ cups of water is medium strength) into heated teapot. Pour freshly boiling water over the leaves and let steep 2 to 3 minutes before serving.

Weaker tea for special tastes. Never dilute the tea in the pot. Instead add hot water to individual cups of tea or provide hot water in a container so a guest or member of your family may help himself.

Real tea connoisseurs abhor the tea bag, but it's undoubtedly a convenience. Just don't serve a cup of hot water with a bag on the side. Instead pour hot water over the bag, in the cup, and allow the drinker to decide when to remove the tea bag.

You can use tea bags in the teapot too. Follow directions for making tea with leaves, and remove bags before serving tea, after tea has steeped as directed. An occasional swish as tea steeps will give you full strength from the bags.

Tea sensation. Next time you serve tea with lemon, stick a small clove into each side of the lemon slice. Changes a taken-for-granted beverage into something really special.

CHOCOLATE

Chocolate or cocoa? Both are derived from the seeds of Theobroma cacao, a tropical evergreen tree. Some of the fat is extracted from chocolate to make cocoa.

You can buy chocolate in solid form unsweetened and semi-sweet. Chocolate bits may also be melted and used, with milk, to make hot chocolate. And always add a dash of salt.

Cocoa's easy to make if you buy it combined with sugar and dried milk, so that all you need to add is boiling water. For richer cocoa, make it with hot milk or combine cocoa and milk and heat together, stirring until it almost reaches the boiling point.

Iced mint cocoa. Make cocoa as usual, increasing sugar for sweet tooths. Strain hot cocoa and chill. When cold add 1 teaspoon vanilla and pour into tall glasses partially filled with crushed ice. Top each glass with whipped cream and garnish with mint leaves.

Iced chocolate mocha. Combine 1 cup strong hot coffee, 3 cups milk, and ½ cup chocolate syrup. Beat with egg beater or electric mixer until frothy. Pour over ice in medium-sized glasses, with whipped cream on top.

EGG AND MILK DRINKS

Fluffy eggnog. This beverage is usually served to people who must gain weight or are on convalescent diets. They're more appealing fluffy. The only difference is in how you treat the egg. Separate egg and beat white first. Then beat the yolk with 2 tablespoons sugar or 2 tablespoons honey. Add a cup of milk or

½ cup milk, ½ cup cream, and ¼ teaspoon vanilla. Beat again. Fold in egg white. Serve cold in tall glass, with a sprinkling of nutmeg on top.

Fruit eggnog. Vary standard eggnog by adding a tablespoon of fruit juice such as orange, cherry, or grape.

Chocolate eggnog. Two tablespoons of chocolate syrup added to eggnog, omitting sugar in the basic mixture, is another interesting variation.

Sherry eggnog. Flavor eggnog with 2 tablespoons sherry or any desired wine.

Frosted chocolate. Use 2 tablespoons chocolate syrup to 1 cup milk. Beat with mixer or egg beater until frothy. Pour over ice in tall glass and serve at once. Whipped cream on top, or ice cream, makes it more popular with the young fry.

Chocolate malted milk. Use 2 tablespoons each of malted-milk powder and chocolate syrup to 1 cup milk. Beat and serve in tall glasses. Some chocolate or coffee ice cream beaten with the liquid makes it richer. Or add a spoonful of ice cream in solid form.

Orange milk shake. Combine in large bowl 2½ cups orange juice, 1½ cups grapefruit juice, 1 cup evaporated milk, 1 cup water, dash of salt, ¼ teaspoon almond extract, additional sugar as desired, and a cup of shaved ice. Beat with electric mixer or egg beater. Serve in tall glasses.

Ginger-ale cream. Combine ¼ cup lemon juice, a mashed banana, ½ cup sugar, and chill. Stir in ½ cup light cream, 1 cup orange ice, and 2 cups ginger ale. Mix well and serve at once. Garnish with orange or lemon slices.

COOL DRINKS FOR HOT DAYS

Sugar syrup. This is a very convenient commodity to have in your refrigerator during cold-drink time since it dissolves, whereas granulated sugar does not do so readily. Simply boil any quantity you want of equal amounts of sugar and water. Stir only until sugar dissolves. Boil it for 10 minutes. Pour into a sterilized jar, cover, and keep chilled in your refrigerator.

Warm-weather fruit drinks need not go flat. Avoid weakening their flavors with ice cubes by adding some of the beverage itself (lemonade, etc.) to the water in your ice-cube tray before freezing the cubes.

Ice cubes for vacuum bottle. To manufacture ice cubes that will fit into the mouth of vacuum bottles, fold long strips of heavy waxed paper into pleats (perhaps milk-container cardboard) and slip the paper into the tray after filling it with water. When frozen, dislodge the cubes by pulling the pleated section apart. (Also gives novel touch to highballs and cocktails.)

Rhubarb flip. Stir 1 cup sweetened rhubarb juice, 1 tablespoon sugar, and a dash of nutmeg into 3 well-beaten egg yolks. Pour over cracked ice in tall glasses. Fill with ginger ale.

Tea punch. Tea is a wonderful extender for punches. Use it many ways. Here's one idea: to 1 cup strong tea infusion add 1 cup sweetened strawberry juice, ½ cup orange juice, and 3 tablespoons lemon juice. Chill. Just before serving, add 1 cup chilled dry ginger ale. Pour into chilled glasses and garnish with whole berries.

Rhubarb tea punch is another recipe using cold tea. Add 6 tablespoons lemon juice, ½ cup sugar, small bunch fresh mint, two cups slightly sweetened stewed rhubarb, and a stick of cinnamon to 1 cup of tea. Chill. When ready to serve, remove cinnamon and add 1 quart cracked ice, 1 sliced orange, 1 quart chilled ginger ale, and 1 pint iced carbonated water. Serve with straws in tall glasses.

Lemonade for one. Allow the juice of 1 lemon for a tall glass of lemonade, add sugar syrup to taste, and fill a glass half full of ice with either water or soda water.

Frozen lemonade is fine for people who like their lemonade pleasantly sweetened. It tastes like lemonade made from fresh lemons.

Make orangeade with frozen concentrated orange juice. Turn orange juice into orangeade by simply combining the 1 can concentrate and 3 cans water with the juice of a lemon or two and serving it over ice in tall glasses.

14

SANDWICHES, BOX LUNCHES, PICNICS, AND COOKOUTS

Some treats and tips for adding variety to informal meals

Sandwich bread should not be too fresh, or it may tear when spread with butter or fillings. Day-old bread is best. And remember, many bake shops and supermarkets feature day-old bread at reduced prices. (It comes out of the freezer like fresh-baked bread, too, after sandwich thaws.)

For neat sandwiches, lay out bread slices so that those next to each other in original loaf (same size) can be paired together. This makes cutting, wrapping, and eating easier.

Avoid monotony in sandwich making. Vary the breads, or even combine slices of different kinds in one sandwich. Rolls or fancy breads also make a nice change. Try cheese bread and raisin bread in the same sandwich.

Ways to grill sandwiches. Butter bottom of lower slice and top of upper slice of bread. Put filling between slices. Toast in broiler, turning once, in electric grill, or toast in skillet, turning with pancake turner.

Or toast, unbuttered, under broiler; or in electric toaster by the slice. Tuck in lettuce after grilling.

Storage tip on sandwich fillings. Keep ground meat and other ground fillings in covered jars in refrigerator. Use within 2 to 4 days. Tart fillings keep better than mild ones. Ground meat, cooked or uncooked, does not keep as well as sliced meat.

Importance of bread spreads. Spreading softened butter (or creamed) or margarine on each slice of bread in sandwiches prevents fillings from soaking into bread and making it soggy. Also makes sandwiches more palatable and easier to handle.

Ice-cream scoop is a perfect utensil for getting standardized portions of sandwich fillings, wonderful when many sandwiches must be prepared at same time for party, bridge club, group of box lunches, or freezer storage. Saves time, avoids waste.

Spreading trick for peanut butter. Add a teaspoon of hot water just before spreading. Also makes the peanut butter go further.

Vary the flavor of mayonnaise with chili sauce, catsup, and prepared mustard to give new taste to sandwich fillings. Honey, jam, or mayonnaise whipped into creamed cheese is another fine treat.

The best meat sandwiches are those containing several thin slices, not one thick slab. They taste better, are easier to handle.

Ground leftover meat, chopped pickle, chili sauce, and a little onion juice make a wonderfully refreshing taste combination for sandwich delight.

Extend leftover sandwiches with chopped hard-cooked egg, lemon juice, and a bit of grated onion, and surprise the person who is bored with sandwiches.

PACK-IN-THE-BOX

Freezer can be box-lunch paradise. Since sandwiches may be stored in the freezer from 2 to 3 weeks, you can make them when you have time, not be plagued by last-minute rush. Nix on hard-cooked eggs, though. (They deteriorate when frozen.)

If several sandwiches of same kind are to be stored in your freezer, after wrapping in moisture-vaporproof material, pack either in top-opening waxed cartons (properly labeled), in metal refrigerator trays with covers, or in plastic bag with top twisted, gooseneck fashion, and secured with string or rubber band.

Pack sandwiches from freezer straight into lunch box. They will thaw in about 3 hours, just in time for lunch.

Like fresh sandwiches? To keep them that way, after you've wrapped them press the ends of the waxed paper together with a hot iron. Keeps them about as fresh as when you made them.

Pack lettuce separately for freezer sandwiches for picnics. But for lunch boxes tuck lettuce into frozen sandwiches and rewrap. Lettuce will stay nice and crisp as the sandwich thaws. You could do the same for picnics, but why do all the work when people can help themselves at a picnic?

For families in which several carry lunches, preparation time can be cut considerably by the assembly-line method. Lay out bread for all sandwiches to be filled in a double row of bread slices. Spread filling in one operation down one line of bread; butter, margarine, or mayonnaise down the second line. Put them together, with lettuce if they're to be eaten that day, without if you're making sandwiches for the freezer.

Speed up sandwich cutting by putting 2 or 3 on top of each other. Cut them all at once with a sharp knife.

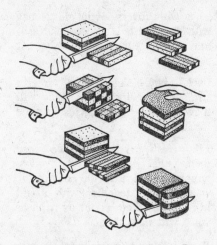

For packing lunch box, cut sandwiches in sizes that are easy to handle. For added novelty, cut them in various shapes.

FOR-FREE AND LOW-COST LUNCH-BOX AIDS

Save the little plastic bags that you'd normally throw out after using the products or food they contained. Excellent for such drippy lunch-box foods as coleslaw and pickles, since they're practically leakproof.

Glass freezer jars and canning jars keep cooked fruits, soups, and other liquids in excellent condition for later use in lunch boxes.

Inexpensive plastic containers, square-shaped and with lids, are excellent for sandwiches, salads, fruits, and cake. Wedge-shaped types are available for pies. Can be washed and used over and over again.

Household aluminum foil does as well in lunch box as in refrigerator or in cooking. Perfect for wrapping irregularly shaped foods. Can be reused if handled carefully.

Disposable containers for lunch box are especially good for person who does not wish to carry containers home. Inexpensive wax-paper bags, waxed cups, and plastic spoons, forks, etc., are easily disposable.

PICNIC TIPS

Afraid to pack ice in picnic basket? Here's a way to keep melting ice from ruining your carefully made picnic-food plans: Fill empty, rinsed milk carton with cold water the day before. Reseal opening carefully. Freeze solid in your home freezer or refrigerator, but leave a 2-inch space at the top of the carton, for water expands when it freezes. Put carton in your picnic box. Even when ice finally melts in carton, it won't drip, for the carton remains sealed.

Why not use that ice? You won't be unpacking your lunch until you're ready to eat, so why not bring along an ice pick when you picnic, chop up the ice in the milk carton (easy to get at by simply slitting the carton away from the ice with a sharp knife you bring along too) and use it to cool the drinks you bring along?

Ice in double boiler? If you want your salads to taste fresh at the picnic, pack them in a double boiler with ice in the bottom container.

Cover of thermos jug stuck? Instead of fretting, insure against it. Before you use jug again, spread a bit of fresh shortening or salad oil over thread of cap. Caution: wash cap after each use, because fat or oil might become rancid.

Ants are allergic to chalk. When going on a picnic, take along a piece of soft white chalk. Use it to draw a heavy mark around edges of picnic table. This magic circle will repel any of the bold crawlers from making their way up the table.

COOKOUT HINTS

Oven shelf for grill. The wire shelf from your oven makes a marvelous picnic stove. Support the corners over the fire with stones or tin cans. It will hold your skillet or frying pan and prove ideal for broiling beef or grilling frankfurters.

Quick-brick picnic fire. To get a quick blaze when you build a picnic fire, soak an unglazed brick in kerosene for a day or two before you plan your outing. The brick will start your fire immediately, will ignite damp logs without kindling, and burn for quite a while on the kerosene fuel alone.

Wear wet gloves in outdoor cookery. Next time you have picnic or outdoor barbecue, have pair of canvas work gloves handy. Soaked in water, they're almost as good as asbestos to prevent hand burns.

Chefs keep a cool head in the hot sun. Line your hat with aluminum foil. Slip edges of foil under sweatband to avoid actual contact with hair or skin.

To roast wienies safely, take along a few extra paper plates and impale them on roasting fork up around edge of handle. They protect hand from scorching heat of fire. Remember, they're made of paper, so don't get them too close to heat.

It's easy to cook chicken on an outdoor grill. Just place chicken (cut into frying-size pieces), mushrooms, and seasonings on a large square of foil. Seal into a tight packet and cook on grate over hot coals. Frozen vegetables with seasonings and butter added may be cooked in same manner.

15

A BOUQUET OF HERBS

Applied properly, these turn flat meals into pleasurable experiences

Herbs are but one of many types of seasoning available—seasonings that range from the familiar salt, pepper, cloves, vanilla, mustard, and garlic to the more exotic such as curry powder, tabasco sauce, or saffron. Here are a few hints about the effective use of herbs.

To be used most effectively, herbs must be applied subtly. You may want to experiment, but the general rule is to use small quantities. A basic measure is ¼ teaspoon dried or crushed herbs or 1 teaspoon chopped fresh ones in a dish to serve four persons.

Fresh herbs, in most cases, definitely are preferable to dried herbs. If you can't buy them fresh, consider growing them at home yourself. Any competent gardener can do so by planting in a sunny plot with good drainage. You might even consider growing them in pots —and indoors. Read up on this in a reputable book, one taste of your own fresh parsley, basil, or chives will make it worthwhile.

Herbs can add magic to your meals. Chives pep up cottage cheese, bay leaf is a natural for chicken or pea soup, chopped parsley enhances a boiled new potato, and your own inventiveness will carry you from experimentation with herbs to a sure touch.

When gravy isn't just gravy. Add a sprinkle of dried dill and stir vigorously. It's a treat all by itself.

An easy trick is to tie together several large sprigs of parsley, a small sprig of tarragon, and one of thyme. Then drop this herb bouquet into a kettle of soup, stew, any meat or fowl dish that is cooked with moist heat. Or try putting an herb bouquet into the cavity of a roasting chicken. It does wonderful things to the flavor of the meat besides eliminating the necessity for stuffing the fowl.

BASIC HERB GUIDE

Basil. This is an easy-to-grow herb with a clover-bloom-like flavor. Use it in any recipe that calls for tomatoes, sprinkle into a green salad or scrambled eggs.

Bay leaf. The versatile leaf with really pungent flavor. Add to homemade vegetable soup, chicken dishes, pea soup, cooking water of beets, onions, and potatoes. Crush and add to tomato juice, soup, or aspic.

Borage. Good only in its fresh form (and its young leaves can even be cooked and served like spinach), this herb provides a subtle, cucumberlike flavor for such delicacies as aspics or fish sauces. It is also used traditionally in punches or lemonades.

Burnet. Like borage, this has a cucumberish flavor and also should be used fresh. Only the tender young center leaves are suitable, but the seeds may be soaked in vinegar that is then used in salad dressings.

Capers. These tiny buds of the caper bush have the sharp taste of a gherkin and add a piquant touch to many a dish. They are especially common in tartare sauce.

Caraway. Both the leaves and seeds of this herb are commonly used, the former in soups and stews, the latter on rye bread, sauerkraut, cheeses, borsch, and in marinades. But never cook the seeds too long with any dish or they become bitter. Used in salads or with vegetables, the seeds should be crushed first to release the flavor.

Chervil. This is a delicate herb that resembles parsley. It goes well with omelets, green salads, Welsh rarebits, cheese spreads, and in the melted butter you pour over green vegetables. Use it, too, on chicken, before broiling.

Chives. Mildest of the onion family, chives are superb in cold potato soup, vichyssoise; potato, fish, and vegetable salads. They blend with cheese for appetizer dip and as a sandwich spread, make a perfect topping, chopped, over cream or clear soups. Stir into cream sauce, omelet, lemon-butter sauce.

Coriander. Only the fresh leaves are used—not the stem—and the whole leaf is placed in soups such as pea or chicken, in stews, or on top of roasts. The seed is also used in such dishes as gingerbread, apple pie, or curry, where its "bite" will not overpower.

Cumin. This is one of the basic herbs of Indian curry powder, but it is also used alone in other foods—cheeses, baked dishes, eggs, beans, rice dishes, chilis, tomato sauces. When it is called for in reputable recipes, try it as directed.

Dill. This herb has feathery green leaves, with a flavor that adds piquancy to many a dish. Add to melted butter as a dip for lobster, crabmeat, or shrimp. Stir into cream or cottage cheese, mashed potatoes. Toss with green, potato, fish, or vegetable salads.

Garlic. Another member of the onion family, garlic has a bad reputation in some quarters. In fact, used properly, it is a fine addition to many foods and is in no way overpowering. Rub a wooden salad bowl with a cut clove of garlic. Soak some cloves in salad dressings if you prefer. Place slivers on meat as it is being cooked, add cloves to stews or sauces. Above all, use fresh garlic whenever possible.

Marjoram. Sweet-smelling as a flower, it's a must on any herb shelf. Use with veal cutlet or Swiss steak. Rub over beef, lamb, or pork before roasting. Add to cheese dishes, omelet, green or vegetable salads, meat loaf, meat pie, stew. Toss with stuffing for chicken or fish.

Oregano. A "natural" with tomatoes. Mix with sauce for spaghetti dishes, add to tomato sauce or soup, meat casseroles. Rub over pork, lamb, or veal before roasting. Use in potato or fish salad.

Parsley. This is certainly one of the most common herbs, flavorful in itself and useful for blending the flavors of other herbs. The stems as well as leaves (even the roots of some of the many varieties available) are used in a wide range of dishes—soups, salads, meats. Aside from being tasty, parsley is also rich in vitamins A and C.

Rosemary. A delicate and versatile herb that has many flavoring possibilities. Add to pan when roasting beef, lamb, pork, or veal. Sprinkle lightly inside poultry before stuffing. Mix into biscuit or dumpling dough before cooking or bak-

ing, to serve with meat. Use in stew or meat loaf. Add to water when cooking peas, potatoes, spinach, turnips.

Saffron. Known mainly for the golden orange color it imparts to rice or other dishes, saffron may also be used for flavoring dressings, cakes, or breads. Use only the small amounts called for in recipes. Saffron, by the way, is the stigma of the autumn crocus.

Sage. Used sparingly, sage adds a welcome flavor to cheeses, chowders, omelets, pork, sausage, duck, or goose. The freshly chopped leaves are far superior to the dried form.

Savory. This herb has a spicy flavor. Use in any dish made with dried peas, beans, or lentils. Mix in stuffing, ground beef, gravy, stew, croquettes, green salad, scrambled eggs, omelet. Sprinkle over baked or broiled fish just before serving.

Tarragon. A tangy and sharp herb that is good chopped for tartare and lemon-butter sauces. Add to fish or egg salads. Toss with green salad or stir into the dressing. Blend with butter to pour over broiled steak or vegetables. Sprinkle over cottage-cheese salad.

Thyme. An aromatic herb that's meant for poultry, meat, and fish stuffing. Add it to dishes made with tomato or cheese. Sprinkle over tomato-clam chowder. Add to meat stew or pot roast. Combine with melted butter to serve over vegetables.

16

THE HOME FREEZER

Ways to save money, food, and time with this storage convenience

Money-saver. You can buy for the freezer when your favorite supermarket or food store runs specials when seasonal large supplies bring prices down. You can often buy in quantity at discount prices. Stow away scraps of this and that until you have enough to make low-cost stews and casseroles.

Better food. Because, on the whole, you buy when prices are in your favor, you can now buy only the best food.

Best food in season and out. Because many foods store as long as a year, you can have strawberries in February, garden-fresh asparagus in November, an oyster cocktail in July. You can eat trout, salmon, and venison—not only after a fishing or hunting expedition, but most any time during the year.

Time-saver. With a home freezer you can buy enough and store enough prepared foods at one time to yield up a complete meal at a moment's notice today—not just for the family but for unexpected guests as well—tomorrow, and day after day.

Work-saver. With a home freezer your cooking side of housekeeping is lightened. You need not shell peas, scrape carrots, or soak spinach in a hurry once the freezer is stocked with foods that need only be brought to the range and cooked, or thawed and eaten.

No more worries. Whether you're late coming back from a downtown shopping trip or company drops in out of the blue, you're saved by the freezer. All you have to do is reach into it and pull out any kind and quantity of the delicious food you like.

Prepare party foods ahead. Why be tired out when your guests arrive if you can have the party food in the freezer days or even weeks before the big day?

If you're without power, your home freezer will hold foods as long as two days if you don't open the door or lid. Longer power delays are rare. But if they occur, dry ice placed on top of frozen foods will keep them in frozen state still longer.

WHICH KIND OF FREEZER?

Smallest freezers today are the frozen-food compartments of combination refrigerator-freezers. They're not so small, either, if you'd like to consider the larger sizes of two-in-one appliances. The freezer section of some runs as large as 5 cubic feet, ample room for regular frozen-food storage for a week or two for a family of four, with some space to spare for home freezing of foods.

Tall and upright, or wide and deep? You have a choice of two styles of plug-in home freezers, upright and chest type. Either type is sized anywhere from a minimum of about 7 cubic feet to 20 maximum for most uprights, sizes going larger in chest-type models.

If you're short of floor space, you'll probably want an upright freezer. And since it's tall, it takes but little wall as well as floor space.

Make sure your flooring is strong enough to hold the weight of an upright freezer, though, since much weight in a filled upright freezer is concentrated in one relatively small floor area.

The top of a chest-type freezer, if you locate the appliance in kitchen or utility room, provides counter space that is sometimes needed and as welcome as the addition of the convenient freezer itself.

A giant home freezer can be built right into your home. It's actually a refrigerated room like the one your butcher disappears into, which is filled with his meat supplies.

The locker plant isn't a home freezer, in the strictest sense, but it does exist primarily to serve the home. It is a commercially operated refrigerated warehouse in which individual families rent space for the freezing and storage of foods.

MANAGING YOUR FREEZER

Freezer management will be more successfully experienced if you proceed gradually. Don't, for instance, fill the freezer with the first products of the season. As the year passes you'll want to add many things. As a guide to help you decide how much space to reserve for various foods, 1 cubic foot will hold about 40 pint cartons or about 35 to 40 pounds of meat (not including whole poultry).

For best results, freeze only specified amounts for the size of your freezer at one time. The use-and-care book which comes with the appliance will give you this information.

Freeze foods as fast as possible. To do this, be sure they are in contact with the sides of a freezer chest or on the permanent refrigerated shelves of your upright freezer.

Once food is frozen you can store it anywhere within the freezer, thus freeing the refrigerated walls or shelves for further freezing.

Organizing your freezer, with special sections for meat, fruit, vegetables, breads, and desserts, simplifies finding items quickly when you are planning a freezer meal. You might also like to have separate storage sections for beef, lamb, poultry, and so forth.

Some combined meals, sometimes called TV dinners, can be stored together for unexpected dinner guests, school lunches, or special diets.

Package carefully to be sure there's as little air as possible between contents and covering, using moisture-vaporproof materials.

Packages should be labeled as to content and date. Since foods have maximum storage time, arrange foods that have been in the freezer the longest time on top and near the front of your freezer.

Reorganize as you shop and add new freezer foods, so you'll keep freezer packages coming out in about the order they went in.

Use your freezer for day-to-day meals so that frozen foods are in prime condition when they become part of your menus. Refer to the following guide for length of storage time for various foods, since some foods do not keep frozen as long as others.

You'll want to keep an inventory to help you remember quantities of various foods and length of time they've been in your freezer. Keep the record accurate so you'll know when to replenish supplies as well as when to use up foods that have reached their time limit in the frozen state.

If you experiment with prepared foods for the freezer, keep a record of the method you used. If it was satisfactory, you can repeat the method; if not, you will try to improve your method.

Take your pick of record keepers. An inventory list on a blackboard near the freezer, with a magnetized pencil that sticks to the metal board; a record book, a card file, a calendar—these are all good ways to keep track of just what you have in your freezer.

RECOMMENDED STORAGE PERIOD AT ZERO° F.*

FRUITS

Apples (sliced), 12 months
Apricots (when packed with ascorbic acid), 12 months
Blackberries (with sugar or syrup), 12 months
Boysenberries (with sugar or syrup), 12 months
Cherries (sour), 12 months
Cranberries, 12 months
Fruit juices (except citrus), 8 to 12 months
Fruits and juices, citrus (in glass jars, with ascorbic acid), 4 to 6 months
Grapes, 8 to 12 months
Huckleberries, 12 months
Loganberries (with sugar or syrup), 12 months
Melon balls, 6 to 8 months
Peaches (when packed with ascorbic acid), 12 months
Pineapple, 12 months
Plums (when packed with ascorbic acid), 12 months

* New techniques develop constantly. If you question storage times listed above, consult your State College Extension Service for latest home-freezing information.

Raspberries (with sugar or syrup), 12 months
Rhubarb, 12 months
Strawberries (with sugar or syrup), 12 months

VEGETABLES

Asparagus, 6 to 8 months
Beans (bush), 8 to 12 months
Beans (Lima), 12 months
Beans (pole), 8 to 12 months
Beans, soy (green), 8 to 12 months
Beets, 12 months
Broccoli, 12 months
Brussels sprouts, 8 to 12 months
Carrots, 12 months
Cauliflower, 8 months
Corn on the cob, 8 to 12 months
Eggplant, 8 to 12 months
Kohlrabi, 8 to 12 months
Okra, 12 months
Parsnips, 12 months
Peas, 8 months
Peppers, 8 to 12 months
Potatoes, sweet, 12 months
Pumpkin, 12 months
Rutabagas, 12 months
Spinach and other greens, 8 months
Squash (summer), 8 to 12 months
Squash (winter), 12 months
Tomatoes (stewed), 6 to 8 months
Turnips, 12 months
Vegetables, mixed, 8 to 12 months

MEAT, MEAT PRODUCTS, FISH

Bacon (not sliced), 3 to 4 months
Bacon (sliced), less than one month
Beef, 8 to 12 months
Beef, ground, 3 to 4 months
Beef liver, hearts, kidneys, 3 to 4 months
Fish, fat (catfish, herring, mackerel, white fish, etc.), 3 to 4 months
Fish, lean (bass, cod, perch, pike, sunfish, etc.), 6 to 8 months
Fish, some fatty (especially pink salmon), 2 to 3 months
Game birds, 8 to 12 months
Geese, 3 to 4 months
Ham, 3 to 4 months
Lamb, 3 to 9 months
Liver, beef or calf, 3 to 4 months
Oysters, 4 to 6 months
Pork, fresh, 4 to 6 months

Poultry (cut up), 4 to 6 months
Poultry (except broilers), 6 to 8 months
Poultry, broilers, 4 to 6 months
Poultry giblets (except liver), 2 to 3 months
Poultry liver, less than 1 month
Rabbit, 8 to 12 months
Sausage (seasoned, not smoked), less than 1 month
Sausage (smoked and seasoned), 2 to 3 months
Shrimp or shellfish, cooked, 2 to 3 months
Turkey, 6 to 8 months
Veal, 6 to 8 months
Venison, 8 to 12 months
Wieners, 1 month or less

PREPARED FOOD

Bread, baked quick, 2 to 3 months
Bread, baked yeast, 2 to 3 months
Cake and cupcakes, baked (frosted), less than 1 month
Cake and cupcakes, baked (unfrosted), 2 to 3 months
Cake, baked fruit, 6 to 12 months
Cheese, Cheddar (and processed), 8 to 12 months
Cookies, 8 to 12 months
Foods, cooked leftover, less than 1 month
Pie, baked and unbaked, 2 to 3 months
Pies, chiffon, less than 1 month
Rolls, baked yeast, 2 to 3 months
Sandwiches, less than 1 month
Soups, stews, 4 months

MISCELLANEOUS

Butter, creamery, 6 to 8 months
Cream, 40 per cent, 3 to 4 months
Cream, heavy (50 per cent), 3 to 4 months
Coconut, shredded, 8 to 12 months
Eggs (not in shell), 8 to 12 months
Ice Cream, 2 to 4 weeks
Lard, 6 to 8 months
Milk, pasteurized homogenized, 2 weeks or less
Nuts, 8 to 12 months

SHORT-TIME STORAGE

Use your freezer fully for short-time (2 weeks or less) as well as longer storage.

Leftover cooked meats and fowl may be stored for a week or two in a covered container. Or wrap in aluminum and tuck into a freezer bag.

Buy a week's supply of bread, take out as much as you need, and freeze the rest in the waxed paper in which it comes. If bread is unwrapped, use waxed paper for storage of 2 weeks or less. Be sure, however, that you use a good grade of paper that is moisture-vaporproof.

Baked goods, such as coffee cakes and rolls, may be stored for a short time in the cardboard sealed containers in which you buy them.

Ground meats for household pets, purchased in quantity to last a week, may be divided into one-day portions and frozen in a covered container. This can be done with frozen meat for pets, too. Let the meat thaw just enough so you can divide it into meal-size portions and refreeze the individually-packaged meat.

Lunch-box foods can be prepared in two ways: a complete lunch may be put in the freezer, or individual items can be packaged and assembled when ready to use.

Use any bread for sandwiches, dark, white, or special kinds of bread or rolls. Each sandwich should be wrapped individually in moisture-vaporproof material. Fillings suitable for freezing include luncheon meats, leftover roast, tuna, cheese, peanut butter, jelly, jam.

Butter both pieces of bread if the sandwich filling is moist, to keep the filling from soaking into the bread.

Don't freeze lettuce, celery, tomatoes, or raw carrots. Add these to the lunch box after it has been taken from the freezer.

Cupcakes, individual pies, a wedge of pie, turnovers, bar-type cookies, or thin cookies can be frozen individually and used as needed for lunch boxes. Even chocolate candy bars can be frozen for the lunch box.

Potato chips, crackers, and pretzels take well to short-time freezing. Remove the amount you need and they'll soon thaw at room temperature.

WRAPPING MATERIALS AND FREEZER CONTAINERS

Food stored in freezers, for whatever length of time, must be covered. You may be able to improvise coverings or containers from materials you find around the home, but you will probably sooner or later want to buy at least a few of the special products designed for just such freezer storage. There are numerous materials and containers sold in houseware stores or supermarkets, and they do the jobs described. The main factors have to do with the nature of your storage requirements: Are the foods liquids or solid, regular or irregular in shape, for short-term or long-term storage, etc.? Read the directions on the side of each product before purchase or use and you should end up doing just the job you want to do. The major materials and containers are described here.

Plastic-coated freezer wrap. This is a special material available under several trade names. It works well in wrapping solid foods. Kept clean and handled carefully, it might be reused, but this is not especially recommended.

Aluminum foil. Very satisfactory for use with irregularly shaped foods such as meat, fish, fowl, cakes, pies. Be sure to buy heavy foil especially made for freezing and so labeled. Use the drugstore fold (see description below) and mold foil around product, eliminating as much air as possible. Freezer foil is reusable if handled carefully.

Plastic film. This is a completely transparent wrapping material that adheres to the substance being covered. It is sold under several trade names (the best known perhaps being Saran Wrap). Plastic film is very durable, needs no overwrap. It is difficult to reuse because of its tendency to cling to materials, but may be reused if successfully smoothed out on a flat surface.

Drugstore fold. Place food in center of wrapping material, allowing enough to cover the food plus an overlap of 3 to 4 inches. Bring longest together over the food and fold over about 1 inch. Continue folding again, over and over, until edges are flat and tight against the food. Press out all air pockets. Fold ends and tuck under package to make secure and tight.

Plastic bags. There are several kinds of plastic bags made for storing dry foods, or you can use any plastic bags that come into your kitchen with other products. Eliminate all air before closing the bag and seal the top with anything such as tape, wire strips, or string. (Do not use rubber bands for long-term storage because they deteriorate in a freezer.) Plastic bags may be reused if handled with care.

Waxed folding cartons. With these, use a bag or liner or some moisture-vaporproof material, or overwrap with cellophane and seal. These are suitable for dry packaging of vegetables and some meats. They come top- and end-opening. Also, special wire racks are available for convenience in filling and opening boxes.

Heavily waxed cartons. Use for liquid or dry-pack foods. No liner necessary. These come in two shapes: round, with slanting sides and disk snap-in lids; and square, tapered cartons with plastic covers. Easily filled, and contents may be removed without complete thawing.

Glass freezer jars. Can be used for liquid or dry pack. Jars have full, open mouths so that contents may be removed with little thawing.

Canning jars. Regular canning jars may be used in the freezer. Because the top opening, however, is smaller than the remainder of the jar, foods must be partially or completely thawed before using. (Be sure to leave 1 to 1½ inches of head space for expansion of liquids.)

Molded or plastic containers. Use for liquid or dry pack. This type of container is easy to label and reusable indefinitely. Its tapered sides make it easy to nest when empty and to stack in the freezer.

Heavy aluminum-foil containers. Can be used for both liquid and dry pack. Some have heavy foil lids that must be sealed with a special device which comes with the containers. Others have covers but can be used for meat or fruit pies. Foods can be heated or baked right in these containers directly from the freezer.

Aluminum containers. Small aluminum dishes with tight-fitting covers may be used for heating goods directly from the freezer. These do not need any sealing device. Follow manufacturer's directions for using.

Stainless-steel containers. These may also be used for heating foods directly from the freezer, but lids are not as tight-fitting as those on aluminum ones and it's well to overwrap with foil or any of the freezer bags, or seal lid edges with tape.

Ice-cube trays. May be used for soup or eggs. Individual servings can be removed one or more at a time in cube form. Must be overwrapped.

Empty waxed cartons. Filled with water and frozen, these make handy chunks of ice to take on picnics for cooling beverages.

Tin cans. May be used for packaging meat patties. Wrap patties individually and place in can. Cover ends with aluminum foil.

Coffee cans. Seal edges with sealing tape.

Paper pie plates. These have metal edges, and pies may be baked in them either before or after freezing, thus freeing other pie plates for nonfreezer baking.

A FEW FREEZING DO'S AND DON'TS

Do use your use-and-care booklet. It can guide you toward best use of your home freezer.

Don't use more than you need. If you want to cook only part of a package of frozen food, remove one end of the package with a sharp knife. (There are special knives made for cutting frozen foods.) Cover the exposed end of remaining frozen food with moisture-vaporproof material and return to the freezer.

To thaw or not to thaw is often the question. Most vegetables should be cooked from the solid state (corn on the cob is an exception). If in doubt, read package directions.

Package family-size servings. Small packages freeze and thaw more quickly than do larger ones.

Always package foods that are to be layered, such as hamburgers, with two thicknesses of packaging material between the layers, so they can be separated easily when frozen.

Cover sharp bones, or other protruding parts that might tear wrapping, with extra patches of material, for extra strength.

Leave head space in containers, especially for liquids, for expansion during freezing. Follow manufacturer's directions and use minimum amount of head space recommended, because air permits dehydration and damages frozen-food quality.

Trap those odors. Be sure that smoked meats, especially, are completely covered and sealed before freezing them. Leaking odors could permeate other foods in the freezer.

Fruit floats? Hold it down with a crushed piece of moisture-vapor-proof material between carton contents and cover. This prevents discoloration and flavor loss of fruit.

Wrap fruit pies after you freeze them. This makes them easier to handle. Don't delay the wrapping, though, or pie will deteriorate in quality.

Label all food carefully. There are several types of inks and pencils on the market for labeling. A china marking pencil or crayon is fine for labeling glass and plastic containers.

Don't refreeze quick-frozen foods once they've thawed. There's usually a loss of quality when thawed foods are frozen, so use them promptly.

When freezing cooked foods, cool them as quickly as possible after cooking. Then package and freeze at once.

Seasonings are fine, but use of some in freezing foods is inadvisable. Onions and sage gradually lose flavor during freezer storage. Cloves and garlic become stronger. Plan to add most seasonings when reheating the food.

Avoid freezing fried foods. They're apt to become rancid even after a very short shortage period.

DEFROSTING

Twice a year is usually often enough to defrost your freezer. It isn't even necessary to shut off the motor. Simply remove the contents, if possible, when you have plenty of room in your refrigerator, and scrape off the frost with a blunt instrument.

Defrost when stocks are low if you want to do a thorough cleaning job within your freezer.

A quick way to melt freezer frost in a horizontal-type machine is to remove all contents, pull the plug, and blow warm air inside with your vacuum-cleaner hose attached at the blowing end. Close the lid on the hose (it's rugged enough to take this for 15 minutes) and the warm air will soon melt the frost. After that you simply sponge out the water into a basin, clean the interior with water and baking soda, rinse with clear water, and wipe dry. Plug it back in and replace frozen foods after temperature is well below freezing (32° F.).

MISCELLANEOUS FREEZER OCCUPANTS

Parsley can be frozen for use in soups, stew, etc., and minced while still frozen and crisp.

Bean coffee, if you grind your own and buy it in quantity, keeps very well in your freezer, better than on the pantry shelf.

Shaved and crushed ice are handy to have stored in moisture-vapor-proof bags, as are a supply of extra ice cubes.

Coffee and ice tea can be frozen in ice-cube trays, the cubes tucked into freezer bags, and you'll have a supply on hand in a minute's notice.

Cigars or cigarettes keep well when frozen, stored in original box and dropped into freezer bags. Remove small amounts as needed or desired.

Furs, if stored at home, can be wrapped in moisture-vaporproof material and placed in the freezer for 2 days. This will kill any moth larvae. Remove and store in cool, dry place, leaving the wrapping material on during storage.

Sprinkled clothes that you haven't time to iron can be wrapped or placed in a moisture-vaporproof laundry bag and stored in the freezer temporarily.

17

KITCHEN APPLIANCES

Ranges, refrigerators, and electrical appliances that make meal-preparation easier and more pleasant

If you're buying a new range, ask about the new surface units that turn the heat down automatically after foods begin to cook. Initial range cost is a little higher than for those not equipped with these units, but you'll have years of economical and carefree cooking if you buy the latest convenience that does some of your work for you.

Your gas-range pilot light is most efficient if you regulate the flame height until it is blue with just a trace of yellow at the top. And keep the assembly clean. Newer gas ranges, with electric pilot ignition, use no gas at all when the range is not in use and provide a cool appliance as well.

Gas-range burner holes should be entirely open. A stiff wire or an opened-up bobby pin is an easy tool to use to keep burner holes open. Yellow flame is usually a symptom of clogged holes. If cleaning them doesn't correct the condition, call your gas company for a service man to adjust the burners.

Your range should be level. If floor unevenness makes your range tilt even slightly in any direction, you'll bake cakes that are uneven because oven shelves are not level.

Check oven-temperature control. If an oven thermometer indicates that your thermostat isn't working efficiently, have it adjusted by your service man.

Know your oven temperatures. Take the guesswork out of oven timing and temperature by knowing that:

Very slow oven means		250°–275° F.
Slow oven	"	300°–325° F.
Moderate oven	"	350°–375° F.
Hot oven	"	400°–450° F.
Very hot	"	475° F. and up

Grandmother's way still works on checking oven temperatures if yours is an old range and has no thermostatic control and you have no thermometer for checking. For a very slow to slow oven, you can hold your hand in the middle of a preheated oven and not feel any discomfort: A moderate oven soon makes you withdraw your hand. A hot oven is immediately uncomfortable, and a very hot one blasts you with heat when you open the oven door. Better invest in an oven thermometer, though, if you haven't one.

Cool hot oven quickly. When a recipe calls for a lower temperature for the second part of the cooking or baking, as for popovers, changing the oven temperature control isn't enough. You have to let the heat out. What's simpler than merely opening the door? Heat spills out in minutes. In a gas range you can tell when it's time to close the door because the gas flame gets larger when temperature drops. Most electric ranges have signal lights to tell you the oven's working again.

TIMERS AND ALARMS

Timer clocks on ranges may seem like intricate contrivances. If you take the trouble to read the range instruction booklet, however, you'll find that that clock will be a great convenience in announcing when things are done on top of the range and when they are ready to come out of the oven. They keep right on calling for you, too, don't just give one "ping" the way a nonelectric minute minder does.

Set the clock for the time you want an oven meal to start cooking, and you can go off for the afternoon knowing it won't even matter if you're a little late because the clock will turn off the heat too. Don't tarry too long, though, because

modern range ovens stay hot a long time and your foods will be too well done.

Alarm in the kitchen. To be sure you don't overbake, underbake, underbeat, or overbeat your cakes, use the clock on your electric or gas range, a small timer clock, or even a regular alarm clock, to let you know when time's up. It's handy for other kitchen uses, too, where timing is of the essence.

"Stop watch." Instead of trying to remember exactly when you started cooking, make a small cardboard clock face with hairpin or bobby-pin hands and hang near your kitchen clock. Set it at starting time, save guesswork and disappointments.

COOK AND SAVE

Cook on retained heat on your electric-range surface-cooking units. Simply turn off the switch and foods will finish cooking with no fuel cost at all. Units stay hot for quite a while after juice is turned off.

Cook with retained heat in either your gas or electric-range modern oven which is so well insulated you have to open the door to let the heat out if a recipe calls for starting high and finishing low-temperature baking or roasting. You can turn the modern range oven off a good half hour before end of cooking time and know your foods will be done to a turn.

Let your oven cook whole meals at once instead of a dish at a time. You'll save fuel costs, time and energy too.

Remove food for broiling from the refrigerator long enough ahead of cooking time so it's no longer chilled through. It will broil more quickly than if cooked directly from the refrigerator.

Pans staggered on your oven shelves, when baking, provide needed air circulation for best baking results and require the least consumption of heat.

Save on gas. Keep a kettle of water over pilot light when gas range is not in use. Kettle keeps warm enough overnight for quick use in the morning. (This applies only to older ranges; new ones have electric ignition, no pilot lights any more.)

Why waste the bottom of your double boiler while cooking in the top? While you make a dessert or sauce in the top, your vegetables can cook simultaneously in the bottom of your double boiler.

Foods boil more quickly if pot covers fit snugly.

Select flat-bottom pans as wide in diameter or wider than cooking burners or heating elements. You simply waste heat around the edges of too-small pans.

Turn down the heat after foods begin to cook on top of the range. You'll cut fuel costs and foods will neither burn dry nor be shaken up and made unattractive because of too rapid boiling.

Add salt to the cooking water for vegetables in the bottom of your double boiler when the water's cold. Water will come to a boil faster.

Heat only as much water as you need, not a whole kettleful, for a cup of tea. In fact, there's a tiny teakettle that holds just enough water for a cup of tea or instant coffee, and a kettleful boils in only a few minutes.

Save fuel as well as vitamins and minerals by cooking vegetables in the smallest possible amount of boiling water for as short a time as possible. They look and taste better if still slightly crunchy when served, are more nutritious too. And short cooking conserves fuel.

Double-boiler food-saver. A jar lid placed in the double boiler will rattle when the water gets too low and thus give you a dependable SOS.

Avoid stirring air into cooking or hot food. Permit food to cool before straining, too. Oxygen destroys some nutritive elements.

Heating baby food quickly. You can heat different kinds at the same time by using a two- or three-cup egg poacher. When food is warm, lift it from tray and feed baby directly from the cups.

Cut-up potatoes, which are to be mashed later, cook in half the time whole ones do, cutting your fuel bill in half. Saves you time too.

Heat the potatoes, when they are ready to be cooked, in hot tap water while the cooking water comes to a boil. Cooking water will return to boiling temperature faster if warm potatoes are added to it.

Don't peel scrubbed potatoes you plan to add to an oven roast. Instead cut them in quarters, parboil for 15 minutes, drain and return to the heat to dry for a few moments. Then roll them in the fat around the roast, and they'll finish cooking in less time than whole potatoes. (Skins left on potatoes make them nutritious and out of this world in flavor.)

Cut large potatoes in half before baking them and lessen baking time. Simply rub the dried cut surface with shortening or bacon drippings, as you do the skin side of a well-pricked baking potato, and the resulting taste thrill will delight you while you save money by halving the fuel bill.

CLEANUP TIME

Don't let foods burn on. Wipe up food spills as fast as they occur and you'll preserve the porcelain-enamel finish of your range.

Stop frying-pan explosions. A little salt sprinkled in the frying pan will keep fat or lard from splattering. Also makes range cleaning easier.

When frying fish or meat, cover skillet with a colander. This allows steam to escape, permits food to brown well, and prevents grease from spattering.

Paper plates keep grease off burners and electric units. When frying food that tends to spatter grease, place paper plates over the burners or surface units not in use.

Surface units or burners should be kept clean. Electric units are, on the whole, self-cleaning, but you'll save yourself cleaning time if you line reflector pans with aluminum foil. Gas burners simply need to have holes kept free of burned-on foods, and burner holes should be kept open.

Foil broiler-pan cleaning with aluminum foil. Line the bottom part with foil to catch the drippings. Cover the top section with foil, too, and cut slits in it where the top part of the broiler pan is slit, to let juices escape to the bottom part.

If you have a corrugated, solid broiler pan, with a collecting trough at one end, shape your foil to fit that pan, with outside edges turned up.

Commercial oven cleaners, both solid and spray type, do a quick job. Be sure to follow container directions for use, however, and be safe by wearing rubber or other moistureproof gloves.

It's easy to clean kitchen-range porcelain. Wait until it's cool, because porcelain enamel is glass-fused on steel and is breakable if misused. Use mild soap and warm water. Avoid cleaning powder and harsh abrasives which may scratch enamel finish.

Range enamel will last longer if you wait until cooking appliance cools before washing it, because water on warm enamel cools it more quickly than the base to which it is fused and may cause the enamel to crack.

In cleaning open-coil oven units, never put them into water. Wipe them off with a slightly damp cloth.

Broiler pan cleans easier the sooner you wash it after using. Don't leave uncleaned pan in oven, for stains will bake on and become difficult to remove.

REFRIGERATORS

Is your refrigerator door airtight? Models with magnetic closings and gaskets are practically permanent. But if yours is an older model, make this simple test: Close the refrigerator door on a piece of paper. If the paper pulls out easily, chances are you are wasting gas or electricity and the door needs a new gasket.

Place your refrigerator on a cool kitchen wall. If it's next to a range or other heat-using appliance, the cold-food-storage appliance works overtime. Besides, it's ideal to have three work centers in your kitchen —refrigerator, range, and sink—as nearly in V formation as possible, so if you separate the refrigerator, as recommended, work will be easier in the room.

When off on vacation or even a week end, save gas or electricity by turning the cold control of your refrigerator down to the lowest operating point, just short of the defrost position on older refrigerator models.

GETTING THE MOST FROM YOUR REFRIGERATOR

Cool foods before you put them in your gas or electric refrigerator. It takes more power to cool hot foods in the refrigerator than it does if you let them come to room temperature first. If yours is a refrigerator that doesn't defrost automatically, you'll also have to defrost oftener because of excess moisture hot foods give off as they cool. With an automatic defroster, it will have to work overtime while hot foods cool.

Allow air space. Avoid crowding refrigerator shelves. To refrigerate properly, air must circulate inside the box.

Save that enamel. Acids corrode enamel. If vinegar, lemon, or tomato spills in the refrigerator, wipe up immediately.

Deodorize inside of refrigerator by washing it with soapy water containing a little baking soda.

Another refrigerator deodorizer. A lump of charcoal in your refrigerator "sponges up" fish, onion, and other strong odors. Prevents them from penetrating butter, cheese, and other sensitive foods.

Ice cubes in a hurry. Store one or more large jars of water in your refrigerator. Use the water to refill ice trays. Since the water is already chilled, you'll have those extra ice cubes in jig-time when you want them for company.

Ice will freeze faster if you pour a little water on the surface where the tray sits. Be sure, however, not to have a heavy coating on the coils. Defrost well in advance of entertaining.

DEFROSTING

Use a reminder when defrosting if your refrigerator is one of the older models that must be defrosted. Are you one of those absent-minded people who forgets the refrigerator is being defrosted? Hang a sign on the handle with the word "defrosting" in large letters, to remind you to turn the knob back when the appliance is completely defrosted.

Some modern refrigerators don't have to be defrosted. All you have to do to make the appliance give you full service is not to overcrowd the interior, clean it thoroughly every week or two, and give the exterior a regular application of a special wax designed for appliances with porcelain-enamel finish. Use it whether yours is white or one of the new colored appliances.

Quick defroster. When your refrigerator needs defrosting but frigid temperature is necessary to keep food from spoiling, try filling your ice-cube trays or pans with hot water. Repeat if necessary. The ice that coats the freezing unit will melt away in record time.

COOKING APPLIANCES

Microwave ovens are relatively new appliances that are still quite expensive to buy but that might prove economical over the long haul by cutting down on your utility bills. But most people will be interested in a microwave oven for its sheer convenience: it cooks foods extremely quickly and eliminates much of the mess of cleaning up. Despite the name, by the way, this appliance is not really a substitute for your oven, for many of the foods it cooks best—such as soups or frankfurters—are those usually cooked on range burners. Government and other tests have declared microwave ovens to be safe so long as the directions for use are followed, and they are not thought to have any side effects on people.

A portable oven makes a wonderful second oven if you have a range with one oven. It's a natural to fill and take along on picnics too, and for camp cookery where electricity is available.

Square or round? You have a wide choice of electric skillets these days. You might be used to nonelectric round ones and prefer that shape. If you'd like to adventure a bit and have a little more cooking surface, there are square ones too. In any case, select one that has the plug at the end of the handle. These are easily washed right in the sink or dishpan.

Electric cookers, designed for deep-fat frying and anything from making soup to stews and more exotic dishes, are fun for cooking at the table. To clean, you simply put water and dishwashing detergent or soap into the cooker, rinse with clear water, and wipe dry. Just be sure that you don't get water into the plug. Outside may be wiped with a damp cloth, polished with a dry one.

Crockpots are a special version of electric cookers designed to cook at low temperatures over long periods. Their main appeal is that you can prepare certain kinds of dishes and leave them to cook in the crockpot while you are away.

When you get a new toaster, check to be sure it is easy to clean. Nothing is more exasperating to a careful homemaker than a toaster with the problem of getting at stale crumbs in inaccessible corners.

To clean a pop-up toaster, never, never shake it or poke into it with a harsh brush. Better use a chicken feather to brush out the crumbs. There's usually a hinged tray at the bottom, however, which you can unfasten by placing the toaster on its hinge, and it's easy to clean.

Toasters have gone big and glamorous. Look for them in decorator colors now. You might as well pick one that pretties your breakfast table as long as you're shopping for a new one. There's a huge one out now that takes two regular-width slices of bread in each slot; turn a knob and you can toast or broil in a tray at the bottom. The heating element turns on its side when you turn the knob.

Your gravy lumpy? Put it in your blender and in seconds it will be smooth as can be. The blender's wonderful, too, for smoothing ap-

plesauce, puréeing vegetables, and many other things you'll find in the recipe and instruction booklet that comes with it.

Electric-mixer blades are easy to clean if they come out easily and if they have no center shaft in the middle of the mixing end.

Here's how to clean your waffle iron: Scrub the grids with a fine wire brush, then brush them with non-salted oil. After this, heat the iron for about 10 minutes to recondition it. Soak up excess oil with a piece of bread placed between the grids.

The safest, most convenient can opener is the wall type. Get the detachable kind that can be removed from permanently mounted bracket for cleaning and storage (and can be folded back toward wall without detaching, when not in use). Among portable can openers, preferred type has circular cutting wheel.

Can openers need cleaning too. The cutting wheel gets gummy with food in time and should be cleaned very thoroughly. There's one can opener that comes with a spare wheel so the one that needs to be cleaned can go right into the dishpan.

You'll have keen knives if you keep an electric knife sharpener handy. A few strokes on each side of the knife and presto, it's sharp and safe to use again. Some sharpeners are even flexible enough so you can use them for sharpening scissors as well.

18

KITCHEN HINTS

Tricks of the trade that save time, work, and money

Food shopping with minimum effort usually means one large shopping trip a week and a second one for fill-ins. By planning an entire week's menu in advance, it's often possible to buy a large quantity of one inexpensive item and use it in several forms during the week. If some foods, such as pot roast, have risen in price since previous week, substitute a less expensive meat.

Fresh food products in season cost less, taste best. Take advantage of peak supply to enjoy fruits and vegetables at their nutritive best and at lowest price. Where surplus supply offers exceptional bargains, buy in bulk for canning and freezing.

Friendliness to merchants pays dividends. Shopper who gains confidence of grocer and butcher can tell him her budget problems. To keep you a loyal customer, he will look for good items you can afford and give you first choice on bargains. Your butcher, too, knows many ways of preparing inexpensive meat cuts and will gladly impart his "know-how."

For economys' sake, read labels on canned foods. Often the same food packed in heavy syrup is more costly (and higher in calories for weight watchers) than that packed in lighter syrup. By checking weights listed, you can choose the product that gives most for your money.

SHORTCUTS WITH FOODS

Use substitute ingredients only after you've tested recipe enough times to know what you are doing. With a new recipe, follow directions to the letter.

Season within reason when doubling a recipe. It is not safe to double salt or other seasonings. Spices should be used sparingly too, adding what is needed only after tasting results first.

A cup of milk, called for in most recipes, may be made from ½ cup of evaporated milk plus ½ cup water, or from ½ cup nonfat dry milk combined with ¾ cup water.

Tip on egg volume when baking. If a superfluffy egg white or meringue is your desire, take eggs from the refrigerator long enough before you bake so that eggs are room temperature. Egg whites give greater volume when not chilled.

How to sour milk or cream. Mix a tablespoon of lemon juice into a cup of sweet milk. Let stand a few minutes, stir, and it's ready for any recipe calling for sour milk or buttermilk. In recipes requiring sour cream, you may sour cream the same way.

To mix liquid and flour, pour them into a small jar, then cover and shake until the ingredients blend. They're used for artful thickening of sauces and gravies. Store unused sauce in refrigerator for future use.

Airy, easy way to chop parsley. Bunch up the parsley, then snip across it in narrow slices, using your kitchen shears. It's much easier than chopping it in a wooden bowl.

COOKING WITH FOIL

Line the bottoms of waste cans with circles of aluminum foil. The foil will prevent the can from rusting and will keep it new.

For an amazing short cut in cleaning silver, lay a piece of aluminum foil in the bottom of a dishpan, add about 2 quarts of warm water and 2 tablespoons each of salt and baking soda. Place silverware in dishpan, touching each piece to the foil. The tarnish will disappear.

Wrapping odorous foods, such as cheese and onions, in aluminum foil for refrigerator storage will prevent them from contaminating other foods. The foil is odor- and moisture-proof.

Line crumb tray underneath surface burners of gas and surface units of electric ranges with aluminum foil. Wipe off the foil when necessary, but if serious boil-overs occur, discard the foil and reline.

When casseroles or pies run over, place a piece of aluminum foil somewhat larger than the utensil holding the food on the shelf beneath the one on which the food rests. Edges of the foil may be turned up. In some ranges this may interfere slightly with browning, but the convenience of catching these drips offsets this. Don't cover the entire shelf or the greater portion of it with foil; this will interfere with heat circulation. And in no way line the oven bottom.

In electric-range ovens having the concealed-heat type of unit, covering the bottom surface reflects the heat back on the enamel finish, causing it to craze. Practically all electric ranges have a bottom unit open in the center. Most gas ranges have openings in the bottom surface of the oven. Closing these openings in either an electric or gas range seriously interferes with heat circulation and may damage the enamel of the oven lining.

To line the broiler pan, join two pieces of 12-inch-wide aluminum foil with a tight double fold. Fit it into the bottom of the broiler pan, letting it extend up the sides nearly to the top. If heavy-duty foil is available, one piece may be used the same way. Place the rack in position, put the meat on the rack, and broil as usual. For good broiling, the melted fats must be allowed to drain into the bottom of the pan. After broiling is finished, pick up foil, drain off melted fat, and discard foil. And you've only the rack to wash in the dishpan.

Many of the latest-model broiler pans have an upper rack or pan on which the meat rests, consisting of wide bars with slits between, or other more or less solid surfaces with openings for the fat to drain through. These are often difficult to wash and may be covered with foil. Mold the foil to conform to the shape of the rack, make openings or slits with a knife exactly like those in the rack. In addition, use the foil in the bottom of pan, to catch the fat.

Will aluminum foil catch fire? Foil does not itself catch fire, but sometimes fat that has drained onto the foil in broiling catches fire, causing smoke. Trim excess fat from meats and follow directions in your range's instruction manual for placing the broiler the correct distance from the broiling unit or flame. There should always be at least 3 inches between the surface of foods being broiled and the source of heat when you're broiling fatty foods.

No matter what size or shape bowl or dish you use for storing food, aluminum foil will form a tight, moistureproof cover. It doesn't need fastening with a rubber band or tying, since it is pliable and clings to whatever it covers. It keeps in the fresh flavor and moisture of foods, prevents them from drying out and discoloring.

Place aluminum foil over roasts to promote even browning and to keep spattered juices from soiling the oven. Remove during last stages of roasting.

Use foil to reheat rolls, coffee cakes, and buns in a 350° F. oven and they'll have a fresh-baked flavor that makes them doubly delicious.

Wrap up potatoes or large juicy apples in foil. Bake them as usual and serve right in the silver jackets.

For bottles that can't be recorked with their own stoppers, keep a supply of corks on hand and build them up to fit by wrapping aluminum foil around them. The foil will fit tightly and will not be affected by the moisture.

Corks can stick in bottles containing sugary liquids (sweetened extracts, etc.). Prevent this by smoothing a bit of waxed paper or aluminum foil around cork before inserting it in opening.

Salt is usually hard to pour in damp or muggy weather. Try this trick: wrap a small piece of aluminum foil tightly around the top of the shaker. Moisture-vaporproof, the aluminum foil keeps dampness out of the salt, allows the salt to pour freely. Replace the "lid" immediately after pouring.

FIRST AID FOR UTENSILS

Spend a little more, save a lot. Buy best cooking equipment; better materials last longer, do a better job, give you tastier foods, cause less waste.

Kitchen tools need oiling? Apply a little glycerine with eye dropper. If any glycerine accidentally gets into food, don't worry. It's harmless.

Scales of household accuracy. Careful homemakers keep a kitchen scale handy. It's helpful in certain cookery and especially helpful in jam and jelly making. Handy for weighing baby, too, with the aid of a well-padded large dishpan.

Measuring liquids is tricky. Undermeasuring is a common fault but can be avoided by setting measuring cup on level surface (otherwise the surface of liquid may slant and deceive you). Fill until liquid flows into correct groove mark of measuring cup.

Best cooking utensils are flat-bottomed, with base just large enough to cover heating unit or range burner. Use pans with relatively straight sides, as those with flaring sides tend to waste heat. Tight-fitting lids prevent heat from escaping, keep cooking time to minimum.

Utensils darkened by heat absorb more heat than bright, shiny ones and often are responsible for over-browned or burned foods.

Brighten dulled aluminum pans by boiling some apple parings in them.

Aluminum dim-out. Don't worry if the bottoms of your aluminum pans aren't too shiny. A dull surface absorbs more heat than a shiny one and cuts down fuel bills.

How to treat new skillets and pans. After greasing them well, place them in a 450° F. oven for about 30 minutes. Scour them well afterward, using fine steel wool, and wash in suds and water. Rinse and dry.

"Season" new enamelware by putting it in water and bringing to a boil slowly. Lengthens its life.

Look for these qualities in a carving set: Hardness of blade and sharpness of steel, initial sharpness of blade (to which it can be returned after it grows dull); resistance to stain and rust, resistance to warping; durability of handles.

Save kitchen knives from damage. Chop and cut foods on wooden cutting board. Protects other work surfaces, too, from being gouged by knife cuts.

Don't soak knives with painted handles. Soaking damages painted surfaces of any kind. In fact, any knife handle is liable to be undermined if soaked, since they are attached to the metal part by a variety of adhesives that don't take to soaking.

How to firm a food chopper. Place a piece of sandpaper under the clamp, with the rough side up, before tightening the screw to the table or pull-out shelf.

To keep whipping bowl from slipping, set it on a folded damp cloth.

For emergencies. A small coping saw of your own can be of great help when the butcher has not quite sawed the bone clear through. It also comes in handy when carving.

Pastry-brush longevity. It will last longer if you wash and dry it carefully after each use. Hang it up to dry where air circulates before putting it away.

New uses for old toothbrushes. Many thrifty homemakers have found them to be wonderfully handy for intricate cleaning chores. The bristles can penetrate into the hard-to-clean spots on numerous household gadgets, such as the gear-type can opener, egg beater, food chopper, grater, etc.

Salt flows freely, even in humid weather, if you keep a few grains of raw rice in the salt shaker.

CLEANUP TIME

Save dish-washing time. Use your china in rotation, so that there's never a group at the bottom of the pile that remains unused. Always take dishes from the bottom of the pile, and when they've been washed and wiped, return them to the top spot. That way none gathers dust.

Soak all cooking utensils if you haven't time to wash them up before dinner. They're much easier to wash later.

Don't rush hand dish-washing. If you use a good dish-washing detergent and plenty of hot water, you'll find dish-washing much easier if you let them soak in the water and detergent for a half hour before proceeding with the job.

The cool treatment. Always let metal cake pans cool before washing, to prevent warping of the metal.

When pot and kettle call each other black. To clean the inside of pot or kettle, slice a lemon and put the slices in an aluminum coffeepot with plenty of cold water. Let it come to a boil and keep it boiling until the inside surface can be made to look like new just by rubbing the surface with a cloth.

How to rescue a burned or greasy pan. Fill the pan with an inch of water, add 1 tablespoonful or more of soda, and heat the water to the boiling point.

Clean greasy frying pans with ease. Put a small amount of soap powder in the pan, add warm water, and simmer slowly for a few minutes. In this way even the greasiest of frying pans can be cleaned in a matter of seconds.

To "de-fish" or "de-onionize" utensils, put a few drops of ammonia in the dish water when washing used dishes. Or put several tablespoons of vinegar in the dish water; fish and onion odors disappear just like that. Another quick deodorizer consists of washing, scalding, then inverting the utensils over a gas flame for about 2 minutes.

Remove teakettle coating. When lime settles on the inside of your teakettle, don't wait until the coating gets thick. Make it a point to use the teakettle every time you want to boil potatoes or boil the peelings from carrots. Either one keeps the inside of your teakettle free of lime coating.

Save lemon skin after squeezing juice. Use rind to remove mineral stains from insides of teapots and other vessels. Fill utensil with lukewarm water. Add cut-up skin of 1 lemon (with pulp still attached) for each pint of water. Allow it to soak for 4 or 5 hours. Rinse kettle with hot water.

Never scour Pyrex cooking utensils with steel wool or scrape them with a knife. In doing so, you may scratch the surface of the glass. Wash glass utensils by soaking them in lukewarm suds, rinsing with lukewarm water. If brown stains appear on the glass, rub them with dry baking soda before washing or use a mild scouring powder on them.

To clean the inside of a Pyrex kettle, half fill it with water, add a few small pieces of lemon. Let water boil, then pour off; finally, rinse in fresh water.

Removing remains of burned food from an enamelware pot. Soak pot overnight with water and washing or baking soda. Wash it the next morning in soapsuds, then rinse carefully with clear water. Don't use a knife to scrape off burned particles if you don't want the enamel to chip; it's glass, you know.

Never soak an earthenware dish or pot if food has scorched in it. Add a teaspoonful of baking soda to the water and let it stand only until particles have loosened.

Crusted casseroles. When burned food is hard to clean from casseroles, fill them with warm water and add a teaspoonful of baking soda. The crusted matter will loosen quickly.

Clean out hard-to-remove sediment that often clings to bottom of bottle or glass vase by filling vessel half full with warm soapsuds, then add a handful of carpet tacks. Shake vigorously and watch the sediment loosen.

After grinding other foods (meats, nuts, etc.), grind through a piece of dried bread. This carries sticky food particles away and makes grinder washing easy.

Toothbrush cleans egg beater. Gets into spots that are difficult to penetrate otherwise. Also handy when cleaning food choppers, graters, etc. (Jewelry too.)

Egg beaters and potato mashers wash easily and quickly if you place them in cold water as soon as you've used them.

Rust remover. Dip rusted metalware in pure cider vinegar, then let it dry for a few days. Wipe away the remaining loosened rust particles.

Rust rings caused by scouring-powder cans sitting on shelves in the bathroom or kitchen can be prevented by covering the bottom edges of the can with strips of Scotch tape.

Keep faucets shiny bright. Rub the brass or other metal with furniture polish after cleaning.

Don't clog your drain with grease. When pouring off fats, lay a few pieces of newspaper over the drain before you pour. The grease will then remain on the paper, while the water will naturally disappear, thus saving you clogged drainpipes and nasty plumbing jobs.

KITCHEN COMFORT

Good-bye to unwelcome cooking odors. Neutralize them by boiling 3 teaspoonfuls ground clove in 2 cups water for 15 minutes. Or heat some vinegar on the range. Works like a charm.

Banish workaday odors from your hands. Remove clinging odor of onions, fish, or oil from hands and dishes by rubbing with moistened salt. Rinse well with clear water, then wash with soap. Or just rinse with vinegar.

Sinks smell better. A handful of baking soda put in the sink overnight will clean and purify that unfragrant drain.

Less noise in the kitchen. Cover work counters or shelves with sound-deadening linoleum, vinyl, Formica, or tile. They are also easily kept clean by wiping with damp cloth.

You can replace existing sink faucets with dish-washing equipment. It works like a faucet, too. There's a brush at the end of a hose, a detergent well behind the faucet part. When you turn on the water it comes through the brush. Press a button and the water and detergent mix. You can thus wash with much hotter water than your hands can stand in the dishpan.

You'll cook in cool comfort if you have an air conditioner in your kitchen as well as a ventilating fan. Your appliance dealer will tell you the best location for each of these luxuries so they'll perform at peak perfection and most economical operating cost.

Save your larger-size paper grocery bags. They make excellent linings for garbage pail or wastebasket, make disposal of refuse easier, keep receptacle clean. Paper-bag-line all your wastebaskets, for the same reasons.

LITTLE THINGS MAKE
A BIG DIFFERENCE

Save screw-top glass containers from coffee, jams, etc., and you'll save money. Use them for storing dry foods such as cereals, flour, and dried vegetables. These foods, if kept in original cardboard containers during warm months, tend to foster growth of bacteria. Not so in airtight covered glass jars.

With glass containers for foods in the pantry, you can always tell when you are running low on an item and can replenish the supply before you're out of stock.

Fasten linoleum to kitchen shelves with linoleum cement and it will practically never come off. It will also look handsome and clean easily with a damp cloth.

Solids won't go through your funnel? Keep a knitting needle handy, the plastic kind that won't rust. It's perfect to use as a plunger in the narrow funnel opening.

Use your sieve or colander when changing flower water. You'll catch the bits of leaves and other deposit in the water that might in time clog up your drain.

Saucy sieve successes. Sauce lumpy? Simply force it through a sieve, using a wooden spoon or rubber scraper to speed the process. Works as well with gravy too.

Paper toweling makes an excellent "blotter" for draining foods that are fried in deep fat.

Candlelight can be beautiful, unless the romantic touches start to drip. Avoid messy candles by putting them in refrigerator for a few hours before using.

Heatproof table mats can be made by mounting colorful lengths of linoleum on pieces of plywood. Ce-

ment linoleum to the plywood, then paint edges a bright color.

Morning time-saver for busy bodies. Set your table for breakfast the night before and save precious time in the morning when every minute counts.

Good breakfasts can be made quickly. If dry ingredients for muffins or pancakes are mixed the night before (and muffin tins greased), many precious minutes can be saved during the breakfast rush.

Toast for invalids. Just before serving eggs on toast to invalids (and children), cut the toast into cubes, leaving the slice in its original shape before putting the egg over it. Easier to handle, and coaxes feeble appetites.

When a convalescent child loses interest in food, try this: paste attractive cutouts to outside bottom of drinking glass, glass bowl, or glass dish. Use any good mending adhesive for pasting on the cutouts. You thus make a game of mealtime and give ailing child a new incentive for "cleaning the plate."

Gift wrappings for the kiddies. Add gala touches by thrusting a few lollipops into the knot of the bow or by wrapping package in comic pages instead of regular gift wrapping. Another idea: attach a dimestore trinket or foil-wrapped cookies to your wrapping ribbons.

If you haven't a low flower bowl but still want a really special

Christmas-table decoration, take one of your cake pans and "turn it into sterling silver" by covering it completely with aluminum foil from your kitchen roll. Mold the foil tightly to the pan and make a deep ruffle of foil to attach to the edge of the pan. Spread chicken wire or lay a frog in the center of the pan and arrange your evergreen sprigs and pine cones.

Attractive hangers for pot-holder hooks. Use plastic shower hooks. They're rustproof, colorful, and allow pot holders to be hung easily from screw hook or nail.

Probation corner for new recipes. Paste a large, strong envelope in the back of your favorite cookbook. Put in untried or clipped recipes until you have time to test them and decide whether you want them in your permanent recipe file.

Cookbook rack. Use a rubber-covered plate rack to hold your cookbooks. It keeps them neat and easy to get at, either at the counter top or in a cupboard.

19

NUTRITION AND DIETING

Losing—or gaining—weight must be based on sound nutrition

The most precious inheritance anyone can give to children is sound eating habits to maintain good health. On every level—from general feelings of well-being to savings on medical bills—a richer life lies in store for them.

"Food problems" for many people in this world, it has been observed, means getting enough to eat, while in our society—with some exceptions—it usually means getting too much to eat. Even when people do not eat such large quantities as to become fat or overweight, they are often eating too much of the wrong kinds of food. This can lead to a form of malnutrition that may not show up in the body's appearance but is just as surely undermining a person's health.

People are right to be concerned about being overweight. Quite aside from appearance—which can have crucial effects on relations with other people, emotional states, and a person's whole attitude toward the world—excess weight has definite links with specific bodily conditions, maladies, and life expectancy.

The complete story of nutrition requires whole books, but it might well be summed up in that old but still true expression, "a balanced diet." Whatever your tastes in food, however much you need to maintain your proper weight, whether you buy only organic foods or take everything prepared from the supermarket shelves, the important thing is to get the proper proportions of the various essential foods.

Even people who have never been able to tell the difference between proteins, fats, and carbohydrates or who cannot be bothered keeping track of minimum daily requirements of vitamins and minerals can at least be aware of the need to vary their daily diet. For general purposes of meeting daily requirements, everyone should try to eat something from each of the seven basic food groupings:

Leafy green and yellow vegetables
Citrus fruits, tomatoes, and raw cabbage
Potatoes and other vegetables and fruits
Milk, cheese, and ice cream
Meat, poultry, fish, eggs, dried peas, and beans
Bread, flour, and cereals
Butter and fortified margarine.

The amounts of food required vary considerably from individual to individual depending on age, body size, daily activities, the environment, and other factors. A handy all-round measure, though, is based on the numbers of calories—the unit of measure that describes the amount of energy potentially available in a given food and also the amount of energy the body must use up to perform a given function. The following charts give general guidelines for the amounts of calories required and expended by people engaged in different levels of activity.

ADULT MALES	CALORIES NEEDED PER DAY
Sedentary	2,500
Moderately active	3,000
Active	3,500
Very active	4,250

ADULT FEMALES	
Sedentary	2,100
Moderately active	2,500
Active	3,000
Very active	3,750

TYPE OF ACTIVITY	CALORIES PER HOUR
Sedentary: reading, sewing, typing, etc.	30–100
Light: cooking, slow walking, getting dressed, etc.	100–170
Moderate: sweeping, light gardening, making beds, etc.	170–250
Vigorous: fast walking, hanging out clothes, golfing, etc.	250–350
Strenuous: swimming, bicycling, dancing, etc.	350 and more

Caloric content of family foods can only be approximated, because many dishes contain a combination of low- and high-calorie ingredients. What you put into salads, for instance, how much dressing you use, and how much you eat of them determine whether they are for weight gainers or weight losers. For people who want to keep track of their food intake, however, the calorie count provides the easiest guide.

Eat a good breakfast. You'll eat less the rest of the day and feel better too. The skip-a-meal routine is for the birds, not you. All it does is make you hungrier; you tend to turn light snacks into heavy ones and wind up consuming more calories than you need before the day is out. Eat the right foods in the right amounts at the right time of day—mealtimes.

LOSING WEIGHT

There is a constant stream of books and articles promising the "secret" of losing weight. Some of these methods may be effective, some may be harmless, but some may be downright dangerous for certain individuals. If it is a matter of cutting down by a few pounds, a small proportion—say, 5–10%—of your total weight, you should be able to do this without any particular method other than eliminating the obviously starchy, sugary, heavy foods. But if you intend to embark on a more serious diet program—whether yours is a weight-losing or weight-gaining problem—then you should first consult a doctor.

The decision that you are overweight or underweight may usually be fairly based on appearance, but there are often other factors. The accompanying chart provides a general guide to desirable weights, taking into consideration both height and the body frame.

Dietetic foods or diet supplements cannot replace sensible low-calorie diet and are unnecessary with such a diet. Reducing candies, capsules, etc., only spoil appetite. High-roughage, low-calorie cracker products often harm sensitive digestive tracts. Danger of reducing drugs is especially high if self-administered. Use of benzedrine and dexedrine must be supervised by a physician to avoid use by people whose systems "can't take it." Laxatives, including mineral oil, should never be used for reducing purposes.

As you battle your bulges, remember that the more you avoid carbohydrates such as sugars and starches (and alcohol), the more of your stored-up fat is used up by your body and eliminated. Limit your carbohydrates to a minimum in the bread and potato department, since both of those foods are

DESIRABLE WEIGHTS FOR MEN AND WOMEN AGED 25 AND OVER [1]

(in pounds by height and frame, indoor clothing)

MEN (in shoes, 1-inch heels)				WOMEN (in shoes, 2-inch heels)			
Height	Small Frame	Medium Frame	Large Frame	Height	Small Frame	Medium Frame	Large Frame
5 ft. 2 in.	112-120	118-129	126-141	4 ft. 10 in.	92- 98	96-107	104-119
5 ft. 3 in.	115-123	121-133	129-144	4 ft. 11 in.	94-101	98-110	106-122
5 ft. 4 in.	118-126	124-136	132-148	5 ft. 0 in.	96-104	101-113	109-125
5 ft. 5 in.	121-129	127-139	135-152	5 ft. 1 in.	99-107	104-116	112-128
5 ft. 6 in.	124-133	130-143	138-156	5 ft. 2 in.	102-110	107-119	115-131
5 ft. 7 in.	128-137	134-147	142-161	5 ft. 3 in.	105-113	110-122	118-134
5 ft. 8 in.	132-141	138-152	147-166	5 ft. 4 in.	108-116	113-126	121-138
5 ft. 9 in.	136-145	142-156	151-170	5 ft. 5 in.	111-119	116-130	125-142
5 ft. 10 in.	140-150	146-160	155-174	5 ft. 6 in.	114-123	120-135	129-146
5 ft. 11 in.	144-154	150-165	159-179	5 ft. 7 in.	118-127	124-139	133-150
6 ft. 0 in.	148-158	154-170	164-184	5 ft. 8 in.	122-131	128-143	137-154
6 ft. 1 in.	152-162	158-175	168-189	5 ft. 9 in.	126-135	132-147	141-158
6 ft. 2 in.	156-167	162-180	173-194	5 ft. 10 in.	130-140	136-151	145-163
6 ft. 3 in.	160-171	167-185	178-199	5 ft. 11 in.	134-144	140-155	149-168
6 ft. 4 in.	164-175	172-190	182-204	6 ft. 0 in.	138-148	144-159	153-173

[1] Adapted from Metropolitan Life Insurance Co., New York. New weight standards for men and women.

highly nutritious. (It takes only a few minutes to eat a rich dessert like pie á la mode, but a long time to get rid of the layer it leaves where you need it least.)

Perspiring causes weight loss, but it's temporary. It only reduces water in tissues, without diminishing fat, no matter what method is used (steam baths, heat treatments, reducing girdles, etc.).

Does exercise help cut down weight? Although good for body tone (if pursued in moderation), exercise tends to stimulate appetite. It is not advisable along with strenuous diet, especially if previously neglected. Sudden indulgence in strenuous exercise may even be dangerous.

GAINING WEIGHT

If you are underweight, don't try to change your diet habits suddenly, or you'll become quickly discouraged. Gradually add extra-fattening foods daily, and start drinking midmorning and midafternoon milkshakes. An important factor is to allow for a relaxation period as often during the day, especially after meals, as you can make time for.

You can even fill up on these vegetables. (Average portions are worth 100 calories apiece.) Corn (1 ear or ½ cup kernel corn; cream style is 125 calories per ½ cup), Jerusalem artichokes (5 small), lima beans, macaroni, potato (1 medium), rice, spaghetti, succotash, sweet potato (½), yam (½). And

every pat of butter you put on lower-calorie vegetables adds 50 calories to your weight-gaining diet. Two tablespoons of cream sauce on a vegetable add another 50 calories.

Food served at home, of course, is seldom measured by cup (let alone on a gram scale, as is necessary when special diets are being prepared, as by hospital dietitians). Would-be weight-gainers should simply try to develop tastes for foods that are higher in calories than others. And as always, if large amounts of weight are involved, all this should be under a doctor's guidance.

NUTRIENTS IN COMMON FOODS

Calories do provide an easy way of keeping track of your diet. But any truly nutritious diet must also consider such nutrients as proteins, fats, and carbohydrates, not to mention vitamins, minerals, and trace elements. In the charts that follow, the common foods are shown with their amounts of calories and of the three major nutrients. Naturally there is variation in the actual foods eaten, depending on the source of the food and other factors. But these figures provide a good starting point.

How many grams of protein, fat, and carbohydrate should a person consume each day? There is no simple answer, because the intake of one is inextricably linked with the intake of the others. But proteins can be used as the starting point. There are extreme needs, of course—from infants who require relatively small amounts, to nursing mothers, who require large amounts (about 75 grams of protein daily). In general, children require 25 to 50 grams of protein daily, while adults require 50 to 65 grams. With these as general guides, the ideal is to assemble daily diets that provide the desired number of calories and proteins with the minimal amounts of fats and carbohydrates. It is not that everyone doesn't need a certain amount of fats and carbohydrates but rather that they tend to take care of themselves if you watch after the proteins and calories.

NUTRIENTS IN COMMON FOODS

	Food energy Calories	Protein Grams	Fat Grams	Carbohydrate Grams
MILK AND MILK PRODUCTS				
Milk; 1 cup:				
Fluid, whole	165	9	10	12
Fluid, nonfat (skim)	90	9	Trace	13
Buttermilk, cultured (from skim milk)	90	9	Trace	13
Evaporated (undiluted)	345	18	20	24
Dry, nonfat	290	29	1	42
Yoghurt (from partially skimmed milk); 1 cup	120	8	4	13
Cheese; 1 ounce:				
Cheddar, or American	115	7	9	1
Cottage:				
From skim milk	25	5	Trace	1
Creamed	30	4	1	1
Cream cheese	105	2	11	1
Swiss	105	7	8	1
Desserts (largely milk):				
Custard, baked; 1 cup, 8 fluid ounces	285	13	14	28
Ice cream, plain, factory packed:				
1 slice or individual brick, 1/7 quart	165	3	10	17
1 container, 8 fluid ounces	295	6	18	29
Ice milk; 1 cup, 8 fluid ounces	285	9	10	42
EGGS				
Egg, raw, large:				
1 whole	80	6	6	Trace
1 white	15	4	Trace	Trace
1 yolk	60	3	5	Trace
Egg, cooked; 1 large:				
Boiled	80	6	6	Trace
Scrambled (with milk and fat)	110	7	8	1

Adapted from *Food: The Yearbook of Agriculture, 1959*, U. S. Department of Agriculture, pp. 243–265. The cup measure used in the table refers to the standard 8-ounce measuring cup of 8 fluid ounces or one-half pint. When a measure is indicated by ounce, it is understood to be by weight—1/16 of a pound avoirdupois—unless a fluid ounce is indicated.

	Food energy Calories	Protein Grams	Fat Grams	Carbohydrate Grams
MEAT, POULTRY, FISH, SHELLFISH				
Bacon, broiled or fried, medium done; 2 slices	95	4	9	Trace
Beef, cooked without bone:				
Braised, simmered, or pot-roasted; 3-ounce portion:				
Entire portion, lean and fat	340	20	28	0
Lean only, approx. 2 ounces	115	18	4	0
Hamburger patties, made with				
Regular ground beef; 3-ounce patty	245	21	17	0
Lean ground round; 3-ounce patty	185	23	10	0
Roast; 3-ounce slice from cut having relatively small amount of fat:				
Entire portion, lean and fat	255	22	18	0
Lean only, approx. 2.3 ounces	115	19	4	0
Steak, broiled; 3-ounce portion:				
Entire portion, lean and fat	375	19	32	0
Lean only, approx. 1.8 ounces	105	17	4	0
Beef, canned: corned beef hash: 3 ounces	120	12	5	6
Beef and vegetable stew: 1 cup	250	13	19	17
Chicken, without bone: broiled; 3 ounces	115	20	3	0
Lamb, cooked:				
Chops; 1 thick chop, without bone, 4.8 ounces:				
Lean and fat, approx. 3.6 ounces	450	24	39	0
Lean only, 2.4 ounces	130	19	5	0
Roast, without bone:				
Leg; 3-ounce slice:				
Entire slice, lean and fat	265	20	20	0
Lean only, approx. 2.3 ounces	120	19	5	0
Shoulder; 3-ounce portion, without bone:				
Entire portion, lean and fat	300	18	25	0
Lean only, approx. 2.2 ounces	125	16	6	0
Liver, beef, fried; 2 ounces	120	13	4	6
Pork, cured, cooked:				
Ham, smoked; 3-ounce portion, without bone	340	20	28	Trace
Luncheon meat:				
Boiled ham; 2 ounces	170	13	13	1
Canned, spiced; 2 ounces	165	8	14	0
Pork, fresh, cooked:				
Chops; 1 chop, with bone, 3.5 ounces:				
Lean and fat, approx. 2.4 ounces	295	15	25	0
Lean only, approx. 1.6 ounces	120	14	7	0
Roast; 3-ounce slice, without bone:				
Entire slice, lean and fat	340	19	29	0
Lean only, approx. 2.2 ounces	160	19	9	0
Sausage:				
Bologna; 8 slices (4.1 by 0.1 inches each), 8 ounces	690	27	62	2
Frankfurter; 1 cooked, 1.8 ounces	155	6	14	1

	Food energy Calories	Protein Grams	Fat Grams	Carbohydrate Grams
Tongue, beef, boiled or simmered; 3 ounces	205	18	14	Trace
Veal, cutlet, broiled; 3-ounce portion, without bone	185	23	9	0
Fish and shellfish:				
Bluefish, baked or broiled; 3 ounces	135	22	4	0
Clams: raw, meat only; 3 ounces	70	11	1	3
Crabmeat, canned or cooked; 3 ounces	90	14	2	1
Fishsticks, breaded, cooked, frozen; 10 sticks (3.8 by 1.0 by 0.5 inches each), 8 ounces	400	38	20	15
Haddock, fried; 3 ounces	135	16	5	6
Mackerel: broiled; 3 ounces	200	19	13	0
Oysters, raw, meat only; 1 cup (13–19 medium-size oysters, selects)	160	20	4	8
Oyster stew: 1 cup (6–8 oysters)	200	11	12	11
Salmon, canned (pink); 3 ounces	120	17	5	0
Sardines, canned in oil, drained solids; 3 ounces	180	22	9	1
Shrimp, canned, meat only; 3 ounces	110	23	1	—
Tuna, canned in oil, drained solids; 3 ounces	170	25	7	0

MATURE BEANS AND PEAS, NUTS

	Food energy Calories	Protein Grams	Fat Grams	Carbohydrate Grams
Beans, dry seed:				
Common varieties, as Great Northern, navy, and others, canned; 1 cup:				
Red	230	15	1	42
White, with tomato or molasses:				
With pork	330	16	7	54
Without pork	315	16	1	60
Lima, cooked; 1 cup	260	16	1	48
Cowpeas or black-eyed peas, dry, cooked; 1 cup	190	13	1	34
Peanuts, roasted, shelled; 1 cup	840	39	71	28
Peanut butter; 1 tablespoon	90	4	8	3
Peas, split, dry, cooked; 1 cup	290	20	1	52

VEGETABLES

	Food energy Calories	Protein Grams	Fat Grams	Carbohydrate Grams
Asparagus:				
Cooked; 1 cup	35	4	Trace	6
Canned; 6 medium-size spears	20	2	Trace	3
Beans:				
Lima, immature, cooked; 1 cup	150	8	1	29
Snap, green:				
Cooked; 1 cup	25	2	Trace	6
Canned: solids and liquid; 1 cup	45	2	Trace	10
Beets, cooked, diced; 1 cup	70	2	Trace	16
Broccoli, cooked, flower stalks; 1 cup	45	5	Trace	8

	Food energy Calories	Protein Grams	Fat Grams	Carbohydrate Grams
Brussels sprouts, cooked; 1 cup	60	6	1	12
Cabbage; 1 cup:				
Raw, coleslaw	100	2	7	9
Cooked	40	2	Trace	9
Carrots:				
Raw: 1 carrot (5½ by 1 inch) or 25 thin				
strips	20	1	Trace	5
Cooked, diced; 1 cup	45	1	1	9
Canned, strained or chopped; 1 ounce	5	Trace	0	2
Cauliflower, cooked, flower buds; 1 cup	30	3	Trace	6
Celery, raw: large stalk, 8 inches long	5	1	Trace	1
Collards, cooked; 1 cup	75	7	1	14
Corn, sweet:				
Cooked; 1 ear 5 inches long	65	2	1	16
Canned, solids and liquid; 1 cup	170	5	1	41
Cucumbers, raw, pared; 6 slices (⅛-inch thick,				
center section)	5	Trace	Trace	1
Lettuce, head, raw:				
2 large or 4 small leaves	5	1	Trace	1
1 compact head (4¾-inch diameter)	70	5	1	13
Mushrooms, canned, solids and liquid; 1 cup	30	3	Trace	9
Okra, cooked; 8 pods (3 inches long, ⅝-inch				
diameter)	30	2	Trace	6
Onions: mature raw; 1 onion (2½-inch diam-				
eter)	50	2	Trace	11
Peas, green; 1 cup:				
Cooked	110	8	1	19
Canned, solids and liquid	170	8	1	32
Peppers, sweet:				
Green, raw; 1 medium	15	1	Trace	3
Red, raw; 1 medium	20	1	Trace	4
Potatoes:				
Baked or boiled; 1 medium, 2½-inch diam-				
eter (weight raw, about 5 ounces):				
Baked in jacket	90	3	Trace	21
Boiled; peeled before boiling	90	3	Trace	21
Chips; 10 medium (2-inch diameter)	110	1	7	10
French fried:				
Frozen, ready to be heated for serving;				
10 pieces (2 by ½ by ½ inch)	95	2	4	15
Ready-to-eat, deep fat for entire process;				
10 pieces (2 by ½ by ½ inch)	155	2	7	20
Mashed; 1 cup:				
Milk added	145	4	1	30
Milk and butter added	230	4	12	28
Radishes, raw; 4 small	10	Trace	Trace	2
Spinach:				
Cooked; 1 cup	45	6	1	6
Canned, creamed, strained; 1 ounce	10	1	Trace	2

	Food energy Calories	Protein Grams	Fat Grams	Carbohydrate Grams
Squash:				
Cooked, 1 cup:				
Summer, diced	35	1	Trace	8
Winter, baked, mashed	95	4	1	23
Canned, strained or chopped; 1 ounce	10	Trace	Trace	2
Sweet potatoes:				
Baked or boiled; 1 medium, 5 by 2 inches (weight raw, about 6 ounces):				
Baked in jacket	155	2	1	36
Boiled in jacket	170	2	1	39
Candied; 1 small, 3½ by 2 inches	295	2	6	60
Canned, vacuum or solid pack; 1 cup	235	4	Trace	54
Tomatoes:				
Raw; 1 medium (2 by 2½ inches), about ⅓ pound	30	2	Trace	6
Canned or cooked; 1 cup	45	2	Trace	9
Tomato juice, canned; 1 cup	50	2	Trace	10
Tomato catsup; 1 tablespoon	15	Trace	Trace	4
Turnips, cooked, diced; 1 cup	40	1	Trace	9
Turnip greens, cooked; 1 cup	45	4	1	8
FRUITS				
Apples, raw; 1 medium (2½-inch diameter), about ⅓ pound	70	Trace	Trace	18
Apple juice, fresh or canned; 1 cup	125	Trace	0	34
Apple sauce, canned:				
Sweetened; 1 cup	185	Trace	Trace	50
Unsweetened; 1 cup	100	Trace	Trace	26
Apricots, raw; 3 apricots (about ¼ pound)	55	1	Trace	14
Apricots, canned in heavy sirup; 1 cup	200	1	Trace	54
Apricots, dried: uncooked; 1 cup (40 halves, small)	390	8	1	100
Avocados, raw, California varieties: ½ of a 10-ounce avocado (3½ by 3¼ inches)	185	2	18	6
Avocados, raw, Florida varieties: ½ of a 13-ounce avocado (4 by 3 inches)	160	2	14	11
Bananas, raw; 1 medium (6 by 1½ inches), about ⅓ pound	85	1	Trace	23
Blueberries, raw; 1 cup	85	1	1	21
Cantaloupes, raw, ½ melon (5-inch diameter)	40	1	Trace	9
Cherries, sour, sweet, and hybrid, raw; 1 cup	65	1	1	15
Cranberry sauce, sweetened; 1 cup	550	Trace	1	142
Dates, "fresh" and dried, pitted and cut; 1 cup	505	4	1	134
Figs:				
Raw; 3 small (1½-inch diameter), about ¼ pound	90	2	Trace	22
Dried; 1 large (2 by 1 inch)	60	1	Trace	15
Fruit cocktail, canned in heavy sirup, solids and liquid; 1 cup	175	1	Trace	47

	Food energy Calories	Protein Grams	Fat Grams	Carbohydrate Grams
Grapefruit:				
Raw; ½ medium (4¼-inch diameter, No. 64's)	50	1	Trace	14
Canned in sirup; 1 cup	165	1	Trace	44
Grapefruit juice:				
Raw; 1 cup	85	1	Trace	23
Canned:				
Unsweetened; 1 cup	95	1	Trace	24
Sweetened; 1 cup	120	1	Trace	32
Frozen concentrate, unsweetened:				
Undiluted; 1 can (6 fluid ounces)	280	4	1	72
Diluted, ready-to-serve; 1 cup	95	1	Trace	24
Frozen concentrate, sweetened:				
Undiluted; 1 can (6 fluid ounces)	320	3	1	85
Diluted, ready-to-serve; 1 cup	105	1	Trace	28
Grapes, raw; 1 cup:				
American type (slip skin)	70	1	1	16
European type (adherent skin)	100	1	Trace	26
Grape juice, bottled; 1 cup	165	1	1	42
Lemonade concentrate, frozen, sweetened:				
Undiluted; 1 can (6 fluid ounces)	305	1	Trace	113
Diluted, ready-to-serve; 1 cup	75	Trace	Trace	28
Oranges, raw; 1 large orange (3-inch diameter)	70	1	Trace	18
Orange juice:				
Raw; 1 cup:				
California (Valencias)	105	2	Trace	26
Florida varieties:				
Early and midseason	90	1	Trace	23
Late season (Valencias)	105	1	Trace	26
Canned, unsweetened; 1 cup	110	2	Trace	28
Frozen concentrate:				
Undiluted; 1 can (6 fl. ounces)	305	5	Trace	80
Diluted, ready-to-serve; 1 cup	105	2	Trace	27
Peaches:				
Raw:				
1 medium (2½- by 2-inch diameter), about ¼ pound	35	1	Trace	10
1 cup, sliced	65	1	Trace	16
Canned (yellow-fleshed) in heavy sirup; 1 cup	185	1	Trace	49
Dried: uncooked; 1 cup	420	5	1	109
Pears:				
Raw; 1 pear (3- by 2½-inch diameter)	100	1	1	25
Canned in heavy sirup; 1 cup	175	1	Trace	47
Plums:				
Raw; 1 plum (2-inch diameter), about 2 ounces	30	Trace	Trace	7
Canned (Italian prunes), in sirup; 1 cup	185	1	Trace	50
Prunes, dried:				
Uncooked; 4 medium prunes	70	1	Trace	19

	Food energy Calories	Protein Grams	Fat Grams	Carbohydrate Grams
Cooked, unsweetened; 1 cup (17–18 prunes and ⅓ cup liquid)	295	3	1	78
Prune juice, canned; 1 cup	170	1	Trace	45
Raisins, dried; 1 cup	460	4	Trace	124
Raspberries, red:				
Raw; 1 cup	70	1	Trace	17
Frozen; 10-ounce carton	280	2	1	70
Strawberries:				
Raw; 1 cup	55	1	1	12
Frozen; 10-ounce carton	300	2	1	75
Tangerines; 1 medium (2½-inch diameter), about ¼ pound	40	1	Trace	10
Watermelon: 1 wedge (4 by 8 inches), about 2 pounds (weighed with rind)	120	2	1	29

GRAIN PRODUCTS

Biscuits, baking powder, enriched flour; 1 biscuit (2½-inch diameter)	130	3	4	20
Bran flakes (40 percent bran) with added thiamine; 1 ounce	85	3	1	22
Breads:				
Cracked wheat:				
1 pound (20 slices)	1,190	39	10	236
1 slice (½ inch thick)	60	2	1	12
Italian; 1 pound	1,250	41	4	256
Rye:				
American (light):				
1 pound (20 slices)	1,100	41	5	236
1 slice (½ inch thick)	55	2	Trace	12
Pumpernickel; 1 pound	1,115	41	5	241
White:				
1–2 percent nonfat dry milk:				
1 pound (20 slices)	1,225	39	15	229
1 slice (½ inch thick)	60	2	1	12
3–4 percent nonfat dry milk:				
1 pound (20 slices)	1,225	39	15	229
1 slice (½ inch thick)	60	2	1	12
5–6 percent nonfat dry milk:				
1 pound (20 slices)	1,245	41	17	228
1 slice (½ inch thick)	65	2	1	12
Whole wheat, graham, or entire wheat:				
1 pound (20 slices)	1,105	48	14	216
1 slice (½ inch thick)	55	2	1	11
Cakes:				
Angelfood: 2-inch sector (1/12 of cake, 8-inch diameter)	110	3	Trace	23
Butter cakes:				
Plain cake and cupcakes without icing:				
1 square (3 by 2 by 1½ inches)	180	4	5	31
1 cupcake (2¾-inch diameter)	130	3	3	23

	Food energy Calories	Protein Grams	Fat Grams	Carbohydrate Grams
Plain cake with icing:				
2-inch sector of iced layer cake (1⁄16 of cake, 10-inch diameter)	320	5	6	62
Rich cake:				
2-inch sector of layer cake, iced (1⁄16 of cake, 10-inch diameter)	490	6	19	76
Fruit cake, dark; 1 piece (2 by 2 by ½ inches)	105	2	4	17
Sponge; 2-inch sector (1⁄12 of cake, 8-inch diameter)	115	3	2	22
Cookies, plain and assorted; 1 cookie (3-inch diameter)	110	2	3	19
Cornbread or muffins made with enriched, de-germed cornmeal; 1 muffin (2¾-inch diameter)	105	3	2	18
Cornflakes: 1 ounce	110	2	Trace	24
Corn grits, degermed, cooked: 1 cup	120	3	Trace	27
Crackers:				
Graham; 4 small or 2 medium	55	1	1	10
Saltines; 2 crackers (2-inch square)	35	1	1	6
Soda, plain: 2 crackers (2½-inch square)	45	1	1	8
Doughnuts, cake type; 1 doughnut	135	2	7	17
Farina, cooked; 1 cup	105	3	Trace	22
Macaroni, cooked; 1 cup:				
Cooked 8–10 minutes (undergoes additional cooking as ingredient of a food mixture)	190	6	1	39
Cooked until tender	155	5	1	32
Noodles (egg noodles), cooked: 1 cup	200	7	2	37
Oat cereal (mixture, mainly oat flour), ready-to-eat; 1 ounce	115	4	2	21
Oatmeal or rolled oats, regular or quick cooking, cooked; 1 cup	150	5	3	26
Pancakes, baked; 1 cake (4-inch diameter):				
Wheat (home recipe)	60	2	2	7
Buckwheat (with buckwheat pancake mix)	45	2	2	6
Pies; 4-inch sector (1⁄7 of 9-inch diameter pie):				
Apple	330	3	13	53
Cherry	340	3	13	55
Custard	265	7	11	34
Lemon meringue	300	4	12	45
Mince	340	3	9	62
Pumpkin	265	5	12	34
Pretzels; 5 small sticks	20	Trace	Trace	4
Rice, cooked; 1 cup:				
Converted	205	4	Trace	45
White	200	4	Trace	44
Rice, puffed or flakes; 1 ounce	110	2	Trace	25
Rolls:				
Plain, pan (16 ounces per dozen); 1 roll	115	3	2	20
Hard, round (22 ounces per dozen); 1 roll	160	5	2	31

	Food energy Calories	Protein Grams	Fat Grams	Carbohydrate Grams
Sweet, pan (18 ounces per dozen); 1 roll	135	4	4	21
Spaghetti, cooked until tender; 1 cup	155	5	1	32
Waffles, baked, with enriched flour: 1 waffle				
(4½ by 5½ by ½ inches)	215	7	8	28
Wheat, puffed: 1 ounce	100	4	Trace	22
Wheat, rolled, cooked; 1 cup	175	5	1	40
Wheat flakes; 1 ounce	100	3	Trace	23
Wheat flours:				
Whole wheat; 1 cup, sifted	400	16	2	85
All purpose or family flour: 1 cup, sifted	400	12	1	84
Wheat germ; 1 cup, stirred	245	17	7	34

FATS, OILS, RELATED PRODUCTS

Butter; 1 tablespoon	100	Trace	11	Trace
Fats, cooking:				
Vegetable fats:				
1 cup	1,770	0	200	0
1 tablespoon	110	0	12	0
Lard:				
1 cup	1,985	0	220	0
1 tablespoon	125	0	14	0
Margarine; 1 tablespoon	100	Trace	11	Trace
Oils, salad or cooking; 1 tablespoon	125	0	14	0
Salad dressings; 1 tablespoon:				
Blue cheese	90	1	10	1
Commercial, plain (mayonnaise type)	60	Trace	6	2
French	60	Trace	6	2
Mayonnaise	110	Trace	12	Trace
Thousand Island	75	Trace	8	1

SUGARS, SWEETS

Candy; 1 ounce:				
Caramels	120	1	3	22
Chocolate, sweetened, milk	145	2	9	16
Fudge, plain	115	Trace	3	23
Hard	110	0	0	28
Marshmallow	90	1	0	23
Jams, marmalades, preserves; 1 tablespoon	55	Trace	Trace	14
Jellies; 1 tablespoon	50	0	0	13
Sugar; 1 tablespoon	50	0	0	12
Syrup, table blends; 1 tablespoon	55	0	0	15

MISCELLANEOUS

Beverages, carbonated, kola type; 1 cup	105	—	—	28
Bouillon cubes; 1 cube	2	Trace	Trace	0
Chocolate, unsweetened; 1 ounce	145	2	15	8
Gelatin dessert, plain, ready-to-serve; 1 cup	155	4	0	36

	Food energy Calories	Protein Grams	Fat Grams	Carbohydrate Grams
Sherbet, factory packed; 1 cup (8-fluid-ounce container)	235	3	Trace	58
Soups, ready-to-serve; 1 cup:				
Bean	190	8	5	30
Beef	100	6	4	11
Bouillon, broth, and consommé	10	2	—	0
Chicken	75	4	2	10
Clam chowder	85	5	2	12
Cream soup (asparagus, celery, or mushroom)	200	7	12	18
Noodle, rice, or barley	115	6	4	13
Tomato	90	2	2	18
Vegetable	80	4	2	14
Vinegar; 1 tablespoon	2	0	—	1

20

WORDS FOR THE KITCHEN

Learning the language of food will help make your meals easier to prepare, tastier to eat

à la (*Fr.*) In the manner or style of.

à la mode (*Fr.*) **1** Served with ice cream: used in the U.S. to describe pie and some other desserts. **2** Marinated, then braised in its marinade, often with vegetables, and served in a rich gravy: used to describe beef prepared in a classic French manner.

al dente (*Ital.*) Cooked until done but still firm: used to describe pasta.

amandine Prepared or garnished with almonds.

à point (*Fr.*) Cooked just until done.

aspic A jelly made with meat, poultry, fish, or vegetable stock, usually with gelatin added.

au gratin (*Fr.*) With a crust; gratiné: used to describe food topped with bread crumbs or grated cheese or both, then baked or broiled until brown.

au jus (*Fr.*) Served in its own juice or gravy: used to describe cooked meat, especially roast beef.

bake To cook with dry heat, especially in an oven.

barbecue 1 To cook on a rack or revolving spit over or in front of a source of heat. Barbecued food is usually coated with a highly seasoned sauce. **2** The food prepared in such a way. **3** A portable device used to prepare barbecued food.

bard To tie suet, pork fat, or bacon around lean meat before cooking. This technique helps to keep the meat moist.

baste To pour or brush liquid on food while it cooks, the purpose being to flavor the food and keep it from drying out.

batter An uncooked mixture, usually of flour, liquid, eggs, seasonings, and a leavening agent, thin enough to pour.

beat To whip ingredients, as with a whisk or electric beater, to mix thoroughly and incorporate air into them.

beurre (*Fr.*) Butter.

bind To add a binder to food.

binder Any ingredient or combination of ingredients, as an egg or a sauce, added to a food mixture to thicken it.

bisque A thick, rich soup, usually made with shellfish.

blanch To plunge food briefly into boiling water to loosen skins or to enhance flavor and set color in preparation for freezing.

blaze See FLAMBÉ

blend To thoroughly mix two or more ingredients.

boil To cook food in a boiling liquid. At normal atmospheric pressure, the boiling point of water is 212° F or 100° C.

bone To remove bones from fish, poultry, meat, or game.

borsch Any of various beet soups, originally from Russia or Poland, some of which are made with meat/or other vegetables. Also spelled borscht.

bouillabaisse A highly seasoned chowder made with several varieties of fish.

bouillon A clear, lightly seasoned broth, usually made with beef.

braise To cook by browning quickly and then simmering in a covered pan.

bread To coat with bread crumbs before cooking.

brine A strong salt solution used to pickle or preserve food.

brochette (*Fr.*) A small spit or skewer. The expression *en brochette* is used to describe food cooked on such a spit.

broil To cook by exposing food to a direct source of heat.

broth 1 A thin, clear soup. 2 The liquid in which meat, vegetables, etc., have cooked.

brown To cook until brown, usually by searing on the top of the stove but also by baking in a very hot oven or by placing under a broiler flame.

butterfly To split food, as shrimp, through the center but not all the way, so that the two connected pieces can be spread out flat to resemble butterfly wings.

café (*Fr.*) Coffee.

canapé An appetizer.

candy To cook, coat, or preserve with sugar or syrup.

caramelize 1 To heat sugar until melted and golden brown. 2 To coat food with caramelized sugar.

casserole 1 A dish of earthenware, glass, or metal, in which food may be cooked and served. The French *en casserole* is used to describe food cooked in such a dish. 2 Food prepared in such a dish.

caviar The salted roe of sturgeon or some other large fish.

chop To cut food into small pieces. Chopped food is more coarsely cut than ground or minced food.

chowder A kind of stew or thick soup, usually made with fish or shellfish and sometimes with vegetables.

chutney A highly spiced condiment of East Indian origin made with various sweet and tart ingredients, as different kinds of fruit.

citron A fruit like a lemon, but larger and less acid, the preserved rind of which is used in making candies and various desserts.

clove of garlic A small, individual section of a garlic bulb.

coat 1 To cover food with a layer of some dry ingredient, as flour or bread crumbs. 2 To cover food with aspic or a sauce. 3 To form a filmy covering layer on a spoon. This is a test of doneness for custards and other egg-thickened mixtures.

cocotte (*Fr.*) A casserole. The expression *en cocotte* is used to describe certain foods cooked in a casserole.

coddle To cook food, especially eggs, in water that is just below the boiling point.

colander A perforated metal or plastic vessel used for draining off liquids.

compote 1 Fruit, usually whole or in large pieces, cooked in a heavy sugar syrup. 2 A bowl, usually with a stem and base, for serving compotes, fresh fruit, etc.

condiment Something, such as a spice or relish, used to season or serve with a food to enhance its flavor.

confectioners' sugar Finely powdered sugar mixed with cornstarch

conserve A preserve made of several fruits stewed together in sugar, often with nuts and raisins added.

consommé A clear, highly seasoned soup made from meat or poultry.

court bouillon A broth for cooking fish and shellfish. It can be as simple as plain salted water, but usually a court bouillon is seasoned with herbs and spices and very often wine is added to make it more flavorsome. (See page 33 for one recipe.)

cream To beat butter or another fat until it is soft and creamy; also, to combine such a fat with sugar or other ingredients.

crêpe (*Fr.*) A pancake. French pancakes are thin, light, and tender, and are often served rolled over a filling, as of jam, seafood, or a savory meat.

crimp To seal the edges of a pie crust decoratively by pinching with the fingers or pressing with the tines of a fork; to flute.

croquette A small cake of minced food, usually bound by an egg or sauce, then crumbed and fried in deep fat.

croûte (*Fr.*) Crust or pastry. Food prepared *en croûte* is wrapped in or topped with crust before being cooked.

croutons Small toasted or fried cubes of bread used as a garnish, as in soups, on salads, or on vegetables.

crown roast A roast shaped like a crown, prepared by frenching two or more rib sections of lamb, pork, or veal, and then skewering or tying them together in a circle.

crumb To coat food with crumbs before cooking.

cure To preserve meat, fish, or cheese by any of several processes, as salting, drying, or smoking.

curry A stewlike dish of East Indian origin that is prepared with curry powder.

curry powder A condiment used in preparing curries. Commercially sold curry powders contain as many as twenty ingredients, usually including coriander, cumin, turmeric, cayenne, and fenugreek.

cut in To cut solid shortening into

small pieces and then incorporate it into a dry mixture, as of flour.

deep fat Hot fat, usually 360° F., used to deep-fry food.

deep-fry To cook food in a quantity of hot fat deep enough to cover it or on which it can float.

deglaze To loosen congealed pan drippings from the bottom of a cooking utensil by stirring in and heating a liquid, as wine or stock.

degrease To remove grease from a cooked liquid, as a soup or gravy. Degreasing can be done by skimming fat off the surface of the liquid with a spoon; by dropping in and retrieving ice cubes to which some congealed fat will cling; or, easiest of all, by chilling the liquid and lifting off the grease which will have risen to the top and hardened.

devil To prepare a food, as eggs or crab, with hot seasonings, usually mustard and cayenne pepper.

dice To cut into small cube-shaped pieces, approximately ⅛″–¼″.

dissolve 1 To pass or cause to pass into solution. 2 To melt or liquefy.

dot To dab the surface of a food with small bits of an ingredient such as butter or another fat.

dough A mixture of flour, liquid, and other ingredients, firm enough to knead with the hands.

drain To remove water or other liquid from food.

draw To take out the entrails of, as poultry; disembowel; eviscerate.

dredge To sprinkle, dust, or otherwise coat, as with flour or fine bread crumbs.

dress To draw and otherwise prepare for cooking, as poultry, game, or fish.

drippings Fat and other juices exuded from meat, poultry, etc., when cooking.

drizzle To pour liquid on food in very small drops or in a very thin stream.

dust To sprinkle or otherwise coat, as with flour or fine bread crumbs. Dusted foods are less heavily coated than dredged foods.

en brochette See BROCHETTE.

en casserole See CASSEROLE.

en cocotte See COCOTTE.

en croûte See CROÛTE.

enrich 1 To add, as vitamins and minerals, to a foodstuff or to food, usually to replace nutrients lost in processing. 2 To add something to a sauce or a prepared food to make it richer or thicker.

escallop See SCALLOP.

essence See EXTRACT.

eviscerate See DRAW.

extract A concentrated flavoring, either natural or synthetic, often in an alcohol solution.

farce (*Fr.*) See FORCEMEAT.

filet (*Fr.*) Fillet.

filet mignon (*Fr.*) A small, choice fillet of beef tenderloin.

fillet 1 A piece of boneless meat or fish. 2 To slice or bone into fillets.

flake To separate, as a cooked fish fillet, into small pieces with a fork.

flaky Rich; short; crumbly: used to describe pastry.

flambé 1 Served in or with flaming liquor or a sauce made with liquor that is ignited. **2** To ignite a liquor-drenched food; to flame or blaze.

flame See FLAMBÉ.

flute See CRIMP.

foie gras (*Fr.*) Fat liver. In cooking the term usually refers to goose liver.

fold in To blend a light, delicate ingredient into a heavier one by mixing with a gentle turning-over-and-over motion.

forcemeat Finely ground or pounded meat, poultry or fish, mixed with other ingredients and served alone or used as a stuffing; farce.

french 1 To cut, as a string or snap bean, into long, lengthwise strips. **2** To cut into pieces, then pound before cooking, as beef tenderloin. **3** To cut off the meat from the end of the bone, as of a rib lamb chop.

French fry To fry, as potato strips, in deep fat.

fricassee 1 To braise pieces of chicken or small game. **2** A dish of pieces of braised chicken or small game, often accompanied by vegetables.

frizzle To fry or bake at very high heat, as thinly sliced meat, until it is crisp and curled at the edges.

fromage (*Fr.*) Cheese.

frost To cover with icing.

frosting See ICING.

fry To cook in a skillet with fat but not deep fat; panfry; sauté.

fumet A very rich stock, as of meat, fish, etc., used to flavor sauces.

garnish 1 A decorative and/or savory accompaniment for a dish. **2** To furnish such accompaniments for food.

gâteau (*Fr.*) Cake.

giblets Edible internal organs of fowl; the heart, liver, and gizzard.

glace (*Fr.*) Ice or ice cream.

glacé (*Fr.*) Glazed or iced.

glaze 1 A coating, as of syrup, aspic, or beaten egg, which when applied to food gives that food a glossy surface; also, the glossy surface so given. **2** To apply such a coating to food.

granulated sugar A pure, refined sugar whose crystals are in the form of small grains.

grate To reduce a food to small particles by rubbing it against a rough surface, as that of a grater.

gratiné (*Fr.*) See AU GRATIN.

gravy 1 The juice exuded from meat during cooking. **2** A thickened sauce made from this juice.

grease To rub a cooking surface with a fat, as oil or butter.

gridiron A framework of metal bars for broiling food.

grill 1 A gridiron or other similar utensil for broiling food. **2** To broil food on a grill, usually over charcoal.

grind To reduce to small particles or powder; to mince or pulverize, as in a food mill or grinder.

hang To suspend meat, especially game, for a period of time to age it, thereby tenderizing it and making it more flavorsome.

herb A plant or part of a plant used, fresh or dried, as a flavoring agent in cooking.

hash To cut, as meat and potatoes, into small pieces.

high Slightly tainted: said especially of game which has been aged by hanging.

hors d'oeuvre (*Fr.*) An appetizer.

husk 1 The outer covering of certain fruits or seeds. **2** To remove such a covering.

ice 1 To chill with or as with ice. **2** To cover, as a cake, with icing.

icing A sweet, flavored, and often creamy coating for cakes, cupcakes, etc.; frosting.

infuse To steep or soak, as tea leaves, so as to make an extract.

infusion A flavorsome liquid produced by steeping or soaking, as tea leaves.

Italian paste See PASTA.

jardinière, à la (*Fr.*) Garnished with vegetables: used to describe a dish, as a rack of lamb served with mixed vegetables.

jell To turn into jelly or a jellylike substance; congeal.

jug To stew, as hare, in an earthenware pot.

julienne Cut into thin strips, as potatoes or carrots.

kipper To cure, as herring, by salting and smoking.

knead To work dough with the hands until it has reached a desired consistency.

kosher Fit for consumption or use according to Jewish ritual laws.

lait (*Fr.*) Milk.

lard 1 Rendered hog fat. **2** To insert strips of fat, as lard or salt pork, into lean meat before it is cooked.

lardoon A strip of fat, as lard or salt pork, with which meat is larded.

leaven 1 See LEAVENING AGENT. **2** To add a leavening agent to batter or dough.

leavening agent An ingredient, as baking powder, soda, or yeast, which produces gas bubbles that lighten and expand the volume of baked goods before and during baking; leaven.

liaison A thickening or binding agent, as flour, cornstarch, or a mixture of cream and egg yolks.

liquor 1 Any of several nonalcoholic liquids, as meat broth, clam juice, gravy, etc. **2** An alcoholic beverage.

macédoine A mixture of vegetables or fruit.

macerate To soak fruit in a liquid, usually spirits, in order to absorb the liquid's flavor.

madrilène A consommé flavored with tomato, served hot, cold, or jellied.

marinade A liquid mixture, as of oil and vinegar mixed with seasonings, in which food (other than fruit) is steeped in order to absorb the mixture's flavor and, in the case of certain meats, to be tenderized.

marinate To steep food (other than fruit) in a marinade.

marrow A soft, fatlike tissue found in the central cavities of most bones, prized as a delicacy by gourmets.

marrowbone A bone containing marrow, especially one rich in marrow, as a beef shinbone.

Marrowbones are frequently used in soups and stews.

mash To crush or beat into a pulpy mass, as with a potato masher.

mask To completely coat food, as with a sauce or aspic.

mealy Having a texture resembling meal; powdery.

medallion A piece of meat, usually beef, cut into a round or oval shape that resembles a medallion.

melt To reduce or change from a solid to a liquid state by heating.

mince To cut food into fine pieces. Minced food is cut more finely than chopped food.

mix To unite or blend two or more ingredients by stirring them together using a round-and-round or over-and-under motion.

mold 1 A container into which food is placed so that it can cook, chill, or freeze into the shape of the container. 2 To cook, chill, or freeze food in such a container.

moutarde (*Fr.*) Mustard.

nap To coat food, as with a thick sauce.

navarin (*Fr.*) Lamb or mutton stew.

noisette A small piece of lean meat, especially lamb.

oeuf (*Fr.*) Egg.

pain (*Fr.*) Bread.

panbroil To cook in a heavy skillet using as little fat as possible and draining off excess fat as it accumulates.

panfry See FRY.

parboil To cook food briefly in boiling water. Parboiled food is usually cooked to completion by some other method.

parch To dry corn, peas, or other starchy vegetables by exposing them to great heat.

pare To cut off the outer layer of a fruit or vegetable

pasta Any of a number of foods made of flour paste or dough, as spaghetti, ravioli, etc.

paste 1 A mixture, as of semolina and water, used to make pasta; Italian paste. 2 Dough, especially the very rich dough used to make cream puffs, eclairs, and the like. 3 Any food that has been reduced to a soft, creamy mass, as anchovy paste.

pastry 1 The dough used to make various baked goods, as pies and tarts. 2 The baked goods made from this dough. 3 Any of various sweet baked goods, as cakes, cookies, etc. See also PUFF PASTRY.

pastry bag. A conical bag fitted with a nozzle through which some foodstuff, as icing or mashed potatoes, is forced. (See page 75 for directions to make one.)

pasty A pie, especially a meat pie.

pâté A paste or spread, usually of liver and/or meat finely ground and seasoned with spices and sometimes alcoholic liquor.

pâté de foie gras A rich pâté made from the livers of force-fed geese.

patty A small flat cake, as of chopped meat or fish.

patty shell A small shell of puff pastry made to hold prepared food, as creamed meat or fish.

peel 1 The outer skin of certain fruits and vegetables. 2 To remove such skin.

pickle To preserve food in vinegar or brine.

pinch The amount of a substance, as salt, pepper, etc., that can be held between the thumb and forefinger, approximately ⅛ of a teaspoon.

pipe To apply, as frosting or mashed potatoes, by forcing through a pastry bag.

pit 1 The hard stone of certain fruits, which contains the seed. **2** To remove pits from.

plank To broil on a wooden plank, as steak or fish.

pluck To pull out the feathers from poultry.

plump To cause dried fruit to soften and swell up by soaking it in water or other liquid.

poach 1 To cook food, as chicken breasts, in simmering liquid. **2** To cook eggs in a poacher.

poacher A cooking vessel in which eggs are cooked over steaming water.

poisson (*Fr.*) Fish.

potage (*Fr.*) Soup.

pot liquor The liquid in which food has been cooked.

poulet (*Fr.*) Chicken.

pound To flatten, as a veal scallop, before cooking.

powdered sugar Sugar ground into a powder that is very fine but less fine than confectioners' sugar.

preheat To bring an oven to a predetermined temperature before putting food into it.

puff pastry A very rich dough used in making napoleons, patty shells, etc.

purée 1 A smooth, thick paste or sauce. **2** To reduce food to a purée, as by forcing through a sieve or food mill or by subjecting to the action of a blender.

quenelle A very light and delicate dumpling made of poached forcemeat.

quiche Any of various savory custards baked in a pastry shell.

ragout A highly seasoned stew of meat and vegetables.

reconstitute To add water to a dehydrated or condensed food, as dry mushrooms or frozen juice.

reduce To boil a liquid until the reduction in volume brings it to a desired consistency and flavor.

refresh To thrust hot food into very cold water to stop the cooking process.

render To melt animal fat, thereby extracting it from the connective tissue to which it is bound; try out.

rice To put food through a ricer.

ricer A perforated container through which foods are forced, the resultant product being in the form of strings having a diameter like that of a grain of rice.

rind The outer coat that may be peeled or otherwise taken off, as of fruit, bacon, cheese, etc.

rissole A small deep-fried pie or turnover with a sweet or savory filling.

roast To cook by exposure to dry heat, as in an oven or by placing in hot ashes.

roe Fish eggs.

roulade A rolled slice of meat stuffed with any of various fillings, as ham and cheese.

roux A cooked paste of flour and

butter used to thicken gravies, sauces, and soups.

sauce To provide or cover with a sauce.

sauté See FRY.

scald 1 To heat a liquid, especially milk or cream to a point just short of boiling. **2** To plunge food briefly into boiling water; blanch.

scale To remove the scales from a fish.

scallop 1 The edible muscle of certain mollusks. **2** A thin, boneless slice of meat, especially veal. **3** To bake food in a white sauce, often with a topping of bread crumbs; escallop.

score To make cuts in, as the surface of a ham or the fatty edge of a steak, often in a crisscross pattern.

sear To brown meat quickly by exposing it to very high heat.

seed To remove the seeds from, as grapes.

set To become firm; solidify; congeal; jell.

shell To remove the shells of, as nuts.

shirr To bake eggs, often in cream.

short Rich; crumbly; flaky: used to describe pastry containing a large amount of shortening.

shred To cut or grate food into thin slivers.

shuck To remove the husk or shell from corn, osyters, etc.

sieve 1 A device consisting of a frame provided with a bottom of wire mesh or perforated metal. **2** To press a substance through such a device.

sift To put a substance, as flour, through a sieve or sifter.

sifter A device similar to a sieve, used for sifting flour, sugar, etc.

simmer To cook food in a liquid at a temperature just below the boiling point.

singe To burn bristles or feathers off plucked poultry, usually by passing it through flame.

skewer 1 A metal or wooden pin used to fasten meat or to hold small chunks of food while cooking. **2** To use such a pin to fasten meat or hold small chunks of food.

skim To remove floating matter from the surface of a liquid, as cream from milk or fat from a sauce.

skin To remove the outer covering of, as a fish.

sliver To cut into thin pieces, as almonds.

smother To cook food in a covered pot or under a covering of another food substance.

soak To let food stand in a liquid, as to reconstitute or flavor it.

soupçon (*Fr.*) A slight taste; dash: used to describe a small amount, as of seasoning added to a food.

souse 1 Pickled food, as the feet and ears of a pig. **2** A pickling liquid; brine. **3** To pickle food.

spit 1 A slender, pointed rod on which meat, poultry, or fish is roasted. **2** To fix meat, poultry, or fish on such a rod.

steam To cook food in the steam produced by a small amount of boiling water under the food.

steam-bake To bake food in an oven in a vessel which has been placed in another, shallow vessel containing hot water.

steep To let a substance, as tea or coffee, stand in a liquid which is usually hot but below the boiling point in order to extract flavor, to soften, etc.

stew 1 To cook food slowly in a simmering liquid. **2** Food cooked in this way.

stir To mix or dissolve a substance by moving a spoon or other utensil through the substance with a circular motion.

stir-fry To cook food very quickly over intense heat with constant, rapid stirring of the ingredients in a small amount of oil.

stock Liquid in which meat, fish, bones, vegetables, etc., have cooked, used after skimming and straining as the base for soups, sauces, etc.

stockpot A pot, usually large and heavy, for preparing stock.

strain To cause food to pass through a strainer, as for the separation of liquids from solids.

strainer Any of various devices for straining foods, as a sieve or a colander.

stud To insert a seasoning ingredient into the surface of food, as cloves into ham.

stuff To fill a cavity, as in poultry, with a stuffing.

stuffing Any of various savory mixtures, as of bread crumbs, celery, onion, sausage, spices, herbs, etc., bound with egg and liquid.

suet The hard, fatty tissue around the kidneys and loins in beef and mutton.

tenderize To break down the tough fibers and connective tissue of meat. This is done by a physical process, as pounding, or by the application of a tenderizing substance, as a vegetable enzyme.

terrine 1 A container, usually of earthenware, in which pâtés and other similar dishes are baked. **2** The dishes baked in such a container.

thicken To make a liquid thicker by boiling it down or by the addition of a thickening agent, as flour, cornstarch, or eggs.

thin To dilute or weaken by the addition of a liquid.

timbale 1 A custardlike mixture, as of meat or vegetables, baked in a mold or served in a pastry shell. **2** The mold or pastry shell in which such a mixture is baked or served.

toast To make crisp and brown by heating.

toss To mix, as a salad, by turning the ingredients over and over with a fork or other implements.

truss To fasten into position for cooking, as with string, skewers, etc.

try out See RENDER.

veau (*Fr.*) Veal.

viande (*Fr.*) Meat.

vin (*Fr.*) Wine.

volaille (*Fr.*) Poultry.

vol-au-vent A large shell of puff pastry, filled with a creamed mixture, as of poultry or seafood, and covered with a lid made of the pastry.

whip To beat vigorously until fluffy or stiff, as eggs or cream.

work To mix by hand or with a utensil.

21

MEASURES AND WEIGHTS

Review familiar measures and get a head start on thinking metric in the kitchen

What is the Metric System? It's a simple way of measuring that is based on the decimal system, with units increasing or decreasing in size by 10s.

How would a change to the metric system affect your cooking habits? Very little to begin with, because a conversion to the system will take many years. But since nearly every country in the world is "thinking metric," it is well to have an idea of what the system is all about. To give you that idea we suggest a look at this chapter on measures and weights. In its pages you will find standard U.S. measures and weights with equivalents in other units of the same system; metric measures and weights with equivalents in other units of the same system; metric equivalents of U.S. measures and weights, and U.S. equivalents of metric measures and weights; conversion tables showing you how to convert common kitchen units from the U.S. system to the metric system and from the metric system to the U.S. system.

As an extra kitchen helper we have provided a temperature conversion table that enables you to convert Fahrenheit and Celsius temperature from one to the other plus a list of the most commonly used oven temperatures in both the Fahrenheit and Celsius scales.

U. S. SYSTEM

UNIT	ABBR.	EQUIVALENTS IN OTHER UNITS OF SAME SYSTEM
LIQUID MEASURE		
gill	gi.	¼ pint (4 fluid ounces)
pint	pt.	4 gills (16 fluid ounces)
quart	qt.	2 pints (32 fluid ounces)
gallon	gal.	4 quarts (128 fluid ounces)
½ cup		gill (4 fluid ounces)
cup		½ pint (8 fluid ounces)
2 cups		pint (16 fluid ounces)
4 cups		quart (32 fluid ounces)

DRY MEASURE

pint	pt.	½ quart
quart	qt.	2 pints
peck	pk.	8 quarts
bushel	bu.	4 pecks

AVOIRDUPOIS WEIGHT

grain	gr.	0.036 dram
dram	dr.	27.34 grains
ounce	oz.	437.5 grains or 16 drams
pound	lb.	7,000 grains or 16 ounces

LIQUID and DRY MEASURES

teaspoon	tsp.	⅓ tablespoon
tablespoon	tbs.	3 teaspoons
¼ cup		4 tablespoons
⅓ cup		5 tablespoons + 1 teaspoon
½ cup		8 tablespoons
⅔ cup		10 tablespoons + 2 teaspoons
¾ cup		12 tablespoons
cup		16 tablespoons

*All measures are level.

WEIGHT OR MASS

milligram	mg	0.001 gram
centigram	cg	0.01 gram
decigram	dg	0.1 gram
gram	g	10 decigrams or 100 centigrams or 1,000 milligrams
decagram	dkg	10 grams
hectogram	hg	100 grams
kilogram	kg	1,000 grams

U. S. SYSTEM WITH METRIC EQUIVALENTS

U.S. UNIT	METRIC EQUIVALENT

LIQUID MEASURE

gill	0.118 liter
pint	0.473 liter
quart	0.946 liter
gallon	3.785 liters

DRY MEASURE

pint	0.551 liter
quart	1.101 liters
peck	8.810 liters
bushel	35.239 liters

AVOIRDUPOIS WEIGHT

| ounce | 28.349 grams |
| pound | 453.59 grams |

METRIC SYSTEM

CAPACITY

UNIT	ABBR.	EQUIVALENTS IN OTHER UNITS OF SAME SYSTEM
milliliter	ml	0.001 liter
centiliter	cl	0.01 liter
deciliter	dl	0.1 liter
liter	l	10 deciliters or 100 centiliters or 1,000 milliliters
decaliter	dkl	10 liters
hectoliter	hl	100 liters

LIQUID and DRY MEASURES

teaspoon	5 milliliters
tablespoon	15 milliliters
¼ cup	60 milliliters
⅓ cup	80 milliliters
½ cup	120 milliliters
⅔ cup	160 milliliters
¾ cup	180 milliliters
cup	240 milliliters or 0.24 liter

METRIC SYSTEM WITH U. S. EQUIVALENTS

	CAPACITY			WEIGHT OR MASS	
METRIC UNIT	U.S. UNIT (liquid)	U.S. UNIT (dry)	METRIC UNIT		U.S. UNIT
milliliter	0.034 fluid ounce		milligram		0.0154 grain
centiliter	0.338 fluid ounce		centigram		0.1543 grain
deciliter	0.21 pint	0.18 pint	decigram		1.543 grain
liter	1.05 quarts	0.908 quart	gram		15.43 grains or 0.03527 ounce
decaliter	2.64 gallons	1.14 pecks	decagram		0.3527 ounce
hectoliter	26.418 gallons	2.84 bushels	hectogram		3.527 ounces
			kilogram		2.2046 pounds

CONVERSION TABLES

The tables below are set up to help you convert the most common kitchen units from one system of measures and weights to the other. The answers you arrive at will be approximate but accurate enough for all but scientific purposes.

WHEN YOU KNOW THE U.S. UNIT	MULTIPLY BY:	TO FIND THE METRIC UNIT
teaspoons	5	milliliters
tablespoons	15	milliliters
fluid ounces	30	milliliters
fluid ounces	0.03	liters
cups	240	milliliters
cups	0.24	liters
pints	0.47	liters
quarts	0.95	liters
gallons	3.8	liters
ounces	28	grams
pounds	454	grams
pounds	0.45	kilograms

WHEN YOU KNOW THE METRIC UNIT	MULTIPLY BY:	TO FIND THE U.S. UNIT
milliliters	0.2	teaspoons
milliliters	0.07	tablespoons
milliliters	0.034	fluid ounces
liters	34	fluid ounces
milliliters	0.004	cups
liters	4.2	cups
liters	2.1	pints
liters	1.06	quarts
liters	0.26	gallons
grams	0.035	ounces
grams	0.002	pounds
kilograms	2.2	pounds

CONVERTING TEMPERATURES

To convert from Fahrenheit to Celsius, subtract 32 from the Fahrenheit reading, multiply the figure left by 5, and divide the product by 9. *Example:* 65° F. — 32 = 33; 33 × 5 = 165; 165 ÷ 9 = 18.3° C.

To convert from Celsius to Fahrenheit, multiply the Celsius reading by 9, divide the product by 5, and add 32. *Example:* 35° C. × 9 = 315; 315 ÷ 5 = 63; 63 + 32 = 95° F.

On the Fahrenheit scale, water boils at about 212° and freezes at about 32°. On the Celsius scale, water boils at about 100° and freezes at about 0°.

THE MOST COMMONLY USED OVEN TEMPERATURES

OVEN TEMPERATURES		FAHRENHEIT SCALE	CELSIUS SCALE
Very slow	=	Below 300°	Below 149°
Slow	=	300°	149°
Moderately slow	=	325°	163°
Moderate	=	350°	177°
Moderately hot	=	375°	191°
Hot	=	400–425°	204–218°
Very hot	=	450–475°	232–246°
Extremely hot	=	500° or more	260° or more

22

PERSONAL APPEARANCE

A natural approach to cultivating good looks also connects with health and happiness

Don't neglect the importance of frequent and regular exercise to the health, well-being, and personal appearance of all the members of the family. Exercise and fresh air improve the circulation and muscle tone, keep figures trim, increase over-all vitality. Tennis, golf, bicycling, hiking, running, badminton, and volleyball are all healthful recreational activities that the whole family can enjoy together, often at moderate cost. Find out if there's a YM-YWCA or community center near your home that offers a program of sports and recreational activities, and apply for a family membership.

Good posture hides waistline bulges. When working, cleaning, or walking, remember to stretch to your full height and keep your shoulders back, tummy in, rear under. Cultivate the good-posture habit and you'll soon be walking in beauty, go much longer before you tire.

Lift your chin off your chest, unfold your neck, and look up for beauty's sake. When you read, walk, write, think, drive your car, or talk, lift up your chin, hold up your head, and unfold the creases of your neck. By doing this you will not only augment the beauty of your neck but you'll add grace to everything you do.

Are you one of those who should eat more? Does it take you twice as long to get rested? Half as long to get tired? Do you feel and look as though you'd lost your luster? Are you a pushover for the first fall sniffles? It may well be that you don't eat enough. Watch your calories if you must watch your weight, but make up for it in vitamins, proteins, and don't go around hungry. Vitality is the most important beauty factor you have.

You have to work on the art of relaxation. Don't think you're relaxing just because you tie on a dressing gown and stretch out full length on a couch. You have to "work at it." Here are two relaxing exercises and seven other energy-saving tips:

1. S-t-r-e-t-c-h-i-n-g: Catch the footboard of your bed with your toes and grasp the headboard with both hands. Pull toward the headboard, sliding your body upward, until your head almost touches it. Repeat until tensions go and a sensation of release spreads over you.

2. Shake like a puppy. Stand up, bend over, let arms hang limply, and shake.

When you feel low, it's not easy to be bright and gay every single day of the week. We are all subjected to moods of depression and an occasional "blue Monday." Don't make the mistake, however, of matching your mood with drab costume colors. Instead bring out the gayest and brightest of all your costumes and deliberately set about to squelch that mood.

When out on the town shopping, you can save your time, feet, your sweet disposition, and have more fun besides, if you'll heed these seven practical tips:

1. Wear shoes with sensible heels, and take a big carryall along. For neighborhood shopping, get a little cart on wheels to "carry" home the groceries, it's much easier to push than carrying bulky sacks of groceries.

2. Sit down at every counter where an empty stool beckons.

3. Either be an early bird or a Jenny-come-lately. Shop before 11:30 A.M. or after 3:30 P.M., thus avoiding the heaviest shopping hours in most stores. When stores stay open every week night, as during Christmastime, pick the three least hectic ones for your stores—Mondays, Tuesdays, and Wednesdays. Friday is best for daytime shopping.

4. Remember that when the weather is bad the shopping room is good.

5. To avoid back-tracking, have your list made out and grouped according to stores.

6. Don't skip lunch. Having it on time, and enough of it, will help to keep you going at full energy.

7. If it's an all-day expedition, take time out to relax in the restroom and kick off your shoes. Refresh your make-up, puff on a refresher from a cream cake, and you'll look and feel as good as new. Carry a vial of perfume, a whiff of which will be electrifying to tired spirits.

FAMILY AFFAIRS

Parents can set the tone—and example—for their children's attitudes toward their personal appearance. Parents who appear at breakfast in pajamas, with faces unwashed and hair uncombed, cannot expect their children to do otherwise.

Besides reminding them of their grooming, parents can aid children by keeping them supplied with all the grooming requisites needed—shoe polishes in several needed shades, razor blades, shaving soaps or creams, after-shave lotion, hair dressing, and deodorant cologne. Parents who take inventory of these items and replace them as needed, just as they do their own grooming materials, will find that they are used, and used successfully.

The direction of the purchase of clothing is another important part of grooming. If parents will study the types of clothing and the colors that look best on each of the children, and help each with these selections until they have learned the art themselves, they will raise a happier, better-looking group of people.

The young women of the family, hopefully, will want to follow the direction and example of Mother. Mothers who begin to teach their daughters to care for their skin, hair, and clothing at a very early age, and set an example of neatness and good grooming themselves, will have little difficulty in raising a well-groomed, lovely woman.

If teen-age sons or daughters seem completely indifferent to fashion and grooming, don't fret too much. Constantly nagging them to get a haircut or wear something besides faded jeans and work boots will only make them cling more stubbornly to these tribal symbols of adolescence. Relax—they'll grow out of it eventually!

BEGINNING YOUNG

You're the fairy godparents who can do it. Avoid pressure on any one spot of baby's skull by simply turning your baby from side to side carefully. It's almost entirely in your hands whether a child will have a beautifully shaped head or one that will have to be camouflaged.

Teeth are so important to future good looks. See that the first full crop of 20 baby teeth get a close review by a trusted dentist. If teeth buck or bolt out of line, put them into braces when the dentist says it is time for them.

Watch out for any thumb-sucking habit. Correcting any habit that threatens to push teeth out of line is the ounce of prevention now worth nine pounds of orthodoritic "cure" later on to try to revamp an ugly mouth.

Training for beautiful posture, which is the dynamic keystone to all future good looks, should begin the moment you start picking your baby up. Firmly supporting Baby's back with one hand, changing often from right to left the arm in which you hold him, are the earliest steps in posture training.

When the baby starts to sit up is another period of posture training. Don't allow him to sit until his spine is strong enough to support him. Pillow-propping Baby's back before he's ready is an invitation to a curved back.

Bowed legs are often due to cooping a baby up in a playpen or other confined area. If he pulls himself up to see what's going on outside, legs not ready for body weight are apt to bow in or out. The same risk is taken if he is encouraged to walk before he's ready to support his weight.

If you want your child to walk gracefully, on two grown-up feet, be vigilant now about shoes and socks. If either are too short or pointed now, a natural future walk will be thwarted. Well-formed feet and toes are being shaped right now, by shoes and socks that are both square-toed and roomy. To make sure they are adequate on both counts, leave the fitting of a baby's shoes—from the first pair on —to a trusted expert on baby shoes. If your baby shows evidence of any foot problems that may require special shoes, consult your pediatrician.

LITTLE THINGS COUNT

Never overlook any detail, from head to toe, that might spoil your appearance. No woman can be truly glamorous—even though her hair and make-up have a look of perfection and her dress is a compliment to her taste—if her shoes are not attractive. Hands that aren't clean and carefully manicured also will cancel an otherwise glamorous impression. By paying attention to these small details you can consistently look your best.

To be serene, and to "feel" well groomed is as important a beauty asset as physical good looks. Avoid clothes and cosmetics that make you do constant checking while you wear them.

Wear a stole that can be anchored, one that fastens with a self-fabric loop or buckle.

If you wear nearly backless shoes, see that they have magnetic soles that grip your feet. Backless shoes that wobble, slip off, or slap up and down not only make the wearer nervous, but also every man who watches helplessly while she clatters by.

Keep the disheveling wind out of your coiffure either by wearing a tie-on veil or spraying on a coating of lacquer that can be brushed out when you get to your destination.

If you wear a shallow hat, keep it in place by sewing to the sweatband small grip-tooth combs to catch your hair, or tie your hat on with a veil.

Sew tiny inside holders to shoulder line of garments so there's not a constant struggle with straps of bras and slips.

If you wear a strapless gown, use double-face adhesive strip to keep it from slipping. Tugging up a gown can become almost as unattractive a public habit as pulling down your girdle or foundation garment.

You have often sat behind a woman wearing a gossamer, transparent blouse that exposed an elegant bra and slip, and the sheer beauty became lost as you read the bra tab that popped up above the lace—"size 34, B cup, style 22." Don't let others see you that way.

FACE THE FACTS

Pick her carefully. Many women, especially the younger set of beauty seekers, secretly select some current beauty of the stage or screen or TV after whom to pattern their beauty scheme. Too often, however, they select an inappropriate model for their own particular kind of beauty, and the results are unnatural and far from lovely.

Find your double. Remember that there are different kinds of blondes, brunettes, brownettes, and redheads, so be sure to find the one who resembles you in many ways.

Never forget that you are you. Use these lovely women of the stage and screen as models from whom to get ideas for your make-up, your coiffure, your fashions, etc., only because they are groomed by experts in the grooming arts and not because you wish to look and act exactly like them. Then adapt the ideas you gather so that they may enhance your own individual personality and make you a more beautiful, well-groomed "you."

Suppose you have a plumpish face and neck that you'd like to lengthen a bit? Bedeck yourself as dazzlingly as Marco Polo in a long necklace of eye-pulling color. Pin it into a V at the neckline with a jewel. That device can be as effective as a lighted road sign in flagging eyes to a longer route.

For another way to achieve a longish effect, wear graduated ropes of beads. Don't have the first rope start too high. Let ropes fall on an open neck or spill their splendor over a dress, shirt or sweater.

If your face is long and your neck a bit angular, the choker or dog collar has a foreshortening effect. A bib of beads is just as effective. Besides reducing apparent length of the neck, the graduated ropes of beads will hide angular neckbones.

Your teeth are important. Your teeth may not be perfect and even, but your mouth can still be attractive if your teeth are sparkling. Regular dental care is the best assurance for keeping teeth in good condition. The most carefully applied lipstick won't hide neglected teeth. When you speak or smile your teeth become a focal point and they can spoil an otherwise beautifully groomed appearance or be the "extra plus" that makes you truly attractive.

Clear-eyed beauty. The best eye care is, of course, lots of sleep and avoidance of overstraining through reading, sewing, movies, or TV. If your eyes get tired easily, bathe occasionally with soothing eye lotion and check with your eye doctor as to whether you need glasses.

"Can't do a thing with your hair?" Try adding this simple ritual to your daily beauty program: Bend over and brush your scalp and hair from back to front until your scalp tingles. Then massage scalp with fingertips and see how easy to manage your hair becomes.

HAIRCUTS

If your face is round, do not cut your hair so short that it fails to add the illusion of length to your face. You will need enough hair on top to add height in waves, curls, etc. Also you will need enough hair to fall down below the lobes of your ears so that the illusion of the perfect oval face is created.

If your face is long, allow for enough hair to curl or dip over the side of your forehead and enough at the side to add width to the sides of your face. You will also need hair falling down below your jawline. In other words, your long face needs complete framing to create the wanted oval contour.

If your face is a triangle, a narrow forehead and wide jaws, your hair must never be cut so short that it causes the jaws to stand out. They should be completely framed by a soft coiffure that falls below them. Furthermore, the narrow forehead should be widened by waves or curls to accentuate the oval illusion.

If your face is an inverted triangle, a wide forehead and narrow chin, your hair should never be cut so short that a pointed chin is left alone. Your hair should be cut and curled so that it is long enough to give width to this chinline, and so that dips and curls may cover part of the forehead to give balance to the contour.

If your face is squarish, wide forehead and wide jaws, be sure to leave your hair long enough to soften its contour into the perfect oval. Never crop your hair so short that jaws and forehead are left standing alone.

If your face is a perfect oval, you are a very lucky person indeed. Show this beauty by wearing the most simple styles possible. Your face type will look lovely with short hair or long. However, avoid extreme styles, for these can distort even a perfect face and lessen its natural glamour.

SKIN CARE

How to outwit your skin's worst foe, dry indoor heat. Considering the drying effects of steam and dry heat on skins that are naturally dry, it's no wonder that so many women and girls lack the lovely freshness of face that is their birthright, for the drying effects are forerunners of premature lines and wrinkles. Here are some combat tactics to defeat this enemy:

Lower the thermostat to 68° F., or under. If you don't believe your skin suffers in an overheated room, watch an ivy plant (the hardiest) wither in a higher temperature.

Place a humidifier, or an ordinary basin of water, in any heated room.

Go easy on soap and water for a couple of months while the heater in the basement is being stoked. Substitute cleansing creams which won't further deplete your skin of natural oils.

Be faithful in use of night cream. See that this oil replenisher is rich in oils.

Don't cancel out the good work your night cream does by wearing a make-up the next day that draws natural moisture from your skin like a dry sponge. Wear instead a creamy type of foundation make-up. There's rejuvenating moisture, all-day protection, and actually a beauty treatment in creamy make-up foundations.

Before you apply one single beauty requisite to your face always make sure it is thoroughly cleansed with your cleansing cream. Use your fingertips or a natural-silk sponge to spread the cream over your entire face. Then allow it to remain on your face long enough to cleanse all dirt and grime from the pores. Removing the cleansing cream from your face is equally as important as its application. So wipe away all traces of the cream, using a soft clean towel or a facial tissue. Complete the cleansing process with an application of a skin freshener or astringent. And for a cooling pickup on hot days, keep your skin freshener or astringent in the refrigerator.

Regular skin care is essential even for the youngest girl. Your daily skin cleansing should become a night and morning habit. Each night remove your make-up with cleansing cream and wash your face thoroughly with a mild soap and warm water. Then follow with an application of skin freshener or astringent. Even though your skin is oily, it needs lubrication, but not as frequently as a dry skin. Use your sleeping hours for this lubrication by applying a night cream before retiring. In the morning your skin care ritual can be a very simple face washing followed by an application of skin freshener or astringent. Then you are ready for your make-up.

BEWARE OF BEAUTY THIEVES!

The most common, most wanton thief of beauty is the blackhead that makes its appearance on the sides of the face where it often cannot be seen when looking into a mirror front view. It first appears as a pinpoint blackhead of no great consequence, and because it cannot be easily seen, it grows until it is big, black, and the size of the head of a pin. Often such blackheads appear just inside of the ears, on the lobes of ears, or along the hairline. They should be removed before they gain large proportions. If, however, in your search you find that such a thief has invaded your beauty territory and has grown to a larger size than you believe it is wise to handle, let your doctor or dermatologist remove it for you, so that a scar may not take its place.

If blackheads have become so large that infection has started, if they are stubborn and will not come out with gentle pressure, or if certain areas of the skin are filled with many blackheads, visit your dermatologist before trouble begins. Never try to remove such blackheads yourself, for your skin is precious, and the lack of professional care and advice may mean the difference between a perfect skin and a scarred one.

After your blackheads are gone, follow a thorough day-by-day cleansing routine, so that your pretty face will be as free and smooth, when school reopens this fall, as the palm of your hand.

Another glamour thief is the wild hair or hairs that often grow out of the chin, nose, or at the sides of the face where they are not too obvious at first glance. Once seen, however, they become an obsession with the observer. Keep these plucked out with tweezers, being sure to apply alcohol or astringent before and after the plucking. Hairs that grow out of the nose, and gain such length that they can be seen, should be snipped with fingernail scissors, not plucked. If hairs are growing out of a mole, consult your doctor before touching them. He will know how you should remove them so they will not rob you of your beauty.

Avoid a red nose from head colds or wintry winds. Best concealment of a leaky nose's unwanted redness is to use a make-up from a neat, compact cake which you can carry with you. For those inevitable repairs, you'll need to carry your make-up and reapply it often.

Camouflage for blemishes. Skin blemishes can be retouched on you much as the negatives of photographs can be retouched to give it a flawless print. The way to do it is with products especially made for this purpose: cream-stick "eraser," or a heavy, dry "coverall" cream. Either should be of the kind that vanishes into the skin while covering up the blemished spot. Slight blending may be necessary. The camouflaging should be applied in a skin-matching or foundation-matching shade to soft-focus any flaws or imperfections in your complexion, whether temporary or permanent. Choose a cover-aid that is smooth and soft, but not greasy. Use it under your make-up if you have cake make-up, but over a cream foundation, covering it all with powder. Beware of applying the "camouflage" heavily, or it will cake and call attention to the imperfection instead of hiding it.

To minimize a vaccination scar, and other spots that seem to grow whiter the darker your skin tans, use a pastel cream rouge over these body marks. Rouge brings up the red pigment that's been lost, blends scar tissue to a pale pink. But practice to get the exact amount of rouge over the scar, since this is the trick of canceling out whiteness. Now apply a cake make-up of a shade that matches your tan and blend around scar. If patchwork is still not perfect, dust some of your tan face powder over the mark in a still wider area.

HOW TO MAKE YOUR EARS MORE ATTRACTIVE

With short and upswept coiffures, your ears should have special make-up consideration. Remember that your ears are actually a part of your face and should be treated as such whenever any part of them is exposed. Here are the make-up rules:

Shiny ears. If you ears are shiny and your make-up is of a matte finish, the contrast will cause your ears to look as though they don't belong to your face, and they will stand out like two gleaming shells. Cut down the shine, therefore, by applying a light touch of face powder with your powder puff. Be sure, however, that the powder application is smooth and doesn't pile up in the little ear folds. After you have gently applied the powder, spread it and blend it evenly with your fingertips or a piece of cotton. Examine the results carefully in the mirror and eliminate any application error.

Face powder may not be enough to tone down shiny ears. If this case, when you are applying your cake make-up, also apply a thin coat of the make-up to your ears and spread it evenly with your fingertips. Then apply a dusting of face powder and blend. The main idea is to apply foundation make-up, powder, or both, until the skin on your ears is the same color and quality as the skin of your face.

If your ears are red, chalk-white, or blotchy. It is not unusual to find a woman with ears that are naturally of a much higher and redder color then her face, or ears that become red at the slightest exposure to the sun or wind. If this is your ear condition, choose a make-up foundation one shade lighter than the one you use on your face. If your ears are chalk-white, you will need a foundation make-up for them that is a shade darker than the foundation you use on your face. If your ears are blotchy, your regular foundation make-up will solve the problem. In all cases, however, be sure to blend the make-up perfectly and check to see that your ears match your face.

When you wear your hair swept away from your ears and neck, remember to extend your make-up behind your ears and blend it down over your neckline. The face, ears, and neck should be all one lovely color. The thinnest application will do the trick and produce untold added glamour.

Fashion's elaborate earrings, which are being worn these days, point up the ear-color difference too. When you wear earrings, therefore, be doubly sure of your ear coloration.

THE NECKLINE

Give your neck as much attention as you give your face. Too many women concentrate so much effort on their faces that by the time they reach the neck area their enthusiasm is diminished and the treatment is scanty. The result is a neck that is older looking than the face.

There are two major causes of the unwanted, old-looking feminine neck that is ravaged with wrinkles, sags, double chins, and blotches. These two causes are "time" and "neglect." We can do little about "time," but so much can be done about "neglect" that the clock seems to stand still and a lovely neck is the result.

During your sleeping hours use your pillows to increase your neck's beauty. If you sleep on your back, push your pillow aside so that your neck will be straight and uncreased. If you sleep on your side, push your pillow under your head next to your shoulder, so that your head does not bend your neck and fall forward, thus causing your neck to fold into dozens of wrinkles.

Exercise your throat. Stretch and pull the muscles and cords of your neck by pointing your chin from a straight-forward position up to the sky and returning to a straight-for-ward position again. Stretch it in all directions in a rotating movement from left to right, and rest. Reverse the movement from right to left, and rest. Repeat until the neck muscles begin to feel tired. Increase this exercise as the days pass until you can easily exercise for about five minutes.

Cleanse your neck with cleansing cream every time you cleanse your face, and with the same enthusiasm. Also, be sure to continue the cleansing by washing your neck with soap and water and rinsing it well, just as you do your face. Stimulate by applying skin freshener or astringent. Use skin freshener for dry skin and astringent for oily skin.

Each night massage your neck for about three or four minutes with the same rich cream you use for your face. Massage with an upward stroke, moving your hands from the base of your neck up to your ears, your jaws, and your chin. Blot off excess cream and retire.

Two or three times a week continue the night treatment, and further stimulate your neck, by following the massage with this procedure: Fashion a piece of cotton into a pad about the circumference of a medium-sized powder puff and about an inch thick. Dampen it with a skin freshener or astringent, hold it by its edge, as you would a powder puff, and pat it against every part of your throat for two to three minutes, or until the skin be-gins to tingle. Then gently rub your throat with the dampened pad and let the liquid dry.

If your neck seems to get dry during the day, apply hand lotion to it in the morning and when you freshen your make-up during the day. Face powder applied over the hand lotion not only takes away the shine but gives your neck additional daytime protection and adds beauty. If you are wearing a white dress, scarf, or white collar, however, puff a small amount of white bath powder over your neck, instead of the tinted face powder, so that your white garments will remain white.

An oily neck is another beauty thief that most women ignore completely. If you find, within a few hours after your bath, that your neck is oily, you will know that a bath is not enough to keep this thief away. After you have dried your neck, therefore, apply astringent or skin freshener with a cotton pad and then further insure yourself against oiliness by patting your face powder over your neck. If you are going to wear a white dress or a dress with a white collar, keep it white by applying white bath powder to your neck instead of face powder.

HANDS ARE GOSSIPS

Whether tapering and thin, plump and dimpled, tanned and trigger-quick, gifted or lazy, hands have one trait in common: they're gossips that will shout out their tales of neglect. And they'll all protest cold weather with ruffled-up skin.

To get the most from your hand lotion, first soak hands in warm water to open skin pores. Massage as you work in the lotion. This manipulation will limber up hands that are never very supple in cold weather.

Gloves were made to be worn, not to carry. Wear gloves, even if the supermarket is only around the corner. Keep a pair of gloves in your car pocket to wear when you drive. Since cold, close-fitting gloves are too easy to push aside, settle for warm, flexible wool knits that fingers like to wriggle into, in which palms have ample room and you are cozily content.

Chapped hands crying for help? Salvage a pair of worn old cotton gloves, apply pure lanolin to your hands, slip on those old gloves, and wear them while you sleep.

If you use strong detergents when you battle with pots and pans, wear rubber gloves into the fray.

For more ways to outwit "dishpan hands," Hollywood's Max Factor, Jr., advises pampering these kitchen slaveys with a hand cream before they climb into rubber gloves, again afterwards, if they run amok with detergent suds.

Using mild soap to spell a strong detergent whenever you can will help to save hands and nails from a scullion's fate. The shorter the contact with either cleaning agent,

however, the better off your hands will be.

If you wear your wedding ring into the dishpan, follow the warning of a dermatologist of the New York University School of Medicine and d-o-n-'t! The warning is that bits of soap captured and confined under wedding bands can cause skin irritations.

Keep your hands beautiful. Paint and paper, run the power saw, dig in your garden to your heart's content, but keep your hands looking as if you'd never lifted a finger. Canvas gloves are a gal's best friend for all out-of-door chores, and rubber gloves are best for inside jobs. Rub plenty of hand lotion on your hands before slipping them into gloves and they'll come out prettier for the extra effort. When gloves interfere with the light touch, just scratch your nails across a cake of wet soap to protect them.

For longer, more attractive nails, make a habit of pushing back cuticles with a towel after each washing.

Brittle, cracked, or split fingernails may often be due to overfrequent applications of nail polish and remover. When nails chip excessively, remove nail polish, treat with vaseline and hand lotion, but leave nail polish off for a few days and watch the nails recover.

Make your own nail-polish remover. Ask your druggist for two ounces of acetone. You'll have a supply that will last two months at a fraction of the usual cost.

FROM KNEES TO TOES

Get your knees on a regular diet of a rich hand and body lotion if knees are going to be exposed under shorts, in a bathing suit or tennis clothes. Rough knee skin can be rough on your over-all appearance. For comfort and for longer-lasting hose, follow this hand-lotion routine on your soles and toes as well.

Sleight-of-hand for slighter ankles and slimmer legs. Wear a neutral hose shade, neither too ruddy a tan nor too ashen a gray, to make your legs look slimmer.

Whatever kind of stockings you wear, keep them tightly tethered. The straighter the seams, the better-groomed your legs look.

Footwork's afoot. Feet clad in stockings as thin as tinted air, shod in a string or two of leather attached to soles, need a lot of care before their unveiling.

Get rid of corns and calluses. Both will go if taken out of shoes with points of friction at toes and heels. To speed the departure of these blemishes, use corn pads on toes until the kernel can be uprooted. With a piece of pumice, work on the calluses every day after your bath.

Give toenails even more care than fingernails until they're out of the rough. Push back soaped-up cuti-cles while you're in your tub. File toenails straight across, but stop short of the toe tip. When you apply polish, align length of toes more perfectly by stopping the color short of the long toes, brushing color to the tips of the shorter ones.

Are toes crooked? The kindest treatment is to skip too-naked sandals in favor of cut-out shoes that more discreetly expose what you want to show.

Roughness of foot skin will yield only to daily creaming with your hand lotion.

Down-at-the-heels on rouge. Dare to carry rouge down to too-white heels. Even after feet are as tanned as nutmegs, the heels continue to stay an off-white. To subdue pallor, use cream rouge around pink-polished toenails in a sure-fire way of making sandalfoot sheers give their money's worth of allure.

How to take summer's pinch out of shoes. When feet feel twice as big as the shoes that pinch them, bathe them in tepid water and rinse with cool water to dwarf their size. Dry, apply bracing cologne, and dust feet with talcum powder. Then dust some more talc inside your shoes to give your feet that glorious silken slide.

The moment shoes are removed, while they're still warm and pliable, is the time to insert shoe trees. Do use shoe trees that can fill shoes like feet, not flimsy sticks. Their use is all the more necessary if shoes are damp when you remove them, for damp shoes, if left to dry without support, will shrink and become real torture for summer's puffier feet.

LIVING WITH MAKE-UP

There are still people who believe that make-up is a luxury, but there are very few women or girls who have such lovely complexions or regularly defined features that they can appear without make-up at all. For the many whose complexions are dull or who have one or more irregular features, make-up is essential. Make-up can be used for corrective purposes. If make-up can help appearance, it is no luxury.

Look natural. Many women are afraid to apply a sufficient amount of make-up and fail to reach their true beauty goal. Also, in the effort to look glamorous, other women apply too much make-up, and fail.

Make-up applied under an electric light may show up quite differently by daylight. Try to apply your make-up in light as close as possible to that in which you expect to be seen.

Don't apply make-up too heavily, even if you have to apply two kinds of foundation, plus rouge, plus powder. "Make down" with the minimum amount of each, spreading evenly, blending perfectly.

Don't be too enthusiastic about make-up. Be sure to apply it immediately after your face powder, so that you will add the color against a rather monotone background. Then, after putting your lipstick and rouge on, apply more eyelash makeup and eyebrow pencil, if necessary.

Avoid mask contour. Although you can't see the area between the edge of your cheeks and your ears when you face the mirror, your critics can. So, don't stop short. Continue your make-up right to your ears, pull it down even to your ear lobes, and see the natural glow your whole make-up takes on.

If your face is too full, apply a foundation of a shade darker than your regular foundation to the outer contours of your face. This shadows the sides and makes your face appear narrower. Be very careful, though, that color line blends smoothly. In choosing another shade, make sure there is not too much difference in depth and that darker shade is of the same tone of warmth as your regular foundation, that it contains the same proportions of pink or yellow overtones. See also that it is the same make and type as the regular foundation.

Your dressing-table drawer will welcome divided cutlery trays. They are excellent for "filing" small items, such as bobby pins, curlers, combs, costume jewelry; everything's in its place and easy to find whenever needed.

Your make-up and make-up accessories should be carried in your purse in a little bag, for the purpose of neatness, and, even more important, for good hygiene. It doesn't have to be an elaborate bag. It can be something you make yourself. But if facial tissues, brush, puff, and sponge are allowed to jangle and mix with keys, coins, well-fingered wallets, etc., you can't expect these make-up tools to be germ-free. When you use them you may be transferring minute germs to your face and cause infections. It is much safer to have a little "cosmetic bag" to hold your make-up and make-up tools. It is more convenient, too, especially when transferring your purse contents from one handbag to another. These bags can be as plain or as fancy as you wish. The new embroidered or brocade zippered eyeglass cases make pretty, as well as handy, cosmetic bags.

Instead of carrying loose powder in your compact, for touch-ups, carry a pressed powder compact, a creamy blend of make-up base and powder all-in-one, which will not spill when it is applied.

Putting a finger to work. To keep a shiny lipstick case from getting scratched in your purse, make a cover for it from a finger cut from an old glove. Make sure the glove is soft on the inside.

THE EYES

Give special attention to your eyes, for they will be the first to reflect your mood. Use eyelash make-up and eye shadow to enhance your eyes, and if you wish to make them appear brighter and clearer, choose a lipstick in a fiery shade of red.

Women with red hair must pay special attention to making up their eyebrows, because they are usually very light in color and therefore do not serve their beauty purpose in giving expression to the face. Eyebrows should be defined with an eyebrow pencil in a shade that blends with the hair color. Girls with light, flaming "carrot-top" hair should use maroon pencil, which is reddish brown in color. Women with medium red hair should use a light brown pencil, and the dark auburn redhead should use a brown pencil. If your hair is one of the in-between shades of red, combine two shades of eyebrow pencil, applying the lighter one first. You should be very careful not to get your eyebrows much darker than your hair, because beautiful red hair should always be the outstanding feature.

Your eyebrows are thin, light, unarched? You want them naturally full and arched? First pluck out all straggling hairs between your eyes and over your eyelids. Then, with a sharp eyebrow pencil, using little, short, hairlike strokes, define and shape the brows into the arch you desire. Begin directly over the inside corner of the eye and sketch the brow in a slight upward curve. Now fill in the eyebrow to the width desired and diminish to a thin, faint line at the outer extension of the brow.

Often two shades of eyebrow pencil create the exact color needed for a soft, natural appearance. For instance, light brown eyebrow pencil is often too light, and dark brown pencil is too dark. When a little of the dark brown pencil is stroked through the lighter shade, however, you often strike the exact color wanted. Black mixed with dark brown becomes a softer shade than black alone. Auburn mixed with maroon often becomes a shade that is perfect for many redheads. Experiment with eyebrow-pencil shades and find the one that will give you a new, more beautiful you.

If eyebrows need correcting, pluck carefully, cool with compresses for a few minutes, then apply your eyebrow pencil with tiny individual strokes that resemble your eyebrow hairs. (Avoid solid line.) In outlining your new "arch of triumph," follow the original line as closely as possible, adding or taking away only at crucial points.

If your eyes are set closely together, pluck eyebrows to start farther apart from each other. Be careful to keep a natural curve and natural "hairline" shape where you pluck. You may also extend outer ends of eyebrows beyond their original length, straightening the curve somewhat.

If your eyes are set far apart, bring eyebrow lines closer together and shorten at outer ends.

To make your eyes appear larger and more exciting, draw a thin eyebrow-pencil line directly above the upper lashes and extend beyond corner of eye. Blend ever so gradually, to avoid a distinct line of demarcation.

To match the stars in your eyes, apply mascara after making up the rest of your face completely. Brush off the excess and let it "set" for a few minutes. Then curl your lashes and add a little more mascara to the tips of your lashes. It's this last "tipping" that does most to give the alluring illusion of length.

Eyelash make-up goes on quicker, looks smoother, stays put longer (even while slicing onions), if you'll use hot instead of cold water to work up a paste.

Use hot water for the application of cake eyeliner and mascara. The warmth of the water seems to cause the make-up to go on more smoothly and lastingly than when cold water is used.

To make the nose appear narrower, apply a drop of dark blue, brown, or gray eye shadow along each side before applying powder. Make sure that you blend the eye shadow to avoid spotty look.

Scarecrow for crow's-feet. Laugh wrinkles in the corners of your eyes come not from age, but from relative skin dryness. So don't neglect daily, or nightly, lubrication with a good eye cream. Don't massage that delicate skin area. Pat cream lightly around outside corners of eyes, under eyes, and on eyelids.

Detract attention from circles under your eyes by adding blue eye shadow on and around your lids, discreetly blending the shade.

Wear glasses if you need them, and look pretty too. Avoid exaggerated bangs, and instead sweep hair to one side, revealing your brow. This is important if you wear glasses. Eyeglass lenses magnify your features, and therefore you should avoid bright-colored eye shadow and wear brown or gray instead. Use eyelash make-up, but in moderation. Emphasize the arch of your eyebrows but still keep them natural looking. And don't use too much rouge. Choose earrings that are in proportion to your face. Your glasses should be the right size and shape for your face, and you should be certain that the frames do not clash in color with your lipstick and rouge shades.

If you wear contact lenses, you may prefer to apply eye shadow before inserting your lenses, and eyeliner and mascara afterward. This method prevents smudging your liner or mascara when the lenses are inserted. Cake or liquid eyeliner applied with a small, fine brush is preferable to pencil eyeliner, which puts more pressure on the eyelid and may dislodge the lens.

If your eyes are extremely sensitive, one of the brands of hypo-allergenic eye makeup on the market may solve your problem.

LIPSTICK

Many women fail to achieve a beautiful lip pattern with their lipstick because they are in a hurry to complete their entire make-up. In the rush they either spread on a heavy layer of lipstick or fail to cover the lip area perfectly. In both instances the lipline, which has often been called the beauty line, is wavy, crooked, and uneven. One extra minute, taken from some lengthy portion of the grooming, would provide sufficient time for this important, brilliant, and mobile feature which is so vital to glamour and to the expression of individual personality.

The color of your lipstick depends on two factors: your natural coloring and the color tones of your costume. Generally speaking, no one should ever wear deep, dark lipsticks of any shade, unless an intentional "exotic" effect is sought. A clear, medium-shade lipstick is any woman's, any girl's, best bet for harmonious beauty. A basic true red should figure in your make-up scheme to wear with all non-blue tones, with white, yellow, beige, tan, brown, black, grays, greens. Wear a soft blue-pink (not purple) lipstick with all blues from powder to navy, with all pinks except peach, with all lavenders and purples, with turquoise, aqua, bluegreens, or with any of the non-blue colors if accented by warm bluetone accessories. Keep on hand an orangy hue for less frequently worn colors such as orange, terra cotta, mustard, persimmon, peach, and for all non-bluish pastels to wear with your summer tan.

Lip contour. Strive for smooth outlines, straightening and blending with one firm stroke of forefinger wrapped in cleansing tissue. You may stay a little inside the outline of a mouth you feel too full or may go just slightly beyond the outlines of thin lips, though not too much. Above all, don't try to change the shape too much. It will always show, and will only look unnatural.

If you'd like your lipstick to stay on, beautifully and naturally, permanently, make sure your lips are dry before you apply lipstick. Apply generously and wait about 2 minutes before blotting with tissue. Puff on a light coat of face powder and apply a second coat of lipstick just as carefully and generously as the first. Wait again before you blot. If you use a lipstick that is really color-fast and apply it as outlined above, your lips can look beautiful after many hours.

All professional make-up artists use a lipstick brush to apply lipstick, and the actresses on whom they apply this beauty requisite soon learn how to use the brush themselves so that their lips look perfectly beautiful all the time.

You can mend a broken lipstick. All you have to do is heat the broken ends over a gas, match, or cigarette-lighter flame until they melt enough to adhere when you press

them together. Then don't use the lipstick until the ends have had enough time to get together and cool.

Lipstick trick. Use a color-fast lipstick, applied with a lipstick brush, so that the lipline stays better put. Then blot, reapply, and blot again. Don't cheat on the time it takes lipstick color to set. It takes 2 full minutes for the first application.

If lips are flaky, use a rich lipstick —rich in lanolin, that is. Lanolin, which almost all dermatologists swear by, most nearly duplicates the skin's natural oils. A lipstick rich with lanolin will be your best assurance of keeping lip tissue smooth, supple, and receptive to make-up, no matter how nippy the fall or how rambunctious the winter.

ROUGE HAS A DUAL ROLE

Rouge is a color artist, a feature builder. Colorwise, you should select just one shade. Rouge should be discreetly applied and correctly blended, and made to appear as part of your own natural coloring. It cannot, therefore, take on various hues that blend with your costume, but must always blend with your skin tone. In selecting your personal rouge color, it's best to take a medium shade with the barest touch of pink in it, to make you look soft and pretty. If you are very fair-skinned, find a lighter shade, still with only a touch of pink in it; a natural blush is never an out-and-out pink. On a darker skin the medium-shade rouge will take on a deeper tone automatically.

Rouge as a feature builder. In this capacity the tutored application of rouge can help correct: the height of a forehead, the distance between the eyes, the length and angle of the nose, the fatness or flatness of the cheeks, the height of the cheekbones, the narrowness or the breadth of the face, the length and shape of the face, the shape of the chin.

Rouge and the forehead. For a low forehead, apply rouge somewhat lower than ordinarily; for a too-high forehead, apply closer to the eyes.

Rouge and the eyes. For eyes too close, apply rouge from point under center of eyes and blend toward and almost into the ears. For wide-apart eyes, start rouging at point directly under inner corner of eye and blend evenly at height of cheekbone.

If nose is broad, start rouging on cheekbone, blend to outer edge of face. If nose is narrow, apply rouge from bridge to point under outer corners of eyes. With a flat nose, treat rouging as if nose were broad, and conversely, with a jutting nose, rouge as if the nose were narrow. If done very discreetly, a too-short nose may be made to look longer by blending a little rouge on its tip before powdering.

Full cheeks should preferably have no rouge at all. If a must for other reasons, be as delicate as possible in its application. Flat cheeks need heavier rouging than any other reason for feature building, but still avoid the clownish, over-rouged look. Height of color should concentrate under eyes and on cheekbones. A narrow face is rouged from nose to ears, the rouge kept on cheekbone height. A long face is rouged in circular blend. A short face is rouged high and narrow under the eyes.

A short chin can be brought to pretty size by round "invisible" rouging. A square chin can be rounded by rouging the center with a well-blended dot; a pointed chin, by rouging its sides.

This trick makes rouging look natural. Apply foundation on freshly washed, just-dried face. Blend in rouge while foundation is still very fresh, almost moist. Allow it to set 1 minute. With fresh cotton, lightly go over rouging, so that any heavy spots are toned down. Powder immediately. Brush. Cushioned between foundation and powder, the rouging looks like the bloom of your own skin. (This method refers to cream or gel rouge and liquid.) Use cake rouge only if you have oily skin, and then over your powder, blending rouge with fresh cotton.

To avoid obviously rouged cheeks, put one dot on the widest part of your rouge areas, grin or smile, and blend the color up and out, according to the natural smiling contour. Under no circumstances should you apply rouge in a circle.

FACE POWDER

Face-powder applications should extend over the entire face. But if too much powder is applied and not brushed off with a face-powder brush so that only a thin film remains, the powder may stray to the clothing and into the hairline. Practice until you learn just the right amount to apply and brush off the surplus.

Start powdering at the lower part of the cheeks. Then pat and blend the powder toward the center of the face. Powder the nose last. Otherwise you are apt to get too heavy an application on this feature, where it will be more obvious than anywhere else. Press the powder into the little skin lines around the eyes, nose, and mouth, stretching these tiny complexion crevices open with the fingertips. First apply face powder liberally with a puff and then use a powder brush to remove the excess. The final result is a superbly smooth finish.

Muddy-looking complexion? Better switch to a powder that closely matches your skin or is, if anything, a little darker. Too light a powder often tends to make the complexion muddy.

HAND LOTION, ONE OF YOUR MOST BENEFICIAL BEAUTY AIDS

Many women believe that just because hand lotion is named "hand lotion" that it has been made for the hands only. It is, however, a softening and beautifying requisite that is most beneficial to the entire skin.

When your limbs are constantly exposed to the elements and become so dry and scaled that the smooth beauty is lost, return them to their natural satin smoothness by applying hand lotion to your feet, legs, arms, and hands. Concentrate the lotion on your elbows and knees, for they will be very dry at this time. While you are about the lotioning task, actually massage the feet, so that the skin and cuticle around your toenails becomes soft and will not tear your expensive hose when you pull them on. You'll find it will put pep in your step too.

Your neck, from jawline to collarbone, is constantly exposed and becomes old-looking simply because it is allowed to get dry. Provide extra moisture for your neck by applying hand lotion to it before you apply your make-up in the morning or before you dress for the evening. Then, when you dust your neck with powder, it will be soft and silken instead of crepe-like. Furthermore, your neck will remain young-looking longer if it is softened with lotion every day.

During the hot summer, or early in the morning, you may wish to apply a very simple make-up, consisting only of face powder and lipstick. A small amount of hand lotion smoothed over your face will correct the dry look and will change your face to satin. Furthermore, it will provide a wonderful base for the face powder.

Shoulders, backs, and chests are made more beautiful when hand lotion is massaged onto them. If you're going to wear a strapless, sleeveless gown or sun dress, massage an abundance of hand lotion on all skin that the gown will expose, just before your shower or bath, and let the warmth of the water help it to penetrate. Then dry with your towel and note the new-looking skin you have acquired.

If your entire skin is extra-dry, try this nightly treatment. Bathe, dry your skin with a towel, apply a film of hand lotion to your entire body, and retire. You'll awaken with the softest smoothest skin you've ever known.

Rough elbows are indicative of incomplete grooming. When you are wearing a sleeveless dress or short sleeves, don't let rough elbows spoil an otherwise perfect appearance. In addition to scrubbing your elbows when you bathe, you should also rub hand lotion on them every time you use the lotion on your hands and in between times too.

THROUGH THE DAY

Whether you have a big day planned or merely household chores, make it a morning ritual to keep yourself glamorous. It isn't necessary to apply complete beauty requisites immediately upon arising. But don't neglect make-up entirely just because you're not going anywhere. For quick, easy application, use an all-in-one make-up, which is a combination of creamy make-up base and compressed powder, and a color-fast lipstick in a pale shade. Both will stay on for hours, and then you're ready to answer the door without looking unkempt or untidy.

In the morning, wear a pale lipstick. That's enough color for 8 A.M.

Make up your face before you dress. Then keep a thin silk scarf for one purpose only: to tie around your face and head so that you can pull tight necklines of sweaters, dresses, and blouses over your head without getting a trace of powder or make-up on them. Keep this scarf clean and it will keep your necklines clean.

If you are going to wear a dark garment, never just dust powder under your arms after your bath. Instead press the powder under your arms and then buff it down with the back of your puff. Take more time when you don your dark garment and you'll not have those unaccountable white splotches appearing on your skirt or bodice.

After you have worn a garment made of dark material, check the neckline to see if some of your powder or the oils from your skin have soiled it. If so, you'll be able to whisk it off in a moment with a clean cloth dampened with one of the popular cleaning solvents. Then your garment will be ready for the next wearing and your good grooming assured.

If you renew your make-up in your outer clothing, tuck clean cleansing tissues around your neckline before you begin so that you won't take any chances with your well-groomed appearance. Tuck them well under the neckline and let more than half of each tissue fall over the outside of your garment. Even wear a make-up cape whenever possible.

When it's time to reach for a late-day lipstick, a blazing red to brighten your face and lift your spirits, it's time for touch-ups. Unlike loose powder, which can look spotty if confined to one area, touch-ups from a creamy cake make-up can be localized. With a cake powder you can freshen your face without fear of building up a layered look. Or you can use your touch-up merely to erase nose shine, to blot up perspiration, hide a blemish, or get rid of lipstick smears.

To banish the pallor of fatigue, smooth on a bit of gel blusher at the end of the day. Brush all powdery traces from eyebrows and give them a once-over-lightly with a sharp eyebrow pencil.

PERSONAL APPEARANCES

Realizing the risk of facing up to powerful cameras, Madam Chairman or the visitor to a TV audience-participation show should learn how to apply a quick TV make-up over the one she's wearing, if time will not permit her to be made up in the television studio with the professional TV make-up shades. Every one of her "emergency" TV make-up requisites can be fished from her purse:

For TV apply a darker foundation over the one you're wearing. This requires a creamy cake make-up, applied with the puff that you carry in your purse compact.

Quickly pencil your brows and outline your eyes, unless they're already made up.

Erase any dark under-eye shadows or lines at the sides of your nose with a cream stick cosmetic eraser (an item Madam Chairman carries in her purse anyway, for platform appearances).

Lighten your lipstick shade, unless you're already wearing a true red shade.

EIGHT SUMMER PICK-ME-UPS

A generous dousing of your body with your favorite cologne (first cooled in your refrigerator for this purpose) feels wonderful on a hot summer day. Especially dab some on your wrists and the soles of your feet. . . . Is that you purring?

Take hot baths, for if you bathe in water that is warmer than the air, you feel cooler when you get out of the bath. Use cologne after the bath, talcum on the soles of your feet to lessen friction between feet and shoes.

Wear cotton eyelet and other self-ventilating fabrics, as cooling as air conditioning in hot weather.

Set your hair with a little cologne. It's cooling and refreshing to your scalp, helps hair waft a heavenly fragrance.

Before repowdering your face, press over it a face towel wrung out in cold, even icy water.

Keep feet cool and comfortable by changing hosiery during the day, even more than once if you happen to stroll by the stocking box.

Keep colognes, skin fresheners, astringent, cotton pads for cooling eyelids in the refrigerator.

Eat summer's lighter-caloried foods: Vegetables and fruits. See that you have sufficient salt in your diet. Drink lots of water and cooling beverages.

TRICKS FOR SPEEDING UP A SUN TAN

In a hurry to look like a gypsy? You'll tan faster if you strike out for the sun's gold in white clothes. White all down the line, from towels to sun hat, will reflect sun rays, enable you to get an even, quicker, more spectacular tan.

Don't wash off that vitamin D. If you dash into a shower bath too soon after your sun bath, you'll risk washing off valuable vitamin D before your skin has had enough time to absorb all of it.

How to repel seepage into your swim cap. If you've tried simply everything to keep your curls dry under a swim cap, maybe you've overlooked the one trick that champion divers use: a chamois band, 4 to 5 inches wide, wound around your head. Hair is pushed over band, the chamois is folded once, wrapped snugly, and fastened with a hook and eye or by tying the string attached to each end.

TEEN-AGE MAKE-UP TIPS

The barest minimum of make-up a youngster needs depends a great deal upon her individual coloring. To create a better color balance between skin and hair is the reason why anyone, young or old, wears make-up in the first place.

The vibrant brunette with fair skin will need only lipstick to complete her color contrast.

The girl whose hair, eyelashes, brows, and skin shades are almost the same tone will need more lipstick to break up the uniformity of color. She should be allowed (note to Mother) to wear a discreet touch of cheek rouge.

If a teen-ager's skin is gray or colorless (regardless of her color classification), she should use a make-up foundation and face powder to enliven her skin tone. Such a cosmetic aid can work wonders in building up a girl's self-confidence. The only time make-up should be ruled out is when the girl's skin is troubled, and this should be handled by a doctor.

The youngster who is to wear a foundation should be given a compressed cake type. This is the perfect blend of make-up base and powder and takes no skill to apply. No matter how inexpert she is, she can't use too much, layer it on, or look obviously made up while wearing it.

Make-up for young diploma takers or young girls otherwise under glaring lights: Nervousness and the auditorium's lighting can conspire wickedly against the girl graduate while all the world is wishing her well. Suppose she goes as pale as her white dress when she steps up on the stage? The remedy for that is prevention—a bluish-pink makeup.

Make-up to make a young girl look delectable is hardly more than a tinted powder. There is, however, a creamy base to make powder cling, to kill the shine on a soap-scrubbed face, to hide, if need be, any adolescent blemishes. With this make-up a pink or coral lipstick shade looks completely correct.

To keep the lighting from casting unwanted shadows, avoid letting strays mar the clean arch of her eyebrows. Remove stragglers and erase any eerie shadows. If brows are nondescript or pale, pencil lightly. Her face will take on more character, even for admirers in the very last row.

Clean up a ragged hairline too. Don't let her hair fall untidily over the brow or spray out in an uneven bang. Any such tuft can collect shadows, distort a face.

If you dress like a little girl, here are some make-up cues. Fashions inspired by a second-grader's bibs, sashes, jumpers, middy dresses, and "baby breath" petticoats call for as artless a look in make-up as in clothes. If a make-up technique is used, it should be almost invisible when the final effect is viewed. For this look of innocence, use a foundation as natural-looking as your skin. Ever so lightly, apply a bright, sunny-red lipstick, eyelash make-up, just a whisper of rouge.

If you're a teen-ager, accent your youth for all it's worth with the freshest appeal you can muster. If you're wearing a dark lipstick, give it away. A party-pink lipstick will bring out your youthful charm.

See that the fresh pink lipstick goes on as clean a face as you can bring up from the basin. If you need to kill a soap shine, puff on powder from a cream cake, which is gentle to a young skin. If there are adolescent blemishes to shush, the palest pink shade will help you keep your secret.

Teen-agers, want a face cleaning?
Cleansing the oily little face with its magnetic power for attracting blackheads often takes more than slushing suds or flourishing a washcloth over your face. To really clean a face when blackheads have burrowed in and caused mischief, there's a ritual to be performed:

Wash your face clean with soap and water. Then steam the blackhead area with a Turkish towel soaked in warm, almost hot, water. With finger covered with cleansing tissue, ever so gently press the flesh in a rather wide area around the blackhead until it eases out. After the eviction, apply strong rubbing alcohol to the opened pore with sterilized cotton as a precautionary measure against any kind of infection. The astringent action will also help the pore to normalize.

HOW TO BE A BEAUTIFUL BRIDE

If you'd be a lucky bride, here are some important suggestions that can help you to look your most beautiful on your wedding day. The most important thing to remember is to look your own, natural self. Never try to look like someone you have seen in pictures or at another wedding. If you are a glamour type, be a glamorous bride. Don't try to be a fragile beauty. If your beauty is of the fragile type, remain true to this beauty and don't try to be a glamour girl.

Plan the coiffure that you'd like to wear several weeks in advance and learn how to handle it properly.

Many girls make the mistake of having their hair set in a brand-new style the day before the wedding, and because it is unfamiliar, their nervous fingers don't know how to handle the curls and waves and the result is anything but beautiful. Often the style you are wearing at present is the best and will look the most beautiful when you don your veil.

Your make-up should appear natural. Apply all the beauty requisites that you usually apply for your own special occasions. Select them in shades that harmonize with your complexion. Your wedding day is no time to play with new tan or rosy foundation make-up shades, exaggerated eyebrows, or lip patterns. Likewise, the girl who is accustomed to applying many beauty requisites should not walk down the aisle looking like a ghost.

Select a fragrance that will surround you with an air of excitement but that will not be too heavy. A floral fragrance in the modern manner will be the best, for it will blend with the many blossoms in your bouquet and in those of your attendants.

Apply all your make-up before you put on your wedding gown. Nervous fingers often drop anything they hold, and a lipstick falling down over your spotless white dress would spell disaster. Allow yourself enough time for your make-up and hair, so that when your bridesmaids adjust your gown and veil, and you hear the music that will float you down the aisle, you'll be one of the most beautiful brides of the year.

Any woman who is going to have a color photograph taken before she weds can have a lovely portrait with the proper use of make-up. Powder or creme-puff your face generously and apply a bit more cheek rouge than you usually use. Make sure that the rouge does not have a blue cast. Blend the rouge carefully so there is no line of demarcation. Lipstick should be in a light or medium-clear red shade. Do not make your application too light, for it tends to turn orange; not too dark, for it will turn to blue or purple. Use eyelash make-up generously to outline your eyes and to make them sparkle.

SO YOU'RE GOING TO BE A BRIDESMAID

Color cues for bridesmaids. Don't take too literally the unwritten law that you must never outshine the bride. The more colorfully and excitingly the bridesmaids are dressed, the more breath-taking and ethereal, by contrast, the white-clad bride.

If the church is dimly lit, be careful of make-up shadows. The way to fight them is to wear a foundation that reflects a maximum of light. That would be a color lighter and brighter than your own skin. With it wear a little pastel cheek rouge (harmonized, of course, with lipstick and color of dress). Be sure, however, there's no blue undertone in your cheek rouge to look dark in

a half-lit church, casting unwanted shadows.

After all your make-up is on, including face powder, sponge your face with an astringent, pat skin with an astringent-dipped sponge wrung almost dry. This will make your skin luminously lovely, give it a sheen that will seem almost to glow in the darkness.

Wear a lipstick shade that's in harmony with the pastel coloring of your gown, but favor the brilliant shades of the clear reds, the bright reds, the pure reds, and the golden-flame shades. With little or no blue undertone, such lipstick shades will fight shadows, keep your lips from looking hard, sometimes black.

If you're a bridesmaid at a springtime or summer wedding in or out of doors, that puts another light on your make-up choice. Your cue, then, is to wear as natural-looking make-up as you would normally use. The more natural it is, the lovelier your skin will look in intense daylight. In that event, lipstick shades can have all the nuances of pink, orchid, coral, and bluish reds that bridesmaids' pastel gowns are apt to have.

MAKE-UP AND YOUR WARDROBE

Make-up plays supporting the color drama. Here's how to complement with make-up fashion colors such as:

Peanut. This fashion prima donna, acting in the gray-beige school of understatement, needs the color punch of a fiery lipstick, a rocket-bursting red. With it wear a radiant but light make-up foundation, green or blue eye shadow.

Scarlet. Give this fashion star a lipstick in an understudy red, pale cream or amber make-up foundation, green or blue eye shadow.

Yellow. Whether as golden as table butter or as greenish as chartreuse liqueur, yellow needs a strong support in make-up. To rout any sallowness from the skin, wear a golden-flame lipstick, a rosy-beige make-up foundation, green eye shadow.

Kelly green. Its perfect color support would be a redhead. Borrow her colors, then, and use a lipstick shade the color of a crushed rose, shamrock-green eye shadow, make-up foundation pink and creamy or magnolia white as a redhead's skin.

With a turquoise-and-violet combination of colors wear lipstick containing blue, a definite warm blue that has a rich overtone of red.

A brown, blue, and orange outfit should be worn with the reddest, hottest orange lipstick you own. Your most aggressive costume color, orange, must be played up with an almost matching bright lipstick of golden flame.

FOR THE TWEEDY TOUCH

When you wear tweeds, by all means wear a tinted make-up foundation. Choose and use it for enliv-ening skin color and glow, not for the thickness of its coating. To veil any little flaws, bring skin tones from hairline to an after-five neckline into one uniform tone; to impart an impeccable finish, all you need to use of it is a film as sheer as chiffon.

Choose a cake-type make-up foundation if your skin is normal or inclined to oiliness; a cream-type if you need a foundation to correct dryness and give you a soft, satin finish.

Wear rouge, too, with tweeds. This is one of the most feminine aids a woman can use to cope with the dull textures or neutral coloring of tweeds.

Best lipstick shade for tweeds is a red as fiery as the costume is "cool."

For the palette-pink, lilacs, honey-toned, and tawny tweeds get out your lipsticks in exactly matching or closely allied shades.

MAKE-UP TIPS FOR SLEEVELESS, STRAPLESS, OFF-THE-SHOULDER FASHIONS

Be sure every square inch of the skin you reveal is scrubbed every day as you shower or bathe. Use a soft bath brush, plenty of mild soap and warm water, and concentrate on the areas between your shoulders, the back and sides of your neck, the tips of your shoulders, the backs of your upper arms, your elbows, and your fingers. When you've finished, rinse off every bubble of soap and pat your skin dry with a soft towel. Before you retire, gently massage this skin area with hand lotion until the moisture disappears.

Until this part of your skin is in perfect condition, give your neck, shoulders, chest, arms, and hands a special dry-skin treatment at least three times a week. After your shower or bath, dot these areas with dry-skin cream and begin to massage it on with a silk sponge that has been dampened with water but pressed almost dry between the folds of a towel. Take about ten minutes for this ritual, or until your skin glows and tingles with renewed circulation. Remove any remaining or excess cream with tissues, pat your skin with bath powder, and retire.

Because all exposed skin must be the same color tone to be glamorous, choose make-up of the same color as your skin when you are going out to sun or swim. If it is of a different color, lighter or darker, you'll look as though you're wearing a mask. However, when you dress for a gala party and you want your skin to look a shade darker to highlight white or pastel gowns, or a shade lighter to emphasize the new feminine look, apply make-up blender or face powder to the exposed skin in the same color tone that you apply to your face. Blend it well below your gown's neckline, however, so that there will be no demarcation line.

BEAUTY FROM YOUR KITCHEN

Fruits, vegetables, and dairy products are not only good for you to eat—they can also do wonders for your skin and hair when applied externally. Your refrigerator and pantry contain the ingredients for homemade beauty preparations as effective as expensive commercial cosmetics—and you can eat the leftovers! Here are some natural beauty recipes you might like to try:

Farm-fresh skin care. Dry, reddened skin can be soothed by an application of the "milk" from scraped corn kernels. If skin is oily, rub a cut slice of tomato on it, allow the juice to dry, then rinse with cool water.

Another good astringent for oily skin is parsley tea. Steep a handful of parsley in boiling water for a few minutes, allow to cool to room temperature, and splash on face and neck.

A paste of steamed and puréed carrots is beneficial against acne and other skin inflammations. Spread the paste on inflamed areas, leave on for 30 minutes, then rinse with cool water.

Give yourself a delightful pore-opening facial by steeping fresh mint leaves in boiling water in a large, shallow enamel pan. Drape a bath towel over your head, bend over the pan, and let your face bask in the fragrant steam.

A **cucumber mask** gently cleanses the skin and, if used regularly, lightens and evens out skin tones. Grind up a large, unpeeled cucumber in the blender and strain the juice through a triple thickness of cheesecloth. Mix the juice with the whites of 2 eggs until smooth, then add 2 tablespoons of 90-proof vodka and 1 tablespoon lemon juice. For extra astringency, ¼ teaspoon of peppermint extract may be added.

Here's a recipe for a delectable, moisturizing avocado-honey mask: In a blender or electric beater, combine 1 tablespoon mashed avocado, 2 tablespoons raw honey, and 2 egg whites or 1 whole egg. Blend at high speed and smooth over your face.

Home treatment for dandruff. Apply hot olive oil several hours before shampooing. Shampoo scalp thoroughly with tincture of green soap, which you can buy at any drugstore.

A well-beaten egg blended with 1 cup of your favorite shampoo will give your hair extra shine and body.

Rinsing your hair regularly with sage tea after shampooing helps curb dandruff and is also said to darken gray hairs.

Lemon juice makes a safe, inexpensive, and easy-to-apply bleach, if your hair is already light. A mild preparation may be made with a cup of 15 percent alcohol, the juice of a lemon, and a drop or two of glycerine.

A natural body rub for soothing sore muscles may be made as follows: In an enamel saucepan, heat ¼ cup lanolin, ¼ cup sesame or safflower oil, and 3 tablespoons oil of wintergreen. Stir well and remove from heat. When cool, add ½ cup water and mix with electric mixer on high speed.

Mix your own delicious tooth powder by combining 2 tablespoons baking soda with 2 tablespoons powdered cinnamon and 2 tablespoons oil of cinnamon.

23

YOUR WARDROBE

How to choose and care for your clothes and shoes to be well-dressed on a budget

Multiply a small wardrobe. Have garments in colors that harmonize with one another and are interchangeable. Variety of removable dickies and scarfs will do wonders. Plan your wardrobe so that you can mix-match various sweaters, skirts, jackets, etc.

Accessory variations make a small wardrobe look like a million. Crochet hats, bags, gloves in season's newest colors. Important tip to budget-conscious gals: keep dresses, skirts, suits simple of line and in good basic colors that take on dressy or tailored look, depending on the trimmings.

Knit your own sweaters. You'll save money, look pretty, have fun making them. Take your old skirt along when you shop for yarn. Try various colors against it until you find the most flattering combination, perhaps even a perfect match.

Stoles and shawls are smart if length is correct for you. Make sure it is. It may even pay you to crochet them yourself. Stores carry mostly standard sizes that may not be the most flattering to you.

SHOP WISELY

Save without skimping. Watch for midseason and end-of-season sales. Make sure that sales are genuine, that reductions are genuine. Rely on the large department stores and on smaller stores with whose regular prices you are familiar.

A ready-made suit can be more costly than one custom-tailored. It happens often enough when a garment requires too many costly alterations. Any jacket needing alterations beyond adjustment of shoulder pads, sleeve length, or collar will usually cost more than it's worth. Skirt (or trousers) should not require anything but minor adjustments.

When buying washables, dresses and blouses that save time and money formerly spent on trips to the dry cleaner, stay away from garments with fussy detail, unless the fabric is permanent-press.

Nonwashable summer clothes need more frequent dry-cleaning than winter clothes because they continuously soak up perspiration and become dirt traps in this condition. Once perspiration stains are pressed into the material they become very hard to remove and cause yellowish-brown discolorations.

There's many a slip that doesn't quite fit your purposes. Inspect seams: double-sewn seams with turned edges are the best in fabric slips; overcast type the strongest in knit materials. Frilly styles may look pretty, but tailored ones last longer, as the fabric is usually stronger than the trim. As to fit, don't depend on strap adjustment for more than one inch. Also, try on the slip before removing label; size markings are not always a reliable guide.

Beware of the "one-way stretch." Sad to relate, the yarn is often deliberately overstretched by a few greedy manufacturers so that they can get more yardage. Any contact with moisture is ruinous because the fabric shrinks back to its true size. Best preventive is to spend a little more for garments of good quality. They usually pay, in longer, better wear and in the nice way they keep their shape. And deal with stores known to stand behind their merchandise.

"Problem" buttons. Some buttons are beautiful, but incompatible with dry-cleaning. These include colored plastic buttons that can't hold their shape or color. They may warp, let loose their coloring and stain the garments. Also beware of polystyrene buttons, which melt in steam; cardboard-base buttons, which get soggy; sharp-edged buttons, which may puncture fabric. If not sure about their composition, coloring, or cleaning safety, take buttons off before bringing garment to dry cleaner. In shopping, give preference to cleanable buttons wherever possible.

Test for lining color-fastness. To know beforehand whether the color of clothes linings will come off, rub a moist handkerchief over the lining. If any color shows on the handkerchief, look for another lining.

When purchasing women's coats, watch out for black interlining—the padding and filling between the lining and outer fabric. It is usually loosely dyed, not color-fast, and can stain the coat badly if steam or water should be necessary to remove a sugar, food, or perspiration spot. To avoid interlining troubles, ask specially for the colorless undyed interlining now made by several leading manufacturers. Nobody sees the padding, so dyes add nothing but possible trouble. Note: watch out, too, for black buckram, particularly in collars.

Synthetic fleece linings can be dangerous. Make sure they have been treated with a fire-retardant, for this so-called fleece can be highly flammable. After a washing or dry-cleaning, the fire-retardant will lose its power. It is best to keep such linings away from flames or heat.

Tight fits didn't "shrink at the cleaners," usually. If you are plump, get the size that gives you breathing space when you buy wools, sweaters, or any loose weaves like crepe, especially acetate crepe. Flat and close weaves are recommended, since they shrink hardly at all when dry-cleaned.

FLATTER YOUR FIGURE

Gently flared skirt is the most practical style, not only because it flatters most figure types but also it is the most versatile. Goes well with dressy or tailored blouses, sweaters, and jacket separates. Easy to make, attractive to wear.

Short girls look taller in straight or princess-style coats, simply tailored, or feminine dresses with straight or slightly flared skirts. Stick to smooth fabrics of solid color, small prints. Stay away from large sleeves, large purses, large-brim hats.

If you're tall, make the most of it. Enjoy wearing large hats and purses, wide sleeves and belts, full skirts. Wear gay plaid jacket with solid-color skirt, flare-back coats, and striking blouses and skirts in patterned fabrics.

Figure flattery for plump gals is achieved with smooth, soft fabrics of darker solid colors; jumpers, straight-line suits, coats with a little flare; V necklines and pointed collars. Avoid strong colors, large plaids, wide belts, full skirts, frilly trimmings.

Dress thin figure smartly in bulky materials, plaids, checks, feminine frills, and drindl skirts. Shun severely tailored, straight-line clothes.

The prettiest colors for you:

For brownettes: Greens, blues, blue-greens add more color. Tan, red, orange will camouflage freckles. Most pastels and dusty colors are more flattering than white.

For brunettes: Vivid shades and stark white do wonders. Bright, clear, warm tones are fine for those with high coloring. Cool green and blue-green tones add more color to the pale-skinned.

For blondes: Because hair tones vary widely, experiment until you find your best colors. Generally, blue, blue-purple, and blue-green are fine. Navy-blue and dark shades are better than gray and beige. Greens heighten natural color, rosy tones make it paler. Dark tones are more flattering than pastels.

For redheads: Deep or dark colors highlight hair, browns and orange-tans tone it down. White, pale blue, pearly gray, and soft, dusty pastels are most becoming. Light redheads should wear deep blues and blue-purple. Note about freckles: less obvious when wearing tan or orange-brown than with blue or green outfit.

A STITCH IN TIME

Save garment with clever embroidery trick. Cover a small hole in a blouse or dress with a pretty bit of colorful embroidery design, and actually profit by an accident to the fabric by giving the garment a new look. Cover frayed cuffs with a closely sewn blanket stitch and add matching touch at neckline.

Chain stitch has many uses as wardrobe-saver. Makes new button loops for those small under-the-collar buttons on coats, dresses, blouses. It's handy for inconspicuous belt loops, makes firm anchor between the coat lining and the outer fabric, allows the lining to hang freely so it doesn't bulge at the hemline.

Don't let yourself be embarrassed by a loose hem. Use the catch stitch to make it secure. Work from left to right on the wrong side of the dress or skirt, catching several threads of material above the seam tape. Pull thread through gently.

Have you a growing daughter? Let out the hems of her dresses at the end of the season, before they're cleaned or laundered and stored. When she's ready to wear them again and needs dresses a little longer, a new hem can be made without any telltale mark to show the position of last year's line.

When that ugly hemline shows, the nap or finish usually has worn off so that the line cannot be removed. Just cover the telltale mark with a narrow ribbon or braid resembling the present trimming. Or make a tuck with the old hemline concealed on the underside. The result is often prettier, smarter than before.

Save your coat from puckering. If it is sewed together at the hem, separate the lining and outer material. One or the other fabric may shrink; ugly, cheap-looking puckers and bulges are then caused by the shrinkage. For a smart, trim look, re-hem both outer material and lining and let them hang free at the hemline.

Friction foiler. Elbows of long-sleeved woolen dresses usually are the first to show wear. Reinforce these weak spots by sewing an oblong piece of lightweight fabric of the same color inside the elbow.

Line the pockets of trousers with chamois to protect them from tears made by nails, bolts, and small tools carried around by some men.

Protect rough-and-tumble knees of children and pants with knee patches that iron on. They're marvelous on playsuits, corduroys, overalls, blue jeans, work slacks, snow suits, ski suits, etc. Get the kind that will wash and dry-clean with garment.

ZIPPER SURGERY

To remesh a zipper that pulls out of the slider, remove the slider to the open end, hold it loosely, and insert end tooth on the pull-out side into the slider where it belongs. Be careful to hold flat the rest of the zipper in front of the slider, so that the two sides are exactly parallel and so close they almost touch. If you are holding them correctly, you can hold the ends of the tape as the slider pulls up and meshes the teeth.

When a zipper jams. You'll probably find that paper or thread particles are interfering with its free play. These must be removed patiently. Wherever an end of thread or fabric protrudes, pull it out gently. If the slider still jams, move it back and forth until you loosen the impediment. Always hold the slider by the tab. Never push, pull, or poke.

Zippers always work smoothly when teeth are rubbed occasionally with a bit of wax.

HOW TO COPE WITH SHINE, LINT, HAIRLINES

Remove shine from wool clothes. Sponge garment with solution of 1 teaspoon ammonia to a quart of water. Press on wrong side.

Another shine remover. Rub with a pressing cloth moistened with a mild vinegar solution, to raise the nap, then again moisten the cloth and use it as a regular ironing cloth for pressing.

Remove shine from serge, as well as worsted gabardines, flannels, and worsted wools in general, by dampening a sponge or cloth slightly and sponging the shiny parts quite thoroughly. While fabric is still damp, go over it, gently, with fine steel wool. Stroke the fabric with this, covering about 6 inches of the suit with each stroke. Results will amaze you, usually giving plenty of new life to an old suit. (Do not try this on cottons or rayons.)

Hairlines are danger lines on men's and women's clothes. Once that oil mark hardens in the fabric, it may prove impossible to remove completely. So, once weekly, clean coat-collar hairlines with a cleanser and brush briskly afterward.

Vaccum-clean clothes. Loose dust and dirt won't harden and cut men's and boys' suits if you take advantage of the small, stiff brush attachment that comes with most vacuum cleaners. (Be sure the brush itself is clean before using it on clothing.) Notice how it sucks out the dirt and, in tweeds and heavy woolens, revives the texture.

You like your serge suit but oh, that lint. Remove hair and lint by rolling up a magazine, wrapping some wide adhesive tape around it, sticky side out, then passing roller over the serge to get rid of annoying lint, threads, and hairs.

Remove lint from small area. Wrap adhesive or Scotch tape around your finger, sticky side out, then use as a pick-up.

ENEMY NUMBER 1 FOR CLOTHES: PERSPIRATION

Prevent underarm "mystery holes." Most deodorants are chemicals that may be gentle on the skin but, when freshly applied, may eat into the fabrics they touch. Remedy: when deodorant dries, dust underarm with talcum powder.

Dress color vs. perspiration. Don't let perspiration ruin those beautiful dress colors or weaken the fabric. Large-size dress shields give real protection, in addition to regular use of an underarm deodorant.

Remove arm shields before cleaning, because, if of doubtful quality, steam may soften and smear the rubberized fabric.

Perspiration can ruin coats, too. Tack lining-cloth shields in armholes of coats to protect against perspiration and wear.

Dress shields for men? Sure thing. Protect wool suits against perspiration rot by stitching over the armholes dress shields covered with fabric to match the coat lining. Remove shields when suit is ready for dry-cleaning.

GETTING THE HANG OF IT

Here's a trick up your nonexistent sleeve. To prevent sleeveless garments from slipping off wire hangers, bend up both ends of the hanger.

Anti-wrinkle tip. While it still retains body heat, put right on a hanger the suit or dress you've just taken off. The wrinkles will fall out more easily.

Prevent a trouser crease where it doesn't belong. To avoid a horizontal midway crease, put a newspaper over the hanger rod, then fold trousers over the paper.

Wire hangers won't rust-stain clothes if you wind cellulose tape around them.

Do wire hangers cave in under weight of heavy garments? Double their strength by binding two hangers together with cellulose or adhesive tape.

To prevent wooden garment hangers from snagging fabric give them a coat of clear shellac. Allow to dry well. Wood won't chip or sliver if protected this way.

STORAGE TIPS

Number the shirts. Shirts should be rotated so that each gets equal wear. Why not number each shirt inside the neckband, to help keep track?

Fade-out on fading. Clothes of aquamarine and some shades of blue, purple, and gray tend to fade. They'll stay their true color longer if you store them between wearings in a black cloth bag or in black wrapping paper.

To protect delicate lace articles, keep them beautiful and durable, wrap them in waxed paper. Prevents threads from rotting.

Angora sweaters, gloves, and scarves are beautiful, but how they shed! Unless you're in on this little secret: keep angoras in your refrigerator between wearings. Works wonders.

Fur protection. Fur will last lots longer, look much better, if the closet in which you keep it is humidified. Place inside the closet a bowl of water in which you've put a sponge. Renew the water before it evaporates.

Give extra protection, not only from moths but also from dust, to babies knit bonnets, winter leggings, jackets, angora mittens, sweaters, woolen hats and caps; to Argyle socks, ski suits. Make sure they're all clean, then wrap in a package of aluminum foil, also including a sprinkling of paradichloride crystals. If the garment is large, join several lengthwise pieces of the foil together, double-folding along the lengthwise edge so it is wide enough to take such things as ski clothes. Use a double fold in joining outer edges together also, forming an envelope that is airtight. This way garments really have absolute protection.

HOW TO STARVE MOTHS

Your mothproofing money's worth. Moth preventatives should be hung as high as possible in the clothes closet, because the fumes filter downward. Otherwise you get only partial protection.

Moths love woolens. Woolens don't love moths. One sure way to keep them apart in summertime is to store unused sweaters and other woolens in large jars stuffed with moth balls, the lid turned down.

Moths love grease spots too. That's why articles ready for storing should be dry-cleaned or laundered first.

Moth balls on a hanger. Drill two or three small holes near top of wooden-hanger beam. Press moth balls into holes and fix in place with strips of tape, so they won't fall out as they grow smaller. Pierce the tape with pinholes.

HOLD ON TO YOUR HATS

A flick of the hat will tell if it's properly dyed. At time of purchase flick the surface. If a cloud of powder rises, the dye job is imperfect.

To clean spot off felt hat. Tackle it while fresh, letting the stain dry, then rubbing lightly over the mark with a piece of fine sandpaper or an emery-board nail file.

To clean black or colored felt hat. Just rub over it with a piece of stale rye bread.

To clean white felt hat. Coat with a mixture of equal parts of corn meal, salt, and flour and let stay on overnight. Next morning brush out thoroughly.

To clean that Panama. Cover it entirely with a paste made of gloss starch. Put it out in the sun to dry. Then brush the hat thoroughly.

Got your hat caught in the rain? Don't hang it on a rack. Push out the dents, turn up the brim evenly, turn out the sweatband. Let hat dry on a level surface, then brush it.

To store hats, so that the crowns won't be crushed out of shape, crumple enough newspaper to fit into the crowns, then pack in boxes.

To keep beret shapely, after washing, put it over a large flat plate or over a pot cover, depending on the size of the beret. Remove when thoroughly dry.

A spare shelf for hats and other light articles can be made by tying rows of cord between screw eyes above the top shelf of your closet.

GLOVE-STRETCHERS

You'll get the most from leather gloves by checking information on label. Superior leathers (blackhead mocha, peccary, genuine kid) are usually marked. Leather should be soft and pliable. Glove should fit your larger (usually the right) hand. If fit is too snug, glove will wear out rapidly.

Stretch gloves. Insert glove stretcher or the metal portion of a curling iron (if you still have one) into each finger separately. Then, slowly and carefully, press stretcher handles so glove finger is taut. Repeat for each finger that needs stretching.

When repairing glove fingertips, slip thimble inside first. Makes sewing easier, assures retention of original shape.

HOSIERY-SAVERS

Cinderella complex is expensive. If you buy stockings too short for the foot, they'll wear through quickly because of strain. Won't be comfortable, either. Correct hosiery fit is yours if you buy hose a half inch longer than the length of your foot. Buy dressy sheers half a size longer than usual.

Wash nylons separately. Nylon has an affinity for dyes and will pick up color from other wet fabrics.

Easy way to prevent hosiery snags. Before washing hose or before putting them on, remove your rings and be sure your fingernails are smooth. A minute with a nail file or cuticle scissors (to get rid of hangnails) will save you stocking money.

Dyeing gives new life. Stockings of different shades can be matched for plenty of extra wear by dyeing them. Get a package of color remover and a package of dye you prefer. Follow instructions on the packages.

Another way to avoid throwing out one-of-a-pair is always to buy at least 2 pairs of the exact same kind at a time. This means you can go through 3 stockings before you are down to one.

Easy to pair. Sew a different colored thread at the top of each pair of stockings. This makes it easy to identify and pair them after washing.

Saves hosiery. If the leather on the inside of the heel of your shoe wears through, cover the hole with a piece of very flatly fitting adhesive tape. You will stop wearing holes in your hosiery.

Rainy-weather protection for sheer hose. Place strips of adhesive tape around inside of boots at top. Keeps them from leaving rings on your stockings.

Boots needn't snap at your hose. If zippers or other fasteners on the inside are roughened, cover those spots with layer of colorless nail polish. Use several coats of polish on fasteners and surrounding lining.

BEST SHOE FORWARD

Shoe-buying tip. One shoe salesman points out that it's best to shop for new shoes late in the afternoon, not in the morning. Reason: your feet spread as the day wears on, especially in hot weather and if you do a lot of standing or walking.

Another tip. Since one foot is often a trifle larger than the other, buy the size that fits the larger foot. If necessary, put an inner sole or a pad in the shoe of the smaller foot.

Double the life of your shoes by changing them daily. It's the airing between wearings that prevents perspiration from rotting the leather.

A shine in time preserves shoe leather and extends wear. Shine shoes before you wear them, and shine regularly thereafter.

Slippery shoe soles. You won't risk sliding around on those new shoes if you sandpaper the soles. Especially worth doing with a baby's new shoes. Or try this: rub a little linseed oil on the sole.

Silence squeaky shoes by piercing several small holes through the sole just in back of the ball of the foot.

Watch out for "builder-uppers." The shoe-repair man who fixes extra-worn sections of shoe sole by building it up beyond original thickness is the wrong man for your family's shoes. Such work is no money-saver. It just throws the shoe, and the wearer's posture, out of line, and can lead to serious problems.

Powder puffs make wonderful shoe-polish applicators. Keep one inside the can of wax shoe polish, where it won't dry out.

Lemon juice as a shoeshine works wonders. Spread a few drops on black or smooth, tan-leather shoes, then rub briskly with soft cloth. Gives elegant sheen.

Don't discard hardened shoe polish. Renew its usefulness by softening it with a little turpentine.

Substitute shoe polish. Use a little paste floor wax when you run out of shoe polish. Can be used on light or dark shoes because the wax color is neutral.

To clean shoebrushes, soak them in warm sudsy water to which a few drops of turpentine have been added.

Leather beautifier. Luggage, belts, chairs, and plain kid-leather shoes can be kept new-looking and clean by rubbing them with egg whites beaten to stiffness.

Simple leather-goods dye. To darken light tan-leather articles, such as belts, shoes, etc., rub with cloth dipped in ammonia. Gives a deep brown finish. Apply uniformly, so finish won't be spotty.

How to waterproof shoes. Apply hot ski wax to the leather, then rub in briskly with a stiff brush. After the wax is set, rub with a cloth. Keeps leather rainproof and springy.

Keep suede shoes new by rubbing them with a piece of stale rye bread or a rubber sponge after each wearing.

Stained suede shoes are easy to clean. First brush them to remove all dust particles, then hold the shoe over a steam-kettle spout long enough to raise the nap but not long enough to get the shoes wet. (A steam iron is wonderful for this, too.) Brush the nap with a soft brush and let the shoes dry before wearing them again.

Rain spots on suede. Rain spots will disappear quickly from suede shoes, bags, or hats if rubbed gently with an emery board such as is used in manicuring.

Stained kid shoes. Ordinary cuticle remover will usually do away with spots on kid shoes when regular cleaning fluid isn't handy. Moisten a cloth with it and rub over the spots, which disappear quickly.

Patent-leather shoes won't crack in cold weather, and they'll look lots better, if you rub a little petroleum jelly (Vaseline) over the surface, then polish with a dry cloth.

Clean fabric shoes, such as those made of satin, linen, etc., by rubbing them with a cloth dipped in a cleaning fluid such as carbon tetrachloride.

Keep white oxfords white by preventing the metal eyelets on the laces from discoloring the leather. Do this by coating the eyelets with a dab of colorless shellac.

If your white shoes have dark heels, apply coat of colorless nail polish to the heels. Allow to dry thoroughly. This prevents white cleaner from rubbing off on dark surface, and a damp cloth is all you need to remove any that spills over onto heels.

Clean white shoes neatly. Make mask out of cardboard cut in shape of shoe sole. Keeps soles free from cleaning material.

Gold, silver, and kid slippers tend to tarnish with exposure to air when not worn. To keep them glamorous and untarnished, wrap them after each wearing in black tissue paper or discarded black socks.

Mildew on leather shoes can be removed. Mildew, which might form if shoes haven't been worn for some time and the storing area is not dry, should be rubbed with petroleum ointment. The marks will disappear quickly.

Shoestring tip. When the metal tips come off the laces, dip the ends into hot paraffin and twist them, or harden tip ends with a little nail polish.

READY FOR A RAINY DAY

Raincoats: waterproof vs. water-repellent. Waterproof garments (plastic, rubber, oilskin) give greater protection but are likely to be uncomfortable in warm weather, since they're airtight. Underarm ventilation may help. Water-repellent coats have the advantage of doubling as topcoats in fair weather. And many of them, especially women's coats, are very stylish.

Dry waterproof coat at room temperature. Sunlight or direct heat tends to crack some raincoat materials. Hang coat from collar strap rather than on hanger, to avoid stretching out of shape or deterioration at points of contact. This is especially necessary for rubberized types.

Rubber footwear will last longer without cracking if, when not in use, it's kept standing erect by inserting rolls of cardboard. Laundry-shirt cardboards are excellent for the purpose.

24

LAUNDERING, CLEANING, IRONING

Laboratory-tested directions for taking good care of fabrics

Fabric, like human skin, deteriorates with dirt. Just as dirt-clogged pores cause skin blemishes, so dirt or perspiration lodged in fabric fiber weakens the threads and damages the texture. You keep fabrics healthy simply by keeping them clean. Let fabrics "breathe." Periodic airings help preserve most materials. Cottons can take the sun in varying degrees. White is always safer in the sun than colored materials of any kind. Silks, rayons, fiber blends are better off in the shade and should not be left outdoors too long.

Follow washing directions. Manufacturers are now required to print washing directions on labels permanently affixed to garments. Follow these directions carefully. Manufacturers spend a fortune in laboratory tests and research to give you the most accurate directions for cleaning your wearables and household fabrics. Lengthen fabric life, save money, avoid disappointment by using this valuable information.

Laundry reminder. Most clothes hampers are too small for large articles of family wash. Fasten memo inside the hamper cover to remind you of bedspreads, curtains, etc. Scotch tape will hold note in place and is easily removed.

If you have a laundry basket, line it with oilcloth or plastic sheeting to protect your wash from soiling or discoloration. Cut one piece to fit the bottom, another to line the sides. Make the side lining wide enough to allow about 2 inches to fold over the edge of the basket.

New things for old. Even the best of fabrics eventually wears out, so make a discard pile when sorting your wash. If that sheet or shirt seems ready for retirement, save the "fare" another trip to the laundry would cost. Salvage the fabric by making it into handkerchiefs, underwear, sun suits, house cloths, and other usefuls.

For best laundering results, sort clothes by grouping thus:

1. White cottons and linens with fast-color pastel cottons.

2. Dark, fast-color cottons and linens.

3. Fabrics requiring special care (wools, silks, rayons, nylons, etc.).

Do the less-soiled articles first, follow with the more heavily soiled pieces.

When sorting clothes before they go into washer, empty the pockets, examine for spots, stains, torn areas. Rips should be mended before washing, to prevent more tearing. Take off all removable trims and shoulder pads.

Cut laundering time. Brush off all loose dirt from surfaces inside pockets and trouser cuffs. Pretreat heavily soiled areas by use of brush dipped in soap or special detergent suds. Avoid overloading washing machine.

A few minutes can prevent many laundry accidents. Take time to close zippers so they won't catch on other articles and rip them. Mend rips, secure loose buttons, replace missing snaps, buttons, and other fastenings beforehand.

Protect the snaps. Have mercy on snap bindings. Fasten them together before putting through the wringer and they'll come out the way they went in.

YOUR LAUNDRY EQUIPMENT

Automatic washers and dryers require very little care other than exterior cleaning except when you use them for special jobs such as dyeing or starching. In that case the washer should have detergent added (not as much as when you have a full load in the machine) and be run through a complete cycle, to be sure you've flushed it out and let it clean itself. Wipe the inside of a dryer after drying starched items in it.

Washer-dryer combinations save space and save you the effort of switching your launderables from one machine to another. Treat them as both a washer and a dryer in caring for them.

Following use instruction booklet that comes with your appliance will give you longest possible service from the machine. Two causes of washer breakdown are overloading and using too much soap or special detergent.

You have a choice of several low-sudsing detergents now on the market and designed especially for automatic washers. For best results use amounts recommended on the package and in the booklet that came with your own machine. Don't guess; use a measuring cup.

Check your dryer lint trap and empty it whenever there's some accumulation of lint. Failing to do this not only decreases the efficiency of the appliance but could also be a fire hazard.

TIME- AND MONEY-SAVERS FOR LAUNDRY DAY

Save time on laundry day. Instead of measuring out soap, bleach, softener, etc., every wash day, put up proper mixtures in glass jars. You can prepare enough to last a few weeks.

Soap thrift. Save leftover slivers of soap in a jar. When jar is half filled, add boiling water, to make a jelly. It will come in handy for lots of pretreating and light laundering.

Remove stains before laundering article, because hot water and suds may set some stains so that they can't be removed later.

Rubbing fabrics with cake soap causes threads to slip or spread. Let the soapsuds and brush do the work instead.

Synthetic detergents have advantage over soap for use in hard water because they don't form curds. Some detergents form suds as readily as soap, others clean with little or no suds. If you live in an area where phosphate detergents are banned, you may need to add a softener to your water to get clothes really clean.

Add softener to rinse water as well as washing water if you have hard water.

Easy test for hardness of water. Hard water makes soap cling to clothes in sticky curd. Add ¼ teaspoon powdered soap to pint of warm water in quart jar. Shake. If no suds form, or if suds do not remain firm, the water is hard.

Solve your hard-water problem by consulting your city water department. Find out degree of water hardness in your area and ask what

chemical compound will most effectively soften the water in your locality. You may be advised, for very hard water, to have a water softener installed in your home.

Damp-weather odors sometimes cling to dish towels and dishcloths, and ordinary washing fails to remove them. As a remedy, try adding a little ammonia to the wash water. Leaves kitchen linens sweet-smelling again.

Too much thrift doesn't pay. Don't use badly soiled wash water at any time. Such saving of water and cleanser is poor economy, because articles in soiled water never look, or are, really clean.

Overwashed clothes may come out soiled. Prolonged agitation of your washing machine often drives dirt back into garments. For lightly soiled pieces, 5 minutes is usually enough. This holds true, not to overwash, even for heavily soiled articles. Never agitate washer longer than 15 minutes.

To soak or not to soak. Twenty minutes is plenty for cottons. Precaution: never soak rayons (swells fibers and traps dirt particles) or colored pieces (colors may run).

To remove clinging soap particles, when laundering at home, put a few tablespoonfuls of vinegar into the first rinsing water.

Chlorine bleaches are most effective in whitening cottons and linens. May also be used on color-fast colored cottons, since bleach, properly used, is not a color remover but a dirt loosener. Overbleaching and long soaking, however, weaken fibers and shorten length of service of articles bleached. So use it with discretion.

Rinse out the "blues." If you've gotten too much bluing into your wash, cheer up. Just rinse the clothes in clear water to which you've added a little vinegar.

Rinsing clothes well promotes health. Insoluble soap curd forms on fabrics not rinsed completely. This not only weakens the cloth but gradually builds a coating that can harbor and protect bacteria which cause skin infections.

There's no such thing as too much rinsing. A thorough job is necessary to wash out yellowing and dirt weakeners of fabric fiber. Water should be fully extracted after each rinsing.

Like velvety-soft bath towels? Who doesn't? Invest in one of the new laundry-conditioning liquids that goes into the final rinse when you launder. Follow container direc-tions for the amount to use. After the towels are dry you'll be amazed at the difference. Other laundera-bles are also improved when rinsed with the conditioner added, but the difference is most startling on bath towels.

Softener in the dryer? Yes, one of the newer washday aids is a prod-uct that you place in each load in the dryer and that makes the clothes feel softer and eliminates much of the "cling" due to the static electricity that builds up in dryers. (Most brands also promise a "fresh, clean smell," but this is merely a perfume.) Another attrac-tion is that you don't have to worry about pouring a softener in a par-ticular phase of the washing or rins-ing cycle.

WASH OR DRY-CLEAN?

In cleaning, follow the fabric's own preference. The following chart tells you whether washing or dry-cleaning is the natural requirement of given materials, also the best ironing procedure for each of the basic fabrics:

FABRIC	CLEANING METHOD	IRONING METHOD
COTTON	Wash. Check label for instructions on textured types.	Minimum pressing for embossed surfaces. While still damp, press on wrong side with hot iron.
LINEN	Wash. Household bleach is all right for white table linens, bedclothes.	Iron on wrong side, while damp. Go easy on crease-resistant lin-ens.
SILK	Outer garments usually dry-cleaned. Wash only if recommended by instruc-tions. Guard against perspiration dam-age. Don't hang in sun to dry.	On wrong side, with moderate iron.

FABRIC	CLEANING METHOD	IRONING METHOD
WOOL	Outer garments usually dry-cleaned. Sweaters, etc., should be washed carefully in lukewarm water, mild suds. Never soak or rub. Dry flat. Air frequently; brush after wearing. Clean before storing.	Steam-press, when necessary. Use cloth between article and iron.
RAYON	Consult label to determine washability. Mild suds, warm (not hot) water. Rinse with extra care. Brush. Air often to avoid mildew.	Moderate iron on wrong side.
ACETATE	Launder at low temperature. To avoid permanent wrinkles, don't wring.	Use low-heat iron.
NYLON	Generally washable, but may be dry-cleaned. White garments will retain whiteness if washed often. Special bleaches available if they begin to "gray." Mild soaps or detergents recommended.	Requires little pressing. Use moderate iron.
DACRON	Used in blends and washable if other fibers in mixture are. Medium-hot water. Check label.	Depends on other fibers in blend. Consult label.
ORLON	Wash in moderate-to-hot water. Drip-dry if pleated.	Low temperature, requires little pressing.
ARNEL or ACRILAN	Wash in moderate-to-hot water. Drip-dry if pleated.	Low temperature, requires very little pressing.

Just how warm should the water be for the various basic fabrics? Here are the easy-to-go-by general rules:

HANDLE WITH CARE

Most woolens may be laundered successfully if not exposed to exces-

FABRIC	WATER TEMPERATURE	OR IN OTHER WORDS:
WHITE COTTONS AND LINENS (machine washing)	140° F. and up.	Much to hot for hands.
WHITE COTTONS AND LINENS (hand washing)	120° F.	As hot as hand can bear.
FAST-COLOR COTTONS, LINENS, NYLONS	110° F.	Warm or comfortable for hands.
SYNTHETICS	100–110° F.	Lukewarm to warm.
SILKS AND WOOLENS	95–100° F.	Lukewarm. Feels neither hot nor cold to wrist or elbow.

sive heat or strong detergents. If still soiled after brief washing, it is best to wash again, for a short period, in fresh suds. Rinse twice in water of same temperature as wash water. Press out moisture by gently squeezing. Do not wring. Roll in bath towel. (Check fabric at time of purchase. Don't try to wash it unless label recommends it.)

When washing sweaters, sew buttonholes together first, so they won't stretch during laundering.

Your hand-knit garments will stay in shape with home care. Wash in mild suds, then pat into proper size and shape. Dry thoroughly. When dry, hold steam iron an inch above garment, then move slowly back and forth over entire surface until steam penetrates it thoroughly, never actually touching the garment with the iron.

To wash corduroy, use lukewarm water and mild suds. Lift up and down in the water. Rub badly soiled parts with a very soft brush or with the palm. Rinse in clear water, then hang up wet without squeezing or wringing out the water. While drying, shake occasionally. When thoroughly dry, raise the nap by stroking with a soft brush in the same direction as the ribs run. An automatic dryer is ideal for drying corduroy, fluffs up the nap as it dries.

Handkerchiefs come out whiter and stay fresh longer if you place a little borax in the laundry water. Borax gives fabric just enough extra body to withstand soiling too quickly.

Whiten discolored handkerchiefs by immersing them in cold water to which you've added a pinch of cream of tartar.

Dainty lingerie and blouses should be hand-washed without soaking. If shoulder straps, band, hems, etc., are more soiled than rest of garment, pretreat with soft hand brush and mild suds.

Laundering of small lace things. To keep from tearing the dainty threads, put collars, cuffs, and other small pieces of fine lace in jar containing lukewarm suds. Shake the lace around in the jar, then empty it and refill with clear water. Return the lace and rinse by shaking the jar again. Rinse several times, until water is clear. Remove and roll the lace in a bath towel until almost dry. Then press gently with a warm (not hot) iron.

A trick in washing delicate lace that insures the best result is to wrap it around an empty milk bottle. Fasten the ends and dip the bottle up and down in soapy water. Then rinse by dipping in clear water.

Best cleansing agents for fine fabrics and hosiery. Mild soap (in soft or softened water) or mild synthetic detergent (in hard or soft water).

Anti-snag suggestions. When washing stockings, remove all your rings other than a plain band. If your fingernails are razor-sharp, better use thin rubber gloves.

White nylon won't yellow from washing to washing if you use bluing when laundering nylon shirts, blouses, underthings, and the like.

To wash leather gloves (when washable) use lukewarm water and mild soap, leaving some soap in the glove to keep the leather soft. Don't rinse too much.

When washing doeskin or chamois gloves, add a few drops of olive oil to the water. Keeps gloves soft and pliant.

Roll gloves off your hands after washing, don't pull them off. Pulling stretches the glove fingers.

To wash feather pillows. Swish them around in the washtub or bathtub in lukewarm water and mild suds. Neither soak nor scrub the pillows. Rinse gently in clear lukewarm water by swishing them around again. Hang outdoors to dry in a spot that is shady and breezy, or dry them in your automatic dryer. Caution: don't overdry.

10 TRICKS IN WASHING BLANKETS

Your blankets will be soft, fluffy, and really clean if simple laundering rules are observed:

1. Select a wash day, if you haven't an automatic dryer, when the sun isn't too hot and the outdoor temperature is above freezing.

2. Measure the blanket.

3. Go over soiled binding areas with soft brush dipped in warm mild suds and water.

4. Dissolve soap or detergent in warm washing water before putting in blanket, if this is possible with your washer. If not, and washer has a soap dispenser at the top, don't add soap or detergent until blanket is wet through.

5. Wash only 1½ minutes, let rinse, and spin-dry 3 minutes.

6. Measure blanket again after washing and stretch it to its original size.

7. Two parallel, taut lines are better than one for blanket drying. Don't fold blanket or use clothespins. For dryer drying, add several dry Turkish towels with the blanket. They act as buffers and speed drying. Don't let blanket become completely dry, regardless of drying method, line or machine.

8. When blanket is almost dry, stretch again and brush the nap all over, on both sides of the blanket, with a stiff brush.

9. Final step. Press the binding with warm iron and pressing cloth.

10. Blanket trick. The next time you wash your wool blanket try this: To the final rinse water add 1 tablespoon of household ammonia. This makes the blanket really fluffy and raises the nap so that it looks and feels like new.

COLOR CARE

Even color-fast fabrics need care in handling. The enemies of color-fastness are: excessively hot water, extended exposure to the rays of the sun, and soaking.

Color-fast articles may lose a little dye in the first laundering. Wash each piece separately the first time, so you won't chance dye transfer to other launderables.

Art of laundering colored garments: Never soak them; the colors may bleed or run. The danger is the same if you leave them lying wet. Don't dry colored fabrics in the sun, as they may fade. Prints or colors should not be ironed in double thicknesses. To avoid streaks and wanderlust colors, don't hang colored garments or iron them while too damp.

Set with salt. Common table salt is good for setting most colors, but Epsom salts are better for washing and rinsing delicately colored materials. Dissolve 1 teaspoonful of the salts to each gallon of water. The most delicate shades will not run or fade.

To make bright colors stay bright. When laundering colored garments, prevent them from graying by adding a tablespoon of vinegar to the next-to-the-last rinse.

Black and blue. When washing black or navy-blue lingerie, add a teaspoon of bluing to the water. This preserves the dye far longer than laundering in plain water.

Don't weep over faded curtains. Renew them by putting a tint dye in the washing machine with the soap or detergent. They also dye more evenly than when dipped.

HANGING HINTS

Hang 'em right. They'll wear longer, iron easier. Hang clothing on line at the strongest part: men's shirts, women's dresses, by the hems; shorts by waistband; men's cotton knit shirts by shoulders; socks and stocking by toes. Avoid hanging any articles by their corners.

For pillowcases, towels, etc., turn about 6 inches over the line and pin. Hang sheets over line with hems together, after shaking them out straight. (To help smooth out sheets, run your fingers down selvage edge while folding.)

Their place in the sun. White clothes dry well in sunshine. Colored clothes are less likely to fade if hung in the shade.

Slow clothes drying preserves color in garments much better than quick-drying methods.

Prevent colored clothes from fading by hanging them wrong side out after laundering.

Sheets won't wrinkle when drying if you hang them on the line dripping wet. The weight of the water pulls them down and practically does the ironing and straightening for you.

Remember to dry all curtains in the shade. Direct sunlight will weaken most curtain fabrics.

Woolens will hate you if you dry them in cold temperature. To keep them soft and pliant, let them dry in a warm atmosphere.

Hang slacks or trousers by the cuffs when they are drying. Weight of the wet garment will take out most of the wrinkles and reduce ironing time.

Two life savers for blankets. Never hang out to dry when the winds are strong. Never hang out in really cold weather.

Blankets won't shrink if, after washing, you dry them on curtain stretchers.

Stockings won't get tangled on an outside clothesline on a windy day if you drop one or two marbles in each stocking before hanging out to dry. The marbles will provide enough weight to stop the wind from tangling the hose but not enough to pull the stockings out of shape.

Avoid humid-weather mildew. Don't leave any dampened articles out longer than 24 hours in damp weather. If you don't plan to iron right way, allow articles to dry completely; sprinkle when ready. Or keep them in your home freezer or refrigerator, after sprinkling, wrapped in plastic sheeting or enclosed in a zippered plastic laundry bag.

New wooden clothespins have longer life if you pour boiling water over them and let them stand until the water is cold. Toughens them and prevents splitting.

Clothesline antifreeze. Does your laundry freeze to the line in winter? Prevent this by dipping a cloth in strong salt-water solution and wiping the line with it. A little salt in the last rinse water will also help.

Rustproof the clothesline. If yours is a wire clothesline, your worst enemy is rust. Disarm the enemy with a nice coat of white varnish at least once a year, preferably in the spring. If the line has already started to rust, sandpaper the rust spots, then use two coats of varnish.

You won't have to keep bending over or move back and forth when hanging up your wash if you'll keep clothespins in a large towel pinned at its ends or in an inexpensive clothespin bag hung over the line. Another trick is to wear an apron with deep pockets and fill them with clothespins before you begin to hang out your wash.

Your hands won't get chilled and stay that way while hanging out clothes in cold weather if you keep a hot-water bottle among the clothes in the basket.

Save your energy when hanging out clothes. Be sure clotheslines are strung at proper height for you. Place clothesbasket on stool or rack.

MORE ABOUT RIGHT DRYING

Unroll garments immediately after towel drying. Leaving them rolled up for any length of time may cause rot, mildew, and other damage.

Streaks will be avoided and moisture will evaporate evenly if you'll dry silk stockings on damp towels.

Washable knit woolens will keep their shape if dried by blocking back to shape on special stretchers. Never put them in automatic dryer.

Knitted garments should never be hung over a line or fastened with clothespins. Let them dry flat and they'll keep their shape.

If you're in a hurry to use the sweater you washed, place it in a Turkish towel and press out excess moisture with a rolling pin.

To make sure knitted mittens and sweaters go back to their original size after laundering, outline them with chalk on a galvanized window screen before laundering. Then stretch back to indicated size, when washed, by pinning down with small nails.

A washed sweater will not stretch if you rinse it in a colander and squeeze out the excess water very gently.

If you haven't a form on which to stretch washed gloves, use an old curling iron. It will do the job of stretching the fingers before they are thoroughly dry.

Or insert ordinary clothespins in the fingers of laundered gloves. This will prevent fingers from shrinking. This is especially true if they have been washed in the usual manner with soap and water.

No stretcher for lace curtains? You'll do all right if you'll put them back on the rods while the curtains are wet, then slip a second rod through the lower hems to weight them down.

To make a drying rack for small articles, sew spring paper clips to tape on an ordinary clothes hanger.

If you use the neighborhood laundromat, take a plastic pillowcase to tote home your damp clothes. They'll stay nicely damp until you get ready to iron them.

SPRINKLING

Sprinkling cuts ironing time, if not overdone. If clothes are too wet, ironing becomes more difficult, takes longer.

An even sprinkling means a smoother finished job. Use a bottle with perforated metal top. Sprinkle with warm water, which spreads more evenly than cold water. Sprinkle pieces individually, folding and rolling each one carefully to eliminate as many wrinkles as possible. If sprinkled wash must remain rolled up overnight, place in the refrigerator to prevent mildew.

A real ironing shortcut is to hang on one line all clothes to be sprinkled. When they're dry, sprinkle with fine-spray garden hose, all at once. Then roll up each piece as you remove it from the line.

Sprinkling small, flat pieces takes less time if all pieces of similar size are shaken out and placed in pile. Sprinkle about every third piece, roll together, smoothing fabric as you go. Roll tightly.

Homemade clothes sprinkler. Punch a few small holes into the screw top of a jar. Fill the jar with water and you have handy ironing aid. Use the same way as a salt shaker.

TIPS FOR IRONING

When ironing fine fabrics, don't use too hot an iron. Hurts the fabric, sometimes badly.

Tablecloth tips. To give a smart professional look to your tablecloths, remember to press the center crease only. All other folds are best made by hand, since ironed creases don't lie flat on the table.

So the fabrics won't split, occasionally change the creases from halves to thirds when ironing tablecloths and other large, flat pieces.

To keep linens neat, insert a piece of cardboard, the size of the folded article, between the folds of each piece. Then, when you remove one article, the others are not wrinkled or disturbed.

To iron embroidery properly, turn it face down on a Turkish towel, then press on the wrong side. Brings out the depth, instead of

flattening it. Use the same method for braided trimming.

Steam iron keeps accessories and high-fashion garments looking lovely longer. Velvet, velveteen, corduroy, and suède, all high in the fashion picture, are pile fabrics. Dresses, coats, hats, bags, and even shoes of these materials will keep their attractive finish longer with steam treatment. Hold steam iron just above fabric and allow steam to penetrate and raise the nap.

Distilled water is best for steam irons. If you run out of it and have the kind of refrigerator that requires defrosting, collect the defrosting water in a bowl or pan to use in your steam iron.

Turkish bath keeps velvet new-looking. Steaming velvet is the easiest way to remove wrinkles and to lift crushed parts. Place the velvet garment on a hanger in a steamy bathroom for an hour, then let it dry. Be sure it hangs free, perhaps from a shower bar, so that nothing touches it until the velvet is entirely dry. Small garments or velvet pieces may be steamed over the spout of a teakettle.

No shine wanted, thank you. When pressing woolen materials with a damp cloth, don't iron until the fabric is completely dry, for this causes shine. Press quickly, then allow the steam to rise. This brings up the nap marvelously.

Collar shiny? Sponge it first with vinegar, then press on the wrong side. No more shine.

Your dark cottons won't pick up lint from ironing board if you use this trick. Before starting to iron, go over the cover with a damp cloth or sponge, a wide piece of cellophane tape, or some adhesive tape wound around your hand, sticky side out.

When ironing double thicknesses, such as collars, cuffs, pockets, hems, iron first on the wrong side, then on the right side.

To prevent wrinkling clothes while ironing, do the small parts first, in this order: trimmings, collar, sleeves, back bodice, front bodice. Skirt part of dress should be the last.

Bias-cut skirts, dresses, will never develop wavy hemline if properly ironed with the weave of the cloth.

In pressing a pleated skirt, keep the pleats flat by using a loop of string attached to a weight object. Press up to the string and then remove it before finishing.

Pin before you pleat. To iron pleated skirts, first press hem on wrong side, then on right. Place on ironing board and pin pleats, at intervals of 3 or 4 inches, to the board pad. Be sure not to catch the fabric where pins will show. Iron from the top to the bottom of the skirt. Remove the pins as you go; do not iron over them.

Another neat trick for pressing pleated skirts: place a sheet of sandpaper, rough side up, on the ironing board, to hold pleats in position. When pleats are formed, re-move the paper, to avoid making impressions in the cloth.

To avoid ridges when pressing heavy seams, slip strips of paper under the loose ends before spreading a damp cloth over the area.

Scorches are not always a tragedy. If you've scorched an article lightly, lay a piece of wet cloth over the scorched spot and iron over it several times. Scorch often disappears, or almost does.

A man's white shirt, when scorched, should be sponged with a cloth dipped in peroxide, then ironed again, over the blemished area, with a clean dry cloth over it.

Scorch on cottons may be removed by wetting the spot with water, then covering it with a thick paste made of starch and water. Let it remain on until dry, then use a clean cloth and peroxide to sponge it off. Press the article again and hang it in the sun for several hours.

Scorched linens. If linen scorches during ironing, cut an onion in half and rub the flat side over the mark. Then soak the linen in cold water for several hours.

Scorched woolens. To remove the blemish, wet the spot and then rub dry cornstarch over it. Brush off the cornstarch when article is dry.

TIPS THAT LIGHTEN LABOR

You needn't get tired ironing. Sit down on the job. If you buy a new ironing board, get an adjustable one and regulate it to the height of your chair. If you use a stand-up board, sit on a stool that is high enough to bring you up to height of board. Be sure the chair or stool has a proper back rest to avoid fatigue. Save steps, too, by placing a board near the table for flatwork and by having a small clothesrack handy for skirts, blouses, etc.

You'll be even less tired if you use an ironer, which speeds up the work. You need only a little practice before you'll be as adept at running an ironer as you are at using your other household appliances.

Save money you'd spend for tailor's services with new "steam and dry" type of iron. You'll recover the purchase price many times over. Steam section will do wonders for woolens. Simple button switch to "dry" provides the best method for ironing linens, heavy cottons, silk, and rayon.

Don't take chances with frayed ends of extension cords. Wrap several rubber bands over the frayed ends, to avoid a short circuit when ironing, or possible further damage.

Prevent breaks in the insulation of an iron cord at the bends where it hangs over the ironing board, or at the wall outlet, by wrapping with cellulose tape at these points.

No crossed wires. Fasten a large blanket pin to the side of the ironing board, put the iron cord through the pin, and it will slip freely back and forth as you iron,

without tangling or getting in your way.

Look at cord-minders too. These clamp on your ironing board, hold the cord a couple of feet above the board, out of the way when you iron.

If your iron sticks during pressing, add a small lump of butter or lard to the starch and the iron will move smoothly.

Remove starch that has collected on your iron. Rub the hot iron over a piece of brown paper on which you've sprinkled salt.

The ironer shoe may occasionally have a little starch stuck to it. You can remove it with a mild abrasive or fine steel wool, but treat it gently.

Keep pressing cloths in a cloth pocket tacked to the ironing board so you won't have to chase around looking for the cloths.

Suspend a whiskbroom underneath your ironing board so that it will always be handy when you have to press garments that have not been brushed.

Sponge rubber is kind to your feet. When special jobs make it necessary to stand while ironing, stand on sponge-rubber mat. You won't get nearly as tired as usual.

If long pieces fall on the floor, try a card table underneath the ironing board and the problem is solved.

You can make a good sleeve board by rolling up several large magazines, tying at the center and ends, then padding with an old Turkish towel and slipping into a cover made of muslin.

Ironing-board holder can be improvised with a towel bar to keep the board standing upright when stored in a closet. Attach bar to wall at a height that will allow the board to be slipped under it easily. Stores board in minimum space.

Make rack for freshly ironed clothes. Twist a wire hanger into a square shape, so that hook part can be secured over the top of a door or a high shelf. You'll have a hanger rod several inches long.

Your ironer roller needs to have its cover laundered occasionally, the padding removed to give it a chance to breathe a little before you reassemble roller covering.

Allow your hand iron to cool before putting it away. Then wind the cord around it neatly, in order to get longest life from the cord.

25

SPOTS AND STAINS

How to remove the most common ones and save many dollars in cleaning bills

With proper attention to the storage of some of the cleaning materials, and respect for them while applying them, removing spots and stains at home can be a safe procedure. But safety must be stressed. Some of the substances are flammable and/or poisonous, and others are at least harmful to the skin. You cannot afford to take the slightest chance, especially if there are children around the home.

For about the cost of dry-cleaning a single garment, you can own a handy kit containing these most often needed:

1. White vinegar, for dissolving acid stains.

2. Ammonia, for "spotting" that requires an alkali.

3. Neutral detergent; there are numerous good ones at your grocery store.

4. Glycerine, a wet-cleaning lubricant.

5. Petroleum jelly or white mineral oil, for use as a dry-cleaning lubricant.

6. Hydrogen peroxide, for stains that require a mild bleach.

7. Amyl acetate (banana oil), available at your drugstore.

8. Mild castile soap, available at your drugstore.

9. Grease solvent; there are several to choose, either by chemical names or by trade names. All are poisonous and some are flammable, so follow directions carefully.

10. Chlorine bleach, for stains requiring a strong bleach.

11. White blotting paper, or paper toweling.

Don't try home cleaning methods on these fabrics: rayon taffeta, heavily sized nets, spun rayons that contain resin or sizing, flock-printed fabrics. In these cases your dry cleaner has better resources than you could possibly command.

Help your dry cleaner do his best. When taking a stained garment to your dry cleaner, be sure to attach a note indicating stained area and explaining type of stain if you know its origin.

KNOW YOUR FABRICS

Know when to stop. Know your fabric and how much punishment it can take; certain fabrics can be rubbed, worked on a good deal without fiber damage, others cannot. If fabric is not the type to respond readily to home treatment, don't even start on it, or you may do more harm than good. If fabric is type to waterspot, don't try a home method calling for use of water.

Wool is least temperamental. This is the easiest fabric to work on, because the fiber is soft and pliable and spots often lie right on the surface. The spongy, elastic quality of the fiber makes it easy to work on without rubbing a hole. Because the weave is relatively porous, stains can usually be "flushed out" without too much trouble. Acid solutions usually work best on wool.

Cottons are usually harder to "spot" than wool, and the dyes generally are not as resistant to the friction involved in spotting. Many cottons can't even be dry-cleaned. One precaution is to check the fabric carefully at time of purchase as to cleaning qualities. Types that have too much sizing don't even wash well, as a rule.

Silks, surprisingly enough, have many of the same easygoing dry-cleaning properties as wool. They respond well to spotting and dry-

cleaning. However, certain shantungs are susceptible to loss of color from rubbing, and others will bleed in plain water.

Synthetic fabrics. Rayon, a soft fiber, is used to a great extent in clothing. Watch out, however, for rayon-taffeta weaves, as considerable sizing is often used to provide added body, making spotting very difficult. In many cases this stiffening dissolves in plain water. Moreover, alkalies often cause rayon dyes to bleed. Acetates, however, have hard fibers and make better material for taffetas. Acetate dyes, however, will bleed in the presence of acid solutions.

Buckram linings. Black buckram will bleed its dye severely in plain water and stain the surrounding fabric badly. The stain will prove just about impossible to remove thereafter. Examine garments for such linings and avoid them where possible.

DO'S AND DON'TS THAT SAVE FABRICS, DOLLARS AND DISAPPOINTMENT

Play it safe. Work in good light. And be sure no flames are present when using flammable solvents.

Test resistance of fabric colors to the cleansing agent being used. Find inconspicuous area in seam or inner layer of double facing, etc., on which to make test. If a separate swatch of fabric happens to be available, so much the better.

Protect your hands, and do a better job when dry-cleaning your own dainties, by using a wire potato masher as a plunger to gently force liquid through the cloth. Or buy a special little cleaning machine equipped with its own no-hands plunger.

Work as quickly as possible. Repeated brief applications of cleansing materials are best. Using too strong a solution and permitting it to remain on stain for too long a time can damage the fabric.

When directions call for small amount of cleansing agent, such as ammonia, vinegar, etc., stretch stained area over a bowl or beaker containing cold water and apply with eye dropper.

Use alkalies warily. Alkalies, especially strong or caustic soaps, should never be used on animal fibers. For instance, alkalies are generally destructive to wool and silk.

Mineral acids are harmful to vegetable fibers like cotton, linen, rayon, etc. Sulfuric and hydrochloric acid are mineral. Nitric and oxalic acid will also attack cellulose fibers if dried into material.

After using any substance for stain removal, rinse it thoroughly from the article before drying or pressing.

To prevent permanent fiber damage, avoid excessive friction, especially with silk and rayon. Apply the necessary stain removers to these fabrics with a soft brush. Where some rubbing or other form of fabric friction is called for, especially on delicate fabrics, work on reverse side of material.

White kid gloves sometimes turn yellowish after several cleanings. Avoid this by adding a teaspoon of powdered borax to the cleaning fluid.

To bleach out dyes that have bled to other portions of garment (usually caused by excessive soaking or the use of too much alkali or acid): Start dye bleeding again. Use ammonia in the rinse water. If it bleeds on acid side, use some white vinegar in the water. In some cases you may be able to do the job by soaking in a solution of detergent and water. Continue until discoloring dye is cleared away. Then rinse thoroughly in cold water to loosen any remaining dye. The dye must then be set with an acid (such as vinegar), or an alkali (such as ammonia), in water. In some cases salt in the water will set the dye. The use of acid or alkali depends on what caused the dye to bleed in the first place. If it bled with an acid, set the dye with an alkali-and-water-solution, and vice versa. For example, if dye bleeding is caused by soap (an alkali), clear away the dye with an alkaline solution (such as ammonia and water), then set the fabric's original dye after rinsing with a slight acid-water solution (such as white vinegar and water).

TERMS USED IN DIRECTIONS FOR STAIN REMOVAL

Bleeding. Loss of dye. If fabric is not color-fast, the dye may be loosened from the fabric under certain conditions (as when soaked in water). The color then is said to "bleed."

Feathering out. A way of treating stains that avoids a spotting ring on fabric. Whether you wet-clean or dry-clean, the outer edge of the saturated area must be allowed to dry gradually toward the center, to eliminate the ring. Do this by wiping the outer edges vigorously with dry cloth. A hand blower or hair dryer is helpful in drying the outer edge before a ring develops.

Flushing out. Removing stain by working it free from fabric by brushing, rinsing, etc.

Sizing. A stiffening agent used in fabrics. Sometimes fabric itself is weighted with resinous or other substances. Sometimes it comes in separate stiffening fabrics, such as buckram, employed to give extra firmness to collars, facing, belts, etc.

Spotting. The actual process of removing spots and stains. Methods of "spotting" include:

Lubrication. Using cleansers with oil bases.

Solvent action. Use of so-called "wet" and "dry" solutions for dissolving stains.

Mechanical action. Scraping, rubbing, brushing, etc.

Wet-cleaning and dry-cleaning. Terms to indicate whether a specific stain responds to treatment by so-called "wet" or "dry" cleansing agents. Wet cleansers are liquids, the most important being water. Dry ones contain no actual moisture, even when in liquid form.

SPECIFIC SPOT-REMOVAL DIRECTIONS

Acids (wet-clean). First rinse with cold water. If any solid substance is imbedded in stain, you may have to flush it out with a fairly concentrated solution of neutral detergent. If acid is strong mineral type (such as hydrochloric or sulfuric battery acid), follow cold-water treatment with application of ammonia to completely neutralize it. Such strong acids will quickly damage cotton, rayon, etc. Wool is more resistant, but sufficient acid concentration can also damage it. Color changes caused by acid stain can usually be neutralized with household ammonia and water.

Adhesive tape (dry-clean). Usually easy to remove with grease solvent or some amyl acetate. After treating stain, rub rather vigorously with clean cheesecloth to avoid ring.

Alcoholic beverages (wet-clean). Rinse immediately from fabric with cold water, especially if fabric is cellulose acetate, because acetate yarns bleed profusely in alcohol and loss of color often results.

Since alcohol is readily soluble in water, it will come out easily. If other food substances are present, remove with neutral detergent.

Ammonia stains (wet-clean). Ammonia may bleed dye or cause color change. Color changes can be corrected by applying white vinegar and water to affected area.

Axle grease (dry-clean). Unless grease spot contains dirt, a grease solvent does the trick quickly. Should stain appear to be rather heavy, lubricate first with white mineral oil, then flush from fabric with grease solvent.

Blood (wet-clean). If fabric can withstand plain water, soak it first in a pan or bowl of cold water, or between two wet towels. Add about ½ teaspoon neutral detergent to soaking bath. When using towels, apply concentrated solution of detergent to the stain itself, this usually being enough to remove it. If stain still persists, apply small amount of household ammonia to area and rub between your fingers (unless fabric is acetate), or use back of comb to help break up stain. Flush from fabric as necessary. Hydrogen peroxide can also be effective, if fabric can stand such bleaching.

Bluing (wet-clean). Soak stain in solution of water to which you've added ½ teaspoon of neutral detergent and about 1 ounce of household ammonia. Soak for about an hour if color of fabric permits, then launder. If any of the stain remains, next step is bleaching. For rayon, cotton, or acetate, use weak solution of chlorine bleach. For silk or wool, use hydrogen peroxide.

Butter (dry-clean). Sponge out with grease solvent. When dry (a matter of seconds), sponge out remaining traces of stain that may be water-soluble (such as salt) with solution of water and neutral detergent.

Candle wax (dry-clean). Scrape off surface wax with dull knife. Heat small amount of grease solvent by placing a little bottle of it in a pan of hot water. Place towel under stain, then apply the warm solvent, flushing out stain onto the towel. Use of small brush to help break up the stain will speed removal. Sometimes such stains can also be removed by placing stained fabric between two pieces of blotting paper and pressing with warm iron.

Candy (wet-clean). Since mostly sugar, candy stains are usually easy to remove by sponging out with plain water. In more stubborn cases a neutral detergent in the water will help. (See also directions for Chocolate Stains.)

Carbon paper (dry-clean). Sponge with grease solvent. To remove remaining traces of dyestuff, flush out with a solution of water, detergent, and small amount of ammonia.

Carrot juice (wet-clean). In washables this stain usually comes out in laundering. If not, treat stained area with solution of water and neutral detergent.

Catsup (wet-clean). Remove as soon as possible, because age makes this one hard to budge. First flush as much of stain as possible in fairly concentrated solution of neutral detergent and water. Lubricate remaining portions of stain with glycerine, working it in with blunt edge of knife or back of comb. Then flush again with detergent-and-water solution.

Chewing gum (dry-clean). Remove heavy portions of gum with blunt edge of knife or similar object. Then sponge area with either grease solvent or amyl acetate. The gum will loosen itself from fabric and remainder can be rolled off with finger or blunt-edged instrument. If some stubborn residue remains, keep saturating area until gum is all dissolved and rinsed from garment. Afterward, rub area thoroughly with dry cloth and allow to dry.

Chocolate (wet-clean). First apply grease solvent to stain to remove oils present in chocolate. When area has dried, apply solution of water and detergent. Unless fabric is taffeta or satin, flex area slightly between fingers to help break up stain, or tamp it with brush. Then launder garment or flush stained area with water and wipe with dry cloth, working to break up wet edge of stain, to prevent ring from developing. This is called "feathering out."

Cocoa (wet-clean). Follow same directions as for chocolate, except that cocoa stain is likely to be more deeply imbedded and require more work.

Cod-liver oil (dry-clean). Treat without delay; this oil tends to oxidize fast. If freshly spilled, flushing out with grease solvent is likely to be enough. Otherwise lubricate stain with a little white mineral oil or Vaseline. Work into stain with back of comb or blunt edge of knife. Then flush out lubricant again with grease solvent. If any trace of stain remains, use soap and ammonia, unless color is likely to bleed.

Coffee (wet-clean). Treat as soon as possible, because tannin compounds in coffee are impossible to remove once they've dried. If possible, soak stained area in bowl of warm water and neutral detergent solution. Watch to detect quickly if any bleeding of dye occurs. If it does, soak immediately in cold water and stop working on it. If no dye bleeds, soak in original solution, then flex between fingers (except taffeta or satin, etc.). If necessary, work some glycerine into stain and soak again. Avoid hot water and alkalies (such as soap). On white cotton, rayon, or acetate, use bleaching solution of chlorine to remove remaining traces. Then wash, if fabric is dyefast. For wool and silk, bleach with a milder agent such as hydrogen peroxide (drug-store variety).

Cooking oil (dry-clean). Follow same directions as for linseed oil.

Crayon (dry-clean). Sponge out stained area with grease solvent, flushing stain out onto towel placed under it. If necessary to lubricate stain, use some vaseline or white mineral oil. Then flush area again. In washables, if traces remain, try removing with soap and ammonia, color permitting.

Cream (wet-clean). Follow same directions as for ice cream.

Egg stains (wet-clean). Scrape any caked-on residue from fabric with dull edge of knife. Apply cold water and neutral detergent and allow to soak in such a solution for few minutes, depending on tendency of dye to bleed. Brush, or flex between fingers to loosen particles imbedded in fabric. If necessary, lubricate area with glycerine or neutral detergent (in heavily concentrated form). Then apply soap or neutral detergent to stain, plus ammonia. Tamp with brush or flex between fingers. Then flush area, wipe it dry, or launder garment.

Fish slime (wet-clean). This is a concentrated albumen stain and can be very difficult to remove, impossible on certain resin-treated or sized fabrics. Soak stained area immediately in pan containing solution of water with some neutral detergent and about a spoonful of salt. Soak about 10 minutes and flex slightly between fingers or tamp with brush. Rinse in plain cold water. Should stain remain, further home treatment is not advisable. Send to dry cleaner, identifying the stain.

Floor wax (for washables and nonwashables). Laundering will remove most of wax stain. Remove leftover traces with grease solvent spotting treatment.

Fruits and fruit juices (wet-clean). Brown or tan stains resulting from fruit juice are due to sugar in the fruit. Often stains don't show at once, but the stain may set as fruit sugar dries and caramelizes (turning brown), the way sugar does under high heat. Once caramelized, such stains become difficult to treat, and practically impossible on wool. Flush stain as soon as possible in a solution of water and neutral detergent. Soaking may also help. If stain remains, try few drops of white vinegar, then flush again in detergent and water. Don't use high heat on the stain, since this speeds up caramelization and only sets the stain faster.

Gelatin stains (wet-clean). Normally laundering will remove such stains, provided water is not over 100° F. Hot suds and rinses tend to set rather than to remove stain.

Glue or mucilage (wet-clean). Soak out stain in hand-warm water and neutral detergent, then apply some household ammonia and tamp with brush or flex between fingers. Rinse, then wipe area with dry cloth.

Grass stains (wet-clean). Test fabric to see if it will withstand alcohol by applying some to hidden area (such as the seam). If this is all right, use alcohol to remove green color, then lubricate area with concentrated detergent solution and flush both alcohol and detergent out of fabric with cold water. Next apply few drops of household ammonia to stain and at the same time work in more detergent solution. Flush again with cold water and launder if possible. Otherwise wipe area with dry cloth and let dry.

Gravy (for washables and non-washables). Because greases will doubtless be present in stain, remove these first by sponging area with grease solvent. Then apply some detergent solution and ammonia (or alkaline soap). Flex, or tamp with brush. Rinse in warm water.

Grease and oil (dry-clean). Mineral oils and greases are readily soluble in dry solvent. Sponge out stained area with grease solvent, which will remove oils quite thoroughly. If water-soluble oil is also present in the stain, remove by sponging the area with solution of soap or detergent and water.

Grease spots on carpets, rugs (dry-clean). Usually easy to remove by rubbing stained area with piece of cheesecloth slightly saturated with grease solvent. Rub over outer edges with dry cloth as spotted area dries, to prevent formation of ring. Be sure to have towel or similar absorbent material under rug and try to avoid letting solvent contact the floor, since it may affect the wood finish.

Ice cream (wet-clean). If stained area is dry, sponge with grease solvent to remove fats. When the solvent has evaporated, apply solution of water, detergent, and few drops of ammonia directly on the stain. Work stain with back of comb or knife and flush it from fabric with cold water.

Ink: India, printer's, ball-point (dry-clean). First put good absorbent material under stain. Then lubricate stain with Vaseline or white mineral oil. Flush lubricant and as much of stain as possible with grease solvent. Repeat until ink stops bleeding. Ball-point ink removes without much trouble. Others may take more work. Back of comb or dull knife edge helps work ink particles free and facilitates stain removal.

Iodine (wet-clean). Quickly remove with sodium thiosulphate crystals (usually called hypo crystals), which are available at drugstores. Place some crystals in piece of cheesecloth, moisten them, and pat stained area with wet crystals. Drop of ammonia tends to speed up action, but stain usually disappears quickly anyway. Rinse with cold water and wipe with dry cloth.

Iron rust. Use either commercial rust remover (hydrofluoric acid) or get oxalic-acid crystals at drugstore. Place a few in cheesecloth, moisten, and apply to stain. After stain is removed, be sure to rinse acid completely from fabric.

Lacquer (dry-clean). If color permits (alcohol bleeds acetate dyes), alcohol is best solvent. As lacquer softens and becomes dissolved, rinse from fabric with grease solvent. If dye bleeds with alcohol (test inconspicuous area to determine this), apply amyl acetate to stain until it tends to dissolve, then rinse with grease solvent.

Lead pencil (wet-clean). Work glycerine or heavy detergent solution into stains with blunt-edged object. Apply few drops of ammonia and gently work into stain. As stains dissolve, flush from fabric with warm water.

Leather stains (dry-clean). Very difficult to remove. Lubricate thoroughly with white mineral oil or Vaseline, then rinse lubricated areas with grease solvent. If garment is white and washable, stains may also be treated with soap and ammonia, rubbing leather-stained areas between hands. Using chlorine bleach on the remaining traces may clear stain. Unless these methods get quick results, turn job over to dry cleaner as soon as possible.

Linseed oil (dry-clean). Very harmful to garment, because once it has been in fabric long enough to oxidize, it's almost impossible to remove. Speed is vital. Lubricate stained area with white mineral oil or Vaseline, working into stain with blunt-edged object. Then rinse with grease solvent. Repeat if necessary. If such measures fail, give to dry cleaner.

Lipstick (dry-clean). If stain is fresh, grease-solvent treatment is often enough. Otherwise lubricate stain well with white mineral oil or Vaseline and flush with grease solvent. Try to do complete job this way. Once the lipstick dye becomes separated from lubricant in the lipstick, its removal requires this further treatment: In a solution of water, ammonia, and detergent, soak stain for hour or two (depending on what the fabric color can stand), then work stain between fingers occasionally while soaking. Finally, rinse thoroughly in warm water.

Liquor stains: alcohol (wet-clean). Alcohol content can be particularly damaging to acetate fabrics because it bleeds their dyes so severely. The longer stain remains, the more the damage. Sponge area immediately with solution of water and neutral detergent. If fruit juices are also present, follow procedure given for their removal after rinsing out the alcohol. It may be necessary to let your cleaner take over further spotting activity.

Machine oil (dry-clean). This is a mineral oil, therefore soluble in grease solvent. Sponge out the stain.

Mascara (dry-clean). Follow same directions as for lipstick stains.

Mayonnaise (dry-clean). Follow same directions as for linseed oil.

Meat juice (dry-clean). First sponge with grease solvent to remove grease. When dry, sponge with either a detergent and ammonia or soap and ammonia.

Mildew (wet-clean). If garment is washable, first launder in soap-and-ammonia solution, then rinse well and dry in the sun. If color will withstand bleaching action of chlorine bleach, use that. Don't try to do job on wool or fancy fabrics. Play safe; give it to your dry cleaner.

Milk (wet-clean). Sponge area with neutral detergent and water, then add few drops of ammonia to area and continue using detergent solution. If necessary, tamp stain with brush or work back and forth across it with blunt-edged object. For old milk stains it may be necessary to use an anzyle (such as powdered pepsin), available at drugstores. Soak in solution of water and pepsin at least 20 minutes at temperature slightly above handwarm. After soaking, repeat above procedure. Milk stains may be impossible to remove on some resin-treated fabrics.

Mud (wet-clean). Allow to dry. Then dry-brush as much as possible from garment. Sponge remaining mud with warm solution of water and detergent. Launder, or flush out with plain water and wipe down with dry cloth.

Mustard (wet-clean). On washables, apply glycerine. After working it into stain, flush with detergent and water. Do not use soap. If stain remains, better let dry cleaner try. Even he, however, may not be able to eliminate yellow stain caused by a chemical in the mustard.

Nail polish (dry-clean). Dissolves in acetone or amyl acetate. However, do not use acetone if fabric is rayon, vinyon, acetate, or nylon, since it damages them. Note: do not use nail-polish remover on above-mentioned fabrics since it, too, often contains acetone.

Oils and fats, other than cooking oils, linseed and similar oils (dry-clean). Generally easy to dissolve in grease solvents. In severe cases lubricate stain with white mineral oil, then sponge with grease solvent.

Paraffin (for washables and non-washables). Laundering is usually sufficient. If stain persists, place towel or fold of absorbent cloth under it and sponge with grease solvent. Piece may then be rewashed as required.

Perfume (wet-clean). Flush from fabric with solution of detergent and water as soon as possible, because alcohol in perfume will severely bleed some dyes, such as acetate. if fabric has no acetate, small amount of alcohol added to detergent solution will help. Test first for color-fastness to alcohol.

Perspiration (wet-clean). When fresh, perspiration is acid in nature. However, bacteria act upon it quickly, turning it alkaline. For fresh stains, flush area with detergent, water, and ammonia in solution. For old stains (by now turned alkaline), use a solution of water, detergent, and vinegar. Sometimes color changes occur from either acids or alkalies. An acid or alkali will restore the color, depending on which agent originally caused the color change.

Plastic stains (dry-clean). Follow same directions as for nail polish.

Resins (dry-clean). Use turpentine, grease solvent, alcohol, or similar organic solvents, but be sure no flame is present anywhere near where you are working. Stain should be softened and well soaked in solvent. Work cleansing agent into stain with glass stirring rod. If fabric has to be rubbed, use soft sponge or brush. Avoid chafing fabric (to prevent combustion).

Rouge (dry-clean). Follow same directions as for lipstick.

Rubber stains (dry-clean). Usually respond to treatment with grease solvent or gasoline (special cleaning type). Do not work near flame.

Salad dressing (dry-clean). Follow same directions as for linseed oil.

Salad oil (dry-clean). Follow same directions as for linseed oil.

Scorch (wet-clean). If fabric is washable, launder first. Scorch itself must be removed by bleach. If fabric will withstand chlorine bleach (rayon, acetate, nylon, etc.), and if dye will also react favorably, bleach as you wash. If scorch is on wool, apply hydrogen peroxide by spray or with a cloth (in this case use rubber gloves). Then place garment so that stained area faces the sun. Watch from time to time until stain is gone. If necessary, apply more hydrogen peroxide as it dries out. If dye begins to lighten, stop procedure and rinse peroxide from fabric.

Shoe polish (dry-clean). Liquid polish stains are usually impossible to remove, because of high tannin content. Paste-type polishes are often easily removable (especially from wool) because of lubricating agents in them. Sponge out area thoroughly with grease solvent. If necessary to lubricate stain further, use white mineral oil or Vaseline, then sponge again with grease solvent.

Soot (wet-clean). Especially tough to remove if soot stain is wet. Soak garment or affected area in heavy solution of detergent and water to lubricate, penetrate, and flush away stain. Watch fabric colors carefully if long soaking is necessary. If severe color bleeding starts, rinse garment or spot the area with cold water. (Some salt in the water usually checks or prevents bleeding.) If bleeding takes place, don't continue; let cleaner take over. Bleaching is ineffective, because soot is primarily carbon.

Sugar syrup (wet-clean). Follow same directions as for candy.

Tar (dry-clean). Catch this stain as soon as possible. Remove heavy portions with blunt-edged instrument. Then sponge thoroughly with grease solvent. If natural tar lubricant has dried out, relubricate with either Vaseline or white mineral oil. Then sponge out with more grease solvent. If stain is stubborn, continue by using glycerine, soap, or a similar agent, working it into the stain. Then flush with water or launder garment. Color-fastness and washability of fabric determine which course you take.

Tea (wet-clean). Normal washing will usually suffice, unless stain has been present a long time. If stain is stubborn, use chlorine bleach on white cotton or linen; hydrogen peroxide on silk or wool (if color will withstand the bleach).

Tin foil (for washables and non-washables). Foil from corsages can leave stains. First lubricate with white mineral oil or Vaseline, working well into stain. Then flush with grease solvent. Wipe fabric vigorously with dry cloth as solvent evaporates from it. When dry, switch to wet-cleaning by lubricating stain with glycerine or soap, then flush well with water.

Tobacco juice (wet-clean). Lubricate with glycerine, then soak garment or stained area in solution of detergent and hand-warm water. On whites, bleaching may be necessary, chlorine bleach for cottons and synthetics, hydrogen peroxide for silk and wool. Tobacco's tannin content makes it a difficult stain to remove.

Tomato juice (wet-clean). Follow same directions as for catsup.

Tooth paste (wet-clean). If dry, most of it can be dry-brushed off. Otherwise, usually easy to flush off with either soap-and-water or detergent-and-water solution. Since some toothpastes contain sodium perborate (a bleach), guard against allowing stain to damage fabric; remove quickly.

Vaseline (dry-clean). Easy to remove with grease solvent. After sponging, wipe area dry with clean cloth.

Water spots on taffeta (wet-clean). If fabric shows spots, it contains considerable sizing, which creates a problem. No home method will work. Dry cleaner has certain facilities that usually solve the situation.

Wine (wet-clean). Work on this stain as soon as possible. Apply concentrated solution of neutral detergent and some glycerine, working it into area. Allow to remain a few minutes, then sponge with clear water, about hand-warm (never hot). Flex stain between fingers while rinsing. If some color of wine remains, apply few drops of ammonia with some detergent to the stain. This may turn it from blue to pink. White vinegar will turn it back to original blue. Such a condition means that a so-called indicator dye is present and there is little you can do unless fabric can withstand bleaching.

26

LUGGAGE

Experience-tested tips on how to pack properly and how to care for your luggage

Smooth sailing with smooth-packed clothes. Whether you sail, fly, board the train, hop a bus, or take the wheel of your car, you travel for a purpose and must look your neatest to further that purpose. Here's the pick of the pack of packing tips.

From the bottom up, pack your suitcase with heavy items on the bottom, getting lighter as you near the top. If you haven't a separate hat and shoe case, pack your shoes first, starting with one corner. Stuff shoes with cosmetic jars, folded gloves, socks, stockings, etc. Saves space, keeps shoes shapely.

Fill out the corners and uneven spaces in your suitcases. This not only utilizes space to the fullest, but prevents your carefully packed clothes from sliding around and becoming wrinkled when carried.

Wardrobe case. Place dresses and suit coats on hangers; either cross sleeves over front or let hang down alongside seams of garment. Pin skirts to hangers and fold side panels toward center. Snap holder bar into position. Tuck hankies, gloves, hose, into corners of bottom section. Fit shoes into bottom of case near hinged side.

Is your beauty in the bag? Careless packing of toiletries and cosmetics can spoil your clothing and luggage. Safeguard the good looks of your clothing against your beauty aids. Suggestions:

Transfer the contents of breakable bottles and jars to plastic containers, or use the original containers with one of the following methods to prevent leaks: Paint a coat of colorless nail polish around the edge of the cap, or seal with wax from a candle. Even faster is the use of aluminum foil, which should be torn from the roll in sheets to fit each bottle or jar. Wrap the foil completely around the article, pressing to the contours of the container. Save the sheets for your return trip. When placing cosmetics in your luggage, try not to have any two pieces of glass touching. Tuck hairbrush, tissues, toothpaste tubes in empty spaces and be certain that nothing moves or shifts about when the luggage is carried.

For perfumes, there are handbag-size containers more practical for traveling, or stick to colognes and sachets, which are good travelers. Refillable purse vials give you an ample supply of your favorite scent and will match your billfold and key case.

If the small soap bars provided by hotels aren't to your taste, don't hesitate to carry your own, plus washcloth, with aluminum foil or a pastic bag to "fence in" the dampness on return.

Last-minute packing, first-minute unpacking. See that your clothes spend as little time in the suitcase as possible. While you may pack shoes, toilet articles, lingerie, and sweaters as much ahead as seems convenient, leave clothes to the last. Even if you start from the house very early in the morning and must pack the night before, at least don't close your suitcase until a few minutes before you begin your journey.

Unpacking. Do this with care, as soon as possible after reaching your destination. It's easy to get wrinkles out of woolen garments. Just put the suit or dress on a hanger, give it a damp brushing, or hang it over a tub of steaming water. Your clothing will be fresh and ready to wear in a matter of minutes.

Bring along a travel iron if you want to press something to wear at once, immediately after unpacking.

Steam travel irons are particularly useful, take up very little packing space.

Use hotel beds as ironing boards for travel pressing. Simply put several thicknesses of smooth hand towels on top of the bedspread and you have an excellent surface for quick pressing as well as a convenient appliance outlet behind the bed for plugging in the iron, where bedside lighting in hotel rooms is usually found.

BAGGAGE WEIGHT

In this era of air travel, the weight of your luggage is more than a matter of saving your strength: it can become quite costly if you have to pay for baggage over the allowed limits. At present, on most domestic flights the limit (except for hand-held items) is two standard-sized pieces; on international flights, that limit is 44 lbs.

How to figure baggage weight. Know the weight of your suitcase. Then the list on page 246 will serve as an approximate guide to the weight of items you pack, so that you may save on the high cost of excess baggage in air travel.

WOMEN—PUT IN THE NEATNESS WHEN YOU PACK YOUR BAG

Best way to pack skirts. For that important, impeccable look, start

Weights for women's clothing items:

Coat	3 pounds	Pair of shoes	1 pound
Suit	2½ "	Hat	¼ "
Dress	1 "	Handbag	1 "
Sweater	½ "	Scarf	¼ "
Blouse	¼ "	Belt	¼ "
Skirt	¾ "	Handkerchiefs	⅓ "
Slacks	1½ "	Lingerie	1¼ "

Weights for men's clothing items:

Tweed suit	4 pounds	Shirt	½ pound
Worsted suit	2½ "	Sweater	1 "
Flannel slacks	1½ "	Socks	¾ "
Topcoat	3½ "	Neckties	½ "
Shoes	4 "	Pajamas	½ "

with skirt hem at one end of your suitcase, making sure that the bottom side of the skirt lies completely smoothed out. If it isn't a straight skirt, smooth out the overhang on both sides and fold back neatly over strips of tissue paper. Another strip of tissue goes under the fold-back you make with the waist extending over the other end of the suitcase. For the next skirt, start procedure from the opposite end of the suitcase, so that the thickness evens out.

Blouses show no folds if folded right—that is, at shoulders, with sleeves under the back, much as new shirts are folded. Again, as with skirts, alternate their position for level packing.

Suit jackets are stuffed shirts, really. They may be packed like shirt blouses, possibly with sleeves folded toward their front, or topside from where you stand. Stuff front with tissue paper. Or turn suit jacket inside out except for the sleeves. Fold jacket in half, tucking one shoulder inside the other. Smooth out folds at collar and lapel.

Dresses are really skirts with blouses, so start as with skirt, the hem of your dress at one end of suitcase. Place strip of tissue paper at other end and fold back the rest of the dress over it. Stuff bodice with tissue paper, fold sleeves over or under, whichever seems to leave dress in a more normal fold. Tuck some tissue under sleeve fold too.

Lingerie. Place each item on several full-length sheets of tissue paper. Roll with tissue on outside. Place lingerie so that it will be at the top of the bag.

MEN—LEAVE OUT THE WRINKLES WHEN YOU PACK YOUR BAG

Unfold shirts to full length and refold with shirttails up over front and tucked under back of collar, and you'll keep collars from crushing when packed.

Pack shirts, shoes, belts, socks, slippers snugly but not crowded.

Travel-wise ties should be folded in half crosswise, of course, then rolled from fold. Stop rolling a few inches from the tip ends. Roll tie over accordion-pleated tissue for wrinkle-proof packing.

Pack your clothes; leave out the wrinkles. For a man's suit, the best home-away-from-home is a "two-suiter," which makes packing a joy. Follow manufacturers' directions.

You're not in it when you pack your jacket. So don't button it, just overlap it as far as the cut easily allows front to lie flat. Stuff shoulders with tissue paper. Curve sleeves over side seams at armholes.

Two-Suiter

Remove hangers. Lay in trousers with front creases toward bag's hinges. Put coats on hangers, and replace. Put in divider board. Fold trousers over board and coats over trousers.

Pack mittened shoes and any other heavy objects near hinges. Put shirts on top of bag. Ties, socks, underwear, dressing case will keep shirts from shifting.

Pullman Case

For trousers and coats, follow same procedure as for two-suiter. Use pleated tissue to cushion folds. Put pajamas and underwear flat in pocket of lid, ties rolled.

Tissue, accordion-pleated, guards against wrinkles. In general, pack so that nothing shifts. Experts of the Luggage and Leather Goods Manufacturers' Association, from whom we got our tips, say, "Be like the Post Office, and don't accept this package if it rattles." But they also advise against packing too tightly: no tighter, they say, than a bureau drawer is packed.

Expandable Brief Bag

It's a good idea to slip in cardboard backs to brace shirts. Put them in collars downward, for this ride.

There's also room, in an expandable brief bag, besides papers, for socks, handkerchiefs, dressing case, razor. Roll pajamas and underwear to save space.

Traveling Garment Bag

Put trousers in first, on hangers. Be sure to curve sleeves over side seams of coat, as shown. Use crushed tissue to fill out sags in coat.

Fold clothing flat for packing pockets. Roll ties and socks and place in collar openings of pajamas. Place shoes so they'll ride at bottom of bag when it's folded for carrying.

HOW TO CARE FOR LUGGAGE

For luggage care, it is most important to be absolutely certain of exactly what material covers the article; for instance, a plastic may look like leather or fabric. No one type of cleaning is best for every kind of material. Most luggage and leather-goods retailers will be happy to identify the material of an article if it is brought to a local store.

Rawhide leather (translucent, mostly white or eggshell in color, brushlike marks in irregular pattern) can be cleaned easily with scouring powder, using steel wool only for stubborn spots. Reseal pores of the leather with several coats of clear shellac or spar varnish, allowing each coat to dry before applying another. Unprotected rawhide is candy to rodents, will encourage mold or mildew.

To clean smooth leather, pigskin (in the brown or tan family, generally), and replenish oils at the same time, use saddle soap according to container directions. Lighten the color of travel-weary leathers in this class with the juice of half a lemon in a glass of water. For larger stains, such as might be caused by water, darken the entire article with thick coats of lemon oil applied for 2 or 3 days until the leather is all of the same color. To finish and protect after cleaning, use paste wax or neutral shoe polish. Preservatives sold in luggage stores are excellent. Bad scratches should be cared for by a professional repairman.

Alligator usually wipes clean with saddle soap. Paste wax or Simonize will restore the sheen.

Colored leathers, grained or smooth, may fade as do fabrics. Use only mild soapsuds and a nearly dry sponge or soft-nap cloth. Rub very gently. Neutral shoe cream is the best polish.

Coated fabric usually looks like cotton, linen, or similar fabric that has been shellacked or varnished; some all-plastic material resembles coated fabric, so be certain before you begin cleaning. Clean with a fairly strong soap or powder. Two tablespoons of household ammonia in a pint of soapy water will help lift heavy soilage. Bleach with the juice of a lemon in a quart of water. Mildew may be removed with a solution such as toluene, a solvent available in small quantities from most hardware stores. Protect against further soiling by applying several coats of self-polishing floor wax.

Fabric. Work "dry" suds into fabric carefully. Rubberized or waterproofed linings may be sponged, dried with soft cloth. Don't use cleaning fluids when fabric is bonded to a lining or backing material.

Plastic. Most plastics wipe clean with a damp cloth. Use soap for stubborn spots. Should require no waxing. Save manufacturers' directions for cleaning when purchasing new items, since new types of plastics often require different methods.

Straw or wicker hamper-type luggage (picnic kits, etc.) may be shellacked to prevent mildew. Remove fittings first.

All-fiberglass luggage of the type that has no additional covering may be wiped with a damp cloth; scratches are smoothed out with fine steel wool.

All-aluminum luggage of the type that has no additional covering is treated as plastic. Hardware stores have preparations that remove stains from aluminum, and these, rather than home experimenting, are recommended.

Combination covering. When an article is composed of more than one type of covering, treat each material separately, as outlined, being certain of positive identification before beginning.

Hardware and locks on luggage. Never oil metal parts. Seepage almost always results, staining lining with spots that can rarely be removed. If coating on metal has become scratched, or rust begins, clean carefully with fine-grade steel wool and recoat entire section of metal with colorless nail polish or clear lacquer. Do not experiment with balky or broken locks; see a repairman before your next trip.

Linings. Avoid use of water or chemicals. More often than not, linings are glued to the body of the article. Moisture and solvents will frequently cause linings to come loose. French powder cleaners will somewhat lessen oil stains. To combat occasional odors that may come from infrequent use, try keeping chlorophyll tablets in the suitcase, or sachets, or wrapped cakes of soap such as are provided by hotels.

GO FURTHER WITH WELL-STORED LUGGAGE

Never store dirty, stained, or soiled suitcase, leather goods, or brief case. Moths, vermin, mice will feast on it and the damage may be beyond repair.

If you nest cases inside one another, make sure the inner pieces are carefully wrapped in paper or luggage covers. Hardware can snag linings, and excessive humidity will promote rust, which causes permanent stains.

Store accessories in normal humidity and temperature. Too much moisture in the air can cause mildew, mold, rust. Too little moisture promotes brittleness and cracking. Use bags of dehumidifying powder in or near articles to combat excessive humidity, particularly if you live near water or in the South. A large open pan of water, replenished from time to time, will help humidify a dry atmosphere, especially if storage space must be near a furnace, radiators, or in an uninsulated attic.

Allow air to circulate. Stand luggage upright on hinged ends with a space between each case. Avoid storing cases on the floor, especially in the cellar. Instead place the cases on a plank raised a few inches on two blocks of wood or bricks. This helps prevent rust, mildew, and mold.

Protect suitcases with luggage cover or heavy paper wraps if you don't anticipate using them for a long period. Wrap small items in tissue.

Folding (traveling) garment bags provide storage for out-of-season garments. Hang them in closet or attic as regular storage bags. Protect tops against dust by making shoulder covers of paper or old plastic tablecloths, etc.

27

SEWING

A mini-course in making, remodeling, and mending clothes, with ingenious tips on saving time and money

Have you ever felt that, for all the many clothes on store racks to choose from, you still can't find exactly what you want? Then why not make your own? With proper preparation and care, anyone can learn how to sew clothes—if not all kinds for all occasions, at least many items of the family's wardrobe. Along with the considerable savings in money, you should end up with exactly what you want in terms of fabric, color, and styling.

Even if you don't choose to make clothes from start to finish, mastery of the basic sewing techniques will allow you to remodel old clothes or mend others, thus getting full value from your purchases. The many sewing aids available today and the ease of operating modern machines make sewing much more accessible to everyone.

Unit construction is a good strategic plan to follow. In plain English, you complete and press each section of your garment before you join it to another section. This plan reduces the handling of fabric

pieces, increases the speed with which you assemble your garment, makes sewing more interesting for you, because each time you have finished a unit you get that glowing feeling of accomplishment.

FABRIC BASICS

Tip to beginners. Start with a fabric that is easy to handle. Choose a solid color material, not a print, stripe, or checked design. The problem of matching design patterns at the seams is a tricky one and is easier to master when you are more experienced. Also, choose your pattern for a style with a minimum of detail work.

Fabric must be preshrunk. Unless you are sure that it is, take your material to your cleaner's and have it shrunk before working with it. Or do it yourself, but be sure to press it smoothly afterward, before cutting into it.

How to shrink colored cottons and linens. Soak material in cold water for 3 to 4 hours. Squeeze out the water; don't wring the fabric. Hang material on your clothesline or, if you have a dryer, dry it in your dryer with several dry Turkish bath towels that will buffer the fabric as it tumble-dries. Buy non-shrunk cottons and linens with the foreknowledge that these materials will shrink anywhere from 1 to 3 inches per yard.

Shrink white cottons and linens the same way, except that you may soak them in either hot or cold water.

To shrink woolens, take a sheet or other large white piece of thin material and wet it. Spread the wet sheet on an even surface. Open the woolen material completely and spread it over the wet sheet. Now clip fabric selvage every few inches. Spread a second wet sheet over the woolen fabric. Pat lightly over the entire area and let stand overnight.

Preshrunk fabrics are of greater importance in tailored garments than in any other kind of feminine clothes. In making a coat or suit that is to have interfacings and a lining, have all materials preshrunk.

What is the role of interfacings? They give the material more body. This is especially important for collars, lapels, center-front sections, cuffs, and the fashionable standout, stiffened short tunic of the suit jacket that makes for smartly rounded hips.

Fabric must be free of folds or wrinkles. If home-shrunk, press and iron fabric carefully before starting work on it. Iron out any folds it may have acquired if it has been lying around in your drawer for some time since you bought it.

Handle your material as little as possible once work on it has begun. Keep it on the work table even when not working on it, or put it away carefully folded. When pinning or basting, don't try to hold it on your lap; keep it on a large work table.

Slippery fabric may make work difficult when you pin on or cut the pattern. If you don't have a special cutting board, spread material on a clean rug or carpet to make it hold still.

CORRECT MEASUREMENTS AND FITTINGS

It isn't enough to know what size you are. You have to know your exact measurements before you buy a pattern, and especially before you undertake to cut your material. Even if you have the correct size pattern, very few women's measurements conform with that of the standard pattern in every detail. Yet you want a dress that will fit with professional perfection, and you will, therefore, need to make certain adjustments in your personal pattern. To know just what adjustments are necessary, you need to know your own measurements; those used in the pattern are indicated on the pattern itself.

The best work plan is to set up a chart, indicating for each measurement: your own measurement; the usual allowance for ease, if any; the measurement of the pattern; and the difference between the pattern and your own measurements.

How to take your own measurements. Have someone do the measuring for you, of course, but be sure your helper understands the rules of this most serious game. The illustrations on page 254 show where the measuring tape is placed in each instance. The numbers correspond with the numbers of the chart on page 255. (Unless you make several garments around the same period, recheck your measurements when you get set for a new season's wardrobe. Your figure may show changes in 6 months, or even less.)

Measurements should be taken from the right side, except where both side measurements are needed.

When checking measurements with those of the pattern, remember to figure in the seam allowance.

The four most important measurements of the feminine figure are, as you well know: the bust, the difference between the bust and the chest, the waist, and the hips. To make sure you get them at the exact right points, the following description will be helpful:

1. The bust is the measurement over the fullest part. Draw the measuring tape just taut, but not so it cuts in, unless you want to look flat.

2. To measure the chest, or "high" chest, take the tape high under the armpits and straight across the chest.

3. At the waist, where you wear your belt most naturally.

4. Hip, approximately seven inches below your waistline, but take largest circumference into due consideration or you may have a tight fit.

Determine right-size pattern from your measurements. Taking the last four types of measurement into consideration, remember that your chest and bust measurements determine the size of the pattern you need. If the bust measures no more than 4 inches larger than the high chest, buy the pattern size nearest to the chest measurement. Substitute, in this case, your chest measurement for the bust measurement that appears on the pattern. In this way you are sure of well-fitting shoulder and bust section. This is important, because these are the pattern lines that are the most difficult to alter.

Let bust measurement lead you to right-size pattern. If bust is more than 4 inches larger than chest, buy pattern size nearest your bust measurement. Waist and hip measurements are less important for this purpose, as pattern alterations are easily made for these simple lines. Often adjustment need not even be made until fitting time.

The custom-made dress form is the easy way to your correct measure-

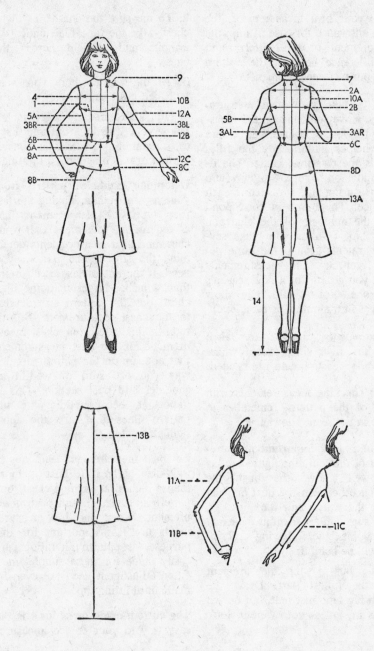

	Your own measurement in inches	Usual allowance for ease in inches	Pattern measurement in inches	* Difference in inches
1. Bust—Fullest part—Slightly higher in back		4	....	......
2. Back—A—Shoulder to shoulder	....	1½ to 1	....	......
B—Under arm to under arm at side seam	....	....	....	......
3. Shoulder to natural waistline—				
A—Back Right....in. Left....in.	....	½ to 2	....	......
B—Front Right....in. Left....in.	....	½ to 2	....	......
4. Chest front—from armseye to armseye	....	....	....	......
5. Armpit to natural waistline—				
A—Right......in.	....	....	....	......
B—Left........in.	....	....	....	......
6. Natural waistline—A—entire	....	....	....	......
B—Front........in.	....	....	....	......
C—Back........in.				
7. Neck circumference	....	....	....	......
8. Hip—A—Inches below natural waistline (fullest part)	....	....	....	......
B—Entire	....	2	....	......
C—Front hip from side to side	....	1	....	......
D—Back hip from side to side	....	1	....	......
9. Shoulder length—Neck to tip of shoulder	....	....	....	......
10. Armseye—A—Right......in.	....	....	....	......
B—Left........in.	....	....	....	......
11. Sleeve length—A—Shoulder to elbow	....	....	....	......
B—Elbow to wrist	....	....	....	......
C—Inside from underarm seam to wrist	....	....	....	......
12. Sleeve Width—A—Upper arm	....	3 to 4	....	......
B—Lower arm	....	....	....	......
C—Wrist	....	....	....	......
13. Full length—A—Back of neck to floor	....	....	....	......
B—Back waistline to floor	....	....	....	......
14. Skirt length—Floor to hem line	....	....	....	......

* Use plus (+) and minus (—) sign. If your bust is two inches larger, mark: +2. If your waist is 1½ inches smaller, mark: —1.

ments and fitting. You may have this made for you at professional dress-form centers. It is a relatively small investment for insuring more perfect dresses you can make for yourself. It makes things easier for you and encourages you to own more dresses at homemade prices.

For measurements taken at home, preferably wear those foundation garments and shoes that you plan to wear, as a rule, with the finished dress.

If you make a straight skirt, take your hip measurement as indicative of the right-size skirt pattern for you, since the waistline will be easy to adjust.

For full or flared skirt (if the skirt is a separate), use your waist measurement to establish what size pattern will be just right for you.

Have a fitting, not a fit. Avoid disappointment; fit carefully on yourself, on your dress form, or have someone competent to fit you. It will still be you who made the dress. Whoever does the fitting, where crosswise grain seems to run upward, ease that side of the section down to restore grain line. Where crossgrain sags, give material a lift. If lengthwise grain goes on the bias, unless it was cut on the bias, open waist basting and adjust into place.

WORKING WITH PATTERNS

For accurate measurement of pattern pieces, iron them with a warm iron. If you use printed paper patterns, trim off the edges. If you use perforated patterns, connect with a heavy ruled line the perforations along the straight-of-goods lines.

Do patterns give you the "creeps"? When cutting patterns with light, thin fabrics, the cloth often "creeps" and spoils the possibility of good fitting. To prevent this, stiffen the cloth temporarily by basting a heavy piece of paper to the underside, then cut through both cloth and paper.

Pins unnecessary. When using paper patterns for cutting garments, run a warm (not hot) electric iron over the pattern, placed over the cloth. You'll not need pins, and you can move the paper easily.

In placing the pattern pieces on the material, it is important to watch the grain of the material, make sure that one edge of the material is straight. If pattern is to be placed in fold of material, cut along one pulled crosswise thread; pin together two selvage edges.

Foundation pieces, such as front, back, skirt, and sleeves, are pinned on material first; patterns for trimmings last.

On straight grain of fabric, perforations or other marking on pattern indicate position of pattern. Check with ruler. See that markings are parallel with selvage.

In considering grain of material, follow pattern instructions for each style. Bias is used for fitted bodices or flared skirt. "True bias" means a bias line a true 45 degrees across the middle of the right angle (90 degrees) formed by straight-of-goods and crosswise thread.

Patchwork and appliqué piece patterns, cut from fine sandpaper, make fast work of your piece cutting. Hold pattern with rough side next to the fabric.

To cut materials smoothly, keep left hand on pattern, cutting along right edge; use sharp, medium shears; take long, smooth strokes; never quite close the shears.

Before you remove the pattern make sure you have put in all the markings for darts, tucks, lengthwise and crosswise grains, and have basting lines run down center front and center back.

Prevent stretching of curve-cut portions of material by running basting around neck and armholes.

Stretching is encouraged, though, before marking the hem. Let dress, once put together, hang for several days before you decide on the exact hem length.

ALTERING PATTERNS

Alteration of pattern pieces to fit each part of you. Don't feel badly if you are bigger here or shorter there than the standard measurements of the pattern. The most beautiful figure is rarely a standard figure. Deviations go unnoticed if your garment fits perfectly. The general rule for alterations is, of course, to let out the pattern piece for larger-than-standard to take it in for smaller-than-standard measurements.

Don't waste the beauty of a long waist. About midway between underarm points and waistline, slash pattern piece straight across. Spread the two new halves as far as the length difference you require. Make sure the edges of the new halves remain parallel. Insert and pin to halves a strip of paper wide enough to be gripped by the pins without slipping out. Lengthen the back similarly.

Don't let waist hang. If waist measurement of pattern needs to be made shorter, make a fold straight across the lower part of the bodice-half pattern, making it shorter by the required length. Alter the back correspondingly.

To narrow shoulder on the pattern, make either 3 or 4 fine tucks that are like narrow darts tapering off at a point above the bustline; or make one wider, short dart. In either case, adjust back to correspond.

If you have a high bust, slash the pattern piece at the bustline from center front toward the underarm. Don't spread in parallel fashion; spread only the front center part, to the fullness required. Pin on paper under it, keep straight front line. Note, however, that this will, at the same time, increase the width at the waistline. If this isn't needed, it can be eliminated on the pattern piece by a series of darts.

Round shoulders are good with fashionable styles. Adjust the pattern to your natural form by slashing pattern toward armhole at round of shoulder. Move front center downward for the extra length required. Pin the pattern at the slash to the paper you have placed underneath. Pin also in lower back. Retain the straight line from neckline to waist.

Sloping shoulders have the right slant on fashion. Here's how to adjust the standard pattern to your particular shoulder: Lay a dart along the shoulder line of the pattern. Begin it at the armhole, taper it off at the neckline. Lower the underarm by following the dotted line on the pattern.

Square your shoulders to look your athletic self. Give yourself a build-up by building up the shoulder line of your pattern. Do it by adding paper the required width just over the armhole, tapering toward the neckline. Raise underarm line correspondingly.

Are you active enough to have to think of preventing the sleeve from pulling and wearing out at the armhole? Then slash long-sleeve pattern at the elbow and spread for the extra length you require. Ease fullness in at the elbow rather than make darts.

Are you long-armed? First find out where the sleeve pattern needs lengthening, above the elbow or below, or both. Accordingly, slash the sleeve pattern straight across at the required point or points, and spread the slashes to the necessary length, keeping pieces parallel. Insert paper strip(s) under the slashes and pin.

Don't let your sleeve hide your hand. To get a shorter sleeve, determine if sleeve is too long above or below the elbow, or both. Make fold(s) in the paper, and pin.

To let out upper part of sleeve, slash pattern from top to sleeve. Carefully spread pattern to the required width. Make darts at the full part of the sleeve and close the slash on top. Pin piece of paper under the slash and at the top, to retain the original sleeve length.

For a slender arm, make a fold in the sleeve pattern, starting at top, tapering toward wrist. Make a small short dart in front and back of armhole, below the shoulder seam.

To lengthen a skirt, cut pattern below the hipline, spread to required length, keep parts parallel, insert strip of paper under it, then pin. Repeat evenly in back. If a skirt much longer than pattern is required, don't spread that much, but rather repeat with another slash about 5 inches above hem of skirt.

To get a shorter skirt, make even fold, below hipline, in front and back, lifting length difference. Again, if pattern is much longer than you need, don't make too wide a fold, but repeat the fold about 5 inches below hemline.

Wider hips in a skirt are achieved by slashing pattern from the lower edge (hemline) toward the waistline, but stopping at least 1 inch short of the waist. Spread both front and back patterns one fourth the width required for the total difference between your hip measurement and the pattern measurement for the hip. The width around the lower edges increases proportionately and automatically, so you need not bother about it.

If you have narrow hips, wait for the first fitting before you cut down your material. There's always time for that.

THE SEWING MACHINE

The modern sewing machine has come a long way from its simple original. With its various automatic features and its many accessories and attachments—special "feet," for instance, that make unusual stitches, buttonholes, etc.—the modern sewing machine allows even a novice to create sewing miracles.

Select your machine with care, then learn all about it. Preferably get it from a dealer or center where its special workings can be explained in detail. Keep your instruction booklet and study it conscientiously.

If you are a beginner, find out how to replace the needle, how presser bar adjustment, length of stitch, and tension adjustment work. Find out about the seams the machine will make with various methods and attachments, and also what attachments are available that you may want right then or in the future.

Manufacturer sewing centers and sewing sections in department stores have a wealth of information that's helpful to you in your home sewing work. They'll give you lessons as well, at nominal charge, if you'd like to sew like a pro.

If you have trouble threading needle, get a special machine needle that has a small slanting slot which admits thread when pulled down on it, but does not release it. Or place a piece of white paper under the needle so its opening is highlighted.

The care and feeding of the sewing machine. Your machine requires cleaning and oiling to function properly. If you use it only a few hours a day, removal of lint, oiling and cleaning are simple once- or twice-weekly assignments. On the other hand, if you keep your machine stitching continuously, care becomes a daily routine.

Your sewing machine is an intricate and sensitive mechanism and, while equipped to withstand continuous hard use, it should not be tampered with by unskilled hands. Beyond simple adjustments and removal of lint, a regular check-up of the machine parts should be made by a skilled mechanic. Replacement of such machine parts as motor brushes, the presser foot, motor belt, and tension spring may also be necessary. Sewing centers throughout the country offer such service. For instance, one of their inexpensive tune-ups includes lubrication of all machine parts, a complete "bath" for the machine head and bearings, a motor tune-up, and polishing of all bright parts.

The grade of oil should be watched. Poor-grade oil can cause almost as much damage as no oiling at all. It may dry on the parts and make them gummy. It may make necessary a complete overhauling of the machine by a competent repair man. The safest bet is to buy oil from the sewing-machine manufacturer. A good general rule for oiling is to apply one drop to each bearing or regular oiling point and each point where there is any friction. Equipped with cheesecloth, a clean, soft 1-inch paintbrush, a large screw driver, a small screw driver, and a stiletto-type instrument, you can give the machine a thorough cleaning and oiling.

Care of the machine head. Before oiling any part of the machine or stand, remove all dust, lint, and threads, giving special attention to the shuttle race. If you have a treadle machine and the treadle works hard, the stand bearing may require cleaning, oiling, and readjustment.

To do a thorough oiling job on machine heads, remove the upper thread, slide plate, bobbin case, needle, and presser foot. Take out the screws and remove the throat plate. This will enable you to clean and oil the shuttle race.

There are two types of machines equipped with an oscillating hook. This oscillating hook is lubricated by oil from a piece of red felt that touches the top of the hook. Remember that this felt wiper should be kept moist with oil.

How to remove gummed oil. If your machine has not been used for several weeks, you may find that it will run hard when you begin using it again. This is probably due to oil that has become gummed in the oil points and other moving parts. To loosen up this accumulation, oil all parts carefully with a few drops of kerosene. Then begin stitching rapidly, wiping off all the excess oil with a piece of cheesecloth. When you are certain that the machine has been freed of the old oil, begin again by oiling all working parts with a regular high-grade sewing-machine oil. Whenever kerosene has been used in this manner, it is advisable to give the machine another oiling after running it for a few hours. Should the machine continue to drag after this treatment, turn it over to a skilled sewing-machine adjuster.

Check the bobbin area for accumulated lint that is evident when the machine seems to work with difficulty even if you've just oiled it. Bobbin holder snaps out so you can clean it and get at the area to clean out the lint under the stitching section of the machine. A fine crochet needle is a convenient tool to use, plus a pair of tweezers. But work carefully so you don't scratch the metal of the machine.

Stitch and tension adjustments are very important for best operation of your sewing machine. If you have difficulty in making the adjustments properly yourself, call in a machine service expert.

ON PINS AND NEEDLES

Keep pins on hand. Be sure to use plenty of pins with sharp points. To keep them always handy, buy a special wrist pincushion you may keep on your left wrist. Or take a plastic bracelet not otherwise being used and glue on it a long piece of foam rubber about 2 inches wide. Or attach a large powder puff to your wrist with a rubber band or ribbon. These clever devices will also prove practical in fittings.

Scraps of wool to stuff pincushions will save your needles and pins from rust.

Lipstick "pincushion." Try an empty lipstick container as a pin-and-needle case. Remove the last trace of lipstick, then pack with cotton for a cushion.

Pin-catcher. A small magnet in your sewing basket will help you pick up pins and needles easily when they go astray.

For velvets and corduroys, use fine needles as "pins," to prevent unsightly marring of the pile.

Remove rust from sewing needle or pin by pressing it, tip first, into a piece of soap. Soap removes the rust, sterilizes needle.

Sewing stiff fabrics becomes easier if you occasionally stick your needle into a bar of soap. The soap lubricates the needle and makes the going far smoother.

If nylon fabrics pucker along stitching lines, try using a sharp, new, finer machine needle and pasting a piece of heavy brown paper over the plate of the machine. This will reduce the size of the hole for the needle and prevent the fabric from being drawn down too far.

To sharpen machine needles. If you have sewing to do and a new needle isn't handy to replace the dull old one, stitch a few inches through sandpaper. Such a difference.

Another way to keep needle "in business." Stick sewing-machine needles in a cork bottle stopper and rest on a wad of oiled cotton deposited at the bottom of the bottle. Keeps them safe, handy, free from rust.

THREAD CARE

Sewing-kit champ. If you have a spare ping-pong paddle, drive nails into it to hold spools for sewing and fix one or two small corks on the handle to hold the thimbles. Choose mercerized threads in colors darker than fabric, because all thread colors appear lighter when sewed.

Save thread; save mess. Rubber bands slipped over spools of thread keep the ends of the thread from unwinding and cluttering your sewing box.

Make a thread holder. Unwind twist of wire hanger. Open short end. Form wire into circle. Slip on spools. Retwist wire to close circle. Hang pincushion from it. Hang circle in your sewing corner. You can then unwind thread as needed without removing spool from hanger.

Spools won't fly off spindles if you clamp a spring-type clothespin on the spindle just before you start winding bobbin on your sewing machine.

Avoid a whirlspool. Keep your spool from unwinding too rapidly on your machine by placing a small rubber faucet washer on top of the spool. Serves as friction brake, saves you time, keeps thread from snarling.

A handy thread cutter that costs you nothing can be improvised with an empty container of dental floss. Wind length of thread on a cut-down drinking straw and slip loose end through opening in the cover of the container. You can store a needle or two with the thread and keep this useful gadget in your purse for emergencies.

Free thread. Unravel the tops of discarded socks and stockings and you'll have a nice supply on hand.

Proper thread thickness gets buttons to stay in place. If you haven't button thread, use double thickness of good mercerized thread in color to match fabric.

Loose ends. A rubber sponge will quickly and neatly pick up the loose threads from a line of stitching that has been ripped out.

Remember the old adage: "The shorter the thread, the faster the seam." Three needlefuls of short thread will go faster and easier than one long needleful.

Use up your odds and ends of colored thread for basting, using a different color for each type of marking.

Strong, slippery nylon thread used on the bobbin when making lines of gathering provides a quick trick for avoiding broken threads and uneven gathers.

Use darning cotton to make tailor-tack markings. It won't slip out of the fabric as easily as sewing thread.

When sewing on fur fabrics, nylon thread will give greater strength and elasticity to the seams. "Picking out" the pile along the seam lines will make them inconspicuous.

BASTING AND HEMMING

Easier basting. One woman has found that as much as 16 inches of material can be basted without moving the fabric, if it is pinned down to a pillow during the basting or hemming. Pillow is held in the lap, leaving both hands free to work.

Another basting short cut. Try strips of masking tape to baste two pieces of cloth together before stitching a seam with the machine. Apply the strips across the seam close together, to keep the edges even. As you sew, remove the strips ahead of the sewing-machine needle, one at a time.

Cut basting thread, not fabric, when removing the thread. Best way: cut between the stitches and pull out in short lengths. You may risk large thread holes, even tear fabric threads in sheer material, if you try to pull out long basting threads.

To get that lining in line, pin lining to garment, so that the wrong sides of both lining and material face each other. Baste in the lining around the armholes and the shoulder seams. Turn under the usual seam allowance. The lining overlaps the edge of the front facing and the back overlaps the front at the shoulder seams. The lining is blind-hemmed to the front-facing shoulder and neckline.

No pinholes, please. If you have a lot of hemming to do and you don't want to use pins because they'll make holes, paper clips or bobby pins will do a good job of gripping the hem while you baste or work the machine.

No hemming and hawing about the way the hem of a long coat should be: Lining should hang free at lower edge and be finished with a narrow hem. The hem of the coat is finished with seam binding.

Ex-hemlines become invisible. When lengthening a dress or skirt, let the old hem out before sending the garment to your cleaner. He can then do a better job of removing the hemline mark.

Lengthening skirts. Before trying to add length to a skirt edge, when there is no hem to let down, ask yourself, "Is the hem edge of the skirt on the straight-of-goods (from selvage to selvage), or does this edge curve?" Bands of contrast fabric which look like an extension of a skirt must cut across a true bias. In other words, it must match the hem edge.

When the hem is down, and you have no matching material to provide good facings, try bandage gauze. It's preshrunk and doesn't pucker when laundered.

Folds and hems. In gathered and pleated skirts with straight edges, a double band, cut from selvage to selvage, can be added to the hem, or a single straight band can be inserted above the hem. But if the edge of the skirt curves, cut your double band on the true bias, the stretchiest part of the fabric. When piecing, take care to join the exact same fabric grains. However, when many pieces are necessary, they must be stitched and pressed and folded in the center, then pressed again. The fold can then be stitched easily to the skirt hem.

PLEATS AND OTHER TRICKY STITCHES

For best pleats, use a fabric that's neither too soft nor too wiry. Make sure the folds of the pleat are exactly on the lengthwise thread of the material. Finish and press the hem of the skirt before ironing the pleats. To prevent bulkiness, and to make sure of a straight-hanging pleated skirt, clip seams in pleats straight across at the top of the hemline and press seam in the open hem.

Accordion pleats should be steam-pleated. It requires 3 times the skirt-width length of material, plus special professional equipment and skill you can get for pennies at places that do just this and make covered buttons, belt, embroidery, etc.

When stitching square corners or sharp points on facings, make a very slight curve at the top of the corner or point. The corner will be less bulky and look more nearly square when the facing has been turned.

When sewing seams on lace or sheer garments, stitch each seam twice, the second stitching ¼ inch from the first. Then trim the seam close to this second stitching. No other finishing will be necessary.

To prevent puckering, when stitching sheer and stiff fabric such as taffeta, place a one-inch-wide strip of paper under the seam line while stitching. The paper easily tears away when the seam is finished.

Attached collars are cut double. Stitch together the outer edges by placing the right sides together. Then trim the seam and turn the collar right side out.

Detachable cuffs must hide (or reveal) a sleeve that has been finished with narrow seam binding or bias facing.

BUTTONS AND BUTTONHOLES

Cut button, not clothing. When removing a button from a garment, slip a fork under the button and insert the scissors over the fork. Prevents cutting the fabric.

Place a large matchstick over the holes of a button when sewing it on. Before fastening the thread, remove match and wind thread several times around threads between button and garment, thus forming a shank that relieves strain on button and prevents it from pulling out.

Dental floss for button thread. Use for attaching buttons to men's work clothes, children's play garments. Much stronger, withstands rough wear.

Self-covered buttons lend elegant custom-made detail, especially when you use imaginative stitching through the perforated holes in button shell. Use buttonhole twist, beads, French knots, embroidery thread, metallic thread, pearls, rhinestones, sequins, braids—indeed, anything that will sew through.

Choose size and type of button before you make the buttonhole, but no matter what shape button you select, make sure it is washable if the dress is, or that it can be dry-cleaned if the dress is made of material that must be dry-cleaned. The self-covered button is your best bet in practicality as well as in style.

Keep black, white, and gray permanent-finish organdy on hand to use as lightweight interfacing and reinforcement for buttonholes and buttons.

And on the buttonhole. It's easier to make buttonholes in thin materials if you first rub a little library paste on the wrong side. (Do this with cottons only.)

Instead of regular, rectangular, bound buttonholes, use triangular ones on occasion. Made the same as rectangular ones, but in the shape of a triangle with the point toward the edge of the garment. These are especially attractive when bound in a color contrasting with the garment.

When making "worked" buttonholes, use thread long enough to finish entire buttonhole; it is very difficult to make a neat joining. Working a trial buttonhole in a scrap of your fabric will enable you to estimate how long your thread should be.

To keep buttonholes from fraying when working them in loosely woven fabrics, apply a thin line of clear nail polish exactly where each hole is to be. Let dry, then cut buttonhole with a blade or buttonhole scissors and work as usual.

When buttonholes pull out, reinforce on the wrong side with paste-patch tape or finely woven narrow tape that you can hem into place. These reinforcements must overlap the buttonholes from neck to hem. They then will hold while you cut and rework the torn buttonhole.

ZIPPERS

Stitch zipper from bottom to top in order to preserve grain in fabric. If placket-seam allowance is narrower than $\frac{5}{8}$-inch width, stitch seam binding to each edge of seam to bring it up to that width or $\frac{3}{4}$ inch.

When measuring length, keep zipper taut.

When stitching zipper, turn its pull tab up.

To turn sharp corners, lower machine needle into fabric, raise the presser foot, and pivot on the needle. Lower the presser foot and continue stitching.

When you get to slider, allow stitching to fan out slightly around it.

When you apply zipper in skirt, trim the tape ends flush with the top of the skirt before attaching the waistband to the skirt.

PRESSING AND IRONING YOUR NEW CLOTHES

The difference between pressing and ironing is this: When pressing, you place your iron on the fabric, lift it, and place it on the fabric again. When you iron, you push the iron back and forth evenly. Pressing is used for all fabrics, ironing only for washable fabrics, also for smoothing out wrinkles and shaping a garment.

While sewing your dress, be sure to keep all seams, darts, tucks, etc., smooth by frequent pressing and steaming. When joining or crossing two seams, first press the one that is ready, and only then make the other seam.

Press side seams of skirt and blouse before the two parts are joined. Press sleeve seams before fitting sleeve into place.

Pressed seam edge may show ridge on outer side of garment. To avoid that non-professional look, follow this tip: Slightly press seam open with the point of the iron only, as in regular underpressing. Place straight-cut wrapping paper under seam allowance, so it runs along the seam. Do this on both sides, toward the body of the garment. Now press seam flat open. Width of seam allowance then cannot show telltale seam-edge line on the outside of your dress.

"Directional" pressing means letting the iron follow the grain of the fabric. It is as important as directional stitching. Also, when pressing stitching, press along with it, not across it.

What is "blocking"? It's the way you press curved parts of your dress, such as shoulder, bust, elbow, hip section. Use a rolled or ham-shaped special blocking cushion.

In addition to your regular ironing board you will also find other aids useful: The point presser for difficult-to-reach seams, for collars, other pointed edges. It looks like an anvil. The pounding block, used to obtain sharp edges the light-touch way. And the pressing mitt to press seams on material with a nap.

A must is the sleeve board. You can't do without it if you want to press and iron sleeves, collars, cuffs, other small pieces.

A pressing need is filled by the press cloth. Ideally, this should be a chemically treated, lintless cloth you can buy. Otherwise damp cheesecloth will do, but never wet. Organdy used as a press cloth also enables you to see what you are pressing.

The dress goes to press. Final pressing is done on the right side of the garment and is the last item in finishing that piece of clothing. Use a press cloth on top to prevent a shine.

Wrong side is right for pressing all tailored garments. Occasionally a heavy fabric will require pressing of both sides of applied sections, such as pockets, back belts, decorative trimming. Final pressing, however, should still be on the wrong side.

Cut down on ironing time by laying a piece of aluminum foil beneath your ironing-board cover. The aluminum reflects the heat onto the reverse side of the fabric being ironed, usually making it unnecessary to iron both sides.

To "heal" bruises on your velveteen jumper or velvet party dress, place the crushed area, pile down, over a brush of many bristles. Now hold a steam iron just above the back of the fabric and let the steam pour down through the pile. Then remove from the brush and shake until partially dry. Leave alone until fabric is entirely dry.

Velvets and other napped and piled fabrics made of rayon, celanese, or nylon should be pressed as follows:

To keep them young even when they're old, buy a pressing pad especially for the purpose, made of a stiff board covered with plush. Place this pad, plush side up, on your ironing board. Place your material right side down, on the pad, so that the nap of the plush and the nap of your material are face-to-face. Place dry press cloth over the wrong side, now topside, of your material. Press lightly with short up-and-down motions.

Silk velvets and other silk fabrics are correctly pressed the same way, except that the press cloth is now slightly moistened.

Wool velours, wool plush, and other napped wool fabrics are pressed similarly, but with two press cloths on top. Be sure, however, that the one next to the fabric is dry, the top linen sheet well-moistened.

Cotton and linen velveteens, corduroys, and all other cotton and linen fabrics must also have two protective press cloths, both of them well-moistened.

Other fabrics to be pressed in the same manner: Crepes, failles, all materials that have a raised surface.

Press these fabrics right side up: Satin, sateen, broadcloth, and other napped fabrics not specifically mentioned elsewhere in this section. Make sure inside seams like flat.

SEWING AND MENDING TIPS

Don't get stuck. Just before taking up that hand sewing, try coating your fingertips with several layers of colorless nail polish as protection against needle cuts.

Size of thimble affects comfort. Buy one large enough, because a small thimble makes finger perspire.

Stiff fingers will find the short needles, known as "betweens," or quilting needles, a great comfort.

Double, double, have no trouble. Next time you sew with double thread, pull through to even length, then knot each end separately instead of both together. Thread will not snarl or break as when two ends are knotted jointly.

Avoid eyestrain when threading a needle. Hold eye of the needle against a light background when using dark thread and against a dark background for light thread.

Eye-saver. A two-tone darning egg is a sight-saver. Paint half the egg black, the other half white. Then use the white half for mending dark-colored hose, the black half for mending light-colored hose.

Easy way to sharpen scissors. Cut through fine sandpaper several times.

Finger-protecting grips for scissors and shears can be made from rubber tape by placing strips around handles lengthwise and pressing the edges.

Ripping long seams. Long seams are easier to rip if you hold the material under the presser foot of your sewing machine, making the presser foot serve as a "third hand."

When ripping machine stitching, a good pair of tweezers is a boon. Thread will pull out easier, make work much faster and certainly less tedious.

Button, button; you've got the button. Before discarding old garments, rip off the buttons. String them to keep handy for future use.

A homemade bank for buttons is a screw-top jar with a slot in the cover. Use a screw driver and a hammer to make the slot.

Save hours of time in mending. While sorting the wash to be done, set a work basket beside you so that you may repair small rips, tears, cigarette holes, or other damage. Minor damage should be repaired before it is so enlarged by washing that a serious mending job is necessary.

Do your own "invisible mending." Paste-on patches (sold by the yard or package) are lifesavers for all sorts of cottons like shirts and sheets. You press them to the torn fabric with a hot iron, according to manufacturer's directions. Properly applied, these paste-ons withstand quite a few launderings.

Darning made easier. Protective gauze strips from small adhesive bandages are excellent backing for darning or mending difficult tears. Starched strips give body during mending job. Starch launders out and leaves fabric soft.

New twist in turning collars. An easy way to save work in turning a shirt collar is to rip it off at the seam where the band and the collar join, not where the band joins the shirt. You can then turn and sew it back without going to all the trouble of making a new buttonhole on the band.

Ribbon ends won't fray if you apply colorless nail polish to them.

Elastic temper-saver. When replacing elastic in a garment, pin the end of the new elastic to the old, then pull in the replacement as you pull out the old. Now it's easy, isn't it?

"Refresher course" for limp tape measure. Place it between sheets of waxed paper and press with hot iron. Wax stiffens the tape.

Knee-and-elbow reinforcement. When material starts to thin, that is the time to prevent weakening on that spot. Disengage ravelings from the inside of garment. Lengthwise ravelings are best taken from the side seams, while the crosswise ravelings should be pulled from the hem. Arrange ravelings on the wrong side of the garment, under the weakened areas. Place a piece of soft bias material over the ravelings. Pin or baste this material into place with a thin, color-matching thread. Now start to darn, going under and over the bias material and ravelings, while lightly catching just a few threads of the garment itself. Go easy, with a light hand. Do not pull, otherwise the right side will pucker. Repeat this back and forth, then across. Press on the wong side.

Mend sheets correctly and they're good for months of extra wear and washings. To make a sturdy muslin patch, use muslin of the same weight as the sheet and cut the patch 2 inches longer and wider than the tear. Pin patch in place, matching the grain line of the fabric. Hem edges by hand or machine, making sure the wrong-side edges are also hemmed.

Bad sheets worn in middle? Slit lengthwise, sew the two former selvage edges together, and run a hem around the new rough edges.

Sad sheet makes gay curtain. When sheets begin to wear they can be cut up and the strong parts tailored into smart café curtains for small kitchen or bathroom windows. Dye them in attractive decorator colors to match the color scheme of the room. Another idea: whip up extra pillow slips or sheets for a child's bed or a baby carriage.

Transferring pillow feathers. A clever way to feather your new pillowcase without mess or muss is to stitch the edge of the old pillowcase to the new one. Then you can shake the feathers into their new home without having them sail madly about. When done, simply cut the stitches to separate the pillowcases and sew up the opening.

Curtain tears. A coat of colorless nail polish applied to a tear in a net curtain, after mending, makes a perfect finish. Press the frayed ends together until the polish dries. Curtain mended in this way should not be stretched after laundering, though. Iron it carefully instead, avoid the mended spots.

Pot holders. Worn or torn Turkish towels make excellent pot holders. Cut and sew together 2 squares for each holder. Inexpensive tape for piping, available at five-and-tens, gives professional finishing touch.

Make an attractive robe from bath towels. Eight of them should be enough, and you can get the towels in beautiful shades. Looks snazzy; launders beautifully.

28

NEEDLECRAFTS

*Crochet, knit, or embroider with the aid of
words-and-pictures directions*

The traditional needlecrafts have never really gone out of fashion among many women, but today they seem to be enjoying greater popularity than ever—even among men. Quite aside from the savings involved, these crafts provide a genuine sense of creativity for many individuals. There are many related forms, of course, such as needlepoint and macramé, but here the three classic techniques—crocheting, knitting, and embroidery—are explained in some detail.

INTRODUCTION TO CROCHETING

Crochet threads. Use the exact threads specified in crocheting instructions. Any substitution will give you a result different from what you expect. Remember, too, to buy the entire amount of thread needed right at the beginning, at the same time, especially if you buy colored thread. In this way you'll get the same dye lot and no shade variation can occur in your work. Preferably, get enough thread not only to finish the article you have in mind but for any matching pieces you might want to tackle later on.

Crochet hooks. Buy steel hooks for fine work with cotton threads or, in the larger sizes, for crocheting wool. Otherwise, bone, composition, and wooden hooks are used with woolens. Each size is especially made for use with a certain size of thread. Again, follow the directions in selecting the hook you'll use.

Gauge your crocheting tensions. Gauge is a measure. It means the number of stitches you make per inch and, crosswise, the number of rows you make per inch. This number, in both cases, varies with each individual, depending on whether you are a "tight" or "loose" crocheter. To find out, make a practice piece at least 2 inches square in size, using the size of hook and thread specified in the instructions. If you make more stitches per inch than are specified in the directions, take a hook a size larger. If you make fewer stitches per inch than the directions call for, use a hook a size smaller. Change your hook until your own gauge corresponds with the gauge in the directions; otherwise you'll never be able to make the crocheting pattern the directions describe.

BASIC CROCHET STITCHES

Chain stitch revisited. The first step in crocheting is learning to hold the hook and thread comfortably. To make a loop, hold the end of the thread in the left hand, main length in the right hand, turn it around and in front of left hand end, hold loop in place between thumb and forefinger.

resting it about midway between the broad bar and top of the hook. With the thread in back of hand, place thread between fourth and little finger, across palm side of fingers and over forefinger, if more comfortable, wind thread over finger once. Do not hold thread too tightly. Hold the loop in left hand, insert hook in loop, pick up the main length of thread on hook (this is termed "thread over"), and pull through loop.

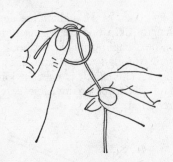

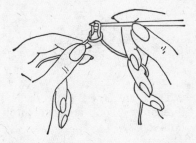

Repeat this chain for required length.

Insert hook in loop, pick up the main length of thread on hook and draw it through loop, pull both lengths of thread to tighten loop on hook.

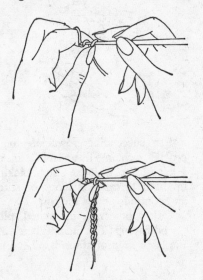

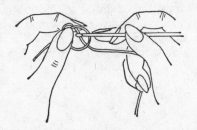

Loop is now ready to make the first chain stitch. Hold the hook in right hand as you would a pencil, bringing the middle finger forward

On this foundation chain may be worked practically any stitch desired. Practice this stitch until you can do it with ease.

Single crochet. Chain for desired length, skip 1 chain, insert hook in next chain, thread over hook and pull through chain.

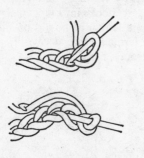

There are now 2 loops on hook; thread over hook and pull through both loops.

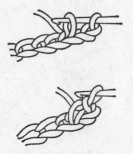

For succeeding rows of single crochet, chain 1 to turn, insert hook in top of next stitch picking up both threads or loops of stitch and continue across the row.

Unless otherwise instructed, pick up both loops of stitch. When only the back loop of stitch is picked up

it forms a rib and is called rib or slipper stitch.

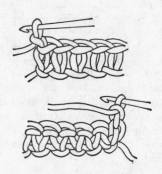

Slip stitch. Make a chain the desired length. Skip one chain, insert hook in next chain, thread over hook and pull through chain and loop on hook. This stitch is used in joining and whenever an invisible stitch is required.

Short double crochet. Chain for desired length, thread over hook, insert hook in 3rd stitch from hook, draw thread through (3 loops on hook), thread over hook and draw through all three loops on hook. For succeeding rows, chain 2, and turn.

Double crochet. Chain for desired length, thread over hook, insert hook in 4th stitch from hook, draw thread through (3 loops on hook) thread over hook and pull through 2 loops, thread over hook and pull through 2 loops. Succeeding rows, chain 3, turn and work next double crochet in 2nd double crochet of previous row. The chain 3 counts as 1 double crochet.

Treble crochet. Chain for desired length, thread over hook twice, insert hook in 5th chain from hook, draw thread through (4 loops on hook), thread over hook, pull through 2 loops, thread over, pull through 2 loops. For succeeding rows chain 4, turn and work next treble crochet in 2nd treble crochet of previous row. The chain 4 counts as 1 treble crochet.

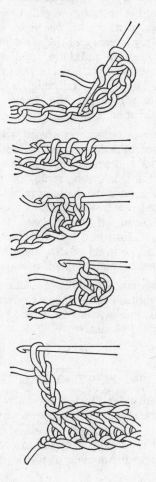

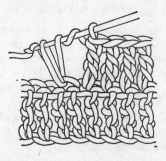

Double treble crochet. Chain for desired length, thread over hook 3 times, insert in 6th chain from hook (5 loops on hook) and work off 2 loops at a time the same as in a treble crochet. For succeeding rows, chain 5, turn and work next double treble crochet in 2nd double treble crochet of previous row. The chain 5 counts as 1 double treble crochet.

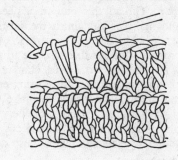

Treble treble crochet. Thread over hook 4 times and work off same as for double treble crochet.

CROCHETING ROSES

Crocheted roses are easy and fun to make. The individual rose motifs are joined together not only with needle stitches but, in addition, with two cross trebles worked into the space between motifs.

Make yourself a bed of roses by joining roses together to form a bedspread. For very practical joining, you may want to try a bedspread of the hexagonal motif, which is easily joined by overcast stitches with a sewing needle. This motif is especially suited for hard, long-lasting wear.

A bouquet of roses can emerge from your hands singly, to strew roses in the path of your best glassware and china.

CROCHETING TIPS

Finish line. Crocheted work must be finished by cutting the thread about 4 inches away from the last loop. Thread this end in a needle and make secure finish by darning it through the solid part of the crochet. Cut the thread close to the work. Before you ever start crocheting, make sure the starting end, too, is sufficiently long to make the right finishing. Let no knots be visible, either, when you join pieces together by sewing. Instead use several over-and-over stitches, and wherever possible darn the thread through the solid portion of crochet for a short stretch.

Blocking, in crocheting language, really means pressing. When your article is finished, you must always press it in a special way. If the piece has become soiled in work, wash it first, then block it. Pin the damp article to a padded ironing board. Use rustproof pins or you'll have rust marks on your work. Gently stretch and shape the article to the size and form specified. If you haven't washed the lace before blocking, press it through a damp cloth with a hot iron. Leave it in position until thoroughly dry.

How to launder crocheted articles. Place in lathery soapsuds and hot water and squeeze in and out until clean. Don't rub, scrub, or twist. Then rinse the piece several times in lukewarm water until all the soap is rinsed off. Now rinse in cold water. Roll in a bath towel and let stand, so towel absorbs most of the moisture. Starch only if necessary.

Store crochet hooks in a discarded toothbrush container. Convenient and prevents hooks from getting snarled in yarn.

BASIC KNITTING STITCHES

Casting the stitches correctly. You need one needle and two threads from one ball of thread. Measure out the length of thread in proportion to the number of stitches to be cast on. Do not cut. Hold the measured thread in your left hand, the thread pulled from the ball in your right hand. Around your left thumb form a loop into which to insert the knitting needle. Pass right thread around the point of the needle and pull out a loop. Now you have made the first stitch. Go on in the same way until you have reached the required number of stitches and you'll have a neat and solid base.

Knit (or plain) stitch. Insert the right-hand needle into the first stitch. Pass the thread around that needle and pull out a loop through the stitch loop that is kept on the right-hand needle, letting the stitch slip off the left-hand needle.

Purl stitch. Pass the thread in front of the work, toward yourself. Insert

the right-hand needle from back to the front and wind the thread downwards. Draw thread through stitch from front to back, letting stitch slip off left-hand needle.

Stockinette stitch. This is produced by knitting one row and purling the next. The result: two entirely different surfaces, ribbed on the right side, like a stocking.

Ribbing is worked by alternating a specified number of knit stitches with a specified number of purl stitches. Ribbing, being elastic, is used most often in waistbands, cuffs, turtle necks on sweaters, tops of socks, winter caps, from all of which you want a snug fit.

How to increase. Usually worked from two to four stitches in from the beginning or end of a row. In shaping, though, increases are often made in the first or last stitches of the row. Knit first into the front of the stitch to make one

stitch. Do not slip off the needle. Knit into the back of the same stitch and slip old stitch off left needle. Now you have transferred two stitches to the right-hand needle instead of one. To increase purling, follow the same method, but, of course, use the purl, not the knit stitch.

How to decrease. In purpose and procedure, decrease is, of course, the opposite of increase. Decreases, though, are also usually made two to four stitches in or, for shaping, on one of the two ends. On a knit row, knit two stitches together, so that you transfer to your right-hand needle one stitch instead of two. Purling decrease is the same, except you merge the two stitches by purling.

knit stitch. At the end of that row, knit two stitches together before last stitch that you knit.

The cable stitch is much easier than it looks and is very decorative. Work up to where you want cable to start. Know how many stitches wide your cable is to be. Transfer first half of these stitches onto a double-pointed spare needle. Place spare needle at back of work. Knit second half of cable stitches first, then knit the stitches on the spare needle, then continue. By reversing the order in which you knot the two halves of the stitches in the prescribed "ribbon," you have achieved the twisted cable effect.

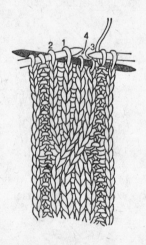

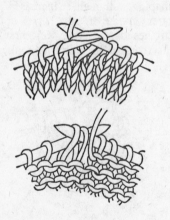

To shape toes for socks, decreasing is handled differently at the beginning of a row. You knit one, slip a stitch, knit two together, then pass slipped stitch over last two-together

Cast on and bind off with a needle a size larger than you intend to knit with. This keeps edge from being taut.

When binding off shoulders, avoid the little bumps by slipping the first stitch.

LACE KNITTING

Lace knitting is different from ordinary knitting since it is lighter. This is due to the use of fine, twisted cotton thread with rather thick needles; to the inclusion of much openwork and combination of stitch decreases to form a design; and to the tension and starching of the finished work. Knitting instructions for each pattern must be followed to a "T."

Knitted lace edging looks elegant on flower-vase mats, tea napkins, tray cloths of fine linen.

The knitted rose motif can be made small to protect furniture tops from marks of ash trays, china figurines, or can be made into a fine round table cover.

To launder and block knitted lace, follow hints given for crocheted lace.

KNITTING TIPS

Thread wool easily by twisting a tiny piece of cotton on the end of the wool. Makes it much easier to slip the wool thread through the needle.

Make swatches of new patterns to familiarize yourself with them before you start the main work.

If you drop a stitch, use crochet hook to pick it up. Catch the loose stitch and work it up on the horizontal thread of each subsequent row. Keep stitch in pattern. Continue until you've caught up with the row you are knitting on.

To reuse yarn from old sweaters, first remove kinks this way: Slip three or four clothespins over the rim of a large dishpan. Wind the raveled yarn around them. Then pour steaming hot water into pan. In a few minutes the steaming straightens the yarn for reuse. Or wash ravel, then dye the wool a fresh new color. Reknit, and there you are!

You can straighten used yarn by drawing it through a slotted hose slipped over the end of a teakettle spout.

To reshape broken edge of plastic knitting needle, sand it to a new point, then pass it through steam from teakettle. Plastic will soften and blend the tiny scratches at the tip into a smooth surface.

Toothpick "needle." When knitting, try a round toothpick, pointed at both ends, as a temporary stitch holder. Avoids having to slip the stitches back onto the knitting needle so they can be knitted back again into the pattern. The toothpick serves as a temporary knitting needle.

"Smoke cure" keeps moths away from yarn. Store knitting yarn in empty tobacco tin. Faint odor repels moths, doesn't damage yarn.

MEND SWEATER HOLES INVISIBLY

Swiss darning does an almost invisible job of mending sweater holes. Clip frayed edges of yarn and free two stitches at each corner of hole so sides can be turned back and hemmed. This makes a rectangular hole, straight at the sides and with loops hanging free at each end of the hole.

Use a blunt embroidery needle, threaded with yarn that matches sweater. Working on right side of garment, slip needle through free loops at upper right-hand corner of hole. Cross vertically and pick up two more at opposite end. Continue across hole until all loops are picked up. Now you have a vertical core of yarn on which to weave crosswise mending stitches.

Start mending at right-hand corner. To weave in stitches, insert needle

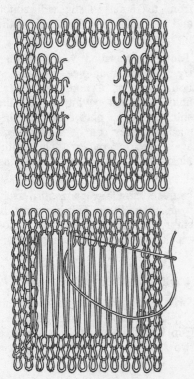

from under side of sweater, into first loop, then around under first two vertical yarns and back into same loop, bringing needle up through next loop. Work across row, making loops the same size as those of sweater. At end of row, catch edge of hole from under side. Turn garment around so you work to the right on the next row. Continue in same manner until all stitches are replaced.

INTRODUCTION TO EMBROIDERING

This section shows how to make—easily and simply—the majority of embroidery stitches used today. From lazy daisy to trapunto, they are all here to decorate your home and your wardrobe.

Threads and yarns. Six-strand, mercerized cotton may be separated for fine or heavier work. On twisted or purled cotton, No. 8 is fine; No. 5, medium, and No. 3, coarse. Loosely twisted candlewick yarn is used for tufting. There are two types of silk embroidery thread: the strand floss type, and the twisted rope type. There is also a linen thread for use on linen embroidery. Loosely twisted crewel yarn and firmly twisted tapestry yarn are two special types of wool.

For neat hand embroidery, start all stitches on wrong side of cloth. Sew two small stitches, one over the other, to anchor thread, then push needle through to right side.

For the thrill of giving your work that artistic, professional touch, follow the step-by-step directions carefully. And, of course, since good threads cost so little, you will want to use the best.

BASIC EMBROIDERY STITCHES

Running stitch. This is used for outlining and paddling. Start stitch on wrong side of material by sewing two small stitches (one over the other) to anchor thread. Then bring out thread on right side. Make small up-and-down stitches on line to be covered.

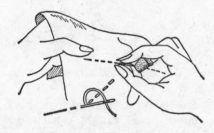

Backstitch. Bring out the needle on the right side of material. Insert it back of the thread and bring it out again in front of the thread. The first stitch determines the length of the second stitch, etc. Stitch in back of the thread again and put needle through the same hole where thread was brought out first.

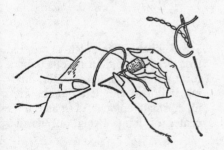

Outline stitch. This stitch is worked from left to right. Bring out the needle on right side of material. Insert it a little further along. Hold the thread with the left thumb and bring the needle out again halfway back of the first stitch made. Hold the thread with the left thumb, insert needle a little further along line to be covered, then stitch back into the same hole where first stitch was completed. Always hold thread with left thumb to the left side. The effect is slightly different if thread is held to the right side. It is important to hold thread to the same side from start to end.

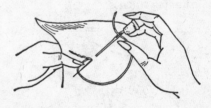

Couching stitch. This is a method of stitching down threads that are carried along the surface of the line to be covered. Variations of couching stitches can be used, such as crisscrossing stitches, slanting stitches, etc.

Long and short stitch. This stitch is made by working one long and one short straight stitch close to one another. It is used as an outline for leaves, flower petals, etc.

Whipped running stitch. Work a row of running stitches (see page 279), and whip the stitches. The whipping does not go through the material, only through and over the running stitches.

Chain stitch. Bring out the thread. Hold it down with left thumb, stitch into same hole where thread was brought out, forming a loop. Bring out the needle below the length of

the stitch desired, over the loop. Repeat as before.

Lazy-daisy stitch. This is really a single chain stitch "A" kept in position by a stitch at round end of loop "B." Start each stitch the same way as chain stitch. End off each chain individually.

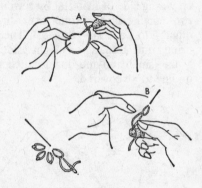

Bundle stitch. This stitch is made up of three straight stitches tied down in the center with a tight overcasting stitch.

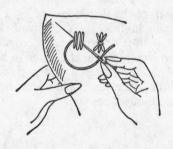

Scroll stitch. This stitch is worked from left to right. Bring out thread, form a loop from left to right, holding it down with left thumb. Pick up a small amount of material in center of loop. Bring out needle.

Release loop slowly. This stitch is very effective when a heavy yarn is used.

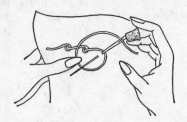

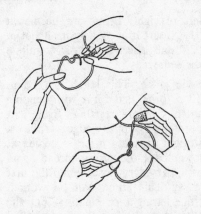

Blanket stitch. Bring out thread on lower edge. Insert it again above, a short distance to the right, while holding thread with left thumb. Bring out the needle above the thread, at lower edge. Continue the same way.

Fly stitch. Bring out thread. Insert needle a small distance to the right. Make a slanting stitch back to the left. Pull out needle over the thread. Fasten stitch with a small straight stitch. Bring out the thread again on same level as first stitch made, a small distance to the right. Continue as before.

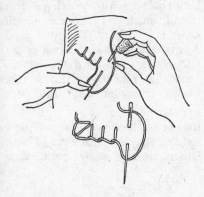

French knot. Bring out the thread. Hold the thread with the left hand a short distance from where thread was brought out. Twist thread around needle twice (or three or four times, according to the size of knot desired). Insert needle right back into same hole while releasing thread slowly with left hand.

Herringbone stitch. This stitch is worked along a double line, from

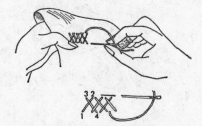

left to right. Bring out needle at "1," insert it at "2," bring it out at "3," and insert it at "4." Continue the same way.

Satin stitch. This stitch is used to fill a form. Pad form with running stitches before starting. Bring out needle at upper edge. Take a straight stitch, insert needle at lower edge. Bring out thread again at upper edge, close beside the first stitch. This stitch can be worked either straight or slanting, but the stitches must always be worked close to one another.

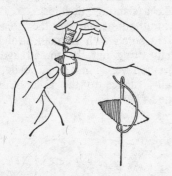

Straight stitch. This stitch is worked by one single stitch in a straight line taken over a small portion of the material.

Buttonhole stitch. This stitch is made exactly the same way as a blanket stitch (see page 281), except that the stitches must be worked close to each other.

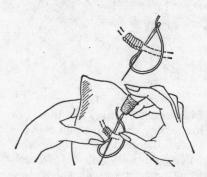

Cutwork. Work a close buttonhole stitch all along double line. Pad the buttonhole stitch by working over a thread, which you carry along until figure is completed. To insure good results, always have the knot of the buttonhole stitch face the cutout. Veins in petals and leaves are worked in outline stitch (see page 279).

Bars across the cutouts are no longer stylish. They are made as follows: Stitch across to cutout twice, close

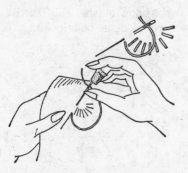

together, forming a bridge. (Don't stitch through the material.) Work a buttonhole stitch all along the "bridge," without stitching through the material. Bars have to be completed before cutwork is started.

Scallops. Scallops are worked in a close buttonhole stitch, starting narrow and getting wider in the center of the scallop.

Cross-stitch. Bring out thread at bottom of cross. Stitch up diagonally from left to right. Bring out needle at bottom of next cross. Work all stitches in the same direction first. Then work all top stitches in the opposite direction. Crosses, when finished, should join at top and bottom.

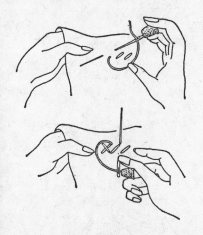

Gobelin stitch. This stitch is used to embroider tapestry and petit point.

It is usually worked over canvas. It is really half a cross-stitch. See enlarged diagram for detail.

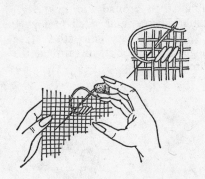

Bullion stitch. Bring out thread at "1." Stitch back to "2," come out at "1" again, leaving needle in material. Twist thread around needle, making enough twists to cover length of stitch. Hold twist in place with left thumb and ease needle through gently. Stitch down through "2." Stitch is then completed.

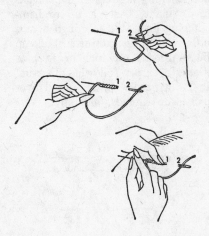

OTHER EMBROIDERY TECHNIQUES

Eyelets. Eyelets are usually punched or cut out. Work a running stitch around the raw edge. Embroider a satin stitch (see page 282) or a buttonhole stitch (see page 282) over it, all around the circle.

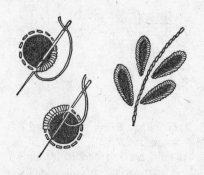

Hemstitching. The material must be perfectly straight, as threads have to be drawn. This stitch is used for narrow hems around handkerchiefs, as decorations on lingerie, etc. Draw as many threads as width of hemstitching desired. If a hem has to be made, baste it up to hemstitching line. Stitch through hem a little below drawn threads. Pick up three threads (or four or five, as desired), as per following diagram. Pull out needle, bring thread over picked-up threads, and stitch ver-

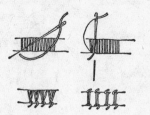

tically through hem. Bring out thread and continue as above. When bottom row has been completed, work top row the same way.

How to make a hem. Baste hem the desired width. Make a knot at end of thread. Stitch through edge of fold and bring out thread. Pick up a small amount of material below fold, slightly to the right where thread was brought out. Stitch through two thicknesses of hem and continue the same as before. This stitch is called slip stitch.

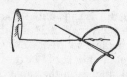

Appliqué work. Cut out appliqué on dash line "A." Bend edges

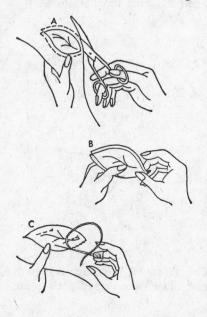

under to solid line "B." Baste or pin appliqué in place and slip-stitch to base material "C." (Slip stitch is shown on page 284 as "How to make a hem.")

Smocking. Stretch the section to be smocked, tacking it on a board. Mark off dots at regular intervals with pencil (about ¼ inch apart) in perfectly straight horizontal and vertical lines. (Fig. 1.)

Take a long thread, fasten the stitch firmly, and gather along the dots, pushing needle from one dot to the next. Do not finish off thread at end of row. All other rows are gathered directly under the first row. (Fig. 2.) Take threads at end of rows, gather up material to form flutes. Insert a pin at end of every two rows and twist threads of these two rows around it. (Fig. 3.) Do not break off threads.

Catch the first two flutes together by sewing two top stitches firmly over them. Next go down one row and catch the next two flutes together. Go up again and continue the same way. (Fig. 4.) Tighten all loose threads and finish off on wrong side.

Faggoting. This stitch is used to join two materials in a decorative way. Prepare both edges by making a narrow hem of materials to be joined, and baste them the desired distance apart to a piece of hard paper. Follow diagram A-B-C.

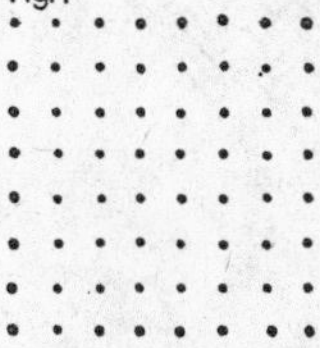

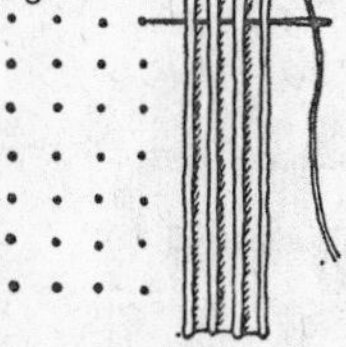

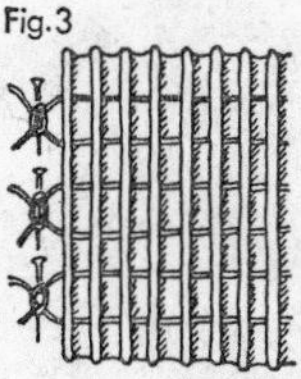

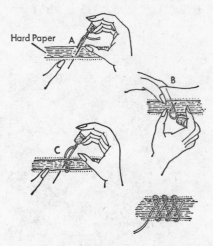

Trapunto. Baste together two layers of material evenly. The design is stamped on the wrong side. Work

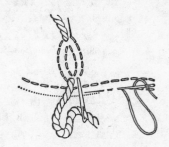

Fig. 1

Fig. 2

Fig. 3

Fig. 4

over design, using a running stitch and working through both layers of material. The design is then padded with heavy yarn that is pulled through on the wrong side. Trim ends of yarn as each pattern is completed.

How to make a tassel. Wind thread around a piece of cardboard "A"; cut thread at one end. Tie a knot around the middle of the threads "B." Then wind threads around cut ends "C," about ⅜ inch below knot, to make the head of tassel. End off thread by stitching through head.

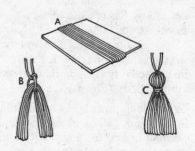

SPACE-FILLING STITCHES

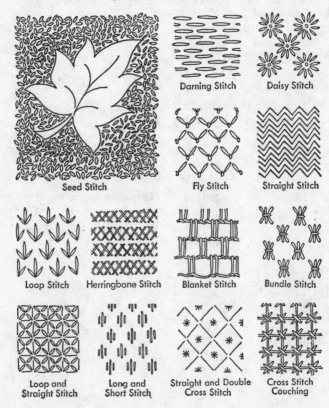

Seed Stitch

Darning Stitch   Daisy Stitch

Fly Stitch   Straight Stitch

Loop Stitch   Herringbone Stitch   Blanket Stitch   Bundle Stitch

Loop and Straight Stitch   Long and Short Stitch   Straight and Double Cross Stitch   Cross Stitch Couching

Quilting. Two layers of material and interlining are basted together evenly. The design appears on the right side of the material. Outline the design in a running stitch on the right side, working through the three layers of material.

gerie. They are fascinating to make and add that distinctive touch that can only be yours and yours alone.

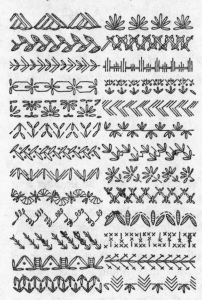

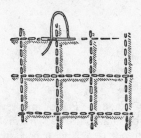

Decorative borders. Use these charming, simple borders for anything from your children's first layette to your very loveliest lin-

29

CHILD CARE

*Hints for raising happier, healthier children—
from infancy to teens*

There is no end to the number and variety of printed words on how best to raise children: the classic texts, the annual best-sellers, magazine articles, government pamphlets, and many more. There is no question that should go unanswered, no problem that should be prolonged, when it comes to the basics of child care. What follows is merely a small selection of hints to suggest the variety of matters parents today might consider in raising children.

The diaper question: Which of the three solutions to the diaper problem will you use—disposables, fabric diapers (which need laundering), or a diaper service? The diaper service is probably the most expensive, but it may be justified for convenience. Most families probably use disposables: there are various brands available, in a range of sizes, thicknesses, etc. Certainly everyone will want to use disposables for trips or in situations when the disposal of soiled diapers is inconvenient.

Fabric diapers. There are several kinds of material used in making such diapers, each with certain advantages and disadvantages. You might like to test each kind on your baby before buying a large supply. Caution: new fabric diapers should be laundered before the first use.

"Ouchless" pins. A decorative pot holder attached to the wall several feet above the crib or dressing table provides a safe, handy place to park open safety pins while changing a baby's diaper.

Safety-first diapering. Stick pins into a cake of soap kept handy on the table or bed where diapers are changed. Makes pin points easier to pierce diapers with, avoiding pinholes in sheets and mattresses. Also keeps pins out of baby's reach.

The decision to use a pacifier is one that each family must make for itself, but if you do use a pacifier make sure it has a large enough shield so that it cannot be swallowed.

What does baby weigh? If you have a bathroom scale, but not one for baby weighing, you still can determine infant poundage. Step on the bathroom scale with baby in your arms, then get off and put baby down. Now step on the scale again. The difference is what baby weighs.

Handy storage for baby's buoy toys. Use net bags from potatoes, onions, or oranges. Hang out of the way on clothesline or bathroom hook. Toys will air-dry quickly and be handy for the next dunking.

Protect baby in the rain. If it's raining when you take baby out in the carriage, cover the blankets with a plastic tablecloth.

Card table protects baby. To keep a small child from going through the open doorway where door can't be closed, open a card table and place it on its side in the doorway. Stand it on the side of the door opening away from the child, well barricaded with heavy objects so table isn't movable by child-strength. A chair backed against it, loaded with telephone book and other heavy books, does the trick nicely.

Bumpers protect your walls from baby's excess energy. Much damage that is caused when your youngster pushes chairs against the walls can be prevented. Drive two or three rubber-headed tacks into the back of the chair, to cushion impact against wall.

Keeping track of the toddler in your house. A tiny bell on the shoelace between the two bottom eyelets of the tot's shoe can save you many steps. You can hear where he is by the tinkle of the bell as he walks. Also, the child will enjoy the sound as he moves about.

Small children's garments should not fit too snugly. The measurements you need are those of length, shoulder width, chest, waist.

In making baby clothes for tiny infants, add that ruffle not at end of hem, but 2 to 3 inches above, so it can't rub against tender skin.

Safeguard that sensitive skin by using only the softest fabrics for babies: batiste, nainsook, fine flannel, cashmere, crepe-de-chine. They need so little material, you can afford the best.

Children's sleepers. Look for garments giving maximum comfort and wear. Knit fabrics are more elastic than wool, also less likely to irritate or to shrink in washing. It is important to be sure of roomy seat, crotch, and armholes, and of legs and feet that are long enough. Snap fasteners are more convenient (also less likely to rip) than buttons. Such garments are far safer than sleeping-blanket devices that fasten to crib.

Economy in two-piecers. While one-piece snow suits are convenient for babies, two-piece types have many advantages for toddlers. Jackets can be worn separately in mild weather; adjustability of trouser straps often permits second season of wear; if pants wear out before jacket, or vice versa, you have only to replace half a suit.

Double-decker snow suits preferred. Select them when made in two layers, a lightweight outer one, plus a warm lining. Combines warmth with lightness and freedom of action. Knitted wool wristlets and anklets are better than cotton; they retain elasticity much longer.

Safety-first buttons on play clothes. Buttons on small-fry clothes that take rough wear should be attached to a tape so they won't pull a hole through the fabric.

On children's clothes use the fewest possible fasteners. You'll make it easy, this way, for tots to learn how to dress themselves at an early age. Give buttons top preference, bound buttonholes ditto. Zippers are fine too.

When children become conscious of what they wear, it always makes them happy when a bit of embroidery or appliqué adorns their clothes: a nursery animal, a storybook character, some small flowers, and most especially their name or monogram.

For female juniors, never just shorten the dress handed down by you or anyone else, no matter how good a condition the garment is in. The adult style is unsuitable, and the young girl will wear it with that hand-me-down feeling. Make the dress over completely, and preferably dye it navy blue, or dark red, or stylish brown. Add a new pocket, a fresh, frilly collar, some braiding or embroidery. For her, too, a monogram is always sure success.

Where there are several children wearing jeans of about the same size, it is sometimes difficult to tell which pair belongs to whom. With an indelible pencil, mark their names or initials on the inside white band or pockets.

CHILDREN'S SHOES

Children will get shoes of proper fit if they try them on while wearing stockings of correct size. Also, try both shoes. When child stands up, with weight evenly distributed, large toe should be about ¾ inch from the tip, with vamp loose enough for you to grasp a small fold of leather. Heel should be snug when shoe is laced up or strap-fastened.

Hand-me-down shoes are poor economy. Shoes shape themselves to the individual's foot, so that a shoe that fits one child will never fit another exactly right afterward and, in fact, can cause great foot discomfort.

Shellac children's shoes. If you've been having trouble with your youngster's habit of scuffing the tips of his shoes regularly, you can calm your nerves and your pocketbook. Just shine the shoes and then brush several thin layers of shellac over the tip. Not only will shoes retain the gloss, but the shellac will protect the leather against careless kicks, scratches, etc.

To keep tots from falling, sandpaper the soles of their new shoes before they are worn. Gives better traction.

Junior won't lose his galoshes at school if you try this: Give him a spring-type clothespin with his name on it. When he takes off his rubbers or overshoes he can clip them together with the clothespin. He'll have no trouble after that.

Your children won't lose their shoelaces if knots are tied to center of each lace between the two lower eyelets.

Junior's shoelaces have raveled tips? He may have lost the tips during a hectic play period. Dip the tips into glue and allow to dry. Simple job saves you price of new laces, keeps old ones looking neat.

FUN FARE FOR CHILDREN

Gift wrappings for the kiddies. Add gala touches by thrusting a few lollipops into the knot of the bow or by wrapping package in comic paper instead of regular gift wrap. Another idea: attach a dime-store trinket to your wrapping ribbons.

Children love party sweets, but . . . when planning refreshments that include ice cream, it is well not to court possible tummy-aches by adding other rich items. Stay away from heavy chocolates or very rich cakes.

For your little girl's birthday cake try using tiny kewpie or baby dolls instead of candles. They're inexpensive and mean an extra gift of a dolly for each of your child's little guests.

Rainbow bath. To make the bath a real treat for the kiddies, add a few drops of vegetable coloring to the bubble suds. The resulting scads of gaily colored bubbles that float about will delight your child.

For budding sculptors. Modeling in clay intrigues most youngsters, and clay-modeling sets are available at reasonable prices. When the clay figure is complete it will keep its form and be greatly enhanced by a thin coat or two of fresh white shellac.

Preserve children's art work. Those precious pencil drawings your child brings home from school can be kept from smudging by dipping them for a few seconds in a pan of skimmed milk. Hang up to dry, making sure no moisture marks or streaks are allowed to form. Takes just a little bit of liquid, costs practically nothing, and it makes a really fine fixative.

Save wear and tear on children's games. Shellac the board of such games as checkers, parchesi, etc. Keeps pasteboard in better condition; it can even be wiped off when soiled by play-begrimed little hands.

Interesting use for old broom handle. Use a hand saw to cut circular disks and save them to replace checker pieces which children so frequently lose. After disks are sanded smooth, paint them to match the missing checkers.

CHILDREN'S FURNITURE

Bunk partitions. Two bunks, one above the other, in children's room can often serve as a partition forming a partially private room for each youngster. Do it this way: Fasten a piece of ¼-inch fir plywood on one side of the lower bunk so that it closes off one side between the lower and upper. On the other side close off the space between the upper bunk and ceiling. The result will be two room areas, one for each youngster.

A gift from your hardware man. Ask him for empty nail kegs. Painted and decorated, with the addition of a cover, they can serve as children's hampers, stools, or as scrap baskets and containers for kindling wood.

Roll-away toy boxes. Ever notice how toys in the children's room tend to accumulate in an untidy pile under the bed? Here's a simple way to eliminate the clutter and to keep the room neat. Put together two or three sturdy plywood boxes, then mount them on casters. Keep the height low enough so that the toy wagons can be rolled under the bed when not in use.

Personalized furniture for children. Paint first name or nickname on the top drawer of chest of drawers, then add favorite décor: animals, cowboys, astronauts, ballerinas, or a circus scene.

Children's wardrobe and desk. Crowding is often unavoidable in a small child's room, but here's a compact little unit that will reduce the crowding to a minimum. Build the doors as high as necessary from ¾-inch fir plywood. Hinge table so it folds up when door is closed. Shelves at right allow space for radio, shoes, and other items. Unit can be constructed to fit any child's height.

FURNISHING GOOD HABITS

Your child will enjoy learning orderly habits when you give him his very own storage shelves for books and toys. An inexpensive, colorfully decorated open bookcase in his room will do the trick. Once he learns the habit of returning objects to their proper place, he'll take pride in continuing the habit.

Your child's clothes closet should be arranged with rods low enough so child can reach the garments.

This encourages self-help, keeps child from developing overdependence on grownups in keeping belongings in place. Besides, tots enjoy having facilities in their rooms scaled comfortably to their own size.

Closet grows too. Children's wardrobes can be planned so that they grow with the youngster. Have for children a plywood wardrobe, where racks and drawers are placed within the youngster's reach. As the child grows taller, the clothes rack can be moved up a peg and the shelves taken out or set down under the clothes. Arrangement of storage facilities for children so that they can use them at an early age not only keeps rooms tidy but teaches neatness early enough for it to become a habit.

House-cleaning primer. Teach your children to divide room into two sections, doing half at a time. First half: start them with dusting brush (desk, knickknacks, window frames, chair section behind bed). Then show them how to use upholstery tool attachment of vacuum cleaner for draperies, bed covering, throw pillows, etc.; a crevice tool for desk drawers, bedsprings, etc.; the floor brush for bare floor sections. Second half: start them with floor brush to complete floor area; then the rug tool for throw rugs, etc.; the dusting brush for dresser, closet shelves, garment and shoe bags, radio, etc.; the crevice tool for dresser drawers and corners of closet; the upholstery tool for remaining chairs.

For that student in your family, a helpful memory aid. A small bulletin board made of builder's wallboard and simply framed, then placed above his desk, is a good place to tack advance assignments or other study memoranda. And a wonderful way to communicate for the kid who loves to exchange notes.

Protect children's eyes. If studying is done at a highly polished table, be sure to place a large blotter under the books to prevent glare.

Your child may be avoiding piano practice because of eyestrain. Make sure keyboard and music stand are well lit by placing two upright lamps, one 34 inches to right of keyboard center and one an equal distance to left. Use 100-200-300-watt three-way light bulbs. Shallow white inside dense reflectors, 12 to 16 inches in diameter, are preferable. Height to reflectors should be 66 inches.

30

HOME FURNISHINGS

How to get better and longer service from the things that make a home

Some people think all knots in wood denote defects. This is not true. Knots that form an integral part of the wood are completely sound, should not be rejected. Sometimes they even make the grain pattern more attractive. However, black knots (dead-wood spots) are likely to drop out as the board weathers. Examine wood carefully.

Overheated rooms will injure your finest pieces of furniture and ruin antiques. Don't store extra table leaves in cellar or other damp areas. Avoid placing furniture against hot radiators or under open windows.

No-snag furniture. If you have any chairs that keep snagging your hosiery, sandpaper away the roughened spots, then coat with clear shellac.

Smooth-sliding drawers. To make those hard-to-budge drawers slide much more easily, put thumbtacks on the runners.

Fresh touch for dresser drawers. Empty them every so often and clean by wiping down inner surfaces with soapy cloth and rinsing with clean damp cloth. When dry, line drawers with waxed paper or plastic sheeting.

Scratchproof furniture casters. Casters will roll quietly and smoothly if rolling surfaces of the wheels are covered with adhesive tape. Ends of tape should meet but not overlap, as this would cause uneven rolling.

Casters stay put. If caster keeps slipping out, wrap a slip of adhesive tape around the stem of the caster until it fits the hole snugly. Or fill the hole with melted paraffin and then insert caster.

Piano-care hints. Extremes of temperature hurt the instrument. Keep pianos away from windows often opened in wintertime, away from radiators and steampipes, away from damp spots. You'll need tuning less often and the instrument will last much longer. In summertime, since the felted hammers attract moths, safeguard them with paracrystals. Note, also, that piano keys need light to retain their sparkling whiteness, so they should not be constantly covered, and that idle pianos do not stay in good condition, so that moving parts should be exercised weekly with several hours of playing.

To clean piano keys, dip a piece of flannel in denatured alcohol and wipe each key carefully. Then dry at once with another piece of flannel.

Rush-bottom chairs won't develop split reeds for a long time if you apply a coat of clear shellac over the seats.

Restore loose cane seats. Cane seats loosened by too much strain quickly tighten up if you do this: Go over the seat with a rag soaked in hot water, then set the chair in the sun to dry.

Ideal care for leather furniture. When leather shows signs of soiling, wash with a thick lather of castile or saddle soap. Remove soap with damp cloth, then wipe dry. Occasionally use leather dressing to keep it pliable and prevent cracking.

To clean leather chair seats, rub each seat with half a lemon. Polish with furniture oil, then shine up with a dry cloth.

Or shine up leather furniture by using a soft piece of cotton dipped in vinegar. First squeeze cotton almost dry, then polish.

To repair cigarette burns in upholstered furniture, select a yarn color to match material, darn hole with close stitches. Place damp cloth over spot and iron the patched area.

Beware the busy moths. Spraying is not enough precaution with overstuffed furniture, even if you use slip covers. Remove covers once a month and check to make sure no stray moth colony has survived the spray. A few moments of effort can avoid lots of damage. Apply more mothproofing if necessary.

When pets shed. Even prize-winning dogs and cats will shed hair on the furniture. You can whisk the hairs off in record time by sliding a piece of adhesive tape very gently over the furniture surface. The hairs will stick to the tape, and your pet will be out of the "doghouse."

Even angora hairs can be removed from furniture by dabbing with a damp sponge.

FURNITURE SURFACES

Fingerprints on furniture can be removed easily with a cloth saturated in olive oil. When applying wax polish, use just as little as possible and rub until you get a surface free of film. If you do, furniture will increase in loveliness.

How to remove heat marks from table tops. Rub the unsightly white marks with a hard paraffin wax candle. Then cover with blotting paper and press with warm iron. Repeat, if necessary. Afterward, rub well with soft cloth to restore finish.

White rings vanish. Unsightly white rings on highly polished furniture (from heat, etc.) will disappear upon applying warm camphorated oil. Rub the furniture until it is dry, then polish with a clean, soft cloth.

Protect your fashionable marble-top furniture. If stains don't respond to soap and water, rub spots with a cotton pad soaked in lemon juice. Rinse surface thoroughly with clean water to prevent damage to marble. Colorless polishing wax is a good conditioner for thoroughly clean marble.

Give mahogany furniture a vinegar rinse. Restore dull or blurred finish to its original luster this way: Wring out a soft cloth in a solution of vinegar and warm water. Wipe the surface of the furniture with it and leave it on for a day or two. Then apply furniture cream or polish.

Paper stuck to table surface can damage finish unless you take this precaution: Put a few drops of oil on the paper scrap. Let it soak through for several minutes, then rub gently with a soft cloth. Paper is then easily removed without damaging wood finish.

Scratchproofer. Beautiful table tops need not be marred by scratches from the bottoms of ash trays or knickknacks if you cushion bottoms with pieces of felt cut to shape. At-

tach with glass cement. For very small areas use pieces of adhesive tape.

Make nicks invisible. During spring cleaning all the nicks and scratches that your furniture has accumulated during the year usually show up all at once. A furniture expert points out that you can first darken these scratches with wood stain, to get back as nearly as possible to the original color of the wood, and then apply white shellac to the scratches, one coat at a time, until they are filled.

Furniture scratches disappear. A little iodine applied to a scratch on dark furniture will nearly always erase the blemish or make it much less noticeable.

Speed up furniture polishing. Since warm polish penetrates wood pores fast, warm your bottle of polish beforehand by placing it in a pan of hot water for a little while.

Wonderful furniture polisher. An ordinary shoe buffer is a tool that's especially good for pieces with curves and molding. Soft pad gets into all uneven surfaces.

When do you wax? New pieces of furniture should be polished with wax or wax polish every two weeks. Later, once a month is enough. Wax protects surface against water or liquor marks.

Wax wise. Polish furniture or floor surface with cloth wrapped around a small sandbag. This adds weight, results in smoother work.

DRAPES, CURTAINS, AND SLIPCOVERS

Even if fabric is washable, it's best to dry-clean slip covers and draperies. Why? In washing, they may get distorted and shrink just enough not to fit well afterward. Some of the heavier fabrics and trimmings, washable-dyed though they are, may contain excess dye that will bleed.

If wash you must, make sure the material, as well as the trimmings, is indeed washable. Use only lukewarm water and only fine mild soaps. If you cleanse in a washing machine, don't let it spin too long. If a color runs while you are washing the article, rinse immediately several times in succession, until the last rinsing water is absolutely clear. Hang to dry so that deep-colored parts can't drip on lighter sections.

To press draperies. Cotton and linen may be ironed on the right side with a hot iron. Rayon should be pressed on wrong side with only a warm iron. No-iron fabrics should be rehung while still slightly damp, so they can be shaped into place by hand.

Snap those draperies. Take this cue from a young lady who sets the pinched pleats at the top of her draperies with snap fasteners. She pins in her pleats and uses a home kit for applying the snaps. Before sending her curtains to the cleaner, she can unsnap the pleats in a jiffy. When her draperies return, she resets and hangs them just as quickly.

Snap when you clean too. Fasten snaps at the bottom and part way up in an unobtrusive spot at each side of drapery panels. When cleaning, simply turn up the drapery and snaps hold the fabric off the floor when you dust it.

Put slip covers back on while still slightly damp. They'll smooth out as they dry, fit better than if you ironed them. Only the ruffles and pleats may need a bit of touching up. Even those, however, you can do after the slip cover is back on the furniture. Put a towel between the cover and furniture when you're pressing the edges of freshly laundered slip cover.

Hand laundering is the rule for sheer curtains. Easy does it. Be equally careful in hanging them to dry, in smoothing them, and finger-pressing the seams, as this will facilitate the ironing job. If it's a straight curtain, slip a rod in the hem and hang at the window to dry.

Your lovely curtains shrank in washing or cleaning? You can add length to them in several ways:

If shrinking is only hem-length, carefully rip hem, let it down, and add a false hem of material of same color and weight (even if you can't match it exactly). Or rip the heading at top, and add a false heading.

If shrinking is more than that, add fringe the length desired (cotton fringe to cotton curtains, rayon to rayon, etc.), for a formal room. In an informal room, curtains may be lengthened by adding a band of a contrasting material at the bottom (and even at the heading if desired).

LINEN AND BEDDING

Pure linen towels are best for drying dishes. They more than make up for the small extra cost since they absorb moisture so readily and leave no lint. Watch for the seasonal "white sales" and buy them at minimum cost.

Towels should be well woven. Test this way: Hold towel up to a bright light. Light should come through in even pin points. If it's in uneven patches, the ground cloth is unevenly woven and will not wear well.

Plain white towels usually cost the least. The addition of color, embossing, or other decorations increases the price as well as laundry upkeep.

The thicker are better. Heavy bath towels are more absorbent.

Grounds for refund. Woven borders sometimes shrink more than the body of the bath towel. This cannot be determined before washing, but it does constitute a defect and should be grounds for returning the towel. Moral: save those sales slips, or buy a reputable brand.

When buying bed sheets, guard against "April fool" fabrics by testing for excess sizing. Rub a portion of the sheet between your fingers. If fine white powder comes off on your hands, look for a better quality. You'll save money in the long run because this powder (called sizing) will wash out in the first laundering.

Economy tip. Heavier muslin sheets wear much longer, tear less easily, than medium weights, cost only a trifle more.

Blue prevents yellowing. To help keep your linens from yellowing, paint the inside of your linen closet a medium shade of blue.

The thicker the blanket, the warmer. High nap is desirable, for low nap often indicates blanket is excessively "felted." When you squeeze a wool blanket the nap should spring back when you remove the pressure. Check the label for washing directions and degree of shrinkage before you buy.

Blankets too short? Relax. Just sew a strip of muslin to the end that is to be tucked in at the foot of the bed.

MATTRESSES

Happy dreams. We hope you don't toss and turn at night, but if you do, squeaking bedsprings won't bring on restful slumber. Instead of oiling the springs and thereby staining sheets, spray on liquid wax and out go the squeaks.

Oh, that aching back. It's often traceable to a lumpy mattress and can be avoided by turning mattress. Turn once a week for nonspring mattresses, every month for innerspring mattresses. Keeps mattress from wearing unevenly and prolongs its usefulness. And you'll sleep better besides.

Handles on the mattress. If there are no loop handles on your mattress, sew on some sturdy strips of ticking. They're very helpful when it's time to turn the mattress.

Protect mattresses with sheet or mattress cover. Never roll a mattress; this is bad for innersprings and coverings. Place in special boxes made for this purpose.

BATHROOM

Cover wire towel hooks with corks to prevent holes from forming in towels when they hang for any length of time.

Double-duty mats. Make bath mats reversible, and use them twice as long, by sewing a Turkish towel on the reverse side.

Shower curtains last longer if soapy water is sponged off with clear water immediately after each use. Spread curtain out and allow it to dry before drawing it back.

Shower curtains stay put. Lightweight curtains don't hang properly and fly around when you're showering. Solve the problem by sewing weights (the kind used by dressmakers) in the bottom hem of the curtain.

MIRRORS

To make mirrors sparkling new. Wash them from a pan of water to which you've added one tablespoon of ammonia. Then dry and polish with tissue paper. They look beautiful.

To keep a mirror from fogging, apply film of soap with moistened finger, then polish the glass with soft cloth or cleansing tissue.

Scratchless mirrors. To protect the back of a mirror from scratches, cover it with a coat of clear shellac. Another reminder: the sun will cause mirrors to become cloudy. Hang them away from direct sunlight.

"Resilvering" mirrors. When a bare spot appears in your mirror, place a piece of smooth tinfoil over it on the back of the mirror. Paint over the tinfoil with shellac.

GLASSWARE

Life insurance for glassware. A glassmaker confides this nice little secret for strengthening glassware and making it less fragile: put it into a vessel filled with slightly salted water that you allow to come slowly to a boil. The slower the boiling, the hardier your glassware.

Glassware shock absorber. Place a silver spoon into any piece of good glassware or chinaware before pouring a hot liquid into it. Absorbs the shock of sudden sharp changes in temperature that may crack the glassware you prize.

Another tip. To avoid breakage, place ice cubes carefully into a glass; never drop them into an empty glass.

If one glass sticks to another, don't try to force them apart. Fill the glass on top with cold water, then dip the outer one in hot. They'll come apart without strain or breakage.

Prevents nicks in glassware. Handle and put glasses away carefully, so that edges do not bump together. Never stack. Store glasses with their rim sides up.

Save that nicked glass. When that hard-to-replace glass does get nicked, wrap a piece of "00" emery paper around the handle of a spoon and rub it back and forth across the nick until you've smoothed it down.

Washing delicate glassware. Glassware often cracks if put into hot water bottom first. Even very hot water will usually not hurt the most delicate glassware if you slip it in sideways or edgewise, slowly.

Give glassware extra sparkle by adding a few pinches of borax to the water when washing glassware.

Making jars and bottles smell fresh. Pour a solution of water and dry mustard into them, letting them stand for several hours; or use a diluted chlorine solution, then rinse in hot water.

Ammonia to the rescue. Use it in the water when washing greasy jars and bottles. Works like a charm.

To clean out the hard-to-remove sediment that often clings to the bottom of a bottle or glass vase, fill the vessel half full of warm soapsuds, add a handful of carpet tacks and shake vigorously.

To clean glass vases that have become stained, add some tea leaves to warm water and let it stand in the vase for several hours. Empty, then wash vase out with hot soapsuds and rinse in clear hot water. Another idea: soak in strong solution of hot vinegar, then wash in clear water. Either way the sparkle returns like magic.

To clean inside of glass drinking straws, run pipe cleaners through them.

CHINAWARE

How to tell real china from earthenware, often described as "china." Hold it up to the light. Earthenware is generally quite thick and porous in texture. China is nonporous and translucent. Through it you can see the light diffused.

Don't be afraid to use your good china. Instead of saving china dinnerware for special occasions, use it often, every day if you like. It's strength makes frequent use practical. Like your good silver, it grows lovelier with use.

China insurance. Never pour hot liquids into china cups just taken from a cold cupboard. First allow them to stand a short time at room temperature. Also, don't put fine china into the oven; the drastic temperature change may cause it to crack.

Care of china is simple. Because of its durability, it's simple to wash fine china. Use a mild dish-washing detergent, washing and rinsing with water as hot as your hands can stand. Avoid harsh detergents, gritty cleansers, and steel wool.

Most china can go into the dishwasher, except for china that is decorated with material that can't be subjected to water as hot as is delivered to a dishwasher.

Stains on china. Clean off the stains but don't take off the decorations with them. Instead of scouring powder, which is hard on decorations, use salt and soda to cleanse away spots.

Keep your china clean. Wrap your best china in cellophane or plastic bag before putting it away, to keep it dust-free for the next use.

Cracked dishes. If the cracks are not too deep, you can probably make them invisible by boiling the dish in sweet milk for about an hour, over low heat. This is often a wonderful way to keep intact pieces that are hard to replace.

Save dish-washing time. Use your china in rotation, so that there's never a group at the bottom of the pile that remains unused for long. Always take dishes from the bottom of the pile. When washed and wiped, return them to the top. That way, none gathers dust.

After washing china, drain on a rubber mat or dish rack. Place the largest plates on the bottom when stacking them on the shelf. Store cups either on separate hooks or stacked by twos.

SILVERWARE

How to clean silver: Place silver in 1 gallon of hot water, using an aluminum pan. Add 1 tablespoon of ordinary salt and 1 teaspoon of soda. Then rinse and dry the silver.

Removing egg stains from silverware. Knives, forks, and spoons discolored by egg stains are easily cleaned by rubbing them with salt before washing, then rinsing in soapy water, followed by a clear-water rinse, and drying.

To prevent tarnishing, keep a piece of alum in the silverware drawer.

Rub furniture polish on silver vases and frames and notice how long it keeps them gleaming new and free of tarnish.

Simplest way to retard silver tarnish is to rinse thoroughly after washing. Even slight soap residue hastens tarnishing.

To clean tarnished silverware, place some boiling water in a large aluminum vessel and add 1 tablespoon of baking soda to each quart of water. Place the silver in this and let stand for 15 minutes. Then rinse with hot water and dry. You'll be delighted with the results. Do not, however, use this method with "antiqued" silverware.

Tarnishproof silver storage. Wrap pieces of silver individually in tissue paper and store in tall potato-chip can. Seal cover with cellulose tape or store in airtight glass jars.

OTHER HOUSEHOLD METALS

Brassware needn't be hard to clean. Instead of polishing frequently, clean once, then apply a thin coat of fresh white shellac. Second coat gives still more protection. After this treatment, brass keeps clean with whisk of dustcloth.

Make your own brass polish. Here's how: Put 2 tablespoons salt into a cup of vinegar. Add just enough flour to form a smooth paste. Dip a damp cloth into the paste. Rub the brass until stains disappear. Rinse with cold water, then dry.

Tarnished brass. A lemon rind dipped in salt will remove most corrosion spots on brass.

To keep pewter brilliant, merely wash with hot suds, rinse, and dry. Silver polish will help.

Copper beautifier. Rub copper with salt and lemon juice or with salt and vinegar and you'll have it clean and sparkling richly in a jiffy.

Copper polish. Use the homemade polish given for brass on this page. But if green spots need removing, rub them with a cloth dipped in a weak solution of ammonia and water. Dry quickly, then polish with the paste mixture.

Keeps aluminum shiny. Aluminum will discolor if cleaned with harsh soaps or powders. Use a cloth moistened with lemon juice, rinse with clear water, dry thoroughly, and your aluminum will really brighten up.

Black's the wrong color for aluminum. If the inside of the aluminum pots starts turning black, slowly stew some acid food (rhubarb, tomatoes, etc.) and watch the sparkle return. The food won't be harmed.

Clean iron like magic. A little vinegar and salt boiled in an iron skillet will remove untidy black spots or burns.

Iron pots and kettles won't rust if, after washing, you wipe them thoroughly dry and then apply a little lard or other grease.

CARE FOR ODDS-AND-ENDS

To clean narrow-neck vases or bottles that have openings too small for a bottle brush, drop some crushed eggshells into the vessel, add a little water, and shake until all film and dust disappear from the glass. After rinsing, it will be crystal-clear.

Ashtray gum. Denatured alcohol does a miracle job of cleaning those black and gummy stains on ashtrays.

To clean plaster ornaments, try dipping them in thick liquid starch. Brush off the starch when dry and the dirt will come off with it, leaving the statuettes or ornaments spotless.

Keep those decorative candles clean with this jiffy treatment: rub them with a soft cloth dampened in a little alcohol.

Leather book covers need care, especially if not in constant use. When dusting, use a slightly oiled cloth occasionally, to restore some of the oil that has dried out of the leather.

Books stay new-looking if you clean soiled top edges, spread covers apart, grip the pages lightly, and rub gently with fine steel wool or sponge eraser.

When washing your lamp shades, prevent the colors from running by turning an electric fan on the shades as soon as you've finished them.

Parchment shades clean easily if you first coat them with a thin film of colorless shellac. Clean, when necessary, with a damp cloth.

31

HOUSECLEANING

How to keep your home clean with less work, less money, and less time

Housecleaning was once a major task that required a lot of physical exertion. Today, with all the special cleaning agents, much of the labor has been removed. Time is also saved—and, if you select properly, so is money. But you must inform yourself so as to know when it is wise to buy a specialized cleaning product and when it is more economical to buy some multipurpose one.

A worker is only as good as the tools brought to the job, and this is true of housecleaning. With all the special tools and gadgets available, most of the hard labor can be eliminated. But as with cleaning agents, you must know which to buy and which not. Often some ordinary household item or little trick will do instead of an expensive appliance.

Scrub brush won't slip from your hand, and will be easier to use, if you fit a drawer knob into the wooden back. Also provides good grip for your hand.

Rack long-handled cleaning tools together. Brooms, mops, carpet sweepers, and even curtain rods should be slipped into spring clips high enough so they do not rest on the floor.

For worn-down sweepers. If the bristles on your carpet sweeper are beginning to wear short and won't pick up the dirt, try winding adhesive tape around the rollers, adhesive side down, facing the floor. This lets the brush down and the sweeper works better than ever. A cinch to do, too.

New mop out of old socks. Instead of discarding worn socks, clamp them into the holder and you've a fine new dry mop.

Sponge hint. Keep household sponges fresh by soaking them in cold salt water from time to time.

When chamois stiffens up, soak it in warm water to which a spoonful of olive oil has been added. Your chamois will emerge as soft and clean as when you bought it.

To move heavy furniture single-handed, lay an old rug or burlap sack on the floor close to it. Lift furniture onto rug, one end at a time. By pulling rug (or sack), furniture can be moved much more easily.

To clean under furniture that is too heavy to move easily, wrap a length of oil-treated cheesecloth to a flat stick (a yardstick will do very well) and slip this under the furniture, making sure that the end of the cloth-wrapped portion of the stick doesn't go all the way under. That keeps cloth from getting caught and remaining under the furniture.

Easy wall or window washing. First tie a sponge to your wrist with a string. Saves getting down from a ladder when the sponge pops out of your hand, also speeds up your work by freeing the same hand for your chamois cloth.

VACUUM CLEANERS

Housekeepers in a hurry sometimes forget that the vacuum cleaner needs brief inspection at frequent intervals. Take a moment every two weeks to put one drop of oil in oilcaps or oil holes (to keep the motor in better working order), and also to empty the dustbag faithfully if it gets too full and the motor has to work against back pressure.

Reassignment for discarded wire hairbrush. Use it to remove hair and dirt from brushes of vacuum cleaners and carpet sweepers, a quick job which keeps these household tools in better working order.

Uprights are best for carpeting, rug and cleaner manufacturers agree. Modern cleaners have disposable bags which make it easy to empty when bags are so full cleaner is no longer able to remove dust and dirt at top efficiency. Don't let the bag get too full, disposable or not. It's hard on you, your rugs, and your cleaner if your machine doesn't work to perfection, because you have to go over the same area so often.

Protect the cleaner cord. Never just throw the cord on top of a tank-type, canister-type, oblong-type, space-ship-type, barrel-type, or any other type non-upright cleaner. It's worth the time it takes to coil the cord neatly around the machine. There are hooks on most uprights to help you store the cord properly. One upright even has a cord that winds up inside the handle when you push a button.

Use those cleaner attachments. They do a very thorough cleaning and dusting job for you for many above-the-floor cleaning tasks, much better and more easily than you could do with dusters, cloths, and brushes.

Clean the attachments, especially the dusting brush. Wipe off all attachments regularly. Wash brushes in suds and water, rinse in clear water, and hang up to dry so bristles won't flatten. Fasten a piece of string or a rubber band to the neck of the brush and hang on any convenient hook. If you haven't a convenient hook, tie the string to a clothes hanger with a rod across the bottom and hook the hanger to a towel or shower rod.

Two cleaners are ideal, especially in larger homes. Reserve your upright cleaner for rug and carpet cleaning. Use the other for smooth floor surfaces and above-the-floor cleaning. If there's an extra old cleaner around the house, don't get rid of it. It's handy around the furnace or other heating unit. The car, the workshop, etc., will benefit greatly.

HOW TO COPE WITH DUST AND DIRT

Your neighbors will love you if you don't shake dust mop out of the window. Lay it on the floor, on a piece of paper, then run the vacuum-cleaner nozzle over the top. Takes up dirt easily, quickly.

To collect the dust, dampen the inside of the dustpan and the broom bristle ends before sweeping. This will prevent dust from flying around. There's also a chemical you can spray on these convenient picker-uppers, as well as on dustcloths, which makes quick and dustless work of dusting. You can buy it in grocery and hardware stores.

Save time and work while dusting. Be sure to dust high objects first, so that any falling dust can be gathered later without your having to dust some things twice.

To keep dirt from accumulating in corners, shellac the baseboards in your room. Not only will this make sweeping far easier, but it will make cleaning the baseboards a relatively simple task of merely running a cloth over the surface from time to time.

Use a small syringe to suck out chips and dust when cleaning out a blind hole or crevice.

Dirt-proof that fireplace. Brick fireplaces that act as dirt catchers can be kept clean easily (and better-looking) if you brush the surface with liquid wax. Dust won't gather nearly as quickly and can easily be wiped off when it does.

Fireplace smoke stains. To clean the smoked areas on brick or stone, cover with a paste made of concentrated ammonia and powdered pumice. Let paste remain on for about 2 hours. Scrub off with hot water and soap. Rinse with clear water and dry.

WAYS TO LIVE BETWEEN CLEAN WALLS

Homemade solution for cleaning painted walls can be conjured up by combining 2 ounces of borax, 1 teaspoon of ammonia, and 2 quarts of water. You'll need no soap. Apply with a soft cloth.

Make wallpaper washable. Go over it first with sizing, then with a clear shellac. A damp cloth will clean it easily thereafter.

When cleaning washable wallpaper, make heavy suds, using warm water and mild soap, and apply with clean cloth. Don't let suds remain on the paper too long.

Protect wallpaper. Hold a cardboard against the wallpaper to prevent staining when you are painting or washing the woodwork.

Grease spots on wallpaper. Make a paste of cornstarch and water, let it remain on the spot until dry, then brush off. Usually works like magic. If it doesn't, try a paste of fuller's earth and carbon tetrachloride and use it the same way.

Wallpaper stained? Try these tricks:

Ink spots. Touch lightly with water and apply blotter, then treat with oxalic acid. If color of paper is affected, touch up with water colors or crayon.

Smudges. Work art gum eraser lightly over area. (Heavy rubbing may damage pattern of paper.)

Finger marks. Dampen with cold water and dust on a little powdered pipe clay or fuller's earth. After a few minutes remove with a soft brush.

Grease spots. Apply blotter over spot and hold it in place with a moderately hot iron. Finish cleansing with pipe clay or fuller's earth, as for finger marks.

Trick for the switch. The space around light switches sees a lot of traffic and, therefore, may be smudged frequently. After the space is cleaned, a thin coat or two of fresh white shellac will make the area around the switch easier to clean. An occasional quick dab with a damp cloth will then keep the space clean.

CARING FOR WOODWORK

To repair deeply scratched woodwork, fill scratches with mixture of fine sawdust and spar varnish. After filler has hardened completely, smooth down with fine sandpaper.

New surface. Small splits or "checks" that sometimes appear in old or weathered piece of plywood can be cleaned up with floor filler. Rub the filler into the cracks with burlap, working across the grain. When the material is dry and sanded, you'll have a smooth, solid base for a new paint coat.

"Starch" your woodwork. To remove smoke and grease stains, paint woodwork with a solution of starch and water. After the solution has dried, rub it off with a soft brush or clean cloth. This also removes the stains. Woodwork treated in this way doesn't harm the paint and stays good-looking for a very long time.

Kitchen-cabinet preservation. A coat of shellac on the interior of wooden kitchen cabinets not only provides protection from the steam and moisture always present in the kitchen, but keeps the wood surfaces of the cabinets from deteriorating. The shellac can be applied either before or after painting, and will work against dry rot and fungus growths as well as against moisture.

Rubber bumper. A chair positioned so it bumps the wall soon leaves an ugly mark. One way out: cushion the contact spot on the chair with a rubber-headed tack. A white one is best because it won't mark the wall.

Save the walls by applying a coat of colorless nail polish to upholsterer's nailheads on back of chairs placed against wall.

WINDOWS AND VENETIAN BLINDS

Window-cleaning hint. After washing a window, dry it on the inside with a sideways motion and on the outside with an up-and-down motion. Then if any streaks remain to be removed, you'll know instantly whether they are on the inside or on the outside of the window by the way the streaks run.

Keep Jack Frost away. On cold days rub alcohol or salt water on the outside of your windows, then polish them with newpapers. Keeps windows defrosted.

Spotless ledges. Window sills can be cleaned with practically no effort if you give them a coating of wax. The wax protects paint. Rain and dirt wipe off in a jiffy.

Beautiful Venetian blinds. To clean and polish slats, first wipe them with a damp, clean cloth, or wash if necessary. Allow to dry. Then put on an old cotton glove, dipping the tips into polishing wax and rubbing the polish into the slats between the fingers.

Chamois is excellent for cleaning Venetian blinds. Soak soft chamois in solution of household detergent and warm water. Wring nearly dry before using. Result: Fast, lint-free job.

Clean white tapes on Venetian blinds from time to time with white shoe polish. They'll always look bright and fresh.

When you clean Venetian blinds, keep a spring-type clothespin handy. If phone or doorbell rings while you're working, slip the pin on the slat you've been cleaning, so you'll know where to resume work.

WOODEN FLOORS

Floor surfaces wear better if you wash them very thoroughly before applying wax or shellac.

Oil treatment for varnished floors. Clean daily with broom covered with a flannel bag, or with floor mop or soft brush (bare broom bristles drag grit along surface, scratch it). Go over the floor occasionally with a cloth or mop moistened in warm, soapy water. The less water on varnish, the better. After using damp cloth, dry floor at once. Then go over it with oiled cloth or mop.

Clean painted floors with a soft brush, then go over them with a floor mop, either dry or dampened with floor oil. If necessary, occasionally wipe with a damp cloth, then with a clean, dry mop. Afterward rub with oiled cloth or floor mop.

Remove floor scratches by rubbing with fine steel wool dipped in floor wax.

Remove rubber heel marks by wiping the spots with kerosene, turpentine, or floor oil.

Fill holes in floor with plastic wood or with wood putty, stained to match. If you mix the wood putty or the plastic wood with weldwood glue you'll get a harder patch.

Silence those floor squeaks by dusting talcum powder or dripping glue into the cracks. (Works like magic.) Shellac the floor when dry.

Your rocker won't scratch waxed floor if you line the rocker arcs with adhesive tape.

Oil is bad for waxed floors. It dissolves the wax. Keep the floor clean with soft brush, dry floor mop, or floor-dusting attachment of your vacuum cleaner. When more thorough cleansing is needed, go over the floor with cloth wrung out of warm suds or one moistened, but not saturated, with turpentine. After every cleaning polish with weighted floor brush or polisher or rub briskly with soft cloth pad.

LINOLEUM

How to clean linoleum. Never flood linoleum surface with water. Use only wax on linoleum, never shellac, varnish, or lacquer.

Inlaid linoleum should be waxed, since varnish would tend to crack where breaks occur between inlaid pattern segments. Liquid wax is preferable to paste type, because it's easier to apply. Aply thin coat. Too much doesn't dry hard and simply becomes gummy.

Protect printed linoleum floor covering with coat of varnish. Some stores have special linoleum varnish; if this isn't available, use thin-bodied, light-colored floor varnish. Must be light or colorless to avoid staining light colors in the print.

To seal linoleum seams, run a strip of cellophane tape down the full length of the crack. Shellac over the tape and the surface will hold up indefinitely. The shellac coat will not only prevent dirt from seeping through but will also prevent tripping.

Loose linoleum edges look terrible and are a safety hazard, but they're easy to fix. Get some linoleum cement at the hardware store and work it under the loosened edge or corner, using a dull knife. Put an iron or a few heavy books over the area for at least 24 hours, until cement has hardened.

FINISHING TOUCHES

Got those ring-around-the-bathtub blues? Add a few drops of kerosene to the suds and watch those telltale markers disappear like magic.

Air purifier. Replace hospital smell of antiseptic cleansers with fresh, perfumed fragrance by pouring a little cologne into a saucer and lighting it. Heating the cologne first makes it burn better.

Are your cellar steps grimy? A little kerosene in the wash water will whiten them.

Discarded auto license plates make fine back-step scrapers. Your kitchen floor remains cleaner if muddy shoe soles are scraped out-of-doors. Nail old license plate to a corner of back doorstep.

32

RUGS AND CARPETS

Hints on increasing the beauty and life of rugs and carpets—and directions for removing the most common stains

Unless otherwise mentioned, the following hints generally apply to cotton and synthetic (artificial) fiber floor coverings as well as to wool.

Three "beauty hints" for floor coverings. For long life and beauty, practice the three rules of rug care recommended by the National Institute of Rug Cleaning:

1. Clean daily with a carpet sweeper or vacuum cleaner. The carpet sweeper is a handy tool and is especially good for frequent light pickups. Light vacuuming is equally recommendable.

2. Carefully vacuum your rugs once or twice a week.

3. Have your rugs professionally cleaned at least once a year.

Cleanliness is the best defense against moth damage. You can effectively discourage moth larvae from feeding on your rugs and carpets by daily vacuuming and by using the professional rug cleaner's services at least once a year. If, for some reason, less frequent use of this professional service is necessary, apply one of the better known moth-repellent sprays around all the edges of the carpet and under all pieces of furniture three or four times a year. Food stains and other fatty or greasy substances should be removed as soon as seen. Under no circumstances roll up a rug and place it in attic, cellar, or storage room without first having it thoroughly cleaned.

CLEANING RUGS

Remove the "cutting edge" from your rugs and carpets. Dirt is the accumulation of heavy soil particles and sooty deposits that either stick to the surface of the rug pile or work their way deep down into it. Under constant footsteps, these sharp-edged particles cut rug fibers like hundreds of tiny knives, thus shortening rug life. They cannot be vacuumed away. The grease in this dirt is often as high as ten per cent, causing particles to cling tenaciously to pile fibers. Your best defense against this enemy is the use of good professional cleaning at least once a year.

If you decide to clean your rugs or carpets yourself, be careful about your choice of cleaning preparations. Read the directions and warnings on the labels before purchasing, and make sure the particular substance is designed for the type of material your rug or carpet is made of. Some of the substances sold are not easily removed from the floor covering after they have been applied. The residue that remains in the rug will cause rapid resoiling and may damage colors or even the fabric. It may also trap dust particles and check their removal by vacuuming.

Go slow in using ammonia or preparations containing ammonia on your floor coverings, or soaps containing alkalies, such as heavy laundry soaps, strong dish-washing and floor-scrubbing compounds, and wall or sink cleaners. The pile of your rug and the dyes with which it has been colored may be sensitive to alkaline solutions; their use may cause discoloration or bleeding of colors, may even damage fibers.

Shampoo your rug. Pick a day when the rug will dry quickly. Good ventilation and an electric fan will speed drying process. Proceed as follows: First vacuum the rug well on both sides. Place newspapers under rug edges to protect the floor. Test a small portion of the rug for colorfastness. Wash foot-square section at a time, being sure to overlap edges when going on to next section. Apply suds with flat, soft-bristled scrubbing brush, using a minimum of water. Rinse with damp (not wet) cloth. Never wet through to the back. Wait until it's all dry before replacing the furniture or walking on the rug.

Unless you really intend to shampoo your rugs regularly, you will probably not find it worthwhile to buy a shampoo machine, especially as it is now possible to rent one at many outlets, including some supermarkets or hardware stores. By saving all your rug cleaning for one session, you can rent a shampooer for a short time and avoid the outlay, upkeep, and storage of owning a machine.

TIPS ON RUG CARE

Turn your rugs around to face in different directions once or twice a year. This helps to distribute the wear over their entire surface.

Dents on carpeting can be fluffed back to shape by covering such spots with damp cloth, then applying hot iron and brushing with a stiff brush.

Keep stair rugs handsome. Make a point of shifting the front edges of stair rugs from time to time, since they receive the greatest wear.

To prevent rugs from slipping on hardwood floors, glue or sew rubber jar rings to each corner. The suction will keep the rugs in place.

Let your professional rug cleaner rebind worn edges of rugs and carpets. Amateur attempts to trim off such edges only result in greater unraveling.

Clip the little tufts or "sprouts" that protrude above the surface of your floor covering with a pair of shears, but don't—no, *don't* pull them out.

Don't let shadows fool you. Most rugs and carpets, as well as other pile fabrics, don't stand up straight. Instead they have a natural slope in one direction known as the "lay" of the pile. Because of pile lay, almost all floor coverings, plain-colored ones in particular, show "shading," or light and dark areas. This is not a defect, but a common characteristic, and results simply from differences in reflections of light between the pile in its smooth normal condition and in its "ruffled" or irregular condition. If for any reason you are bothered by such shading, you can retard it to some extent by always finishing off each session of vacuuming by running your cleaner with the pile lay.

REMOVING STAINS

In case of accident. The following describes steps you can take to remove or check stains when they occur, using common household products from your kitchen cabinet or medicine chest. The methods described here are not those of the professional rug cleaner, who uses specialized stain-removal technique based on textile chemistry; they are emergency methods that you, as a homemaker, can apply when the inevitable spill takes place.

Treat stains while still fresh or wet. Unfortunately some stains can be effectively treated only with specialized skill and knowledge, while inexperienced attempts at removal can result in permanent damage. Therefore, while the emergency treatments suggested in the following pages may not always produce the desired results, they at least will not contribute to making a stain permanent. In other words, by following these suggestions you can be confident of not doing the wrong thing.

Caution. Several of the treatments suggested in the following pages call for the use of nonflammable, home dry-cleaning solvents that may be applied by sponging or with a spray-type product. Many tufted rugs are manufactured with rubber backing, and solvent applications should be light to prevent any possible damage to the rubber. Paper (fiber) rugs are easily damaged by spot-removal techniques. Mechanical action, especially when fiber is wet, must be kept to a minimum.

The "how" of emergency stain removal. First of all, don rubber gloves to protect your hands from acquiring the stain. Then arm yourself with one or more pieces of clean, white, unstarched cloth, white absorbent tissue, or white paper towels. "Sponge out" as much of the spill as possible with these. If you can, place an old bath towel or uncolored cloth under the stained area.

Always begin the first-aid operation at the outer edges of the stained area and gradually work in from the edges toward the center. If you work from the center out, you may enlarge the area of stain. Don't at any time brush or rub stained area vigorously, as this action tends to distort the pile; even if the stain is removed, the disturbed pile may be more objectionable than the stain. If a stain will respond to treatment at all, it will respond readily without harsh rubbing. Whenever possible, apply the solution recommended for removal of the stain with a medicine dropper, and apply it directly to the stain, not to the area outside the stain.

Quick formulas for stain removal. With one of these formulas, or, where indicated, the right combination of formulas, you can proceed to tackle a variety of common stains resulting from accidents. If a mishap occurs, refer to the specific cause of the stain in the following list. It indicates the formula to use and how to use it.

Formula 1. Put a teaspoonful of detergent in a jar, mixing bowl, or other container. Add a cup of water and stir vigorously until you have a clear solution with no residue. (The amount of suds has no bearing on the effectiveness of the formula.) Apply this solution, where recommended, directly on the stain with an eye dropper. Using a rotary mo-

tion, sponge the stained area with a clean, white, unstarched cloth, beginning at the outer edge and working in. Try to keep inside the stained area at all times. Blot up remaining moisture with damp cloths, sponging in the direction of the pile lay. Finally, with another cloth dampened in clean, lukewarm water, sponge the area again several times. Finish by blotting up remaining moisture with damp cloths.

Formula 2. Mix a teaspoonful of white vinegar with 2 teaspoonfuls of lukewarm water. Apply this solution directly to the stained area with a medicine dropper. Using a rotary motion, gently agitate the saturated area with a clean, white, unstarched cloth. Allow the solution to remain on the stain for about 15 minutes. Blot up remaining moisture with damp cloths. With another cloth dampened in clean, lukewarm water, sponge the area again several times. Finish by sponging in the direction of the pile, blotting up remaining moisture with damp cloths.

SPECIFIC STAINS

Animal urine. In homes with pets, floor-covering accidents are not only the most common but the most serious. As stated previously, the fibers and dyes in wool-pile floor coverings are sensitive to strong alkaline solutions. And when the moisture content of the urine evaporates, a highly concentrated alkaline deposit remains. This alkaline concentration then reacts to cause an actual change of color. However, when animal stains are properly treated as soon as they occur, color change can be held to a minimum.

Treatment. Sponge the stained areas with several applications of clean, lukewarm water. Use a damp, clean, unstarched cloth or cellulose sponge to absorb as much of the moisture as possible. Apply Formula 2 as directed. Allow to dry thoroughly and apply Formula 1. Allow to dry thoroughly. Apply Formula 2 again, as directed. This treatment is effective in a great percentage of cases. Where a color change actually takes place, however, no further treatment can restore the color. Your professional rug cleaner, nevertheless, can have the rug redyed if it is a solid color rug. Or if it is a pattern rug, he may be able to improve its appearance by spot-dyeing the affected areas.

Beverages—alcohol, coffee, tea, soft drinks. Sponge the area with lukewarm water, using clean, white unstarched cloth or cellulose sponge. Absorb and repeat several times. Follow with Formula 1 as directed. If necessary, follow with Formula 2. Most beverages contain a certain kind of sugar that is colorless when first deposited on a fabric. After it has been exposed to air for some time, however, this invisible sugar stain undergoes a chemical change called caramelization and it sets permanently in the rug fibers. Later on, after exposure to direct sunlight or heat used for drying cleaned rugs, the stain may appear as a delayed-action tan or brown discoloration. Consequently, treat such spills immediately.

Blood. Sponge with cool water. Follow with Formula 1. If a yellowish stain results, apply a few drops of peroxide. Allow to remain 2 or 3 minutes. Follow by sponging with clear, cool water.

Butter and fats. Apply any nonflammable household dry-cleaning fluid to the stain with an eye dropper and sponge with a clean, white, unstarched cloth. Observe "Caution," page 313.

Cosmetics. Apply a nonflammable household dry-cleaning fluid, then follow with Formula 1 as directed. Observe "Caution," page 313.

Egg, gelatin, mucilage. Apply Formula 1 as directed. If stain remains, apply Formula 2, as directed.

Foodstuffs, general. If it's a "crusty" food, gently scrape off as much as possible with a dull knife or spatula. Follow by sponging with lukewarm water, using a clean, white, unstarched cloth, then apply Formula 1. If any trace of stain remains after area dries, apply a nonflammable household dry-cleaning fluid with an eye dropper and sponge dry with a clean cloth. Observe "Caution," page 313.

Fruits and fruit juices. Sponge with a clean white cloth dampened with lukewarm water. Follow with Formula 1.

Furniture polish. Removal of furniture polish is one of the more difficult stain-removal tasks. Very often these stains are insoluble because the polish contains a dye that has an affinity for the fibers of the rug and the chemical action necessary to remove the stain may often remove the color of the rug as well. Apply a nonflammable household dry-cleaning fluid, and sponge with a clean cloth. If this is ineffective, allow the solvent to evaporate and apply Formula 1 as directed. Observe "Caution," page 313.

Furniture stains. Spots from wood dyes and stains from bottoms of chairs and table legs sometimes occur. These are often difficult or impossible to remove. Consult your professional rug cleaner.

Grease. Apply a nonflammable drycleaning fluid and sponge with a clean cloth. Repeat until the cloth shows no further evidence of discoloration. Observe "Caution," page 313. If any stain remains, apply Formula 1.

Ice cream, milk, desserts. Sponge with lukewarm water, using a clean, white, unstarched cloth. Follow with Formula 1.

Ink (ball-point pen). Apply a nonflammable household dry-cleaning fluid, and sponge with a clean, dry cloth. Observe "Caution," page 313.

Ink (other than ball-point). Ink stains are another common source of trouble to the homemaker. Since there are many kinds of inks, there have been hundreds of formulas suggested for ink removal. While many of them produce satisfactory results, their misuse often causes a small stain to spread over a larger area of the floor covering. Nearly all household inks, except ballpoint pen inks (see above), are soluble in soap and water. However, excessive use of soap and water will extend the stain over too large an area of the carpet for an inexperienced person to tackle. Where the stain or stains are small, do this:

Use clean white tissues to blot up as much of the stain as possible. Have an abundance of these or clean white rags available and be sure to don your rubber gloves. Sponge the stain from its outer edges in toward the center. Repeat the spongings as long as you can see evidence of the stain on the cloths you are using. Follow by using Formula 1, again being careful to work in toward the center of the stain. Changing cloths frequently, repeat until all evidence of the stain is removed. Don't use milk.

If a brown or yellow stain remains, this is evidence that iron was incorporated in the ink formula. Its removal is a job for your rug cleaner.

Removing large ink stains can be a very messy chore. It is best to merely blot up as much ink as you can, then call your professional rug cleaner. Permanent-ink stains, however, usually can't be removed.

Iodine. Apply a few drops of white vinegar to stain. Mix a solution, using 1 teaspoon of hypo crystals (obtainable from drug or photography-supply store) in a glass of warm water. Apply with an eye dropper, a drop or two at a time, and carefully sponge with a clean white cloth from the outside to the center. Repeat as often as necessary. Follow by sponging with clean lukewarm water. Blot up remaining moisture with damp cloths.

Medicine (general). Sponge with lukewarm water and clean, white, unstarched cloths, changing cloths as often as necessary and working from the outer edge toward the center. Apply one drop of Formula 1 to the stain and immediately apply a cloth to that area. If there is evidence of the stain transferring to the cloth, continue with Formula 1. If not, follow the same procedure with Formula 2. If the stain still doesn't respond, find out from your physician or druggist the chemical content of the medicine. Then call your professional rug cleaner and pass on to him the information as to chemical content. With this information he can determine the best way to remove the stain.

Nail polish, household cement, dope. Nail polish, household cement, or airplane dope may damage a rug or carpet made of synthetic fibers or blends. Home treatment of these stains with agents such as nail-polish remover or thinner may also be very damaging. Apply chemically pure amyl acetate directly to the stain with an eye dropper. After a few minutes sponge with a clean, white, unstarched cloth, working from the outer edge in toward the center.

Oil. Most oil stains will respond to the use of a nonflammable household dry-cleaning fluid, applied by eye dropper to the stained area and sponged with a clean, white, unstarched cloth. Where such stains cover a large area and are caused by an appreciable amount of oil, the cost of attempting to remove them in the home is prohibitive. Send the rug to your professional rug cleaner or call him into your home. Observe "Caution," page 313.

Paint, varnish, shellac. Where a small quantity of such material has been dropped on the rug, apply turpentine with an eye dropper and sponge it from the outer edge of the stain toward the center. Follow by applying a nonflammable dry-cleaning fluid in the same manner. If the stain remains, contact the paint manufacturer for a thinner or remover made especially for the product involved. Where the stains are caused by considerable spillage, the cost of home removal makes the effort impractical. Better let your professional rug cleaner remove the stain. Observe "Caution," page 313.

Rust. Removal is no job for an amateur. Better call your professional rug cleaner.

Shoe polish, liquid. If the stains are in small local areas in the floor covering, apply a nonflammable dry-cleaning fluid with an eye dropper and sponge the area from the outer edge in toward the center of the stain. Repeat as often as necessary and while there is evidence that the stain is being transferred to the cloth. Observe "Caution," page 313. If not entirely successful, apply Formula 1, as directed.

Shoe polish, paste. Scrape off any crusty surface, using a dull knife or spatula. Apply a nonflammable dry-cleaning fluid with an eye dropper, sponging from the outer edge toward the center of the stain. Repeat as often as necessary and while there is evidence that the stain is being transferred to the cloth. Observe "Caution," page 313. If not entirely successful, apply Formula 1.

Sugar stains (candy, chocolate, syrup, etc.). Scrape off any crusty surface with a dull knife or spatula. Sponge with lukewarm water, working from the outer edge of the stain toward the center. Follow with Formula 1 as directed.

Wax. Scrape off as much as possible with a dull knife or spatula. Apply a nonflammable dry-cleaning fluid and sponge with a clean cloth. Observe "Caution," page 313.

Stains of unknown origin. Any attempt to remove a stain of unknown origin with a patent cleaning preparation may set the stain and make it impossible for even your professional rug cleaner to remove. If you insist on attempting the removal of a "mystery" stain, it is wise to confine your activity to the following:

Apply a nonflammable household dry-cleaning fluid with an eye dropper and sponge with a clean, white, unstarched cloth, working from the outer edge toward the center. Observe "Caution," page 313. If the cloth picks up some of the stain, repeat the application until either the stain is removed or there is no further transfer to the cloth. Follow with Formula 1. If still unsuccessful, phone your rug cleaner.

33

REDECORATING THE HOME

Be your own interior decorator—work wonders and save money while making your home more pleasant

To make a good beginning, whether you are planning a new room or replanning an old one, start by drawing your own version of a blueprint, or floor plan, to see what goes where. Prepare your floor plan to scale, and use cut-out pieces of cardboard to represent pieces of furniture, also cut to scale.

When in doubt, keep it simple. Take your time about deciding on the decorating schemes. After all, you'll have to live with it, and so will your family, day in, day out, 365 days a year, probably for years. In deciding, use color swatches in various parts of the room, both in daylight and under electric light at night.

Proceed with caution in mixing formal and informal articles in your home. For instance, an oriental rug would be out of place with most informal Colonial furniture; a cotton rag rug would never do with a velvet sofa.

Use the same caution with curtains, draperies, pictures. Think of your house as if it were something to wear. You wouldn't wear satin evening slippers with a housedress, or bedroom slippers with an evening dress. Apply the same principle to the interior decorating scheme.

Fit the fabric to the style. For modern rooms, select draperies and matching slip covers for a chair or two, or a sofa and a chair, from the following materials: chintz, organdy, mohair, linen, slipper satin, plastic fabrics, raw silks, novelty cottons, fiberglas fabric.

Early American furniture requires draperies of small-patterned chintz, calico, voile, or novelty cottons.

Period-style rooms in Queen Anne, Chippendale, Hepplewhite, or Sheraton look best with rich silk brocade, moire, damask, or chintz draperies.

CHOOSE WELL YOUR BASIC COLOR SCHEME

Avoid vivid colors for your basic color scheme. Softer, neutral shades are more restful and you are more certain not to tire of them. Reserve your bright color favorites for accent only.

Color is the easiest tool of illusion. Make a small room look larger by painting it a light color, cool shade, either plain or of unobtrusive pattern. Make your large room look cozy by applying a darker, warm shade to its walls. Pull down that high ceiling with wallpaper bearing a definite horizontal repeat pattern. Lift a low ceiling by painting it a pastel shade and by putting vertical stripes on your walls.

A north room, with little sunlight, is cheered no end with a little light paint. Cover the walls with a pastel pinkish gray or a light yellow.

A south room, receiving too much sunlight, may need walls that absorb, rather than reflect, the glare. Here, darker shade is best.

There are four basic color schemes to choose from:

1. Monochromatic uses various shades of one color. The effect is subdued modern.

2. Related motif uses consecutive colors in the rainbow. For example: groups of green, blue-green, blue, blue-violet, and violet. The effect is modern and slightly more daring.

3. Complementary is usually complimentary as well. Don't use complementary colors, however, in equal strength. Decide which is to be your major color and select a softer, lighter shade within its complementary color range. The color-choosing chart on pages 322–325 will help select the right complementary colors.

COMPLEMENTARIES

4. Split complementary. The chart will be helpful in selecting two colors complementary to your major color. This is especially necessary in large rooms where your dominant color may be very bold

SPLIT COMPLEMENTARIES

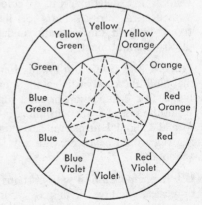

by virtue of large wall space. A warm wall color must then be balanced by two cool colors, and vice versa.

When undecided about color combinations, and to assure the final result you really seek, refer to the detailed color guide on pages 322–325. It may help you.

PAINTING AND PAPERING

Paint away those blemishes. If the room has architectural eyesores, such as beams that jut out, paint the walls and the woodwork (doors, window frames, baseboards, moldings) all one color. Or if you use wallpaper, select one that has an allover pattern but is not striped. This will camouflage the structural faults in the room.

Another room stretcher is to use one color paint for the walls and ceilings of small, low-ceilinged rooms. It is a good idea, too, to use the same color paint (or enamel) for the wood trim such as doors, windows, moldings. The one-color scheme creates an illusion of both height and width in a small room.

A high-ceilinged room may be made to appear lower by painting walls a dark color, the ceiling very light or white.

Patterned ceiling. A handsome joint pattern can be created in the ceiling by cutting fir plywood in squares and beveling the edges. Squares should be about 2 feet square. The beveled edge makes a nice V joint,

and if the grain direction in each square is turned at right angles to adjacent squares, the result is a handsome visual effect.

Paint plus paper. A tricky way to give a room individuality is to combine painted walls with papered ones. For example, paint three walls and paper the fourth wall in a harmonizing color scheme. Or, paper three walls; paint one. The one wall that is decorated independently of the other three should be the "important" wall, such as the one where you place the beds in the bedroom, or the couch, or piano, in the living room.

Distinctive is the word for walls whose uniformity is broken by one wall done differently from the other three, although related to them in color and design. For example: with three patterned walls, one plain-color wall picking up the colors in the pattern of the other three. Or with one wall covered by a large, handsome design, three walls of plain color or simple stripes may pick up one or two of the colors on the patterned wall. Pick-up colors should be exact matches. Caution: decorate only one room in your house or apartment in this way.

A better-furnished appearance is achieved by walls with patterned wallpaper than by plain walls. In selecting patterns, large designs are safe even for a small hall, since that part of the wall usually is barest of furniture. Small patterns used in

COLOR-CHOOSING CHART
BASED ON UPHOLSTERY AND WALL COLORS,
AND ON FLOOR COVERING AND DRAPERY COLORS

If your UPHOLSTERY IS	USE WALLS OF	USE DRAPERIES OF	USE FLOORS OF	USE ACCENTS OF
Cinnamon	A. Soft yellow	A. Yellow	A. Deep brown	A. Chartreuse
Brown	B. Deep beige	B. Pale, clear blue	B. Dark brown	B. Pale, clear blue
Light tan	A. Light chartreuse	A. Light tan and brown	A. Dark brown	A. White
	B. Soft, light shade of old red	B. Striped in tones of old red, beige, and white	B. Deep old red	B. Copper
Golden yellow and white	A. Soft dark gray	A. Golden yellow	A. Deep gray	A. White
	B. Deep, soft green	B. Golden yellow lined with white	B. Light brown	B. White
Soft blue and gray	A. Gray-and-white corduroy-stripe wallpaper	A. Soft blue with deep red trimming	A. Dove gray	A. Silver
	B. Dusty blue	B. Gray trimmed with soft blue	B. Dark burgundy	B. Crystal
Burgundy and natural	A. Burgundy	A. Natural	A. Deeper burgundy than walls	A. Chartreuse
	B. Warm beige	B. Burgundy background with white and beige design	B. Warm beige	B. White
Shell pink, green, and off-white	A. Off-white	A. Off-white trimmed with soft green and pink	A. Soft light green	A. Crystal
	B. Soft green	B. Off-white lined with soft green	B. Off-white	B. Shell pink and white
Light green	A. Warm gray	A. Gray background, dark green design	A. Dark green	A. Yellow
	B. Pickled pine	B. White chintz with off-white and light green design	B. Light green	B. Brown
Off-white and Wedgewood green	A. Light brown	A. Off-white	A. Deep brown	A. Gold
	B. Lighter tone of carpet color	B. Off-white	B. Deep, soft green	B. Yellow

IF YOUR WALLS ARE	USE UPHOLSTERY OF	USE DRAPERIES OF	USE FLOORS OF	USE ACCENTS OF
Beige with pink cast	A. Brown and off-white check	A. Brown, beige, and white stripe	A. Light beige	A. Sky blue
	B. Shell pink	B. Chintz with shell-pink and burgundy design	B. Burgundy	B. Grayed white
Sable brown	A. Shell pink and off-white	A. Off-white with turquoise trimming	A. Off-white	A. Turquoise
	B. Chartreuse with white pattern and plain chartreuse	b. Bright yellow	B. Warm, deep beige	B. Earth brown
Jonquil yellow	A. Warm gray and white	A. White trimmed with Chinese red	A. Gray	A. Chinese red
	B. Soft blue, green, and white	B. White with yellow dots	B. Soft, blue-green	B. White
Grayed soft green	A. Deep beige	A. Same color as walls	A. Chinese red	A. Light beige
	B. Grayed green and off-white	B. Corn yellow	B. Darker shade of wall color	B. Pine green
Powder blue	A. Yellow and powder-blue stripe	A. Canary yellow	A. Delft blue	A. Off-white
	B. Old white and dusty pink	B. Old white trimmed with dusty pink	B. Burgundy	B. Delft blue
Old white	A. Sharp, clear yellow	A. Sharp, clear yellow	A. Royal blue	A. Silver
	B. Emerald green and white	B. Emerald green	B. Black and white marbleized	B. Black
Slate gray	A. Empire yellow and slate gray	A. Empire yellow	A. Lime green	A. Silver and crystal
	B. Bluish white	B. Bluish white with soft crimson trimming	B. Soft crimson	B. Gold
Dusty mulberry	A. Pale, clear blue	A. Clear blue chintz, and deep brown design	A. Mahogany	A. White
	B. Creamy peach	B. Creamy peach chintz, gray, old rose, and ebony design	B. Ebony	B. Black

IF YOUR FLOOR COVERING IS	USE WALLS OF	USE UPHOLSTERY OF	USE DRAPERIES OF	USE ACCENTS OF
Burgundy	A. Warm gray with pinkish cast	A. Pale grayed blue and white	A. Primrose yellow	A. White
	B. Pale, clear yellow	B. Burgundy and white	B. White with burgundy valances	B. Gold
Crimson	A. Bone white	A. White chintz, floral design in red and soft green	A. Same chintz as upholstery	A. White
	B. Soft gray	B. Crimson, gray, and white stripes	B. White edges with crimson	B. Black
Brown	A. Warm beige with brown cast	A. Brown and old white	A. Chintz with tones of brown, beige, dusty pink	A. White
	B. Grayed yellow	B. Yellow, beige, and moss green	B. Brown and beige stripe	B. White
Beige	A. Tobacco brown	A. Clear yellow chintz, beige, dark brown design	A. Same chintz as upholstery	A. White
	B. Dusty pink, beige flowered paper	B. Deep dusty pink, pale olive green	B. Old white and beige	B. Terra cotta
Ivy green	A. Clear beige	A. Clear beige of walls and chintz with dark and light green floral design	A. Same chintz as upholstery	A. Black
	B. Pale, soft grayed green	B. Golden yellow and white	B. Same color as upholstery	B. Lacquer red
Foam green	A. Slate gray	A. Lemon yellow and gray	A. Lemon yellow and white	A. Gold
	B. Soft dusty blue	B. Soft dusty blue, dusty pink, and white	B. Bone white	B. Crystal
Dark blue	A. Striped wallpaper in tones of light blue, medium blue, and white	A. White and wine	A. White with wine trimming	A. Crystal
	B. Grayed blue	B. Lemon yellow	B. Blue and white stripe	B. Dark blue

IF YOUR DRAPERIES ARE	USE WALLS OF	USE UPHOLSTERY OF	USE FLOORS OF	USE ACCENTS OF
Light blue	A. Shell pink	A. Powder blue and shell pink	A. Off-white trimmed with powder blue and shell pink	A. Italian red
	B. Dusty blue	B. Thistle, beige, and dusty blue	B. Chintz with eggshell, pale blue, and thistle tones	B. Crystal
Wine red	A. Soft grayed blue	A. Wine red and grayed white and blue of walls	A. Deep gray	A. Silver
	B. Cream	B. Grayed green and off-white	B. Wine red	B. Crystal
Dusty rose	A. Deeper dusty rose	A. White and brown	A. Brown	A. Silver
	B. Pickled wood	B. Foam green and natural	B. Pinkish beige	B. Pale green
Soft golden yellow	A. Pale turquoise blue	A. Golden yellow and white	A. Dark turquoise	A. White
	B. Deep Georgian green	B. Golden yellow and white	B. Dark green	B. Gold
Deep sea blue	A. Pale yellow	A. Deep sea blue	A. Natural	A. White
	B. Deep blue	B. Canary yellow	B. Deep blue	B. White
Apple green	A. Same color of draperies	A. Gold, yellow, and ivory	A. Plum	A. Gold
	B. Gray with green cast	B. Grayed green and white	B. Deep green	B. Salmon
White with dark green pattern	A. Ivory green	A. Old red, off-white, and dark green	A. Dark green	A. Black
	B. White	B. Dark green and white	B. Deep green	B. Yellow
Chintz in green blue, soft red	A. Dark green	A. Chintz of draperies and soft reds	A. Tan	A. Copper
	B. Light beige	B. Chintz of draperies and soft green	B. Soft red	B. Soft green
Pure white	A. Ashes of roses	A. Pure white	A. Café au lait	A. Strong blue
	B. Chocolate brown	B. Chartreuse, brown, and eggshell	B. Eggshell	B. Chartreuse

large rooms become background and texture. This is desirable if the room has a lot of furniture; otherwise, the walls should play a larger-patterned part.

To select wallpaper. Remember that patterns look larger in the sample book than when actually viewed on the wall from across the room. Also, once the paper is hung, the colors seem lighter. To be sure of final result, hang a large sample against the wall, then step way back and decide.

Where an old house has patched, uneven walls, neither paint nor plain paper will be able to cover these defects suitably for long. It is best to use patterned, especially textured patterned, papers, as these aren't perfectly smooth themselves.

Don't let a spoiled patch of wallpaper get you down. If you can't get matching piece of paper to cover the spoiled area, get enough mahogany-veneered plywood and cover the wall. Frame with fine beaded molding. Cost is very low, and appearance of room is vastly improved.

Add richness to your room with wallpaper murals. Paint the wall first for background. Then apply the murals.

Wallpaper may be used as camouflage. To make a low-ceilinged room look higher, use wallpaper with a vertical stripe, or any narrow design that runs up and down.

To make small room look big, try wallpapering three walls in a plain, modest pattern, with the fourth wallpapered in a predominant, bold pattern.

Over-large room seems cozier. Wallpaper with bold patterns or large figures tends to bring the walls closer together and gives that homey, compact feeling to an otherwise over-large room.

Wallpapering dark rooms. "The darker the room, the lighter the paper color" is a good rule to follow. If only one wall is dark, you can use a lighter paper on that wall and a darker shade on the other three; this makes that part of the room appear lighter.

Improving wide rooms. Wallpaper with a vertical striped design will tend to foreshorten rooms that are too wide, by making the ceilings appear higher. Works even better when used on one wall, or on opposite walls, with another pattern on the other two.

Rooms too narrow? Ceiling too high? Follow same rule as for the over-wide room, but substitute a horizontal pattern, or one with a large figured pattern that gives the illusion of a horizontal pattern. This makes the room seem wider, the ceiling lower.

Rooms should blend. If you use wallpaper throughout the house, relate one room to the other, including the hallways. It becomes confusing to the eye when each room is papered in a color and design that has no relationship to the others. A good decorator strives for harmony in color and design throughout the house. The blending of neutral colors is conducive to eye ease and relaxation, besides being decoratively pleasing.

CARPETS AND RUGS

Room-stretching illusion can be achieved by carpeting which covers the entire floor. This also ties together the furniture groups that have various functions and makes for a harmonious, unified setting.

Cut down a large rug for a small room. Turn rug on left side, with chalk mark the size and shape you want it to be (oval is usually a good shape in which to remodel). Cut rug on left side, using a sharp razor blade. Buy inexpensive cotton rug binding, or rug fringe, and sew it around the cut edges. (There are rug bindings that are simple to iron on, too.) If rug has a central design, watch out to be sure it remains in the center of the cut-down rug.

Add luxury to your rugs and carpets by putting a pad underneath them. It makes them softer to walk on, and prolongs wear. Felt pads, and foam-rubber ones, are available commercially. Or you may use a discarded old rug for that purpose, cutting it down (if it's too large) one inch smaller than the rug all around.

SCREENS AND PARTITIONS

Folding screens are versatile aids in decorating. Use them to separate kitchen and dinette sections of one room, or to form a dining section in a living room that needs to do double duty. Screens are also attractive and useful in a hall that leads into the living room in a wide, open archway that has no door.

Want something attractive in folding screens? Use three or four shutters you took off your windows. Paint or enamel them to match or contrast with your walls. Buy double hinges to be screwed into the separate shutters that form the "leaves" of the screen. They are sturdy, and give a modern touch to your decorating scheme, besides being useful.

A clever partition is achieved by hanging a Venetian blind from the ceiling. Ideal, for instance, when you have a large kitchen and want to partition off a dining area. The blind should be the same color as the walls or should match the basic wallpaper color.

Venetian blind works also to hide kitchenette. If you live in a small place with a built-in kitchenette, hang a Venetian blind over it to provide an interesting decorative effect. Conceals yet keeps kitchenette constantly aired.

Also a Venetian blind works wonderfully when you want a good "door" to hang in front of a doorless closet or cupboard which you want to cut off from the view while providing for ventilation.

Scrapbook on your screen. Those pictures, greeting cards or play programs you've been saving to put into a scrapbook someday will make attractive decorations on a wooden or plywood screen. Arrange them interestingly and fix in place with good household cement. Press smooth, from center outward, before cement hardens. When all pieces have been mounted and allowed to become firm in place, rub away excess cement and cover entire surface with clear shellac.

FOCUS ON FIREPLACE

In summer the unused fireplace may produce a void in the room. Here's where your originality steps in. Build a trellis of wood or metal bars, place it in front of the fireplace, and have growing vines over it. Or place three or four large flowerpots, with tall leaves in them, to cover the gaping hole. A fire screen, covered with wallpaper or painted to match the wall, or more luxuriously covered with needlepoint, is also a way to hide the fireplace when it's not in use.

Retrieve that old coal scuttle. Give it a place of honor beside your fireplace after you've treated it to a coat of paint to suit the color scheme of your room and added a cheerful design to its exterior.

CLEVER WAYS WITH WINDOWS

The view of your window can be as important as the view from it. Draperies and curtains can do much to correct the construction work of the harder materials that go into a building. For instance:

To increase window height. Place upright across the top of the window a board high enough to reach the desired height. This extension is screwed on the wall and finished like the woodwork of the window. A valance may cover this. The draperies are hung from the top of the new height.

To increase window width. Place a block of wood outside the frame at each side of the top of the window, about 2 to 4 inches wide. Place curtain fixture in the new, increased window width.

Valances tend to make the ceiling seem lower. Use only when that is your purpose, and exercise caution in small rooms.

A short, squat window, in a room where ceilings are high, can easily be remodeled to look tall and narrow, so its proportions are more suitable for the size of the room and the ceiling height. A solution for this is a swagger drapery treatment with a companion straight-hanging drawstring curtain in non-transparent fabric. Measurements for the curtain are taken from approximately 8 inches above the top of the window frame and down to the floor. Two lengths of fabric are used, the full width, either 36 or 50 inches, depending upon the window width. Narrow hem at the top should be reinforced with stiff backing, then attached to a pulley arrangement, placed above the window frame at the point where the curtain measurement was taken. Directly over it goes a cylindrical wooden curtain rod. The swagger valance in contrasting fabric is draped over the rod.

Side-by-side windows with wall space between can be made into an important single unit by dressing them up in picture-frame fashion with double ruffling across the top and down both sides of each window. The wall space between the windows is then dramatized with a single row of three pictures, hung one below the other. A crisp fabric in bright color, such as glazed chintz, is a perfect choice for this remodeling project, and the sewing machine's ruffler attachment will transform the straight strips into an even mass of fluffy ruffles in short order.

A triple-bay window can be made into an effective, cozy corner unit with double-tiered sash curtains. A deep valance of flower-printed cotton across the top unites the three windows. Below are double-decker drawstring curtains of the same fabric, which can be drawn closed at night and pulled back during the day to let the sunshine in. Both top and bottom tiers have straight-hanging windowpane fabric undercurtains, to eliminate that bare look

when the overcurtains are pulled back.

Offside corner windows are a common apartment ailment and can be an eyesore in a small room unless you introduce the simple expedient of an unbroken sweep of fabric from the outside window frame on one wall to the outside window frame at right angles on the other wall. To begin with, join the two windows into a single unit with a pleated valance. Next make two single drapery panels, each 50 inches wide and from window top to floor in length. Hang one panel along the outside frame of each window. Then use double panels for the inside, right-angle corner. The double panel, besides presenting a dramatic sweep of fabric, also helps to cover the bleak wall corners between the two windows.

A small dressing alcove is formed by draw curtains hung from a ceiling traverse rod. Also make an attractive room decoration. Such an alcove can house a dressing table and one or two chests that do not fit in with other bedroom furniture pieces. Chintz is used for drapery panels that are lined with polished cotton.

The lost window is one that never gets direct sunlight, or is inconvenient or too small. Since it doesn't serve its intended purpose, give it a delightful new one. Build a few shelves across it on which to display your favorite bric-a-brac or crystal.

Picture-window privacy. Living behind a picture window that looks out on the street can give those in the house a goldfish-bowl feeling. Too much sun and insufficient privacy often occur. Here is one solution: Build a framework over the glass area, providing for squares two feet large, or for rectangles that fit the dimension of the window or glass area. Then cut ¼-inch panels of plywood to fit the squares, placing them in a checkerboard design or other pattern. If the plywood is handled so it is removable, it can be taken out during dark fall and winter months. In the summer, the squares can be replaced to cut off the sun. Paint the plywood to harmonize with the rest of the room.

A dormer window in a bedroom can be made to produce an excellent effect, especially if used for dressing-table purposes. Build a convenient-height shelf under the window, to go from wall to wall. A simple board with two brackets underneath it will do. Enamel the surface or cut a glass or mirror to cover the shelf top. Sew a "skirt" to reach from wall to wall. Attach it to the shelf, place a standing mirror on the table top, and you have something that is both ornamental and useful. If possible, use the same material for the dressing-table skirt as for the curtain on the dormer window, to produce the effect of a well-planned unit.

Dramatize close-together small windows and make one unit of them. If you have two or three small win-

dows with only a slim panel of wall between, hang draperies only at the extreme outer end of the group of windows (no draperies between them), and make one long continuous valance or cornice across the tops of all the windows. Each window in this unit may have its own curtains or shades. Or you may use one large Venetian blind or wide window shade to go across the windows, instead of individual curtains.

Create an interesting treatment of two small windows on the same wall by hanging or attaching an unframed mirror on the wall space between the windows. This tends to relate the windows to each other, adds interest to the wall, and the mirror reflects and makes the room seem larger. This is a good way to use up a large mirror you have, that may be cut, if necessary, to fit the space between windows.

DRAPES AND CURTAINS

Loose-weave draperies. In buying draperies, remember that loose-weave fabrics naturally tend to shrink. To avoid the risk of having those lovely peasant-style crashes and basket weaves hang short after cleaning, buy the longer lengths. Or look for the extra-shrinkage hem which gives you an extra tuck that is easy to press out.

Think of dress materials as fabric for curtains, draperies, and bedspreads. If you can't find what you want in the upholstery department make a shopping tour of dress materials and you may find just what you want. Bear in mind, though, that most dress fabrics don't run wider than 39 inches, as a rule.

In making draperies, finish them at the top, then hang them at the windows on fixtures already mounted. Let the draperies hang for a few days before you put in the lower hems. Materials may give a little under their own weight. Then, too, the measurements may not have been exact, or the seams may prove wider than you provided for.

Include some bottom weight, once you put in the final lower hem, to keep the curtain down and make it hang evenly. The pin-on weight is easiest to put in and remove for washing. 1. It is placed in the corner of the lining. Note especially: 2. The round disk weights should be covered with the curtain fabric and tacked into place or stitched to the edge of the hem. 3. Yardage weights are used for lightweight fabric draperies. 4. Round string weights are most suitable for glass curtains (the very sheer curtains that hang directly against the glass).

Pleats complete the drapery top not finished by valance or cornice. Pleats should be made in groups of uneven numbers: 3, 5, 7, depending on the width of the material. With 36-inch-wide fabric, 3 or 5 pleats are sufficient on each side. But 50-inch-wide materials take up

to 5, 7, or even 9 pleats on each side.

French pleats are used most often. At the lower edge of the heading, divide each pleat into 3 smaller pleats, drawing up the thread and fastening it securely on the underneath side.

Pinch pleats. Evenly divide large pleat into 3 smaller pleats and firmly press in each smaller pleat. Stitch all 3 folds evenly across the lower edge of the heading.

Use pleater facing and hooks, available at drapery fabric stores and department stores, if you don't want to take the time to make the pleats the needle way.

If you shirk shirring, there's another drapery aid you can buy at your notions counter: a shirring tape that is quick and easy on the draw as well as on your time and energy.

Don't align the lining. Lining should be cut 3½ inches shorter and 6 inches narrower than the draperies themselves. Remove selvage from both drapery and the lining fabric.

Work with ready-to-use cornice material made of buckram. Here's a trick to make a perfect instant-scallop cornice. Measure width of window and cut enough yardage to make cornice cover both ends of the curtain rod. Cut the width you want for your cornice. Now simply draw a pencil line across the length of it, about 2 inches from the bottom edge of the cornice. Use a dinner plate to make the scallops up to the 2-inch line.

Curtain rings in a jiffy. Save time by getting poultry rings (in colors to match the materials in the room) and, without a single stitch, slipping them into the tops of lightweight or wash curtains. Takes only a few minutes to ring all the curtains in a room. You can also lacquer the brass curtain rods to match the room or curtains.

Clip-on curtain rings. There are very elegant curtain rings in brass and other metals that clip on without stitching, which go wonderfully with brass window-curtain rods and other fittings. Most department stores will order them for you if they don't stock them regularly.

When your tie-back curtain ruffles show signs of wear, cut them off and replace with ruffles of a colorful contrast to the curtain. Use tie-backs of same new material.

Dress up tie-back curtains, by using gay ribbon (grosgrain usually lasts longest), and include an artificial flower in the bow when the ribbon is tied.

Sew window cornices to match the draperies. Use left-over material. Cut a paper pattern and fit it over top of window; then cut a piece of stiff muslin or other heavy material. Cut the drapery material at least one inch wider all around the muslin piece. Turn under this one-inch material, pin it down, baste into place, then attach it to the lining with a cross stitch that can't be seen on the right side. Cut a lining (also good to use some left-over material of any color) one inch wider than pattern. Bend under, pin and baste on wrong side, and finish with overcast stitch. The cornice may be straight, have a scalloped edge, or be finished with a narrow moss fringe.

WINDOW SHADES

Beautify windows with remnants. Left-over material from slipcovers or draperies may be converted into colorful, attractive window shades. Remove old shade material, keeping it intact for use as pattern. Cut fabric a bit larger than pattern, to allow for hems. Bottom hem should be wide enough to hold wooden slat from old shade. Attach fabric to roller with small tacks. Transfer pullcord to bottom of new shade.

New window shade for old. A clever way to renew, even to prettify old shades is to daub them with ordinary flat paint that you have first thinned down. If you merely want to clean it, stretch the shade out flat, rub with cornstarch, then carefully brush off.

Window shade to match wall covering. When a kitchen or bathroom or even bedroom is papered with washable wallpaper, save a vertical piece as large as the window shade. Replace the shade with that piece of wall covering, stapling it to the roller.

Rolled-down window shade helps you see the light. Make a decorative and highly practical container for sewing-fashion aids by borrowing an idea from the window shade. Attach fabric panel to a roller, then add pockets of convenient size to hold patterns, tape measures, scissors, threads, etc. Apply colorful cutout appliqués and contrasting binding. Hang to the inside of closet door and you'll find all sewing aids conveniently displayed.

SELECT CAREFULLY FOR FURNITURE FIT

Use a critical eye when selecting the size furniture to match your room. A very large room should not have small-scale furnishings, especially the important pieces like the sofa and desk.

A tiny room should not be crowded with large-scale pieces of furniture. Use a love seat instead of a long couch; provide smaller tables and desk and lamps.

The well-balanced room doesn't have too much gaping wall space, nor is it so crowded that you need a shoehorn to wend your way between the furniture.

Small house or apartment will look spacious with the help of smart built-in furniture. What's more, rooms will be free, uncluttered and attractive. Also, built-in pieces cost about a third as much as orthodox, movable furniture.

Keep 'em balanced. Be sure all furniture pieces balance with one another. It's all right to use one large piece as "focal point" in small room, but if you do, other pieces should be modest; don't mix delicately designed styles with heavy ones.

To arrange the living room. The homey feeling is half taken care of when you allow for one or more fixed seating arrangements in your living room, so that at least three people can sit together and talk and see each other easily. Add convenient small tables near all chairs and sofas, whether the seating is in groups or singly. Add soft lighting, or a good reading lamp, whichever the arrangement calls for.

Arrange living-room furniture around a focal point of interest. If you have a fireplace, that's the answer. Otherwise, you may create a focal point of a large window or group of windows, a large desk or breakfront bookcase.

Group your seating arrangements at all times to allow for ease of conversation. Don't make your family or guests shout across to each other.

In a very large room, have two focal points of interest, with two ease-of-conversation groupings of chairs and tables.

You may combine furniture of different woods in one room. It is not necessary to have only mahogany or only maple. Light and dark woods blend together well.

Does your large upright piano dominate your small room? Change its color to match the wall or blend with your wallpaper, by giving the piano two coats of flat paint or enamel. Don't forget to include the stool or bench, too. This seems a daring idea, but it does wonders for the decorating scheme of a room.

Catty-cornered arrangement of furniture must be done with caution. Don't place desks, cabinets, large tables, sofas, or bookcases catty-cornered. Use that arrangement for chairs, their accompanying tables, or other small pieces of furniture.

Arrange special corners, not only for good conversation, but also for good music, radio, television, record player, piano; for good work, desk and bookcase; or for good card playing. Provide them all with adequate seating, table space, lighting.

REDOING OLD FURNITURE

New furniture, practically free. Many old pieces, such as kitchen chairs, will take on new life and beauty if all the finish that hides the natural wood is removed right down to the wood and the piece then refinished so that the grain is visible. Those who have done this (and more are doing it all the time) feel that they have gained "new" furniture at practically no cost.

Did you inherit tables and chairs that don't match? If you want to use them together, paint them all one color so they'll be related to each other. Quick-drying enamel is a boon to the furniture painter; often only one coat is needed.

An informal dinette, or small dining room, will look cheerful and distinctive if you paint the table one color, the chairs another, to contrast. This is a good way to use up the old kitchen table and chairs and produce a charming, colorful decorative result.

Make flowers grow on furniture. Rescue some of the well-constructed but worn-looking chairs, toy chests, etc., from dingy exile in the attic. Sand them down, add fresh coat of paint, then add floral or other designs that will make them different-looking.

Cut them down for a new lease on life. That old table or chest of drawers can be cut down and painted the same color as the walls of the room, to achieve a new, built-in look. Replace old metal drawer handles with solid flat brass pulls, yours at the five-and-ten.

Two chests for one. Chests that are too high can be sawed in half and made into two small ones that fit into spare corners.

That old sewing-machine, which still has years of service in it but is in an outmoded cabinet, may be turned into a double-duty piece of furniture. When not in use, turn it into a dressing table by means of a slip cover. Hang a mirror on the wall over the camouflaged machine and you have a decorative item that is more eye-pleasing than the old machine.

Victorian desk goes modern. Remove upper-shelf section for conversion into a hanging "whatnot" cabinet by removing the pigeon-holes. Lower half becomes a modern secretary.

"Roll out the barrels." At practically no cost, create a gay kitchen nook with old barrels as chairs, and gay fringes everywhere to add color and co-ordination.

Find a kitchen cupboard in the attic. An out-of-date chest of drawers makes a perfect base cabinet, after legs are sawed off to bring top surface down to worktable height. Then add shelves with plywood back and sides.

Two files equal one desk, like so: Set a plywood top across the surface of twin two-drawer files, separated by enough space for your legs

to fit comfortably. Let your imagination and personal taste guide you in decorating it.

Boudoir note. Same idea can give you a serviceable dressing table if you use two small chests instead of files and add a pretty chintz skirt.

Hanging bookshelves. A clever, easy way to put in bookshelves is to cut them from fir plywood to the length and width desired. Then suspend them from the ceiling with black or white Venetian-blind cord at the desired height. The weight of the books and other articles insures sufficient solidity and the cord makes a handsome line pattern against the wall. Closed plywood cupboards can be handled very effectively in the same way.

HOW TO MAKE SLIP COVERS

If you're making your first slip cover for a chair or sofa, be sure to make a muslin pattern first. If you find your first try easy, go ahead and cut right into the material of subsequent ones. But even professionals make muslin patterns for any unusual design.

Center the pattern on your material when you place your muslin pattern pieces on the yardage or when you lay out the material on the chair to be slip-covered. In using materials with a large motif, repeat design, taking care to place motif to best advantage on the center back, center seat, and on the arms and side. Always begin at the top, with the front and back sections, and work

from the center to the sides and down.

Plain fabrics cut easiest. Next easiest is the allover design, particularly if there is no up-and-down in the pattern or fabric.

Grain directions. Lengthwise grain of the fabric should always run up the back, the arm sides, and from front to back of cushion. Crosswise grain should run across each section of the chair.

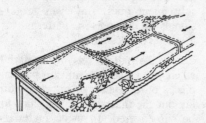

Center pattern on both sides of cushion, so it can be reversed. Match pattern on the inside of the arms. No need to match the outside, since no one ever sees both sides of the chair at once.

Striped fabrics need matching. Locate a stripe at exact center of the chair, running through center and back, front, and cushion. Place center of muslin pattern on that stripe. Locate stripe at given point of arm and side pieces and match them for opposite side. If you don't use a muslin pattern, simply locate a center stripe and block each section accordingly.

Pieces cut from fabric after muslin pattern should be pin-fitted to chair before sewing, just to check fit. Work with the right side of the fabric out. Mark lines that are to be the seam lines.

If one arm of chair is stuffed fuller than the other, fit arm sections separately. To fit curves of arm, run a row of gathers with needle and thread between the notches. Fasten thread securely. Or instead use darts, but make them inconspicuous. Don't stretch the fabric.

Choose a closely woven fabric, so it won't give like a loosely woven material and will, therefore, not become stretched and baggy after brief use. A closely woven fabric, moreover, gives better protection from dust. Many of the new linens, chintzes, and other standard slip-cover fabrics are made in a dust-proof weave. As an extra precaution, be sure that the fabric is both preshrunk and sunfast.

How much material will you need for what? Below is an approximate yardage chart for slip covers.

Caution: Repeat-pattern yardage may be higher. In any case, go to the store armed with measurements and consult the salesclerk.

Allow for seams. Make a 1-inch allowance on all seams. Leave 5-inch tuck across back of seat, on each side of seat, and at back corner where arms join.

Silk materials rate matching silk thread. In fact, this is a must. For all other slip-cover materials use boil-fast, mercerized cotton thread of matching color. Watch for right-

SLIP-COVER MEASUREMENTS CHART

TYPE		48-inch wide PLAIN	48-inch wide FIGURED OR STRIPED	36-inch wide PLAIN	36-inch wide FIGURED OR STRIPED	WELTING OR TRIMMING
	3	14 yds.	15½ yds.	21 yds.	23 yds.	36 yds.
Sofa	1LC	13½	15	20½	22½	33
	0	10	11	15	17	21
	2	10	11	15	16½	24
Love seat	1	10	11	15	16½	23
	0	8½	9¼	12¾	14¼	14
Armchair	1	7½	8¼	11¼	12½	18
	0	6	6¾	8⅓	9½	13
Boudoir chair	1	5	5¾	7¾	8¾	15
	0	4½	5¼	6½	7½	12
Wing chair	1	8	9	12	13	18
	0	6½	7¼	9¾	10¾	13
Cogswell chair	1	7	8	10½	12	16
	0	5½	6	8¼	9	11
Day bed and	3	14½	16	21¾	23¾	42
mattress	0	11	12	17½	19½	27
Day bed	3	11	12	16½	18	29
	0	7½	8¼	11	12¼	14
Ottoman	0	2	2½	3	3½	6
Chaise lounge	1	10	11	15	16½	23
	0	8	9	12	13¼	16
Dining-room chair	0	1½	1¾	1⅚	2⅙	5½
Extra cushion	1	1¼	1¾	1⅚	2⅙	5

Add an extra yard if the fabric has a design that must be centered.

To estimate yardage, add up lengthwise measurements of pieces and divide by 36".

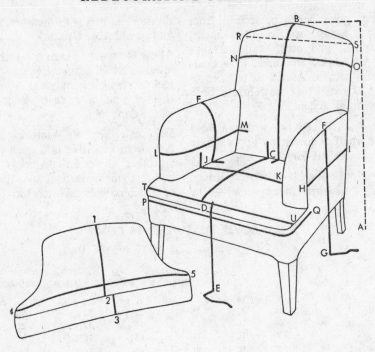

YARDAGE
FOR

Back length (floor to top)—A to B plus 2″ seam allowance.......... inches.........inches

Back width—R to S plus 2″ seam allowance...................... inches

Front back length—B to C plus 2″ seam allowance, plus 3″ tuck-in.. inches.........inches

Front back width—N to O plus 2″ seam allowance............... inches

Back width—O to N plus 2″ seam allowance.................... inches

Seat length—C to D plus 2″ seam allowance, plus 3″ tuck-in....... inches.........inches

Seat width—across—J to K plus 2″ seam allowance, plus 3″ tuck-in.. inches

Seat width—across—T to U plus 2″ seam allowance.............. inches

Front length—D to floor at E plus 2″ seam allowance............. inches.........inches

Front—across P to Q.. inches

Side length (arm to floor)—F to G plus 2″ seam allowance.......... inches×2=....inches

Side (front to back)—H to I plus 2″ seam allowance.............. inches

Arm length (inside) F to J plus 2″ seam allowance plus 3″ tuck-in.... inches×2=....inches

Arm (inside) front to back—L to M plus 2″ seam allowance,

plus 3″ tuck-in........ inches

Cushion: Length—1 to 2 plus 2″ seam allowance.................. inches×2=....inches

Width—4 to 5 plus 2″ seam allowance................. inches

Depth of box—2 to 3 plus 2″ seam allowance.......... inches.........inches size needle, considering both thickness of thread and weight of material.

Slip covers may protect or conceal. An old-slipper chair that may have legs and a back that welcome camouflage can still be dressed up with a smart slip cover made from your drapery material, or in a plain color picking up one of your room's basic colors. Make it even more decorative by adding tassels to match the welting.

Eye-deceiving width with eye-pleasing ruffles. This newly gained lower width is further enhanced by using moss fringe on outer seams, etching out the frame of the chair in the strongest color of the pattern. On the inside chair seams use matching small welting.

Give your bedstead a slip cover. If yours is an old-fashioned bedstead (perhaps you even have a brass bed), modernize it by making a slip cover for the headboard and footboard, of the same material as your bedspread, or a contrasting material. Use cretonne or chintz if spread is plain-colored, solid color for slip cover if spread has a design.

It's best, however, if you have sufficient material, to use the same for slip covers as for bedspread. Cut a pattern of the headboard and footboard on a large piece of wrapping paper. Cut your material (plus a lining, for added strength and better appearance) one inch wider all around. Baste and stitch on wrong side. Finish the bottoms with a hem or a binding. Quilted material is excellent for such slip covers, and needs no lining.

LIGHTS AND LAMPS

Remodel home lighting at little cost. Use inexpensive adapter equipment, specially designed light bulbs, and lamp modernization for better lighting. In the kitchen, for instance, an old center ceiling fixture can be replaced with a new shielded fluorescent unit or smartly styled incandescent fixture. Lights over the sink and range and under the wall cabinets speed culinary tasks immeasurably.

Light the way ahead when revamping your home lighting. You should be able to flip a wall switch at the entrance or entrances of any room so that you can see to enter or pass through. Since safety is one reason for good lighting, be sure you can turn the hall and stair lights on and off from both the foot and head of all stairways. Light the way ahead at front and back entrance steps, too, and to and from the garage.

See your electric push buttons in the dark. Simply coat them with a layer of luminous paint and you'll never have to grope to find a switch.

Eyesore into indirect lighting. An unsightly ceiling light fixture can easily be concealed by cutting a square of fir plywood and hanging it from the ceiling so it hides the fixture or globe. Paint the plywood or give it a natural finish. The square of plywood directs the light outward and provides for a simple, smart indirect lighting setup at practically no cost.

As glamorous as candlelight, but not as bothersome, is an indirect-lighting unit over your dining-room table. No spluttering candles to worry about or prevent guests on opposite sides of the table from seeing each other. And it's far less glaring than direct lighting.

Unused light brackets offer a wonderful decorative idea: trim them with artificial hanging vines.

Add a circular lamp shade covered with same or matching material as slip cover. Circular lamp shades should be lined with fabric. For good stretch, both fabrics should be cut on the bias.

To avoid rusting of lamp-shade frame, paint it with a primer, then with a coat of flat white paint. Allow to dry thoroughly.

Match-dress lamp shades by adding tassels, moss fringe, or welting to match chairs near which they stand.

Don't throw away the worn-out lamp shade. Sew a "skirt" over it, by ruffling a piece of fabric, finishing it at the bottom with a ribbon binding, and at the top with a heading of the same ribbon trim. Sew the top of this "skirt" to the top of the old lamp shade, let it hang loose (coming to the bottom of the old shade). You may use organdy or lace or net for bedroom lamps, leftover rayon or silk or nylon materials for the lamps in the living room, pieces of gingham or other cotton fabrics for the child's or teenager's room.

PICTURES

Uniformity in pictures on the wall, especially in a small room, is desirable. Don't sprawl every size and shape and type of picture on your walls. This creates confusion in the eye of the beholder. Hang pictures at eye level. If not the same size, have the bottoms of the picture frames at one level.

Grouping of pictures of various sizes may be made to look uniform, by buying frames all the same size (that is, the size of the largest picture), then cutting the mats of different size to accommodate the measurements of the picture itself. In such cases, it is best to have simple frames, and mats of white or other light tints, like egg-shell or pearl-gray.

You need no fortune to own attractive pictures. Make your own oil paintings from magazine prints, etc. Glue picture to heavy cardboard, smoothing out all air bubbles. Lay cheesecloth over picture, fold edges over the back, pull cloth taut, and attach with large stitches across the back of picture, keeping mesh of cloth parallel to edges. Apply coat of white shellac (not too thickly) with soft brush across surface of picture. Presto! There's your "oil" painting.

Corking cutouts. Cutouts in various designs, made from sheeting cork (the kind used for automobile gaskets will do), are attractive finishing touches for homemade Masonite cabinets. Animal figures or characters from nursery rhymes are excellent in child's bedroom; fruit, vegetable, and floral motifs will look attractive in your kitchen.

Maps look important. Here's an inexpensive decoration idea for your den or TV room: put up a large pictorial map with colored pin markers to remind you of the places you have traveled to or want to see. It's a smart idea that complements any library or television set.

Make individual picture mats, to suit the room in which they are hung. In a child's room, cut the mats from left-over pieces of gingham or chintz, or gay wallpaper. In other rooms, you may also use dress materials, or even colored desk blotters, to produce interesting mats for your pictures.

Faded gold frames should be rubbed with a sponge or soft cloth dipped in turpentine to bring back luster.

Antique that old gilt frame this easy way: Buy a small tube of oil paint (burnt umber) at any artist's supply store. Daub small amount on piece of clean cloth and rub into gilt wooden frame until you get the mellow shade you want.

DECORATING TIPS

Wallpaper leftovers see action. There's no need to throw away that leftover strip. Cover a shabby wastepaper basket with it, then protect with coat of clear shellac.

Left-over linoleum pieces do not go to waste. Cut them to fit the tops of shelves or mantels, paste the linoleum down with cement made for the purpose. This is especially recommended for children's rooms, kitchens, and utility rooms that receive hard wear.

Save draperies that are no longer used at your windows. The time will come when you can cut them down for cushions, seats and backs on dining chairs, and for clothes-closet conveniences. Make shoe bags, covers for hangers, large bags for your evening clothes.

Attractive telephone directories. Cover them, too, with leftover swatches of wallpaper to match the decorative scheme of your room.

Unusual glossy finish for ceramic figurines can be achieved with a coating of white shellac. Coating protects finish of bric-a-brac too.

Another decorating trick. Use interesting cutouts from magazine covers on utility jars. Then coat with colorless shellac for permanence. These make the humdrum jar an attractive decoration as well as a charmingly personalized gift.

Bridge-table top worn? A simple renovation job can be done with a piece of left-over floor linoleum. Cut it to fit the top of the table, right to the edge, and secure with linoleum cement. Your table will reward your work with long life, unusual appearance, and an easy-to-clean surface.

Alphabet book ends. If your youngster no longer has need of his alphabet blocks, you can make very nice book ends with them. Glue four of the blocks together for each book end and give them one or two thin coats of pure white shellac. The book ends can be made heavier by putting flat weights at the bottom, or they can be glued to a felt bottom.

Flatirons into book ends. If you have a pair of old-fashioned flatirons, turn them into picturesque, colorful book ends. Paint them a gay color, add a design if you like, then stand them up with the flat sides against the books and handles facing outward.

Make your own shoe rack. Nail a metal curtain rod on the back of the closet door. Hang shoes by their heels over this rod. If necessary, use the whole back of the closet door, nailing several rods one below the other and allowing sufficient space between the rows so that shoes don't touch.

NEED SPACE? MAKE ROOM FOR MORE

To get more floor space, replace swinging doors with sliding or folding doors. You can buy complete kits for almost any size door wanted. In fact, you can even buy kits that include the door frame, so that there is no work to hanging and fitting the new door closing. How much easier can you have things?

Handy headboard. Storage space in a headboard puts articles needed for relaxing in bed right where they are needed, within arm's reach. This design can be built quickly and easily with fir plywood. Flat surfaces at head of bed can be hinged to provide storage of additional pillows and blankets.

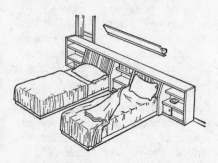

Bedstead drawer space. Plywood drawers, built in under a bed, make use of usually wasted space. They are simple to install and provide extra storage for sheets, pillows, and blankets.

More living space. Adequate storage area in the living room leaves more space for living, eliminates clutter, gives you more flexibility in furniture arrangement. One way to get it is the modern storage wall, built either against an existing partition or as a free-standing unit that forms a partition of its own.

Linen trays. Your linen closets will be far easier to use if the shelves are installed as trays. Make the combination drawer-trays from ¼-inch or ⅜-inch fir plywood, depending on the size of the closet. Trays should slide easily in any kind of track or slide arrangement that is adaptable to the closet in which they are installed. By adding extra slides, the height of the trays can also be adjusted.

Shelf-door storage. Don't let usable storage space on the back of your wardrobe doors go to waste. In this award-winning shelf-door wardrobe the designer has used every inch of space. You can do the same for just the small cost of the plywood. Shelves are movable, can be used

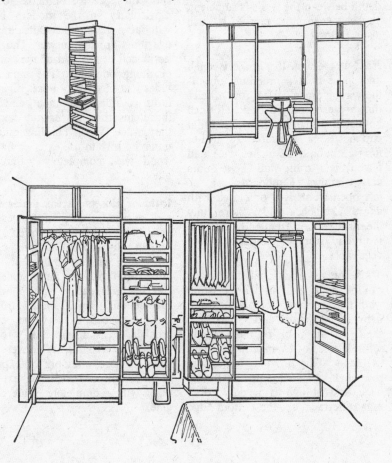

for purses, lingerie, handkerchiefs, odds and ends. In man's unit one shelf is left vacant so that there is space for him to empty his pockets at night.

Build a doorway closet. If a doorway between two bedrooms is not used, close one side in with wallboard and build shelves for storage of small objects. The space won't be very deep but it can be put to good use for a variety of purposes. In rare cases, where the existing depth between the walls is sufficient, you can even store clothes in such a spare closet.

High-up storage. If a house is small and space is at a premium, out-of-the-way storage units for articles that are used only occasionally can be installed high on the walls. Build cupboards of plywood 24 inches long and about 12 inches wide and fasten them to the wall above doors and windows. Cupboards can be left open as shelves or closed with doors 12 inches wide. Store only the articles not frequently needed. Everyday storage should be more accessible.

Wall storage. Additional shelf space can be built right into an existing wall. Cut wallboard or plaster away between two studs and fasten in a shelf. At the back of the opening set in a piece of ¼-inch fir plywood as facing. This provides for a narrow shelf, 14 inches to 16 inches wide, and as high as needed. For a magazine rack, set the bottom edge of the plywood backing piece near the outside edge of the shelf and slant it toward the back at the top. In this way magazines can be stood on edge without falling forward. The wall shelf works equally well in the living room, the kitchen, or the bedroom.

Carport storage. With the increasing popularity of the carport, and the construction economy it makes possible, home owners are often short of space for outdoor storage, particularly in the modern home without a basement. Outside storage units are the answer. They can be placed at the end of the carport or along one side. The area provides storage for hoses, garden tools, camping equipment, and similar items that are usually kept in the garage. When building outdoor units, be sure to use exterior fir plywood with completely waterproof glue.

Outdoor closets. Areas under wide roof overhangs, or along fences and exteriors of the home, offer space for an all-purpose outdoor closet for tools, garden equipment, outdoor furniture. The outdoor closets can be built easily with plywood. Free-standing units similar to this can be placed to serve as windbreaker or as a screen to provide privacy in a patio. Wherever plywood is used outdoors or exposed to moisture, it should be exterior type with completely waterproof glue.

34

PAINTING AND WALLPAPERING

Practical hints and directions that show how to paint and wallpaper the interior and paint the exterior

Painting—inside or outside—and wallpapering are jobs that many people will prefer to pay others to do. There is no denying that in return for considerable savings in money, you must expand considerable amounts of time and energy. Yet many people find it worthwhile. In the case of painting the exterior of a house, of course, there are two major factors to consider—safety and equipment. If the shape of the house presents a lot of special problems, you may not be able to do the job. And if you have to invest in expensive ladders or other equipment, you may also decide to hire professionals. But when it comes to painting or papering your interior rooms, observing some tips and shortcuts should make the job well worth your while.

Paint like a "pro." Prepare for the job by moving everything to the center of the room before you begin painting.

A cheap brush or an undersized one tends to cause the painter to try to carry too much paint in his brush, the excess dripping off exactly where you don't want it.

Paint daub identifies color in can. Save yourself time and wasted effort when hunting among your stored paints for the color you want. Apply a daub of the color at the level of the remaining paint in the can. That way you can also tell whether you have enough for the job you want to do.

Tin cans helpful treasures make. When opening can, don't perforate cover completely. Leave attached area of about 1 inch. Wash and use as rinse bath for paintbrushes. Bend cover back at angle, so that can will "stand" at a slant. Pour in turpentine or other paint cleaner, then insert brush. Brush will be able to lie flat and keep bristles straight (standing brush upright in container causes bristles to bend).

Inexpensive glue stirrers and paint applicators. Wooden tongue depressors do a good job and are so cheap you can afford to discard them after one use. Available in most drugstores.

Convenient, disposable paint containers can be made from empty milk cartons. Cut container in half, rinse, and dry. Wonderful for holding small amounts of paint or varnish. Straight side of carton is fine wiping edge for the paintbrush.

Paint won't slop over sides of the can when you replace lid if you take this precaution: Before using paint, tuck a piece of heavy twine in the lid groove of the can. Remove this just before replacing lid and there won't be any paint in the groove to drip over.

WHICH PAINT FOR WHICH JOB?

Most interior surfaces are now painted with water-based paints of various kinds—latex, rubber, vinyl latex, acrylic vinyl, and such—which are applied with rollers rather than brushes. A major exception are surfaces exposed to much water, steam, grease, or other soilants—which in practice means the walls of bathrooms and kitchens.

Water-based paints are undoubtedly easier to use especially in the cleaning-up stage. But read the directions carefully and make sure the paint you use does not require some special thinner. Also, water-based paints do not go well over enamel, oily, or greasy surfaces. Nor do they stand up to scrubbing —which is why they are not recommended for kitchen walls.

Rolling your own may be fun, but for really satisfactory results, observe these pointers:

Keep roller clean and the paint well mixed (especially the water paints, which settle very rapidly).

Don't roll too fast or you'll spatter.

Don't dip roller too deeply or paint will drip off.

Use a large size, generously felted or furred. An undersize roller is as bad as a poor-quality brush.

For getting into tight spots, use a small brush.

The most water-resistant paint, according to the experts, still is oil-base enamel. Although water-base paints are more convenient to handle, regular enamel is voted number one for durability.

Best ceiling paint still is calcimine. It was the first water paint discovered, yet remains the top favorite today. To do a real good job, rent a big, fat calcimine brush or a roller and go to it.

Calcimine will go on calcimine or plaster, but not over paint. Excess calcimine can be removed with a damp sponge. (By the way, always start room painting with the ceiling.)

ADDITIVES FOR SPECIAL CHORES

To control drying speed, add japan dryer to your paint, as needed—more on cool days, less on warm, dry days.

Lingering paint odors are passé. Kill odors as you paint by adding a special chemical now available at your paint shop.

Insects add nothing to a paint job. Keep them from settling on painted surfaces that are still wet. Add citronella, cedar or pine oil to final coat of paint. Teaspoonful or two in full pail of paint is enough, and won't injure the consistency of the paint itself.

MIXING PAINT

Make paint mixing easier. For a few days before it is to be used, keep the paint can inverted. It will mix well with less stirring.

Keep mixing your paint thoroughly. Its ingredients have a tendency to separate and settle. You must keep "boxing" your paint even though the machine at the store has mixed it for you. To do this properly, start with a container as large as the paint can. Pour half the paint into it. Mix both cans. Pour back and forth. Keep on mixing. Then take off just about the amount you expect to use. Remix the remaining paint at least twice a day until it is all used up.

Easy on the colors! You can always add a little more color to your mix, but you can't remove it once added. A drop of black added to a gallon of white makes a gray. Add several gallons of white to even pale gray and it is still—gray. Moral: follow the paint-store chart when mixing —don't fight it! Some of the colors may surprise you. For instance, brown added to white makes a gray, etc.

Eliminate guesswork when matching area already painted. Make small swatch by applying new mixture to piece of wood or scrap metal, allow to dry. Then check against surface to be matched. Alternate method: find spot on wall that won't show and apply sample there. Check when it's dry.

PREPARING SURFACES

To keep the paint from crawling off your kitchen wall, be sure to wash the wall down carefully with special cleaner and have the wall thoroughly dry before you apply the paint. (Remember, paint won't "stay put" on a greasy surface.)

For best results when painting over enamel or varnish, first either wash the surface down with special "bonding" solution or roughen it with sandpaper or steel wool. Otherwise subsequent coats will not adhere properly because enamel and varnish have a slippery finish.

Before you paint walls, a first coat of fresh shellac will form a nice even base for the paint. The shellac will also prevent uneven absorption. Because shellac dries very quickly, the paint should go on the same day.

Quick way to remove old varnish or paint finish. Make saturated solution of oxalic-acid crystals and warm water in 1-quart bottle. Pour half into another quart bottle and fill both to the top with warm water. (Unused portion can be stored in covered jar for future use.) Tie soft rag to a stick, dip rag into mixture and swish over furniture. Sprinkle sawdust or wood shavings over it (to absorb excess remover). Let furniture stand a few minutes, until old finish softens, then wash off with hot suds. Rinse off suds and dry immediately with soft cloth. Wear rubber gloves throughout operation, as solution is strong.

Before applying enamel to brass, prepare metal surface carefully. Wash thoroughly with any household cleaner that doesn't contain soap, then wipe down with denatured alcohol. Otherwise paint won't stick.

Useful use for burned-out fuses. When spray-painting, screw an old fuse into each socket within the area to be sprayed. Keeps sockets clean.

Before painting doors and windows, smear locks with Vaseline, so surplus paint will be easy to remove.

Sandpaper's important before you paint furniture. Why? It removes film of dirt and grease sometimes invisible to the naked eye. It gives better gripping surface for paint application, prevents blistering or cracking of paint. Use sandpaper even on new unpainted pieces, unless store guarantees surfaces as ready for paint.

When sanding painted surfaces, dust on a little fine pumice first. Helps prevent paint from clogging sandpaper, also adds to abrasive action and makes job go faster. Sandpaper lasts longer, too.

BRUSH CONTROL

Good brushes make house painting easy. If you're going to paint your home or any other large area, you'll save time and do a better job if you buy the best brushes you can afford. They hold more, lay the paint down better, last longer. Experts agree, by the way, that animal-hair brushes are still the best.

To keep your brush soft overnight, if you're going to use it again the next day, don't bother cleaning it. Give it a drop or two of turpentine or linseed oil, wrap it tightly in wax paper or aluminum foil, and lay it flat.

Hold your brush short, don't wear gloves, and paint first with one hand, then with the other, to avoid premature fatigue. Gloves do keep your hands clean but they tend to keep slipping, thus wasting your energy on merely gripping the brush as you try to paint.

Reshape worn paintbrushes. Soak the bristles in water-soluble glue, shape and allow to dry. Then rub bristle tips over coarse sandpaper to the form desired. Remove the glue by setting brush in hot water.

Single greatest cause of spatter is the beginner's tendency to flip the brush at the end of the stroke. Other causes are the habit of dipping the brush too deeply and failure to clean the brush by pressing the paint out of the brush heel frequently.

A wipe in time saves nine. While painting, keep a clean rag handy. Use it to pick up the stray drops as they form. If you wait till the job is finished, or if you use a paint-filled rag for the wiping, you'll simply be piling up a lot more work for later on.

TRICKS OF THE TRADE

Fasten a stiff wire across the center of your paint pail or can. To do this, drill holes just under the top rim at opposite sides of container. Wire goes through the holes, is crimped around rim on both sides. Use the wire to wipe excess paint off brush. Use it, too, when you want to rest the brush over the paint. (If you use a double length of wire, you can have one fastening by looping the wire singly through one hole, fastening the double ends at the other. Makes it easier to unfasten if you want to remove the wire.)

Mix putty and paint to make a color-matching hole filler. It really works.

Large paper plate, glued to bottom of paint can, catches all drippings and provides convenient resting place for brush.

Banish paint odors. In a freshly painted room place a large open pan of cold water containing a large onion cut in half. This time the onion goes to work for you. Paint odors will sponge up within a few hours.

Skip a step. When painting steps, paint every other one, then let them dry. Later paint the remaining ones. In this way the dry steps may be walked on without injuring the paint.

Dust specks won't cling to newly varnished furniture if it is suspended upside down to dry.

When painting small pieces of furniture, turn them upside down and paint the underneath portion first. Much more convenient.

To paint a straight line, use a ruler to mark out the line exactly, then some masking tape on each side of the line to be painted. Now brush the paint between the parallel rows of masking tape. It doesn't matter, of course, if some of the paint wanders onto the tape. When the paint has dried, lift the tape off gently and there you are. Remove the tape promptly after paint dries, however, or you may lift away some of the paint that has hardened.

To paint border designs like an artist, simply rent or buy border stencils and dab the paint over the openings.

Painting flowerpots is easy if you rest them upside down on suitable-size tin can. Can permits rotating pot without touching it and provides good support to hold pot while it dries.

Painting a floor? You need not develop housemaid's knee and an aching back to do the job. Use a new pushbroom as your brush, and get a large shallow pan to hold your paint, and save yourself a lot of strain.

Powder puff protects linoleum. Use new puff as "brush" to apply plastic-base linoleum varnish. Spreads varnish smoothly.

SPECIAL FINISHES

Wipe finish. Fir plywood can be finished in color tones that harmonize with any color scheme and at the same time retain the striking visual pattern of the real wood grain. Here's how to do it: Apply a coat of white Rez or undercoat to the plywood and wipe or dry-brush to the desired grain show-through. Then sand it lightly. Next apply a color coat and wipe this to the desired grain show-through. Sand it when dry and finish with a coat of varnish. A steel-wool rub will make the finish glow. This kind of finish softens grain contrast but retains the rich beauty of real wood paneling. Experiment first with various paint consistencies to get exactly the tone you want.

How to create a smart limed-oak furniture finish. Stir 1 pound unslaked lime into 2 quarts of water. Rub across grain of wood and wipe when partly dry (to prevent accumulation of excess lime). Seal with two coats of thin white shellac and finish with thin coat of paraffin wax.

Low-cost wood stain. Strong tea diluted with a little water makes an excellent antique-like stain for pine wood. When dry, cover with two thin coats of fresh white shellac. When dry, wax for a fine finish.

Face-lift discolored brick walls this way: Dissolve 1 ounce of glue in a gallon of hot water. Add a piece of alum the size of an egg, plus a half pound of Venetian red and a pound of Spanish brown. Apply the mixture to the brick surface with a brush and bricks will look as bright as when new.

HINTS ABOUT EXTERIOR PAINT AND PAINTING

How many coats of paint does your new home really need? At least three coats of good paint for every bare-wood surface exposed to the weather. It's the third coat that adds years of good grooming to your nice new home.

But don't overdo it. Enough is just right. In fact, most older homes suffer from too much paint. Such buildings are repainted when all they need is washing down. There's a special chemical that you add to water for this purpose.

Good paint is good for about four years on exteriors. Exposed paint wears down only about 1/1000 of an inch per year. If the paint isn't permitted to thin, or if your house is repainted too frequently, the paint layer becomes so thick it will peel and crack with no assist from you.

Why cheap paint costs too much. Eighty per cent of the cost of house painting is—labor. "Saving" on the cost of the paint is a waste of expensive labor. Good paint costs more only because its ingredients cost more. Bargain paints simply don't exist. Government surplus paint is fine stuff, but it was made for some special purpose, such as painting landing barges or airplanes, and, in most cases, is worthless for exterior home painting.

When stalling pays off. Never paint when the temperature is below 50° F., when it is raining, or when the wood is wet. The results will be unsatisfactory if you do.

Thin outside paint with linseed oil and you'll improve its quality. Incidentally, linseed oil is in itself a very fine wood preservative. Turpentine, on the other hand, evaporates.

THE CLEANUP

Paint spattered on tiles may be removed with a cloth dipped in turpentine.

Paint-spattered floors. Even when paint spatters have hardened on your floor they are fairly easy to remove if moistened with nail-polish remover, allowed to soak in for a few minutes, then rubbed off with a cloth and washed with warm suds. They usually disappear no matter how long the spots have been there.

Paint spills on concrete. To remove paint spilled on concrete floors or driveway, scrub with a strong solution of lye water, then rinse the floor well with clean water.

A new role for erasers. Hard pencil erasers will remove paint or varnish that has dripped onto window glass.

Paint all over your hands? Don't despair. Use a little cooking oil on your hands before you scrub them with soap and water. Works wonders; won't dry or injure skin as turpentine might (especially if your skin is sensitive).

Lost the cover of that leftover paint? Here's a trick borrowed from the kitchen. Melt paraffin and pour it over the surface of the paint (the way you do over jellies and preserves). Paint will remain soft until needed again.

WALLPAPERING

Vinyl wallpaper has become more popular than the traditional all-paper wall covering. The vinyl wall coverings tend to be sturdier and can be cleaned more readily. With a little practice, either type can be hung by the amateur. Both come with trimmed or untrimmed edges (depending on price, brand, etc.), the latter variety requiring that the hanger cut along the edge to avoid a bulging overlap. Each type of paper uses its own kind or distinctive mixture of glue. You should therefore specify the type when you are buying glue. Follow the directions carefully for mixing the powdered glue with the recommended proportion of water.

Papering-equipment needs. The first thing you'll need is a paperhanger's table, or any large table having a flat, smooth surface, at least 6 feet long and 2 feet wide. If wider wallpaper is to be hung, get a table as wide as the paper plus about 4 inches. You can also use two sawhorses and a sheet of plywood of suitable size. You'll also need a straight-edge about 5 feet long, which may be rented along with the table. A length of hardwood that has had one edge trimmed absolutely true makes an adequate substitute for a straightedge. A metal ruler or straight-edge is even better. These types are sold in many art-supply stores.

How much paper do you need? You estimate how much paper you'll need by measuring the height, width, and length of your room and referring to the chart on page 353.

PREPARING THE WALLS

Before wallpapering a painted wall, examine the wall for grease spots. Clean the wall thoroughly, and if grease seems to persist, coat those spots with white shellac before sizing and papering the wall.

Preparing wall for papering. Examine existing wall surface. If walls are calcimined, they should be washed down with a wet sponge until all the calcimine has been re-moved. Walls that have a very glossy surface should have the gloss dulled. To do this, wash the surface with a solution of one part ammonia and five parts water.

If there is paper on the walls, it should be removed where there are more than two layers or if the old paper is coming loose. When in doubt, it is always safer and wiser to remove the old wallpaper.

To remove old wallpaper, use a pail of warm water and a brush or sponge to wet the wall thoroughly. (Work from the top down, as the water will seep into lower areas as you work.) It's best to go over the wall several times and allow it to soak and be thoroughly wet before you attempt to remove the paper. When soaked, use a stiff-bladed putty knife to scrape the paper off. Be careful not to gouge the wall with the scraper, as such scratches will only have to be patched up later.

An easier and quicker way to remove paper is by a machine that can be rented from many paint and wallpaper stores. The machine applies the moisture in steam form, applies it so evenly that the paper comes off in large sheets and you'll need to use your putty knife hardly at all.

When paper is off or wall washed, carefully fill in all cracks and holes with patching plaster or spackling putty, using a flexible, wide-bladed putty knife. When patches are hard, smooth them with medium to coarse sandpaper. Next mix a package of prepared size with water, according to manufacturer's directions. Apply this solution to the wall with brush or sponge. Do not apply too heavily, and try to avoid runs. Also be careful not to leave unsized spots, working the size into all corners and along the edges where the wall meets the woodwork. Let dry for an hour.

If ceiling is to be painted, do this before you paper. Also paint woodwork before applying your wallpaper.

TRICKS OF THE TRADE

Mixing the paste. Mix the paste and lukewarm water in a clean pail, according to the manufacturer's directions. Use a good grade of paste

HOW TO ESTIMATE REQUIRED NUMBER OF SINGLE ROLLS

SIZE OF ROOM	SINGLE ROLLS FOR WALLS HEIGHT OF WALL			SINGLE ROLLS FOR CEILING
	8-foot	9-foot	10-foot	
4×8-foot	6	7	8	2
4×10-foot	7	8	9	2
4×12-foot	8	9	10	2
6×10-foot	8	9	10	2
6×12-foot	9	10	11	3
8×12-foot	10	11	12	4
8×14-foot	11	12	14	4
10×14-foot	12	14	15	5
10×16-foot	13	15	16	6
12×16-foot	14	16	17	7
12×18-foot	15	17	19	8
14×18-foot	16	18	20	8
14×22-foot	18	20	22	10
15×16-foot	15	17	19	8
15×18-foot	16	18	20	9
15×20-foot	17	20	22	10
15×23-foot	19	21	23	11
16×18-foot	17	19	21	10
16×20-foot	18	20	22	10
16×22-foot	19	21	23	11
16×24-foot	20	22	25	12
17×22-foot	19	22	24	12
17×25-foot	21	23	26	13
17×28-foot	22	25	28	15
18×22-foot	20	22	25	12
18×25-foot	21	24	27	14

Note: Deduct one single roll of sidewall paper for every two ordinary-sized doors or windows, or every 36-square-foot opening.

and be careful to avoid lumps. Tie a string across the top of the bucket to rest the paste brush on. Set the bucket on top of a box to save unnecessary bending.

A trick to avoid dry spots on ready-pasted wallpaper is to get it all wet by inserting a metal rod in the roll before you submerge it in the water box.

Cutting the paper. You'll want to take the curl out of the paper to enable easier handling. To do this, draw the paper across the edge of the table with one hand while lightly pressing with your other hand. Examine the pattern carefully before you begin cutting, so you can cut it with the least waste. If your pattern has figures or animals in it, try not to tear off in such a way that the figures will be cut in two. Instead tear off a few inches higher up and cut off the excess at the beginning of the strip.

The wrinkles that plague paper wallpaper are often caused by not allowing the paste to soak sufficiently into the paper, which should be flexible from moisture before you start to hang it. When applying the paper to the wall, ease out the wrinkles with a broad smoothing brush. A whisk broom might be substituted, but not if it is too rough.

Wrinkles should be less of a problem with the vinyl wallpapers if you have used the right glue and applied it properly. You can smooth the paper with a mildly-damp sponge.

It's a good idea to start hanging wallpaper on the most prominent wall of the room first. Center pattern on that wall, being very sure it hangs absolutely straight.

An easy way to fit wallpaper behind window sill is to saw a slot for it. This saves hours of tiresome trimming. Slip paper in slot as you fit it next to window casing.

An easy way to fit the top of wallpaper is to fold it back to mark. Trim while paper is dry. Trim the bottom of the strip last.

35

HOUSEHOLD HANDYMAN

A miscellany of helpful tips for all those little things that need doing

Don't waste shoe polish. To get the polish that clings to sides of tin after center part has been used, hold tin over low heat. The wax will melt and form new cake of polish.

Did you ever think of a bottle cap as an umbrella tip? It's really quite an idea. Plastic bottle tops (from cologne, nail polish, etc.) are colorful and practical replacements for lost umbrella tips. Fasten in place with household cement.

For wet umbrellas. A large sponge placed in the bottom of your umbrella stand will absorb the dripping water.

Newspaper rug pad. If you haven't a regular rug pad, use newspapers under your large rugs. Spread several layers flat under the rugs and you'll save wear, make the rugs look and feel better underfoot, make the floor warmer, provide a soft, luxurious tread.

Thumbtacks prevent dust marks. Place one thumbtack in each lower corner at the back of a picture frame and the tack heads will provide air space between picture and wall, thus preventing dust line from soiling the wall surface.

A fair deal with cards. If playing cards stick together, rub some talcum powder over them and you'll have a smooth new deal.

Precondition your new toothbrush by soaking it in cold water for 24 hours before using. This preserves the bristles for a longer time.

Fireplace magic transforms kindling wood into logs. With one or two nails, fasten together several pieces of wood otherwise useful only as kindling. They'll become as long-burning as a regular log.

A colorful touch for your open fire. Soak pine cones in chemical solution and add to your firewood. Dry cones thoroughly after soaking, before you burn them. Copper nitrate produces emerald green, potassium nitrate gives you orange, lithium chloride gives a purple glow.

MINOR MENDS AND REPAIRS ABOUT THE HOUSE

Remove broken light bulb safely. Press a large cork into the base of the bulb and unscrew it easily without having to touch the jagged edges of the bulb.

Extracting key if broken. If you break off a key in a lock, run an old jigsaw blade into the cylinder alongside the broken piece and twist it so that the teeth bite into the key. Pulling on the blade while in this position usually will remove the broken piece.

Outwit the lid. Those frustrating struggles with a jar lid that won't come loose can be eliminated by lining your hand with sandpaper before turning. You'll be able to grip like mad.

Glue lid opens easily. After opening a new bottle of glue, rub a little lard or oil on the bottle top before putting back the lid. It will come off quickly the next time you want to open it.

Mend breaks in your toothpaste tube (or any other kind of tube) with a strip of sturdy Scotch tape wrapped twice around the tube. Saves you money, keeps tube neat.

Use modeling clay, in mending chinaware or glass, to hold chipped pieces together while the mending cement is hardening.

To remove dents from pots, pans, trays, place dented surface against firm, level object (upturned flatiron often works), with bumpy surface facing you. Using medium-heavy hammer, tap the protruding dent with slow, light raps (heavy hammer blows will mark up the surface around the dent). A dozen blows or so will turn the trick.

Hot-water bag mended fast. If the hot-water bag springs a leak, tamp adhesive tape down over the tear. For a permanent mend, however, apply an inner-tube patch (same as is used on tire tubes).

Emergency home shoe repairing. Run-down rubber heels, cuts, and other worn spots can be built up with rubber-base tire-cut filler, available in tube containers. Spread over worn area, allow to dry overnight. This material is self-adhering and self-vulcanizing.

Tape keeps plaster from chipping. When driving a nail into a plaster surface there's always danger of chipping. Before you start stick a bit of Scotch tape over spot where nail is to be driven in and you are more likely to prevent the chips from flying.

Rag rugs stay put. Those little rag rugs are attractive but are such a nuisance when they curl. Dipping the ends in weak starch after they have been washed will keep them on the straightaway.

Sticking metal to wood. First soak the metal in acetone. When dry, use household cement to attach it to the wood. Don't touch the cleaned area of the metal before cementing.

Repair holes or short tears in canvas by using rubber cement to apply the patching material. Weight the patch for several hours to be sure it will stay in place.

FABRIC CARE

Permanent-wave solutions. Usually stains from these do not show up immediately upon contact. It may take days, weeks, before they do. So, when having a home permanent, protect garment completely. Not even your dry cleaner can guarantee removal results.

White furs that have yellowed. Many white furs are originally bleached with a "reducing bleach." After a time they take on oxygen from the air and start turning yellow. This can be overcome, usually, by spraying on a solution of hydrogen peroxide or by brushing with a soft brush. Sometimes hanging fur in the sun afterward will speed up the rebleach job.

"Pilling" of fabric. Surface yarns (as in bouclés and poodle cloth) sometimes roll themselves up into a small accumulated ball (sometimes happens with smooth-surface fabrics too). Brush with coarse, dry brush. If you're very careful, you may be able to remove the pilling by stretching fabric tight and "shaving" surface with safety razor. But take care not to cut the cloth itself.

Suède glove freshener. Put gloves on and rub hand with thick slice of stale bread, changing to another slice as bread becomes soiled.

If careless you, or one of your guests, burned a cigarette hole in your lovely bridge cloth, don't be dismayed. Cover that hole with an appliquéd design or monogram, of a contrasting color, using thread to match the appliqué. Or if the hole is minute, embroider a little design or monogram over it with same or contrasting thread.

If party guests leave coats on your bed, protect both spread and wraps by covering spread with sheet of pliofilm or plastic tablecloth. Keeps coats from picking up lint, protects spread from soiling.

PERSONAL COMFORT

Tired feet mean a tired you. Two handfuls of ordinary salt in a basin of hot water give you new feet for old. Epsom salts, bicarbonate of soda, or ordinary brown laundry soap make a mighty refreshing foot bath too.

Clean eyeglasses. Opticians recommend an occasional soap-and-water bath for your glasses to remove the film of oil that gathers from the skin. Rinse, then polish with soft tissue paper.

When particles of adhesive stick to your skin after removing bandage, rub with acetone and rinse with water. Use absorbent cotton to apply acetone.

Smoke disperser. Soak a towel in water, swish it around the room, and watch how quickly smoke disappears. Another idea: dispel smoke and other odors by leaving a saucer of vinegar in the room.

Soundproofing the sickroom. Cover watch or small clock on bedside table with large glass tumbler. Patient can see the time when wanted, but won't be disturbed by sound. Muffle telephone bell with thick cloth covering.

Keep phone easy to reach. Have telephone connected in spot that saves the most steps. If house has two floors, place phone on stair landing rather than remote room on either floor, if you can't afford the luxury of an extension phone.

DEALING WITH ANIMALS

When dog has his bath his hair won't clog the drain if you place a wad of steel wool in the drain opening. Steel wool strains out hair that might otherwise cause clogging.

Don't tip them off. When a mousetrap has caught its prey and you spring it for the next victim, other mice will stay away once they scent the previous occupant. To remove this secret signal, be sure to scald the mousetrap thoroughly before reusing it.

Fly repellent. A few drops of oil of lavender in a glass of boiling water not only chases away those flies but quickly fills a musty room with a pleasant odor.

Ants will hate you. If ants are invading your household, it will help you to know that they are allergic to cucumber skin. Keep bits of it where ants congregate and they'll scram.

CANDLES

No-drip burning candles. Place candles in refrigerator for a couple of days before using. They'll burn twice as long, won't drip.

A candle to the rescue. When addressing packages in ink for mailing, protect addresses from smearing and becoming illegible by rubbing a candle over the writing. The wax coating forms a weatherproof protective surface.

Candles just for "show." Candles used for decorative purposes only can be treated against drooping by giving them a coat of shellac. To clean, simply wipe with a damp cloth.

A Christmas use for old lipsticks. First melt down wax from old candles, shave the lipstick ends into the melted wax, and, while it is warm, dip inexpensive white candles into it. They'll be beautiful and burn long.

CORKS

Homemade corks. Satisfactory substitute for a lost cork is an inch or two of candle. Soften up the wax a bit and your candle "cork" is sure to fit. Or, if a cork's on hand but it's too large for the bottle, cut a small V in the side and, presto! it fits.

Corks frequently stick in bottles containing sugary liquids (sweet extracts, etc.). Prevent this by smoothing a bit of waxed paper around the cork before inserting it in the bottle opening.

Removing cork from inside bottle. A cork that has lodged inside a bottle or decanter can be removed in this way. Pour enough ammonia into the empty bottle to make the cork float, then put the bottle away for a few days. By then the ammonia will have chewed down the cork to size where it can be poured out of the bottle.

AT THE DESK

A note about inks. Permanent inks are for documents meant to last a long time and withstand possible exposure to water or strong light; if spilled, chances are they can't be removed without fabric injury.

Washable ink is for general use. If spilled on color-fast material, soak up as much as possible with blotter. (See stain-removal chapter for specific instructions.)

Inkstains on fingers. To remove them, moisten the stain, then rub with the sulphur end of a match and wipe with a dry cloth.

When you open a new box of stationery, paste a small envelope inside the cover. Use it to hold stamps and air-mail stickers and you'll have them handy as needed.

When adhesive on envelope flap doesn't stick, try quick application of nail polish. Dries quickly, leaves no smudge. Can't even be steamed open.

Novel key ring at very lost cost, especially valuable to people who have to remove keys from ring frequently, is a simple metal shower-curtain hook.

Paper clip does double duty as a pencil clip. Straighten out one end and wrap it around pencil.

Make your own rubber bands. When you discover holes in your rubber gloves, convert them into rubber bands instead of throwing them out. With a pair of scissors cut across the width of each finger, the palm, and the wrist. You'll have quite a few first-class rubber bands of different sizes, cut just the thickness you want.

STORING TIPS

What's in it? Label each package before you put things away in your attic, basement, or extra closet. This will save you needless unwrapping, bewilderment, and time when you finally do want some of the contents. Sounds obvious, but the reminder seems needed.

Speed up packing job. Packing cardboard cartons goes faster if flaps are held open by small sections of garden hose, split apart on one side to form rubber clamps. Saves your temper as well as your time.

To tie tight, secure package, use wet string. It shrinks as it dries and thus gets tighter.

Shelf paper won't tear as quickly if you secure it with transparent adhesive tape instead of thumbtacks.

Save egg cartons for Christmastime. They make excellent containers in which to store your colorful tree ornaments.

Newspapers have many uses, even after the family has finished reading them. Save for packing clothes out of season or rolling in rugs put up for the summer. Newsprint also discourages moths. A well-crumpled newspaper is also handy for wiping windows dry, leaves no linty coating.

Store garden shoes and rubbers in the garage. Off in a free corner, hammer several large nails into the wall. Use these as pegs for the footwear. Keeps them in shape; they gather less dust, too.

Before storing overshoes, wash outside surface with warm water to remove oil and grease spots as well as encrusted dirt. Stuff with crumpled newspaper and store in dark, cool, dry place.

Use sandwich bags for wool storage. Small items—balls of yarn, mittens, etc.—can be mothproofed for storage by placing them in plastic bags together with some mothballs or moth flakes. Seal the open end of the bag with adhesive or transparent tape.

To store tennis racquets for the winter, cover them first with a coating of petroleum jelly. Prevents strings from snapping when not in use.

It's easy to slide heavy storage boxes if you tack four or more metal bottle caps to the base of the box. Caps raise the box and reduce friction between it and the floor. Saves "elbow grease," costs you nothing.

A stored card table won't flop on its side if kept in place with a homemade cleat. An inexpensive towel bar, fastened to the wall on a diagonal line, serves beautifully.

MOVING AIDS

Shred old newspapers as packing filler for bric-a-brac, dishes, stemware, and even lamp shades. Pack each shade separately after first wrapping in tissue paper.

Packing liquid preparations for travel. Bind corks or stoppers with adhesive or Scotch tape before packing. This keeps the containers leakproof, prevents costly damage to clothes.

For safety and ease of handling, pack books on end and one row deep in strong cartons or boxes. If box is wide enough for two rows, pack with books back-to-back. Saves the bindings.

Dresser drawers won't rattle or break, when moved, if packed with lightweight things. Best idea is to double-fold pillows into the drawers.

Don't lose the screws. When you take down the curtain rods, towel racks, etc., for moving, fasten all the screws to them with pieces of Scotch tape. Then they'll be handy when you put the piece back in place.

HOBBIES AND SPORTS

Develop your own photos with trays? To ensure excellent agitation while developing your prints, place a round pencil or piece of dowel under your developing tray. You can roll your tray back and forth without spilling any solution.

Good news for record collectors. Restore that warped disk to life. Don't discard that treasured collector's item. Place record between two sheets of glass and allow to set in the sun. Heat will soften disk, and weight of glass will flatten it back into shape.

Record albums will stand up, when some are removed from shelf, if you glue a sheet of corrugated cardboard inside back of cabinet. The cardboard ridges will keep remaining albums upright.

Advice to amateur wood carver. To harden wood that has been cut out or sculptured in the shape desired, boil the pieces in pure olive oil for 8 to 10 minutes.

Old fork becomes leather crafter's tool. It's especially good for scoring lines on heavy belt leather. Place leather on a wood block with perfectly straight edge. Bend up an outer tine of the fork and draw this tine over the leather. The neighboring tine acts as a guide, keeping the line uniform.

Shoe polish waxes golf clubs. This is a trick used by professionals in the game. Rub new clubs with a little polish and they'll retain their original luster. Rub thin coating of Vaseline over metal parts to prevent rusting.

Going fishing? Moistureproof your wrist watch by wrapping it tightly with cellophane.

Line your fishing box with rubber to protect the enameled surface of casting plugs and the plated surface of spoons and spinners. Use inner-tube rubber for the purpose and attach it with tire-patching cement.

Bait minnows used for ice fishing will not freeze and become brittle if kept in a jar filled with glycerine.

A live minnow is a good minnow. They'll stay alive much longer when being transported if you add 6 to 8 drops of iodine to the water, as the minnows show need for more oxygen.

36

INDOOR AND OUTDOOR GARDENING

How to make your home and garden more beautiful

PLANNING YOUR LANDSCAPING

Whether you've just moved into a newly built house on a bare lot or want to enhance the attractiveness of a house where you've lived for many years, careful planning before you seed the lawn or plant shrubs and trees will pay off in the long run and give you many years of enjoyment.

First, consider the size of your house and lot, its location, and the social and recreational needs of your family. Is there heavy traffic on your street? A hedge planted along the street line will muffle traffic noises and block the glare of headlights at night. Do you want a play area for your children, with swings, slide, and sandbox? It should be fully visible from the house, and a safe distance from the street and driveway.

Take advantage of natural features of your property—streams, slopes, outcroppings of rock—and landscape around them to show them off. A planting of spring bulbs around a large rock in the lawn provides a charming accent. A steep, sandy bank where no grass will grow could be a perfect site for a rock garden.

When you've decided on the main features of your landscaping plan, take a piece of graph paper and make a scale drawing of your property, including all buildings—house, garage, tool shed—and all trees and shrubs that are to be left in place. This will enable you to see at a glance what will and won't fit within the space at your disposal.

As the next step in your landscaping plan, you can make a scale model of your property as you want it to look, using pieces of paper or cardboard to represent fences, lawn furniture, and garden areas. Move the pieces around until you have the most pleasing and convenient arrangement.

When you're ready to begin the actual work of landscaping, the best procedure is to plant trees and shrubs first, then construct walks and driveways, then seed the lawn areas and flower borders.

When planning or remodeling your driveway, remember to leave extra space at the end nearest the house for a parking and turn-around area.

If you're planning to grow vegetables, remember that they need about 6 hours of direct sunlight every day in summer; don't put your vegetable garden close to the house on the north side, or on the shady side of a large tree.

Small trees, shrubs, or flower beds scattered at random all over the lawn make mowing difficult and give an aimless, untidy appearance to your landscaping. Group your plantings attractively—perennials bordering a path, spring bulbs in front of low evergreen shrubs—for the most pleasing effect.

KNOW YOUR SOIL

Acid or alkaline? If plants fail to thrive in your soil, a chemical imbalance may be at fault. Take a pH reading, using a simple soil-testing kit available in garden centers. A pH reading of 7.0 is neutral; below 5.5, soil is strongly acid; above 8.0, strongly alkaline. Soil is more likely to be acid in regions with moderate to heavy rainfall.

Most plants prefer soil that is neutral or very slightly acid. A few, such as azaleas, rhododendrons, oaks, and blueberries, do best in strongly acid soil.

To increase soil acidity, apply 10 to 20 pounds of dusting sulfur per 1,000 square feet, depending on the density of the soil. To "sweeten" soil (decrease acidity), add 35 to 70 pounds of ground limestone per 1,000 square feet.

The texture of your soil is just as important as its pH, if not more so. You can judge this factor by turning over a spadeful of soil and sifting it through your fingers. If it is very light and sandy, it needs organic matter. If it is heavy and does not crumble readily, it needs to be lightened with sand or cinders.

Plant roots need oxygen in order to absorb water from the soil. If soil is so heavy and compact that there is little air between particles, plants will not thrive no matter how much they are watered.

Steam cinders, the residue of hard coal burned in high-pressure boilers, are the best material for lightening soil. Before mixing them with your soil, let them stand outdoors for six months to get rid of harmful chemical residues, then sift them through a wire mesh screen.

ENRICH SOIL WITH COMPOST

All types of soil will benefit from the addition of humus, or decayed organic matter, and the cheapest source of humus is your own compost pile. It's an excellent way to recycle wastes, and see the direct results in the increased productivity of your garden.

What goes into the compost pile? Anything that will rot, including bones, vegetable and fruit peelings, grass clippings, fallen leaves, even scraps of used clothing (providing they're made of natural fibers only).

A compost pile may be useful, but it's not a thing of beauty, so put it behind the garage or shed, or screen it from view with a stake fence planted with climbing vines. The site chosen should be well drained and in light shade; too much direct sunlight will kill the bacteria needed to enrich the soil.

If you live in a rural or suburban area, you may find that skunks, raccoons, and other animals are attracted to your compost pile. In that case, you'll need a sturdy fence, perhaps electrified if necessary, to keep them out.

Build your pile by sprinkling finely ground limestone on the ground, then laying down alternating 4-inch-thick layers of organic material and garden soil. (Use soil as the top layer to confine odors.) Sprinkle alternate layers with 5-10-5 fertilizer and ground limestone. The pile should be turned over and the layers thoroughly mixed about once a month. If the odors are extremely ripe, add a little superphosphate.

Protect the pile from high winds and heavy rains by covering it with a sheet of black plastic. During long dry spells, the pile can be wetted down with a hose when it is turned over.

If your compost pile is started during the summer, it will probably be ready for use in about three months; if started in fall or winter, wait until spring before using it.

When compost is thoroughly decomposed, remove sections from the pile by cutting vertically with the edge of a spade. Sift through a coarse screen and mix with three to four parts garden soil. Apply a 1½-inch layer of this mixture to the area to be fertilized and work it into the top six inches of soil.

If space is at a premium in your yard, try composting on a small scale by keeping organic garbage, grass clippings, pulled weeds, etc., in plastic trash bags.

FERTILIZER FACTS

While many home gardeners prefer to use only organic fertilizing agents, such as manure and compost, the fact remains that the chemical fertilizers available in garden stores provide nourishment to plants quickly and directly, and are economical in the long run, since only small quantities need to be used at each application.

What do the numbers mean? The three figures found on bags of complete commercial fertilizers refer to the percentages of three essential plant nutrients—nitrogen, phosphorus, and potash—in the mixture. Thus, 5-10-5, a common mixture, contains 5 per cent nitrogen, 10 per cent phosphorus, and 5 per cent potash.

What do these nutrients do for plants? Nitrogen aids rapid growth and is an essential element of chlorophyll. Phosphorus produces sturdy stems and aids seed formation. Potash is necessary for the production of roots, especially in vegetables.

Wood or leaf ashes are a good organic source of potash. They also contain lime, which hastens the decomposition of organic matter in the soil.

Avoid fertilizer "burn" by watering soil thoroughly after applying chemical fertilizer.

CULTIVATING AND MULCHING

Cultivating, or stirring up the top layer of soil before planting seeds, permits air to enter the soil and makes nutrients readily available to roots. Wait until soil is fairly dry before cultivating. If a handful of soil, squeezed in the fist, remains in a moist, compact ball without crumbling, it needs to dry out some more before cultivation.

After plants are established, cultivate the soil around them to a shallow depth with a light hoe to avoid injuring their roots. This will keep the soil aerated and prevent weeds from getting a foothold.

A mulch is any material, such as grass clippings, hay, or plastic sheeting, applied around the base of plants to hold moisture in the soil, protect roots from alternate freezing and thawing of the ground in winter, and prevent the growth of weeds. The advantage of using organic materials for mulches is that

their eventual decay will enrich the topsoil.

Avoid using fallen leaves as a mulch. They form a heavy sodden mass when wet, preventing air from reaching the soil.

TREES AND SHRUBS ADD BEAUTY TO YOUR HOME

When choosing trees to plant around your house, keep in mind their growth rate, their full height at maturity, and the amount of shade they'll cast. A sycamore or sugar maple may reach a full adult height of 60 feet. As a general rule, choose trees that will grow to a full height of no more than 2 to 3 times the height of your house (measured from ground to ridge pole).

Flowering trees such as magnolia, crab apple and dogwood are an excellent choice for landscaping around a new house. They grow fairly quickly to their full height, provide a moderate amount of shade, and have lovely blossoms in spring.

If you have an older house of two or more stories, set on a cement foundation, a foundation planting of evergreen shrubs will improve its appearance. Around ranch houses, such plantings are not necessary; they can make the house look as if it's sinking into a sea of foliage.

Highlight your front door with a tree or shrub on each side, preferably asymmetrical—perhaps a low shrub on one side and a small, conical evergreen tree on the other.

When planting a tree, dig a hole deep enough and wide enough to hold the roots without crowding. If roots are balled and burlapped, make the hole at least 12 inches wider than the diameter of the ball.

Burlap can be left on the root ball when planting—it will eventually decay in the ground—but remember to loosen the string around the base of the tree.

Wrap burlap or brown paper around the trunk of a newly planted young tree to prevent injury from direct sunlight.

The best time to transplant trees and shrubs is in late fall, after leaves are gone, or early spring, before leaves appear.

To compensate for loss of part of the root system when a tree is dug up for transplanting, prune back about one third of the branches.

Fertilizer should not be applied to newly planted or transplanted trees or shrubs until they have been in their new location for at least one year.

A slow, thorough soaking once a week in summer is better for the roots of trees and shrubs than a light sprinkling once a day.

Sprinkle the foliage of evergreens and deciduous trees in the evening during hot weather.

Fertilizer does the most good when it is applied to the roots of trees in a circular pattern about halfway in from the maximum spread of the branches. Make holes in the soil 8 to 10 inches deep, about two feet apart, all around the tree, apply fertilizer to the holes, fill in with soil, and water well.

When extra soil is heaped up around the base of a tree, the roots may suffocate. If the grade of your lawn is being changed, it may be necessary to build wells around the base of trees so roots will get enough air.

LAWNS AND GROUND COVERS

A smooth green lawn planted with the same strain of grass throughout may look beautiful, but is an easy prey to diseases and insect pests. It's better to seed the lawn with two compatible varieties that are resistant to different diseases.

The best time to seed a lawn is late summer or early autumn. Soil is usually drier then and easier to cultivate.

Birds won't eat your grass seed if you color it with bluing before spreading it. Soak seeds in solution of bluing and water until well colored, then scatter. Birds won't touch them, and coloring doesn't affect fertility of seed.

It isn't necessary to water the lawn too frequently, except in very arid climates or during a long drought. Too much water encourages the growth of weeds.

Let new grass reach a height of about 3 inches before mowing it. This gives the roots a chance to take firm hold in the soil.

Grass that has turned brown over the winter can be mowed very short in early spring, before new growth starts, to let sunlight penetrate to the soil.

Reduce erosion damage to your lawn and grounds by setting a large, flat stone under your rainspout. This will spread the rainwater over a larger area and help to prevent the wearing away of your precious topsoil.

Don't use a chemical weed killer on lawns that children and pets use for play. Many of these chemicals are dangerous. Better remove the weeds by hand, and do it early in the spring before the weeds flower and seed. If you wait, your weed crop will multiply tenfold or more.

There are some spots where grass just won't grow—on steep banks, for instance, or around the roots of large trees. The best substitute for grass in these areas is an attractive, hardy ground cover such as pachysandra or English ivy.

FLOWERS TO BEAUTIFY YOUR LIFE

It's easy to have a succession of colorful blooms in your garden from early spring through late autumn. Plant borders of paths or "island" gardens with spring bulbs and perennials that bloom at different seasons, e.g., lily of the valley and iris for spring, day lily and hollyhock for summer, chrysanthemums and hardy asters for autumn.

Annuals such as petunias, marigolds, and snapdragons can be grown from seed in flats or pots and transplanted to the outdoor garden when their first leaves are established.

Best results with narcissus bulbs. When starting them for indoor growth you'll be assured a hardier plant by not putting them in full light until rooted.

Annuals grown in peat pots can be set directly in garden soil if the pot is first cracked in a few places so the roots will penetrate the soil.

Most flowers grow best in a light, well-drained soil in full sun.

Plant a "children's row" of flowers in your garden. Youngsters can pick their own bouquets for teacher, for you, or for a friend. They'll enjoy the pride of something all their own and very likely won't go snipping any of your favorite blooms.

Test your leftover seed. Before using leftover garden seed make sure it will germinate. Lay a few seeds between two sheets of dampened paper toweling. Allow to stand in warm room 5 to 10 days. Keep towels moist. If three-quarters of the seeds begin to sprout, it's safe to plant them in your garden.

DECORATING WITH CUT FLOWERS

Always cut flowers with sharp tool, whether with knife, garden shears, or scissors. Dull tools produce clogged stems that don't let water flow freely, and they harm the plant from which the flower is cut.

Tools you need to make effective flower arrangements efficiently: a small, sharp knife; needle-point holders; fine wire; sharp shears (for stems); waterproof clay (to anchor holders); shears (for wire); twist ties from plastic bags (to tie stems); scissors; chicken wire (to put into containers and to anchor flowers).

Basic designs of flower arrangements. Consider the container, the style of the room, the spot in which arrangement is to stand. Then arrange flowers and plants by taking your cue from simple shapes such as arcs, ovals, triangles, etc. Here are a few ideas to start you off:

Don't overlook the proper foliage. Flowers look best when set off by foliage and branches. Don't use too many flowers in your arrangements, either. Crowding them detracts from their charm and beauty.

Container must be scrupulously clean, otherwise the soil, dirt, vegetable matter that accumulate, or are left over, will reduce the life span of fresh flowers.

Ideal temperature for keeping flowers is 40° to 50°F. High temperature and low humidity make for short-lived flowers. It's the low humidity that harms them when kept in the home refrigerator.

Dress up flower arrangements with added color, when using clear glass vase or bowl. A few drops of vegetable coloring added to the water,

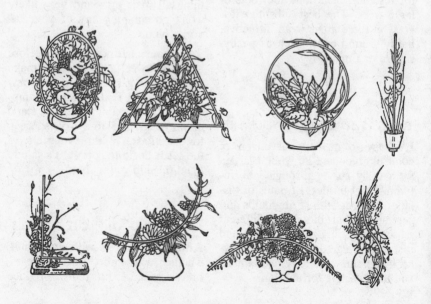

in shade to match or contrast with flowers, does the trick.

Short-stemmed flowers can be used in tall vases. Just "extend" the stems by inserting them in plastic drinking straws. You'll be amazed at the graceful arrangements you can create.

Pipe stems and flowers. To preserve a short-stemmed flower in a deep vase, slit the stem and wrap one end of a wired pipe cleaner around it to serve as a wick and extend into the water.

Stems ends of flowers should never rest against the bottom of the container or the sides. Leave stem end free so water can get to it and, through the stem, to the flowers. If you use proper holder, you can avoid not only this danger but the necessity to recut stems every day.

Cut off leaves below water level. Leaves quickly decompose when submerged.

Woody and semi-woody stems of lilacs, chrysanthemums, etc., live longer if the stem ends are scraped and split.

Zinnias and marigolds should be stripped of their foliage. These leaves are coarse and have a pungent odor. Substitute other greens with these flowers.

Flowers stay fresh longer in a vase if you put about a teaspoon of salt in the water.

Wilting flowers are a headache? Use aspirin to revive them. Cut flowers stay fresh longer than usual if you drop a couple of aspirins into the water.

Charcoal, too, preserves freshness of cut flowers. Many thicker-stemmed blossoms develop unpleasant odors after a day in the water, due to decay of the thick stems. A piece of charcoal in the water will retard their decay considerably.

Did you know fresh flowers are good for fabrics? Cut flowers and growing plants not only bring life and color into your room, but the water you give them will add moisture to the air. This is healthy for you and your family as well as for your furniture, draperies, carpets, and other textiles in the room.

Table flower pond. Here's a cute idea. Stand a candle in a deep saucer, anchoring it with wax drippings. Then pour some water in the saucer and float a few fresh flowers in it.

Are flowers in their cups at your party? They can be, and what a charming arrangement you get. Decorate your lunch table by placing at each setting an egg cup filled with daisies. For an afternoon party, fill period teacups with small bunches of violets, placing them next to each setting. At dinner, grace your setting by arranging garnet roses in champagne goblets at each guest's place. And floating a full-blown rose, or a camellia, inside a large sifter makes another attractive table decoration.

YOUR HOME VEGETABLE GARDEN

On a plot 30 by 50 feet you can grow enough vegetables to keep your family for the whole summer and have enough left over to give to friends or freeze for winter.

First, decide what kinds of vegetables you wish to grow, based on your family's preferences and the kind of soil you have. Most vegetables do best in fairly light, well-drained soil. If you have very heavy clay soil, give up your hopes of growing carrots, parsnips, and other large-root vegetables; the effort of pushing through the clay will make them tough and woody.

Plant quick-growing crops, such as radishes and lettuce, in rows between slow-maturing vegetables, such as tomatoes.

After cultivating the soil in your vegetable plot, let it settle for three or four days before sowing seeds.

Ideally, vegetable rows should run north and south to get the maximum amount of sunshine.

Make sure your seed rows are straight by stretching a cord along the ground between two stakes. When digging the seed furrow with a hoe or pointed stick, draw the tool along the cord as a guide.

In the northern United States, sow hardy vegetables such as beets, carrots, lettuce, cabbage, and onions between mid-March and mid-April. Tender crops such as beans, corn, tomatoes, eggplant, and peppers can be sown between May 1 and June 1. Sow a second crop of hardy vegetables from mid-June through late July for your late-summer and early-autumn table.

TIPS ON HOUSE PLANT CARE

House plants bring a welcome breath of the outdoors into your home all year round. Use them as decorating accents and room dividers wherever a touch of green is needed.

For beginning gardeners, the easiest house plants to grow are spider plant, philodendron, Swedish ivy, snake plant, asparagus fern, piggyback plant, and wax begonia.

Most house plants, especially flowering ones, need direct sunlight in order to thrive. (African violets are an exception—they do very well in north windows.) If your home gets little or no sun in winter, try growing plants under fluorescent lights. For best results, the light should be 8 to 10 inches above the topmost leaves, and should be left on 12 to 14 hours a day.

Indoor heat and low humidity are hard on plants. They prefer a location where the daytime temperature averages around 65° F., dropping into the 50s at night. On very cold winter nights, plants can be moved back from windows, or pieces of cardboard can be placed between the plants and the window glass.

To counteract the drying effects of steam heat in winter, keep plants in a tray on a 2- to 3-inch layer of pebbles, and keep the pebbles constantly moist.

Most plants should be watered when the top of the soil feels dry. Keep pouring until you see water begin to run out of the drainage hole. Some plants, such as cactuses and snake plants, need less water and can be allowed to dry out for several days between waterings. Plants in clay pots will need water more often than those in plastic pots.

Let cold tap water warm up to room temperature before using it to water plants.

Plants water themselves. To keep potted plants watered while you're away on vacation, make a 3-inch strip of flannel for each plant. Fasten a small bolt on each end of the strips. Then place a bucket of water on a chair or shelf behind the pot and several inches above it, and put one end of the strip in the bucket, the other end in the pot close to the plant. The "wick" will carry sufficient moisture to the plant to keep it in adequately watered condition as long as the water lasts.

Plants with glossy leaves can be refreshed by placing them under running water once a month. This also helps remove any insect pests that may be hiding on the under side of the leaves. Fuzzy leaves can be dusted with a camel's-hair brush dipped in warm water.

Milk bath for plant leaves. Sponge leaves of house plants with milk to remove dust and give foliage beautiful luster.

Oil the leaves. From time to time rub a little mineral oil or castor oil on the leaves of your house plants. Gives them nice shiny look and stimulates growth.

Put your plants on an egg diet. Save eggshells, put them in water, and let stand for several hours. Water plants with this liquid. The lime extracted from the eggshells will greatly benefit the plants.

Plants need good ventilation, but that doesn't mean a draft of cold air blowing directly on them. Opening a window in a nearby room for a few hours a day should do the trick.

How can you tell if a plant needs repotting? Wait until the soil is dry, then turn the pot upside down, cupping one hand over the base of the plant. Rap the rim of the pot against the edge of a table; the soil should slide out easily. If the soil ball is covered with a fine web of dry root hairs, a larger pot is needed. Even if repotting isn't necessary, the plant will benefit from having its pot scrubbed and washed and its roots loosened.

Don't put flowering plants in pots that are too large; their roots need to be crowded in order to produce abundant blooms.

"Precondition" your plant boxes. Before adding the soil, be sure to paint inside surface with a wood preservative and spread an inch-thick layer of gravel in the bottom of the box after paint dries. Mark off the inch-high level and you'll be sure to have the right amount.

Flowerpots made of eggshells. It sounds odd. It really isn't. Start seedlings in eggshell halves filled with loam. Shells can be stored in egg cartons and moved easily to any sunny spot. Later transplant them, shell and all. Roots will break through and be supplied with fertilizer as shell decomposes.

Inner tube mends flowerpot. Instead of discarding a cracked flowerpot, make it useful again by holding it together with a wide band of rubber cut from an old inner tube. Stretch a section of the tube up over the base of the pot. You can even paint patch to match color of pot, to make it decorative.

Fireplace garden. An empty fireplace in the summer isn't very attractive. Fill up the space with a few potted plants, especially those with tall, heavy foliage.

Give your house plants a summer vacation by "plunging" them outdoors in the garden as soon as the weather turns warm. Dig a bed 3 inches deeper than the largest pot, put a 3-inch layer of pebbles in the bottom, set pots in, and pack light soil around them, almost up to pot rims. Water when soil seems dry. Take them in before frost, and give pots a good scrubbing to get rid of insects.

Create a miniature landscape in a terrarium by arranging soil and stones on a slope instead of a flat surface. Put mosses and creeping plants at the bottom, erect plants and tree seedlings higher up.

MORE HANDY GARDENING IDEAS

Convert a corner of the garage into a tool shed and potting area. A wide shelf at waist height can be used for potting. Drawers underneath will hold pots and labels. A rack along one wall for rakes and

PLANT	HARDINESS	SOIL MIXTURE	LIGHT
African violet *Saintpaulia ionantha*	Fair	Commercial African violet mixture; or loose mixture of sand and peat moss.	No direct sunlight; north or east window in summer, south or west in winter.
Aralia (false) *Dizygotheca elegantissima*	Good	Equal parts loam, peat moss, and sand.	Partial shade; east or west window.
Asparagus fern *Asparagus sprengeri*	Good	Equal parts loam, peat moss, and sand or perlite.	Partial shade; east or west window.
Avocado *Persea americana*	Good	Equal parts loam, peat moss, and sand.	Bright, but not direct sun.

hoes, and a pegboard for small tools, will keep the area neat. A bracket protruding from the wall can hold the garden hose.

Rack keeps gardening tools handy. Tack strips of leather to side of wheelbarrow to form loops. Loops are excellent holders for various tools.

For your steppingstone garden walk use slates at least 2 inches thick and you'll save yourself the cost and trouble of providing a concrete foundation. Simply lay the stones in place and encourage the grass to grow around them.

Make a low-cost patio in the same fashion. If you want a continuous surface, place the stones closer together and cement the joints. You'll have to reset and recement the stones every few years if you want the patio to remain perfectly level, but you'll save about 90 per cent of what concrete paving would cost you.

Sagging garden gates can easily be pulled into square by using a turnbuckle. You can buy a buckle-and-rod set to fit your gate, or you can save a little by using two loops of heavy galvanized wire and a turnbuckle. Use the buckle to pull the high side, where the hinges are, to the low side (the corner that swings free).

Wire coat hangers take to the out-of-doors. When you want to direct a light spray of water on shrubs, flower beds, etc., and have nothing on which to support the hose nozzle, bend a wire coat hanger into shape as a stand and use the hook to hold the hose in place.

Safe perch for a birdhouse. Birdhouses can be fastened to the top of a pole in your yard with help of a large tin can. Screw the house to the underside of the can, slip the can on the top of the pole, and nail it in place.

TEMPERATURE AND HUMIDITY	WATERING	SPECIAL CARE
60°+; high humidity.	Keep soil moist, but don't let pot stand in water, use tepid water.	Keep in small pot; roots must be crowded if plant is to bloom. Avoid drafts.
60°+; high humidity.	Keep soil moist, not soggy	Cut back stems to prevent legginess. Mist foliage frequently.
60–70°; moderate humidity.	Soak soil thoroughly; allow to dry out between waterings.	Mist foliage frequently.
60–70°; moderate humidity.	Keep soil moist; use tepid water.	Mist foliage frequently.

PLANT	HARDINESS	SOIL MIXTURE	LIGHT
Begonia, wax *Begonia semper- florens*	Good	Equal parts loam, peat moss, and sand; add lime or charcoal to counteract acidity if necessary.	Bright, but not direct sun.
Boston fern *Nephrolepis exaltata*	Fair	Rich mixture of peat moss and sand; add charcoal to prevent acidity.	Partial shade.
Cactus varieties	Excellent	Sandy, alkaline.	Full sun in fall, winter and spring; partial shade in summer.
Chinese evergreen *Aglaonema simplex*	Excellent	Equal parts loam, peat moss, and sand.	Partial shade, north or east window; grows well under artificial light.
Coleus *Coleus blumei*	Good	2 parts sand, 1 part loam, 1 part peat moss.	Full sun or partial shade.
Dieffenbachia *Dieffenbachia seguine; Dieffen- bachia maculata*	Good	Porous mixture of loam, peat moss, and sand.	Partial sun; east or west window.
Dracaena varieties	Good	Commercial potting soil with drainage material (pebbles or broken pieces of clay pot) added.	Partial sun.
English ivy *Hedera helix*	Excellent	Equal parts loam, peat moss, and sand.	No direct sunlight; north window.
Gardenia *Gardenia radicans floriplena*	Fair	Acid mixture of peat moss, loam, and manure; sand or perlite for drainage.	Needs good light to bloom, but direct sunlight may burn foliage.
Geranium *Pelargonium domesticum*	Good	2 parts sand, 1 part loam, 1 part peat moss.	Full sun in summer.
Gold-dust plant *Aucuba japonica*	Good	2 parts sand, 1 part loam, 1 part peat moss.	Partial shade.
Grape ivy *Cissus rhombifolia*	Excellent	Loam, peat moss, and sand with added organic matter.	Full or partial sun.
Impatiens *Impatiens holstii*	Good	Loam, peat moss, and sand with limestone.	Full sun in winter, partial shade in summer.

TEMPERATURE AND HUMIDITY	WATERING	SPECIAL CARE
60–70°; high humidity.	Soak soil thoroughly; allow to dry out between waterings.	Pinch back frequently to keep shapely. Phosphate-potash fertilizer will increase blooms.
65–70°; high humidity.	Keep moist but not soggy.	Keep in fairly small pot with good drainage.
65–70°; low to moderate humidity.	Very infrequently in winter, more often in summer.	
60–70°; moderate humidity.	Keep soil moist, but not soggy.	Wash leaves regularly.
65–70°; high humidity.	Keep soil moist but not soggy.	Pinch back frequently to keep bushy. Wash leaves frequently to discourage insects.
65–70°; low to moderate humidity.	Let soil dry out between waterings.	Mist foliage frequently. Leaves and stem are poisonous; keep away from small children and pets.
60–70°; high humidity.	Let soil dry out between waterings.	Sponge leaves frequently. Keep away from hot air drafts.
60° in summer, 45–50° in winter; high humidity.	Keep soil moist to roots.	Pinch back frequently to keep bushy; can be trained to climb on supports.
65°+; high humidity.	Set in bucket of water for half an hour or until soil surface becomes moist.	Avoid drafts. Mist foliage daily.
65–70° for best bloom, 50° over winter.	Keep moist in summer; decrease water in winter.	Pinch back frequently for good bloom. Fertilize in fall and spring.
55–60°; moderate humidity.	Let soil dry out between waterings.	
60–70°; increase humidity at higher temperatures.	Soak soil thoroughly; allow to dry out between waterings.	Mist foliage frequently. Can be trained to climb on supports.
60–70°; moderate humidity.	Keep soil moist but not soggy.	Pinch back frequently to keep shapely.

PLANT	HARDINESS	SOIL MIXTURE	LIGHT
Jade plant *Crassula arborescens*	Excellent	Loam, peat moss, and sand with drainage material added.	Partial shade; east or west window.
Kalanchoe *Kalanchoe uniflora*	Good	Equal parts loam, peat moss, and sand.	Full or partial sun.
Maranta (prayer plant) *Maranta leuconeura*	Good	Rich mixture of loam, peat moss, and sand.	Partial shade; east or west window.
Parlor palm *Chamaedora elegans*	Fair	Equal parts loam, peat moss, and sand, well drained.	Partial shade, no direct sun.
Peperomia *Peperomia sandersi*	Good	Commercial potting mixture.	Partial sun; east or west window.
Philodendron varieties	Excellent	Commercial potting mixture plus perlite or vermiculite	Partial sun; east or west window.
Poinsettia *Euphorbia pulcher-rima*	Fair	Equal parts loam, peat moss, and sand.	Full sun during growing season, partial shade rest of year.
Purple-velvet plant *Gynura aurantiaca*	Good	Equal parts loam, peat moss, and sand.	Full or partial sun (sun brings out purple color).
Rubber plant *Ficus elastica*	Excellent	Equal parts loam, peat moss, and sand, well drained.	Full or partial sun.
Schefflera *Schefflera actino-phylla*	Good	Equal parts loam, peat moss, and sand, well drained.	Filtered sunlight, shaded east or south window.
Snake plant *Sansevieria trifas-ciata*	Excellent	Equal parts loam, peat moss, and sand.	Partial shade; will bloom in full sun.
Spider plant *Chlorophytum elatum*	Good	Equal parts loam, peat moss, and sand.	Partial sun; east or west window.
Wandering jew *Tradescantia fluminensis; Zebrina pendula*	Excellent	Commercial potting mixture.	Moderate sun; too much sun will burn foliage.
Zebra plant *Aphelandra squar-rosa*	Fair	2 parts peat moss, 1 part loam, 1 part sand.	Partial sun; east or west window.

TEMPERATURE AND HUMIDITY	WATERING	SPECIAL CARE
65–75°; moderate humidity.	Soak soil thoroughly; allow to dry out for several days between waterings.	Will not bloom unless roots are crowded; repot only every 3 to 4 years.
60–70°; moderate humidity.	Soak soil thoroughly; allow to dry out between waterings.	Will bloom if exposed to light for 12 hours or less per day.
60–80°; moderate humidity.	Keep moist but not soggy; decrease water in winter.	
60–75°; high humidity.	Frequently in summer; less often in winter.	Mist foliage frequently.
55–75°; high humidity.	Soak soil thoroughly; allow to dry out between waterings.	Good plant for terrariums.
60–70°; moderate humidity.	Keep soil moist but not soggy; don't let pot sit in water.	Mist and sponge foliage frequently. Pinch back to avoid legginess.
65° during growing season, lower rest of year.	Keep moist till plant is through blooming, then allow to dry out during dormant season.	
65–70°; high humidity.	Keep soil moist but not soggy.	Mist foliage frequently. Pinch back often to avoid legginess.
60–70°; moderate humidity.	Water only when soil is completely dry; can be set in bucket of water until soil surface feels moist.	Clean leaves with a damp cloth every 2 weeks. Don't use artificial "shine" preparations on leaves.
55–75°; high humidity.	Soak soil thoroughly; allow to dry out between waterings.	Wash leaves once a week.
60–70°; low to moderate humidity.	Only when soil is bone-dry.	Wash leaves every 2 weeks. Avoid chills and sudden temperature changes.
65–70°; moderate humidity.	Soak soil thoroughly; allow to dry out between waterings.	"Spiders" can be rooted in soil in a small pot and detached from parent plant when new growth appears.
65–70°; high humidity.	Keep soil moist but not soggy; decrease water in winter.	Pinch back frequently to avoid legginess.
65–70°; high humidity.	Keep soil moist but not soggy.	Mist foliage daily. Avoid drafts.

37

THE HOUSE

Directions and tips for the basics of care and repair of a house, inside and out

Proper maintenance of the basic fabric and fixtures of a house not only makes living there more pleasurable. Such care is what keeps the house's value rising over the years, so that in financial terms, too, you get your investment back. Not everyone will be able to do all the major jobs over the lifetime of a house, but everyone can certainly undertake some of the simpler chores. Both types are explained here, interior and exterior, roof to cellar, from hints on tools to directions for electrical repairs.

SAFETY FIRST

The basic rule for the home handyman is "safety first." Otherwise all the pleasure and profits are of no account. Every tool and material has potential dangers, but if you will follow the instructions there should be no problems. Chapter 44 deals with safety in the home, but here are some special hints for those working on home repairs.

Ladder safety hint. When placing a stepladder on a smooth, slippery surface, such as a highly polished floor, have the ladder rest on a piece of asphalt shingle and be sure of a solid grip.

Hammering nails? Save your fingers. Place a small pad of sponge rubber over spot where nail is to go into wood. It anchors the nail, protects wood surface from hammer marks, and can be removed easily just before you drive the nail home.

Get a good grip. Fit rubber tubing over handles of pliers and they'll be easier to handle. Also insulates them for safer use when making electric repairs.

Repair your roof in safety. Attach triangular wooden cleats on each side of your stepladder halfway between each of the rungs. The cleats serve as stops on which you can rest your load at intervals as you climb. That way you won't lose your balance.

Play safe when making roof repairs. Never stand, always move around on hands and knees, when repairing the roof of your home. Have a safety line looped around the chimney or strung right across the roof and fastened to the ground at both sides of the house.

TIPS ON TOOLS

Improvise a neat holder for small tools. Small files, pliers, screw drivers, etc., can be held in place and carried around conveniently while you work if you rack them into the closely packed bristles of a scrubbing brush. The inverted brush back makes an excellent stand to keep them upright.

Hardware-storage tip. Store bolts, screws, washers, etc., in compartments of plastic ice-cube tray. Compartments are deep enough to prevent mixing of contents.

Keep cutting tools keen. To keep rust from forming on your chisels, bits, and similar tools, wrap them in an oil-soaked rag before putting them away. This wrapping will also keep the tools from being dulled or injured as a result of striking each other in a drawer.

Another anti-rust trick. Keep few cones of carpenter's blue chalk in toolbox to absorb moisture. Every two months dry chalk thoroughly in an oven to renew its effectiveness.

To clean a file, place a strip of adhesive tape lengthwise over it. Rub finger over tape, to press it firmly between file teeth. Then pull it off. Imbedded shavings, dust, etc., come off easily with tape.

Preserve hardware labels from mold that may form after several months. Coat labels with spar varnish when you buy supplies; then, no matter how long you have them, label will be easy to read. White shellac works too.

Handy holder for tape measures can be made from empty adhesive-tape spool. Use the spool cover to keep the tape measure free from dust.

Run your drill through the bottom of a cheese or ice-cream carton to catch the chips when you drill overhead holes.

Increase usefulness of old brushes with lacquer. By applying lacquer at the base of a brush you keep bristles from shedding.

Protect an outdoor padlock by nailing a rectangle of stiff leather on the door above the padlock. This little "roof" over the lock keeps ice or snow from dripping into the lock, where mechanism might rust or freeze in cold weather.

Make your flashlight see around corners. Clamp bicycle mirror to flashlight. Directs beam of light at angle and reflects article at which it is directed. A clever convenience when doing repair work on a car or on plumbing installations.

No one to hold your flashlight? Improvise a holder with a funnel. Invert the funnel, slip a rubber band over its neck, then use the rubber band to hold the flashlight in place. You can slide the light backward and forward until it's just where you want it.

NAILS AND SCREWS

Soap to the rescue. Before driving a nail into wood, push it through a cake of soap. Nail will then go through wood without danger of splitting it.

To drive nails easily into hard wood, dip point of each nail in oil or hard grease beforehand.

Nails are the wrong answer when linoleum floor covering starts to break near the doorway. Either make a clean cut, removing broken section and cementing new piece securely into place, or place a metal edge over the ragged part. (Nails only damage the linoleum.)

To remove headless nails that have been driven into hardwood, grip end of nail with pliers. Then use claw hammer to lift both pliers and nail.

When picture nails come loose from the plaster, all you need to get them back in place is a strip of cloth and some glue. Wrap narrow strip of cloth around shank of nail, dip into glue, and replace in the hole in the plaster. Allow glue to dry for 24 hours before replacing picture.

Screw won't give? Try this. Don't give up if you've tried with all your might to loosen a screw that refuses to turn. Try again with the heated edge of a screw driver.

Screw loose? If a screw has worked loose in its hole, remove it, insert solid wire solder, and retighten.

Another way with loose screws. Insert wooden slivers or tamp wood putty into the old hole before replacing the screw.

To salvage screws with mangled heads, reslot head with hacksaw.

Steel wool, packed in screw hole, will also tighten loose screws.

WORKING WITH GLUE

A powerful homemade glue. If you've been having trouble finding a glue that will stick glass to glass, leather to metal, or other unusual combinations, burn some shellac in a dish to get rid of the alcohol. The remainder will be one of the strongest and best all-purpose glues you've ever used.

Prevent after-mess in gluing jobs. Place a piece of waxed paper on top of glued article before putting on weights, to help hold pieces together as glue hardens. Prevents weight from clinging to glued object.

"Combing in" the glue. To apply a thin coat of glue uniformly over a large surface, use a fine-tooth comb as a spreader. Especially handy when working on large pieces of veneer.

Soften up hardened glue by placing a few drops of vinegar in the container.

PLASTER WORK

To keep that crack from reopening when you patch plaster, first scrape the crack clean, then wet it thoroughly before you plaster. When dry, coat the patch with shellac.

Use two putty knives instead of one when you patch with plaster. By using one wide and one narrow knife, you can keep both clean and much easier to work with.

Slow that plaster down so that you don't have to race against its inclination to harden fast. How? Simply add a little sugar or vinegar when mixing.

Always add the plaster to the water. Don't ask why. You'll have trouble getting a good mix if you do it the other way around.

Patching a giant hole? Use a section of plasterboard to fit the hole. You'll need less plaster and do a much better job.

Plaster wall turning to powder? Usual cause: the plaster was first applied in a dry, hot room so that it dried out before it could set. To mend this condition, try a gentle water spray with an insecticide gun.

Plaster holes disappear. Small nail or screw holes in a plastered wall are annoying. An easy way to fill them is to sharpen a piece of ordinary chalk to a point, then press the point into the hole and cut it off. Next sandpaper the chalk flush with the wall and coat it with fresh shellac. Match the wall color with a little paint.

Another plaster-saver. Heat the nail first before driving it in. It will go in smoothly and won't take a chunk of plaster with it.

DOORS

Modernize that old door easily by gluing and screwing (or nailing) a plywood panel over it. You'll have to remove the paint from the door so the glue will hold tight. If you use paint remover, don't forget to wash afterward with alcohol. Use common 1/4-inch plywood, or, if you wish, choose a ply with a handsome hardwood face.

So you're going to do it the easy way. Hang a door? Slip some pieces of wood of the correct thickness under your door when you stand it up to locate the hinge cutouts.

Doors drag? Try tightening the screws that hold the hinges in place. If they just won't tighten, fill the screw holes with plastic wood and try again when dry.

Cardboard solves problem of door that won't shut. If a door won't stay closed, this may be caused by shrinkage of the wood in the door. To eliminate this nuisance, unscrew hinges and place one or more thicknesses of cardboard behind leaf of hinge that is fastened to the doorframe. Then fasten hinges in place again.

Doors won't latch as easily as they should when there is an accumulation of paint or dirt in the doorframe corner, when the bolt is sticky and won't extend easily, or when the latch has been pushed back out of place.

A shot of graphite powder into the door lock at least once a year will keep it in fine operating condition for the life of the house. Pencil-point shavings will do the trick fine too.

If driving rain seeps in under one of your outside doors, you can stop the leakage by making a shallow saw cut in the lower edge of the door where it stands on the sill. When the water gets to this little crack it has a tendency to run back out-of-doors instead of coming on in. The saw cut, of course, must be on the outside edge of the door.

STAIRS

Creaky stairs are nearly always caused by loose treads. If you can conveniently get underneath the step, tighten the guilty wedges. If you can't, drive long finishing nails at an angle into the risers, through the treads.

To save the price of new stair treads, remove the worn ones carefully, turn them over, and renail. This is easy to do in almost all cases.

To banish nicked edges on stair treads, patch with one of the commercial brands of synthetic woods or make your own filler with glue and sawdust. If it is an especially large hole, drive a couple of nails beneath the surface to help hold the patch in place.

FLOORS

Don't expect new floors to lie perfectly flat. Even the best grade of flooring is usually slightly imperfect. Figure the cost of sanding the floor down as part of the normal cost of a new floor.

Before you invest in power-sanding your old floor, try washing it down with special, high-power floor soap. Use rubber gloves. In many cases the soap will restore the lightness and brightness of your dark floor.

Floors may be covered with a number of liquid applications, but the most popular coating if you are interested in preserving the wood's natural grain and color is polyurethane. This synthetic resin varnish has generally replaced such traditional coatings as shellac. Polyurethane has several qualities that recommend it: durability, long life, waterlike clarity, good flexibility, and a fast drying time. The wood should be as clean and free from any other substances as possible. (Never, in any case, apply wax to untreated wood, for it will penetrate without protecting the surface.) Follow the directions on the can of polyurethane and you should end up with fine, natural wood floors.

Baseboard or wood trim warped? Try drilling a clearance hole through the board at its greatest bulge and running a flat-headed wood screw into the stud underneath. If you can't pull the board up all the way, fill the space between the board and the wall with putty or plaster and paint.

Quick trim for damaged woodwork.
It's not necessary to replace wood
trim that has been damaged along
the edges. Most times you can
plane a new edge and repaint. Even
though the repaired trim may be
narrower and of different edge
shape than its neighbors, the
difference will be scarcely noticeable.

THE BATHROOM

To rewhiten blackened cracks between ceramic tiles, scrub clean
with a stiff brush. Mix white tile cement and water to make a paste.
Rub this paste into the soiled joints,
but wipe the tile clean before putting on the paste. In this way you
can renew an entire wall in just a
few minutes.

Bathroom fixtures can be mounted
quickly by using any of the many
cements made for this purpose. It is
no longer necessary to remove the
old tile and bolt the fixture to the
wall.

The seal between the tub and wall
often crumbles away and leaves an
unattractive open space. Make your
own resealer out of white tile cement. Simply mix until it forms a
paste and apply.

Ceramic tiles are easy to use, and
you can get them in all sizes and
colors. Use white tile cement to set.
On wood surfaces first nail a wire
screen into place (about ½ inch
square), then apply cement and
tile.

New tile sinks. When your tile sink
becomes chipped, touch it up with a
wax crayon in matching color, then
coat with a transparent mending cement. This will stand up nicely
under many washings and can easily be renewed.

**Chipped porcelain-enamel sink or
tub?** Cover it with special enamel
made for the purpose. It will still
look somewhat patched, but looks
much better white, in kitchen or
bathroom, than black or rusty. You
can find sink enamel at your hardware store.

BASIC PLUMBING REPAIRS

Only a drop in the bucket? A faucet
that leaks one drop per second
means a loss of 700 gallons of
water a year. Check and repair immediately.

To stop that faucet drip, resurface
the valve seat before you replace
the washer. (This can be done with
a handy tool that sells for a modest
price at your hardware store.) Shut
off the water. Take apart the faucet.
Screw the tool into the faucet and
turn a few times. (When replacing,
be sure to use red washers for the
hot water, black for cold.)

You can stop a drainpipe leak for
years with a "plumber's poultice."
Wrap layers of cloth and wet plaster around the leak. Use strong
string to tie the "bandage" in place.
Let dry hard before using.

To stop a leaky pipe quickly (but
temporarily) cover the hole with
plenty of black tape. Or clamp a

split hose over the source of the leak. Or clamp on a length of inner tube and a curved metal plate.

Leaking pipe joints can often be repaired, without taking the pipe apart, by smearing the joint with any of several prepared pipe cements, which cost very little and are for sale at hardware stores.

When drainpipes are badly clogged they may need "the full treatment." For this, rent a full-size plumber's snake and probe it all the way through. Simply poking down the drain with a stiff wire will only nudge nearby pieces.

To prevent stoppage in your drainpipes, avoid letting grease go down the drain. It's a good idea always to run hot water down your drain for a few minutes after you do the dishes. Be sure, too, to clean the lint in your washing-machine trap before it gets into the drain. As a headache preventive, give your drain the lye treatment every six months or so.

Infrared lamp does plumbing job. If your sink trap clogs, especially when it's because of too greasy waste, turn your infared lamp on the pipes. This will start things moving. A commercial drain cleaner will finish the job.

Silence that embarrassing bathroom flush by installing one of the silent valves now available. These replace the old-style rubber bulbs and muffle the sound of flushing.

Hard water will ruin your pipes and cooking utensils more quickly than you may realize. A few dollars a month rents a water softener, complete with the necessary chemicals. In addition to preventing the collection of sludge in your pipes and pots and pans, it will make washing yourself, your dishes, and your clothes lots easier and pleasanter.

To keep pipes from freezing, don't leave windows open during the winter near uninsulated pipes. Take the time and trouble to wrap all exposed pipes with insulation made for the purpose. Drain all exposed valves through the little valve drain holes in their sides.

Quick rescue for frozen pipes. Too much heat will make frozen pipes burst because heat makes the ice inside the pipe expand. To thaw properly, fill bucket with very hot water and put heavy cloths in it. Wring out cloths and wrap around the pipes. As soon as cloths chill, reheat them and reapply.

ELECTRICAL REPAIRS

Put your house in a new light. If light outlets are poorly placed or insufficient, invest in a good wiring job to assure adequate, more comfortable lighting. You'll cut down eyestrain for the whole family and the rooms will look better.

A bad fuse may look good. When the "juice" goes off and you can't find a blown fuse, try replacing the fuses one by one. A fuse may go bad without showing it.

Give yourself time. Install time-delay switches to permit you to walk out of the garage or hall with the lights still on. These switches will automatically turn the lights off for you a few moments after you have snapped them.

To replace a defective wall switch, turn off the main power switch and remove the plate by loosening the plate screw or screws. Then loosen the switch by removing the screws that are set into the box at the sides of the switch. Pull the switch out gently, back of the bolts holding the wires. Install the new switch by replacing these wires under the new screw heads. Now tighten and replace switch and plate.

If your fluorescent tube keeps flickering, it's time for a change. You have either the wrong tube for the fixture or the wrong starter. Check and replace.

If your fluorescent light gets dark at one end, reverse the tube. This often corrects the fault.

WINDOWS

Windows stick? Paint the window slides with no-polishing floor wax or rub them down with the end of a candle. Tight windows are sometimes caused also by the divider moving out of place. To fix easily rap the divider to one side.

When a window gets stuck, try running a knife around all the joints. No? Try tapping the window edges with your fist. No? Try using a pry bar on the outside of the window.

Rotted window sills can be repaired by covering decayed parts with aluminum sheeting or corners made of plywood. One piece should cover the top, another the side. Nail fast. When plywood is used, seal the edges with varnish.

Petroleum jelly opens windows. Once a year take this precaution against hard-to-budge windows: Dip a small brush in Vaseline and "paint" the ointment on casing and parting strips of windows. If windows have become stuck, pry open from outside by inserting wedge or chisel under the sash. Before prying up, grease sash runners with Vaseline.

No need to remove the window trim when you have to replace a sash-weight rope. Simply open the little trap door in the side of the slide. Loosen the screw you see there. Now use the old rope or a length of wire through which to feed the new rope. (Use sash chain for minimum trouble.)

Loose windowpanes will rattle in the wind, admit cold air, and eventually break. Save a lot of heat, fuel, and trouble by puttying all loose windows at the first rattle.

A cracked pane of glass can be temporarily held together and weather-proofed with a coat of fresh white shellac on the inside. Vision won't be obstructed by the shellac coat. Breezes and rain will be kept out until the pane is replaced.

To cut glass straight and easy, wipe clean the path of the cutter on the glass, then paint this line with turpentine or any thin oil.

Wax crayons aid glass cutting. Make heavy marks on the glass with wax crayon. Wax will hold your ruler or straight-edge in place as you cut.

SCREENS

Small holes in window screens can be patched by using a few drops of fast-drying model-airplane cement. Larger holes can be repaired by cutting a patch from a discarded screen and gluing it in place.

Use a vacuum cleaner on window screens to remove dust thoroughly and easily. If you don't have the canister type of vacuum cleaner, turn your upright machine on its back and run the screen over its mouth.

Weak or broken screen corners can be repaired by using angle-iron mending plates and long wooden screws driven through the corners.

The fastest way to paint a screen is to use a rag or a paint roller. First clean each screen thoroughly, then place it flat so that the paint won't run while drying.

Magic privacy trick. To fix screens so that you can see out without passers-by seeing in, use white paint thinned with turpentine.

Be sure screens fit tight. If window screens are a bit loose, tack weather stripping along the edges that fit loosely in the window frame. Then you'll be sure to keep out undesirable insects, flying leaves, etc.

AWNINGS

Stretch life of awnings. After a rain, lower the awnings until they are thoroughly dry. This will greatly retard the mildew and rot that result from exposure to moisture.

"New" awnings for old. Repaint faded awnings and you practically have sparkling new ones. Use a canvas paint, also good for outdoor chairs and umbrellas. Lower the awning all the way, get up on a ladder if necessary, and paint with a wide brush and quick, even strokes. Finish the painting in one session, to avoid streaks that may result from doing the job in installments. To make upper-story awnings accessible, adjust each to the most convenient lower-story window, then paint, dry, and replace.

HOUSE SIDES

Split wood siding is easy to fix and doesn't even have to be removed. Simply spread waterproof glue on the split edges and clamp them together firmly.

Proceed with care if you must remove a section of siding. Here's how to prevent further splits: With a hacksaw, saw the board at the ends of the section to be replaced.

Use a metal-cutting keyhole saw to cut nails holding the section. Use a ¼-inch wood chisel to split the section and to remove wood that is under the next higher strip of siding. Use a very sharp chisel and be very careful near the edges. Cut the new section to fit. Slip it into place and nail.

Don't break good shingles in order to remove a bad one. Instead cover the broken shingle with another one cut to the right size. This will save you the trouble of removing the old shingle and the danger of breaking the good ones around it. This "cover-up" may be noticeable near a doorway or at ground level, but not in most other places. The second shingle adds less than ¼ inch in thickness.

If you accidentally split a shingle while tacking it into place, cut piece of tar paper the size of the shingle. Shove it up under split area and nail the corners.

To replace a split shingle, crack it up into slivers and pull them out. Cut the new shingle short, slip into place, and nail.

Asbestos shingles broken at the corners? Make them look as good as new by gluing the broken piece back into place with white or matching calking cement.

Don't paint asbestos shingles, or you will have to repaint every few years. A special cleanser, now available, will clean them like new.

To raise wood shingles so you can repair or replace them, use a garden spade. The long, flat metal blade will let you get safely under the shingles. Press the handle down slowly.

ROOF WORK

You can plug a roof leak from the inside quickly, in an emergency, by using roof cement on small holes, a rag and cement on those of medium size, and a board cut out to fit between the rafters for larger holes. Seal with roof cement.

Loose asphalt roof shingles can be glued back into place by daubing some roofing cement beneath them and pressing them back where they belong. If a shingle is torn, cut a new one to fit, or nail the pieces in place. Goo up the nailheads with cement.

To fix split-shingle roof leaks, do it the easy way by slipping a strip of roofing paper beneath the split. Use a strip as wide as you can without its showing, and at least several times longer than it is wide. This strip won't then be seen from the ground. Use #4 or #5 galvanized nails and place them well back, to prevent further splitting. Two or three nails are usually enough.

A little asphaltum in creosote will stain your replacement shingle to match the others on your roof that have already been darkened by weather exposure.

The one important leak-stopper in your home is flashing. This is the strip of metal that helps join the roof to the chimney or side wall. Small holes in copper flashing usually found near chimneys, and caused by the chemical reaction from nearby galvanized nails, can be closed by soldering. Use small patches if necessary. Spaces between the flashing and a wall can be closed temporarily with roofing cement. When the flashing is badly damaged by storm or time, it should be carefully and promptly replaced.

To waterproof the trough of a wood gutter, or to resurface one that has rusted, use roofing cement. If there are small holes, use special mastic-glass or plastic cloth strip made for the purpose. If the hole is very large, slip a section of matching gutter over the old.

"Stitch in time" for tin roofs. To avoid costly repairs resulting from extensive rust, keep surface covered with protective coat of special paint.

CELLARS

Damp cellar walls can be dehydrated by painting with one or two coats of special cellar waterproofing paint.

To smooth rough cellar walls, try this mix: two parts mortar cement to one part sand containing some calcium chloride. Add water to get a thin mud consistency. This produces a waterproof cement and

may be applied before the waterproofing paint with a large metal mason's trowel.

Don't drill a hole in your cellar floor until you consider the possibility that you may let in a stream of water. This is especially likely in damp areas where the cellar has been waterproofed carefully from the outside.

The cheap way to pave an old-fashioned dirt cellar floor is with soil cement. Do this: Loosen the dirt to a depth of 4 inches. Remove all stones larger than ¼ inch, as well as pieces of wood and debris. Spread a bag of Portland cement in with every 2 to 3 square yards of floor. Mix the cement and the dirt thoroughly, wet down and pack down hard with a tamper. Keep off the floor for a couple of days, meanwhile giving it a light spray of water every day. This will give you an almost concrete-hard floor, that is dust-free and can be tiled or otherwise treated like a regular concrete floor.

Are plants piping water into your cellar? Look carefully around the area outside your home. Dig up roots of trees or vines that may have penetrated the foundation walls, thus carrying moisture to them.

FOUNDATIONS

SOS Urgent. Large cracks in the foundation of your home signal serious trouble. Better hurry and call for the immediate attention of a competent building man.

When an individual house pier begins to crumble, repair or replace it easily by borrowing or renting a large building jack. Use it to raise this section of your home an inch or two above the pier, then rebuild the pier. Lower the building only after sufficient time has been allowed for the concrete to set.

How to patch concrete like an expert. First clean out cracks with a wire brush, then wet down thoroughly. A mix of one part mortar cement and two parts sand is used for the fill. Use a putty knife for small holes, a trowel for large. If you are resurfacing a garage or cellar floor, you'll need to roughen the old concrete by pounding it with a hammer. If there is any grease, you'll secure a better bond by washing with muriatic acid before you patch. (This is important when you have to lay down a large but thin patch.) If you are filling a hollow spot, lay down the concrete and use a long, straight-edged board to level the patch with the old floor. If you are repairing a broken corner on a step, or something similar, build a form of boards around the patch. To get better adhesion and bonding between the old and new concrete, drive some steel-cut nails into the old concrete, roughen it, then wet it down.

To make quick-setting concrete, add calcium chloride or "antihydros" to the mix. Either of these chemicals makes the concrete waterproof and should be added for outside work. Include enough of these chemicals and you can make a cement that sets in five minutes. Such cement is especially useful for patching very wet areas, or even such damp ones as leaking cellar floor surfaces.

Pointing a stone or brick wall consists of removing all the loose cement from between the bricks or stones with a cold chisel and replacing with new. Dust the cracks with a brush and wet the stones down before applying the new cement. Use a length of dowel to secure an indented half-round joint.

Lead drain water as far as possible from your home. Galvanized, aluminum, and, of course, copper drains can be run safely under your lawn or walk for quite a distance. They'll carry ordinary traffic without bending and will do their job for years without rusting. Tile, of course, will last indefinitely.

WALKS, DRIVES, AND OUTDOOR WORK

Make your own walks and drives, and save at least half the cost, with the help of a friend and a rented power mixer. Dig deeply enough to provide room for 6 inches of cinders, 2 to 4 inches of concrete for walks, and 6 inches for drives. Set boards the width of the concrete along the side. Now pour cement and level to these guides.

For an interesting walk of concrete steppingstones, such as cloverleaf, diamond, heart, or other attractive shape, bend a light sheet-metal strip around a wooden form of the desired shape and screw it to the form. Place concrete mixture into the form and let it set. When the mixture has hardened, set the stones in the ground and arrange in whatever order you prefer.

Gravel mixed with fine sand makes sand-sifting easier. A couple of shovelfuls of coarse gravel mixed with the sand tends to break up lumps and the sand falls through the screen readily.

Speed screening of damp sand with chain. If sand is damp or lumpy, place length of chain on sifting screen before pouring in load of sand. Weight of chain breaks lumps and forces sand through screen.

Don't ruin your tires by running them over a hole in your asphalt driveway. It's easy to patch the holes with a bagful of stone and tar mix. Leave the bag in the sun or near a warm radiator to soften it up, and be sure the cavity to be filled is clean and dry. Tamp your patch firm with the end of a two-by-four.

To patch a large hole in a concrete driveway, fill the bottom with clean, good-sized stones, then cover them with cement mix. (For small jobs you can buy cement and sand already mixed.)

Save the price and trouble of a replacement gate or fence post by sawing the post in two above the rot line, removing the rotted post end and leaving a hole. Fill the hole with concrete and clean stones. Set two lengths of strap iron with some holes drilled in their upper halves into the concrete. When set, use lag bolts to fasten the post end between the iron straps.

Use glass bottles to make openings in concrete steps into which pipes are to be inserted for holding a railing. After concrete has set, break out the bottles. Or bend a rectangular piece of tin into a cylinder, lapping edges about two inches. Fill cylinder with sand and set it in the forms where the opening is wanted. Fill concrete around cylinder, which keeps its shape because of the sand. When cement hardens, remove sand and the cylinder is easily collapsed and removed.

38

HEATING THE HOME

Simple ways to cut down heating bills without sacrificing comfort

A home heating plant powered by natural gas, oil, or electricity delivers heat quickly when it's needed—a desirable feature on chilly fall and spring mornings. Gas and electric heat are also clean and non-polluting. These advantages should be weighed against the rising costs of fuel and electricity and the possibility of fuel shortages.

An electric furnace needs no chimney, and requires no maintenance except for the fan, motor, and filters.

For health and economy, your thermostat should be set during the day between 70° and 72° F., normal indoor temperature throughout the winter. An overheated house saps your strength, wastes fuel and money.

Raise humidity, not temperature, if house seems chilly at 72° F. Don't raise temperature; that just increases fuel cost unnecessarily. Inexpensive automatic humidifiers or water pans placed on or near radiators will correct the trouble.

When to turn thermostat down:

1. If windows are open for any length of time, while airing rooms during house cleaning.

2. When you go to bed.

3. If room in which thermostat is located is closed off for airing, in order to prevent rest of house from overheating.

Set it at 70° F. You'll cut your fuel bills by as much as 15 per cent if you select that healthful indoor temperature instead of one only 5 degrees higher.

So you've added a basement rumpus room? Have you checked to make sure your heating unit is still adequate? Whenever you add a room or convert house space to new uses, check on this. You may be putting your present unit to extra strain, thus cutting its efficiency. Also, if you have cut off a room, you may need less heating.

HOW TO CUT HEATING COSTS

Close off a room that's seldom used and don't heat it. Such a room must be sealed off well, however, to keep the cold air in and the hot air from seeping into it. It's a good idea to close off the room in the house that is hardest to heat. Be sure, however, to drain off water in any pipes in the outside walls of unheated rooms or they may freeze, even burst. In extreme weather allow some heat in closed-off rooms to protect the paper and plaster.

The attic doesn't need warmth. Close doors leading to the attic to keep the burner from working overtime. The warm air rises, can escape up the stairs and keep the warmth from where it is needed most.

If your basement isn't heated, you'll have cold floors and resulting cold feet in first-floor rooms. For maximum warmth, finish off basement with a full ceiling.

Don't overheat garage. Antifreeze is cheaper than coal. If you do heat the garage, keep it down to 40° F. It's better for your car, better for your pocketbook.

Pull down the shades at dusk and leave them down overnight. This saves fuel and gives you desired nighttime privacy as well. Fuel is saved because the shade partially insulates the window. (In the summertime drawn shades help keep your home cool.)

Rugs and furniture can cause fuel waste if placed where they block radiators or registers.

If you are away from home for some time during winter, set thermostat down to minimum nighttime temperature of about 55° F. Never turn burner off entirely, because sudden drop in temperature might cause pipes to freeze. Besides, it costs more to bring temperature back up to normal after the thermostat has been turned off and heater idle than to bring it up from lower temperature.

FIREPLACES

Use your fireplace. It not only makes a room cozy in winter but raises the temperature in the room by as much as 10 per cent, especially if coal is burned in the fireplace. When fire is dead and fireplace has cooled, remember to close the damper tight, as it should be when the fireplace is not in use.

Much, in fact most, of the heat in a fireplace goes up the chimney, but there are now available some methods of getting more heat into the room. One type is built into the fireplace itself, with interior vents that circulate the hot air into the room. The other method involves fans attached to special grates; these direct more of the hot air into the room. If you intend to make regular use of your fireplace you might consider some such device.

A piece of asbestos board placed over the fireplace opening saves the heat should you retire before a fire is completely burned out.

Close fireplace dampers when not in use. If dampers are missing and the fireplace isn't used, close the chimney opening.

All fireplaces are safer if protected with a screen.

FIGHTING BACK AT HARD WINTERS

Check list for winterizing your home. Remove screens, then repair; paint and store them flat. Clean window frames, metal screen hangers, and paint. Fit storm windows and doors. Calk around all windows and door frames. Sweep out eavestroughs and give inside a coating of protective paint. Scrape out sidewalk cracks and fill with cement mortar. Insulate exposed plumbing pipes that might freeze. Insulate warm-air ducts and furnace jacket. Get a supply of fuses and store near fuse box.

Cut fuel bills 8 to 20 per cent. Cracks and crevices around doors and windows cost you a lot in wasted heat. The best weather stripping is a metal strip built right into the window sash or door. A less expensive type can easily be put on without special tools. The commonest and by far the cheapest type is felt stripping, and anyone can put it on.

Stop drafts in the house and it will be less costly to heat. Calk door frames and window frames with wood putty compounds. Cover mail slots and door buttons with strips of old leather or beaver board.

Spend once for years of savings. Install storm doors and windows during heating season; be sure doors and windows are adequately equipped with weather stripping. These insulation methods keep the house more comfortable and heating costs down. On stone construction or metal casement windows have the space around the window frames calked to prevent heat leakage.

Those wasteful windows. Engineers figure that glass lets heat escape four time as fast as ordinary uninsulated wall space. The best heat-savers you can get are storm windows and doors that give you a "dead-air" pocket between themselves and your regular windows and doors. This reduces heat loss by as much as two thirds. Experts figure they can easily save you up to 25 per cent in fuel bills.

Insulation means heating thrift. Insulate the hot-water tank and pipes that carry the heat through the house. The materials cost little and mean year-round economy as well as constant hot-water supply and a cooler cellar in summer.

MAINTAINING THE HEATING PLANT

Unless you're a heating expert, don't attempt repairs to heating units yourself. It's better economy to call in a qualified service man.

"Preventive medicine" for heating units. Just as you need an annual check-up by your doctor, so your furnace and boiler should be checked and cleaned once a year by a heating expert. Summertime is best. Have excess soot and scale removed; keep heating costs down. Additional summer treatment: leave furnace doors ajar for free air circulation through firebox. Inexpensive "patch jobs" can be done with putty.

Twin symbols of furnace-fuel waste are black smoke and very hot chimney gases. They're a fire hazard too. Call in your service man if your heating plant doesn't function with at least 70 to 75 per cent efficiency and economy. A trained fuel supplier will give you the efficient and economical service your heating system requires.

Preventing chimney loss. The greatest waste in home heat is up the chimney. You automatically reduce this loss by keeping the turn damper (the disk-shaped damper in the smoke pipe) as nearly closed as possible. To find the just-right setting for the turn damper, first move the handle $\frac{1}{16}$ inch toward the closed position. If the fire continues to burn freely, close the damper still more. Repeat this until the damper is as nearly closed as possible without keeping the fire from burning freely. This will give you the most heat and the least waste of money taking off through the chimney.

Control the draft and save. During heat combustion certain waste materials are formed. These are elimi-

nated by "draft" through the furnace smoke pipe, flue, and chimney. Keep draft passage clear and working well to prevent needless fuel waste. Best solution: have automatic stack-draft control installed.

Install a heat regulator for automatically controlled heat. It saves you steps and money at the same time you keep your home at a desired even temperature.

The nail test. To test the smoke pipe of your home heating plant for weak spots, jab the surface lightly with a heavy nail. If the point penetrates the pipe surface, repair is needed. If only a small section is weak, standard-size, low-priced pipe sections are available at the hardware store. Make the test before the heating season starts. You'll save time, discomfort, higher repair costs, and possible danger of fire.

Your basement runs a temperature? Check your furnace; if it's hot, too, call a service man. Danger signals are browned warm-air ducts and scorched floor joints over the heater.

False economy. Don't connect two heaters to the same chimney flue. This retards the draft and causes poor heat. If you have a separate gas water heater, a separate chimney will save you money.

Check the chimney, too, for loose bricks and breaks, especially in the attic.

Chimneys and flues should be cleaned at least once a year. If the services of a chimney sweep are not available, they can be cleaned by mechanical methods in preference to chemical.

Put several bricks in a burlap bag. Attach bag firmly to strong cord. Working from the top of the chimney, move up and down until soot is removed. Since you need two hands for this, use an extension ladder and hook your leg around a rung.

STEAM AND HOT-WATER SYSTEMS

On steam and hot-water systems, check water for scale and dirt and drain off if necessary. Refill boiler with clean water.

"Pitching" the pipes. Check "pitch" of all steampipes. If incorrectly sloped, they may block heat circulation.

Hot-water and steam boilers should always be equipped with safety valves.

Keep radiators at maximum efficiency. Check vent valves frequently. Open them as often as once a month, if necessary, to let out excess air and assure thorough heat circulation. If valves aren't operating properly, replace them at once.

Radiators give more heat if you place a piece of aluminum foil behind each one. It will reflect more heat back into the room instead of allowing the wall to absorb it.

When radiators go bang! Knock! Wham!!!! Take a look, quick, at the air-vent valves when noisy radiators refuse to get hot. They may be clogged up so that they won't let the cold air out, and if the cold air can't get out, the steam can't get in. Try blowing through the valve to clean it out, or take it off and boil it in a solution of washing soda and water. Defective valves should be replaced, of course.

Try this for knock in radiators. Tilt the radiator slightly downward toward the end at which the steam enters. This permits the water to flow back to the boiler where it belongs. To test the tilt of the radiator, use an ordinary carpenter's level. If it doesn't slope toward the intake end, push a thin wooden wedge under the other end.

If a hot-water radiator won't "hotten," the trouble may come from air trapped in the radiator. Let the trapped air out by using the key provided for opening the radiator. This may take some time, perhaps as much as a half hour, in a house that has been unheated through the summer. Close the key when water squirts out, and stay out of its path because it may be very hot.

To clean out a gummed-up vent, soak it overnight in grease solvent; that will often let the cold air out, while keeping the steam in. Turn off the steam at the valve before removing. If, after cleaning, your radiator still has cold spots, better get a new vent.

If the main valve leaks, remove the handle, loosen and remove the large nut, use a metal pick to remove the old packing, and replace with new. It's O.K. to have the heat on while you do this.

less heat, causing lowered efficiency of heating unit, etc. It pays to buy fuel from a reputable, reliable source.

OIL BURNERS

Oil burner won't start? Check the setting of the thermostat. It must be five degrees higher than the thermometer reading or it won't start. Give it a tap, on the chance that it may be merely dust-filled. Check the burner fuse. Check for oil. Check the water gauge, because lack of water will shut off some set-ups.

Why the fuel tank should be full, even during summer months. It prevents the tank from "breathing and sweating" (caused by water condensation), accumulation of wasteful dirt and dust, avoids needless repair expenses. Exterior underground tanks left empty during a heavy summer rain tend to "float" to the surface. Economy tip: Remember, fuel prices usually are lower in summer than during the heating season; another reason for filling tanks at that time.

The right fuel saves money. A grade that's too heavy may cause excess smoke and soot; if too light, it will usually increase your fuel costs. Let a qualified heating man advise you.

Those bargain-price fuels are often of such cheap quality that they cost you more in the long run by giving

COAL BURNERS

Check damper chains and ashpit dampers to see that they work properly. Caution: Be sure the regular arm is connected by chains to the check and ash dampers.

Keep that firebox full. A thin, skimpy fire burns up much faster, goes out more easily, wastes coal, and keeps you running to the basement.

Don't burn garbage or trash in the furnace. Doing so gives you a dirty furnace, clinkers, and poor heat. It also deposits a thick coating on the heating surfaces which absorbs the heat that ought to be warming your rooms.

Right way to "coal up." Shake the grates gently until the ashes in your ashpit begin to glow. (To shake the daylights out of the fire only wastes good coal.) Then, with shovel or rake, pull the live coals from the back of the fire bed upward toward the feed door. You thus form a cavity sloping downward toward the back of the firebox. Into this cavity put your fresh coal, taking care to leave a spot of live coals showing in the front, just inside the fire door. This "pilot light" quickly ignites the gases from the fresh coal and eliminates "puffs."

To recoal properly. Keep the turn damper in its normal closed position, the ashpit damper open, and the check damper closed. Open the slide in the fire door about the thickness of a wooden match to admit the air above the fuel bed that is needed to burn off any gases.

Another coal-saver. The check damper and the ashpit damper control the burning speed of your fire. When one is open the other should be closed. When you want a slow fire, shut off the furnace's breath by setting the check damper wide open and setting the ashpit damper closed like a clam. When you want more heat, open the ashpit damper and close the check damper.

Open the chimney clean-out door near the floor and carefully clean out the base of the chimney.

Don't jail that heat. John Barclay, a top authority on heating, warns: "To illustrate what dirt can do to slow down a furnace, take the simple matter of fly-ash on its heating surfaces. This fly-ash acts as an insulator five times as powerful as asbestos. If the heating surfaces on a boiler have an accumulation of $\frac{1}{16}$ inch of fly-ash, there is a 26.2 per cent loss of heating efficiency; a $\frac{1}{8}$-inch deposit will cause a loss of fully 45.3 per cent." Moral: A dirty furnace is a terrible coal waster, and you can't tell if a furnace is dirty by looking at the outside of it. It is the inside that gets fouled up. The best time to clean out your furnace is in summer or early fall

when it isn't normally in use. This simple tip is worth many, many dollars to you. Use it to save a big chunk of your heating bill.

Leave door open a little after banking a coal furnace. The chimney damper should also be partly open, or the unburned gas will escape into the house.

To give your furnace "the works." All you need are a wire brush, a scraper, a small supply of asbestos, furnace putty, black asphaltum, paint, and white cold-water paint. Get them at any hardware store or heating-supply house. Then:

Clean smoke pipes first. Remove and clean thoroughly with a stiff wire brush. (Needless to say, old clothes or bathing trunks are best for this work.)

Open furnace clean-out doors, then, with wire brush and scraper, clean out all soot from the heating surfaces, gas passages, and firebox walls.

Remove ashes from the grates, then check to see that all grate segments or sections shake evenly.

After adjusting grates, cover them with a layer of clean ash about 2 inches thick.

Save those grates. Never bank the fire with ashes. This not only results in poor heat but shoots the heat downward, causing clinkers to form and often warping the grates. This tip will save you some good hard-earned cash.

Clean and seal all clean-out doors tightly and seal all cracks around doors. (This is where you need that furnace putty.) You can locate leaks by passing a lighted candle around. If there is a leak, the flame will be sucked in.

Before replacing smoke pipe, seal all leaks at the flue-pipe opening in the chimney with asbestos and furnace putty. After the smoke pipe is put in place, carefully seal all connecting joints.

39

UTILITIES AND SERVICES

Reduce those monthly bills with these simple but all-too-often-overlooked tips

How's your wiring? Any of the conditions listed here is a symptom of inadequate wiring. And with it you won't get full convenience and pleasure from your modern electrical appliances. Your home is probably not wired to give convenient, safe, and efficient use of your electrical equipment if your answer to any of these questions is yes:

1. Do your fuses blow? Do your circuit breakers trip open often?

2. Do your electric lights dim noticeably when appliances are in use?

3. Must you disconnect one appliance before plugging in another, for fear of either overloading circuits or decreasing the efficiency of another appliance working at the same time (such as a TV receiver), or both?

4. Must you connect simultaneously used appliances by means of several double or triple sockets because outlets are scarce?

5. Does your iron, toaster, or waffle iron take overlong to heat up?

6. Are you limited in the use of small portable appliances in kitchen, laundry, or dining areas because there aren't enough outlets?

7. Are you limited to using no more than two plug-in appliances at a time before you blow a fuse or trip your circuit breaker?

8. Must you grope your way into a dark room because there is no wall switch near each entrance?

9. Do you pay more for your electric power than seems consistent with the number of appliances you have and the length of time you use them?

10. Do you try to prevent overloading of circuits by using oversize fuses, thereby risking permanent damage to circuit wires within walls, ceilings, and floors, which may lead to fire?

Branch circuits are the small wires through which electricity is distributed to the outlets in your home. These branch circuits serve the same function that pipes do in carrying water through your plumbing system; the electrical outlets, where you plug in your appliances, correspond to water faucets.

Your home's wiring system should contain three kinds of branch circuits:

1. *General-purpose.* These circuits serve light fixtures all over the house (except the kitchen, laundry, and dining areas) and convenience outlets for lamps, radios, TV sets, phonographs, vacuum cleaners, and the like in every part of the house (except kitchen, etc.).

2. *Small-appliance.* These circuits bring electricity to the kitchen, laundry, and dining-area convenience outlets that serve your refrigerator, toaster, mixer, coffeemaker, and other plug-in relatively small appliances. On one of these small-appliance branch circuits you can connect, at one time, a total of 2,400 watts. How many of this type of circuit you need depends upon the total number of watts required by the appliances you now have and those you plan to add later. Most homes should have at least two of these small-appliance circuits. A large home may require three or more of them.

Note: Kitchen, laundry, and dining-area lights require a circuit of their own. This separate circuit may, in addition, serve lights in other areas of your home.

3. *Individual branch circuits.* These circuits must supply power for many of your large appliances.

Each piece of electrical equipment listed here requires an individual circuit of its own:

1. Automatic heating plant (for all types of fuel).
2. Electric range (a double-oven range needs a larger individual branch circuit than does a single-oven range).
3. Electric water heater.
4. Automatic washer.
5. Combination washer-dryer.
6. Electric clothes dryer.
7. Summer cooling fan (attic fan).
8. Home freezer.
9. Air-conditioning unit.
10. Built-in space heater.
11. Electric workshop and workbench equipment.

Look ahead when wiring. Consider the appliances you have now and those you plan to buy in the future. Figure out from the outline above how many electrical outlets you will need in the future and where they'll be most convenient to use. Then call in an experienced electrical contractor and let him wire your home in such a way that electricity serves you conveniently, safely, efficiently.

MODERN APPLIANCES NEED LITTLE CARE

Manufacturers are your friends. When you buy household appliances don't throw out the descriptive booklets provided by the manufacturers. They'll give you helpful hints on the "ounce of prevention" that will keep the appliance in shape for maximum time. Keep instruction booklets in handy drawer or kitchen file and refer to them until you are completely acquainted with your new appliances.

They're longer-lasting than you think. Many household appliances appear to have outlived their usefulness before they really have. If toaster, cleaner, washer, or other appliance gives you much trouble, don't immediately discard it for a new one. Instead consult your dealer and see if replacement of some parts can make the appliance as good as new again.

They run themselves these days. All you have to do is turn on the switch and your appliance takes over your work for you. Because this automation requires intricate mechanism to operate, however, don't try for home repairs if something goes wrong. Any large manufacturer, and they are numerous, has factory-trained and skilled repair men who will save you money and lengthen the life of your appliance if you call them in at the first sign of faulty operation. Simply consult the classified section of your telephone directory to find the right repair service.

If any automatic appliance becomes noisy, it's time to call a service man. In fact, you can often prevent trouble from threatening or developing if you have an arrangement with your service man to check all your home appliances once a year.

EFFICIENT LIGHTING

Get in the habit of turning off lights when you leave a room and are not planning to return to it for a while.

Cut down on light bulbs by using one high-wattage one instead of several smaller bulbs. A 100-watt bulb gives 50 per cent more light than four 25-watt ones yet costs only a few pennies more per bulb than the small size.

Don't skip the bulbs when you're dusting. Few homemakers realize that a few swipes with a cloth over a dusty light bulb can increase light by as much as 50 per cent. Be sure lamp shades are dusted on the inside as well as outside.

Colored bulbs, except the pale pink ones you use for atmosphere rather than for illumination, serve no good purpose. They greatly lessen the bulb's potential light yield.

Best light from table lamp is assured if the base is at least 12 inches high.

Check your lamp shades. Solid dark shades and dark shade linings reflect less light than light transparent ones. You'll see better with the light shades and room has a cozier look.

Wall-reflected light is free. When you repaint, use white or light pastel shades. Rooms so painted require far less artificial lighting than those with dark walls.

Basement walls painted a light color or whitewashed reflect more light than dark walls. If overhead joists are exposed, you'll increase amount of illumination from ceiling fixture without using a higher-watt bulb this way: Nail to the joist several painted white boards or piece of plywood or white cardboard.

TELEPHONE THRIFT

Numbers are elusive. Check the telephone directory before you dial. Wrong guesses, in most telephone booths, cost you a dime apiece. At home, overages raise your phone bills.

When you shop by phone, write out your list first. This saves ordering time and call-backs on the things you're likely to forget without a check list.

Discount periods for long-distance calls. It was once easy to remember that night calls were cheaper than day calls for long-distance calls.

Now it is a bit more complicated, for the phone company has "discount periods" that depend on whether the calls are being made on weekdays or weekends as well as on the time of day. The rule of thumb, though, is still as before.

Direct dialing for long-distance calls. By looking up the area code in a telephone directory, you can make almost all long-distance calls by yourself. Operator-assisted calls cost more.

Long-distance overtime soon runs into money. Make yourself a conversation guide, before you dial, by jotting down the main points you want to talk about. You'll be surprised at how many minutes this saves on a costly call.

Trick for long-distance calls. Place an egg timer next to the phone. The hourglass kind works on a three-minute schedule, will warn you when your lowest-cost three minutes are used up.

40

CAR CONSERVATION

*Add years and enjoyment, reduce costs and headaches
by following these basics of car maintenance*

The automobile becomes more so-
phisticated year by year, and care
and maintenance of the most complex parts and systems must now be
left to professionals. But the basics
of car checkups can still be performed by anyone capable of driving a car. In the case of the most
fundamental maintenance, in fact,
only the owner-driver can really be
responsible.

A car today costs several thousand
dollars when purchased new. But
that is only the beginning of its
cost. Most people will average another $100 a month—on fuel, in-
surance, registration and other fees,
parking, tolls, maintenance, parts,
repairs. Over the life of the car—
say, five years—this means another
$6,000. You owe it to yourself to
protect this investment—not to
mention your safety and life—by
giving the car frequent checkups.

People often tend to become careless about the basics. Using the car
day after day, they take it for
granted. One of the best ways to
break this pattern of neglect is to
take any longer trip as the occasion
for a full inspection and some preventive maintenance by the owner-
driver. This has a double advantage. Assuming your longer-than-
usual trip is going to put some extra
strain on the car, it may assure that
you don't end up with a breakdown
miles from help. And it is a way of
performing all those little checkups
you have been neglecting.

BASIC MAINTENANCE

Check all lights. Headlights (bright
and dim), tail lights, brake lights,
turn signals (front and rear), back-
up lights, and license-plate light. If
any don't work, replace or repair
them as necessary.

Inspect the wiper blades. The
rubber shouldn't be dried or
cracked, and the wiper arms
shouldn't be bent. Replace if necessary.

To check wiping action, spray the
windshield with a garden hose, or if
no garden hose is available, take a

bucket of water and throw it on the windshield. Then turn the wipers on. You can tell after the wiper blades make a couple of sweeps across the windshield whether they streak or smear.

Make sure the windshield washer is full of fluid. And make sure it works. If you're traveling where the temperature will be below freezing, make sure you use windshield-washer fluid with antifreeze added. Pure water may freeze in the lines. Never use the antifreeze intended for your engine's cooling system to make your own windshield solvent. Use only windshield-washer antifreeze.

Check your brakes if car tends to pull to the left or right. Check both front brakes, not just the one on the side toward which the car pulls.

Look for tire wear. Worn tires can cause an accident. And that's the last thing you want. To check tread wear, stick a penny between the treads, with the top of Mr. Lincoln's head pointed toward the tire. If the tire tread doesn't reach the top of his head, replace the tires—the tread is worn down too much for safety.

Uneven tire wear, often indicated by bald spots around tire edges, can mean that you've got a wheel alignment or balancing problem. Have the wheels aligned and balanced before beginning your trip.

Inflate tires properly. Improperly inflated tires wear faster and can adversely affect the handling of your car. Look at your owner's manual to see what the proper pressure is for your tires and then check their pressure down at the local gas station. Remember, if you're going to be carrying a lot of passengers and luggage, you'll want more pressure than when the car is carrying only one or two persons. Your owner's manual will tell you how much pressure is required for the car when fully loaded.

Don't forget the spare tire. It's embarrassing to replace one flat tire with another one. Check to make sure the spare's inflated and that it has a decent amount of tread left.

Check the jack, too. You can't change a flat tire if the jack is missing or inoperative. Make sure all the parts are there, and jack the car up just to make sure the jack works.

Open the hood. Check all the fluid levels: brake master cylinder, power-steering pump reservoir (if you have power steering), engine oil, and automatic transmission. Check the automatic-transmission fluid level when the engine is warm; otherwise you may get a false reading.

Check the fluid level in the battery and add distilled water if needed. The fluid should reach the bottom of the filler neck in each cell. Although distilled water is best, you can use tap water if distilled water isn't available.

Trouble's abrewing if you look under the hood and see worn or frayed wiring. Have something done about this at once by your garage mechanic.

Look at all the belts. They should have proper tension and not exhibit wear. To check for wear inspect the edges of each belt and the V part of the belt that fits in the pulleys. Belts shouldn't be frayed, cracked, or glazed. Replace any that are. A loose belt can contribute to decreased engine performance, and a worn belt that breaks can cause all kinds of problems, from a discharged battery to leaving you stranded in the country.

To check belt tension—grasp the belt midway between two pulleys with your thumb and forefinger. Pull up and push down on the belt. If you can deflect it more than half an inch, it's too loose. Loosen the appropriate pulley and take up the slack until you can deflect the belt about half an inch.

Check the heater and radiator hoses. Hoses shouldn't be brittle or cracked. And all clamps should be tight. As a rule of thumb, all hoses should be replaced every two years. If you're going on a long trip and the hoses have been in your car more than two years, don't even bother to inspect them. Replace them with new ones. And unless the clamps are reusable screw clamps, replace the clamps too. Keep hosing, as well as wiring, as far from hot engine parts as possible.

Keep an eye on the oil level if you would spare yourself the cost and torture of burned-out bearings.

Remove the top of the air cleaner and inspect the air-filter element. Hold the filter element up to the light. You should be able to see the light through it. If it's blocked and dirty, replace it. A clogged air filter cuts down on engine performance and gas mileage, and in general does nothing good for your engine.

Crawl under the car. Make sure nothing is loose or hanging down, such as part of your exhaust system. If you see anything either underneath or elsewhere that you're in doubt about, run your car over to your local service station and get a professional opinion.

Leave nothing to chance. If your car is overdue for a tuneup, oil change, grease job, brake inspection, or wheel-bearing repacking, have these services performed.

Put together a "trouble kit." Include in the kit a couple of road flares, a flat-tipped screwdriver, a Phillips-head screwdriver, an adjustable wrench, a single-edge razor blade or sharp knife, some electrical tape, and some wire. It's also a good idea to take along an empty container that can be used for carrying gas or water, plus a funnel to make pouring easier.

When preparing for a long trip, remember the ancient proverb, "A stitch in time saves nine." On the highway that might be nine dollars, nine miles, or nine hours.

KEEP YOUR COOLING
SYSTEM COOL

Coolant must always be at its proper level. There's a lot of heat generated inside your engine as the spark plugs fire hundreds and sometimes even thousands of times a minute to ignite the highly combustible fuel-air mix inside the engine's cylinders. The coolant flowing through your engine helps dissipate much of this heat. If you let the coolant level drop, though, the cooling system can't do its job. As a result, metal parts overexpand, there's a loss of lubrication because the oil becomes too hot to adhere to metal surfaces, and in severe cases expensive engine seizure occurs. Even minor overheating contributes to a shorter engine life.

How do you keep the cooling system cool? By checking the coolant level each time you fill up with gas. It only takes a few seconds to check it, and a few more seconds to add coolant if it's low.

Checking engines with coolant reservoir. Look for a transparent or semi-transparent plasticlike container close to the radiator with a small hose running from the container to the radiator. A coolant reservoir usually has two lines on it. The top line indicates where the coolant level should be when the engine is hot, the bottom line where the coolant level should be when the engine is cold.

To add water to the coolant reservoir, remove the cap from the reservoir, pour in enough water to bring the coolant up to the proper level, and replace the cap. Don't worry about steam as you must do when removing a radiator cap; the coolant is not under pressure.

Checking engines without a coolant reservoir. If your car has only a radiator with an overflow hose and no coolant reservoir, then you must check the coolant level in the radiator. Always check the coolant when the engine is cold. Otherwise you can get a face full of hot coolant. Coolant level should be about three inches below the filler neck. If it's not, add water until it is.

If you must remove the radiator cap when the engine is hot, cover the cap with rags to keep from burning your hand. Press down on the cap and turn it counterclockwise until you feel a "click" (about ¼ of a turn). Gradually release your downward pressure on the cap and allow the cooling system pressure to release. When the hissing completely stops, then finish removing the cap. (On some caps there's a little lever you can pull up to release pressure before you twist the cap.)

Replace coolant every two years. And flush the cooling system. Also have cooling-system pressure checked to make sure it is holding proper pressure. Coolant boils at a higher temperature under pressure.

TIPS ON FUEL SAVINGS

Have tuneups performed at intervals recommended in owner's manual. This assures maximum engine performance, best mileage, and longer engine life.

When starting, it's important to have the engine catch the first time you step on the starter. Why? Because restarting consumes fuel needlessly. Five false starts, for instance, will eat up as much as two miles of normal driving. Before stepping on the starter, therefore, prepare the engine by pumping the accelerator a couple of times to charge the intake system with fuel —unless your car's direction manual says otherwise.

Never race a cold engine. It wastes gasoline and increases motor wear.

Change oil regularly. Spending a little here can save a lot in terms of added power, better gasoline mileage, longer bearing life, and many other less tangible results.

Excessive oil consumption can sometimes be traced to an overzealous gas-station attendant who fills the crankcase above the recommended level. Always keep the oil between the "add oil" and "full" marks, not above and not below.

If the clutch slips, have it checked. A slipping clutch robs the engine of power and uses gasoline needlessly.

If your automatic transmission acts up, take your car to a mechanic at once. Correcting the failure is a job for factory-trained experts.

Make sure your automatic choke is working correctly. A malfunctioning choke decreases engine performance and can waste a lot of gas.

At all times start, drive, and stop smoothly. Fast acceleration at any times wastes gas. So does pumping on the accelerator when waiting at a traffic light. And so, believe it or not, does hard braking, because it means that you have used fuel needlessly to build up too high a speed for the conditions under which you're driving.

Moderate speed consumes much less gas per mile than high speed.

Proper engine heat is important. If the engine runs cold, a rich mixture is needed, and a rich mixture burns more gasoline than a lean one. Consequently you should have your thermostat repaired or replaced when the engine runs colder than usual.

A weak spark plug may prevent complete combustion of the fuel. To prevent this, have spark plugs, distributor, battery, ignition coil, wiring, and connections checked regularly.

Incorrect ignition timing, too, can cause fuel to be wasted by making the spark occur at the wrong moment. You should, therefore, have the timing checked at least twice a year.

The carburetor can waste gas by providing too rich a mixture. So have the carburetor and fuel pump adjusted either twice a year or every 5,000 miles, and keep the air filter clean.

Sticking valves, those that are warped and do not seat properly or have excessive carbon deposits, cause "pinging" and loss of compression and thereby waste fuel. This is overcome by having the valves ground and the carbon removed.

Worn piston rings should be replaced because they also cause loss of compression and allow valuable gasoline to escape unburned.

HOW TO GET MORE MILEAGE FROM YOUR TIRES

Keep tires properly inflated. If 30 pounds of pressure is recommended, don't drive around on 24 pounds unless you want to cut tire life by at least 20 per cent. See that each tire has a valve cap and that the cap is screwed on tight. Never drive on a flat.

Eliminate jack-rabbit starts and avoid screeching stops if you'd like to get full use from your tires. One 10-foot skid can burn off enough tread to reduce tire life by 20 miles or more.

Moderate speed is much more beneficial to tires than high speed, especially around curves, where high speed can multiply tire wear by as much as ten times.

Steer clear of obstructions such as curbs, holes, and rocks in the road. These can greatly shorten tire life by crushing the tire fabric against the rim, snapping cords within the tire, or cutting or bruising the sidewall.

Examine tires once a week for cuts and embedded nails or glass. Even small cuts tend to grow deeper with the passage of time. And they provide a means of entrance for dirt and water, which will eventually destroy the cord structure.

Rotate wheels (including the spare) from one hub to another twice yearly, to insure even tread wear and thus increase tire life. After five switches each tire will have been in use on each hub and will also have been temporarily retired to the trunk for a spare-tire rest.

Have wheel alignment, wheel balance, and steering-wheel play checked once a year. Misaligned wheels can decrease tire life by one quarter to one half; out-of-balance wheels will shimmy and cause tires to wear unevenly; and too much play in the steering wheel will let wheels weave back and forth, producing spotty tread wear.

Wheel balancing calls for special skill. Beware the mechanic who installs many balance weights. He may be trying to correct his own mistakes.

BATTERY CARE

Inspect the terminal connections of the battery if it won't hold a charge. To avoid corrosion, the terminals should be kept clean and bright.

Corrosion can be prevented by covering the terminals with petroleum jelly (Vaseline). If corrosion has already set in, disconnect the terminals from their posts and clean both the terminals and the posts with a solution of water and baking soda. Make sure everything is thoroughly dry before putting the terminals back in place.

Unless you drive several miles every day, the alternator may not keep the battery charged. If you don't drive regularly, have the battery checked often and recharged when necessary.

When you lay the car up for any length of time, have your garage mechanic remove the battery and connect it to the garage's trickle charger. This is also known as standby charging or set storage. It will guarantee that the battery won't be dead when you want to recommission your car.

BODY MAINTENANCE

Use car wax or other preservative to protect paint, thereby improving the car's appearance, increasing its life, and preventing rust. Always wax when car is just washed and dried.

Scratch-free car washing made easy. Cover metal hose nozzle with short length of rubber hosing. Allow to project about ¼ inch beyond nozzle tip; this prevents the nozzle rubbing against paint surface when working at close quarters.

Wax the radio antenna occasionally. You'll then have no trouble raising it during the winter.

Mysterious body noises (rattles, squeaks, "birdies," thumps, knocks, rumbles, etc.) can sometimes be traced to one or more of the following sources: loose hood hardware (tighten all bolts and oil all moving parts); loose license plates (especially evident when picking up in high gear from low speed); loose bumper; loose tailpipe assembly; broken engine mount (may thump either when engine idles or when speed is changed); loose flywheel (heavy and sharp knock when speed is changed); or bent or damaged fan blades (these also encourage overheating).

A noisy door sometimes can be quieted by greasing the striker and bumpers with stick lubricant especially made for the purpose. If the door is actually loose, insert rubber pads between the hinges and post.

Undercoating affords excellent protection against the salt that many cities use on icy streets during the winter and against fresh tar-covered pebbles when driving over a street recently resurfaced with tar and small stones. But it should not be applied to catalytic converters or heat shields under the car body.

For a sticking lock, squeeze powdered graphite into the keyhole. If you have no graphite, go over the blade of the key thoroughly with a soft lead pencil. Never use oil; it will gum up the delicate lock mechanism and collect dirt.

For a frozen lock, heat the key with a match or cigarette lighter before inserting it in the lock. The hot key usually melts the ice in the lock in about 30 seconds or so. Reheat the key as necessary.

HARD-WINTER HINTS

If it's extremely cold, have your mechanic change the spark plugs for ones a step higher in heat range, to prevent fouling while the choke is in operation.

Car hard to start? It may be running too cold because antifreeze makes the engine operate at a lower temperature than it does with tap water. A winter-range thermostat will overcome this.

When stuck in deep snow or ruts, with no chains available, let most of the air out of the rear tires. This increases traction enough to allow you to pull out. Then drive very slowly (to prevent damage to tires and rims) to the nearest service station and pump the tires back up again.

On ice or in snow, drive with no sudden throttle changes, no jazzing of the accelerator, no panicky leadfooting or braking. Instead maintain a moderate, steady speed, using the engine to brake as well as to accelerate.

Power brakes may cause the wheels to lock and skid. To prevent this,

always dab at the pedal rather than apply a steady pressure. This is especially true in winter driving.

Proper following distance is even more important in snow than it is on clear, dry roads; so increase the distance between your car and the one ahead from one car length per 10 miles per hour to several car lengths.

During the winter keep the battery completely charged. A partly charged battery can freeze at 20° F. and a discharged battery can freeze at 32° F. Nine times out of ten a frozen battery has had it, can't be resuscitated.

Even a well-charged battery may not prove sufficient when it is a matter of starting a car that has sat for any length of time in truly frigid weather. There are, of course, electrical devices to keep the whole motor warm. But one trick that might be used by anyone expecting an exceptionally cold spell is to bring the battery in and place it by the furnace. Just be sure to refasten the cables firmly to the terminals and you should get full power from your battery through the coldest weather.

Don't use heavy oil in cold weather. The needless friction it causes can be conquered only by using extra fuel.

Put a can of gas-line antifreeze in the fuel tank at every fillup to prevent gas-line freezeup.

BUYING A USED CAR

Don't sign anything before you drive. If the owner won't let you drive it or inspect it carefully, he's probably got something to hide, and hidden things will end up costing you money.

Use your eyes for more than admiring a low price. Check for rust, especially in hidden or hard-to-see areas of the body. A car that's starting to rust probably indicates a car that was not affectionately cared for, and may indicate more serious problems, especially if attempts have been made to conceal the rust with fresh paint. At the very least, rust lowers a car's resale value.

Open the doors. Open the hood and trunk lid. All should open and shut easily.

Climb in the car. Sit in each seat to check for things like broken springs. Look for tears in the headliner, worn carpets, missing floor mats, worn pedals, or missing control knobs. Any of these can indicate hard usage.

Push, pull, twist, and slide every control on the dash. Otherwise how will you know if they all work? And don't forget to try the heater—even if it's summer. Check all lights. You'll have to fix any that don't work if you buy the car. Check hoses and belts. Check the tires, including the spare, to see if they're badly worn. If any have to be replaced, that's extra expense for you.

Check the shock absorbers. Stand at a corner of the car and repeatedly push it down. Keep doing this until you've got that corner of the car rocking up and down vigorously. Then release your hands on a downward push. The car should rebound once and stop. If it continues bouncing up and down, that shock is bad and must be replaced. Repeat this test at each corner of the car.

The engine should start quickly and idle smoothly. An engine that is hard to start is an engine that needs work done on it.

Raise the hood. Check the oil level. If the oil level is low, that may indicate an oil-burning condition.

Rub your fingers across the dipstick and feel the oil. It's okay if the oil is dark; that's normal after a few hundred miles, even with fresh oil. But if you can feel sludge and grit with your fingers, that's not normal. That can mean a lot of things, none of them good. Also if the oil is extremely thick, that can mean a heavier oil has been added to conceal knocks and squeaks the owner doesn't want you to hear.

Check all fluid levels. If any are low, that means, at the very least, that the previous owner didn't pay much attention to his car. At worst it can signal an expensive problem.

Take the car out for a drive. Check the brakes when you're driving. They should not pull the car to one side when you depress the brake pedal.

Find a level, isolated stretch of roadway. When you release your grip on the wheel for a few moments, the car should not pull to either side. If it does, this indicates a wheel misalignment problem. Also there should be no shimmy in the front end or vibration in the steering wheel.

Find a bumpy section of road. The car should not "bottom" as you ride over bumps. Nor should it sway excessively when traveling around smooth or bumpy curves. If it does, this indicates bad shocks.

While traveling along an isolated level stretch of road at about 30 mph, release and depress the accelerator quickly a couple of times. Listen for noises. If you hear any, especially coming from underneath and to the rear, this may indicate excessive wear in some parts of the drive train.

Check that automatic. In a used car with an automatic transmission you can tell something about the condition of this important unit by noticing if the car accelerates properly on a normal upgrade. Slippage is cause for further checking. In addition, try backing the car up a short grade to see if the action is smooth.

An automatic transmission should shift smoothly. There should be no clunking or jerking as the transmission shifts up or down. And the transmission should not "hang" in one gear for an excessive time.

With a manual transmission, or stick shift, notice how far in you

have to push the clutch. If it goes in all the way, there isn't much clutch left. The pedal, however, should have about an inch of play when it's completely released.

Remember, when you're buying a used car, any parts that require immediate replacement add to the cost of the car. Unless the seller is willing to slash the price to allow for this cost, you're going to end up paying a lot more for the car than you should.

If you're in doubt about anything, have a mechanic check it. The few dollars he'll charge can save you a lot of dollars in the long run.

When you buy on the installment plan, have the seller put in writing all the terms of the transaction, including down payment, monthly payments, interest charges, etc. All repairs and accessories that are promised to you should be itemized on the bill of sale or contract and should be acknowledged by the dealer's signature. If you're offered a service guarantee, make sure you understand it, since such guarantees can be tricky, seeming to mean one thing and actually meaning another.

THINK METRIC IN YOUR CAR

A change from the U.S. to the metric system of measures and weights seems to be a future inevitability. To help you adjust to this change, Chapter 21 listed common kitchen measures and weights in both the U.S. and metric systems, and also tables showing how to convert units from one system to the other.

Since metric measurement applies as much to driving a car as it does to working in a kitchen, this chapter includes information on those U.S. and metric units which apply to length (distance) and capacity (liquid measure), and also pertinent conversion factors for both measures.

CONVERSION TABLES

The following tables are set up to help you convert units commonly used when driving a car. The answers you arrive at will be approximate, but accurate enough for non-scientific purposes.

WHEN YOU KNOW THE U.S. UNIT	MULTIPLY BY:	TO FIND THE METRIC UNIT
Miles	1.6	Kilometers
Gallons	3.8	Liters
Miles per gallon	0.42	Kilometers per liter

WHEN YOU KNOW THE METRIC UNIT	MULTIPLY BY:	TO FIND THE U.S. UNIT
Kilometers	0.62	Miles
Liters	0.26	Gallons
Kilometers per liter	2.4	Miles per gallon

U. S. SYSTEM

LENGTH

Unit	Metric Equivalent
Inch (in.)	2.54 centimeters
foot (ft.)= 12 inches	30.48 centimeters or 0.3048 meter
yard (yd.)= 3 feet or 36 inches	0.9144 meter
rod (rd.)= 5.5 yards or 16.5 feet	5.0292 meters
furlong= 220 yards or 40 rods or ⅛ mile	201.168 meters
mile (mi.)= 5,280 feet or 1,760 yards or 8 furlongs	1.6093 kilometers

CAPACITY

Unit	U.S. Equivalent in Cubic Inches	Metric Equivalent
gill (gi.)=4 fluid ounces	7.219	0.118 liter
pint (pt.)=4 gills	28.875	0.473 liter
quart (qt.)=2 pints	57.75	0.946 liter
gallon (gal.)=4 quarts	231	3.785 liters

METRIC SYSTEM

LENGTH

Unit	Equivalent in Meters	U.S. Equivalent
millimeter (mm)	0.001	0.03937 inch
centimeter (cm)=10 millimeters	0.01	0.3937 inch
decimeter (dm)=10 centimeters	0.1	3.937 inches
meter (m)=10 decimeters or 100 centimeters or 1,000 millimeters	1	39.37 inches or 3.28 feet or 1.09 yards
decameter (dkm)=10 meters	10	32.81 feet or 10.93 yards
hectometer (hm)=10 decameters	100	328.08 feet or 109.36 yards
kilometer (km)=10 hectometers	1,000	0.6214 mile or 1,093.6 yards or 3,280.8 feet

CAPACITY

Unit	Equivalent in Liters	U.S. Equivalent
milliliter (ml)	0.001	0.034 fluid ounce
centiliter (cl)=10 milliliters	0.01	0.338 fluid ounce
deciliter (dl)=10 centiliters	0.1	3.38 fluid ounces
liter (l)=10 deciliters or 100 centiliters or 1,000 milliliters	1	1.05 liquid quarts or 33.814 fluid ounces or 0.908 dry quart
decaliter (dkl)=10 liters	10	2.64 gallons or 0.284 bushel
hectoliter (hl)=10 decaliters	100	26.418 gallons or 2.838 bushels
kiloliter (kl)=10 hectoliters	1,000	264.18 gallons

41

MANAGING YOUR MONEY

Sound tips to ensure that your money comes—and goes— in more reasonable ways

Money may not be the root of all evil but no one will deny that it affects people in many, often strange, ways. The challenge is to put money into its proper perspective, to treat it as no less, but no more, important than it should be. One way to do this is to think of money as you would of a favorite tool: take care of it and it will last a long time and do the job it is designed for. With this attitude, you should be able to make money work for you—not end up working for money.

Long before there was money, of course, people bartered actual goods and produce. Gradually metals coins and then paper money replaced such goods in most transactions. But even today, money comes in many different forms— checks and bonds, just to name two. Even people with the most modest incomes may deal with government checks. And people who would never think of themselves as "investors" may buy government savings bonds. Everyone should be informed of the best ways to take care of these variations of money.

Special paper. Money, by the way, is printed on special paper that can't be used by anyone but the Government. But even this strong paper wears out with time and constant handling. The Treasury, therefore, requests banks to send back old, worn, torn, or mutilated bills to be exchanged for new ones. What's the average working life of a dollar bill? Nine months.

Bills scorched or partly burned? The Treasury Department will still redeem them at full value if its experts conclude that real money has been destroyed. No matter what fragments are left, don't despair until you've sent the actual fragments to the Treasury for analysis. Sometimes new money is given for what may seem to be slight evidence because the Treasury's facilities for scientific analysis are often unbelievably ingenious.

As for mutilated bills. If you have ⅗ or more of a mutilated genuine bill, you may redeem it for its full value through the Treasurer of the United States. If you have less than ⅗, but clearly more than ⅖, you can exchange it for ½ of its face value. To redeem fragments not more than ⅖ of the original bill, you must send them with satisfactory proof that the missing portions have been totally destroyed. Take mutilated bills to your bank or send by registered mail, accompanied by the proper affidavits, to the Bureau of the Public Debt, Treasury Department, Washington, D.C. 20226.

It is against the law to print or otherwise reproduce "any impression in the likeness of any obligation of security or postage stamp, or any part thereof, without permission of the Secretary of the Treasury or other authorized officer of the U.S."

It is also unlawful to use any such picture for advertising. However, there is no law against photographing or publishing coin illustrations.

HOW TO PROTECT YOUR GOVERNMENT CHECKS

Our federal government issues hundreds of millions of checks a year, to social-security beneficiaries, old-age pensioners, war veterans, families and other dependents of those in our armed forces, farmers, taxpayers entitled to income-tax refunds, federal employees, and others. Checks are sometimes stolen from letterboxes, and because many storekeepers and businessmen fail to insist on positive identification, thousands of these checks are forged and cashed by thieves every year. If you receive government checks, avoid loss by:

1. Trying to have a member of the family at home on days when checks are likely to arrive.

2. Making sure that your mailbox has a good lock and is clearly identified with your name.

3. Not endorsing your check until you are in the presence of the person who will cash it.

4. Cashing your check at the same place each time, to make identification easier.

Social Security checks mailed directly to your own bank account. Under a relatively new procedure, individuals who so request may have their Social Security checks sent directly to their personal bank accounts, thus avoiding any risks, loss of time, or inconvenience in having to deposit the checks. If you are interested, contact your nearest Social Security office or your own bank to see how you can make such an arrangement.

If you cash government checks:

1. Insist that a person presenting a government check identify himself as the person entitled to the check and endorse it in your presence.

2. Ask yourself this question: "If the check is forged, can I locate the forger and recover my loss?"

3. Test the holder of the check with catch questions such as these: "I see you live at 26 Elm Street?" (Give an address different from that on the face of the check.) If the passer of the check has stolen it, he'll agree because he's not sure which is correct. Or ask about a fictitious neighbor, using your name or that of a friend. For instance, "Oh, 26 Elm Street. You must live next to John Jones. How is he?" Or mention a nonexistent landmark. For instance, "Why, this address is next door to the new Third National Bank. How's their new building coming?"

4. Be sure to initial all checks and to make a note of the kind of identification offered.

THE RIGHT WAY TO SAFEGUARD YOUR SAVINGS BONDS FROM LOSS

Series E savings bonds are safer than cash, and their value grows while that of cash in your pocket or household doesn't. Despite this, savings bonds have been forged, stolen, and fraudulently cashed. But you can't lose if you take sensible precautions. The Treasury Department will replace any savings bonds lost, stolen, mutilated, or destroyed. All you have to do is:

1. Keep your bonds in a safe-deposit box or other safe place.

2. Record the serial numbers, amounts, and dates purchased in a place separate from the bonds themselves. (Use convenient record form on page 418.)

3. Give immediate notice of your loss—including serial numbers, purchase dates (month and year), denominations (values at maturity), and name and address of the owner—to the Bureau of the Public Debt, 203rd Street, Parkersburg, West Virginia 26101.

By the way, Series E savings bonds do not have to be cashed in when they fall due. The bank will be glad to arrange your holding on to them at compound interest.

MAKING A BUDGET

A budget can't save and spend your money for you. It can't work miracles. It can't change very much the basic family realities of income and outgo. But a budget can help you keep better track of your money and it can help you guide the way you spend and save your money. To translate Charles Dickens into our own contemporary terms: "Income, $15,000, expenditures, $15,100, unhappiness. Income, $15,000, expenditures, $14,900, happiness." A budget can help make that little difference.

The "money manager" described here is based on one prepared by the Institute of Life Insurance, which drew on the experience of life-insurance companies with their millions of policyholders. You'll find this money manager easy to set up. It doesn't involve a lot of unnecessary bookkeeping or ask you

RECORD OF U.S. SAVINGS BONDS

Date Purch'd	Serial No.	Name(s) (initials)	Denomination	Date Cashed	Amount Received

to keep track of every dime, nickel, and penny. But the money manager does give you a system of money management, a system of planned spending and saving that will mean more happiness and less worry for you and your family.

One major change has occurred in American families' budgets in recent years, and that is the impact of the working wife. On the one hand, she has added new and larger sources of income. On the other hand, the inflationary trends and increased obligations of family life have made new demands on incomes. The net effect, though, seems to be more money for what the economists call "discretionary spending." In any case, all references to income in the money manager that follows include both the wife's and husband's incomes.

FOUR SIMPLE STEPS

There are just four things to do to put your money manager into operation:

1. *You'll figure out* what your average weekly income is going to be for the next 12 months.

2. *You'll estimate how much* your fixed expenses and obligations are going to be. When you add these up and divide by 52, you'll know how much of your income you must put aside every week to meet these expenses and obligations. Naturally, if you are paid twice a month, rather than weekly, you should divide by

24. Or if your income is received monthly, divide by 12.

3. *Decide how much money* you'll need for day-to-day family expenses.

4. *Start a "rainy-day" emergency fund* by deciding to put away a definite amount each pay day.

While these steps are, actually, set up here in one, two, three, four order, it is likely that you'll arrive at your final estimates by considering them as a group, adjusting the amounts in each step until you have what you feel is a workable plan. And, finally, you'll total all these estimates to find how much (or how little) is left for regular savings.

It's easy to see how a system such as this helps take the worry out of handling money. Every week your regular set-asides will go into a special fund, and whenever a major expense or obligation comes due, you'll pay it out of this fund. Some weeks you may have a lot of money in your fund and in other weeks very little. But if your system is operating and you are conscientious about putting your weekly set-asides away, there will always be enough money to pay these major expenses and obligations when they come due.

In the meantime you'll have a regular, steady "salary" for your family's day-to-day living and spending. You'll pay yourselves this money each week and do everything you can to see to it that it lasts until the next week rolls around. This will be your money, to spend and to save as you and your family please.

MONEY IS A FAMILY AFFAIR

No family budget is ever really successful unless everyone in the family agrees that it is a good budget. For this reason, if for no other, everyone should take a hand in family money planning. Most children in their teens, and some children who are even younger, are mature enough to help.

No matter how you start your budget, on the first try you and your family may find you have been too liberal in certain estimates or have forgotten some major future expense. In this case you must go back and work your budget out again. For a few weeks you may have to keep close watch over your expenses, jotting them down a nickel or a dime at a time until you find out where your money is going.

Before you apply your money-manager system, you'll have to remember one final thing: If, when you start your budget, you owe no one and have cash in the bank, making your money manager work will be easy. But it won't be very easy if you are starting a few dollars in the red, or if you have big expenses immediately ahead of you. In that case it will take quite a lot of patient budgeting and extra setasides before your emergency fund will begin to show a balance.

STEP 1: INCOME

Write down in this chart all the cash you expect to receive in the next 12 months. If your income is from wages or salary, include only your and your spouse's take-home cash pay. If it is from a business, farm, or trade, make the best estimate you can.

Don't forget to include any extra cash income you may receive: interest or dividends from bonds and other investments, money that the children may turn in to the family, rent you may get from property you own, etc.

STEP 2: FIXED EXPENSES AND OBLIGATIONS

The secret of the money manager is this: It allows you to save ahead to meet fixed expenses and obligations, so when they come due you'll have enough money to pay them.

Here, under Step 2, write down what these fixed expenses and obligations are in your household: rent or mortgage payments, life-insurance premiums, taxes other than payroll taxes, installment payments, and so on. Indicate in what months these outlays will come due.

Plan ahead. If you know you are going to have a big fuel bill in October or a clothing bill for the children in the spring or some expensive dental work in the winter, write down these expenses. But don't try to guess all your doubtful future expenses, for you'll find it's too diffi-

ESTIMATED FAMILY INCOME

INCOME OBTAINED FROM	JAN.	FEB.	MAR.	APR.	MAY	JUNE	JULY	AUG.	SEPT.	OCT.	NOV.	DEC.	YEARLY TOTAL
Husband's employment													
Wife's employment													
Other family member's employment													
Interest													
Dividends													
Other (rent, bonus, capital gains, etc.)													
Totals for month													

Total ANNUAL Income _____ $ _____

Total WEEKLY Income (Divide Annual Income by 52) _____ $ _____

This is the money which we have to spend and save during the next 52 weeks.
Enter the amount in the "Family Balance Sheet" on page 425.

ESTIMATED FIXED EXPENSES

INCOME EXPENDED FOR	JAN.	FEB.	MAR.	APR.	MAY	JUNE	JULY	AUG.	SEPT.	OCT.	NOV.	DEC.	YEAR'S TOTAL
Rent or mortgage payment													
Fuel bill													
Telephone bill													
Gas and electricity bills													
Water bill													
Installment payments													
Income taxes													
Real estate taxes													
Insurance premiums (life, home, auto, theft, etc.)													
Other payments (child care, tuition, etc.)													
Totals for each Month													

Total for the year _____ OUR WEEKLY SET ASIDE (Divide by 52) _____

This is the money we shall put in a special fund every week to meet future expenses and obligations. Enter it on the "Family Balance Sheet", page 425.

cult. Put down only the major expenses and obligations that you can estimate fairly closely in advance.

Add up all your items, divide by 52, and you'll have your weekly set-aside. This money goes into a special fund every pay day. When your fixed expenses and obligations come due later on, they'll be paid out of this fund.

STEP 3: WEEKLY LIVING ALLOWANCES

How much does it cost you and your family to live? Unless you have kept family books over a period of years, you won't be able to tell to the penny. But if you have been moderately careful in the past, you'll be able to make a pretty good estimate. Here, under Step 3, is the place to do it.

Exactly how you divide your living expenses into different classifications is up to you. In this chart, they are divided into ten sections:

1. *Food and beverages.*

2. *Household operations.*

3. *Clothing.*

4. *Transportation.*

5. *Medical and dental care.*

6. *Personal needs.*

7. *Education.*

8. *Recreation.*

9. *Gifts and contributions.*

10. *Miscellaneous.*

There won't be anything final in these estimates of yours. After a

month or two you and your family will probably want to come back and rework everything, according to the lessons you have learned under your new money manager.

Now you're ready to add all your estimates and find your total expenditures. When you subtract these from your total income, have you anything left? If so, this amount may be placed in your regular savings account, in savings bonds, or in other investments.

STEP 4: EMERGENCY FUND

One of the most important steps, if your money manager is to work smoothly, is to provide for an emergency fund.

There are two kinds of savings:

1. *Regular family savings* are for long-range projects: family security, the children's education, a new house, a new television set, a new car, or a good vacation.

2. *Emergency set-asides* are something else. It's money you put aside every week to help you buy things you simply must buy but haven't provided for.

It's a comfort to have a lot of extra money left over after all your bills are paid and all other obligations are met. But most families haven't a lot of extra money. After all, there are other things more important than extra money: good diet and good housing, adequate clothing, and the other things that spell out a warm, happy, healthy family life.

ESTIMATE FOR FLEXIBLE EXPENSES

DAILY EXPENSES (BY THE MONTH) FOR	JAN.	FEB.	MAR.	APR.	MAY	JUNE	JULY	AUG.	SEPT.	OCT.	NOV.	DEC.
Food and beverages												
Household operation (furnishings, laundry, services, etc.)												
Clothing												
Transportation												
Medical and dental care												
Personal needs (cosmetics, hair styling, etc.)												
Education (books, stationery, etc.)												
Recreation												
Gifts and contributions												
Miscellaneous												
Totals for each month												

OUR WEEKLY ESTIMATE FOR LIVING EXPENSES _____

This is the amount we shall pay ourselves every week and try to make last until the next week begins.
Enter it on the "Balance Sheet", page 425.

You'll need something for an emergency fund, just the same, if your money manager is going to work properly. You can't estimate in advance all your future expenses. You can't know how much or how little you may have to pay for things like doctor bills and repairs for the car six months or a year in advance. By putting money every week into your emergency fund, however, you'll be building up a fund that will help meet these unexpected bills when they come due. At this point, therefore, set up a definite amount that will be placed each pay day in your emergency fund.

Curb that emergency fund. It shouldn't be allowed to grow too big. When it reaches two or three months' income, put the extra money into regular savings or into something else your family wants and needs.

ESTIMATE OF EMERGENCY FUND

To meet unexpected expenses we shall put aside each week $ _____

Enter in "Balance Sheet"

This fund will be allowed to accumulate until it reaches $ _____
after which we shall pay into it merely enough to keep it at that level.

OUR FAMILY "BALANCE SHEET"

Our weekly income is_____(Step 1)_____

Our weekly set-asides amount to_____(Step 2)_____

Our weekly living allowance is_____(Step 3)_____

Our emergency fund_____(Step 4)_____

And this is what's left for regular savings_____

42

YOUR BANK

The dollars and sense of its many services

Banks perform an important function in receiving, safeguarding, and making available, where and when needed, the money of the community. They furnish us with a convenient place for the safekeeping of our funds, where we can put into actual practice a program of thrift and reap the benefits of interest on our money. They provide numerous practical plans for helping us to acquire our own homes, to finance needed improvements, to make our dreams come true in many different ways.

When about to make a financial move, you'll find your banker's knowledge and experience a genuine help. And it will pay you to become acquainted with the many other services a bank provides in addition to the one or two you may be using now. For instance:

Checking accounts. Because anyone can have one, and because the advantages are so great, this is a "must" service that repays the depositor in many ways. A checking account is the convenient, economical way to pay bills. It saves fares,

auto expense, and traveling to the places where accounts are to be paid. It saves you money-order fees when paying out-of-town bills. (A $12 money order, for example, costs you 70¢.) Every canceled check is automatically a receipt, an immediate proof of payment endorsed by the person or the company to whom you paid the money. Your checks also provide an ideal record that helps make it possible to claim all the deductions and exemptions to which you are entitled when filing your income-tax returns.

Loans. "Buying money" should be done with as much care as buying anything else, and your bank has all the facilities for "selling" you its use on favorable terms. When such loans will benefit the borrower, your bank is able to offer a variety of plans best suited to different needs and situations. These include mortgage loans, collateral loans, loans to small businesses, loans to veterans, personal loans, and various other kinds. Banks are eager to help you work out the type of loan most favorable to you. Their officers will be glad to discuss your borrowing problem with you confidentially.

Your safe-deposit box. Every family has some possessions that should be kept under lock and key in the armored protection of a safe-deposit box. Some of these possessions represent financial values that may be lost, stolen, or destroyed. Others are priceless personal things of sentiment. Such personal treasures should be kept in a safe-deposit box. Your bank makes this important service available to you at very little cost.

Banking by mail. When it is inconvenient to visit your bank, you need not risk loss or theft of your money by keeping it in the house. You can do your banking by mail. Your bank will gladly supply you with forms to use in making deposits or withdrawals by mail. (Be sure, however, to send currency by registered mail only.) Endorse all checks, as soon as received, with a "special" endorsement that should read, "For deposit only to the account of ———— ————." Under this you sign your name. When so endorsed, no unauthorized person can cash the checks, even if they are lost or stolen. Mail deposits and withdrawals receive prompt bank attention.

Traveler's checks. At a relatively small cost, and with complete safety, traveler's checks make it possible for you to carry any amount of money even when traveling to distant points abroad. They are generally cashed as readily as currency and require no identification other than your own signature. If lost or stolen, the traveler's checks' full value is refunded to you at an authorized institution. Just make sure to keep a list of the numbers of your traveler's checks in a separate place; should your checks be lost or stolen, you can report their numbers immediately and thus speed the process of reimbursement.

Interest-bearing accounts. To encourage thrift and provide maximum safety for your funds, most banks offer their depositors the service of accumulating the depositor's dollars at a profit to the depositor. This profit is paid out as interest. Such accounts have the advantage of giving you an incentive for regular deposits and being available for withdrawal in case of emergency. Interest-bearing accounts can be started with small amounts. You can also deposit small or large amounts. *Under one roof,* your bank can provide all the banking services you need in order to handle your financial affairs efficiently. Use them to the advantage of your financial-security program.

THE RIGHT WAY TO WRITE CHECKS

To make sure the right person gets the money:

1. Fill the "payee" line completely when you write the name of the person or firm to whom you are ordering the bank to pay your funds.

2. Begin writing the name close to the printed words, "Pay to the order of."

3. If the name doesn't fill the line to the dollar sign ($), fill the rest of the space with two or three heavy straight or wavy lines.

4. Leave no extra spaces between words or initials in which the "check artist" could write in letters to change the name of the payee.

To make sure payee receives the right amount:

1. Put the first numeral so close to the dollar sign ($) that no other numeral can be written in front of it.

2. Write each additional numeral so close to the previous one that no other numeral can be inserted between them.

3. Use large numerals to represent dollars.

4. Place numerals representing cents even with top of the numerals representing dollars and make them half as large, or smaller.

5. Draw two or more lines under the cents numerals, beginning each line close to the dollar numerals.

6. Begin writing the amount at the extreme left of the "filling" line, so that no letter or word can be inserted in front of it.

7. Write the words so close together that no other letter or word can be inserted.

8. Write the word "and" before the cents amount in a slanting position and close to the previous word, so that it can't be used as part of a word that might increase the amount.

9. Write the number of cents above a line with "100" below that line and put this fraction close to the previous word.

10. Draw two or three heavy or wavy lines from the fraction to the word "dollars."

11. If the check is for less than one dollar, write the fraction close to the dollar sign and write the word "only" close to the fraction.

12. On the "filling" line (close to the left end) write the word "exactly" in front of the fraction and follow the fraction with two or three heavy or wavy lines to the word "dollars."

13. Follow these same rules if the check is written on a typewriter.

14. If a check protector is used, you'll run no risk of having the amount raised. It is still necessary, however, to write the numeral amount with great care and to make sure that this amount is exactly the same as that printed with the check protector.

ANSWERS TO QUESTIONS OFTEN ASKED ABOUT CHECKING ACCOUNTS

Q. Must I sign my check in any particular way?

A. Yes. You must sign every check exactly the way you signed the signature card when you opened your account. If you signed it George S. Smith, you must not sign your checks G. S. Smith, or in any other way except George S. Smith.

Q. Must I make out my own deposit ticket?
A. You protect both yourself and your bank by making out your own deposit ticket. Moreover, when you leave it to the teller to enter the items on a ticket, you delay yourself and others who may be waiting.

Q. How should I stop payment on a check?
A. It is better not to stop payment unless absolutely necessary. If it does seem absolutely necessary, talk the matter over with a bank officer. If he agrees that it should be done, you'll be asked to sign a stop-payment order which he'll provide.

Q. Is it wise to draw on a check deposited before it has had time to be sent to the bank on which it is drawn?
A. If you keep a liberal balance in your account, this won't happen. Banks, naturally, can't allow the use of money that has not yet been collected by them from other banks.

Q. If my name is misspelled, how do I endorse a check made out to me?
A. Endorse it the way it is spelled on the face of the check. Then, under that endorsement, sign your name correctly.

Q. What should be done with a check that is altered when received?
A. Banks do not cash or accept for deposit checks that have been altered. The thing to do is to take it back to the person who gave it to you and ask that a new check be drawn that doesn't show any alteration.

Q. If the amount in figures does not agree with the amount in writing on a check I receive, what shall I do with it?
A. It should be returned to the person who gave you the check with the request that a new check be issued, properly made out. It is not wise to try to cash it with that discrepancy on the face.

Q. If the date is missing on a check to be deposited, should I fill it in?
A. The law allows you to do this, and it probably would be wise to enter the current date.

Q. What is a certified check?
A. When a check is taken to the bank to be certified, the teller puts a certification stamp on the face of your check and immediately deducts the amount of the check from your account. Therefore a certified check should never be destroyed if it is not used for the purpose intended, but should be redeposited in the bank with the notation written across the back of it, "Not used for the purpose intended." Under that, endorse the check for deposit to your account and handle it as a regular deposit. This will get the money back into your account.

Q. Should every check have a number?

A. Yes, the same number should be on the stub of the check and on the check itself. This is a quick way to connect the check with the stub and helps in reconciling your account.

Q. Is a check valid when written with a pencil?

A. It is legal, but it is more easily altered. Always use ink.

Q. Is a check valid if dated on a Sunday or a holiday?

A. Yes. Always use the date of the day on which you write the check.

Q. Is a check valid if deposited two months after it is drawn?

A. Yes, but don't hold a check. Deposit it as soon as you receive it. Checks presented for payment that are more than three months old will be returned by most banks for "stale date." Then you will have to get a new check before you can get your money.

Q. Is a check valid if it is dated two or three weeks in the future (postdated)?

A. Yes, but don't accept a postdated check. It won't be cashed before its date.

Q. What is the right way to endorse a check?

A. Never endorse a check simply by signing your name, unless you are in the bank where you wish to cash or deposit it. Use a "special" endorsement. Then, if it is lost or stolen, the bank will not pay it. A "special" endorsement has a line above your signature that reads, "Pay to the order of —— ——" or "For deposit only to the account of —— ——." If you make a mistake in writing a check or deposit slip, burn it and make out a new one.

HINTS ABOUT CHECKING ACCOUNTS THAT SAVE YOU TIME AND MONEY

Never sign a check until the name of the payee and the amount are carefully written on the check. In other words, never give anyone a check signed "in blank." Deposit promptly the checks you receive. Doing so will maintain your balance and save considerable time in getting misplaced or lost checks replaced. Remember that your bank can't pay against deposits made to your account until the checks you deposit have been collected by your bank. The sooner you deposit your checks, therefore, the sooner the collected funds become available for your use.

File your canceled checks like receipts. They are the best evidence that you paid the debt. The bank and the person or company whose endorsement appears on the check certify that payment was received.

Enter complete information on the stub of each check written, to show for what it pays.

Indicate the source of each deposit item individually, either on your validated machine receipt or on a duplicate deposit ticket. Without further work, a file of these will serve as a record of the source of your income.

Enter the number of the check used to pay each bill on the face of the invoice. When this is done it is not necessary to ask for a receipt. The check is evidence that the amount of the check was applied to payment of the bill. Your creditor admits such payment when he endorses the check. The bank certifies payment when it returns your canceled checks to you, and your statement shows the checks charged against your account.

THE EASY WAY TO RECONCILE YOUR MONTHLY STATEMENT

1. Compare the amount on your duplicate deposit slips, your passbooks, or machine validated receipts with the amount credited on your statement in the column labeled "Deposits." Check each item in that column with a pencil as you verify it. Also check the balance forwarded from your previous statement.

2. Check with a pencil each amount in the column labeled "Checks" as you find the canceled check for the amount.

3. Sort checks in numerical order, or in the order of the dates, if they are not numbered.

4. Go through your checkbook stubs and check with a pencil each stub for which a paid check was returned. Also check the deposits recorded in your checkbook against those appearing in your statements.

5. As you do this, compare the amount and name of the payee with the stub to be sure no check was raised and no payee's name was changed.

6. Most statements contain space, often on the back of the form, for "outstanding checks." As you come across a stub for which the check has not been returned, write the number and amount in this space.

7. Now add up the amounts of the outstanding checks. This total represents checks written by you that were not paid before your statement was mailed to you.

8. Subtract this amount from the last balance on your statement.

9. If you have made a deposit since the statement was closed, add that to the balance in Step 8.

10. At the bottom of your statement write the checkbook balance as of the last day of the month. From this balance you must add or subtract any additional justified credit memos or debit memos the bank has made that you have not entered in your checkbook. After making these adjustments on your statement you must make the same adjustments in your checkbook, otherwise these adjustments will show up as differences on your next statement when you try to reconcile your account.

11. *Now compare this balance* with the last balance shown in your checkbook.

12. *If there is any difference,* go over your figures carefully to see if you find an error in addition.

13. *If the balance in your checkbook* agrees with the bank, write "OK" on the statement and sign your initials.

14. *File the statement and checks* where no stranger is likely to find them. Canceled checks are your legal receipts for paid bills.

15. *Should you find that a deposit* was not credited, or if you think there is any other error, bring the statement, canceled checks, and your checkbook to the bank and ask for an officer. Show what you think is an error. Do this the very day you receive the statement or as soon after as possible. In any event, do not wait over ten days.

43

INSURANCE

Sage counsel and handy hints that put insurance into proper perspective

Americans are probably the most insured people in history. Whatever the pros and cons of this phenomenon, you should at least consider insurance in its fullest perspective. Properly handled, insurance is far more than paying premiums on the chance that some accident might befall you or your property. Insurance in the fullest sense means ensuring the well-being of yourself and all those dependent on you— especially your immediate family. In this sense, insurance is taking responsibility for all your valuables— from the simplest documents to the full extent of your estate.

No matter how much or how little money you have, you do have important documents and papers. If they cannot be located, you create unnecessary problems for yourself and your heirs. Take a moment to fill out the chart provided for your convenience on page 434.

LIFE INSURANCE: THE BASICS

Practically everyone owns some life insurance. It is the most widely owned form of thrift in America today. But not everyone gets the most out of life insurance. In countless cases considerable savings or increased protection can be secured through some simple detail in handling your policies. To make sure that both you and your family will at all times be getting every possible value out of your life-insurance dollars, go over these often-neglected pointers and do something about those that apply to your own situation.

What kind of policy is best? Of the scores of kinds of life-insurance policies in existence, there is one that is the best for your particular needs and will give you maximum value for your insurance dollars. But this cannot be determined by any rule; it requires careful analysis by your agent. Be sure and let your agent make this analysis so you'll get maximum value.

One type of insurance commonly recommended for young families is term insurance—a low premium is paid for a stated term, or period,

DIRECTORY OF VITAL FAMILY RECORDS

Do we have it? Where is it? Who has it? Where can we find it in a hurry? Not to have the answers at your fingertips in an urgent moment can cause no end of grief, loss, hardship. To keep your house in order, record the exact location of these priceless family valuables and correct the record as necessary.

Birth & baptismal certificates	Marriage records
Child relationship proofs	Naturalization papers
Military discharge papers	Organization membership records
Social security card	Passports
Insurance policies	Premium receipts
Bank passbooks	Cancelled checks and stubs
Safe deposit box	U.S. Savings bonds
Stocks and bonds	Tax return records
Will	Business documents, contracts
Real estate documents	Cemetery plot deed
Receipts & receipted bills	Bills of sale
Jewelry	Licenses
Warehouse	Miscellaneous

but no equity is built up. At a stage when income may be low, young children are present, and family obligations many, this often provides the most manageable type of life insurance.

Check your insurance for inflation losses. Maybe it was a "complete" program five or ten years ago, but how about today? Especially income plans; they've been badly hit by inflation. The $500-a-month setup some years ago might have been enough, but is it today? Perhaps you should shorten the income period and increase the income amount, if you can afford additional insurance to make up the needed protection.

Save on premium payments. If you're paying premiums monthly on any of your policies, you can save 5 to 6 per cent by making payment once a year. (On a $10,000 policy that saving might be enough to enable you to buy another $500 of insurance.) If your policy is on quarterly premiums, you can save about 4 per cent by changing to annual payments.

Let your policy dividends earn interest. If you have any "participating" policies that pay dividends to you, a very nice rate of interest may be earned if you leave them with your insurance company to accumulate at interest. More than a fourth of all dividends are now left in this way.

Valuable collateral for loans. If you are ever in need of a bank loan, don't overlook the value of your life-insurance policy as collateral to help you get the lowest possible rate of interest.

Is a will necessary for life insurance? No, the life-insurance payments may all be arranged in the policy itself. Everyone, however, should have a will to cover whatever else is left at death, to make certain everything will work out as planned.

A CHECKLIST FOR YOUR POLICY

Valuable service—no charge. At least once a year you should have your agent check over your policies and make certain nothing has become out-of-date and therefore not up to full value. These check-ups may save you many dollars, and they cost you nothing. They are part of the free service that goes with your policy.

Have you named the right beneficiary? You bought your insurance for the benefit of certain persons, to meet specific needs. Make certain those needs won't be overlooked because some beneficiary change should have been made since you first took out the insurance.

How about a common disaster clause? Have you considered what will become of your life insurance if both you and your wife are involved in the same fatal accident? Unless you have a "common disaster" clause written into your policy (at no extra cost) you may not be providing for your beneficiary as you desire, and may unknowingly change the tax status of your "estate."

If you can wait, you save money. If your income is not likely to be affected by a short period of sickness or disability, consider the advisability of having your personal accident policy written with a "waiting period" of 7, 14, 21, or 28 days. The difference in premium cost is considerable. You may be more interested in the premium savings that a "waiting period" gives you than in receiving coverage from the first day of disability.

Don't let short-term commitments endanger your family plans. If you take out a loan or add some temporary financial responsibility, be sure to cover it with a low-cost "term" insurance policy for the duration of the commitment. This is also true of a home mortgage. Large numbers of families take out a special policy just to pay off the mortgage if the income producer dies before all payments are finished.

Pay off policy loans and save. If you have any policy loans outstanding, plan to pay them off on some regular basis. As long as they are there, they represent a costly interest and also a lien on your family's insurance protection. They must be met, in the event of your death, before the proceeds are paid out. This may mean, for instance, that a planned $500 monthly income could turn out to be a $300

income for the family because a policy loan was outstanding at death.

Don't overlook the "death costs." Practically everyone will have one fifth or more of the value of what he leaves at death lost to his heirs through "death costs." In big estates this may be a much larger per cent loss. Be sure you have provided enough life insurance to cover these costs: unpaid bills, installment accounts, loans, mortgages, doctor bills, burial costs, taxes; or your other plans may go awry. These death costs must be met first, out of immediate cash, even if property has to be sold to meet them.

Protect the extra needs of your family's younger years. If you have young children, your wife's needs will be greater in the next few years than later. To make sure she can be free to give them the proper care through the early school years, you will want added income for her. For this you might change your regular policy into a "family-income plan" by adding a rider that will give income until 20 years from today of $10 for each $1,000 of insurance, and then pay out full face amount of policy.

SPECIAL CASES

Life insurance has traditionally conjured up a husband and father, but today a wife and mother's death may have equal financial impact on a family. Now is the time for all women to consider life insurance.

If your job or career has a short duration potential, consider stepping up the premium payments now, while your income is larger and more certain, so that they may be smaller, or even eliminated, later.

So you're a pole sitter? There are a few occupations, but just a handful, that stand as a bar to life insurance. Today people in practically every occupation are insurable. If you have difficulty in getting a policy, keep looking and you'll probably find a company to insure you.

If you have a medical impairment, don't give up looking for insurance. Today most companies insure persons in impaired health at an extra premium. Each company has its own standards of qualification. Don't take a single "no" as final. Keep looking and you'll probably find a company to accept you. And remember, if you cut down or eliminate that impairment, your premium will go back to the lower standard rate.

Does the sole proprietor of a business need any special kind of life insurance for his widow? No, the regular life-insurance policies are used to set up his "business insurance needs," but he should be sure, if his plans are to work out, that he leaves a will allowing for his widow's discretion to continue the business, since it may otherwise have to be sold by law.

Business partners beware. If you are a partner in a business enterprise, be certain you have provided through life insurance for both your own and your wife's interests in the event of the death of any partner. Without this protection the entire business equity could be lost or at least badly impaired.

If you want to be sure your children will go to college, you can probably take care of their education if you live. But what if you die before they reach college age? An educational policy will provide a school-year income plus initial expense money if you should die before they reach age 18.

LIFE INSURANCE AND RETIREMENT

Count your life insurance in on retirement planning. Remember that your regular life insurance, used for protection, has large cash values by retirement age. If the needs for protection have been greatly reduced, some of these cash values could be used to buy retirement income. For instance, most straight life policies have about $500 in cash value at age 65 for each $1,000 of insurance.

Plan in terms of income where possible. You'll probably need some life insurance to be paid off "in case." But a large part of your insurance needs are to provide your family with an income. You can often add a much greater total "payoff" for your family by using one of the income "options" in the policies. This also guarantees a regular family income without investment worries.

You can "stretch" your life insurance with an income policy. For instance, a $50,000 policy might provide some $250 monthly for 20 years, which would be $10,000 more in payments than the face amount of the policy.

In recent years the Federal government has allowed two groups of individuals to set up their own pension plans—specifically, individuals whose employers provide no pension plan, and individuals who are self-employed. There are a number of different ways of setting aside money so as to remove it from taxable income, but one possibility is to combine this plan with life insurance. Check with your insurance company or local banks, as such plans must be officially approved to qualify.

Don't gamble with a gamble. If you are setting up a retirement income or family income plan or annuity, don't let yourself reduce the possible income just because you don't like the idea of not getting back at least as much as you put in. Life insurance depends upon averages, and if some get less than average, others get more. You might be the one to get more, much more. By using a plan that guarantees to return at least the amount paid in, or the face amount of the policy, you may cut sharply into the income to be paid.

Don't strait-jacket your beneficiary. If you have any policies on the income plan, be sure loopholes are left to allow the withdrawal of principal in limited amounts. A guaranteed life income of $600 monthly is fine, but it loses much of its advantage if some $6,000 cash emergency arises with no money available. This can easily be met by a release clause, permitting withdrawal of a limited amount of principal from time to time.

INSURANCE AND TAXES

Watch the tax collector. If you add either life insurance or other wealth to your family financial protection program, be sure you haven't pushed up the total of what you own into inheritance or estate-tax brackets, without adding protection to offset that too.

Do you pay an income tax on life-insurance proceeds? No, providing the proceeds are paid by reason of the death of the insured.

Can income taxes on endowment or cash value proceeds be cut? Yes, if an income option is chosen prior to date of maturity, only a small portion (3 per cent of total net cost) is taxable for a great many years.

Are life-insurance premiums deductible for income-tax purposes? Not for Federal income taxes, but for some state income taxes they may be deducted up to a percentage of the policyholder's total income.

Is all life insurance a part of one's "estate" for tax purposes? All life insurance on which premium payments were made by the policyholder or in which he has any ownership interest is a part of that policyholder's estate.

Is life insurance tax-exempt at death? There is a general tax exemption of $60,000 under the Federal Estate Tax, and life insurance is a part of the general estate to which this exemption applies. As for state inheritance taxes, some states exempt life-insurance benefits entirely; others have exemptions of varying amounts.

CAR INSURANCE

Car insurance involves tremendous variables, depending particularly on the individuals and their state requirements. One question, though, should concern everyone: How much is enough? States require minimum coverage in certain categories, but other types are left to you. Ask yourself whether you are under- or overinsured.

One way to save on car insurance is to take higher deductibles on coverage of repairs. This means that you assume higher initial payments and save the insurance for major bills. Many people find considerable savings in this approach.

If you own more than one automobile, insure them all with the same company. Why? You get the advantage of automatic coverage for the additional auto you may someday acquire. (Caution: notice of the additional car must be given to the company within 30 days.)

HOME INSURANCE

Too little or too much insurance? That is the crucial question. You are wasting dollars if your home is insured for an unrealistic value. The basic rule is to keep your house insured for at least 80 per cent of its replacement value.

Every few years you should make an appraisal of your home's value. You need not pay a professional, but you can at least get advice from your insurance agent when your policy comes due for renewal. You might also consider having one of the new "inflation guard endorsements" written into your policy: you pay an extra percentage in premiums, but you get automatic increase in your coverage as home replacement costs increase.

Did you know that your fire-insurance policy may be extended to cover most of the major hazards to which your residence is subject, including windstorm, hail, explosion, riot, falling aircraft vehicles out of control, smudge damage, water damage from plumbing or heating systems, bursting of steam or hot-water pipes, glass breakage, and other perils? Your agent will show you how to do this.

To simplify any claims you might make on damage or loss of your house's contents, take a moment and fill out the inventory (pages 442–443).

INSURANCE RECORD

LIFE INSURANCE POLICIES

Insured's Name	Date of Birth	Beneficiary	Date Issued	Policy No.	Amount	Company

FIRE–BURGLARY–PERSONAL PROPERTY–PUBLIC LIABILITY POLICIES

Policy No.	Amount	Premises or Property Covered	Date Issued	Expires	Agent's Name and Address	Company

AUTOMOBILE INSURANCE

Policy No.	Date Issued	Expires	Amount	Type Policy	Agent's Name and Address	Company

MEDICAL INSURANCE

Contract Holder's Name	Certificate No.	Group No. (If group plan)	Effective Date	Persons Covered	Company

BURIAL PROPERTY

Owner of Record	Cemetery	Section	Lot or Crypt No.	No. of Interment Spaces	Care Provisions

BANK ACCOUNTS

Depositor	Type Account	Account No.	Bank	Address	Date Opened

Note: Check and revise these records from time to time, as necessary. See that you, your family and perhaps a close friend know where original documents and these records are kept. A safety deposit vault is low in cost, very advisable.

HOUSEHOLD INVENTORY

POSSESSIONS	NO. OF PIECES	ORIGINAL COST	DEPRE-CIATION	PRESENT VALUE
Sofas, Couches				
Tables, Chairs				
Desks, Bookcases				
Bureaus, Chests				
Occasional Pieces				
Beds				
Mattresses, Springs				
Lamps and Shades				
Cabinets, Built-ins				
Porch Furniture				
Radios, TV				
Phonographs, Piano				
Books, Records, etc.				
Pictures, Paintings				
Mirrors, Ornaments				
Fireplace Equipment				
Floor Coverings, Rugs				
Hobby Equipment				
Drapes, Curtains				
Slip Covers				
Bedwear, Blankets				
Linens				
Luggage				
Children's Playthings				
Food and Liquor Stocks				

TOTALS THUS FAR . . . .

POSSESSIONS	NO. OF PIECES	ORIGINAL COST	DEPRE-CIATION	PRESENT VALUE
Elec. Appliances (Small)				
Kitchen Applicances (Large)				
Kitchen Utensils				
Cutlery				
Silver, Pewter, etc.				
Clocks				
China, Glassware				
Bric-a-Brac				
Vacuum Cleaners, etc.				
Laundry Equipment				
Garden Equipment				
Women's Clothing				
Men's Clothing				
Children's Clothing				
Furs				
Jewelry				

FINAL TOTALS . . . .

OTHER INSURANCE

Protection away from home. It is wise to make sure that your residence theft policy includes protection against "theft away from premises." This will cover your personal property at hotels, camps, dormitories, fraternity or sorority houses, while traveling, or while residing at a temporary residence. For a small additional charge this "away from home" coverage may be extended to include theft from unattended automobiles.

Big insurance bargain. Experts point out that one of the best insurance "buys" today, and a "must" whether you own a home or rent an apartment, is a comprehensive personal liability policy. This contract insures you and members of your family who live with you against many risks, such as liability for bodily injury to domestic employees and the public in general, damage to others' property occurring on the insured's premises, etc. It also protects you against liabilities arising from your personal activities, including sports; the ownership, maintenance, or use of saddle animals or teams, dogs, small boats (of specified power and length), and bicycles not used for business purposes. Also insures liability that you may have assumed under the terms of a lease for your premises.

Save a half year's premium on your comprehensive liability insurance by renewing it for a 3-year term if now written for only 1 year. The same is approximately true of fire insurance. Furthermore, in most states the 3-year premium may be paid in annual installments.

44

SAFETY AT HOME

Hints for avoiding accidents at major trouble spots around the home

HOW TO PREVENT FIRES

Home fire losses are higher than they should be, in spite of educational and engineering work that's done to prevent them. Here are some basic practices to observe and you'll avoid fire losses.

Smokers should be careful when putting out lighted cigarettes and cigars. Smoking in bed should be absolutely taboo.

Matches should be kept away from younger children and should be used with care by older children and adults.

Furnaces, chimneys, and flues should be inspected and cleaned at least once a year.

Use nonflammable dry-cleaning fluids, and only in well-ventilated rooms. Any other type should not be used inside the house. Gasoline, naphtha, and other flammables should be stored either in the garage or, preferably, in a separate storage building. Use only approved containers.

Combustible waste materials should not be permitted to accumulate in the home, basement, or garage.

Flammable articles such as celluloid and some plastic materials have a low ignition point, burn very rapidly. They should be kept away from flame or heat. Even the heat of a steam radiator may be sufficient to cause ignition.

Rags covered with oil, wax, and paint should be disposed of or kept in approved containers.

Burn trash or rubbish in outdoor fireplaces or metal baskets, away from the house.

When cleaning floors use nonflammable solvents, with the room well ventilated.

A fire alarm could be included in your home with little extra cost and much increase in safety, especially in homes with young children and elderly persons. Alarm bells should ring on the main floor and in each second-floor bedroom.

Fire extinguishers should be placed on each floor, installed between the probable source of flames and the nearest exit. In the basement, place it near the stairs. In the kitchen, near a door. On the second floor, in the hallway near the stairs.

A soda-acid or water-type extinguisher is adequate for ordinary fires of wood, paper, or rubbish.

A foam extinguisher will also handle fires caused by flammable liquids—grease, oil, gasoline, kerosene, and paint.

A small extinguisher of the carbontetrachloride type is advisable for fighting electrical fires and is handy for fires resulting from flammable liquids.

A faucet threaded to take the garden hose is also helpful in fighting fires. Such threaded faucets should be installed in the basement or laundry and outdoors on either side of the house.

TAKE NO CHANCES WITH ELECTRICITY

"Electro-caution" instead of electrocution. It costs you nothing to play safe in caring for electric cords:

1. Watch for signs of wear. Repair or replace worn cords at once.

2. Keep cords away from heat, water, grease.

3. Never handle cords with wet hands. If you must touch a wet cord, protect your hands with a dry cloth or with gloves and wear rubber overshoes or boots.

4. Don't run cords where friction can fray them, especially under rugs, where they may be tripped over, or where weakened insulation might cause fire.

5. Don't let any cord develop a permanent kink. If it must be hung, use two wooden pegs rather than a nail.

6. Never pull on its cord to detach a plug from the wall. This weakens connection between cord and plug. Pull on the body of plug instead.

7. Never use a cord beyond its current-carrying capacity (lamp cord in heating appliance, etc.).

Safety measure for electric cords. To prevent strain on cord when it is pulled from a socket, even though you pull by the plug, wrap rubber tape around the wire, starting close to the end.

Lamp-cord coverings vary in safety. Rayon fabric is least durable, cotton-and-rayon mixture is somewhat better, and solid rubber or plastic is the best.

For safety's sake, avoid permanent use of extension cords.

Bright idea for light bulbs. By joining a light bulb to its socket with Scotch tape you can prevent youngsters from removing the bulb and possibly getting an electric shock.

When lamp or radio is close to electrical outlet there's usually an untidy length of slack wire to create a safety hazard. Wind the cord around a broomstick. Pull the broom away and you have a neat, tight coil of wire that won't be in the way.

A handy spot for storing spare fuses would be a shelf placed near the fuse box itself. Then, when you need to change a fuse in a hurry, there's no confusion or waste of time.

APPLIANCE CARE

Household appliances with exposed gears should have them so enclosed that fingers or clothing will not be caught.

Washer wringers should have guards to prevent fingers from getting into the rolls. The wringer should also have a release device.

Electric fans and heaters should always have metal guards.

Motor-driven appliances should always be stopped when oiling or making repairs.

Defective appliances, switches, and all electrical devices should be repaired promptly.

To avoid danger of overload, additional circuits should be added to take care of electrical apparatus. Major installations should be made by licensed electricians.

AROUND THE HOUSE

Check the danger spots and act quickly. Instead of complaining about dark cellar stairways or leaky drainpipes that create icy spots in winter, do something about them. Give the whole house periodic inspections and take the necessary precautions immediately, instead of waiting until someone gets hurt. Repair materials usually aren't costly; accidents can be very costly.

Safety in home cleaning of furniture, rugs, etc., can be achieved if plenty of fresh air carries off any dangerous fumes. Work outdoors if possible. Otherwise let in plenty of ventilation from open windows. Fan placed near a window helps too. Never use cleaning fluids in an unventilated basement. The vapors can travel a long distance over the floor to the heating unit and start a fire.

When is a chair a hazard? If you stand on it to reach for something on a shelf. Solution: Every home should have a safety ladder. It pays for itself many times over, in accidents avoided.

Highly polished floors need not cause broken legs. Be sure that scatter rugs, and especially small rugs at the foot of stairways, are lined with nonslip rug material.

KITCHEN SAFETY

How to prevent kitchen cuts. Keep sharp knives on wood holders, in plain view, instead of among other utensils in a drawer.

Sharp knives are safe knives. Many more knife cuts occur in the kitchen as a result of dull knives slipping than from sharp ones that do their job efficiently and safely.

Never try to open a can when your hands are wet. In fact, never handle implements with cutting edges unless hands are dry.

When a glass shatters, pick up the pieces with moistened cotton. This will protect your fingers, and even tiniest splinters of glass are caught in the meshes of the cotton.

SOME PRECAUTIONS WITH GAS

Unburned gas contains poisonous carbon monoxide. Care must be taken so flames on ranges aren't extinguished by drafts, liquids boiling over, or other mishaps.

Never sleep in a room where gas is used unless there is good ventilation.

If you smell gas, check the valves. If they're closed, it's best to shut the main valve and call the gas company. The windows should always be opened.

To locate a leak in a gas pipe, brush pipe with thick suds. If hole is present, escaping gas will cause bubbles to form at the leaky spot.

Gas water heaters have safety fuses that blow if the water gets too hot. These can be replaced, but have the gas company check the cause of overheating.

When going on vacation it's best to turn off gas water heaters and turn off your range pilot light if it's not one of the new ones that has electric ignition.

HOME BASEMENTS

Stairs should have handrails and should be well lighted. Paint the lowest step white for maximum safety.

Avoid storing paints and varnishes near heating plant. Gasoline or other fuels should not be kept in the basement. Store them elsewhere, in safe containers.

Mount appliances on a platform if the floor in the laundry or laundry area tends to be damp. Proper grounding of appliances is important.

Rafters and other woodwork near the heating plant should be protected by noncombustible material such as asbestos.

Check furnace pipes that lead to the chimney regularly. They should be in good condition and shielded from flammable materials by metal or asbestos insulation.

SAFE POWER MOWING

The dangers and precautions in using power lawn mowers apply equally to hand models or sitdown models. But there is at least one particular precaution that must be observed with sitdown mowers: if there is anything more than the mildest slope to the area being mowed, do not attempt to move parallel to this slope but mow up and down it. And in general, take every precaution possible to avoid tipping a sitdown mower.

Inspect the lawn to be mowed and clear it of stones, wire, or debris. This protects the mower as well as the operator.

Shoo children and pets before you run your power mower. And don't let them play around the mower even when it's not running.

Stop the motor before you work on it, adjusting its performance or removing objects.

Make sure you know how to disengage the clutch quickly in case of emergencies.

Never leave a mower with its motor running for even the briefest moment.

With hand mowers, be especially sure of the terrain: don't let the machine pull you off balance.

Don't smoke when refilling the mower with fuel, and turn the motor off.

It is advisable not to mow wet grass, both for safety's sake and for the proper functioning of the mower.

45

FIRST AID

For the home. In every home there should be specific first-aid materials, carefully selected, labeled, and kept in a special cabinet or box. This container should be placed well out of the reach of children. If first-aid supplies are kept in the medicine cabinet, a definite part of it should be set aside for the purpose. All boxes and bottles containing a substance that would be poisonous if swallowed should be labeled "poison" and kept on a special shelf.

Precaution for medicine cabinet. To make sure labels don't come off those important medicine bottles, "paint" over the labels and label edges with a layer of colorless nail polish. This protects labels from damage and keeps them easy to read.

Don't be a medicine-cabinet squirrel. Throw out anything that is not currently in use. Old medicine, particularly, can be lethal rather than medicinal if it has too long a shelf life.

FIRST-AID SUPPLIES

A clinical thermometer. For taking temperature.

First-aid dressings. Sterile gauze for wound dressings in sealed packages, bandages to hold compresses in place, and a roll of adhesive plaster. A number of 1-inch compresses on adhesive in individual pages will be found very useful. All these supplies are found in drugstores.

Rubbing alcohol (70 per cent), 1 pint. Use externally to relieve the pain of sprains, strains, bruises, and to refresh the skin during an illness.

Aromatic spirits of ammonia, 2 ounces. One half teaspoonful in some water as a stimulant.

Sodium bicarbonate (baking soda), 4 ounces. To make a solution for use as an eye wash, dissolve 1 scant teaspoonful in a glass of hot water and allow the solution to cool.

Petrolatum, 1 tube.

Sterile castor oil or mineral oil. For use in the eyes. Sterile oil may be obtained in small tubes at drugstores.

Oil of cloves. For toothache.

Mild tincture of iodine. (2 per cent solution) in a bottle with a rubber stopper or individual ampoules.

A hot-water bottle or heating pad, and an ice bag.

Other supplies, such as salt and flour, are found in any kitchen or may be obtained from a drugstore as needed.

For traveling. A small first-aid kit that can be bought from a drugstore will be useful and will occupy little space in a traveling bag. A first-aid kit should always be carried in an automobile and on camping or hiking expeditions.

For small workshops. A metal cabinet containing the following minimum equipment, placed in a conspicuous location and under the definite supervision of some member of the family who has had first-aid training, is suggested:

Individual package-type sterile dressings.

Individual package-type finger dressings, 1½-inch compresses.

Individual package-type 3-inch compresses (also a few 4-by-6-inch).

Assorted gauze roller bandages of various widths.

Triangular bandages.

Tourniquet.

Scissors, pair.

Absorbent cotton, package or roll.

Aromatic spirits of ammonia, individual ampoules.

Iodine, individual ampoules.

Adhesive tape, safety pins, and any special equipment for the particular type of treatment found necessary in certain work accidents.

SOME HANDY HINTS

Ice cubes to the rescue. Removing a splinter from a finger is less painful if an ice cube is held against the injured spot before an "operation." When flesh is thus numbed with cold, you hardly feel anything.

If your doctor prescribes medicine that's unpleasant, don't fret. Hold an ice cube in your mouth for a little while to desensitize your taste buds. Remove the ice and take your medicine with a smile. You'll barely taste it.

Sterile compresses are important in first aid to help prevent infection. So keep a supply in the medicine cabinet at all times. If you should run out and an emergency occurs, use a clean handkerchief or clean cloth. If there's time, press it first with a hot iron to sterilize either handkerchief or cloth.

When filling a hot-water bottle, avoid burning your hand this simple way: flatten the bottle to expel the air in it, then hold it creased while pouring in the hot liquid.

AN ALPHABETICAL LISTING OF COMMON MEDICAL EMERGENCIES

Artificial respiration. Act fast. The mouth-to-mouth technique of artificial respiration is easy to learn and easy to do. It must be given right away when someone stops breathing. This may happen after rescue from drowning, suffocation, electric shock, or gas poisoning.

How to do it. Lay the victim on his back, remove any foreign matter from his mouth, and wipe the inside of the mouth clean with a handkerchief. Proceed as follows:

1. Tilt the victim's head back as far as it will go, with the jaw pushed upward, and open his mouth.

2. Take a deep breath and hold it. Open your mouth and place it firmly over the victim's mouth, pinching his nostrils shut at the same time.

3. Blow your breath forcefully into the victim's mouth. When you see his chest rise, remove your mouth so he can exhale. If the chest doesn't rise, tilt his head farther back and force another breath into his mouth.

4. Repeat the process every three seconds.

The Nielsen method of artificial respiration is also useful. Begin by laying the victim on his stomach with his cheek on his hands. Remove any foreign matter from his mouth. Pull his tongue out. You can do all these things as you put him in position or soon afterward. Have someone call a physician.

Position 1. Kneel on either your right or left knee, or on both, in front of the victim's head. Put your hands—thumbs almost together and fingers spread out—on his back just below his shoulder blades.

Position 2. Rock forward and keep elbows straight. Press slowly and evenly downward on his back, adjusting your pressure to the size of his body. This empties the lungs.

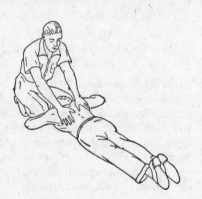

Position 3. Rock back, easing up on the pressure slowly. At the same time take hold of the victim's arms just above the elbows.

Position 4. Lift his arms up toward you until you meet resistance at his shoulders. Raising the arms pulls air into the lungs. Keep your elbows straight while you do it. Then let the victim's arms fall back into place and drop your own arms. Repeat these motions steadily from 10 to 12 times a minute. They should take about 1½ seconds with a short pause in between.

Asphyxiation (breathing stopped). Get patient to fresh air. Send for physician. Start artificial respiration at once (see page 451).

Asthma attack. Remove any constricting clothing, provide a place for the person to lie down, and see that there is proper fresh air. If it is a first attack or exceptionally severe, get person to a physician as soon as possible.

Bite from animal. Wash wound with soap under running water and take victim to doctor at once. Have the animal caught alive so that it can be tested for rabies.

Bleeding. If it is a light flow from a surface wound, wash thoroughly with water, then cover with a sterile bandage. If flow is more severe, press *hard* with a sterile bandage directly over the wound until bleeding stops, then fasten a clean bandage in place. If bleeding persists, keep pressing hard over the wound and transport the victim as quickly as possible to a hospital or to a physician for the application of a tourniquet: the improper use of a tourniquet by untrained people can sometimes cause more harm than good.

Boils. These result from infection within the hair follicles or pores of the skin. The infection causes redness, swelling, and pain. The germs responsible are especially apt to get a foothold on skin surface constantly irritated by the rubbing of clothing—the neck, armpits, and buttocks, for example. Do not squeeze a boil or pimple, as this may spread the infection. Hot saltwater applications may be used to relieve pain and to help in bringing the boil to a head. A doctor should always be consulted for a severe boil. Successive outcroppings of boils may accompany a systemic disease, particularly diabetes.

Bruises. A bruise is an injury usually caused by a fall or a blow. The skin is not broken, but the tissues under the skin are injured, resulting in the breaking of small blood vessels. Pain, swelling, and black-and-blue marks occur. A black eye is a bruise. Apply cloths wrung out of cold water or ice packs to relieve the pain and swelling. If the blow was severe, have a doctor examine the injured person.

Burns.

Mild burns (skin unbroken, no blisters). Hold burned part under cold running water for 2 to 3 minutes. If pain persists, apply petroleum jelly or mild burn ointment and bandage.

Severe burns. Send for physician. Apply wet sterile compresses. Do not break blisters or try to clean burn. Keep patient quiet and comfortably warm until the doctor arrives.

Chemical burns. These are caused by strong acids and alkalies. Immediately strip off all clothing that has come in contact with the chemical and flood the skin with large quantities of clean water. Then give first aid according to the depth and extent of the burn. If there has been delay in giving first aid, don't use water. Get medical aid at once.

Cardiac arrest (heart attack).

Heart attack is a term popularly used to describe several conditions, but in all cases it calls for immediate professional help. The victim should not be moved (unless he is in a dangerous place) and an ambulance should be summoned. Keep the victim calm and administer oxygen if available.

In severe cases, the victim may lose consciousness and the heart stop. Until relatively recently, this usually condemned the victim to death unless professional help and equipment appeared instantly. But increasing numbers of people now owe their lives to emergency administration of cardiac massage—often by nonprofessionals. Clearly, it is recommended only as a last resort, but the massage is given as follows: The heel of one hand is placed on the bottom third of the breastbone; the heel of the other hand is pressed down on it with a force that moves the breastbone about 2 inches toward the spine. (Do not apply pressure on the ribs.) The hands are then relaxed to allow the chest to expand, and this alternate compression and expansion is maintained at about 35–40 times per minute and until the pulse is restored. If there is a second person available to help, mouth-to-mouth resuscitation (see ARTIFICIAL RESPIRATION, page 451) should also be given simultaneously; otherwise a single massager should stop about every 30 seconds to administer four deep breaths to the victim.

Choking. A relatively new way of helping people who are known for sure to be choking on food or some foreign object is known as the Heimlich maneuver (after its developer, Dr. Henry J. Heimlich).

But anyone planning to administer this aid must be positive of the causes of strangulation, for a person suffering a heart attack can exhibit much the same symptoms and the maneuver might be fatal if administered to such a victim.

To perform the maneuver, the rescuer stands behind the victim and clasps his hands firmly over the victim's abdomen, just below the victim's rib cage. The rescuer makes a fist with one hand and places his other hand over the clenched fist. Then the rescuer forces his fist suddenly and sharply inward and upward against the victim's diaphragm. If the food does not pop out on the first try, the maneuver should be repeated until the air passage is unblocked. If the victim cannot stand, he should be placed on his back on the floor; the rescuer kneels astride him and uses the heel of one open hand instead of the clenched fist, placing the other hand over the first and then pressing upward (toward victim's head) quickly to compress the lungs.

A person alone and choking on food can also press his own fist into the abdomen or force the edge of a chair or sink against his abdomen.

Convulsions. Place the patient face up on a rug or bed where he can't hurt himself. Loosen clothing. If the convulsions subside within a minute or so, there is little else to be done. If the person's mouth is open, you might place a wad of cloth between the jaws while raising and pulling the lower jaw forward. But do nothing to interfere with his breathing, and never force anything into his mouth. If the convulsions seem to subside and then go on again, or if they continue for more than a few minutes, call for a doctor.

Croup. This is most commonly a childhood condition in its serious form. A croup attack is characterized by a hoarse, barking cough, with choking spasms (and sometimes a mild fever). Prompt exposure to a mechanical vaporizer or humidifier is called for. Or improvise a croup tent by boiling water on a hotplate under a blanket draped over a chair: but an adult must be present at all times. Another alternative is to take a child into a bathroom, close the door and windows, and let hot water from the shower and/or sink taps run until room is filled with steam.

Cuts. Wash minor cuts with soap under warm running water. Apply mild antiseptic and sterile compress. Apply right-size adhesive tape and gauze covering, preferably of the waterproof kind, so cut stays clean as it heals.

Drowning. See ARTIFICIAL RESPIRATION, page 451.

Ear problems.

Earache. A doctor should be consulted as soon as possible for earache or for a discharging ear. Loss of hearing or mastoid infection may result if you neglect this. If there is delay in getting a doctor, the pain may be relieved by applying an ice bag or hot-water bottle.

Foreign objects. Children sometimes put small objects into their ears. Don't put water or other liquid into the ear, since it causes some objects, such as beans, to swell, making their removal difficult. Occasionally an insect enters the ear. To stop its buzzing it can be killed by putting a drop or two of castor oil or sweet oil into the ear. Plugs of wax formed within the ear canal may also give trouble. In every case have the object removed by a doctor. Don't try to do it yourself by using sharp instruments such as matches, toothpicks, or hairpins.

Electric shock. Turn off electric power if possible. Don't touch patient until contact is broken. Pull him from contact, using rope, wooden pole, or loop of dry cloth. If breathing has stopped, start artificial respiration. Send for physician.

Epileptic attack: See CONVULSIONS, page 455.

Eye problems. The eyes are such important and delicate parts that no chances should be taken in a medical emergency: professional help should be sought as soon as possible. But until such help is available, there are some things that may be done.

Wounds of eye. If the eye is wounded by a foreign body, such as a splinter of glass, metal, or wood, or by a particle blown into it with great force, loosely bandage both eyes and get medical aid at once. Keep the victim lying down until the doctor arrives.

If acid, lime, or other chemical enters the eye, immediately wash out with great quantities of clean water. Don't use water, however, if there has been any delay in giving first aid. In any case, send for the doctor at once.

Foreign bodies in eye. If object can be seen, touch it lightly with moistened corner of handkerchief. If object does not come out after two or three attempts, or if it cannot be seen, take patient to physician. Never rub the eye, as this may force the foreign body in even deeper.

If you splash an irritating liquid in your eye, wash eye first with cool tap water, then drop a little mineral oil into your eye with an eye dropper. If the pain persists, or if substance splashed was acid or caustic, see a doctor.

Sties. These are infections of a small gland opening at the edge of the eyelid. Irritating the eyelids by frequent rubbing, as a person suffering from fatigue may do, paves the way for the development of sties. Compresses wet with hot water will help to bring a sty to a head. Continue hot applications until the sty opens and discharges spontaneously. Do not squeeze. If sties occur in crops, a doctor should be consulted.

Fainting. If patient feels faint, seat him and fan his face. Lower head to knees. If he becomes unconscious, lay him on his back with coat or blanket under hips. Loosen clothing. Open windows. Wave smelling salts or aromatic spirits of ammonia under nose. After consciousness returns, keep patient lying quiet for at least 15 minutes. If faint lasts for more than a few minutes, send for the doctor.

Falls. If patient complains of continued pain, send for physician. Stop severe bleeding if it is present and cover wound with sterile dressing. Keep patient as warm and comfortable as possible. If a broken bone is suspected, don't move patient unless absolutely necessary (as in case of fire, etc.).

Firearm accident. A surface bullet wound accompanied by bleeding should be covered with sterile gauze and the flow of blood stopped. *Do not* try to clean the wound, but contact a doctor at once for further instructions. If the wound is internal, call an ambulance at once; meantime, keep the victim lying down and warmly wrapped, and if respiration is impaired, give mouth-to-mouth resuscitation (see ARTIFICIAL RESPIRATION, page 451).

Frostbite. This occurs when a part of the body is frozen. Signs of frostbite are a lighter skin color, coldness, and numbness of the flesh. The victim should be taken indoors, into a warm room, if available, and given a warm drink.

Warm the frozen part as rapidly as possible by placing it in a basin or tub of lukewarm water—not hot—or by wrapping it in blankets until thawing occurs. Avoid exposure to heat from a stove, hotwater bottle, heating pad, or hot lamp. Handle the frozen part very gently to prevent further injury. Don't rub the area, since tissues are easily torn or bruised. If it isn't possible to bring the victim indoors, cover the frozen part carefully with wool or other clothing or with a warm hand or some other part of the body until circulation is restored.

Heat exhaustion. This condition may occur during protracted heat waves or in foundries, kitchens, bakeries, engine rooms, and similar places where heavy work is done in high temperatures. The victim is very pale, his skin cold and moist, his breathing rapid and shallow, and his pulse weak and rapid. The body temperature may be subnormal or slightly elevated. The victim is usually conscious.

What to do. Call a doctor. Lay the victim in a reclining position in a cool, quiet place. Loosen his clothing. Keep him comfortably warm with blankets or coats placed under and over him. If conscious, give him a stimulant—tea, coffee, or aromatic spirits of ammonia (½ teaspoon in ½ glass of water). It may also be helpful to give him sips of salt water (1 teaspoonful of salt to a pint of water).

Heart attack. See CARDIAC ARREST, page 454.

Insect bites. The bite or sting of such insects as bees, mosquitoes, flies, wasps, or spiders often causes swelling and inflammation. To relieve the discomfort, apply weak ammonia water or a paste of baking soda and water.

Nose problems.

Nosebleed. Slight nosebleed does no harm and usually stops by itself. If bleeding continues, put the victim in a chair and loosen his collar. Apply cloths wrung out in cold water over his nose. Pressing the nostril on the bleeding side against the central partition of the nose for 4 to 5 minutes may help. Plugging the nostril with a bit of cotton or gauze may also help. If bleeding doesn't stop in a few minutes, call a doctor. Don't blow the nose for a while after the bleeding stops.

Foreign objects. Children may poke small objects up the nose as well as into the ears. If the object is one likely to swell (a bean or a grain of corn), a few drops of olive oil or mineral oil will relieve the swelling and irritation. Take the child to a doctor at once. The nose may be blown, but not forcibly and not with one nostril closed.

Plant poisoning. Skin poisoning occurs in most people after direct contact with any part of the poison ivy, poison oak, or poison sumac. Within a few hours to several days the skin becomes red and swollen, and an eruption of blisters occurs, accompanied by painful itching and

burning. In severe cases fever may be present.

Prevention. The only sure way to escape poisoning by these plants is to stay away from them. After exposure, poisoning can often be prevented by washing the exposed skin areas thoroughly with yellow laundry soap and water followed by an application of rubbing alcohol.

Poison ivy (common east of the Rocky Mountains) grows as a vine or low shrub. It has leaves divided into three leaflets and has grayish-white berries in season.

Poison-ivy extract, administered by a doctor, in some instances may give temporary immunity against ivy poisoning.

Eradication of poison ivy and poison oak is made possible now by the development of chemical weed killers (ammonium sulfamate and 2,4-D) sold under various trade names. Ammonium sulfamate destroys both poison ivy and poison oak; 2,4-D kills the whole poison-ivy plant, roots and all. Directions for applying the chemicals are on their containers.

Poison oak. Poison oak, a vine or bush common on the Pacific Coast, has leaves divided into three leaflets.

Poison sumac (a low tree found in bog lands) has a compound leaf of from 7 to 13 leaflets and pale, waxy berries in season.

To relieve skin poisoning, any of the following applications may be applied:

1. Calamine lotion or pyribenzamine ointment (available in drugstore).

2. Compresses soaked in cold baking soda or Epsom-salts solution.

3. A 5 per cent solution of ferric chloride, applied with a cotton sponge and allowed to dry on the skin. (Lemon juice will remove the ferric-chloride stain.)

4. Zirconium in ointment form has recently been found effective in some cases.

In severe cases of ivy, oak, or sumac poisoning, see a doctor.

Poison swallowed by mouth. Call a doctor at once. But until professional help is available, use the antidote recommended on the label of the container. If the victim is conscious, try to find out the exact substance swallowed. If it is one of the poisons listed in the following section, use the antidote recommended. If the poison is classified as an acid or caustic alkali—see below—do not induce vomiting, but follow the directions. If it is not an acid or caustic alkali and the victim is conscious, but the exact nature of the poison is unknown, give the universal antidote obtainable at the nearest pharmacy, or substitute burned toast, milk of magnesia, or strong tea.

Acids or caustic alkalies.

Strong acids. Hydrochloric, nitric, sulphuric, etc.

Caustic alkalies. Ammonia, caustic lime (quicklime), caustic acid, caustic potash, lye, etc.

When a strong acid or caustic alkali in a concentrated form has been swallowed, the victim's lips, mouth, and tongue are stained and burned. Usually it is unwise to force vomiting if the poison was taken in concentrated form, for fear of rupturing the corroded walls of the esophagus and stomach. After diluting and neutralizing the poison as described below, give a soothing drink, such as a wineglassful of olive oil, a glass of milk, or flour and water.

To dilute and neutralize swallowed acids, give 2 glassfuls of diluted milk of magnesia, or 2 tablespoonfuls of baking soda in a pint of water, or finely divided chalk in water, or lime in water.

To dilute and neutralize swallowed alkalies, give a wineglassful of vinegar or the juice of 4 lemons in a pint of water.

INDUCING VOMITING.

Emetics that are easy to prepare:

1. Warm salt water: 1 tablespoonful of table salt to 1 glass of warm water

2. Soapy water: a piece of mild soap shaken up in warm water to make good suds.

If neither substance causes vomiting, a cup of warm water containing 1 teaspoonful of dry mustard may be given.

Vomiting should be induced repeatedly until the fluid coming from the stomach is clear. If it is necessary to induce vomiting after the person has had several glassfuls of the emetic, tickle the back of the throat.

ANTIDOTES FOR COMMON POISONS.

Arsenic and materials containing arsenic (insect poison, rat poison, Paris green, etc.). Induce vomiting repeatedly by giving several glassfuls of an emetic. Meanwhile, send to the drugstore for freshly prepared hydrated oxide of iron and magnesia, the official arsenic antidote. When it comes, give the victim a wineglassful and induce vomiting again.

Barbiturates (sleep-inducing drugs —allonal, amytal, barbital, phenobarbital, etc.). If the victim is conscious, induce vomiting by giving several glassfuls of an emetic. If the victim is unconscious (in a coma or stupor), keep him warm until the doctor arrives. Give artificial respiration if breathing stops. Injections of picrotoxin or metrazol may be helpful in the coma stage, but they can be administered only by a doctor.

Bichloride of mercury (corrosive sublimate). Give the whites of from 3 to 5 eggs immediately, and then induce vomiting repeatedly by giving an emetic.

Carbolic acid (phenol and preparations containing it). Immediately give soapsuds or 2 tablespoons of Epsom salts in a pint of water, and follow with enough lukewarm water to induce vomiting. Then give flour and water to soothe the injured tissues. Don't give oils or fats. Burns on the skin caused by carbolic acid should be washed with large amounts of running water.

Iodine. Give several glassfuls of a thin paste of cornstarch and water or flour in water and induce vomiting until the vomited material no longer has a blue color.

Kerosene. Induce vomiting by giving several glassfuls of an emetic. Then give a dose of Epsom salts. If the stomach is emptied immediately, no serious complications are likely to occur. However, if the kerosene is breathed into the lungs, the results may be serious. Hence it is extremely important to warn the victim to inhale as little as possible while vomiting.

Opium and its preparations (codeine, laudanum, morphine, paregoric, soothing syrups, etc.). If the victim is conscious, induce vomiting by giving several glassfuls of an emetic. Do everything possible to keep him awake. Wash his face with cold water, keep him moving, but not to the point of exhaustion, and give quantities of strong black coffee. If the victim is unconscious, keep him warm until the doctor arrives. Give artificial respiration if breathing stops.

Phosphorus (rat poisons that contain phosphorus). Induce vomiting by giving several glassfuls of an emetic. If copper sulphate is on hand or can be obtained quickly from a drugstore, a weak solution consisting of a scant penknifepointful of copper sulphate (3 grains in a tumbler of water should be given every 15 minutes until vomiting occurs. The copper sulphate forms a coating over the phosphorus so that it can't be absorbed. Then give lukewarm water and induce vomiting again to get the coated phosphorus out of the stomach. Do not give oils or fats.

Salts of fluorides, barium carbonate, or thallium sulphate (rat poisons that contain any of these substances). Induce vomiting by giving an emetic. Call a doctor at once. No specific antidote is known.

Strychnine (nux vomica, medicines, and vermin-killers containing strychnine). The prevention of convulsions is the main object of first-aid treatment. If it is possible to obtain powdered active charcoal (bone black) from a drugstore, give 1 tablespoonful stirred into water. Keep the victim very quiet in a dark room. Do not give an emetic or a stimulant, because doing this is apt to bring on convulsions.

Wood and denatured alcohol. Induce vomiting by giving an emetic. Follow with bicarbonate of soda (2 teaspoonfuls in 1 pint of warm water). Continue to induce vomiting until there is no odor of alcohol on the breath. Then place the patient in a dark room and give a glass of milk to which 1 teaspoonful of bicarbonate of soda has been added.

Shock. This condition, characterized by inadequate blood supply, may result from any one of several causes, such as loss of blood, extreme pain or fright, an allergy, a heart condition, etc. A doctor should be called immediately. See to it that the patient lies on his back, his head slightly lower than his feet. Loosen any constricting clothing and cover the patient enough to keep him warm but not hot.

Snakebite. The bite of a poisonous snake must be treated by professionals at once, but if such help is not immediately at hand, keep the victim still and lying down, with the wounded part lower than the rest of the body. Tie a constricting band above the wound—between it and the heart—tight enough to slow but not stop blood circulation. Sterilize a knife or razor blade in a flame; make shallow cuts in the wound, deep enough to draw blood; then suck out the venom as rapidly as possible (it is not toxic if swallowed); keep this up until swelling subsides or professional help arrives.

Sprains. When ligaments supporting a joint of connecting bones are torn, a sprain is the result. There is pain, swelling, and usually discoloration. What seems like a bad sprain may be a fracture. A doctor should be called, therefore, unless a sprain is slight.

What to do. Raise the injured joint, so it will get less blood. Apply cold cloths or ice packs for several hours. As the swelling recedes, hot applications are beneficial in hastening return of the tissues to normal. Gentle massage also is helpful.

Strains. A strain is like a sprain, but it is the muscles, not the ligaments, that are injured. Relieve the pain by putting the part to rest. The application of heat and light massage (rubbing the limb upward and toward the body) are helpful. For a severe strain consult a doctor.

Sunburn. This may be treated like any other mild burn characterized by reddened skin or surface blisters. Petrolatum or olive oil may lessen the discomfort. If sunburn is severe or the victim feels sick, consult a doctor. Sunburn usually can be prevented by applying a protective preparation to the skin before exposure or if a protective coat of tan is acquired by frequent short exposures.

Sunstroke. Despite its apparently mild name, this is a life-or-death emergency. Although a doctor should be called, no time should be lost in cooling the victim.

Sunstroke symptoms: The victim feels dizzy, sometimes becomes nauseated, and has acute pain in the head. In true heatstroke or sunstroke these symptoms are rapidly followed by unconsciousness. The victim's skin is dry and hot and his face red or purple. He has stopped sweating. He breathes with difficulty, his pulse is rapid, and he has a high fever.

What to do. Call a doctor. If possible, immerse the victim fully in cold water. Give no stimulants. If immersion is not possible, remove him to a cool, shady place. Lay him on his back and remove as much clothing as possible. Apply an ice bag or cold cloths (iced, if possible) to his head. To reduce his temperature, wrap him in a sheet and spray or sprinkle it repeatedly with cold water, or sponge his body with cold water. Do anything you can to lower his body temperature until professional help can be summoned.

Tick bites. The tick is a blood-sucking insect prevalent in the spring and summer. It is responsible for the spread of several serious diseases, including Rocky Mountain spotted fever. The danger of infection is somewhat lessened by the early removal of the tick. The tick pierces the skin and fastens upon the flesh with a small, toothed probe on its head. In removing the tick, make sure that the probe doesn't break off and remain embedded in the tissues. The insect may be induced to withdraw its probe by holding a hot needle or a lighted cigarette near its rear end, or with cotton or cleansing tissue moistened by alcohol. Then pick up the tick with forceps, tweezers, or a bit of cotton held between the fingers, and destroy it. Don't crush the tick between your bare fingers. After removal of the tick, paint the wound with iodine.

Unconsciousness. Keep the patient warm and lying down. Send for physician. If breathing stops, give artificial respiration. Never give an unconscious person food or liquids.

INDEX

Accordion pleats, 264
Acetate, 222, 233
Acids: burns, 454; in eyes, 456; stains, 232, 234, 235; swallowed, 459, 460
Acne, carrot paste for, 205
Acorn, baked, 46
Adhesive tape: as first aid supply, 450, 451; stains, 235, 359
African violets, 370, 372
Air purifiers, 309–10
Alcohol: rubbing, first aid, 450; wood or denatured, antidote for, 461
Alcoholic beverage stains, 235–36, 240, 243, 315
Alkalies (alkaline solutions), 234, 312; burns, 454; care in using, 234, 312; stains, 232, 233, 234, 312; swallowed, first aid for, 459
Almonds, 11, 103, 111
Alphabet book ends, 342
Aluminum: care and cleaning, 144, 249, 302; containers for freezing food, 131; luggage, 249; pans, 144
Aluminum foil, uses for: cooking and food, 8, 9, 10, 18–19, 34, 47, 101, 131, 142–44, 149; decoration, 149; ironing clothes, 266–67; reflecting heat, 395
Angel-food cake, 72, 74, 94, 102
Animal bites, first aid, 453
Animal urine stains, 460
Antidotes for poisons, 460
Antiquing gilt frames, 341
Ant repellents, 121, 358
Apple(s), 104, 158; applesauce, 107; baked, 107, 143; -ball sauce, 107; dumplings, nippy, 93; -mince pie, 88; pies, 87–88
Appliqué embroidery, 284–85
Apricot-cheese pie, 88
Armchair slip covers, 337–39
Arsenic, antidote for, 460
Artificial respiration, 451
Ashtrays, cleaning, 302
Asparagus, 46, 49, 58, 156
Asphyxiation, 453
Aspics, 35, 41–42
Automobile care and maintenance, 403–14
Avocado, 158; cocktail dip, 407; growing, 372; -honey facial mask, 206; and leftover turkey, 107; mayonnaise, 107; side

dish, 108–9; soup topping, 63
Awnings, care of, 386
Axle grease stains, 26

Babies (see also Children): bowed legs, 180–81; child care, 288–92; clothing, 288–90; diapers, 288; food, 136; head shape, 180; pacifiers, 288; posture, 180; shoes, 181, 290–91; weighing, 289
Bacon, 3, 11, 13–14, 46, 58
Baggage (luggage), 244–50
Baking (baked), 64–69; acorn or butternut squash, 46, 47; Alaska, 76; apples, 107, 143; beans, 43–44; breads, biscuits, rolls, 64–69; cakes, 70–81; chicken, 18–19; egg volume and, 142; fish, 32–33, 34; freezing and, 129; ham, 7, 8; kidney beans, 43–44; nutrients, 160–61; pies, 82–91
Baking powder (baking soda), uses for, 71, 91, 147, 207, 450; measuring, 71; two speeds, 71
Balloon cake, 77
Bananas, 158; desserts, 76, 92, 101; storing, 107
Banks (banking services), 426–32; loans, 426–27, 435; by mail, 421
Barbiturate antidotes, 460
Basements: heating, 391, 392, 399; lighting, 402; rumpus room, 391; safety, 448
Basil, 122–23
Batteries, car, 404, 408–10
Bay leaf, 123
Beans, 43–45, 58, 156
Beds (bedsteads, bedding), 298–99; drawer space, 342; mattresses, 298–99; sheets, 225, 269, 298; slip covers, 337, 339
Beef, 1–2, 4–5 (see also Meat): broiling, 8–9; carving, 23–26; chopped, 11–12; chuck, 1, 4–5; cooking, 1–2, 4–5; cuts, 1; gravy, 13–14; leftovers, 12–13; nutrients, 155; rib roast, 4; roasting, 7–8; stew, 10–11; storing, 14–15; -and-vegetable chowder, 60
Beets, 37, 38, 156; borsch, 61, 63; growing, 370
Begonia, wax, 370, 374
Belts, car, 405
Berries (see also specific kinds): freezing, 107,

108; nutrients, 158, 160
Beverages, 112–17, 162; stains, 315. See also specific kinds
Birthday cakes, 77, 291
Biscuits, 66–67, 160
Bites, first aid for, 453, 461, 462
Black-and-white creams, 92
Black bean soup, 44, 60, 63
Blackheads, 185, 202
Blankets, 224, 226, 298
Blanket stitch, 281
Bleeding, first aid, 453
Blemishes, skin, 186, 201, 205
Blocking: crocheting, 274; knitting, 277; pressing clothes and, 266
Blood stains, 236, 315
Blouses, 222, 246, 266
Blueberry pie, 88
Blue-cheese pinwheels, 53
Bluing, 225; stains, 236
Boils, 453
Bonds, care of, 417, 418
Books, care of, 303, 360
Bookshelves, hanging, 335
Borage, 123
Borax, 223, 224, 301
Borsch, 61, 63
Boston baked beans, 43
Bowed legs, 180–81
Box lunches, 119–20
Braised meat, 2, 3, 10
Bras, use of, 181–82
Brass(ware): care of, 302; enamel painting, 348
Brazil nuts, 111
Bread, 64–65, 160; canapés, 68; crumbs, rolling, 65; flour, 64; freezing, 129; keeping fresh, 64, 65; pudding, 65; sandwiches, 118–20; slicing, 65; spreads, 118–19; sticks, 62, 67
Breathing emergencies, 451–54
Brides and bridesmaids, 202
Bridge cookies, 99
Brioche, 66
Broccoli, 39, 41, 46, 156; and potato casserole, 48
Broiling, 8–9, 136, 142–43, 165; cleanup and, 137, 138; meat, 1, 8–9; pan, 9–10; poultry, 19; seafood, 32
Broken glass, handling, 448
Bruises, first aid, 453
Budgeting, money and, 417–25
Bulbs, electric, 401, 446
Bullion stitch, 283
Burns: first aid, 454, 462; sunburn, 462
Bust measurement, sewing and, 253, 255, 257

Butter, 53–54, 71, 75; spreading, 54, 118; stains, 236, 315; storing, 53
Butterfly cakes, 77, 78
Butternut squash, 46, 47
Buttonholes, 265, 282
Buttons, 208, 290; problems, 208; "self-covered," 264; sewing and, 264–65, 268

Cabbage, 40, 157, 370
Cable stitch, 276
Café au lait, 114
Cakes, 70–81, 160–61; baking hints, 73–74, 78–79; birthday, 77, 291; cupcakes, 78; cutting, 79–81; flour and baking powder, 71; ice cream, four-layer, 102; measurements, 70–71; mixes, 70; oven, 73; pans, 72, 73; party (special occasions), 77–78; pastry bags, 75–76; plates for, 79; special-shaped, 72; toppings (frostings), 74–76
Calories, 151ff., 154ff.
Canapés, 68
Candles, 358, 369; cleaning, 303; decorative, 303, 358, 369; dripless and droopless, 148, 358; wax stains, 236, 241, 318
Candy, 162; stains, 236, 318
Can openers, 50, 148, 448
Capers, 123
Capons, 17
Caraway leaves and seeds, 123
Carbohydrates, 152, 153, 154
Carbolic acid antidote, 460
Carbon paper stains, 236
Cardiac arrest, 454
Carpets (see also Rugs); sweepers, 304, 311
Carport storage, 344
Carrots, 38, 39, 40, 157, 370; juice stains, 237; paste for acne, 205
Carving meat, 23–27, 144
Casserole(s), 165; bacon and lima bean, 58; black-eye peas in, 44; cleaning, 146; soups and, 57–58; squash, 46–47
Casting stitches, 274–75
Cats. See Animals; Pets
Catsup stains, 237
Cauliflower, 41, 45, 46, 48
Caustics, first aid, 454, 459
Ceilings, 321, 346, 353
Celery, 37, 39, 40, 57
Cellars: repairs, 388; steps, cleaning, 310
Celsius scale, 174, 177
Cement: concrete (see Concrete); household, 317, 383
Ceramic: bathroom tiles, 383; figurine decorations, 341
Certified checks, 429
Chain stitch, 210; crocheting, 271–74; knitting, 280
Chairs, 295, 333, 335–39, 447
Chalk, and picnic ants, 121
Chamois: for cleaning Venetian blinds, 308; removing stiffness from, 304
Chapped hands, 189
Checkers (cookies), 99
Checking accounts, 426, 427–32
Cheese, 52–53, 154; -apricot pie, 88; -chicken chowder, 60; cutting, 52; and fruit, 53; fruit cheesecake, 76; grating, 52; as meat stretcher, 53; mold, removing, 52; pinwheels, 53; pudding, 53; puffs, 53; serving temperature, 52; sticks, 53; storing, 52; Welsh rarebit, 53
Chemical burns, 454
Chemicals in eyes, 456
Cherries: freezing, 108; ice-cream dessert, 103
Chewing gum stains, 237
Chicken, 16–22; baking, 18–19; broiling, 19; buying, 16–17; carving, 26–27; -cheese chowder, 60; cooking, 16–22; cooking outdoors, 121; -corn chowder, 60; deep-fat frying and freezing, 19; fricasseeing, 20; frozen, 16–17; gravy, easy, 62; gumbo soup meal, 57; herbs and, 21; oven-barbecued, 19; roasting, 17, 20, 21; sautéing, 19; soups, 57, 58, 59, 61; stewing, 19–20; storing, 21; stuffings, 20–21
Chiffon pies, 88–89, 90
Children, 288–298 (see also Babies; Teen-agers); child care, 288–92; clothing and shoes, 289–91; croup, 455; and flower gardening, 367; furniture, 292–93; games and toys, 291–92; and housecleaning, 293; insurance protection and education, 436, 437; nutrition, 154; personal appearance, 179–81; safety at home, 445, 446, 449
Chili: con carne, 61;

lima-bean, 44
Chimney and flues, maintenance of, 394–95, 396, 397
China, care of, 300–1, 356
Chives, 63, 123
Chlorine bleaches, 220–21; for stains, 232
Chocolate, 115; cake frostings, 74; cakes, testing for doneness, 73; chiffon pie, 88–89; cookies, no-bake, 98; eggnog, 116; freezing and thawing, 90; frosted, 116; hot, 115; iced coffee with, 114; malted milk, 116; mocha, iced, 115; mousse, 95; parfait, 102; puddings, 95; soufflé, 95; stains, 237; velvety frosting, 74; whipped cream, 74–75; whipped-cream cake, 76
Choking, first aid, 454–55
Cigarettes (cigars): burns and stains, 295, 357–58; fire safety, 445; freezer storage, 133; smoke disperser, 357–58
Citrus fruits, 105–6; drinks, 117; nutrients, 159
Clams, 28–31, 34, 60
Cleaning tips (see also Stains; specific items, kinds): furnace chimney and flues, 394–95, 397, 398; furniture and furnishings, 294–303 (see also specific items); house, 304–10 (see also Housecleaning); laundering and dry-cleaning, 218–27; rugs and carpets, 311–18
Clothes (clothing, wardrobe), 207–17 (see also specific kinds, problems, uses); accessory variations, 207; baggage weight, 245, 246; care and selecting, shopping, 207–10; children and teen-agers, 288–90; cleaning, 208, 211–12, 218–31; colors, 203–5, 209–10; figure-flattering, 209–11; hanging, 212–13; laundering, cleaning, ironing, 281–31, 232–43, 265–67; luggage care and packing, 244–50; make-up and, 203–5; mothproofing and storage, 212–13; personal appearance and, 180, 181–82, 203–5, 213–14; rainy-day, 217; sewing,

210, 251–69; spots and
stains, 232–43
Clothespins and
clotheslines, 226
Coal-burning furnaces,
396–98
Coats, 208–10, 212, 217
Cocoa, 115, 118; stains, 237
Cod-liver oil stains, 237
Coffee, 112–14; beans,
freezing, 133; café au lait,
114; decaffeinated, 114;
grinding, 113; iced, 114,
133; instant, 113–14;
keeping fresh, 113;
making, 113, 114; stains,
237; substitutes, 114
Collars: attached, sewing,
264; turning, 268
Cologne, 199, 200, 310
Colored fabrics, shrinking
to sew, 251–52
Colors, home redecorating
and, 319–27
Colors, wardrobe (clothes),
207, 208–10; care in
washing, 225; cleaning
and, 218–19, 220, 225;
make-up and, 203–5;
stains, 233, 234, 235;
testing, 208, 233
Compost pile, 363–64
Compote: defined, 166;
fresh grapefruit, 105–6
Comprehensive personal
liability insurance, 444
Compresses, first-aid, 450
Concrete (cement): house
foundations, 388–89;
paint spills on, 35;
patches, 389, 390;
quick-setting, 389;
railings in, 390; stone or
brick walls, pointing, 389;
walks or driveways,
389–90
Contact lenses, 194
Convulsions, 455
Cookbooks, 149; rack, 149
Cookies, 97–101, 161;
refrigerator, 100;
roll-and-cut, 99
Cooking, 1–15, 16–22,
28–38; appliances,
134–40; carving, 23–27;
definitions, 164–73; heat
conservation, 135–37;
herbs and, 122–24; home
freezers and, 125–33;
kitchen hints, 141–49;
measures and weights,
174–76; nutrition and,
150–63; outdoor, 121;
temperatures, 134–35
Corduroys, 223, 261, 267
Corks: cutouts, 341;
making, 143; stuck, 143,
359
Corn, 38–39, 49; growing,
370; "milk" for skin care,

205; nutrients, 157;
popcorn, 49, 62–63;
soups, 60
Corn muffins, 67
Corns and calluses, 190
Cornstarch pudding, 95
Cosmetic stains, 315
Cottons: laundering,
221–22, 228–31, 267;
scorch, 229; shrinking to
sew, 251–52; stains, 233
Court Bouillon, 166;
poached fish in, 33
Crabs, 28, 30, 31, 35
Cranberries, 44, 104
Crayon stains, 237
Cream: cakes, 76–77;
-cheese spread, 53;
curdling, avoiding, 52;
desserts, 92, 93; prune,
93; sauce, for peas and
string beans, 48; souring,
142; stains, 238; whipped
(see Whipped cream)
Crocheting, 270–74
Crockpots, 140
Croup, 455
Croutons, 62
Crown roast, defined, 166
Crow's-feet, 193
Cucumber(s), 41, 63; facial
mask, 206; mock
eggplant, 46; nutrients,
157
Cupcakes, 78, 129
Curdling, preventing, 52, 76
Curtains (see also
Draperies): laundering,
225–27, 297–98; mending,
269; rings, 332; ruffles,
tie-back, 332; shower,
299; shrinking, 297
Custard, 96; curdled, 76;
garnish for soup, 63;
no-bake, 96; sauce, 96
Cutouts, decorative, 341–42
Cuts, first aid for, 455
Cutting tools, care of, 379
Cutwork (embroidery), 282

Dairy products, 51–54 (see
also specific kinds); home
freezer storage timetable,
128; storing, 51
Dandruff treatment, 206
Darning, 268–69, 277–78
Defrosting: home freezers,
132–33; refrigerators,
132–33, 137
Dents, removing, 356
Deodorants (see also
Odors; Perspiration): and
clothing care, 211–12
Desks, 292, 335, 359
Desserts (sweets), 92–103;
cakes, 70–81; cookies,
97–101; custards, gelatins,
and puddings, 95–97;
freezing, 129; fruits, nuts,
and jellies, 104–11;

ice-cream, 101–3;
nutrients, 154, 162–63;
pies, 82–91
Devil's-food sandwich cake,
68
Diapers, 288
Diet (dieting). See
Nutrition
Dietetic food, 152
Dogs. See Animals; Pets
Doors: added storage, 342,
343, 344; auto, noisy, 409;
care and repair, 381–82;
locks (see Locks);
painting, 348; winterizing,
399
Double crochet stitch, 272;
short, 272; treble, 273
Doughnuts, 93
Drains (drainpipes):
clogged, 147, 384; and
house foundations, 389;
leaks, 383
Draperies, 330–32;
cleaning, 297; color
choosing chart, 322–25;
fabrics, 330–31; home
redecorating and, 322–25,
330–32; making, 331–32;
pleats, 331
Dream pudding, 95
Dressers (chests), 294, 316,
318, 334–35, 360–61
Dresses, 207, 253–56, 290;
baggage weight, 246;
hems, 210, 262–63;
ironing, 229, 266–67;
packing, 246; sewing and
measurements, 252ff.
Dressing alcove, 329
Dressings (stuffings), 162;
fish, 33; giblet, 20, 21;
low-calorie, 108; orange
(for duck), 20–21; pork
sausage, 20; salad, 41,
108, 162, 242; stains, 242
Drills (tools), 379, 383
Drip coffeemakers, 113
Driveways, 363, 389–90
Drop cookies, 99–100
Dry-cleaning, 221–23;
fluids, care in use of, 445,
447; slip covers, 297;
stains, 235, 242–43;
washing vs. (fabric
chart), 221–23
Dry-flour gravy, 13
Dry skin, care of, 184, 198
Duck, 17–18; orange
stuffing, 20–21; roast,
17–18
Dumplings: mincemeat, 93;
nippy apple, 93
Dusting powder, use of, 198
Dyes and dyeing (see also
Colors): bleaching out,
234; care in washing
fabrics and, 225;
leather-goods, 216; stains,
233, 234; stockings, 214

Ears, care of, 186–87; problems, first aid, 455–56
Earthenware, 201
Education insurance, 437
Eels, 35–36; smoked, 29
Eggnogs, 115–16
Eggplant, 317; mock, 46
Eggs, 54–56; beaters, cleaning, 146; cartons as storage containers, 360; Chinese omelet, 60–61; cookery, 55; and milk drinks, 115–16; nutrients, 154; shampoos, 206; shells as fertilizers, 371; simmering, 55; and soup, 58; stains, 238, 301; starting seeds in shells, 372; volume in baking, 142
Elbows: care of, 197, 198; clothes, reinforcing, 210, 268–69
Electric cords, 230, 446
Electricity: care and safety, 446–47; first aid for shock, 456; and home heating, 391–98; kitchen appliances (see Electric kitchen appliances); lights (see Lights); overload dangers, 447; repairs, 384–85; utility and service costs, 399–402
Electric kitchen appliances, 112, 139–40 (see also specific kinds); ranges (see Electric ranges); repairs, 384–85; utility costs and efficient use of, 399–402
Electric ranges (ovens), 134–38; care and cleaning, 135, 137–38, 142; microwave, 139; portable, 139; saving on heat, 135–37; temperature checking, 134–35; timers and alarms, 135; wiring and utility costs, 400
Embroidery, 278–87; appliqué, 284; basic stitches, 279–83; decorative borders, 287; eyelets, 284; faggoting, 285; ironing, 228; quilting, 287; repairs, 210; smocking, 285; stitches, 279–83, 286; tassels, 286; threads and yarns, 278; trapunto, 285–86
Emetics, 359–60
Enamelware: cleaning, 137–38, 146; "seasoning," 144
Epilepsy. See Convulsions
Epsom salts, for setting colors in wash, 225
Eyes: and eyebrows, care

of, 182, 192–94, 196, 201; glasses and contact lenses, 194, 357; problems, first aid for, 454, 456; strain in child, 293

Fabric luggage, care of, 248
Fabrics (see also specific kinds): for babies, 289; burns and stains, 295, 357, 359; clothing and (see Fabrics, clothing); drapes, curtains, and slip covers, 297–98, 330–32, 335–39; floor covers (see Rugs); home decorating, 319, 330–31, 335–39; needles for, 261; patterns and, 256–57; "pilling," 351; preshrinking, 251–52; pressing and ironing, 266–67; sewing, 251–52, 256–57, 260–61, 264, 266; stains, 357
Fabrics, clothing, 207, 208–9, 210, 216, 218–31, 233–43; care, cleaning, and ironing, 216, 218–31; sewing and, 251–52, 256–57, 260–61, 264, 266; spots and stains, 232–43; washing or dry-cleaning, kinds and methods, 221–22
Face, care of, 182–84ff., 191–99, 201–2, 203, 205
Fahrenheit scale, 174, 177
Fainting, 457
Falls, first aid for, 457
Family records, 433, 434
Fats (oils), 49–50, 162–63; in common foods, 162–63; removing from soup, 57; stains, 236, 237, 239, 240, 241, 315; storing, 49–50
Faucets, 147; leaks, 383
Feathering out stains, 235
Feet, care of, 181, 190–91, 200, 357
Fertilizers, 364–65, 371
Fiberglass luggage, 249
Finger mark stains, 307
Fingernails, care of, 189
Fire, picnic, 121
Firearm accidents, 457
Fire extinguishers, 446
Fire-insurance policies, 439
Fireplaces: gardens, 372; safety, 393; uses, 306, 355, 372, 392–93
Fire prevention, 445–48; first aid, 454
First aid, medical emergencies and, 450–62; alphabetical listing, 451–62; supplies, 450–51
Fish, 28–36; chowder, 60, 63; cooking, 32–36; fishing handyman tips,

361; freezing, 128; local descriptive terms, 29–30; nutrients, 28, 156; odors, 145–46, 147; slime stains, 238
Flashing, for leaks, 388
Flashlights, 379–80
Flatirons, as book ends, 342
Floors: accidents and safety, 447; care, cleaning, and repair of, 308–9, 310, 382–83; coverings, 311–18, 322–25; painting, 349–50; stains, 238, 308–9, 313–18, 351
Flour, 64; all-purpose, 82; bread, kinds, 64; cake, kinds, measuring, 71; mixing liquids with, 142; nutrients, 160–61; -paste gravy, 13; pie, 82
Flowerpots, painting, 349
Flowers and plants, 367–71ff.
Fluorescent tubes, 385
Flushing out stains, 235
Fly repellent, 358
Food, 150–63 (see also Cooking); definitions, 164–73; freezing (see Freezing food; Home freezers); kitchen hints, 141–49; measures and weights, 174–77; nutrition (dieting), 150–63; stains, 236–43 passim; storage period table, 127
Foreign bodies in eyes, 456
Foreign objects in ears, 456
Foundation cracks, 388–89
Four-layer ice-cream cake, 102
Fowl (see also Poultry; specific kinds): carving, 26
Frankfurters, 62, 121
Freezing food: baked goods, 64, 78, 79; chicken, 16, 17, 119; cooking and, 45–46; fish, 30, 31; fruit, 107–8, 127, 132; home freezers for, 125–33; meat, 14–15; milk, 51; sandwiches, 119; vegetables, 38, 45
French bread, 65, 67
French pleats, drapery, 331
Frostbite, 457
Frostings, cake, 74–76, 79, 94
Frozen locks, 379; auto, 410
Frozen peach whip, 94–95
Frozen pipes, 384
Fruit juices, 104, 105, 159; stains, 238, 315
Fruits, 104–11 (see also specific kinds): basket (dessert), 94; cake,

storing, 79; cheese and, 53; cheesecake, 76; cobbler, 93; cooling and freezing, 107–8, 127, 132; drinks, warm-weather, 116–17; gelatin desserts, 96–97; jellies and jams, 109–11; juices (see Fruit juices); medley mold, 109; nutrients, 158, 159; pies, 87–88, 90, 132; rice, 94; salads, 108–9; storage, 123

Fudge frosting, 74

Fuel conservation: auto, 407; cooking, 135–37; heating, 391–92, 393, 394, 396–97; refrigerators, 138; utilities and services, 399

Furnaces, 393–98; cleaning, 394–95, 397, 398; safety, 445, 448

Furniture (furnishings), 294–303, 333–35 (see also specific kinds, problems, uses); care, cleaning, and precautions, 294–303, 447; children's, 292–93; color choosing chart, 322–25; home redecorating and, 319, 322–25, 333–39; insurance inventory, 442–43; moving for housecleaning, 304–5; painting, 348, 349

Furs, 133; protecting, 213; sewing, 262; yellow, 357

Fuses, 384, 399, 447

Galoshes, 217, 291, 360

Games (toys), 289, 291–92

Gardening, 362–77, 444–48; fireplace, 372; flowers, 367ff.; house plants, 370–77; landscaping, 362–63; lawns and ground covers, 362, 363, 365–67; patios and walks, 373; safe mowing, 444–48; soil and, 363–65; temperature, light, and humidity, 368, 370–71, 372–77; tools and storage, 372–73; trees and shrubs, 362, 363, 365–66; vegetables, 363, 370; watering, 366, 371

Garlic, 123–24

Gas: cooking, 134–38; heating, 391–98, 448; leaks, 134–38; precautions, 448

Gas ranges (ovens), 134–38

Gates, care of, 373, 390

Gelatin (desserts), 95, 96–97, 101, 109, 162; fruits in, 96–97, 109; ice cream, 101; molds, 96;

nutrients, 162; in salad molds, 41–42

Giblet dressing, 20, 21

Gift wrappings, 148, 291

Ginger-ale cream, 116

Gingerbread, 93–94

Glass windows, 385–86, 393

Glassware: broken, 448; care and cleaning, 299–300; containers, 147–48; freezer jars, 120, 130; mending, 356

Glazes, baked ham, 8

Gloves, 121, 189, 214; fingertip repairs, 214; stains, 234; stretching, 214; suede freshener, 351; washing, drying, 224, 227

Glue: bottles, opening, 356; homemade, 380; stains, 238; working, 380

Golden fruit salad, 108

Goose, roasting, 17–18

Government checks and bonds, safeguarding, 416–17, 418

Graham-cracker crust, 85

Grapefruit, 159; compote, 105

Grapes, frosted, 106

Grass, 366, 448; stains, 238

Gravies, 13, 21, 61–62; lumpy, 13–14, 140; stains, 239

Grease, in drains, 147, 384

Grease and oil stains, 145, 236, 239, 240, 241, 307

Grease solvent, 232

Green beans, 43, 46, 47, 48

Grilled sandwiches, 118

Hair, appearance and care of, 181–87 passim, 192–93, 200, 201, 206, 207

Ham, 3, 6–7, 8, 14, 25, 62, 63; carving, 25; storing, 14

Hamburgers, 11–12, 53, 132

Hand irons, 228–31

Handkerchiefs, washing, 223

Hands, care of, 188–90, 197

Handyman tips, 355–61, 378–90; safety and, 378–79

Hangers, clothing, 212; as pot-holder hooks, 149

Hanging bookshelves, 335

Hardware, care and storage of, 379, 380

Hard water, 220, 384; test for, 220

Hats, 181, 207, 209, 213–14

Hawaiian pudding, 95

Heart attacks, 454

Heat exhaustion, 457

Heating the home, 391–98; coal burners, 396–98; cutting costs, 391–97; fireplaces, 392–93;

maintaining the furnace, 393–94; oil burners, 396; steam and hot water systems, 395–96; thermostat settings, 391, 392; winterizing, 393

Heat marks, table-top, 295

Heimlich maneuver, 454–55

Hems, 210, 262–63, 284

Herbs, 122–24; kinds, guide, 122–24; and poultry, 21

Hobbies and sports handyman tips, 361

Hollandaise sauce, 48

Home freezers, 125–33; advantages, 125–26; defrosting, 132–33; recommended food storage time table, 127

Home insurance, 439–44

Home redecorating, 319–44; carpets and rugs, 327; choosing basic color scheme, 319–21; color choosing chart, 322–25; decoration tips, 341–42; drapes and curtains, 330–32; fireplaces, 328; furniture, 322–25, 333–35; lights and lamps, 339–40; painting and wallpapering, 321–27, 345–54; pictures, 340–41; screens and partitions, 327–28; space and storage room, 342–44; windows and window shades, 328–33

Honey, 92; -avocado facial mask, 206

Hot-cross buns, 65

Hot-water bags and bottles, 356, 451

Housecleaning, 294–303, 304–10; furniture and furnishings, 294–303; linoleum, 309; moving furniture, 304–5; vacuum cleaners, 305–6; walls, 306–7; windows and Venetian blinds, 308; wooden floors, 308–9; woodwork, 387

House repairs and maintenance, 378–90; awnings, 386; bathroom, 383; cellars, 388; doors, 381; electricity, 384–85; floors, 382; foundations, 388; nails and screws, 380; plaster work, 381; plumbing, 383–84; roofs, 387–88; safety and, 378–79; sidings, 386; stairs, 382; tools, 379; walks and drives, 389–90; windows, 385

Ice (ice cubes), 116, 120, 131, 138–39; coffee and tea, 133; to desensitize skin and taste buds, 451
Ice cream, 76, 101–3; stains, 316; storing 102
Inks, 359; spots and stains, 239, 307, 316, 359
Insects: bites, 458; repellents, 347, 358
Insulation, heating, 393
Insurance, 433–44; auto, 439, 441; fire (home), 439–44; life, 433–39, 440; personal liability, 444; records and inventories, 433, 440–43; and retirement, 437–38; and taxes, 438–39
Iodine: first aid, 450, 460; stains, 239, 316–17
Ironing, 221–22, 227–31, 245, 265–67, 297; boards, 229–30, 231, 245, 266; pressing and, 265–66
Iron rust stains, 239
Ironware, cleaning, 302

Jellies and jams, 109–11, 162
Joints, pipe leaks, 384

Kerosene antidote, 460
Keys, 356, 359. See also Locks
Kidney beans, baked, 43–44
Kitchen (household) appliances, 134–40; care and cleaning, 144–47; cooking, 139–40; electric (see Electric kitchen appliances); ranges (ovens), 134–38; refrigeration, 125–33, 138–39; safety and, 447
Kitchen hints, 141–49; safety, 447–48; terms, 164–73
Knees, care of, 190; clothing, 210, 268–69
Knitting, 274–78; lace, 277; stitches, 274–75
Knives, 79; care of, 140, 144; safety, 447–48

Lace, 223, 227, 277
Lacquer stains, 239–40
Ladders, 378, 447
Lamb, 2–3, 5, 10–11, 26, 155
Lamps (lampshades), 303, 339–40, 356, 401; care, 303, 401; safety, 356, 446–47
Laundering, 218–31; color care, 225; crocheting, 274; drapes, curtains, and slip covers, 297–98; vs. dry-cleaning (fabric chart), 221–23;

equipment, 219; hanging and drying, 225–26, 227; safety, 447, 448
Lawns, 362, 363, 365–67; safe mowing, 448–49
Layer cakes, 72, 80; cutting, 76; lemon cream, 76
Lead pencil stains, 240
Leaks, gas, 448
Leaks, water, 382, 383–84, 387–89, 396, 398
Leather: care of, 214–17, 224, 227, 248–49, 295, 303; dyeing, 296; stains, 216
Leftovers, uses for, 12–13, 35, 48, 57–58, 65, 66, 119; fruits and juices, 104; meat, 12–13
Leg of lamb, 3, 5, 26
Legs, care of, 180–81, 190–91; bowed, 180–81
Legumes. See Beans
Lemonade, 117, 159
Lemon juice, 105; hair bleach, 206; shoeshine, 215
Lemons, 105, 106; cakes and pies, 76, 87; for cleaning pots, 145, 146
Lentil soup, 62
Lettuce, 40, 119, 157, 370; growing, 370; kinds, 40
Liability insurance, 444
Life-insurance policies, 433–39, 440; beneficiaries, 435, 438; common disaster clause, 435; "death costs," 436; interest on, 435; kinds, 433–35; loans and, 435, 436; premiums, 433, 435, 440; and retirement, 437–38; taxes and, 438–39; term, 433–35; and wills, 435
Lights (lighting), 399, 400, 401–2, 446–47, 448; auto, 403; costs, 339, 400, 401–2; electrical repairs, 356, 384–85; indirect, 340; safety and, 446–48
Lima beans, 38, 43, 44, 58; and bacon casserole, 58; chili, 44; with mushrooms, 44
Linen(s), 251–52, 298, 342; laundering, 221, 222, 229, 267
Lingerie, 223, 246
Linings (fabric), 208–10, 233, 235, 263; luggage, 249; stains, 233, 235
Linseed oil: paint thinner, 351; stains, 240
Lint, 211, 229, 260
Lips, care of, 194–95, 198
Lipstick, 194–95, 198, 201, 203–4, 240, 358; stains, 240

Liquids, measuring, 144, 174
Loaf cakes, cutting, 81
Loans, bank, 426–27
Lobsters, 28, 30–32, 35
Locks, care of, 379, 382; auto, 409–10; frozen, 379, 410; sticking, 410
Low-calorie dressings, 108
Lubrication stains, 235
Luggage, 245, 246, 248–50
Lunches, box, 119–20

Machine oil, 260; stains, 240
Make-up, 191–99; for camera or TV, 199; for teen-agers, 200–2; wardrobe and fashion colors and, 203–5
Malted milk, chocolate, 116
Malt topping, ice-cream, 103
Maps, as decoration, 341
Marjoram, 124
Mascara, 193; stains, 240
Mats, bathroom, 299
Mats, picture, 341
Mattresses, 298–99
Mayonnaise, 119; avocado, 107; stains, 240
Measurements (sizes), sewing clothes and, 252–57
Measures and weights, 174–76, 412–14
Measuring liquids, 144, 174
Meat, 1–15, 155 (see also Beef; Ham; Lamb; Pork; Veal); -ball garnish, 63; braising, 10; broiling, 8–10; carving, 23–27; cuts 1, 2, 3; extenders 12, 53; freezing (table), 128; frozen, 14, 15; gravies, 13–14; leftover, 12–13; loaf, 12, 13; -and-mushroom muffins, 12; pan-frying, 10; roasting, 7–8; sandwiches, 119; slow simmering, 11; stains, 240; stew, 10–11; stock, 13; storing, 14–15; variety, 7; -and vegetable shortening, 82
Medical emergencies, first aid for, 450–62; alphabetical listing, 451–62; supplies, 450–51
Medicines, poisoning and antidotes for, 460–61
Medicine stains, 317
Melon balls, 106
Mending tips, 267–69; "invisible," 268, 277; knitting, 277–78
Meringue pies, 86–87
Metric system, equivalents and conversion tables, 174, 175, 176, 412–14

Microwave ovens, 139
Mildew stains, 216, 226, 240
Milk, 51–52, 141; boiling, 51; cartons, uses for, 120, 346; dry, 141; and egg drink, 115–16; evaporated, 51, 52, 141; frozen, 51; nutrients, 154; souring, 142; stains, 241, 316; storage, 51
Mince-apple pie, 88
Mincemeat: dumplings, 93; flaming, 103
Mineral acid stains, 234
Mineral oil, and stains, 240
Minnows, bait, 361
Mint, facial, 205
Mint cocoa, iced, 115
Minted cake, 77
Mirrors, "resilvering," 299
Mixes: biscuit, 67; cake, 70; cookie, 97
Mocha: iced chocolate, 115; peach cream, 95
Mock: eggplant, 46; pumpkin pie, 88
Molds: defined, 170; for gelatin desserts, 96; vegetable salads, 41–42
Money management, 415–25; banks, 426–32; budgeting, 417–25; burned or mutilated bills, 415–16; insurance and, 433–44
Mops, cleaning, 304, 306
Mortgages, insurance on, 436
Mothproofing: clothes, 213; furniture, 295; rugs, 311
Mousetraps, 358
Mousse au chocolat, 95
Mouth-to-mouth artificial respiration, 451–52
Moving aids, 360–61
Mucilage stains, 238
Mud stains, 241
Muffins, 148; corn, 67; English, 67; meat-and-mushroom, 12, -pan rolls, 69
Mulching, 365
Murals, wallpaper, 326
Mushroom(s), 40–41; chowder, 60; cream soups, 57, 58, 59, 60, 62; disks, in salad, 40; lima beans with, 44; -and-meat muffins, 12
Mustard stains, 241

Nail polish: envelope adhesive, 359; stains, 241, 317
Nails (fingernails), 189–90
Nails and screws, use of, 292, 361, 378, 380, 381
Narcissus bulbs, 367

Neck (throat) care, 187, 197
Needlecrafts, 270–87
Needles, 259, 261, 267, 276, 277, 278; kinds, 267; sharpening and care of, 261; threading, 259, 267
Newspaper, uses for, 355, 360
Nielsen method of artificial respiration, 452–53
Nitrogen fertilizer, 364–65
No-bake: cookies, 98; custard, 96; graham crust, 85
Nose, care of, 186, 193, 196; problems, first aid, 458
Nutrition (and dieting), 150–63; nutrients in common foods, 153–63; requirements and basic food groups, 150–51; weight loss and gain and, 151–53
Nuts, 85, 103, 156, 158
Nylon: fabrics, 261, 262, 267; laundering, 222, 224, 267; sewing, 261, 262; stockings, 214–15

Oats, quick, leftover, 48
Odors: air purifiers, 309–10; baking, 34; cleaning fluid safety and, 447; cooking, 145–46, 147; fish, 30, 33, 34, 145–46; freezing food and, 132; gas, 448; hands, 147; kitchen utensils, 145–46; laundry, 220; oil of lavender for, 358; onions, 39, 145–46, 147; paint, 346; refrigerator, 138, 142; sinks, 147; smoke, dispersing, 358; vinegar for, 358
Oil, auto, 405, 407, 410–11
Oil and grease stains, 236, 237, 239, 240, 241, 317
Oil burners, 391, 396
Oiling floors, 308, 309
Olive oil, 49; for dandruff, 206
1-2-3 pie, 88
Onions, 39, 46, 157, 370; juice, 39; odors, 39, 145–46, 147
Opium, antidote for, 460
Orange(s), 105, 106, 159; duck stuffing, 20–21; fizz, 105; fluff, 92; milk shake, 116; peel flavoring, 106; whipped-cream frosting, 75
Orangeade, 117
Orange juice, 105, 117, 159
Oregano, 124
Outside storage units, 344
Ovens (ranges), 134–38;

care and cleaning, 134, 137–38, 142; electric, 134–38, 139, 142, 400; gas, 134–38; microwave, 139; portable, 139; saving on, 135–37, 400; shelf for cookout grill, 121; temperature checking, 134–35; temperatures (conversion table), 177; timers and alarms, 135
Oysters, 28, 31, 34–35

Pacifiers, use of, 288
Packing, 359–60; moving aids, 360–61; storing tips, 359–60; and unpacking luggage (clothing), 244–50
Painting (paint), 345–51; brush control, 348–49; cleanup, 351; color choosing chart, 322–25; equipment, 350–52; exterior, 350; home redecorating and, 321–27, 334; roller, 346; safety, 448; stains, 317; storage, 448; straight lines, 349; window screens, 386
Pancakes, 61, 91, 148; raspberry, 91
Pan-fried: fish, 33; meat, 10
Panned vegetables, 47
Pans, use and care of, 136, 137, 143–46; cake, 72, 73; greasing, 86; pie, 86
Paraffin stains, 236, 241
Parchment shades, 303
Parsley, 38, 39, 124, 133; chopping, 39, 142
Pastry, defined, 170
Pastry bag, 170; for cake frostings, 75; making, 75–76
Pastry brush, care of, 145
Patio, and gardening, 373
Patterns, measurements and sewing and, 252–59; for slip covers, 335–36
Peaches(es) : cake, 76; fluff, 94; frozen whip, 94–95; ice cream, 101; mocha cream, 95; nutrients, 159
Peanut(s), 156; brittle ice cream, 103; butter sandwiches, 118–19
Peas, 38, 43, 44, 46, 48, 157; soup, 61, 62, 63
Pectin, use of, 109, 111
Peppers, 157, 370; stuffed, 47, 50
Perfumes, 245; stains, 241
Permanent-wave solution stains, 357
Personal appearance, 178–206; clothing and fashion colors, 203–5, 209–10; face, 182–84ff.,

191–99, 201–2, 203, 205–6; hair (see Hair); make-up, 191–99, 200–5; skin care, 184–88
Personal liability insurance, 444
Perspiration: clothing, 208, 211–12, 241; stains, 247
Petits fours, 77
Pets: bites, 453; food, 129; hairs from bath, 358; shedding, 295; urine stains, 314–15
Pewter, care of, 302
Phenol, antidote for, 460
Philodendron, 370, 376
Phosphorus antidotes, 460–61
Photo development tips, 361
Pianos, 334; care of, 294–95; and eyestrain, 293
Picnic tips, 120–21
Pictures, wall, 340–41
Pies, 82–91; apricot-cheese, 88; blueberry, 88; chocolate-chiffon, 88; crusts, 82–85; deep-dish apple, 88; freezing and thawing, 89–90; instant apple, 87; meringue shells, 86; mince-apple, 88; mock pumpkin, 88; shaping, edgings, 84; shortening, 82; storage, 90–91; strawberry-rhubarb, 88; trellis, 84–85
Pillows (pillowcases): laundering, 224, 225; transferring feathers, 269
Pimiento cream soup topping, 63
Pinch pleats, drapery, 331
Pineapple, 106, 129, 131, 132, 161; cake, 77; -shrimp salad, 108
Pinwheel cookies, 98
Pizza, kitchenette, 67
Planked fish, 34
Plant (skin) poisons. See Skin poisons, plant
Plants. See Gardening
Plaster repair, 302, 356, 381
Plastic stains, 242
Pleats, 229, 264, 331
Plumbing repairs, 383–84
Poaching fish, 33
Pointing stone or brick walls, 389
Poisons, antidotes for, 458
Polyurethane floors, 382
Popcorn, 49, 62–63
Pork, 3, 5–7, 155; chop suey, 6; cuts, 3; roast, 5–6, 7, 25, 61; sausage dressing, 20; steaks, 6; storing, 14–15
Posture, appearance and, 177

Potash fertilizer, 364, 365
Potatoes, 42–43, 46, 48, 49, 136, 143; mashers, cleaning, 146; nutrients, 157; skins, use of, 49, 137
Pot holders, 149, 269
Pot roast, 4, 5, 13, 24
Pots, cleaning, 145–46, 302
Poultry, 16–22, 155; baking, 18–19; carving, 26–27; chicken (see Chicken); cooking, 17–20; duck, 17, 20; fried, 19; frozen, 16; giblet dressing, 21; goose, 17; roasting, 17–18, 20; storing, 17–18, 20; stuffings, 20–21; turkey (see Turkey)
Preshrunk fabrics, 251–52
Press cloth, use of, 266–67
Pressing: clothes, 265–67; crocheting, 224; drapes, 297; "directional," 266; knitting, 277
Property insurance, 439–44
Prune cream, 93
Pudding, 93–96, 97; bread, 65; cake, 77; cheese, 53; chocolate soufflé, 95; cornstarch, 95; dream, 95; Hawaiian, 95; mousse au chocolat, 95
Pumpkin pie, "mock," 88
Punch: rhubarb, 117; tea, 117
Purée, 171; fruit, 107

Quilting, 287

Radiators, auto, 405–6
Radiators, steam, 395–96
Rainbow bath, 291
Rainwear, 217
Raspberry pancakes, 91
Rat poison antidotes, 460–61
Rayon: laundering, 222, 267; stains, 233, 234
Records, restoring shape to, 361
Refrigerator cookies, 100
Refrigerators, 126, 138–39; defrosting, 132–33, 139; deodorizing, 138, 142
Relaxation (exercises), 178
Resin stains, 242
Retirement insurance, 437
Rhubarb: flip, 116–17; -strawberry pie, 88; tea punch, 117
Ribbing, 275
Rib roast, 1, 2, 4, 23–24
Rice, 45, 46, 161
Roasts (roasting), 1–6 passim, 12–14, 17–18, 155; carving, 23–24, 25, 26–27; leftovers, 12; method, 7–8; storing, 14
Roll-away toy boxes, 292
Rollers, paint, 346

Rolls, 64, 65–66, 69, 161
Roly-poly (cake), 78
Roof work, 378–79, 387–88
Roquefort cheese, 53
Roses: crocheted, 274; knitted, 277
Rouge, 190, 195–97, 204; stains, 242
Rubber cement use of, 356–57
Rubber footwear, 217, 291, 360
Rubber stains, 242, 309
Rugs: care and cleaning, 311–18, 447; color choosing chart, 322–25; curling, 356; home redecorating and, 322–25, 327; pads, 327, 355; safety, 447; stains, kinds, 239, 313–18
Rust stains, 146, 239, 317, 340, 361, 379

Safe-deposit boxes, 427
Safety precautions, 378–79; basements, 448; children, 288, 289–91, 293; cleaning materials, 232, 234; electricity, 339–40, 356, 446–47; fire-prevention, 445–46; first aid and, 450–62; gas, 448; kitchen, 447–48; power mowers, 448
Salads, fruit, 108–9; dressings, 41, 108, 162
Salads, vegetable, 39–42; dressings, 41, 108, 162, 242
Salt, 65, 143–44, 145; for setting colors, 225; sweet flavors enhanced by, 105
Sanding floors, 382
Sandpaper, uses, 348, 356
Sandwich(es), 118–20; bread for, 119; cake, 68, 98, 102; cutting, 119; frozen, 129; grilled, 118; spreads, 118–19; storing, 119
Sardine three-decker, 68
Sausage, 155; pork dressing, 20
Sauté(ing), 1, 2, 19, 33
Scales, kitchen, 144
Scallops, 31, 32
Scissors (shears), 50, 268
Scorch, ironing, 229; stains, removing, 242
Scratches (nicks): floor, 309; furniture, 296; glass, 300; mirror, 299; woodwork, 307
Screens, 327–28, 386, 393
Seams, long, ripping, 268
Seasonings, herbs as, 122–24
Seeds, 366–67, 370, 372

Serge, lint or shine on, 211
Series E bonds, 417, 418
Service and utility costs, saving on, 399–402
Seven-layer sandwich, 68
Seven-minute cake frosting, 74
Sewing, 251–69; altering patterns, 257–59; basting and hems, 262–63; buttons and buttonholes, 264–65; drapes, 331–32; fabric basics, 251–52; measurements and fittings, 252–57; mending tricks, 267–69; pins, threads, and needles, 261–62; pleats and other stitches, 264; pressing and ironing, 265–67; slip covers, 335–39; zippers, 265
Sewing machines, 259–61, 335
Shampoo, dandruff, 206
Shampoos, rug, 312
Shelf-door storage, 343–44
Shellac, uses for, 290–91, 295, 299, 303, 306–7, 341, 347, 358, 385
Shellac stains, 317
Shellfish, 28–32, 34, 156
Sherbet, 101, 162
Sherry eggnog, 116
Shingles, care of, 387
Shirts: laundering, 223, 225, 229; numbering, 212; packing, 246
Shock, first aid for, 461
Shoelaces, 217, 291
Shoe polish, 296, 355, 361; stains, 242, 317–18
Shoes, 181, 215–17, 246; buying, 215, 289, 290–91; care and repairs, 190, 215, 356; packing, 246, 247; rack, 342; rubber, 217, 291, 360; storing, 246, 247
Shortcake, 77; strawberry, 93
Shortening, 70–72, 82; measuring, 70–71
Shoulder measurements, sewing and, 253, 255, 257–58
Shoulders, care of, 198
Shower curtains, 299
Shrimp, 28, 30–32, 35; Bombay, 61; cooking, 32, 35; -pineapple salad, 108; and soup meals, 57, 59, 61
Shrinking: adding length after, 297; curtains, 297; fabrics for sewing, 251
Siding repairs, 386–87
Sieves (colanders), uses for, 148, 166, 172
Silks, care of, 221–22, 267
Silver, care of, 142, 301
Simmer(ing), 2, 3, 11, 19

Sink odors, 147
Sizing stains, 235
Skillets, 139, 144, 302
Skin care, 184–88; blemishes, 186, 201, 205; homemade beauty preparations, 205; make-up, 191–99; wardrobe and, 204–5
Skin poisons, plant, 458–59; ivy, 458; oak, 458; sumac, 458
Skirts, 207; packing, 245; pressing, 229, 266; sewing, 256, 258–59, 263–64
Slate garden walk, 373
Sleeve ironing board, 231
Slip covers, 297, 335–39
Slips, 208; seams, 208
Smocking embroidery, 285
Smoke disperser, 357–58
Smoked meats, 14–15, 132
Smoke stains, fireplace, 306
Snakebite, 461
Snap fasteners, drape, 297
Snowballs (dessert), 102
Snow suits, babies', 289–90
Social Security checks, safe-guarding, 416
Sodium bicarbonate, as an eye wash, 450
Sofa slip covers, 335–39
Soft drink stains, 315
Soil, garden, 363–65, 367, 370–72ff.; acid or alkaline, pH and, 363
Soot: cleaning, 395, 397; stains, 242
Soundproofing sickrooms, 358
Soup, 57–63; borsch, 61; chili con carne, 61; chowders, 60, 63; cold, 59; "company," 59; in gravies, 61; as a meal, 57–59; nutrients, 163; omelet with, 60; for party dips, 59–60; pea, 61; removing fat, 57; scrambles, 58–59; shrimp Bombay, 61; stock, 57; toppings (accompaniments), 62–63; vichyssoise (make-believe), 61
Souring milk or cream, 142
Spices, for baking, 79
Spider plant, 370, 376
Spinach, 39, 46, 157; and waffles, 48
Splinters, first aid for, 451
Sponge cake, 72, 74, 79
Spools, thread, 261, 262
Spotting, 235
Sprains, 461–62
Square cakes, cutting, 81
Squash, 34, 46, 158; butternut baked, 46, 47; casserole, 46; pie, 88
Squid, 36

Stains and spots, removing, 232–43 (see also specific items, kinds); fabrics and methods, 233–34; kit for, 232; specific kinds and directions (listed), 235–43; terms used in, 235
Stairs (steps): care and repair of, 310, 349, 382–83; safety precautions, 448
Standing rib roast, 2, 4; carving, 23–24
Star cake, 76
Steaks, carving, 24
Steam and hot-water systems, 395–96
Steam irons, 228, 230–31
Sties, eye, 456
Stitches: chain, 210; crochet, 271–74; embroidery, 279–83; 286; knitting, 274–75; sewing clothes and, 264; space-filling, 286
Stockings (hosiery), 190, 214–15, 223–24, 226–27, 276, 304
Stoles, 181, 207
Storage tips, 359–60 (see also specific items); adding space at home, 342–44; clothing, 212–13; fire and safety, 445, 447; food, home freezers and, 125–33; luggage and accessories, 249–50; meat, 14
Storm windows and doors, 393
Strains, first aid for, 462
Strawberry, 10; -rhubarb pie, 88; shortcake, 93
Straw (wicker) luggage, 249
Strychnine, antidote for, 461
Stuffed peppers, 47, 50
Suede, care of, 216, 357
Sugar (sugar syrup), 92, 109, 111, 116, 162; brown, 92; cookies, 98; measuring, 92; stains, 214, 318
Suits, 207; packing, 246–47
Sunburn, 462
Sundaes, ice-cream, 103
Sunstroke, 462
Sun tan, 200
Sweaters, 207, 209, 212, 277; angora, 212; knitting, 207; laundering, 223, 227; mending, 277–78; storage, 212
Sweet potato, 42, 158; pie, 88
Sweet sixteen cake, 77
Swim caps, seepage, 200
Swiss darning, 277–78

Swiss steaks, 5
Switches, electric, 307, 385

Taffeta, 243, 264
Tape measures, 252–57, 268, 379
Tapioca, marbled, 94
Tarnish, 301–2
Tar stains, 242
T-bone steak, carving, 24
Tea, 114–15; ice cubes, 133; making, 114–15; punch, 116; stains, 243, 315; toasties (cake), 76
Teakettles, cleaning, 146
Teen-agers (see also Children): clothes, 210, 290; make-up tips, 200–2; and personal appearance, 179–81, 184–87, 200–2
Teeth, care of, 180, 206
Telephones, 341, 358; savings, 402
Temperatures, oven: checking, 134–35; conversion table, 177
Thermos jugs, 116, 121
Thimbles, sewing, 261, 267
Thread, 259, 261–62, 264, 267; crochet, 210; cutter, 262; embroidery, 278; slip covers, 337–39; threading needles, 259, 267
Tick bites, 462
Tic-tac-toe (cake), 77
Tiles, care of, 351, 383
Tin foil stains, 243
Tires, auto, 404, 408
Toast, 67–68; de luxe, 68; petite, 67–68; and toaster cleaning, 140
Tobacco juice stains, 243
Tomato(es), 40, 158, 370; aspic, 41–42; and cranberry beans, 44; facial, 205; stains, 243
Tools, 379, 405
Toothbrushes: for cleaning chores, 145, 146; preconditioning, 355
Toothpaste: stains, 243; tubes, mending, 356
Toppings: cake, 74–76, 79, 94; ice-cream, 102, 103; soup, 62–63
Towels, 221, 225, 269, 298
Trapunto, 285–86
Traveler's checks, 427
Trees and shrubs, 362, 363, 365
Trellis pie, 84–85
Trousers: care of, 210, 218, 226; packing, 246, 247
True bias, 256–57
Tubes, mending, 356
Tuna fish chowder, 60
Turkey, 16–22, 107; broiling, 17, 20; carving, 26–27; stuffing, 20–21
Tutti-frutti rice, 94

Umbrellas, 355
Unconsciousness, 462
Urine stains, 314–15
Utensils, kitchen, 144–45
Utility and service costs, saving on, 399–402

Vacuum bottles, 116, 121
Vacuum cleaners, 305–6, 311; for clothes, 211; kinds, uses, 305; for screens, 386
Valves: auto, sticky, 408; bathroom flush, 384; steam radiator leaks, 396
Variety meats, 7, 14
Varnish: removing before painting, 347; stains, 317
Varnished floors, 308–9
Vaseline stains, 243
Veal, 2, 7, 10–11, 156; cuts, 2; roast, 7; stew, 10–11
Vegetable(s), 37–50; beans, 43–45; buying, 37, 38; cooking, 42–49; freezing, 38–39, 128, 129, 131; frozen, 45–46; gardening, 363, 370; hints, 45, 49–50, 136; leftovers, 48–49; nutrients, 156–58; oils, 49–50; potatoes, 42–43; preparing, 39; salads, 39–42; sauces, 48; scallop, 47; soups, 57, 58; storing, 37–38
Velvet, 228; pressing, 267; steaming, 228
Venetian blinds, 308, 327–28
Vichyssoise, 61, 63
Vinegar, uses for, 49, 211, 296; odors and stains, 145–46, 147, 232, 314, 316
Vinyl wallpaper, 351–52
Vomiting (emetics), 459–60

Waffles, 48, 91, 140, 162
Waist measurements, sewing and, 253, 255, 257
Waldorf salad, 108
Walks (walkways), 389–90
Wallpaper, 351–54; care and cleaning, 306–7; color choosing chart, 322–25; cutting, 354; home redecorating and, 321–27
Walls: adding shelf space, 344; cellars, smoothing, 388; cleaning, 305, 306–7; electrical repairs, 384–85; lighting and, 401, 402; painting and

wallpapering, 321–27, 345–54; pictures for, 340–41; plaster work, 381; stone or brick pointing, 389
Washer-dryers, 218
Washer-wringers, guards, 447
Water softeners, 220, 221
Water spots, removing, 243
Waxing: autos, 409; and cutting glass, 386; floors, 308–9; furniture, 296; stuck windows, 385
Wax stains, 236, 241, 318
Weather stripping, 393
Weed killers, 367
Weight gain or loss, 151–53
Weights and measures, 174–76, 412–14
Welsh rarebit, 53
Wet cleanser stains, 235
Whipped cream, 52; cakes and frosting, 74–75, 76–77; on soup, 63
White vinegar (see also Vinegar): for stains, 232–34, 314, 316
Wills, insurance and, 435
Windows: care and repair of, 305, 308, 385–86, 393; home redecorating and, 328–33, 348, 351; shades, 332–33
Wine: balls, no-bake, 98; stains, 243
Wiring, electric, 399–400; auto, 405; branch circuits, 399–400
Wood(work), care and repair of, 307–8, 321, 345–54, 356, 382–83, 386–87; exterior, 350–51; painting and papering, 321, 345–54; siding and shingles, 386; "starching," 307
Wood (or denatured) alcohol, antidote for, 461
Wooden floors, care and cleaning of, 308–9, 382
Wooden furniture, care of, 294–96
Wool(ens): care and cleaning of, 211, 213, 222–23, 226–29, 311–18, 360; embroidery yarn, 278–79; floor coverings, 311–18; shrinking to sew, 252; stains, 233, 234
Wrapping materials and freezer containers, 129–31

Yarns: embroidery, 278–79; knitting, 277

Zippers, 210–11, 265

S